THE COLLECTED WORKS OF CHÖGYAM TRUNGPA

VOLUME ONE

Born in Tibet • *Meditation in Action* • *Mudra* • Selected Writings

VOLUME TWO

Glimpses of Abhidharma • *Glimpses of Mahayana* • *Glimpses of Shunyata* • *The Path Is the Goal* • *Training the Mind and Cultivating Loving-Kindness* • Selected Writings

VOLUME THREE

Cutting Through Spiritual Materialism • *The Heart of the Buddha* • *The Myth of Freedom* • Selected Writings

VOLUME FOUR

The Dawn of Tantra • *Journey without Goal* • *The Lion's Roar* • An Interview with Chögyam Trungpa

VOLUME FIVE

Crazy Wisdom • *Illusion's Game* • *The Life of Marpa the Translator* (Excerpts) • *The Rain of Wisdom* (Excerpts) • *The Sadhana of Mahamudra* (Excerpts) • Selected Writings

VOLUME SIX

Glimpses of Space • *Orderly Chaos* • *Secret Beyond Thought* • *The Tibetan Book of the Dead:* Commentary • *Transcending Madness* • Selected Writings

VOLUME SEVEN

The Art of Calligraphy (Excerpts) • *Dharma Art* • *Visual Dharma* (Excerpts) • Selected Poems • Selected Writings

VOLUME EIGHT

Great Eastern Sun: The Wisdom of Shambhala • *Shambhala: The Sacred Path of the Warrior* • Selected Writings

THE COLLECTED WORKS OF
CHÖGYAM TRUNGPA

VOLUME THREE

Cutting Through Spiritual Materialism
The Myth of Freedom
The Heart of the Buddha
Selected Writings

EDITED BY
Carolyn Rose Gimian

SHAMBHALA · *Boston & London* · 2003

Shambhala Publications, Inc.
Horticultural Hall
300 Massachusetts Avenue
Boston, Massachusetts 02115
www.shambhala.com

Page i: Chögyam Trungpa teaching "The Battle of Ego" at the Wesley Foundation, Boulder, Colorado, 1971. Photographer unknown. From the collection of the Shambhala Archives.

See pages 587–88 for a continuation of the copyright page.

9 8 7 6 5 4 3 2 1

First Edition

Printed in the United States of America

♾ This edition is printed on acid-free paper that meets
the American National Standards Institute Z39.48 Standard.

Distributed in the United States by Random House, Inc.,
and in Canada by Random House of Canada Ltd

Library of Congress Cataloging-in-Publication Data

Trunpga, Chögyam, 1939–
[Works. 2003]
The collected works of Chögyam Trungpa / edited by Carolyn Rose Gimian; forewords
by Diana J. Mukpo and Samuel Bercholz.—1st ed.
p.   cm.
Includes bibliographical references and index.
ISBN 1-59030-025-4 (v.1: alk. paper)—ISBN 1-59030-026-2 (v.2: alk. paper)—
ISBN 1-59030-027-0 (v.3: alk. paper)—ISBN 1-59030-028-9 (v.4: alk. paper)—
ISBN 1-59030-029-7 (v.5: alk. paper)—ISBN 1-59030-030-0 (v.6: alk. paper)—
ISBN 1-59030-031-9 (v.7: alk. paper)—ISBN 1-59030-032-7 (v.8: alk. paper)—
1. Spiritual life—Buddhism.   2. Buddhism—Doctrines.   I. Gimian, Carolyn Rose.   II. Title.

BQ4302.T7823   2003
294.3'420423—dc22   2003058963

CONTENTS

CONTENTS

THE HEART OF THE BUDDHA

CONTENTS

SELECTED WRITINGS

INTRODUCTION
TO VOLUME THREE

With Volume Three of *The Collected Works of Chögyam Trungpa*, we come to a collection of writings that are quintessentially American. The volume opens with the two books that put Chögyam Trungpa on the map of the American spiritual scene: *Cutting Through Spiritual Materialism* and *The Myth of Freedom*. The third book included in this volume, *The Heart of the Buddha*, was published posthumously. However, a number of the core writings that make up that book were originally published in the early 1970s. Many of them appeared in the *Garuda* magazines put together as in-house publications by Trungpa Rinpoche's senior students. Following *The Heart of the Buddha* are a number of articles and interviews. Several of these are also based on or taken directly from *Garudas I* and *II*, while others are from early talks given by Trungpa Rinpoche about the path of Tibetan Buddhism, the problems of spiritual materialism, and the means for overcoming these problems through meditation. There are also three excerpts from *Chögyam Trungpa Rinpoche at Lama Foundation*, discussions published after a visit the author made in 1973 to a New Age spiritual community in northern New Mexico. These capture the eclectic spiritual flavor of the early seventies. Other preoccupations of the era are addressed in two interviews with Chögyam Trungpa conducted in the 1970s: "Freedom Is a Kind of Gyp," an interview in *East West Journal*, includes Rinpoche's thoughts on natural foods, ecology, and EST (Erhard Sensitivity Training); and "The Myth of Don Juan," an interview in the *Shambhala Codex*, deals with the fascination with Carlos Castaneda's books on the Yaqui Indian shaman Don Juan. Finally, seven forewords to works by other authors complete this volume.

On the one hand, material for this volume was selected because it represents Chögyam Trungpa's exposition of spiritual materialism as a primary obstacle for Westerners seeking a spiritual path. On the other hand, much of the same material provides an overview of the Tibetan Buddhist path. In a way that was characteristic of much of his teaching, the problem here is also the promise: a view of all the possible sidetracks to genuine spirituality also provides the opportunity to lay out the real path of awakening, in remarkable depth and with considerable subtlety.

Cutting Through Spiritual Materialism is based on lectures given by Chögyam Trungpa in Boulder, Colorado, during the first year after he arrived there. With the establishment of his seat in Boulder, the axis of his teaching activity shifted westward. When he arrived in the United States in May of 1970 after a brief stay in Canada, he was first based at Tail of the Tiger in Barnet, Vermont. (This center was renamed Karmê-Chöling, the Dharma Place of the Karma Kagyü, by His Holiness Karmapa in 1974.) A number of his students from England had preceded him to Tail, as it was fondly called, in preparation for his arrival. In the 1977 epilogue to *Born in Tibet*, he wrote: "At Tail of the Tiger we [Rinpoche and his wife, Diana Mukpo] found an undisciplined atmosphere combining the flavours of New York City and hippies. Here too people still seemed to miss the point of Dharma, though not in the same way as in Britain, but in American free-thinking style." Nevertheless, according to his wife, Rinpoche was delighted by the freshness of the American students he encountered, and he was tremendously cheered up by their openness and genuine interest in the dharma.[1]

Tail was his home base for the first few months, but within weeks of coming to America, he set out on his first teaching tour across the country. It took him all the way to California, where he met the founder of Zen Center San Francisco, Shunryu Suzuki Roshi. This meeting had a powerful impact on the content and style of his teachings. Seeing how Roshi worked with his students and the importance he placed on sitting meditation, Trungpa Rinpoche began to put a great deal more emphasis on the sitting practice of meditation, especially group practice, which was rare in Tibet. The importance of sitting meditation for all of his students, at whatever level of practice, became a constant theme in his teachings. While in California, he also made the acquaintance of his

---

1. Communication from Diana J. Mukpo to Carolyn Rose Gimian in discussions of "Mukpo," an unpublished memoir.

American publisher, Samuel Bercholz of Shambhala Publications, which was the beginning of a long and fruitful relationship.[2]

While still in England, Trungpa Rinpoche had received a postcard from a group at the University of Colorado, inviting him to teach there, and he was attracted—he said later—by the beauty of the Flatirons, mountains outside of Boulder that were shown on the card. They reminded him of the mountains of Tibet. His wife encouraged him to visit there, and she wrote back on his behalf, saying that they would visit when they arrived in America. In the fall of 1970, Rinpoche traveled to Boulder for the first time. He was first put up in a rustic cabin in the mountains, but within a few weeks he moved to a larger house in Four Mile Canyon, closer to town.

Rinpoche's home soon became the center of a beehive of activity. He held personal interviews there, sometimes in his bedroom or on the deck outside the house. Students meditated in his living room in the evenings, and some of them lived on the top floor of the house, above the quarters for Rinpoche and his family. Several people lived in trailers on the property. Rinpoche and his wife sometimes woke up to find that a student was meditating in their bedroom while they slept—she wanted to experience the guru's body, speech, and mind at close range, he said. Diana Mukpo reports that there were always lots of people around, "from the day that we moved to Four Mile Canyon. The whole sangha, at that point, would come over to the house, and I would often cook dinner for people. We used to make big roasts and curries and things. Visitors would never go home; people would never go to bed. They would hang out with Rinpoche, and then he wouldn't come to bed, and you know it just went on and on. Sometimes I got so claustrophobic, although he never seemed to. Once, it was Easter Day, and I told everybody that we were going to have an Easter egg hunt in the garden. They all went out to look for the eggs, and I locked all the doors and windows. I was finally alone with him and I said, 'You're mine now!' He found it quite amusing."[3]

---

2. Shambhala Publications had already published *Meditation in Action* for the American market, but Rinpoche and Samuel Bercholz had never met. For additional information on both the meeting with Suzuki Roshi and how Shambhala came to be Trungpa Rinpoche's publisher, see the introduction to Volume One of *The Collected Works*.

3. Diana Mukpo in conversation with Carolyn Rose Gimian, for "Mukpo," an unpublished memoir.

Boulder became Trungpa Rinpoche's home for the next sixteen years. Perhaps it is partially the feeling of settling down and becoming established that communicates itself in *Cutting Through Spiritual Materialism*, which is based on talks that he gave to new students in Boulder during 1970 and 1971. He gave many of these talks in the evenings in a rented hall in a recently built Christian church in Boulder. He sat on a raised stage behind which was a large stained-glass backdrop, modern in design, which looked a bit as though the open mouth of a large bird had been filled with colored glass. The audience—the long-haired, barefoot or sandal-clad, paisley-garbed, and beaded youth of the era—sat on the floor at his feet. I attended one of these early talks. Rinpoche seemed utterly at home in this atmosphere. *Cutting Through* is, to my mind, one of the most relaxed and spacious books ever written by Chögyam Trungpa. It is written as though the author had all the time in the world to tell us about the spiritual path, which was very much the flavor of the original talks. It is an energetic book, to be sure, filled with the enthusiasm of its times. Yet in addition to being penetrating, it is also thorough and gentle, reminiscent of a painting by Monet, perhaps, which shows all the details of light, color, and shading that make up a scene. It is as though Chögyam Trungpa had finally arrived; he had found the place where he could settle down and spread out. From that expansive seat, he tells us about the intricacies of the student-teacher relationship and lays out the path that lies ahead if one is game to undertake the journey.

In England, he had difficulty finding students, or they had difficulty finding him. A fair number of people were interested in hearing him lecture, but not so many of them were ready to become his students. In America, he began to attract many students who came, listened, and stayed. It was due partially to the era, partially to the social and political climate, but something about Chögyam Trungpa really connected with the spiritual scene in America at that time, and something about that scene really connected with him. *Cutting Through Spiritual Materialism* reflects part of what drew the audience to him: the intimacy that Chögyam Trungpa conveyed in his talks. In *Cutting Through*, he speaks very directly to the reader, often about surprising topics, considering that this is a book on the Buddhist path. Topics such as self-deception and sense of humor were hardly the standard fare of religious discourse at that time, but they were chapter titles in his new book.

It would seem that Chögyam Trungpa had indeed found his voice: a truly American voice, at home not just in the English language but in the American idiom, a voice ready to mold the language to express the teachings of Buddhism, ready to share a subtle experience and understanding of the Buddhist path, ready to tell stories and share secrets, ready to play, ready to rock. It was this voice that drew Hindu sannyasins, Zen monks, Jewish radical intellectuals, New York actors, Beat poets, California experimental druggies, Buddhologists looking for meditation instruction, and so many others.

Chögyam Trungpa had a poet's sensibility; in fact, he was a poet— mostly in the English language, which was not his native tongue. He used that poetic sensibility in crafting the language to describe the Buddhist teachings. He had a real feeling for the right word, the *mot juste*. *Cutting Through Spiritual Materialism* is the first place that one can truly see that genius—starting with the title.

There is no exact equivalent for "spiritual materialism" in the Buddhist teachings, no comparable Sanskrit or Tibetan term. Yet it precisely defines a tendency to pervert spiritual teachings to support or maintain one's ego-oriented view of reality. Defining this tendency is immensely helpful to students setting out on the path. The idea of *cutting through* spiritual materialism points out exactly what the challenge to the meditator is and why surrendering one's arrogance and unmasking one's self-deception are essential to any genuine experience or progress on the path. In coining this term, Chögyam Trungpa took one of the first steps in creating a truly American Buddhism, a Buddhism that is completely true to its origin and heritage yet completely fresh and up-to-date.

Yet at the same time that he coined new terminology and used good English words to describe ancient techniques of meditation and stages on the Buddhist path, he also respected the integrity of terms for which no English equivalent existed. In *Cutting Through Spiritual Materialism,* one finds that more of these Sanskrit terms are used in chapter titles toward the end of the book, whether that was coincidental or planned. In the first eleven chapters of the book, the only foreign term to appear in the chapter titles is the word *guru*, which certainly needs no translation today and probably didn't even in 1973 when the book appeared. (Since *guru* is a term now laden with connotations, not all of them positive, the chapter was retitled "The Teacher" when it was reprinted in the year 2000 in *The Essential Chögyam Trungpa*.) The last four chapter titles of *Cutting Through* all feature Sanskrit words: "The Bodhisattva

Path," "Shunyata," "Prajna and Compassion," and finally "Tantra." Not all of those terms are yet, nor may ever be, common parlance in America.

When a term was best left in Sanskrit, in Sanskrit it remained. When he used a foreign term, Trungpa Rinpoche preferred to use Sanskrit rather than Tibetan—although there are some important exceptions, such as his adoption of the Tibetan *yidam* rather than the Sanskrit *heruka* as the term for vajrayana deities. Again, he had a real intuition for how the West would best be won. Although it may not have seemed so obvious at the time, it seems almost self-evident in hindsight that Sanskrit was the better choice. That may be because many English and Sanskrit words share a common Indo-European root. But, from a simple perspective, Sanskrit is generally, although not always, a much easier language for Americans to pronounce; it sounds not nearly so foreign to our ears. For example, the Sanskrit *tantra* trips more easily off the tongue than the Tibetan *gyü.*[4]

Almost thirty years after its publication, *Cutting Through Spiritual Materialism* continues to be a standard text in introductory university courses on Buddhism and Eastern religion, and still finds its way into the hands of many inquiring readers. It suffers a bit from its reputation as a classic of the '70s. Not that it didn't earn that reputation—it brought thousands to the study and practice of Buddhism in that day. But aside from a few dated references and passages, it remains applicable and up-to-date. There are few places where one can find Chögyam Trungpa so expansive, so open, and so relaxed in print. One must pay tribute to the book's editors, John Baker and Marvin Casper, who also edited *The Myth of Freedom.* They had not known Chögyam Trungpa in England, so they

---

4. Scott Wellenbach, one of the senior members of the Nālandā Translation Committee, provided some other comments on Trungpa Rinpoche's preference for Sanskrit. He wrote: "There were a number of other reasons for Rinpoche's choice: (1) Sanskrit is the lingua franca of Buddhism; by using Sanskrit, you show that Tibetan Buddhism is indeed Buddhism and not some esoteric 'lamaism.' (2) Many Tibetan teachers love things Indian, especially since India was Buddha's homeland, and Chögyam Trungpa shared that feeling to some extent. Using Sanskrit for him seemed to have a sense of bringing Buddhism back home, and he liked the fact that now, in the diaspora, Sanskrit could be used correctly. (3) Also linked to this, Sanskrit was considered to be a sacred language, as is reflected in its use in Buddhist mantras. Though these days we don't think that Buddha himself exactly spoke Sanskrit, I think that Trungpa Rinpoche felt that, to some small extent, using Sanskrit could only enhance the power of what we were doing."

had been studying with him for no more than a year or two when they undertook to edit the first book. In *Cutting Through Spiritual Materialism*, they produced a real classic, a text that is elegant and intimate at the same time.

John Baker has kindly supplied information on the editing of *Cutting Through*, which also gives a further portrait of the times, including Rinpoche's relationship with Alan Watts and a meeting with one of Ram Dass's gurus:

> *Cutting Through Spiritual Materialism* was based mostly on a seminar Rinpoche gave in early 1971, which I think was called the Battle of Ego. There was a second seminar used as well, but I am no longer sure which it was: it might have been "Mandala" or perhaps "American Karma," both given at a church called the Wesley Foundation out on 28th Street [in Boulder, Colorado].
>
> Some of Rinpoche's students (including Henry Schaeffer, my brother Steve, and Polly Wellenbach, née Monner) had rented a house in Boulder at the corner of Alpine and 9th Street. It was the first community house in Boulder, and Rinpoche named it Anitya Bhavan, which means "House of Impermanence." I guess he figured it wouldn't last long, and it didn't (maybe a year). It belonged to a yoga instructress, a very blond, fit woman of maybe forty who had converted the garage into a yoga studio. It was perfect for the first Boulder seminar, which was attended by thirty to forty people.
>
> These were the hippy-dippy days, and I remember penniless youths frequently offering banana bread in payment for their seminar fees and complaining that Christ never charged for *his* teachings. That first seminar lasted about seven or eight nights, and Marvin Casper and I agreed that we could turn it into a book.
>
> I had met Marvin at Tail where I had decided that he was not my type at all and then had become so close with him in Colorado that six-year-old Jesse Usow thought us one person, calling us interchangeably "John-Marvin." So you see, I can't remember whose idea the book was, but only that we both worked on it pretty much equally. Marvin and I were completely blown away by devoted to in love with amazed at Rinpoche. . . . I think I can speak for both of us on that point. . . . As you might expect, . . . the transcripts were quite difficult to understand. . . . None of us knew much about Buddhism, which also made the transcripts challenging, to say the least. So Marvin and I vetted absolutely

everything we did with Rinpoche. We would read him the transcripts, asking questions until we felt we understood that talk under discussion fully. Then we would do an edit which, depending on the particular talk, might involve more or less rewriting. Then we would read him the edit, eliciting his comments, and do a re-edit. We did this until we were all satisfied with the result, a process which usually required several iterations.

Later, when we put together *The Myth of Freedom* out of a number of seminars, we just read him everything we did and received much less input from him. But *Cutting Through* was an extraordinary learning experience for us. We sat with him for hours, many times, over a period of many months, discussing the material, rewriting it, and then asking for his comments and corrections, which he gave freely. For instance, the chapter on shunyata was especially opaque in its original form. We discussed the idea with him and then completely rewrote the chapter a number of times, resubmitting it to him until we were all satisfied. In the course of creating the book, I received my education into Buddhist thought. He had given me the heart of the matter in an instant at Tail. It was in the hours of discussion over *Cutting Through* that I learned to relate doctrine to that core experience and to see how all Buddhist thought circles around it.

In the spring of 1972 Rinpoche, Marvin, and I went into retreat together in Jenner, California, for three weeks and pretty much finished the editing. We had gone up to Teton Village, Wyoming, to visit the Snow Lion Inn and Trungpa Rinpoche's students running it, and then we drove to Jenner in an ancient yellow Karmann Ghia. . . . Rinpoche dictated a number of poems in Jenner, we dropped acid, went to see a Mexican mystical western movie, the name of which escapes me, made many cooking experiments (Rinpoche loved to concoct weird food, such as baked oranges), I somehow contracted and got rid of crabs, and we drove around in the foggy redwood forest and along the coast of northern California. And we edited: Marvin and I writing, reading the text to him, rewriting. Then we drove down the coast to San Francisco, stopping along the way to visit Hari Das Baba (one of Ram Dass's teachers, living in a stylish seaside development) and José and Miriam Argüelles (who showed us paintings of "guardians" they had met in dreams). In San Francisco we immediately went shopping, and Rinpoche bought Marvin a double-breasted blazer because he told him it made him look thicker, less slight, more substantial. Marvin, so Buddha, who never thought about his personal appearance, beamed with pleasure.

One side note: my father, Edward J. Baker, had input into the manuscript. He had been educated at Yale and Harvard Law, was quite literate, had taught me to write years ago, and I sent him the text for his comments, which he gave, and some of which were incorporated into the finished book. He was also friends with Rinpoche and Diana, as was my mother. . . . In sum, I feel of *Cutting Through Spiritual Materialism* that it is one of the events/products of my life of which I am most proud, for which I am most grateful. It was part of the revolution Rinpoche worked in my being, a personal teaching to me.

A final note regarding *Cutting Through*. In the fall of 1973 the book had just been published. Rinpoche had done two seminars for Alan Watts on his houseboat in Sausalito and had been on a panel with him for Bob Lester (head of the Religious Studies Department) at the University of Colorado. . . . Alan was in awe of Rinpoche. We had invited him to come and teach at Naropa Institute [which was in the planning stages at this point] and he had accepted, and we also wanted him to write a review of the book for the *New York Times Book Review* or a similar [venue]. So I was sent to visit him in his Zen retreat cabin on Mount Tamalpais outside San Francisco. He met me at the door in Zen robes, and we sat on zafus as he agreed to write the review. When I asked him how much he would charge to teach at Naropa, he smiled knowingly and said that he would do it for free, that he knew we were inviting him because he was a "draw." He had become a friend. Sadly, he died that winter of a heart attack in his sleep.[5]

When *Cutting Through* was published in 1973, it was an almost overnight success. It was *the* book to be reading, at least in certain circles. Following its publication, lectures by Trungpa Rinpoche, which might previously have drawn an audience of a hundred, now might draw an audience of a thousand in a major American city. Since his arrival in America in 1970, he had crisscrossed the continent many times, developing a following in many cities, including Boston, New York, Washington, D.C., Toronto, Montreal, Chicago, Boulder, Los Angeles, San Francisco, and Vancouver. By 1973, he had students in these and other locales who helped host his visits to their area. They set up lectures—and sometimes "dharma festivals" or other special events—in large venues that would accommodate all those who wanted to hear him speak.

---

5. From a letter by John Baker to Carolyn Rose Gimian, February 17, 2002.

While he talked about serious topics and warned listeners of the many pitfalls of spiritual endeavors, he did so with warmth and unconventional humor, in a way that generally charmed the audience. The atmosphere surrounding his public appearances was sometimes more like a happening than a lecture. I can remember young women dancing and a band of Hare Krishnas chanting, with much audience participation, as we waited for Chögyam Trungpa to arrive and speak at a lecture hall in San Francisco around 1972. After the main part of his address, he was always patiently and delightedly open to questions and audience participation. He loved to be challenged and seemed to draw energy from the interaction with the crowd.

To be sure, there was a more serious side to all this. Public lectures almost always were a prelude to weekend, sometimes longer, seminars, which generally were attended by fifty to one hundred participants. Here students sat and practiced meditation, had private interviews, and heard in-depth talks on topics from "Mahamudra" to "Buddhism and American Karma."

Although not published until 1976, *The Myth of Freedom* was largely drawn from public talks and seminars that Trungpa Rinpoche gave in many parts of the country between 1971 and 1973. While in some ways it is a continuation of the themes articulated in *Cutting Through, The Myth of Freedom* is also a departure. Rather than painting a detailed picture on a vast canvas, which was the style of the first book, here Chögyam Trungpa's approach is to provide many snapshots of the steps on the path. The chapters are short and pithy and largely self-sufficient; one can start almost anywhere in this book, read a chapter or two, and feel that one has gained something valuable, something that stands on its own merits.

In the intervening years between the publication of *Cutting Through Spiritual Materialism* and *The Myth of Freedom*, several events occurred in Trungpa Rinpoche's world that affected *The Myth of Freedom*. In 1973, the first Vajradhatu Seminary was held. It was the training ground for introducing vajrayana practice to Rinpoche's senior students. Before that time, all of his students were solely practitioners of sitting meditation.[6] By 1976, he had more than three hundred students engaged in ngöndro,

---

6. He had started some students on the practice of ngöndro in England, but he later asked most of them to repeat those practices after a thorough grounding in sitting meditation.

or the foundation practices, to prepare them to receive empowerment, or initiation, in the practice of tantric sadhanas. In 1974, the first session of Naropa Institute (now Naropa University), the first Buddhist-inspired university in North America, drew eighteen hundred students to Boulder, much to the shock of Rinpoche's students who had been organizing the institute on his behalf. They had been expecting a maximum of five hundred participants. Although there were a number of reasons that people came to Naropa that summer, the success of *Cutting Through Spiritual Materialism* and interest in its author were major contributing causes. Also in 1974, the head of Trungpa Rinpoche's lineage, His Holiness the sixteenth Gyalwang Karmapa, visited the United States for the first time and gave his blessing to Rinpoche's work, noting his great accomplishments in transmitting the vajrayana teachings in the West. His Holiness proclaimed Chögyam Trungpa "a Vajra Holder and Possessor of the Victory Banner of the Practice Lineage of the Karma Kagyü."

All of these events had an impact on *The Myth of Freedom*. First, the success of Naropa Institute and Rinpoche's general celebrity encouraged him and his editors to undertake a second popular volume of his teachings. Second, in *The Myth of Freedom*, he chose to acknowledge and honor His Holiness Karmapa: the only photograph in the book is a portrait of the Karmapa, accompanied by one of Rinpoche's poems, entitled "Enthronement." This lends a sense of lineage and heritage to the book— not a lineage in the distant past but a lineage right at hand. Finally, although all of the talks in *The Myth of Freedom* were given to public audiences, there is much vajrayana or tantric content, including the translation of a short but important tantric text, "Mahamudra Upadesa," at the end of the volume. This was, in part, simply the natural outgrowth of the fact that Rinpoche's students—and his editors—were themselves becoming familiarized with and steeped in vajrayana. John Baker commented on this and other aspects of the editing of *The Myth of Freedom*:

> With regard to *Myth of Freedom*, I never liked it quite as much as *Cutting Through Spiritual Materialism*, felt it too much a synthesis from too many seminars, that it was overedited and had lost punch, lost some of the sound of his voice. Nevertheless, it has its moments, for sure, as for instance, the chapter on love. At some point I realized that it was pure Anu Yoga [an advanced stage on the tantric path]. I went to Rinpoche and asked him if he really wanted it in the book as it was, if it wasn't

revealing teachings he only wanted to present to students intimately, at [the Vajradhatu] Seminary. He laughed and said it was all right, that no one would "get it" anyhow. However, with regard to Tilopa's "Mahamudra Upadesa," the poem Rinpoche translated for the conclusion of the book, he did edit out the references to tantric sexual yoga, deeming them too precious and esoteric for this venue.[7]

The year 1976, when *The Myth of Freedom* was published, was a turning point in Chögyam Trungpa's Buddhist community. With the coming of the Karmapa in 1974, Rinpoche's students had discovered that they were part of a large family. Having already found religion, in His Holiness Karmapa's connection to the community they found tradition. And with tradition came responsibility. The end of the party was in sight. Although there were certainly further celebrations to come, the careless freedom and sometimes wild atmosphere that characterized the earliest years began to fade after the Karmapa's visit. Similarly, although the first summer at Naropa Institute seemed like one huge happening, it also had implications. By 1975, what might have seemed like a lark just a year before now clearly held the potential to build an enduring and important institution of higher learning. There were departments to build, programs to plan, degrees to offer. And as Rinpoche's students began their ngöndro, entering the vajrayana path in earnest, they *felt* more personally the preciousness of the teachings they were receiving, and they discovered firsthand how much discipline and devotion were vital parts of their training. Also in 1976, Chögyam Trungpa appointed an American student, Ösel Tendzin (Thomas Rich) as his dharma successor, or Vajra Regent. Tradition was now an intensely personal affair for Rinpoche's students: it was theirs to carry on. As if to underscore this point, Rinpoche announced that he would be taking a year's retreat in 1977, leaving the administration of his world to his Vajra Regent and all his other students.

That things began to settle down and take shape for the future was all for the good, for otherwise the community might have been marooned in the seventies. Still, there was an unfettered exuberant quality that was difficult to leave behind, and indeed some students left around that time, unable to make the transition from emptiness to form. It was

---

7. John Baker, ibid.

a bit like the change from adolescence to maturity—necessary but poignant. The changes in the community also made room for many others to explore their interest in Buddhism and meditation, for there were many who were not attracted to the formlessness of the early years. While some had found it liberating, for others it had appeared merely messy and chaotic.

If one reads *The Myth of Freedom* now, most of this surrounding cultural history is invisible—happily so. The book speaks to readers today who have no relationship to the era from which it sprang. The directness of the prose is hard-hitting, and the fact that the chapters are short makes the book almost more digestible for current readers than it was for its original audience.

The Heart of the Buddha, edited by Judith L. Lief and published in 1991, is a collection of fourteen articles, sixteen if one counts the appendices. "The Four Foundations of Mindfulness," "Taking Refuge," and "The Bodhisattva Vow" all appeared first in issues 4 and 5 of the *Garuda* magazine. Although *Garuda* was originally published by Vajradhatu, Chögyam Trungpa's main Buddhist organization, the last three issues were co-published by Shambhala Publications, with limited sales to the general public. These three articles are meaty, in-depth discussions of the topics, and they deserve the wider audience they enjoy by being incorporated into *The Heart of the Buddha*. The same is true for the chapter "Devotion," which was edited from one of Trungpa Rinpoche's seminars, "The True Meaning of Devotion," to be the main text in *Empowerment*, a beautiful, slim book with many photographs, commemorating the first visit of His Holiness Karmapa in 1974. "Devotion" and the three articles previously mentioned each give a comprehensive view of their topic. Each incorporates material from many of Rinpoche's talks on the same subject. Both "Taking Refuge" and "The Bodhisattva Vow" are based on talks that he gave when he presented Refuge and Bodhisattva Vows, committing his students to formally becoming Buddhists and then to treading the mahayana path of selfless compassion for all beings. These articles thus have a very personal and direct quality to them.

"Sacred Outlook: The Practice of Vajrayogini" was an article that I edited for inclusion in a catalog for the exhibit "The Silk Route and the Diamond Path: Esoteric Buddhist Art on the Trans-Himalayan Trade Routes." This exhibit, which opened at the UCLA art gallery in November of 1982 and then traveled to Asia Society in New York and to the

National Museum of Natural History at the Smithsonian in Washington, D.C., in 1983, was curated by one of Trungpa Rinpoche's students, Deborah E. Klimburg-Salter. For the exhibit, Rinpoche supervised the design and construction of an actual shrine setup for the practice of the Vajrayogini Sadhana, displayed with all its attendant ritual objects. Some of the material in the article was dictated by Rinpoche; some of it was taken from earlier talks he had given. It is material that is not available in any of his other published writings.

The other articles in *The Heart of the Buddha* cover a wide range of topics, including "Relationship," "Intellect and Intuition," and "Dharma Poetics." "Acknowledging Death," another article included here, was originally edited as a contribution to a book on healing. A later version also appeared in the *Naropa Institute Journal of Psychology*. Although health professionals have found it extremely helpful, it is not just aimed at professional caretakers but speaks to anyone dealing with sickness— their own or that of others. "Alcohol as Medicine or Poison" is a penetrating discussion of the positive and negative aspects of relating to drink, written by a man well known to have been a serious drinker. While he acknowledges the problems that can arise with the use of alcohol, Rinpoche expresses not a moral but a spiritual viewpoint of the subject. Altogether *The Heart of the Buddha* brings together important and provocative articles by Trungpa Rinpoche on a broad range of topics.

The other articles in Volume Three of *The Collected Works* are gathered from many sources. "The Wisdom of Tibetan Teachings," published in the *American Theosophist* in 1972, is a pithy piece on both the history of Buddhism in Tibet and the three yanas of Tibetan Buddhism. Part of the article is based on "The Meditative Tradition of Tibet," which appeared in *Garuda I*. The next article, "Transcending Materialism," is reprinted here directly from *Garuda I*. It describes the "three lords of materialism" in a unique context, relating their conquest to the communist takeover of Tibet, forcing many great Tibetan teachers to leave the country in order to preserve the wisdom of their culture. Out of these dire circumstances, some good sprang, Rinpoche tells us, for the Tibetan wisdom subsequently found its way to the West, where there was genuine interest in Eastern spirituality along with many misconceptions about its practice. "Cutting Through," the next article in Volume Three, was originally published in 1972 in *Garuda II*. It looks at the early history of American interest in non-Western spirituality and some of its roots, including Theosophy, the influence of Anagarika Dharmapala on the translation of Pali texts into English and Gendün Chöphel's[8] attempts to translate Pali sutras back into Tibetan, as well as Aleister Crowley's fascination with the magic and mystery of Tibet and Egypt. Then Trungpa Rinpoche relates all of this to the modern fascinations with and sidetracks of spirituality. This article is like nothing else written by Chögyam Trungpa that I know of. It covers interesting territory that he rarely discussed.

The next article, "The Tibetan Buddhist Teachings and Their Application," first appeared in the inaugural issue of *The Laughing Man* magazine. The version reproduced here is based mainly on a later version, which appeared in an in-house Vajradhatu periodical called *Buddhadharma*. The questions and answers are based on the earlier version published in *The Laughing Man*. Trungpa Rinpoche talks once again about the problems of spiritual materialism, overcoming self-deception through the practice of meditation, and meditation as making friends with oneself.

This is followed by a short piece, "The Three-Yana Principle in Tibetan Buddhism," which was published in another in-house organ, *Sangha*, in 1974. It does, in fact, give a brief synopsis of the three major yanas, or stages of the Buddhist path: the hinayana, mahayana, and vajrayana. Next there is the talk "Cynicism and Warmth," which first appeared in *The Vajradhatu Sun* in 1989. Given by Rinpoche at Tail of the Tiger in 1971, it is about cynicism as a tool for recognizing and cutting through spiritual materialism, and warmth as a tool for cutting through the obstacles of doubt and skepticism produced by the cynical approach. It is practice-oriented and powerful teaching.

"Dome Darshan," "Tower House Discussions I and II," and "Report from Outside the Closet" are all reprinted from *Chögyam Trungpa Rinpoche at Lama Foundation*, published in 1974. This publication is a record of a dialogue between Rinpoche, the representative of the Buddhist tra-

---

8. In the original article, Trungpa Rinpoche refers to Gendün Gyamtsol as the Tibetan monk who translated Pali texts back into Tibetan. Rinpoche's description makes it likely that he was referring to the well-known, brilliant, and unconventional Gelukpa scholar Gendün Chöphel. Gyamtsol may have been another name by which he was known, or it may have been improperly rendered by Rinpoche's students at that time. After consultation with members of the Nālandā Translation Committee, the monk's name has been changed in the article "Cutting Through" and here in the introduction as well.

dition, and the students at Lama Foundation, the inhabitants of a hippie commune in northern New Mexico. In some ways the audience at Lama was not that different from an audience of Rinpoche's own students at the time. In fact, soon after his visit to Lama, a number of residents from that community left to study with him. Lama was a melting pot for the new American spirituality, hosting seminars by teachers from many different traditions. For example, Ram Dass, a former Harvard psychology professor (born Richard Alpert) who had become a teacher of Hindu spirituality, helped to found Lama and was a resident teacher there in the 1970s. After making Trungpa Rinpoche's acquaintance there, he came to Naropa Institute for the first summer session in 1974 as one of the main teachers.

Though the group at Lama may have been similar to Rinpoche's students, *Chögyam Trungpa Rinpoche at Lama Foundation* is not like any of his books. Since these talks and discussions took place in the Lama Foundation environment, rather than in one of Rinpoche's practice centers, and since the people from Lama were responsible for the editing and publishing of the material, there is a distinct flavor to the book they produced. After all, the people at Lama were the editors of Ram Dass's best-selling *Be Here Now*, which presents quite a different approach from Rinpoche's view of the spiritual path, to say the least. Nevertheless, the people at Lama produced *Chögyam Trungpa Rinpoche at Lama Foundation* with Trungpa Rinpoche's blessing, and it does not mask his basic message: beware of spiritual materialism. At Lama, he was presenting meditation in what was a respectful but rather vague and eclectic spiritual environment. Rinpoche chose to talk about developing a cynical or critical attitude as an important part of the genuine spiritual path. Discussions of the Hindu experience of bhakti and the dialogue about Christianity and Teilhard de Chardin are interesting highlights in these articles. Readers will have to make what they will of "Report from Outside the Closet," which is a sort of short story or parable, which Trungpa Rinpoche wrote for the Lama Foundation publication. Joshua Zim, one of the residents at Lama who became a close student of Chögyam Trungpa's, was fond of writing rather cryptic short stories, a volume of which were later published as *Empty Heart*. "Report from Outside the Closet" may have been Rinpoche's way of communicating, or playing, with Zim.

"Freedom Is a Kind of Gyp" is an interview conducted and published by *East West Journal* (now *Natural Health*) in 1975. The interview was done during the Nalanda Festival in Boston, which was a kind of mini–Naropa Institute on the road, featuring poetry readings, Buddhist talks, music, and other cultural activities, including the opening of an exhibit of Tibetan art at the Hayden Gallery at M.I.T., for which Rinpoche wrote the catalog (see "Visual Dharma" in Volume Seven of *The Collected Works*).[9] In 1974, a Dharma Festival organized by Rinpoche's students in the Bay Area in California had created the model for the festival that took place in Boston. The interview itself covers a wide range of topics, including Rinpoche's thoughts on EST and ecology. He is critical of Erhard Sensitivity Training, yet points out that Werner Erhard, its founder, is a "friend of ours." Participants in Erhard's training program attended specially EST-sponsored Vajra Crown ceremonies conducted by His Holiness Karmapa in 1976, so there was some genuine interest there in Kagyü spirituality. Trungpa Rinpoche was suspicious of Erhard's approach but also, typically for him, saw the potential of what Erhard was doing with EST.

Next there is an interview with Chögyam Trungpa conducted by Karl Ray on behalf of *Codex Shambhala*. The *Codex* was a small journal started by Shambhala Publications in 1971 as a forum for discussion of its books and as a showcase for its authors. The interview reprinted in Volume Three, "The Myth of Don Juan," appeared in 1975. Karl Ray, then a long-time Shambhala employee, had just assumed the editorship of the magazine, a position that he held throughout the remaining years of its publication. Later in 1975, the *Codex* became *The Shambhala Review of Books and Ideas*. It ceased publication altogether in 1976.[10] There were interesting reviews and excerpts from Shambhala's new books in the magazine; but to my mind, the best of the *Codex/Review* were the original interviews.

In "The Myth of Don Juan," Trungpa Rinpoche criticizes Carlos Cas-

---

9. This festival was sponsored under the umbrella of Nalanda, the nonprofit educational organization that was the corporate parent of Naropa, as well as of other educational and cultural activities initiated by Trungpa Rinpoche, including Shambhala Training and Dharma Art. A few years later, Naropa became a nonprofit corporation in its own right.

10. Philip Barry, the owner of Shambhala Booksellers in Berkeley, California, says that "Karl [Ray] told me some years later that they stopped [publishing the *Shambhala Review*] because it had become too labor-intensive and was not cost-efficient" (e-mail communication from Philip Barry to Carolyn Rose Gimian, February 16, 2002). Back issues of this journal are now a rare commodity. I had to search far and wide for them in compiling *The Collected Works*. Philip has a complete set of the *Codex/Reviews* and supplied most of the historical information about these publications.

taneda for making something of a personality cult out of the figure of Don Juan, rather than emphasizing the teachings themselves—although Rinpoche remains unconvinced that Don Juan actually exists. There is a discussion of the problems with trying to use drugs to shortcut genuine spiritual discipline. Finally, Trungpa Rinpoche contrasts shamanistic teachings—as well as other religious traditions that are based on identifying with the magic contained in particular physical locations—with the approach of both Christianity and Buddhism, which he suggests are both fundamentally based on a mendicant or homeless approach. This, he suggests, is part of their universal appeal.

Volume Three concludes with a group of forewords written by Chögyam Trungpa over the years. They are arranged here chronologically. Two are forewords to translations of important Tibetan Buddhist texts. The first, *The Jewel Ornament of Liberation*, is Gampopa's great work on the stages of the Buddhist path, which was translated by Herbert V. Guenther and published originally in 1959. Rinpoche wrote a foreword to the edition that Shambhala Publications brought out in 1971, and through this made the acquaintance of Dr. Guenther.[11] Trungpa Rinpoche greatly admired this classic text and had studied it thoroughly as part of his own education. One of the first seminars he taught in America was a series of seventeen lectures on the *Jewel Ornament*, which regrettably has not yet been edited for publication. The other text for which he wrote the foreword, *Mahamudra: The Quintessence of Mind and Meditation* by Takpo Tashi Namgyal, was published in 1986, the year before Rinpoche died. He was very happy that this book was being published in translation; his foreword was one of the last things he ever dictated, just a few months before he became quite ill. He used this text as his own study material—in Tibetan, of course—for many of his talks on the Shambhala tradition of warriorship. This may be startling to some readers, since one does not popularly think of his Shambhala teachings as having a direct correlation to the advanced tantric teachings of mahamudra. Rinpoche also used this text in the preparation of many of his Buddhist lectures and seminars. This translation, by Lobsang P. Lhalungpa, was a valiant effort. It is quite a difficult work, and the translation is not

---

11. Chögyam Trungpa and Herbert Guenther collaborated on a book entitled *The Dawn of Tantra*, which grew out of a seminar they taught jointly in 1972. This appears in Volume Four of *The Collected Works*.

easygoing. The book is now out of print, and one hopes that this text will once again be available in English in the not too distant future.

There are also three forewords included here that Trungpa Rinpoche contributed to books about other Buddhist teachers. The first is Jack Kornfield's *Living Dharma: Teachings of Twelve Buddhist Masters*, published in 1975. Next is *The History of the Sixteen Karmapas of Tibet*, which was published in 1980 by Prajñā Press. The third is Tsultrim Allione's *Women of Wisdom*, first published in 1984 by Routledge & Kegan Paul. Undoubtedly Trungpa Rinpoche was delighted to introduce these books, which would broaden the public's knowledge of the history and lineages of Buddhism. It was probably his personal connection to the authors that led them to ask him to contribute a foreword and that led him to comply. Karma Thinley, the author of the book on the Karmapas, was a Tibetan Buddhist teacher in Toronto whom Rinpoche met when Karma Thinley visited Samye Ling in Scotland. Trungpa Rinpoche was very grateful for the hospitality Karma Thinley extended to him and his wife, and also respected him very much as a dharma teacher. As well, several of Trungpa Rinpoche's close students had originally studied with Karma Thinley. Tsultrim Allione was also a student of Rinpoche's in the early 1970s, and he had tremendous fondness for her. Jack Kornfield had been a colleague of Rinpoche's at Naropa Institute; both he and his fellow teacher of insight meditation Joseph Goldstein taught at Naropa in 1974, when they were largely unknown. Rinpoche respected them both for their dedication to the Buddhist teachings. Also included in Volume Three is the brief foreword that Trungpa Rinpoche contributed to José and Miriam Argüelles's '70s classic *Mandala*. Both José and Miriam were early students of Rinpoche's in California. (See John Baker's comments earlier in this introduction.) The Argüelleses extended much personal hospitality to Rinpoche and Diana Mukpo in the early years, and he was grateful for both their friendship and their commitment to the Buddhist path.

Finally, Volume Three includes the foreword that Chögyam Trungpa wrote to *Buddha in the Palm of Your Hand*, by his Vajra Regent, Ösel Tendzin. Trungpa Rinpoche was delighted that Ösel Tendzin produced a book edited from his own lectures, talks he gave between 1976 and 1980, the first four years after he was confirmed as Trungpa Rinpoche's dharma heir. Rinpoche tells us that these are not "self-proclaimed wisdom" but that Ösel Tendzin "reflects here only the study and training he has gone through with my personal guidance." I had the opportunity to work with the Vajra Regent and his editor, Donna Holm, on the preliminary selection of material and some of the editing of this book. I remember how diligently the Regent worked on these talks and how carefully he and Donna Holm scrutinized each word that went into the manuscript.

Trungpa Rinpoche also used his foreword to reflect on the importance of his decision to appoint an American student as his dharma heir: "Many Oriental advisors have said to me, 'Do not make an Occidental your successor; they are not trustworthy.' With the blessings of His Holiness the sixteenth Gyalwa Karmapa, and through working with Ösel Tendzin as my Regent, I have come to the conclusion that anybody who possesses tathagatagarbha [buddha nature] is worthy of experiencing enlightenment. . . . I have worked arduously in training him [the Regent] as my best student and foremost leader."[12] It is now fifteen years since Chögyam Trungpa's death and more than ten years since the death of the Vajra Regent in 1990. Yet Trungpa Rinpoche's belief that buddhadharma can fully take root in America remains alive, untarnished by all doubts and difficulties. There is no doubt that he bequeathed the stainless, pure tradition of awakened mind to the West, and it seems doubtless that it will be carried forward. There will be twists and turns, but the ultimate truth is fearless. This was the motto that Chögyam Trungpa gave to Vajradhatu, the main Buddhist organization that he founded. Readers who never met him can still be touched and transformed by what he taught. In that lies great promise.

CAROLYN ROSE GIMIAN
April 18, 2002
Trident Mountain House
Tatamagouche Mountain, Nova Scotia

---

12. P. 578 of this volume.

CUTTING THROUGH
SPIRITUAL MATERIALISM

Edited by JOHN BAKER
and MARVIN CASPER

To
Chokyi-lodrö the Marpa
Father of the Kagyü lineage

Foreword

THE INSPIRATION to find the truth, to see what is real, and to lead a genuine life—the culmination of which can be enlightenment—is what underlies every spiritual journey. However, embarking on this journey is rarely as straightforward as we may wish. The journey toward enlightenment ultimately may be both profound and simple, yet the process of understanding that simplicity tends to be multidimensional, if not downright complicated. For in order to understand a spiritual path, we must acknowledge and understand our own mind, now, as it pertains to the journey. What misunderstandings and concepts we may have about a spiritual practice, we must overcome so that we're not merely practicing according to our own conceptualized idea. Ego, and the myriad games it plays to unravel our inspiration for enlightenment, must always be monitored.

To understand the essential qualities of the spiritual path, especially what obstacles or conundrums might lie ahead, we need a clear sense of direction. We need teachings, instructions, and guidance from someone who has traveled the path and therefore can give valid and confident advice about how others could travel this same path. This is what is offered by my father, Chögyam Trungpa, in *Cutting through Spiritual Materialism*.

These lectures and teachings were given in the early 1970s, at a crossroads of heightened awareness and spiritual awakening in the United States. East was beginning to meet West. Having turned away from their parents' values, a whole generation was investigating newly available spiritual paths—many of them quite traditional. People wanted a path that would help them rise above life's mundane trappings to see a more

3

expansive view, a view that would dissolve their feeling of alienation and penetrate life's very meaning. At the same time, many of these seekers were still trying to figure out what a genuine path to liberation was. There was a quality of freshness, exuberance, excitement, and youth, as well as naiveté.

People were naive about the many pitfalls possible on any path. Spiritual awakening is not a happy-go-lucky endeavor. The path of truth is profound—and so are the obstacles and possibilities for self-deception. No matter what the practice or teaching, ego loves to wait in ambush to appropriate spirituality for its own survival and gain. Chögyam Trungpa—who had just arrived in the States from Scotland—tried to clarify these issues. He wanted to raise people's awareness to a level where they could distinguish between what is genuine spiritual progress and what is ego hijacking spirituality for its own purposes. He wanted to help them learn to recognize the grip of the three lords of materialism—strategies that ego can use any time, any place, in order to seduce us from a bigger view back into its self-limiting perspective.

From an early age, Chögyam Trungpa had undergone an arduous education in the monasteries of Kham, on the high plateau of Tibet's eastern region. Even the medieval culture of Tibet was not immune to the perils of spiritual materialism. His teachers had trained him in recognizing the wiliness of ego and in avoiding seduction into seemingly beneficial activities that are really just mundane material pursuits in sacred garments. Here was a teacher who clearly understood the materialistic dilemma of the spiritual path, one who had been steeped and trained in the ancient wisdom of the past—and who could also understand the nuances of modern-day Western-style spiritual blockage. The teachings in this book represent a milestone in the introduction of buddhadharma into American culture.

In part because of the playfulness with which my father taught his young American students, Cutting Through Spiritual Materialism has become a classic. For those in the audience who were experimenting with rejecting society in order to pursue an idealistic, transcendental path, his teachings shed new light on working with themselves in the context of their own country, family, and culture. As an enthusiastic newcomer to the West and a spiritual elder as well, he was able to introduce to them the basic workability of their own situation as part of the spiritual path. Rejecting everything was not the solution. Training one's mind, body, and speech in accordance with the truth would bring about the understanding and wisdom that produces peace. Many of those students followed his advice, continuing on their spiritual journeys and at the same time becoming parents, teachers, business people, and even dharma teachers. These people have now become the elders for a new generation of inquisitive minds.

Even though the message of this book was addressed to a particular group at a particular time in history, it is not only for that generation. These teachings will never be dated or pigeonholed. In the last thirty years, in our continuing pursuit of whatever will distract us from the truth of pain and suffering, we have become even more materialistic. In the spiritual realm, there are now even more paths and possibilities to explore than when this book was first published—not just the classic spiritual disciplines, but also many hybrids. This book continues to have the power to sharpen our awareness of spiritual materialism. It deserves our careful attention, as its message is more applicable now than ever.

SAKYONG MIPHAM RINPOCHE
October 2001

Introduction

THE FOLLOWING SERIES of talks was given in Boulder, Colorado
in the fall of 1970 and the spring of 1971. At that time we were just
forming Karma Dzong, our meditation center in Boulder. Although
most of my students were sincere in their aspiration to walk on the spiritual path, they brought to it a great deal of confusion, misunderstanding,
and expectation. Therefore, I found it necessary to present to my students an overview of the path and some warnings as to the dangers
along that path.

It now seems that publishing these talks may be helpful to those who
have become interested in spiritual disciplines. Walking the spiritual path
properly is a very subtle process; it is not something to jump into naively. There are numerous sidetracks which lead to a distorted, ego-
centered version of spirituality; we can deceive ourselves into thinking
we are developing spiritually when instead we are strengthening our
egocentricity through spiritual techniques. This fundamental distortion
may be referred to as *spiritual materialism*.

These talks first discuss the various ways in which people involve
themselves with spiritual materialism, the many forms of self-deception
into which aspirants may fall. After this tour of the sidetracks along the
way, we discuss the broad outlines of the true spiritual path.

The approach presented here is a classical Buddhist one—not in a
formal sense, but in the sense of presenting the heart of the Buddhist
approach to spirituality. Although the Buddhist way is not theistic, it
does not contradict the theistic disciplines. Rather the differences between the ways are a matter of emphasis and method. The basic problems of spiritual materialism are common to all spiritual disciplines. The

7

Buddhist approach begins with our confusion and suffering and works toward the unraveling of their origin. The theistic approach begins with the richness of God and works toward raising consciousness so as to experience God's presence. But since the obstacles to relating with God are our confusions and negativities, the theistic approach must also deal with them. Spiritual pride, for example, is as much a problem in theistic disciplines as in Buddhism.

According to the Buddhist tradition, the spiritual path is the process of cutting through our confusion, of uncovering the awakened state of mind. When the awakened state of mind is crowded in by ego and its attendant paranoia, it takes on the character of an underlying instinct. So it is not a matter of building up the awakened state of mind, but rather of burning out the confusions which obstruct it. In the process of burning out these confusions, we discover enlightenment. If the process were otherwise, the awakened state of mind would be a product, dependent upon cause and effect and therefore liable to dissolution. Anything which is created must, sooner or later, die. If enlightenment were created in such a way, there would always be the possibility of ego reasserting itself, causing a return to the confused state. Enlightenment is permanent because we have not produced it; we have merely discovered it. In the Buddhist tradition the analogy of the sun appearing from behind the clouds is often used to explain the discovery of enlightenment. In meditation practice we clear away the confusion of ego in order to glimpse the awakened state. The absence of ignorance, of being crowded in, of paranoia, opens up a tremendous view of life. One discovers a different way of being.

The heart of the confusion is that man has a sense of self which seems to him to be continuous and solid. When a thought or emotion or event occurs, there is a sense of someone being conscious of what is happening. You sense that *you* are reading these words. This sense of self is actually a transitory, discontinuous event, which in our confusion seems to be quite solid and continuous. Since we take our confused view as being real, we struggle to maintain and enhance this solid self. We try to feed it pleasures and shield it from pain. Experience continually threatens to reveal our transitoriness to us, so we continually struggle to cover up any possibility of discovering our real condition. "But," we might ask, "if our real condition is an awakened state, why are we so busy trying to avoid becoming aware of it?" It is because we have become so absorbed in our confused view of the world, that we consider it real, the only possible world. This struggle to maintain the sense of a solid, continuous self is the action of ego.

Ego, however, is only partially successful in shielding us from pain. It is the dissatisfaction which accompanies ego's struggle that inspires us to examine what we are doing. Since there are always gaps in our self-consciousness, some insight is possible.

An interesting metaphor used in Tibetan Buddhism to describe the functioning of ego is that of the "three lords of materialism": the "lord of form," the "lord of speech," and the "lord of mind." In the discussion of the three lords which follows, the words "materialism" and "neurotic" refer to the action of ego.

The lord of form refers to the neurotic pursuit of physical comfort, security, and pleasure. Our highly organized and technological society reflects our preoccupation with manipulating physical surroundings so as to shield ourselves from the irritations of the raw, rugged, unpredictable aspects of life. Push-button elevators, pre-packaged meat, air conditioning, flush toilets, private funerals, retirement programs, mass production, weather satellites, bulldozers, fluorescent lighting, nine-to-five jobs, television—all are attempts to create a manageable, safe, predictable, pleasurable world.

The lord of form does not signify the physically rich and secure life-situations we create per se. Rather it refers to the neurotic preoccupation that drives us to create them, to try to control nature. It is ego's ambition to secure and entertain itself, trying to avoid all irritation. So we cling to our pleasures and possessions; we fear change or force change; we try to create a nest or playground.

The lord of speech refers to the use of intellect in relating to our world. We adopt sets of categories which serve as handles, as ways of managing phenomena. The most fully developed products of this tendency are ideologies, the systems of ideas that rationalize, justify, and sanctify our lives. Nationalism, communism, existentialism, Christianity, Buddhism—all provide us with identities, rules of action, and interpretations of how and why things happen as they do.

Again, the use of intellect is not in itself the lord of speech. The lord of speech refers to the inclination on the part of ego to interpret anything that is threatening or irritating in such a way as to neutralize the threat or turn it into something "positive" from ego's point of view. The lord of speech refers to the use of concepts as filters to screen us from a direct perception of what is. The concepts are taken too seriously; they are used as tools to solidify our world and ourselves. If a world of nameable things exists, then "I" as one of the nameable things exists as well. We wish not to leave any room for threatening doubt, uncertainty, or confusion.

The lord of mind refers to the effort of consciousness to maintain awareness of itself. The lord of mind rules when we use spiritual and psychological disciplines as the means of maintaining our self-consciousness, of holding on to our sense of self. Drugs, yoga, prayer, meditation, trances, various psychotherapies—all can be used in this way.

Ego is able to convert everything to its own use, even spirituality. For example, if you have learned of a particularly beneficial meditation technique of spiritual practice, then ego's attitude is, first to regard it as an object of fascination and, second to examine it. Finally, since ego is seemingly solid and cannot really absorb anything, it can only mimic. Thus ego tries to examine and imitate the practice of meditation and the meditative way of life. When we have learned all the tricks and answers of the spiritual game, we automatically try to imitate spirituality, since real involvement would require the complete elimination of ego, and actually the last thing we want to do is to give up the ego completely. However, we cannot experience that which we are trying to imitate; we can only find some area within the bounds of ego that seems to be the same thing. Ego translates everything in terms of its own state of health, its own inherent qualities. It feels a sense of great accomplishment and excitement at having been able to create such a pattern. At last it has created a tangible accomplishment, a confirmation of its own individuality.

If we become successful at maintaining our self-consciousness through spiritual techniques, then genuine spiritual development is highly unlikely. Our mental habits become so strong as to be hard to penetrate. We may even go so far as to achieve the totally demonic state of complete "Egohood."

Even though the lord of mind is the most powerful in subverting spirituality, still the other two lords can also rule the spiritual practice. Retreat to nature, isolation, simplicity, quiet, high people—all can be ways of shielding oneself from irritation, all can be expressions of the lord of form. Or perhaps religion may provide us with a rationalization for creating a secure nest, a simple but comfortable home, for acquiring an amiable mate, and a stable, easy job.

The lord of speech is involved in spiritual practice as well. In following a spiritual path we may substitute a new religious ideology for our former beliefs, but continue to use it in the old neurotic way. Regardless of how sublime our ideas may be, if we take them too seriously and use them to maintain our ego, we are still being ruled by the lord of speech.

Most of us, if we examine our actions, would probably agree that we are ruled by one or more of the three lords. "But," we might ask, "so what? This is simply a description of the human condition. Yes, we know that our technology cannot shield us from war, crime, illness, economic insecurity, laborious work, old age, and death; nor can our ideologies shield us from doubt, uncertainty, confusion, and disorientation; nor can our therapies protect us from the dissolution of the high states of consciousness that we may temporarily achieve and the disillusionment and anguish that follow. But what else are we to do? The three lords seem too powerful to overthrow, and we don't know what to replace them with."

The Buddha, troubled by these questions, examined the process by which the three lords rule. He questioned why our minds follow them and whether there is another way. He discovered that the three lords seduce us by creating a fundamental myth: that we are solid beings. But ultimately the myth is false, a huge hoax, a gigantic fraud, and it is the root of our suffering. In order to make this discovery he had to break through very elaborate defenses erected by the three lords to prevent their subjects from discovering the fundamental deception which is the source of their power. We cannot in any way free ourselves from the domination of the three lords unless we too cut through, layer by layer, the elaborate defenses of these lords.

The lords' defenses are created out of the material of our minds. This material of mind is used by the lords in such a way as to maintain the basic myth of solidity. In order to see for ourselves how this process works we must examine our own experience. "But how," we might ask, "are we to conduct the examination? What method or tool are we to use?" The method that the Buddha discovered is meditation. He discovered that struggling to find answers did not work. It was only when there were gaps in his struggle that insights came to him. He began to realize that there was a sane, awake quality within him which manifested itself only in the absence of struggle. So the practice of meditation involves "letting be."

There have been a number of misconceptions regarding meditation. Some people regard it as a trancelike state of mind. Others think of it in terms of training, in the sense of mental gymnastics. But meditation is neither of these, although it does involve dealing with neurotic states of mind. The neurotic state of mind is not difficult or impossible to deal with. It has energy, speed, and a certain pattern. The practice of meditation involves *letting be*—trying to go with the pattern, trying to go with the energy and the speed. In this way we learn now to deal with these factors, how to relate with them, not in the sense of causing them to mature in the way we would like, but in the sense of knowing them for what they are and working with their pattern.

There is a story regarding the Buddha which recounts how he once gave teaching to a famous sitar player who wanted to study meditation. The musician asked, "Should I control my mind or should I completely let go?" The Buddha answered, "Since you are a great musician, tell me how you would tune the strings of your instrument." The musician said, "I would make them not too tight and not too loose." "Likewise," said the Buddha, "in your meditation practice you should not impose anything too forcefully on your mind, nor should you let it wander." That is the teaching of letting the mind *be* in a very open way, of feeling the flow of energy without trying to subdue it and without letting it get out of control, of going with the energy pattern of mind. This is meditation practice.

Such practice is necessary generally because our thinking pattern, our conceptualized way of conducting our life in the world, is either too manipulative, imposing itself upon the world, or else runs completely wild and uncontrolled. Therefore, our meditation practice must begin with ego's outermost layer, the discursive thoughts which continually run through our minds, our mental gossip. The lords use discursive thought as their first line of defense, as the pawns in their effort to deceive us. The more we generate thoughts, the busier we are mentally and the more convinced we are of our existence. So the lords are constantly trying to activate these thoughts, trying to create a constant overlapping of thoughts so that nothing can be seen beyond them. In true meditation there is no ambition to stir up thoughts, nor is there an ambition to suppress them. They are just allowed to occur spontaneously and become an expression of basic sanity. They become the expression of the precision and the clarity of the awakened state of mind.

If the strategy of continually creating overlapping thoughts is penetrated, then the lords stir up emotions to distract us. The exciting, colorful, dramatic quality of the emotions captures our attention as if we were watching an absorbing film show. In the practice of meditation we neither encourage emotions nor repress them. By seeing them clearly, by allowing them to be as they are, we no longer permit them to serve as a means of entertaining and distracting us. Thus they become the inexhaustible energy which fulfills egoless action.

In the absence of thoughts and emotions the lords bring up a still more powerful weapon, concepts. Labeling phenomena creates a feeling of a solid definite world of "things." Such a solid world reassures us that we are a solid, continuous thing as well. The world exists, therefore I, the perceiver of the world, exist. Meditation involves seeing the transparency of concepts, so that labeling no longer serves as a way of solidifying our world and our image of self. Labeling becomes simply the act of discrimination. The lords have still further defense mechanisms, but it would be too complicated to discuss them in this context.

By the examination of his own thoughts, emotions, concepts, and the other activities of mind, the Buddha discovered that there is no need to struggle to prove our existence, that we need not be subject to the rule of the three lords of materialism. There is no need to struggle to be free; the absence of struggle is in itself freedom. This egoless state is the attainment of buddhahood. The process of transforming the material of mind from expressions of ego's ambition into expressions of basic sanity and enlightenment through the practice of meditation—this might be said to be the true spiritual path.

Sengge Dradrok. The aspect of Padmasambhava, who teaches with the lion's roar that subdues the heretics of hope and fear.
DRAWING BY GLEN EDDY.

Spiritual Materialism

W E   H A V E   C O M E   H E R E to learn about spirituality. I trust the genuine quality of this search but we must question its nature. The problem is that ego can convert anything to its own use, even spirituality. Ego is constantly attempting to acquire and apply the teachings of spirituality for its own benefit. The teachings are treated as an external thing, external to "me," a philosophy which we try to imitate. We do not actually want to identify with or become the teachings. So if our teacher speaks of renunciation of ego, we attempt to mimic renunciation of ego. We go through the motions, make the appropriate gestures, but we really do not want to sacrifice any part of our way of life. We become skillful actors, and while playing deaf and dumb to the real meaning of the teachings, we find some comfort in pretending to follow the path.

Whenever we begin to feel any discrepancy or conflict between our actions and the teachings, we immediately interpret the situation in such a way that the conflict is smoothed over. The interpreter is ego in the role of spiritual adviser. The situation is like that of a country where church and state are separate. If the policy of the state is foreign to the teachings of the church, then the automatic reaction of the king is to go to the head of the church, his spiritual adviser, and ask his blessing. The head of the church then works out some justification and gives the policy his blessing under the pretense that the king is the protector of the faith. In an individual's mind, it works out very neatly that way, ego being both king and head of the church.

This rationalization of the spiritual path and one's actions must be cut through if true spirituality is to be realized. However, such rationalizing is not easy to deal with because everything is seen through the filter of ego's philosophy and logic, making all appear neat, precise, and very logical. We attempt to find a self-justifying answer for every question. In order to reassure ourselves, we work to fit into our intellectual scheme every aspect of our lives which might be confusing. And our effort is so serious and solemn, so straightforward and sincere, that it is difficult to be suspicious of it. We always trust the "integrity" of our spiritual adviser.

It does not matter what we use to achieve self-justification: the wisdom of sacred books, diagrams or charts, mathematical calculations, esoteric formulae, fundamentalist religion, depth psychology, or any other mechanism. Whenever we begin to evaluate, deciding that we should or should not do this or that, then we have already associated our practice or our knowledge with categories, one pitted against the other, and that is spiritual materialism, the false spirituality of our spiritual adviser. Whenever we have a dualistic notion such as, "I am doing this because I want to achieve a particular state of consciousness, a particular state of being," then automatically we separate ourselves from the reality of what we are.

If we ask ourselves, "What is wrong with evaluating, with taking sides?", the answer is that, when we formulate a secondary judgment, "I should be doing this and should avoid doing that," then we have achieved a level of complication which takes us a long way from the basic simplicity of what we are. The simplicity of meditation means just experiencing the ape instinct of ego. If anything more than this is laid onto our psychology, then it becomes a very heavy, thick mask, a suit of armor.

It is important to see that the main point of any spiritual practice is to step out of the bureaucracy of ego. This means stepping out of ego's constant desire for a higher, more spiritual, more transcendental version of knowledge, religion, virtue, judgment, comfort, or whatever it is that the particular ego is seeking. One must step out of spiritual materialism. If we do not step out of spiritual materialism, if we in fact practice it, then we may eventually find ourselves possessed of a huge collection of spiritual paths. We may feel these spiritual collections to be very precious. We have studied so much. We may have studied Western philosophy or Oriental philosophy, practiced yoga, or perhaps have studied under dozens of great masters. We have achieved and we have learned. We believe that we have accumulated a hoard of knowledge. And yet, having gone through all this, there is still something to give up. It is extremely mysterious! How could this happen? Impossible! But unfortunately it is so. Our vast collections of knowledge and experience are just part of ego's display, part of the grandiose quality of ego. We display them to the world and, in so doing, reassure ourselves that we exist, safe and secure, as "spiritual" people.

But we have simply created a shop, an antique shop. We could be specializing in Oriental antiques or medieval Christian antiques or antiques from some other civilization or time, but we are, nonetheless, running a shop. Before we filled our shop with so many things the room was beautiful: whitewashed walls and a very simple floor with a bright lamp burning in the ceiling. There was one object of art in the middle of the room, and it was beautiful. Everyone who came appreciated its beauty, including ourselves.

But we were not satisfied and we thought, "Since this one object makes my room so beautiful, if I get more antiques, my room will be even more beautiful." So we began to collect, and the end result was chaos.

We searched the world over for beautiful objects—India, Japan, many different countries. And each time we found an antique, because we were dealing with only one object at a time, we saw it as beautiful and thought it would be beautiful in our shop. But when we brought the object home and put it there, it became just another addition to our junky collection. The beauty of the object did not radiate out anymore, because it was surrounded by so many other beautiful things. It did not mean anything anymore. Instead of a room full of beautiful antiques we created a junk shop!

Proper shopping does not entail collecting a lot of information or beauty, but it involves fully appreciating each individual object. This is very important. If you really appreciate an object of beauty, then you completely identify with it and forget yourself. It is like seeing a very interesting, fascinating movie and forgetting that you are the audience. At that moment there is no world; your whole being is that scene of that movie. It is that kind of identification, complete involvement with one thing. Did we actually taste it and chew it and swallow it properly, that one object of beauty, that one spiritual teaching? Or did we merely regard it as a part of our vast and growing collection?

I place so much emphasis on this point because I know that all of us have come to the teachings and practice of meditation not to make a lot of money, but because we genuinely want to learn, want to develop ourselves. But, if we regard knowledge as an antique, as "ancient wisdom" to be collected, then we are on the wrong path.

As far as the lineage of teachers is concerned, knowledge is not handed down like an antique. Rather, one teacher experiences the truth of the teachings, and he hands it down as inspiration to his student. That inspiration awakens the student, as his teacher was awakened before him. Then the student hands down the teachings to another student and so the process goes. The teachings are always up-to-date. They are not "ancient wisdom," an old legend. The teachings are not passed along as information, handed down as a grandfather tells traditional folk tales to his grandchildren. It does not work that way. It is a real experience.

There is a saying in the Tibetan scriptures: "Knowledge must be burned, hammered, and beaten like pure gold. Then one can wear it as an ornament." So when you receive spiritual instruction from the hands of another, you do not take it uncritically, but you burn it, you hammer it, you beat it, until the bright, dignified color of gold appears. Then you craft it into an ornament, whatever design you like, and you put it on. Therefore, dharma is applicable to every age, to every person; it has a living quality. It is not enough to imitate your master or guru; you are not trying to become a replica of your teacher. The teachings are an individual personal experience, right down to the present holder of the doctrine.

Perhaps many of my readers are familiar with the stories of Naropa and Tilopa and Marpa and Milarepa and Gampopa and the other teachers of the Kagyü lineage. It was a living experience for them, and it is a living experience for the present holders of the lineage. Only the details of their life-situations are different. The teachings have the quality of warm, fresh baked bread; the bread is still warm and hot and fresh. Each baker must apply the general knowledge of how to make bread to his particular dough and oven. Then he must personally experience the freshness of this bread and must cut it fresh and eat it warm. He must make the teachings his own and then must practice them. It is a very living process. There is no deception in terms of collecting knowledge. We must work with our individual experiences. When we become confused, we cannot turn back to our collection of knowledge and try to find some confirmation or consolation: "The teacher and the whole teaching is on my side." The spiritual path does not go that way. It is a lonely, individual path.

Q: Do you think spiritual materialism is a particularly American problem?

A: Whenever teachings come to a country from abroad, the problem of spiritual materialism is intensified. At the moment America is, without any doubt, fertile ground ready for the teachings. And because America is so fertile, seeking spirituality, it is possible for America to inspire charlatans. Charlatans would not choose to be charlatans unless they were inspired to do so. Otherwise, they would be bank robbers or bandits, inasmuch as they want to make money and become famous. Because America is looking so hard for spirituality, religion becomes an easy way to make money and achieve fame. So we see charlatans in the role of student, *chela,* as well as in the role of guru. I think America at this particular time is a very interesting ground.

Q: Have you accepted any spiritual master as a guru, any particular living spiritual master?

A: At present there is no one. I left my gurus and teachers behind in Tibet, physically, but the teachings stay with me and continue.

Q: So who are you following, more or less?

A: Situations are the voice of my guru, the presence of my guru.

Q: After Shakyamuni Buddha attained enlightenment, was there some trace of ego left in him so that he could carry on his teachings?

A: The teaching just happened. He did not have the desire to teach or not to teach. He spent seven weeks sitting under the shade of a tree and walking along the bank of a river. Then someone just happened along and he began to speak. One has no choice; you are there, an open person. Then the situation presents itself and teaching happens. That is what is called "buddha activity."

Q: It is difficult not to be acquisitive about spirituality. Is this desire for acquisitions something that is shed along the way?

A: You should let the first impulse die down. Your first impulse towards spirituality might put you into some particular spiritual scene;

but if you work with that impulse, then the impulse gradually dies down and at some stage becomes tedious, monotonous. This is a useful message. You see, it is essential to relate to yourself, to your own experience, *really*. If one does not relate to oneself, then the spiritual path becomes dangerous, becomes purely external entertainment, rather than an organic personal experience.

Q: If you decide to seek your way out of ignorance, you can almost definitely assume that anything you do that feels good will be beneficial to the ego and actually blocking the path. Anything that seems right to you will be wrong, anything that doesn't turn you upside down will bury you. Is there any way out of this?

A: If you perform some act which is seemingly right, it does not mean that it is wrong, for the very reason that wrong and right are out of the picture altogether. You are not working on any side, neither the "good" side nor the "bad" side, but you are working with the totality of the whole, beyond "this" and "that." I would say there is complete action. There is no partial act, but whatever we do in connection with good and bad seems to be a partial act.

Q: If you are feeling very confused and trying to work your way out of the confusion, it would seem that you are trying too hard. But if you do not try at all, then are we to understand that we are fooling ourselves?

A: Yes, but that does not mean that one has to live by the extremes of trying too hard or not trying at all. One has to work with a kind of "middle way," a complete state of "being as you are." We could describe this with a lot of words, but one really has to do it. If you really start living the middle way, then you will see it, you will find it. You must allow yourself to trust yourself, to trust in your own intelligence. We are tremendous people; we have tremendous things in us. We simply have to let ourselves be. External aid cannot help. If you are not willing to let yourself grow, then you fall into the self-destructive process of confusion. It is self-destruction rather than destruction by someone else. That is why it is effective; because it is *self*-destruction.

Q: What is faith? Is it useful?

A: Faith could be simple-minded, trusting, blind faith, or it could be definite confidence which cannot be destroyed. Blind faith has no inspiration. It is very naive. It is not creative, though not exactly destructive. It is not creative because your faith and yourself have never made any connection, any communication. You just blindly accepted the whole belief, very naively.

In the case of faith as confidence, there is a living reason to be confident. You do not expect that there will be a prefabricated solution mysteriously presented to you. You work with existing situations without fear, without any doubt about involving yourself. This approach is extremely creative and positive. If you have definite confidence, you are so sure of yourself that you do not have to check yourself. It is *absolute* confidence, real understanding of what is going on now, therefore you do not hesitate to follow other paths or deal in whatever way is necessary with each new situation.

Q: What guides you on the path?
A: Actually, there does not seem to be any particular guidance. In fact, if someone is guiding you, that is suspicious, because you are relying on something external. Being fully what you are in yourself becomes guidance, but not in the sense of vanguard, because you do not have a guide to follow. You do not have to follow someone's tail, but you sail along. In other words, the guide does not walk ahead of you, but walks with you.

Q: Could you say something more about the way in which meditation short-circuits the protective mechanisms of the ego?
A: The protective mechanism of ego involves checking oneself, which is an unnecessary kind of self-observance. Meditation is not based on meditating *on* a particular subject by checking oneself; but meditation is complete identification with whatever techniques you are employing. Therefore there will be no effort to secure oneself in the practice of meditation.

Q: I seem to be living in a spiritual junkyard. How can I make it into a simple room with one beautiful object?
A: In order to develop an appreciation of your collection you have to start with one item. One has to find a stepping-stone, a source of inspiration. Perhaps you would not have to go through the rest of the items in your collection if you studied just one piece of material. That one piece

of material could be a signpost that you managed to confiscate in New York City, it could be as insignificant as that. But one must start with one thing, see its simplicity, the rugged quality of this piece of junk or this beautiful antique. If we could manage to start with just one thing, then that would be the equivalent of having one object in an empty room. I think it is a question of finding a stepping-stone. Because we have so many possessions in our collection, a large part of the problem is that we do not know where to begin. One has to allow one's instinct to determine which will be the first thing to pick up.

Q: Why do you think that people are so protective of their egos? Why is it so hard to let go of one's ego?

A: People are afraid of the emptiness of space, or the absence of company, the absence of a shadow. It could be a terrifying experience to have no one to relate to, nothing to relate with. The idea of it can be extremely frightening, though not the real experience. It is generally a fear of space, a fear that we will not be able to anchor ourselves to any solid ground, that we will lose our identity as a fixed and solid and definite thing. This could be very threatening.

Surrendering

AT THIS POINT we may have come to the conclusion that we should drop the whole game of spiritual materialism; that is, we should give up trying to defend and improve ourselves. We may have glimpsed that our struggle is futile and may wish to surrender, to completely abandon our efforts to defend ourselves. But how many of us could actually do this? It is not as simple and easy as we might think. To what degree could we really let go and be open? At what point would we become defensive?

In this lecture we will discuss surrendering, particularly in terms of the relationship between work on the neurotic state of mind and work with a personal guru or teacher. Surrendering to the "guru" could mean opening our minds to life-situations as well as to an individual teacher. However, if our lifestyle and inspiration are working toward an unfolding of the mind, then we will almost certainly find a personal guru as well. So in the next few talks we will emphasize relating to a personal teacher.

One of the difficulties in surrendering to a guru is our preconceptions regarding him and our expectations of what will happen with him. We are preoccupied with ideas of what we would like to experience with our teacher: "I would like to see this; that would be the best way to see it; I would like to experience this particular situation, because it is in exact accordance with my expectation and fascination."

So we try to fit things into pigeonholes, try to fit the situation to our expectations, and we cannot surrender any part of our anticipation at all. If we search for a guru or teacher, we expect him to be saintly, peaceful, quiet, a simple and yet wise man. When we find that he does not match our expectations, then we begin to be disappointed, we begin to doubt.

In order to establish a real teacher-student relationship it is necessary for us to give up all our preconceptions regarding that relationship and the condition of opening and surrender. Surrender means opening oneself completely, trying to get beyond fascination and expectation.

Surrender also means acknowledging the raw, rugged, clumsy, and shocking qualities of one's ego, acknowledging them and surrendering them as well. Generally, we find it very difficult to give out and surrender our raw and rugged qualities of ego. Although we may hate ourselves, at the same time we find our self-hatred a kind of occupation. In spite of the fact that we may dislike what we are and find that self-condemnation painful, still we cannot give it up completely. If we begin to give up our self-criticism, then we may feel that we are losing our occupation, as though someone were taking away our job. We would have no further occupation if we were to surrender everything; there would be nothing to hold on to. Self-evaluation and self-criticism are, basically, neurotic tendencies which derive from our not having enough confidence in ourselves, confidence in the sense of seeing what we are, knowing what we are, knowing that we can afford to open. We *can* afford to surrender that raw and rugged neurotic quality of self and step out of fascination, step out of preconceived ideas.

We must surrender our hopes and expectations, as well as our fears, and march directly into disappointment, work with disappointment, go into it, and make it our way of life, which is a very hard thing to do. Disappointment is a good sign of basic intelligence. It cannot be compared to anything else: it is so sharp, precise, obvious, and direct. If we can open, then we suddenly begin to see that our expectations are irrelevant compared with the reality of the situations we are facing. This automatically brings a feeling of disappointment.

Disappointment is the best chariot to use on the path of the dharma. It does not confirm the existence of our ego and its dreams. However, if we are involved with spiritual materialism, if we regard spirituality as a part of our accumulation of learning and virtue, if spirituality becomes a way of building ourselves up, then of course the whole process of surrendering is completely distorted. If we regard spirituality as a way of making ourselves comfortable, then whenever we experience something unpleasant, a disappointment, we try to rationalize it: "Of course this must be an act of wisdom on the part of the guru, because I know, I'm quite certain the guru doesn't do harmful things. Guruji is a perfect being and whatever Guruji does is right. Whatever Guruji does is for me, because he is on my side. So I can afford to open. I can safely surrender. I know that I am treading on the right path." Something is not quite right about such an attitude. It is, at best, simple-minded and naive. We are captivated by the awesome, inspiring, dignified, and colorful aspect of "Guruji." We dare not contemplate any other way. We develop the conviction that whatever we experience is part of our spiritual development. "I've made it, I have experienced it, I am a self-made person, and I know everything, roughly, because I've read books and they confirm my beliefs, my rightness, my ideas. Everything coincides."

We can hold back in still another way, not really surrendering because we feel that we are very genteel, sophisticated, and dignified people. "Surely we can't give ourselves to this dirty, ordinary street-scene of reality." We have the feeling that every step of the path we tread should be a lotus petal, and we develop a logic that interprets whatever happens to us accordingly. If we fall, we create a soft landing which prevents sudden shock. Surrendering does not involve preparing for a soft landing; it means just landing on hard, ordinary ground, on rocky, wild countryside. Once we open ourselves, then we land on *what is*.

Traditionally, surrendering is symbolized by such practices as prostration, which is the act of falling on the ground in a gesture of surrender. At the same time we open psychologically and surrender completely by identifying ourselves with the lowest of the low, acknowledging our raw and rugged quality. There is nothing that we fear to lose once we identify ourselves with the lowest of the low. By doing so, we prepare ourselves to be an empty vessel, ready to receive the teachings.

In the Buddhist tradition, there is this basic formula: "I take refuge in the Buddha, I take refuge in the dharma, I take refuge in the sangha." I take refuge in the Buddha as the example of surrender, the example of acknowledging negativity as a part of our makeup and opening to it. I take refuge in the dharma—dharma, the "law of existence," life as it is. I am willing to open my eyes to the circumstances of life as they are. I am not willing to view them as spiritual or mystical, but I am willing to see the situations of life as they really are. I take refuge in the sangha. *Sangha* means "community of people on the spiritual path," "companions." I am willing to share my experience of the whole environment of life with my fellow pilgrims, my fellow searchers, those who walk with me; but I am not willing to lean on them in order to gain support. I am only willing to walk along with them. There is a very dangerous tendency to lean on one another as we tread the path. If a group of people leans one upon the other, then if one should happen to fall down, everyone falls down. So we do not lean on anyone else. We just walk with each other, side by side, shoulder to shoulder, working with each other, going with each other. This approach to surrendering, this idea of taking refuge, is very profound.

The wrong way to take refuge involves seeking shelter—worshiping mountains, sun gods, moon gods, deities of any kind simply because they would seem to be greater than we. This kind of refuge-taking is similar to the response of the little child who says, "If you beat me, I'll tell my mommy," thinking that his mother is a great, archetypically powerful person. If he is attacked, his automatic recourse is to his mother, an invincible and all-knowing, all-powerful personality. The child believes his mother can protect him, in fact that she is the only person who can save him. Taking refuge in a mother- or father-principle is truly self-defeating; the refuge-seeker has no real basic strength at all, no true inspiration. He is constantly busy assessing greater and smaller powers. If we are small, then someone greater can crush us. We seek refuge because we cannot afford to be small and without protection. We tend to be apologetic: "I am such a small thing, but I acknowledge your great quality. I would like to worship and join your greatness, so will you please protect me?"

Surrendering is not a question of being low and stupid, nor of wanting to be elevated and profound. It has nothing to do with levels and evaluation. Instead, we surrender because we would like to communicate with the world "as it is." We do not have to classify ourselves as learners or ignorant people. We know where we stand, therefore we make the gesture of surrendering, of opening, which means communication, link, direct communication with the object of our surrendering. We are not embarrassed about our rich collection of raw, rugged, beautiful, and clean qualities. We present everything to the object of our surrendering. The basic act of surrender does not involve the worship of an external power. Rather it means working together with inspiration, so that one becomes an open vessel into which knowledge can be poured.

Thus openness and surrendering are the necessary preparation for working with a spiritual friend. We acknowledge our fundamental richness rather than bemoan the imagined poverty of our being. We know we are worthy to receive the teachings, worthy of relating ourselves to the wealth of the opportunities for learning.

The Guru

COMING TO THE STUDY of spirituality we are faced with the problem of our relationship with a teacher, lama, guru, whatever we
call the person we suppose will give us spiritual understanding. These
words, especially the term *guru*, have acquired meanings and associations in the West which are misleading and which generally add to the
confusion around the issue of what it means to study with a spiritual
teacher. This is not to say that people in the East understand how to
relate to a guru while Westerners do not; the problem is universal. People always come to the study of spirituality with some ideas already fixed
in their minds of what it is they are going to get and how to deal with
the person from whom they think they will get it. The very notion that
we will *get* something from a guru—happiness, peace of mind, wisdom,
whatever it is we seek—is one of the most difficult preconceptions of all.
So I think it would be helpful to examine the way in which some famous
students dealt with the problems of how to relate to spirituality and a
spiritual teacher. Perhaps these examples will have some relevance for
our own individual search.

One of the most renowned Tibetan masters and also one of the main
gurus of the Kagyü lineage, of which I am a member, was Marpa, student of the Indian teacher Naropa and guru to Milarepa, his most famous
spiritual son. Marpa is an example of someone who was on his way to
becoming a successful self-made man. He was born into a farming family, but as a youth he became ambitious and chose scholarship and the
priesthood as his route to prominence. We can imagine what tremendous effort and determination it must have taken for the son of a farmer
to raise himself to the position of priest in his local religious tradition.

Marpa, founder of the Kagyü lineage.
DRAWING BY SHERAB PALDEN BERU.

There were only a few ways for such a man to achieve any kind of position in tenth-century Tibet—as a merchant, a bandit, or especially as a priest. Joining the local clergy at that time was roughly equivalent to becoming a doctor, lawyer, and college professor, all rolled into one.

Marpa began by studying Tibetan, Sanskrit, several other languages, and the spoken language of India. After about three years of such study he was proficient enough to being earning money as a scholar, and with this money he financed his religious study, eventually becoming a Buddhist priest of sorts. Such a position brought with it a certain degree of local prominence, but Marpa was more ambitious and so, although he was married by now and had a family, he continued to save his earnings until he had amassed a large amount of gold.

At this point Marpa announced to his relatives his intentions to travel to India to collect more teachings. India at this time was the world center for Buddhist studies, home of Nalanda University and the greatest Buddhist sages and scholars. It was Marpa's intention to study and collect texts unknown in Tibet, bring them home, and translate them, thus establishing himself as a great scholar-translator. The journey to India was at that time and until fairly recently a long and dangerous one, and Marpa's family and elders tried to dissuade him from it. But he was determined and so set out accompanied by a friend and fellow scholar.

After a difficult journey of some months they crossed the Himalayas in India and proceeded to Bengal where they went their separate ways. Both men were well qualified in the study of language and religion, and so they decided to search for their own teachers, to suit their own tastes. Before parting they agreed to meet again for the journey home.

While he was traveling through Nepal, Marpa had happened to hear of the teacher Naropa, a man of enormous fame. Naropa had been abbot of Nalanda University, perhaps the greatest center for Buddhist studies the world has ever known. At the height of his career, feeling that he understood the sense but not the real meaning of the teachings, he abandoned his post and set out in search of a guru. For twelve years he endured terrific hardship at the hands of his teacher Tilopa, until finally he achieved realization. By the time Marpa heard of him, he was reputed to be one of the greatest Buddhist saints ever to have lived. Naturally Marpa set out to find him.

Eventually Marpa found Naropa living in poverty in a simple house in the forests of Bengal. He had expected to find so great a teacher living in the midst of a highly evolved religious setting of some sort, and so he was somewhat disappointed. However, he was a bit confused by the strangeness of a foreign country and willing to make some allowances, thinking that perhaps this was the way Indian teachers lived. Also, his appreciation of Naropa's fame outweighed his disappointment, and so he gave Naropa most of his gold and asked for teachings. He explained that he was a married man, a priest, scholar, and farmer from Tibet, and that he was not willing to give up this life he had made for himself, but that he wanted to collect teachings to take back to Tibet to translate in order to earn more money. Naropa agreed to Marpa's requests quite easily, gave Marpa instruction, and everything went smoothly.

After some time Marpa decided that he had collected enough teachings to suit his purposes and prepared to return home. He proceeded to an inn in a large town where he rejoined his traveling companion, and the two sat down to compare the results of their efforts. When his friend saw what Marpa had collected, he laughed and said, "What you have here is worthless! We already have those teachings in Tibet. You must have found something more exciting and rare. I found fantastic teachings which I received from very great masters."

Marpa, of course, was extremely frustrated and upset, having come such a long way and with so much difficulty and expense, so he decided to return to Naropa and try once more. When he arrived at Naropa's hut and asked for more rare and exotic and advanced teachings, to his surprise Naropa told him, "I'm sorry, but you can't receive these teachings from me. You will have to go and receive these from someone else, a man named Kukuripa. The journey is difficult, especially so because Kukuripa lives on an island in the middle of a lake of poison. But he is the one you will have to see if you want these teachings."

By this time Marpa was becoming desperate, so he decided to try the journey. Besides, if Kukuripa had teachings which even the great Naropa could not give him and, in addition, lived in the middle of a poisonous lake, then he must be quite an extraordinary teacher, a great mystic.

So Marpa made the journey and managed to cross the lake to the island where he began to look for Kukuripa. There he found an old Indian man living in filth in the midst of hundreds of female dogs. The situation was outlandish, to say the least, but Marpa nevertheless tried to speak to Kukuripa. All he got was gibberish. Kukuripa seemed to be speaking complete nonsense.

Now the situation was almost unbearable. Not only was Kukuripa's speech completely unintelligible, but Marpa had to constantly be on guard against the hundreds of bitches. As soon as he was able to make a relationship with one dog, another would bark and threaten to bite him. Finally, almost beside himself, Marpa gave up altogether, gave up trying to take notes, gave up trying to receive any kind of secret doctrine. And at that point Kukuripa began to speak to him in a totally intelligible, coherent voice and the dogs stopped harassing him and Marpa received the teachings.

After Marpa had finished studying with Kukuripa, he returned once more to his original guru, Naropa. Naropa told him, "Now you must return to Tibet and teach. It isn't enough to receive the teachings in a theoretical way. You must go through certain life experiences. Then you can come back again and study further."

Once more Marpa met his fellow searcher and together they began the long journey back to Tibet. Marpa's companion had also studied a great deal and both men had stacks of manuscripts and, as they proceeded, they discussed what they had learned. Soon Marpa began to feel uneasy about his friend, who seemed more and more inquisitive to discover what teachings Marpa had collected. Their conversations together seemed to turn increasingly around this subject, until finally his traveling companion decided that Marpa had obtained more valuable teachings than himself, and so he became quite jealous. As they were crossing a river in a ferry, Marpa's colleague began to complain of being uncomfortable and crowded by all the baggage they were carrying. He shifted his position in the boat, as if to make himself more comfortable, and in so doing managed to throw all of Marpa's manuscripts into the river. Marpa tried desperately to rescue them, but they were gone. All the texts he had gone to such lengths to collect had disappeared in an instant.

So it was with a feeling of great loss that Marpa returned to Tibet. He had many stories to tell of his travels and studies, but he had nothing solid to prove his knowledge and experience. Nevertheless, he spent several years working and teaching until, to his surprise, he began to realize that his writings would have been useless to him, even had he been able to save them. While he was in India he had only taken written notes on those parts of the teachings he had not understood. He had not written down those teachings which were part of his own experience. It was only years later that he discovered that they had actually become a part of him.

With the discovery Marpa lost all desire to profit from the teachings. He was no longer concerned with making money or achieving prestige but instead was inspired to realize enlightenment. So he collected gold dust as an offering to Naropa and once again made the journey to India. This time he went full of longing to see his guru and desire for the teachings.

However, Marpa's next encounter with Naropa was quite different than before. Naropa seemed very cold and impersonal, almost hostile, and his first words to Marpa were, "Good to see you again. How much gold have you for my teachings?" Marpa had brought a large amount of gold but wanted to save some for his expenses and the trip home, so he opened his pack and gave Naropa only a portion of what he had. Naropa looked at the offering and said, "No, this is not enough. I need more gold than this for my teaching. Give me all your gold." Marpa gave him a bit more and still Naropa demanded all, and this went on until finally Naropa laughed and said, "Do you think you can buy my teaching with your deception?" At this point Marpa yielded and gave Naropa all the gold he had. To his shock, Naropa picked up the bags and began flinging the gold dust in the air.

Suddenly Marpa felt extremely confused and paranoid. He could not understand what was happening. He had worked hard for the gold to buy the teaching he so wanted. Naropa had seemed to indicate hat he needed the gold and would teach Marpa in return for it. Yet he was throwing it away! Then Naropa said to him, "What need have I of gold? The whole world is gold for me!"

This was a great moment of opening for Marpa. He opened and was able to receive teaching. He stayed with Naropa for a long time after that and his training was quite austere, but he did not simply listen to the teachings as before; he had to work his way through them. He had to give up everything he had, not just his material possessions, but whatever he was holding back in his mind had to go. It was a continual process of opening and surrender.

In Milarepa's case, the situation developed quite differently. He was a peasant, much less learned and sophisticated than Marpa had been when he met Naropa, and he had committed many crimes including murder. He was miserably unhappy, yearned for enlightenment, and was willing to pay any fee that Marpa might ask. So Marpa had Milarepa pay on a very literal physical level. He had him build a series of houses for him, one after the other, and after each was completed Marpa would tell Milarepa to tear the house down and put all the stones back where he had found them, so as not to mar the landscape. Each time Marpa ordered Milarepa to dismantle a house, he would give some absurd excuse, such as having been drunk when he ordered the house built or never having ordered such a house at all. And each time Milarepa, full of longing for the teachings, would tear the house down and start again.

Finally Marpa designed a tower with nine stories. Milarepa suffered terrific physical hardship in carrying the stones and building the house and, when he had finished, he went to Marpa and once more asked for the teachings. But Marpa said to him, "You want to receive teachings from me, just like that, merely because you built this tower for me? Well, I'm afraid you will still have to give me a gift as an initiation fee."

By this time Milarepa had no possessions left whatsoever, having spent all his time and labor building towers. But Damema, Marpa's wife, felt sorry for him and said, "These towers you have built are such a wonderful gesture of devotion and faith. Surely my husband won't mind if I give you some sacks of barley and a roll of cloth for your initiation fee." So Milarepa took the barley and cloth to the initiation circle where Marpa was teaching and offered them as his fee, along with the gifts of the other students. But Marpa, when he recognized the gift, was furious and shouted at Milarepa, "These things belong to me, you hypocrite! You try to deceive me!" And he literally kicked Milarepa out of the initiation circle.

At this point Milarepa gave up all hope of ever getting Marpa to give him the teachings. In despair, he decided to commit suicide and was just about to kill himself when Marpa came to him and told him that he was ready to receive the teaching.

The process of receiving teaching depends upon the student giving something in return; some kind of psychological surrender is necessary, a gift of some sort. This is why we must discuss surrendering, opening, giving up expectations, before we can speak of the relationship between teacher and student. It is essential to surrender, to open yourself, to present whatever you are to the guru, rather than trying to present yourself as a worthwhile student. It does not matter how much you are willing to pay, how correctly you behave, how clever you are at saying the right thing to your teacher. It is not like having an interview for a job or buying a new car. Whether or not you will get the job depends upon your credentials, how well you are dressed, how beautifully your shoes are polished, how well you speak, how good your manners are. If you are buying a car, it is a matter of how much money you have and how good your credit is.

But when it comes to spirituality, something more is required. It is not a matter of applying for a job, of dressing up to impress our potential employer. Such deception does not apply to an interview with a guru, because he sees right through us. He is amused if we dress up especially for the interview. Making ingratiating gestures is not applicable in this situation; in fact it is futile. We must make a real commitment to being open with our teacher; we must be willing to give up all our preconceptions. Milarepa expected Marpa to be a great scholar and a saintly person, dressed in yogic costume with beads, reciting mantras, meditating. Instead he found Marpa working on his farm, directing the laborers and plowing his land.

I am afraid the word *guru* is overused in the West. It would be better to speak of one's "spiritual friend," because the teachings emphasize a mutual meeting of two minds. It is a matter of mutual communication, rather than a master-servant relationship between a highly evolved being and a miserable, confused one. In the master-servant relationship the highly evolved being may appear not even to be sitting on his seat but may seem to be floating, levitating, looking down at us. His voice is penetrating, pervading space. Every word, every cough, every movement that he makes is a gesture of wisdom. But this is a dream. A guru should be a spiritual friend who communicates and presents his qualities to us, as Marpa did with Milarepa and Naropa with Marpa. Marpa presented his quality of being a farmer-yogi. He happened to have seven children and a wife, and he looked after his farm, cultivating the land and supporting himself and his family. But these activities were just an ordinary part of his life. He cared for his students as he cared for his crops and family. He was so thorough, paying attention to every detail of his life, that he was able to be a competent teacher as well as a competent father and farmer. There was no physical or spiritual materialism in Marpa's lifestyle at all. He did not emphasize spirituality and ignore his family or his physical relationship to the earth. If you are not involved with materialism, either spiritually or physically, then there is no emphasis made on any extreme.

Nor is it helpful to choose someone for your guru simply because he is famous, someone who is renowned for having published stacks of books and converted thousands or millions of people. Instead the guideline is whether or not you are able actually to communicate with the person, directly and thoroughly. How much self-deception are you involved in? If you really open yourself to your spiritual friend, then you are bound to work together. Are you able to talk to him thoroughly and properly? Does he know anything about you? Does he know anything about himself, for that matter? Is the guru really able to see through your masks, communicate with you properly, directly? In searching for a teacher, this seems to be the guideline rather than fame or wisdom.

There is an interesting story of a group of people who decided to go and study under a great Tibetan teacher. They had already studied somewhat with other teachers, but had decide to concentrate on trying to learn from this particular person. They were all very anxious to become his students and so sought an audience with him, but this great teacher would not accept any of them. "Under one condition only will I accept you," he said. "If you are willing to renounce your previous teachers." They all pleaded with him, telling him how much they were devoted to him, how great his reputation was, and how much they would like to study with him. But he would not accept any of them unless they would meet his condition. Finally all except one person in the party decided to renounce their previous teachers, from whom they had in fact learned a great deal. The guru seemed to be quite happy when they did so and told them all to come back the next day. But when they returned he said to them, "I understand your hypocrisy. The next time you go to another teacher you will renounce me. So get out." And he chased them all out except for the one person who valued what he had learned previously. The person he accepted was not willing to play any more lying games, was not willing to try to please a guru by pretending to be different from what he was. If you are going to make friends with a spiritual master, you must make friends simply, openly, so that the communication takes place between equals, rather than trying to win the master over to you.

In order to be accepted by your guru as a friend, you have to open yourself completely. And in order that you might open, you will probably have to undergo tests by your spiritual friend and by life situations in general, all of these tests taking the form of disappointment. At some stage you will doubt that your spiritual friend has any feeling, any emotion toward you at all. This is dealing with your own hypocrisy. The hypocrisy, the pretense, and basic twist of ego, is extremely hard; it has a very thick skin. We tend to wear suits of armor, one over the other. This hypocrisy is so dense and multileveled that, as soon as we remove one layer of our suit of armor, we find another beneath it. We hope we will not have to completely undress. We hope that stripping off only a few layers will make us presentable. Then we appear in our new suit of armor with such an ingratiating face, but our spiritual friend does not wear any armor at all; he is a naked person. Compared with his nakedness, we are wearing cement. Our armor is so thick that our friend cannot feel the texture of our skin, our bodies. He cannot even see our faces properly. There are many stories of teacher-student relationships in the past in which the student had to make long journeys and endure many hardships until his fascination and impulses began to wear out. This seems to be the point: the impulse of searching for something is, in itself, a hang-up. When this impulse begins to wear out, then our fundamental basic nakedness begins to appear and the meeting of the two minds begins to take place.

It has been said that the first stage of meeting one's spiritual friend is like going to a supermarket. You are excited and you dream of all the different things that you are going to buy: the richness of your spiritual friend and the colorful qualities of his personality. The second stage of your relationship is like going to court, as though you were a criminal. You are not able to meet your friend's demands and you begin to feel self-conscious, because you know that he knows as much as you know about yourself, which is extremely embarrassing. In the third stage when you go to see your spiritual friend, it is like seeing a cow happily grazing in a meadow. You just admire its peacefulness and the landscape, and then you pass on. Finally the fourth stage with one's spiritual friend is like passing a rock in the road. You do not even pay attention to it; you just pass by and walk away.

At the beginning a kind of courtship with the guru is taking place, a love affair. How much are you able to win this person over to you? There is a tendency to want to be closer to your spiritual friend, because you really want to learn. You feel such admiration for him. But at the

same time he is very frightening; he puts you off. Either the situation
does not coincide with your expectations or there is a self-conscious feeling that "I may not be able to open completely and thoroughly." A love-
hate relationship, a kind of surrendering and running away process develops. In other words, we begin to play a game, a game of wanting to
open, wanting to be involved in a love affair with our guru, and then
wanting to run away from him. If we get too close to our spiritual friend,
then we begin to feel overpowered by him. As it says in the old Tibetan
proverb: "A guru is like a fire. If you get too close, you get burned; if
you stay too far away, you don't get enough heat." This kind of courtship takes place on the part of the student. You tend to get too close to
the teacher, but once you do, you get burned. Then you want to run
away altogether.

Eventually the relationship begins to become very substantial and
solid. You begin to realize that wanting to be near and wanting to be far
away from the guru is simply your own game. It has nothing to do with
the real situation, but is just your own hallucination. The guru or spiritual friend is always there burning, always a life-fire. You can play games
with him or not, as you choose.

Then the relationship with one's spiritual friend begins to become
very creative. You accept the situations of being overwhelmed by him
and distant from him. If he decides to play the role of cold icy water,
you accept it. If he decides to play the role of hot fire, you accept it.
Nothing can shake you at all and you come to a reconciliation with him.

The next stage is that, having accepted everything your spiritual
friend might do, you begin to lose your own inspiration because you
have completely surrendered, completely given up. You feel yourself reduced to a speck of dust. You are insignificant. You begin to feel that the
only world that exists is that of this spiritual friend, the guru. It is as
though you were watching a fascinating movie; the movie is so exciting
that you become part of it. There is no you and no cinema hall, no
chairs, no people watching, no friends sitting next to you. The movie is
all that exists. This is called the "honeymoon period" in which everything is seen as a part of this central being, the guru. You are just a useless, insignificant person who is continuously being fed by this great,
fascinating central being. Whenever you feel weak or tired or bored, you
go and just sit in the cinema hall and are entertained, uplifted, rejuve-
nated. At this point the phenomenon of the personality cult becomes

prominent. The guru is the only person in the world who exists, alive and vibrant. The very meaning of your life depends upon him. If you die, you die for him. If you live, you survive for him and are insignificant.

However, this love affair with your spiritual friend cannot last forever. Sooner or later its intensity must wane and you must face your own life-situation and your own psychology. It is like having married and finished the honeymoon. You not only feel conscious of your lover as the central focus of your attention, but you begin to notice his or her lifestyle as well. You begin to notice what it is that makes this person a teacher, beyond the limits of his individuality and personality. Thus the principle of the "universality of the guru" comes into the picture as well. Every problem you face in life is a part of your marriage. Whenever you experience difficulties, you hear the words of the guru. This is the point at which one begins to gain one's independence from the guru as lover, because every situation becomes an expression of the teachings. First you surrendered to your spiritual friend. Then you communicated and played games with him. And now you have come to the state of complete openness. As a result of this openness you begin to see the guru-quality in every life-situation, that all situations in life offer you the opportunity to be as open as you are with the guru, and so all things can become the guru.

Milarepa had a vivid vision of his guru Marpa while he was meditating in very strict retreat in Red Rock Jewel Valley. Weak with hunger and battered by the elements, he had fainted while trying to collect firewood outside his cave. When he regained consciousness, he looked to the east and saw white clouds in the direction where Marpa lived. With great longing he sang a song of supplication, telling Marpa how much he longed to be with him. Then Marpa appeared in a vision, riding a white snow lion, and said to him something like, "What is the matter with you? Have you had a neurotic upheaval of some sort? You understand the dharma, so continue to practice meditation." Milarepa took comfort and returned to his cave to meditate. His reliance and dependence upon Marpa at this point indicates that he had not yet freed himself from the notion of guru as personal, individual friend.

However, when Milarepa returned to his cave, he found it full of demons with eyes as big as saucepans and bodies the size of thumbs. He tried all kinds of ploys to get them to stop mocking and tormenting him, but they would not leave until Milarepa finally stopped trying to play games, until he recognized his own hypocrisy and gave in to openness. From this point on you see a tremendous change of style in Milarepa's songs, because he had learned to identify with the universal quality of guru, rather than solely relating to Marpa as an individual person.

The spiritual friend becomes part of you, as well as being an individual, external person. As such the guru, both internal and external, plays a very important part in penetrating and exposing our hypocrisies. The guru can be a person who acts as a mirror, reflecting you, or else your own basic intelligence takes the form of the spiritual friend. When the internal guru begins to function, then you can never escape the demand to open. The basic intelligence follows your everywhere; you cannot escape your own shadow. "Big Brother is watching you." Though it is not external entities who are watching us and haunting us; we haunt ourselves. Our own shadow is watching us.

We could look at it in two different ways. We could see the guru as a ghost, haunting and mocking us for our hypocrisy. There could be a demonic quality in realizing what we are. And yet there is always the creative quality of the spiritual friend which also becomes a part of us. The basic intelligence is continuously present in the situations of life. It is so sharp and penetrating that at some stage, even if you want to get rid of it, you cannot. Sometimes it has a stern expression, sometimes an inspiring smile. It has been said in the Tantric tradition that you do not see the face of the guru, but you see the expression of his face all the time. Either smiling, grinning, or frowning angrily, it is part of every life-situation. The basic intelligence, tathagatagarbha, buddha nature, is always in every experience life brings us. There is no escaping it. Again it is said in the teachings: "Better not to begin. Once you begin, better to finish it." So you had better not step onto the spiritual path unless you must. Once you have stepped foot on the path, you have really done it, you cannot step back. There is no way of escaping.

Q: Having stumbled around various spiritual centers, I feel that a personality like Marpa must be a very troublesome phenomenon for most addicts along these lines. For here is a man who seems not to be doing any of the things that everybody says will get you there. He's not ascetic, he doesn't abnegate. He looks after his everyday affairs. He is a normal human being and yet, apparently, he is a teacher of enormous capability. Is Marpa the only one who has made the most of the possibilities for a normal man without going through all the tremendous pain of asceticism and the discipline of purification?

A: Of course, Marpa is an example of the possibilities open to us. However, he did experience tremendous discipline and training while he was in India. By studying strenuously under Indian teachers he prepared his path. But I think we must understand the true meaning of the words *discipline* and *asceticism.* The basic idea of asceticism, leading a life according to the dharma, is to be fundamentally sane. If you find that leading an ordinary life is a sane thing to do, that is dharma. At the same time you could find that leading the life of an ascetic yogi, as described in the texts, could become an expression of insanity. It depends upon the individual. It is a question of what is sane for you, the really solid, sound, stable approach to life. The Buddha, for example, was not a religious fanatic, attempting to act in accordance with some high ideal. He just dealt with people simply, openly and very wisely. His wisdom came from transcendental common sense. His teaching was sound and open.

The problem seems to be that people worry about a conflict between the religious and the profane. They find it very difficult to reconcile so-called "higher consciousness" with practical affairs. But the categories of higher and lower, religious and profane, do not really seem relevant to a basically sane approach to life.

Marpa was just an ordinary person, involved in living every detail of his life. He never tried to be someone special. When he lost his temper, he just lost it and beat people. He just did it. He never acted or pretended. Religious fanatics, on the other hand, are always trying to live up to some model of how it all is supposed to be. They try to win people over by coming on very strong and frantic, as though they were completely pure and good. But I think that attempting to prove that you are good indicates fear of some kind. Marpa, however, had nothing to prove. He was just a very sane and ordinary solid citizen, and a very enlightened person at the same time. In fact, he is the father of the whole Kagyü lineage. All the teachings we are studying and practicing spring from him.

Q: There is a Zen expression: "At first the mountains are mountains and streams are streams. Then the mountains are not mountains and streams are not streams. But in the end, mountains are mountains again and streams are streams again." Well, aren't we all in the stage where mountains are not mountains and streams are not streams? Yet you are emphasizing this ordinary quality. Don't we have to go through this "not ordinary" period before we can really be ordinary?

A: Marpa was very upset when his son was killed, and one of his disciples said, "You used to tell us that everything is illusion. How about the death of your son? Isn't it illusion?" And Marpa replied, "True, but my son's death is a super-illusion."

When we first experience true ordinariness, it is something very extraordinarily ordinary, so much so that we would say that mountains are not mountains any more or streams streams any more, because we see them as so ordinary, so precise, so "as they are." This extraordinariness derives from the experience of discovery. But eventually this super-ordinariness, this precision, becomes an everyday event, something we live with all the time, truly ordinary, and we are back where we started: the mountains are mountains and streams are streams. Then we can relax.

Q: How do you take off your suit of armor? How do you open yourself?

A: It is not a question of *how* you do it. There is no ritual or ceremony or formula for opening. The first obstacle is the question itself: "How?" If you don't question yourself, don't watch yourself, then you just do it. We do not consider how we are going to vomit; we just vomit. There is no time to think about it; it just happens. If we are very tense, then we will have tremendous pain and will not really be able to vomit properly. We will try to swallow it back, try to struggle with our illness. We have to learn to relax when we are sick.

Q: When the situations of life start to become your guru, does it matter what form the situation takes? Does it matter what situation you find yourself in?

A: You have no choice at all. Whatever happens is an expression of the guru. The situation could be painful or inspiring, but both pain and pleasure are one in this openness of seeing the situation as guru.

Tilopa the Guru, the teacher of Naropa.
DRAWING BY GLEN EDDY.

Initiation

MOST OF THE PEOPLE who have come to study with me have done so because they have heard of me personally, of my reputation as a meditation teacher and Tibetan lama. But how many people would have come had we first bumped into each other on the road or met in a restaurant? Very few people would be inspired to study Buddhism and meditation by such a meeting. Rather people seem to be inspired by the fact that I am a meditation teacher from exotic Tibet, the eleventh reincarnation of the Trungpa Tulku.

So people come and seek initiation from me, initiation into the Buddhist teachings and the sangha, the community of meditators on the path. But what does this initiation really mean? There is a long and great tradition of handing down the wisdom of the Buddhist lineage from one generation of meditators to the next, and this transmission is connected with initiation. But what is it all about?

It really seems worthwhile to be cynical in this regard. People would like to receive initiation: they would like to join the club, receive a title, obtain wisdom. Personally, I do not wish to play on people's weakness, their desire to get something extraordinary. Some people will buy a painting by Picasso simply because of the artist's name. They will pay thousands of dollars without considering whether what they are buying is worthwhile as art. They are buying the painting's credentials, the name, accepting reputation and rumor as their guarantee of artistic merit. There is no hard intelligence in such an act.

Or someone might join a club, be initiated into a particular organization because he feels starved, worthless. The group is fat and wealthy and he wants someone to feed him. He gets fed and becomes fat as he expected, but then what? Who is deceiving whom? Is the teacher or guru deceiving himself, expanding his ego? "I have such a large flock of followers who have been initiated." Or is he deceiving his students, leading them to believe that they have become wiser, more spiritual, simply because they have committed themselves to his organization and have been labeled monks, yogis, whatever titles they may have received? There are so many different titles to receive. Do these names, credentials bring us any real benefit? Do they really? Half an hour's ceremony does not bring us to the next stage of enlightenment; let's face facts. I personally have tremendous devotion to and faith in the Buddhist lineage and the power of the teachings, but not in a simple-minded way.

We must approach spirituality with a hard kind of intelligence. If we go to hear a teacher speak, we should not allow ourselves to be carried away by his reputation and charisma, but we should properly experience each word of his lecture or each aspect of the meditation technique being taught. We must make a clear and intelligent relationship with the teachings and the man teaching. Such intelligence has nothing to do with emotionalism or romanticizing the guru. It has nothing to do with gullibly accepting impressive credentials, nor is it a matter of joining a club that we might be enriched.

It is not a matter of finding a wise guru from whom we can buy or steal wisdom. True initiation involves dealing honestly and straightforwardly with our spiritual friend and ourselves. So we have to make some effort to expose ourselves and our self-deceptions. We have to surrender and expose the raw and rugged quality of our ego.

The Sanskrit equivalent for "initiation" is *abhisheka*, which means "sprinkle," "pour," "anointment." And if there is pouring, there must be a vessel into which the pouring can fall. If we really commit ourselves by opening to our spiritual friend properly, completely, becoming a vessel into which his communication may fall, then he will also open and initiation will occur. This is the meaning of abhisheka or "the meeting of the two minds" of teacher and student.

Such opening does not involve ingratiation, trying to please or impress our spiritual friend. The situation is similar to that in which a doctor, realizing that there is something wrong with you, takes you from your home, by force if necessary, and operates on your body without an anesthetic. You might find this kind of treatment a bit too violent and painful, but then you begin to realize how much real communication—being in touch with life—costs.

Monetary donations to a spiritual cause, contributions of physical labor, involvement with a particular guru, none of these necessarily mean that we have actually committed ourselves to openness. More likely these kinds of commitment are simply ways of proving that we have joined the side of "right." The guru seems to be a wise person. He knows what he is doing and we would like to be on his side, the safe side, the good side, in order to secure our well-being and success. But once we have attached ourselves to his side, the side of sanity, the side of stability, the side of wisdom, then to our surprise we discover that we have not succeeded in securing ourselves at all, because we have only committed our facade, our face, our suit of armor. We have not totally committed *ourselves*.

Then we are forced to open from behind. To our horror we find that there is no place to run. We are discovered in the act of hiding behind a facade, exposed on all sides; the padding and armor that we have worn are all stripped away. There is no longer any place to hide. Shocking! Everything is revealed, our petty pretense and egotism. At this point we might realize that our clumsy attempt to wear a mask has all along been pointless.

Still we attempt to rationalize this painful situation, trying to find some way to protect ourselves, some way to explain our predicament to ego's satisfaction. We look at it this way and that way, and our mind is extremely busy. Ego is very professional, overwhelmingly efficient in its way. When we think that we are working on the forward-moving process of attempting to empty ourselves out, we find ourselves going backward, trying to secure ourselves, filling ourselves up. And this confusion continues and intensifies until we finally discover that we are totally lost, that we have lost our ground, that there is no starting point or middle or end because our mind has been so overwhelmed by our own defense mechanisms. So the only alternative seems to be to just give in and let be. Our clever ideas and smart solutions do us no good, because we have been overwhelmed with too many ideas; we do not know which ideas to choose, which ideas will provide us with the best way to work on ourselves. Our mind is overcrowded with extraordinary, intelligent, logical, scientific, and cunning suggestions. But somehow there are too many and we do not know which suggestion to take.

So at last we might really give up all these complications and just allow some space, just give in. This is the moment when abhisheka—sprinkling and pouring—really takes place, because we are open and are really giving up the whole attempt to do anything, giving up all the busyness and overcrowding. Finally we have been forced to really stop properly, which is quite a rare occurrence for us.

We have so many different defense mechanisms fashioned out of the knowledge we have received, the reading we have done, the experiences we have undergone, the dreams we have dreamed. But finally we begin to question what spirituality means really. Is it simply a matter of attempting to be religious, pious, and good? Or is it trying to know more than other people, trying to learn more about the significance of life? What does it really mean, spirituality? The familiar theories of our family church and its doctrine are always available, but somehow these are not the answers we seek; they are a bit too ineffective, not applicable. So we fall away from the doctrines and dogmas of the religion we were born to.

We might decide that spirituality is something very exciting and colorful. It is a matter of exploring ourselves in the tradition of some exotic and different sect or religion. We adopt another kind of spirituality, behaving in a certain way, attempting to change our tone of voice and eating habits and our behavior in general. But after a while such self-conscious attempts to be spiritual begin to feel too clumsy and obvious, too familiar. We intend these patterns of behavior to become habitual, second nature, but somehow they do not completely become a part of us. Much as we would like these "enlightened" behavior patterns to become a natural part of our makeup, neurosis is still present in our minds. We begin to wonder: "If I have been acting in accordance with the sacred scriptures of the such and such tradition, how could this happen? This must be due to my confusion, of course. But what do I do next?" Confusion still continues in spite of our faithful adherence to the scriptures. Neuroticism and discontent go on. Nothing really clicks; we have not connected with the teachings.

At this point we really need "the meeting of the two minds." Without abhisheka our attempts to achieve spirituality will result in no more than a huge spiritual collection rather than real surrender. We have been collecting different behavior patterns, different manners of speech, dress, thought, whole different ways of acting. And all of it is merely a collection we are attempting to impose upon ourselves.

Abhisheka, true initiation, is born out of surrender. We open ourselves to the situation as it is, and then we make real communication with the teacher. In any event, the guru is already there with us in a state of openness; and if we open ourselves, are willing to give up our collections, then initiation takes place. There is no "sacred" ceremony necessary. In fact, considering initiation "sacred" is probably seduction by what Buddhists refer to as "the daughters of Mara." Mara represents the neurotic tendency of mind, the unbalanced state of being, and he sends his daughters to seduce us. When the daughters of Mara take part in initiation in which the meeting of the two minds is actually taking place, they will say, "You feel peaceful? That is because you are receiving spiritual instruction, because this is a spiritual thing that is happening to you, it is sacred." They have very sweet voices and bring a lovely, beautiful message, and they seduce us into thinking that this communication, this "meeting of the two minds" is a "big deal." Then we begin to give birth to further samsaric patterns of mind. It is similar to the Christian idea of biting the apple; it is temptation. When we regard abhisheka as sacred, then the precision and sharpness immediately begin to fall away because we have begun to evaluate. We hear the voices of the daughters of Mara congratulating us that we have managed to do such a holy thing. They are dancing around us and playing music in the pretense of honoring us on this ceremonial occasion.

The meeting of the two minds really takes place very naturally. Both the instructor and the student meet in a state of openness in which they both realize that openness is the most insignificant thing in the whole world. It is completely insignificant, truly ordinary, absolutely nothing. When we are able to see ourselves and the world in this way, then transmission is directly taking place. In the Tibetan tradition this way of seeing things is called "ordinary mind," *thamal gyi shepa*. It is the most insignificant thing of all, complete openness, the absence of any kind of collection or evaluation. We could say that such insignificance is very significant, that such ordinariness is truly extraordinary. But this would just be further seduction by the daughters of Mara. Eventually we must give up trying to be something special.

Q: It seems that I cannot get away from trying to secure myself. What should I do?

A: You want so much to be secure that the idea of trying *not* to secure yourself has become a game, a big joke, and a way of securing yourself. You are so concerned about watching yourself and watching yourself watching, and watching yourself watching yourself watching. It goes on and on and on. It is quite a common phenomenon.

What is really needed is for you to stop caring altogether, to completely drop the whole concern. The overlapping complications, building an extremely fine lie detector and a detector for the lie detector as well, such complicated structures have to be cleared away. You try to secure yourself and, having achieved security, then you also attempt to secure that as well. Such fortifications could extend to an infinite empire. You might just own a tiny little castle, but the scope of your protection could extend to cover the entire earth. If you really want to secure yourself completely, there is literally no limit to the efforts you can make.

So it is necessary to drop altogether the idea of security and see the irony of your attempts to secure yourself, the irony of your overlapping structure of self-protection. You have to give up the watcher of the watcher of the watcher. In order to do this, one has to drop the first watcher, the intention of protection itself.

Q: I don't know what nationality to bring up, but if we were Indians, for instance, you wouldn't speak to us this way, would you? I mean, it's because we are Americans and are so much into *doing* things that you have to speak to us this way. If we were given to doing nothing, just sitting around, you wouldn't speak to us like this.

A: That is a very interesting point. I think the style in which the teachings are presented depends upon how much the audience is involved with the speed of materialism. America has achieved an extremely sophisticated level of physical materialism. However, the potential for being involved in this kind of speed is not limited to Americans; it is universal, worldwide. If India reaches the stages of economic development that America has attained, where people have achieved and have become disillusioned with physical materialism, then they will be coming to listen to such a lecture. But at this time I do not think there would be an audience for this kind of lecture anywhere other than in the West, because people elsewhere are not yet tired enough of the speed of physical materialism. They are still saving money to buy bicycles on the way to automobiles.

Self-Deception

SELF-DECEPTION IS A constant problem as we progress along a spiritual path. Ego is always trying to achieve spirituality. It is rather like wanting to witness your own funeral. For instance, in the beginning we might approach our spiritual friend hoping to get something wonderful from him. This approach is called "hunting the guru." Traditionally, it is compared to hunting the musk deer. The hunter stalks the deer, kills it, and removes the musk. We could take this approach to the guru and spirituality, but it would be self-deception. It would have nothing to do with real opening or surrender.

Or we might falsely assume that initiation means transplantation, transplanting the spiritual power of the teachings from the guru's heart into our own. This mentality regards the teachings as something foreign to us. It is similar to the idea of transplanting a real heart or, for that matter, a head. A foreign element is transplanted into us from outside our body. We might tend to appraise our potential transplant. Perhaps our old head is not suitable, perhaps it should be thrown into the rubbish heap. We deserve a better head, a fresh one, a more intelligent one with lots of brains. We are so concerned with what we are going to get out of our potential operation that we have forgotten the doctor who is going to perform it. Have we stopped to make a relationship with our physician? Is he competent? Is the head we have chosen really suitable? Might not our doctor have something to say about our choice of heads? Perhaps our body would reject that head. We are so concerned with what we think we are going to *get*, that we ignore what is really happening, our relationship with our doctor, our illness, what this new head really is.

Pig, snake, and rooster. They represent stupidity, aggression, and passion.
DRAWING BY GLEN EDDY.

This approach to the process of initiation is very romantic and not at all valid. So we need someone personally concerned with us as we really are, we need a person to play the part of mirror. Whenever we are involved with any kind of self-deception, it is necessary that the whole process be revealed, opened. Any grasping attitude must be exposed.

Real initiation takes place in terms of "the meeting of the two minds." It is a matter of being what you really are and of relating to the spiritual friend as he or she is. This is the true situation in which initiation might occur, because the idea of having an operation and fundamentally changing yourself is completely unrealistic. No one can really change your personality absolutely. No one can turn you completely upside down and inside out. The existing material, that which is already there, must be used. You must accept yourself as you are, instead of as you would like to be, which means giving up self-deception and wishful thinking. Your whole makeup and personality characteristics must be recognized, accepted, and then you might find some inspiration.

At this point, if you express a willingness to work with your physician by committing yourself into the hospital, then the doctor for his part will make available a room and whatever else is needed. So both sides would be creating a situation of open communication, which is the fundamental meaning of "the meeting of the two minds." This is the real way of uniting the blessing or adhishthana, the spiritual essence of the guru, and your own spiritual essence. The external teacher, the guru, opens himself and, because you also are open, because you are "awake," there is the meeting of two elements which are identical. This is the true meaning of abhisheka, initiation. It is not a matter of joining a club, of becoming one of the flock, a sheep with your owner's initials branded on your behind.

So now we can examine what comes after abhisheka. Having experienced the meeting of the two minds, we have established real communication with our spiritual friend. We have not only opened ourselves, but we have also experienced a flash of insight, an instant understanding of part of the teachings. The teacher created the situation, we experienced this flash, and everything seems to be fine.

At first we are very excited, everything is beautiful. We might find that for several days we feel very "high" and excited. It seems we have already achieved the level of buddhahood. No mundane concerns bother us at all, everything goes very smoothly, instantaneous meditation occurs all the time. It is a continuous experience of our moment of openness with the guru. This is quite common. At this point many people might feel that they do not need to work further with their spiritual friend, and possibly they might leave, go away. I heard many stories of this happening in the East: certain students met their teacher and received an instant enlightenment experience and then left. They tried to preserve that experience, but as time went on it became just a memory, words and ideas which they repeated to themselves.

Quite possibly your first reaction after such an experience would be to write it down in your diary, explaining in words everything that happened. You would attempt to anchor yourself to the experience through your writings and memoirs, by discussing it with people, or by talking to people who witnessed you having the experience.

Or a person might have gone to the East and had this sort of experience and then come back to the West. His friends might find him tremendously changed. He might look calmer, quieter, wiser. Many people might ask him for help and advice with their personal problems, might ask for his opinion of their experience of spirituality. In the beginning, his way of helping other people would be genuine, relating their problems to his own experience in the East, telling people beautiful and genuine stories of what happened to him. It would be very inspiring for him.

But at some stage in this sort of situation something tends to go wrong. The memory of that sudden flash of insight that a person has experienced loses its intensity. It does not last because he regards it as being external to himself. He feels that he has had a sudden experience of the awakened state of mind and that it belongs to the category of holiness, spiritual experience. He valued the experience highly and then communicated it to the ordinary and familiar world of his homeland, to his enemies and friends, parents and relatives, to all those people and attachments which he now feels he has transcended and overcome. But now the experience is no longer with him. There is just the memory. And yet, having proclaimed his experience and knowledge to other people, he obviously cannot go back and say what he said previously was false. He could not do that at all; it would be too humiliating. Moreover, he still has faith in the experience, that something profound really happened. But unfortunately the experience is no longer present at this very moment, because he used and evaluated it.

Speaking generally what happens is that, once we have actually opened, "flashed," in the second moment we realize that we are open and the idea of evaluation suddenly appears. "Wow, fantastic, I have to catch that, I have to capture and keep it because it is a very rare and valuable experience." So we try to hold onto the experience and the problems start there, from regarding the real experience of openness as something valuable. As soon as we try to capture the experience, a whole series of chain reactions sets in.

If we regard something as valuable and extraordinary, then it becomes quite separate from us. For instance, we do not regard our eyes, body, hands, or head as valuable, because we know they are a part of us. Of course, if we lost them, any of them, our automatic reaction would be that we had lost such a valuable thing—"I have lost my head, I have lost my arm, it is impossible to replace!" Then we realize that it is a valuable thing. When something is removed from us, we have the opportunity to realize that it is valuable. But when we have it with us all the time, when it is part of our entire makeup, then we cannot value it particularly; it is just there. The evaluation comes from the fear of being separated, which is just what keeps us separated. We consider any sudden inspiration to be extraordinarily important, because we are afraid of losing it. That very point, that very moment, is when self-deception comes in. In other words, we lost faith in the experience of openness and its relationship to us.

Somehow we lost the unity of openness and what we are. Openness became a separate thing, and then we began to play games. It is obvious that we cannot say that we have lost the openness. "I used to have it, but I have lost it." We cannot say that, because that will destroy our status as an accomplished person. So the part of self-deception is to retell the stories. We would rather tell stories than actually experience openness, because stories are very vivid and enjoyable. "When I was with my guru, such and such happened; he said such and such things and opened me in such and such a way, etc., etc." So self-deception, in this case, means trying to recreate a past experience again and again, instead of actually having the experience in the present moment. In order to have the experience now, one would have to give up the evaluation of how wonderful the flash was, because it is this memory which keeps it distant. If we had the experience continuously it would seem quite ordinary, and it is this ordinariness that we cannot accept. "If only I could have that wonderful experience of openness again!" So we keep ourselves busy not having it, remembering it. This is self-deception's game.

Self-deception needs the idea of evaluation and a very long memory. Thinking back, we feel nostalgic, getting a kick from our memories, but we do not know where we are at this very moment. We remember the "good times," the "good old days." We do not allow our depression to emerge at all, we do not want to accept the suspicion that we are out of touch with something. Whenever the possibility of depression arises and the feeling of loss is about to occur, the defensive nature of ego immediately brings to mind memories and words we have heard in the past in order to comfort us. Thus ego is continually looking for inspiration which has no root in the present; it is a continual running back. This is the more complicated action of self-deception: one does not allow depression to come into being at all. "Since I have received such great blessings and been fortunate enough to have these wonderful spiritual experiences, how can I possibly say that I am depressed? Impossible, there is no room for depression."

There is the story of the great Tibetan teacher, Marpa. When Marpa first met his own teacher, Naropa, Naropa created an altar which he said was the embodiment of the wisdom of a particular *heruka*. Both the shrine and Naropa contained tremendous spiritual energy and power, and Naropa asked Marpa to which one he would prostrate in order to experience the sudden realization of enlightenment. Marpa, being a scholar, considered that the guru lives in the flesh, an ordinary human body, while his creation, the altar, is a pure body of wisdom, having nothing to do with human imperfection. So Marpa prostrated to the shrine. And then Naropa said, "I am afraid your inspiration is going to fade. You have made the wrong choice. This shrine is my creation, and without me the shrine would not be here at all. The issue of human body versus wisdom body is irrelevant. The great display of the mandala was merely my creation."

This story illustrates the principle of dream, hope, wish, as self-deception. As long as you regard yourself or any part of your experience as the "dream come true," then you are involved in self-deception. Self-deception seems always to depend upon the dream world, because you would like to see what you have not yet seen, rather than what you are now seeing. You will not accept that whatever is here now *is* what is, nor are you willing to go on with the situation as it is. Thus, self-deception always manifests itself in terms of trying to create or recreate a dream world, the nostalgia of the dream experience. And the opposite of self-deception is just working with the facts of life.

If one searches for any kind of bliss or joy, the realization of one's imagination and dream, then, equally, one is going to suffer failure and depression. This is the whole point: a fear of separation, the hope of attaining union, these are not just manifestations of or the actions of ego or self-deception, as if ego were somehow a real thing which performed certain actions. Ego *is* the actions, the mental events. Ego *is* the fear of losing openness, the fear of losing the egoless state. This is the meaning of self-deception, in this case—ego crying that it has lost the egoless state, its dream of attainment. Fear, hope, loss, gain—these are the ongoing action of the dream of ego, the self-perpetuating, self-maintaining structure which is self-deception.

So the real experience, beyond the dream world, is the beauty and color and excitement of the real experience of *now* in everyday life. When we face things as they are, we give up the hope of something better. There will be no magic, because we cannot tell ourselves to get out of our depression. Depression and ignorance, the emotions, whatever we experience, are all real and contain tremendous truth. If we really want to learn and see the experience of truth, we have to be where we are. The whole thing is just a matter of being a grain of sand.

Q: Would you talk some more about the mechanics of this force of despair? I can understand why despair might occur, but why does bliss occur?

A: It is possible in the beginning to force oneself into the experience of bliss. It is a kind of self-hypnosis, in that we refuse to see the background of what we are. We focus only upon the immediate experience of bliss. We ignore the entire basic ground, where we really are at, so to speak, and we work ourselves up to an experience of tremendous joy. The trouble is, this kind of experience is based purely upon watching oneself. It is a completely dualistic approach. We would like to experience something, and by working very hard we do actually achieve it. However, once we come down from our "high," once we realize that we are still here, like a black rock standing in the middle of an ocean of waves, then depression sets in. We would like to get drunk, intoxicated, absorbed into the entire universe, but somehow it does not happen. We are still here, which is always the first thing to bring us down. Later all the other games of self-deception, of trying to feed oneself further, begin because one is trying to protect oneself completely. It is the "watcher" principle.

Q: You speak of people experiencing something and then grasping it intellectually, labeling it saying, "That's fantastic." This seems to be an almost automatic reaction. Could you go through the ways in which people begin to get away from doing this? It seems to me that the more you try to stop evaluating, the more you are evaluating.

A: Well, once you realize that you are actually doing this and are not getting anything from it, then I think you begin to find your way out. One begins to see that the whole process is part of a huge game which is not really profitable, because you are continuously building rather than coming to an understanding of anything. There is no magic or trick involved. The only thing to do is to quite painfully unmask.

Perhaps you will have to build and build until you realize the futility of attempting to achieve spirituality. Your entire mind might become completely overcrowded with your struggle. In fact, you might not know whether you are coming or going, to the point where you become completely exhausted. Then you might learn a very useful lesson: to give up the whole thing, to be nothing. You might even experience a yearning to be nothing. There seem to be two solutions: either to simply unmask, or else to build and build, strive and strive, until you reach a crescendo and then drop the whole thing.

Q: What happens when one says, "Wow, I've made it." That doesn't blow the whole trip, does it?

A: Not necessarily. But then, what happens next? Do you want to repeat your experience again and again, rather than working with the present situation of what is? One could experience tremendous joy in the first flash of openness, which is quite beautiful. But what comes afterward is important: whether one is working to grasp and recreate that experience or whether one is letting be, allowing that experience to be just one experience, not attempting to recreate the first flash.

Q: You are ambitious, building all the time, and the more you think about it, the worse it gets. So you try to just run away from the whole thing, try not to think about it, try to lose yourself in all sorts of escapes. What does this mean and how can one get over the fact that, the more one thinks about enlightenment and tries to find out about it, the worse things become and the more conceptualizations accumulate? What do you do?

A: That is very obvious. You drop searching for anything altogether, drop trying to discover anything, trying to prove yourself.

Q: But sometimes one might have an active feeling of running away, and that is not the same thing as not doing anything at all.

A: Once you try to run away, you find that not only are you being chased from behind, but there are also people coming towards you from the front as well. Eventually there is no room to run. You are completely trapped. Then the only thing to do is really, simply to give in.

Q: What does that mean?

A: Well, one has to experience it. It means to stop trying to go anywhere, both in terms of getting away from and of running to, because both are the same thing.

Q: Is self-remembering or observing oneself incongruent with giving in and being here?

A: Self-remembering is quite a dangerous technique, actually. It could involve watching yourself and your actions like a hungry cat watching mice, or else it could be an intelligent gesture of being where you are. The whole point is that, if you have any idea of relationship—I am experiencing this, I am doing this—then "I" and "this" are very strong personalities, equally. Somehow there will be a conflict between "I" and "this." It is rather like saying that "this" is the mother and "I" the father. With two such polar extremes involved you are bound to give birth to something. So the whole idea is to let "this" not be there, and then "I" will not be there. Or else, "I" is not there, therefore "this" is not there. It is not a matter of telling it to yourself, but of feeling it, a real experience. You must take away the watcher, the observer of the two extremes. Once the watcher is removed, then the whole structure falls apart. The dichotomy remains in existence only so long as there is an observer to keep the whole picture together. You must remove the watcher and the very complicated bureaucracy he creates to insure that nothing is missed by central headquarters. Once we take away the watcher, there is a tremendous amount of space, because he and his bureaucracy take up so much room. If we eliminate the filter of "I" and "other," then the space becomes sharp and precise and intelligent. Space contains the tremendous precision of being able to work with the situations in it. One does not really need the "watcher" or "observer" at all.

Q: Does the watcher exist because you want to be living at what seems a higher level, whereas if you just let go, perhaps you would be *here?*

A: Yes, that is true. When the watcher disappears, the notion of higher and lower levels does not apply, so there is no longer any inclination to struggle, attempting to get higher. Then you just are where you are.

Q: Can you remove the watcher by force? Wouldn't that be the game of evaluation again?

A: You do not have to regard the watcher as a villain. Once you being to understand that the purpose of meditation is not to get higher but to be present, here, then the watcher is not efficient enough to perform that function, and it automatically falls away. The basic quality of the watcher is to try to be extremely efficient and active. But total awareness is something you already have, so ambitious or so-called "efficient" attempts to be aware are self-defeating. As the watcher begins to realize that it is irrelevant, it falls away.

Q: Can there be awareness without a watcher?

A: Yes, because the watcher is only paranoia. You could have complete openness, a panoramic situation, without having to discriminate between two parties, "I" and "other."

Q: Would that awareness involve feelings of bliss?

A: I do not think so, because bliss is a very individual experience. You are separate and you are experiencing your bliss. When the watcher is gone, there is no evaluation of the experience as being pleasant or painful. When you have panoramic awareness without the evaluation of the watcher, then the bliss becomes irrelevant, by the very fact that there is no one experiencing it.

The Hard Way

INASMUCH AS NO ONE is going to save us, to the extent that no one is going magically to enlighten us, the path we are discussing is called the "hard way." This path does not conform to our expectation that involvement with the Buddhist teaching will be gentle, peaceful, pleasant, compassionate. It is the hard way, a simple meeting of two minds: if you open your mind, if you are willing to meet, then the teacher opens his mind as well. It is not a question of magic; the condition of openness is a mutual creation.

Generally, when we speak of freedom or liberation or spiritual understanding, we think that to attain these things we need do nothing at all, that someone else will take care of us. "You are all right, don't worry, don't cry, you're going to be all right. I'll take care of you." We tend to think that all we have to do is make a commitment to the organization, pay our initiation fee, sign the register, and then follow the instructions given us. "I am firmly convinced that your organization is valid, it answers all my questions. You may program me in any way. If you want to put me into difficult situations, do so. I leave everything to you." This attitude supplies the comfort of having to do nothing but follow orders. Everything is left to the other person, to instruct you and relieve you of your shortcomings. But to our surprise things do not work that way. The idea that we do not have to do anything on our own is extremely wishful thinking.

It takes tremendous effort to work one's way through the difficulties of the path and actually get into the situations of life thoroughly and properly. So the whole point of the hard way seems to be that some individual effort must be made by the student to acknowledge himself,

Lohan. *An arhat in meditation posture, a disciple of the Buddha.*
WILLIAM ROCKHILL NELSON GALLERY OF ART, KANSAS CITY, MO.

to go through the process of unmasking. One must be willing to stand alone, which is difficult.

This is not to say that the point of the hard way is that we must be heroic. The attitude of "heroism" is based upon the assumption that we are bad, impure, that we are not worthy, are not ready for spiritual understanding. We must reform ourselves, be different from what we are. For instance, if we are middle-class Americans, we must give up our jobs or drop out of college, move out of our suburban homes, let our hair grow, perhaps try drugs. If we are hippies, we must give up drugs, cut our hair short, throw away our torn jeans. We think that we are special, heroic, that we are turning away from temptation. We become vegetarians and we become this and that. There are so many things to become. We think our path is spiritual because it is literally against the flow of what we used to be, but it is merely the way of false heroism, and the only one who is heroic in this way is ego.

We can carry this sort of false heroism to great extremes, getting ourselves into completely austere situations. If the teaching with which we are engaged recommends standing on our heads for twenty-four hours a day, we do it. We purify ourselves, perform austerities, and we feel extremely cleansed, reformed, virtuous. Perhaps there seems to be nothing wrong with it at the time.

We might attempt to imitate certain spiritual paths, such as the American Indian path or the Hindu path or the Japanese Zen Buddhist path. We might abandon our suits and collars and ties, our belts and trousers and shoes in an attempt to follow their example. Or we may decide to go to northern India in order to join the Tibetans. We might wear Tibetan clothing and adopt Tibetan customs. This will seem to be the "hard way," because there will always be obstacles and temptations to distract us from our purpose.

Sitting in a Hindu ashram, we have not eaten chocolate for six or seven months, so we dream of chocolate, or other dishes that we like. Perhaps we are nostalgic on Christmas or New Year's Day. But still we think we have found the path of discipline. We have struggled through the difficulties of this path and have become quite competent, masters of discipline of some sort. We expect the magic and wisdom of our training and practice to bring us into the right state of mind. Sometimes we think we have achieved our goal. Perhaps we are completely "high" or absorbed for a period of six or seven months. Later our ecstasy disappears. And so it goes, on and on, on and off. How are we going to deal with this situation? We may be able to stay "high" or blissful for a very long time, but then we have to come back or come down or return to normal.

I am not saying that foreign or disciplinary traditions are not applicable to the spiritual path. Rather, I am saying that we have the notion that there must be some kind of medicine or magic potion to help us attain the right state of mind. This seems to be coming at the problem backward. We hope that by manipulating matter, the physical world, we can achieve wisdom and understanding. We may even expect expert scientists to do it for us. They might put us into a hospital, administer the correct drugs, and lift us into a high state of consciousness. But I think, unfortunately, that this is impossible, we cannot escape what we are, we carry it with us all the time.

So the point we come back to is that some kind of *real* gift or sacrifice is needed if we are to open ourselves completely. This gift may take any form. But in order for it to be meaningful, it must entail giving up our hope of getting something in return. It does not matter how many titles we have, nor how many suits of exotic clothes we have worn through, nor how many philosophies, commitments and sacramental ceremonies we have participated in. We must give up our ambition to get something in return for our gift. That is the really hard way.

We may have had a wonderful time touring around Japan. We may have enjoyed Japanese culture, beautiful Zen temples, magnificent works of art. And not only did we find these experiences beautiful, but they said something to us as well. This culture is the creation of a whole lifestyle completely different from that of the Western world, and these creations spoke to us. But to what extent does the exquisiteness of culture and images, the beauty of the external forms really shake us, deal with us? We do not know. We merely want to savor our beautiful memories. We do not want to question our experiences too closely. It is a sensitive area.

Or perhaps a certain guru has initiated us in a very moving, extremely meaningful ceremony. That ceremony was real and direct and beautiful, but how much of the experience are we willing to question? It is private, too sensitive to question. We would rather hoard and preserve the flavor and beauty of the experience so that, when bad times come, when we are depressed and down, we can bring that memory to mind in order to comfort ourselves, to tell ourselves that we have actually done something worthwhile, that, yes, we are on the path. This does not seem to be the hard way at all.

On the contrary, it would seem that we have been collecting rather than giving. If we reconsider our spiritual shopping, can we remember an occasion when we gave something completely and properly, opened ourselves and gave everything? Have we ever unmasked, stripping out of our suit of armor and our shirt and skin and flesh and veins, right down to the heart? Have we really experienced the process of stripping and opening and giving? That is the fundamental question. We must really surrender, give something, give something up in a very painful way. We must begin to dismantle the basic structure of this ego we have managed to create. The process of dismantling, undoing, opening, giving up, is the real learning process. How much of this ingrown toenail situation have we decided to give up? Most likely, we have not managed to give up anything at all. We have only collected, built, adding layer upon layer. So the prospect of the hard way is very threatening.

The problem is that we tend to seek an easy and painless answer. But this kind of solution does not apply to the spiritual path, which many of us should not have begun at all. Once we commit ourselves to the spiritual path, it is very painful and we are in for it. We have committed ourselves to the pain of exposing ourselves, of taking off our clothes, our skin, nerves, heart, brains, until we are exposed to the universe. Nothing will be left. It will be terrible, excruciating, but that is the way it is.

Somehow we find ourselves in the company of a strange doctor. He is going to operate on us, but he is not going to use an anesthetic because he really wants to communicate with our illness. He is not going to allow us to put on our facade of spirituality, psychological sophistication, false psychological illness, or any other disguise. We wish we had never met him. We wish we understood how to anesthetize ourselves. But now we are in for it. There is no way out. Not because he is so powerful. We could tell him goodbye in a minute and leave. But we have exposed so much to this physician and, if we have to do it all over again, it will be very painful. We do not want to have to do it again. So now we have to go all the way.

Being with this doctor is extremely uncomfortable for us because we are continually trying to con him, although we know that he sees through our games. This operation is his only way to communicate with us, so we must accept it; we must open ourselves to the hard way, to this operation. The more we ask questions—"What are you going to do to me?"—the more embarrassed we become, because we know what we are. It is an extremely narrow path with no escape, a painful path. We must surrender ourselves completely and communicate with this physician. Moreover, we must unmask our expectations of magic on the part of the guru, that with his magical powers he can initiate us in certain extraordinary and painless ways. We have to give up looking for a painless operation, give up hope that he will use an anesthetic or sedative so that when we wake up everything will be perfect. We must be willing to communicate in a completely open and direct way with our spiritual friend and with our life, without any hidden corners. It is difficult and painful, the hard way.

Q: Is exposing yourself something that just happens, or is there a way of doing it, a way of opening?

A: I think that if you are already committed to the process of exposing yourself, then the less you try to open the more the process of opening becomes obvious. I would say it is an automatic action rather than something that you have to do. At the beginning when we discussed surrendering, I said that once you have exposed everything to your spiritual friend, then you do not have to do anything at all. It is a matter of just accepting what is, which we tend to do in any case. We often find ourselves in situations completely naked, wishing we had clothes to cover ourselves. These embarrassing situation always come to us in life.

Q: Must we have a spiritual friend before we can expose ourselves, or can we just open ourselves to the situations of life?

A: I think you need someone to watch you do it, because then it will seem more real to you. It is easy to undress in a room with no one else around, but we find it difficult to undress ourselves in a room full of people.

Q: So it is really exposing ourselves to ourselves?

A: Yes. But we do not see it that way. We have a strong consciousness of the audience because we have so much awareness of ourselves.

Q: I do not see why performing austerities and mastering discipline is not the "real" hard way.

A: You can deceive yourself, thinking you are going through the hard way, when actually you are not. It is like being in a heroic play. The "soft way" is very much involved with the experience of heroism, while the hard way is much more personal. Having gone through the way of heroism, you still have the hard way to go through, which is a very shocking thing to discover.

Q: Is it necessary to go through the heroic way first and is it necessary to persevere in the heroic way in order to continue on the truly hard way?

A: I don't think so. This is what I am trying to point out. If you involve yourself with the heroic way, you add layers or skins to your personality because you think you have achieved something. Later, to your surprise, you discover that something else is needed. One must *remove* the layers, the skins.

Q: You speak of the necessity to experience excruciating pain. Can an understanding of the unmasking process make it unnecessary to go through the pain?

A: That is a very tricky proposition. Understanding does not mean that you actually do it; you just understand it. We can understand the physiological process of how someone is tortured and how they experience pain, but the actual experience would be altogether different. The philosophical or intellectual understanding of pain is not enough. You must actually feel something properly. The only way to get to the heart of the matter is to actually experience it for yourself, but you do not have to create painful situations. These situations will occur with the help of a spiritual friend who is a doctor with a sharp knife.

Q: If you are in the process of surrendering and your spiritual friend at that point seems to point his scalpel at you and take away your anesthesia, then that is an extremely terrifying situation. Your spiritual friend seems to be very angry and disgusted and you want to run. Would you explain this?

A: That is just the point. It is a matter of an operation without the use of anesthetics. You have to be willing to do it. If you run away, it is like a man who needs an appendectomy running out of the operating room; his appendix might burst.

Q: But this is at a very early stage in your relationship with your spiritual friend; you have barely been with him for five minutes. Suddenly the roof falls in and he just leaves you to deal with it. Perhaps he is saying, "I am not going on this trip with you. Five minutes have passed. Surrender it, give it all up, deal with it yourself, and when you have cut it all loose, then I will talk to you." That is how I have experienced it.

A: You see, it does not matter whether you are a beginning or advanced student. It is a question of how much a person has been with himself. If he has been with himself, then he must know himself. It is like an ordinary illness. Suppose you are traveling from one country to another and you feel ill and decide to see a doctor. He can barely speak your language, but he can feel your body and see what is wrong with you, and he decides to take you immediately to the hospital and operate. It depends upon how far the disease has developed. The intensity of the operation depends on the maturity of the illness in your body. You might explode completely. If you have appendicitis and the doctor waits too long, perhaps in order to become friends with you, then your appendix is going to explode. You would not say that was a very good way of practicing medicine.

Q: Why does someone take that first step on the path? What leads him to it? Is it an accident, is it fate, karma, what is it?

A: If you expose yourself completely, then you are already on the path. If you give yourself halfway, then you are only part way on the path. It is going to bounce back on you. If you give less information to your doctor, then you are going to recover much more slowly because you have not told him your whole case history. The more you tell your doctor, the sooner he will be able to cure you.

Q: If the truly hard way is to expose myself, then should I allow myself to be exposed to what I judge to be evil, knowing I might get hurt?

A: Opening is not a matter of martyring oneself to every threat that comes along. You do not have to stand in front of an oncoming train to open yourself to it. That would be the way of heroism, the false hard way.

Whenever we confront something we regard as "evil," it poses a threat to the self-preservation of ego. We are so busy preserving our existence in the face of this threat that we cannot see the thing clearly at all. To open we have to cut through our desire to preserve our own existence. Then we can see and deal with the situation clearly, as it is.

Q: This is not a one-shot deal, is it? I mean you can open yourself in one context, and yet when you find yourself in some other situation suddenly you take hold of a mask and put it over your face, even though you really do not want to do it. It would seem that achieving complete openness is a difficult thing.

A: The whole point is that struggle is irrelevant to opening. Once you have stepped on the path, if you give up the struggle itself, that takes care of the whole problem. Then there is no longer any question of wanting or not wanting to be involved with life-situations. The ape instinct of ego dissolves because it is based upon secondhand information rather than upon direct experience of what is. Struggle is ego. Once you give up struggle, then there is no one left to conquer struggle; it just disappears. So you see, it is not a matter of achieving a victory over struggle.

Q: When you feel angry, should you just express that anger in order to open?

A: When we speak of opening and surrendering as, for instance, in the case of anger, it does not mean we should actually go out and hit someone on the spot. That seems to be more a way of feeding ego rather than a way of exposing your anger properly, seeing its real living quality. This applies to exposing yourself in general. It is a matter of seeing the basic quality of the situation, as it is, rather than trying to do something with it. Of course if one is completely open to the situation without any preconceptions, then one would know which action is right and which is unskillful. If a particular course of action would be clumsy and unskilled, then you would not take that fork in the road; you would take the road of skillful and creative action. You are not really involved with judgment as such, but you choose the creative way.

Q: Is collecting things and defending disguises an inescapable stage?

A: We collect things and later it is painful to give them away. It is similar to having stitches in our skin after an operation. It is frightening to have them taken out, we are apprehensive, we have become accustomed to a foreign element in our system.

Q: Do you think it is possible to begin to see what is, to see yourself as you are, without teacher?

A: I do not think it is possible at all. You have to have a spiritual friend in order to surrender and completely open yourself.

Q: Is it absolutely necessary that the spiritual friend be a living human being?

A: Yes. Any other "being" with whom you might think yourself communicating would be imaginary.

Q: Would the teachings of Christ in themselves be a spiritual friend?

A: I would not say so. That is an imaginary situation. It is the same with any teachings; they do not have to be the teachings of Christ necessarily. The problem is that we can interpret them ourselves. That is the whole point: written teachings are always open to the interpretation of ego.

Q: When you speak of opening and exposing yourself, it reminds me a great deal of certain schools of psychotherapy. What do you think is the function of the sort of things people do in psychotherapy?

A: In most forms of psychotherapy the problem is that, if you regard the process as "therapeutic," then you do not really mean it but it is the therapeutic thing to do. In other words, your therapy is a hobby. Moreover, you see your therapeutic situation as being defined by your case history. Because something went wrong in your relationship with your father and mother, you have this unhealthy tendency to . . . Once you begin to deal with a person's whole case history, trying to make it relevant to the present, the person begins to feel that he has no escape, that his situation is hopeless, because he cannot undo his past. He feels trapped by his past with no way out. This kind of treatment is extremely unskilled. It is destructive because it hinders involvement with the creative aspect of what is happening now, what is here, right now. But on the other hand, if psychotherapy is presented with the emphasis on living in the present moment, working with present problems, not just as regards verbal expression and thoughts alone but in terms of experiencing the actuality of emotions and feelings, then I think that would be very balanced style. Unfortunately there are many kinds of psychotherapy and many psychotherapists involved with trying to prove themselves and their own theories rather than working with what is. In fact they find it very frightening to work with what is.

We must simplify rather than complicate the problem with theories of any kind. The situation of nowness, this very moment, contains whole case histories and future determinations. Everything is right here, so we do not have to go any further than this to prove who we were or are or might be. As soon as we try to unravel the past, then we are involved with ambition and struggle in the present, not being able to accept the present moment as it is. It is very cowardly. Moreover, it is unhealthy to regard our therapist or guru as our savior. We must work on ourselves. There is really no other alternative. The spiritual friend might accentuate our pain in certain circumstances. That is part of the physician-patient relationship. The idea is not to regard the spiritual path as something very luxurious and pleasurable but to see it as just facing the facts of life.

The Open Way

I T SHOULD BE CLEAR by now that in order to find the open way we must first experience self-deception as it is, exposing ourselves completely. We may even be hesitant to consider such a hopeful subject as the open way, because we are so wary of our ambition. But our caution is a sign that we are ready to think about it. In fact, hesitation at this point could be another form of self-deception: ignoring the teachings with the rationale of trying to be perfect and extremely careful.

The approach to the open way lies in the experience of exposing oneself—an experience we discussed in the lecture "Initiation"—opening oneself to life, being what you are, presenting your positive and negative qualities to your spiritual friend, and working your way through. Then having presented yourself, having experienced initiation, the meeting of the two minds, you might tend to evaluate your credentials. You have experienced such an extraordinary incident; you were able to open, and your spiritual friend opened, and you met both yourself and your spiritual friend in the same moment. It was exciting, beautiful.

The problem lies in the fact that we are always trying to secure ourselves, reassure ourselves that we are all right. We are constantly looking for something solid to hang on to. The "miraculous" situation of the meeting of the two minds is such a fantastic experience that it seems to confirm our expectation of miracles and magic.

So the next step on the path of self-deception is the desire to see miracles. We have read many books describing the lives of great yogis and swamis, saints and avatars. And all these seem to speak of extraordinary miracles. Either someone walked through a wall or someone turned the world upside down—all these miracles. You would like to prove to yourself that such miracles do exist, because you would like to be sure that you are on the side of the guru, the side of the doctrine, the side of the miracles, sure that what you are doing is safe and powerful, sensational in fact, sure that you are on the side of the "goodies." You would like to be one of those few people who have done something fantastic, extraordinary, super-extraordinary, one of the people who turned the world upside down: "I actually thought that I was standing on the floor, but I found myself standing on the ceiling!" The sudden flash of the meeting with the spiritual friend, the meeting of the two minds, is definitely real, a genuine experience, quite sensational, a miracle in fact. Perhaps we are not quite *absolutely* sure, but certainly such a miracle must mean that we are on to something, that we have found the true way at last.

Such intense attempts to prove to ourselves that what we are doing is right indicate a very introverted state of mind; one is very aware of oneself and the state of one's being. We feel that we are a minority and that we are doing something very extraordinary, that we are different from everyone else. This sort of attempt to prove our own uniqueness is just an attempt to validate our self-deception. "Of course I experienced something extraordinary; of course I saw the miracle; of course I had the insight; therefore I am going on." Which is a very closed-in, introverted situation. We have no time to relate to anyone else, our friends or relatives, the outside world. We are concerned only with ourselves.

Eventually this approach becomes tedious and stale. We begin to realize that we have been deceiving ourselves and we begin to move closer to the genuine open way. We begin to suspect that all our beliefs are hallucinatory, that we have distorted our experience by evaluating it. "True, I had a flash of instant enlightenment, but at the same time I tried to possess it, grasp it, and it went away." We begin to discover that self-deception does not work at all, that it is simply trying to comfort oneself, trying to contact oneself inwardly, trying to prove something to oneself rather than really being open. At this point one might begin to punish oneself saying, "If I am trying not to deceive myself, then that is another kind of self-deception; and if I try to avoid doing that, then that is self-deception too. How can I possibly free myself? And if I am trying to free myself, then that is another form of self-deception as well," and so the chain reaction goes on and on and on, the chain reaction of overlapping paranoia.

Having discovered self-deception, we suffer from tremendous paranoia and self-criticism, which is helpful. It is good to experience the hopelessness of ambition, of trying to be open, of trying to cheer ourselves up, because this prepares the ground for another type of attitude toward spirituality. The whole point we are trying to get to is—when are we going to open, *really*? The action of our mind is so overlapping, an ingrown toenail, introverted: If I do this, then that is going to happen; if I do that, then this is going to happen. How can I escape the self-deception? I recognize it, I see it, but how am I going to get out of it?

I am afraid each of us has to go through this individually. I am not giving a guided tour to enlightenment. I do not guarantee anything. But I am just suggesting that perhaps there is something wrong with this approach.

Perhaps we do feel that something is wrong with this approach and we seek advice from our guru.

"I am completely convinced that this path is right for me, of course—we do not even have to discuss that. But something seems to be wrong. I have worked and worked on myself, and yet I find myself involved in a chain reaction of overlapping defeats."

"Okay then, what next?"

"Well, I am too busy to do anything else because I am so obsessed with all this."

"Okay, relax yourself."

"What can I do? Haven't you got any suggestions?"

"I am afraid I cannot give you an immediate solution to your problem. I have to know what is actually wrong with you, to start with. That is what all professional people would say. If there is something wrong with your television set, you do not immediately plug in a new tube. First you must examine the entire set. Which part does not function? Which tubes do not work?"

"Well, there doesn't seem to be anything wrong exactly. But the minute I try to touch on the subject it just goes berserk, it doesn't click anymore. When I try to do something to correct it, I get no results at all. Something seems to be fused."

"Big problem."

"You see, each time I try to work my way out, as you and other gurus told me to do, I try and try and try but there doesn't seem to be an end to the problem at all. Things keep going wrong all the time. If I start practicing asanas, pranayama, zazen, anything, much as I try to do it correctly, still the same familiar problems come back again and again and again. I have great faith in these doctrines, teachings, methods—of course I do. I love the teachers. I love the methods, I really do. I have complete faith in them. I know that a lot of people turn out beautifully as a result of traveling the same path I am attempting, but what is wrong with me? Maybe I have bad karma, maybe I am the black sheep of the family. Could that be so? If it is so, then I will go on a pilgrimage on my knees to India, I will make any sacrifice needed. I could starve myself. I will take any vow, but I just want to get it, really get into it. What can I do? Isn't there anything else in your sacred books prescribing something appropriate for a person like me? Isn't there something appropriate for a person like me? Isn't there some medicine I can take, a sacrifice I can perform?"

"I'm not sure. Come back later tomorrow and see me. Perhaps we can find something."

That is what a spiritual friend might say: "See me again tomorrow or on the weekend. Let's talk it over but don't worry." You go again, you see him, you think that you have some tremendous problem and that he has all the answers worked out especially for you. And again he will ask:

"How are you? How are you getting on?"

"What do you mean? I was waiting for *your* answer. You know how I am—I'm in terrible shape!"

You become very grumpy, and quite rightly in a way. Nothing happens, as usual, and then weeks and weeks go by as you come back again and again and again. You despair, suspecting nothing will come of the whole thing, entertaining the secret wish that maybe this is the time, maybe the fourth week or the fifth week or the seventh week. Seven is very symbolic, a mystic number. Time goes on: complete despair. You are about to investigate the possibility of other solutions. "Maybe if I go and see someone else," you think. "Perhaps I should return home and work with my own people; this situation is too alien to me. There seems to be no communication between him and me. He is supposed to have some kind of communication with me, but it is very disappointing, nothing happens at all." So you sit and wait. Whenever you see him, you almost immediately know what his words to you are going to be: "Go back and meditate," or "How are you? Have a cup of tea." It is the same thing, again and again.

What is wrong? In fact nothing is wrong at all, absolutely nothing. The situation is quite beautiful, as far as your spiritual friend is concerned. But this period of waiting on your part, trying to get over something, is in itself wrong, because a waiting period means so much concentration into yourself, working inward rather than working outward. There is a tendency toward centralization and there is the notion of the "big deal" involved with your psychology, your state of mind. That is what is wrong.

Perhaps I should tell you the story of Naropa and his teacher Tilopa, the great Indian sage. Tilopa was a guru who spent twelve years with his student Naropa doing practically the same kind of thing we have been discussing here. "If you fetch me soup from that kitchen, I will teach you, I might teach you," Tilopa would say. Then Naropa would bring the soup, having endured a terrible beating at the hands of the kitchen staff and householders in order to get it. He would arrive bloody but happy, and when he had presented the soup, Tilopa would say, "I want another cup, go and fetch it." So Naropa would go and fetch the soup, returning half dead. He did this because he yearned so for the teachings. Then Tilopa would say, "Thank you, let's go somewhere else." This sort of incident occurred again and again until Naropa's sense of expectation had reached its crescendo. At just this point Tilopa took off his sandal and slapped Naropa in the face. That was the abhisheka, the highest and most profound, the greatest—you could use many more adjectives to describe it—the greatest abhisheka. The slapping of a sandal against a man's cheek and suddenly there was nothing more for Naropa to work with.

But we must not get carried away with this mystical scene. The whole point is the open path, the open way. We have thoroughly examined and experienced self-deception. We have been carrying such a heavy burden, like a tortoise carrying its shell. We have continually attempted to seal ourselves into this shell, trying actually to get into "somewhere" with such aggression and speed. We must give up all our speed and aggression, the whole demanding quality. We must develop some compassion for ourselves, and then the open way just begins.

At this point we should discuss the meaning of compassion, which is the key to and the basic atmosphere of the open way. The best and most correct way of presenting the idea of compassion is in terms of clarity, clarity which contains fundamental warmth. At this stage your meditation practice is the act of trusting in yourself. As your practice becomes more prominent in daily life activities, you begin to trust yourself and have a compassionate attitude. Compassion in this sense is not feeling sorry for someone. It is basic warmth. As much space and clarity as there is, there is that much warmth as well, some delightful feeling of positive things happening in yourself constantly. Whatever you are doing, it is not regarded as a mechanical drag in terms of self-conscious meditation, but meditation is a delightful and spontaneous thing to do. It is the continual act of making friends with yourself.

Then, having made friends with yourself, you cannot just contain that friendship within you; you must have some outlet, which is your relationship with the world. So compassion becomes a bridge to the world outside. Trust and compassion for oneself bring inspiration to dance with life, to communicate with the energies of the world. Lacking this kind of inspiration and openness, the spiritual path becomes the samsaric path of desire. One remains trapped in the desire to improve oneself, the desire to achieve imagined goals. If we feel that we cannot achieve our goal, we suffer despair and the self-torture of unfulfilled ambition. On the other hand, if we feel that we are succeeding in achieving our goal, we might become self-satisfied and aggressive. "I know what I'm doing, don't touch me." We might become bloated with our knowledge, like certain "experts" we meet who know their subject thoroughly. If anyone asks questions, especially stupid or challenging questions, they get angry rather than trying to explain anything. "How could you say such a thing, how could you even dream of asking such stupid questions? Don't you see what I know?"

Or we might even succeed at some form of dualistic concentration practice and experience a kind of "mystical state." In such cases we might appear quite tranquil and religious in the conventional sense. But we would constantly have to charge up and maintain our "mystical state" and there would be a continual sense of appreciation, the repeated act of checking and indulging in our achievement. This is the typical distortion of the hinayana practice of self-contained meditation, self-enlightenment, and it is in some sense a form of aggression. There is no element of compassion and openness because one is so focused on one's own experience.

Compassion has nothing to do with achievement at all. It is spacious and very generous. When a person develops real compassion, he is uncertain whether he is being generous to others or to himself because compassion is environmental generosity, without direction, without "for me" and without "for them." It is filled with joy, spontaneously existing joy, constant joy in the sense of trust, in the sense that joy contains tremendous wealth, richness.

We could say that compassion is the ultimate attitude of wealth: an antipoverty attitude, a war on want. It contains all sorts of heroic, juicy, positive, visionary, expansive qualities. And it implies larger scale thinking, a freer and more expansive way of relating to yourself and the world. This is precisely why the second *yana* is called the mahayana, the "great vehicle." It is the attitude that one has been born fundamentally rich rather than that one must become rich. Without this kind of confidence, meditation cannot be transferred into action at all.

Compassion automatically invites you to relate with people, because you no longer regard people as a drain on your energy. They recharge your energy, because in the process of relating with them you acknowledge your wealth, your richness. So, if you have difficult tasks to perform, such as dealing with people or life situations, you do not feel you are running out of resources. Each time you are faced with a difficult task it presents itself as a delightful opportunity to demonstrate your richness, your wealth. There is no feeling of poverty at all in this approach to life.

Compassion as the key to the open way, the mahayana, makes possible the transcendental actions of the bodhisattva. The bodhisattva path starts with generosity and openness—giving and openness—the surrendering process. Openness is not a matter of giving something to someone else, but it means giving up your demand and the basic criteria of the demand. This is the dana paramita, the paramita of generosity. It is learning to trust in the fact that you do not need to secure your ground, learning to trust in your fundamental richness, that you can afford to be open. This is the open way. If you give up your psychological attitude of "demand," then basic health begins to evolve, which leads to the next act of the bodhisattva, the *shila* paramita, the paramita of morality or discipline.

Having opened, having given up everything without reference to the basic criteria of "I am doing this, I am doing that," without reference to oneself, then other situations connected with maintaining ego or collecting become irrelevant. That is the ultimate morality and it intensifies the situation of openness and bravery: you are not afraid of hurting yourself or anyone else because you are completely open. You do not feel uninspired with situations, which brings patience, the kshanti paramita. And patience leads to energy, virya—the quality of delight. There is the tremendous joy of involvement, which is energy, which also brings the panoramic vision of open meditation—the experience of dhyana—openness. You do not regard the situation outside as separate from you because you are so involved with the dance and play of life.

Then you become even more open. You do not regard anything as being rejected or accepted; you are just going along with each situation. You experience no warfare of any kind, neither trying to defeat an enemy nor trying to achieve a goal. There is no involvement with collecting or giving. No hope or fear at all. This is the development of *prajna*, transcendent knowledge, the ability to see situations as they are.

So the main theme of the open way is that we must begin to abandon the basic struggle of ego. To be completely open, to have that kind of absolute trust in yourself is the real meaning of compassion and love. There have been so many speeches about love and peace and tranquillity in the world. But how do we really bring love into being? Christ said, "Love thy neighbor," but how do we love? How do we do it? How are we going to radiate our love to the whole of humanity, to the whole world? "Because we must, and that's the truth!" "If you don't love, you are condemned, evil; you are doing a disservice to humanity." "If you love, you are on the path, you are on the right track." But how? Many people get very romantic about love, in fact get high on it at the very word. But then there will be a gap, a period when we are not high on love. Something else takes place which is embarrassing, a private matter. We tend to seal it off; it is "private parts," shameful, not part of our divinity. Let's not think about that. Let's simply ignite another love explosion and on and on we go, trying to ignore those parts of our being we reject, trying to be virtuous, loving, kind.

Perhaps this will put off a lot of people, but I am afraid love is not really the experience of beauty and romantic joy alone. Love is associated with ugliness and pain and aggression, as well as with the beauty of the world; it is not the recreation of heaven. Love or compassion, the open path, is associated with "what is." In order to develop love—universal love, cosmic love, whatever you would like to call it—one must accept the whole situation of life as it is, both the light and the dark, the good and the bad. One must open oneself to life, communicate with it. Perhaps you are fighting to develop love and peace, struggling to achieve them: "We are going to make it, we are going to spend thousands of dollars in order to broadcast the doctrine of love everywhere, we are going to proclaim love." Okay, proclaim it, do it, spend your money, but what about the speed and aggression behind what you are doing? Why do you have to push us into the acceptance of your love? Why is there such speed and force involved? If your love is moving with the same speed and drive as other people's hatred, then something appears to be wrong. It would seem to be the same as calling darkness light. There is so much ambition involved, taking the form of proselytizing. It is not an open situation of communication with things as they are. The ultimate implication of the words "peace on earth" is to remove altogether the ideas of peace and war and to open yourself equally and completely to the positive and negative aspects of the world. It is like seeing the world from an aerial point of view: there is light, there is dark; both are accepted. You are not trying to defend the light against the dark.

The action of the bodhisattva is like the moon shining on one hundred bowls of water, so that there are one hundred moons, one in each bowl. This is not the moon's design nor was it designed by anyone else. But for some strange reason there happen to be one hundred moons reflected in one hundred bowls of water. Openness means this kind of absolute trust and self-confidence. The open situation of compassion works this way rather than by deliberately attempting to create one hundred moons, one in each bowl.

The basic problem we seem to be facing is that we are too involved with trying to prove something, which is connected with paranoia and the feeling of poverty. When you are trying to prove or get something, you are not open anymore, you have to check everything, you have to arrange it "correctly." It is such a paranoid way to live and it really does not prove anything. One might set records in terms of numbers and quantities—that we have built the greatest, the biggest, we have collected the most, the longest, the most gigantic. But who is going to remember the record when you are dead? Or in one hundred years? Or in ten years? Or in ten minutes? The records that count are those of the given moment, of now—whether or not communication and openness are actually taking place now.

This is the open way, the bodhisattva path. A bodhisattva would not care, even if he received a medal from all the Buddhas proclaiming him the bravest bodhisattva in the entire universe; he would not care at all. You never read stories of the bodhisattvas receiving medals in the sacred writings. And quite rightly so, because there is no need for them to prove anything. The bodhisattva's action is spontaneous, it is the open life, open communication which does not involve struggle or speed at all.

Q: I assume that being a bodhisattva means helping people, and people make specific demands. So a bodhisattva must perform specific acts. But how does this idea of being totally open fit in with the need to perform specific acts?

A: Being open does not mean being unresponsive, a zombie. It means being free to do whatever is called for in a given situation. Because you do not want anything from the situation, you are free to act in the way genuinely appropriate to it. And, similarly, if other people want something from you, that may be their problem. You do not have to try to ingratiate yourself with anyone. Openness means "being what you are." If you are comfortable being yourself, then an environment of openness and communication arises automatically and naturally. It is like the idea of the moon and the bowls of water which we have been discussing: if the bowls are there, they will reflect your "moonness." If they are not there, they will not. Or if they are only half there, then they will reflect only half a moon. It is up to them. You are just there, the moon, open, and the bowls may reflect you or not. You neither care nor do you not care. You are just there.

Situations develop automatically. We do not need to fit ourselves into special roles and environments. I think many of us have been trying to do that for a long time, limiting ourselves, pigeonholing ourselves into narrowly defined sets of circumstances. We spend so much energy focusing our attention in just one place that to our surprise we discover that there are whole areas we have missed.

Q: Can one act with compassion and still get things done as they need to be done?

A: When there is no speed or aggression, you feel that there is room enough in which to move about and do things and you see the things which need to be done more clearly. You become more efficient and your work becomes more precise.

Q: I believe, Rinpoche, that you made a distinction between the open path and the internal path. Could you amplify what differences you see between the internal and the external?

A: Well, the word *internal,* as you are using it, seems to imply struggle, turning back into yourself, considering whether or not you are a sufficiently worthy, functional, and presentable person. In this approach there is too much "working on oneself," too much concentration inward. Whereas the open path is a matter of working purely with what is, of giving up altogether the fear that something may not work, that something may end in failure. One has to give up the paranoia that one might not fit into situations, that one might be rejected. One purely deals with life as it is.

Q: Where does the attitude of warmth come from?
A: It comes from the absence of aggression.

Q: But isn't that the goal?
A: As well as the path, the bridge. You do not live on the bridge. You walk over the bridge. In the experience of meditation there is automatically some sense of the absence of aggression, which is the definition of dharma. *Dharma* is defined as "dispassion" or "passionlessness," and passionlessness implies absence of aggression. If you are passionate, you want to get something quickly to satisfy your desire. When there is no desire to satisfy yourself, there is no aggression or speed. So if a person can really relate to the simplicity of the practice of meditation, then automatically there is an absence of aggression. Because there is no rush to achieve, you can afford to relax. Because you can afford to relax, you can afford to keep company with yourself, can afford to make love with yourself, be friends with yourself. Then thoughts, emotions, whatever occurs in the mind constantly accentuates the act of making friends with yourself.

Another way to put it is to say that compassion is the earthy quality of meditation practice, the feeling of earth and solidity. The message of compassionate warmth is to not be hasty and to relate to each situation as it is. The American Indian name "Sitting Bull" seems to be a perfect example of this. "Sitting Bull" is very solid and organic. You are really definitely present, resting.

Q: You seemed to say that compassion grows, but it was implied that you do not have to cultivate it.

A: It develops, grows, ferments by itself. It does not need any effort.

Q: Does it die?

A: It does not seem to die. Shantideva says that every uncompassion-ate action is like planting a dead tree, but anything related to compassion is like planting a living tree. It grows and grows endlessly and never dies. Even if it seems to die, it always leaves behind a seed from which an-other grows. Compassion is organic; it continues on and on and on.

Q: There is a certain kind of warmth that comes when you start to relate with someone, and then somehow that energy becomes over-whelming and catches you up in such a way that there is no longer any space or room to move.

A: If the warmth is without implication and self-reassurance, then it is self-sustaining and fundamentally healthy. When you make yogurt, if you raise the temperature or try to nurse the yogurt more than neces-sary, you do not make good yogurt at all. If you leave it at the right temperature and just abandon it, it will be good yogurt.

Q: How do you know when to abandon it?

A: You do not constantly have to manage yourself. You must disown rather than attempt to maintain control, trust yourself rather than check yourself. The more you try to check yourself, the greater the possibility of interrupting the natural play and growth of the situation. Even if what you are doing is chancy, even if it seems possible that the whole affair will blow up and become distorted, you do not worry about it.

Q: What happens when someone creates a situation and you do worry about it?

A: Worrying does not help at all. In fact it makes things worse.

Q: It seems the process we are talking about requires some sort of fearlessness.

A: Yes, very much so. It is positive thinking, the mentality of wealth.

Q: What if you feel the necessity for a violent act in order ultimately to do good for a person?

A: You just do it.

Q: But if you are not at that point of true compassion and wisdom?

A: You do not question or worry about your wisdom. You just do whatever is required. The situation you are facing is itself profound enough to be regarded as knowledge. You do not need secondary resources of information. You do not need reinforcement or guidelines for action. Reinforcement is provided by the situation automatically. When things must be conducted in a tough manner, you just do it because the situation demands your response. You do not impose toughness; you are an instrument of the situation.

Q: What do you do for a bridge when you don't feel compassionate?

A: You do not have to *feel* compassion. That is the distinction between emotional compassion and *compassion* compassion: you do not necessarily feel it; you *are* it. Usually, if you are open, compassion happens because you are not preoccupied with some kind of self-indulgence.

Q: Does the bridge of compassion require continual maintenance?

A: I do not think so. It requires acknowledgment rather than maintenance. That is the mentality of wealth; that you acknowledge that the bridge is there.

Q: What do you do when you are afraid of someone, perhaps with reason? For me, this destroys compassion.

A: Compassion is not looking down upon somebody who needs help, who needs care, but it is general, basic, organic, positive thinking. The fear of someone else seems to generate uncertainty as to who you are. That is why you are afraid of that particular situation or person. Fear comes from uncertainty. If you know exactly how you are going to handle this frightful situation, then you have no fear. Fear comes from panic, the bewilderment of uncertainty. Uncertainty is related to distrust in yourself, feeling that you are inadequate to deal with that mysterious problem which is threatening you. There is no fear if you really have a compassionate relationship with yourself, because then you know what you are doing. If you know what you are doing, then your projections also become methodical or predictable, in some sense. Then one develops prajna, knowledge of how to relate to any given situation.

Q: What do you mean by projections in this context?

A: Projection is the mirror reflection of yourself. Because you are uncertain about yourself, the world reflects that uncertainty back to you and the reflection begins to haunt you. Your uncertainty is haunting you, but it is merely your reflection in the mirror.

Q: What do you mean by saying that, if you are compassionate toward yourself, then you know what you are doing?

A: These two aspects of meditation always appear simultaneously. If you are opening to yourself and have a positive attitude toward yourself, then automatically you know what you are doing because you are not a mystery to yourself. This is jnana, "wisdom," "spontaneously-existing-awareness-wisdom." You know that you are spontaneously existing, you know what you are, therefore you can afford to trust yourself at the same time.

Q: If I really were to make friends with myself, then I wouldn't be afraid of making mistakes all the time?

A: That's it. The Tibetan word for wisdom is yeshe, which means "primordial intelligence." You are yourself at the beginning of any beginning. You could almost call it "unoriginated trust in yourself." You do not have to find the beginning at all. It is a primordial situation, so there is no point in trying to logically find the beginning. It is already. It is beginningless.

The coil of joy.
DRAWING BY GLEN EDDY.

Sense of Humor

I T WOULD BE INTERESTING to examine this subject in terms of what is *not* a sense of humor. Lack of humor seems to come from the attitude of the "hard fact." Things are very hard and deadly honest, deadly serious, like, to use an analogy, a living corpse. He lives in pain, has a continual expression of pain on his face. He has experienced some kind of hard fact—"reality"—he is deadly serious and has gone so far as to become a living corpse. The rigidity of this living corpse expresses the opposite of a sense of humor. It is as though somebody is standing behind you with a sharp sword. If you are not meditating properly, sitting still and upright, there will be someone behind you just about to strike. Or if you are not dealing with life properly, honestly, directly, someone is just about to hit you. This is the self-consciousness of watching yourself, observing yourself unnecessarily. Whatever we do is constantly being watched and censored. Actually it is not Big Brother who is watching; it is Big Me! Another aspect of me is watching me, behind me, just about to strike, just about to pinpoint my failure. There is no joy in this approach, no sense of humor at all.

This kind of seriousness relates to the problem of spiritual materialism as well. "Inasmuch as I am part of a particular lineage of meditators, associated with the church and its organization, because of my religious commitment, I must be a good boy or girl, an honest, good, churchgoing person. I must conform to the standards of the church, its rules and regulations. If I do not fulfill my obligations I will be condemned, reduced to a shrunken body." There is the threat of solemnity and death—death in the sense of an end to any further creative process. This attitude has the felling of limitation, rigidity; there is no room to move about at all.

85

You might ask then, "What about the great religious traditions, the teachings? They speak of discipline, rules and regulations. How do we reconcile these with the notion of a sense of humor?" Well, let's examine the question properly. Are the regulations, the discipline, the practice of morality really based on the purely judgmental attitude of "good" as opposed to "bad"? Are the great spiritual teachings really advocating that we fight evil because we are on the side of light, the side of peace? Are they telling us to fight against that other "undesirable" side, the bad and the black? That is a big question. If there is wisdom in the sacred teachings, there should not be any war. As long as a person is involved with warfare, trying to defend or attack, then his action is not sacred; it is mundane, dualistic, a battlefield situation. One would not expect the great teachings to be as simple-minded as that, trying to be good, fighting the bad. Such would be the approach of the Hollywood western movie—even before you have seen the conclusion, you already know precisely that the "goodies" will not be killed and the "baddies" are going to get smashed. This approach is obviously simple-minded; but it is just this type of situation that we are creating in terms of "spiritual" struggle, "spiritual" achievement.

I am not saying that a sense of humor should be wildly unleashed. I am speaking of seeing something more than just warfare, struggle, duality. If we regard the path of spirituality as a battlefield, then we are weak and feeble. Then our progress on the path will depend upon how great an area we have conquered, upon the subjugation of our own and others' faults, upon how much negativity we have eliminated. Relative to how much dark you have eliminated, that much light you have been able to produce. That is very feeble; one could hardly call it liberation or freedom or mukti or nirvana. You have achieved liberation by defeating something else: it is purely relative.

I do not want to make a "sense of humor" into something solemn; I am afraid that people are going to do that. But in order to really understand rigidity, that which is represented by the corpse, one cannot avoid the danger of making a sense of humor into a serious thing. Sense of humor means seeing both poles of a situation as they are, from an aerial point of view. There is good and there is bad and you see both with a panoramic view as though from above. Then you begin to feel that these little people on the ground, killing each other or making love or just being little people, are very insignificant in the sense that, if they begin to make a big deal of their warfare or lovemaking, then we begin to see the ironic aspect of their clamor. If we try very hard to build something tremendous, really meaningful, powerful—"I'm really searching for something, I'm really trying to fight my faults," or "I'm really trying to be good,"—then it loses its seriousness, becomes a paper tiger; it is extremely ironic.

Sense of humor seems to come from all-pervading joy, joy which has room to expand into a completely open situation because it is not involved with the battle between "this" and "that." Joy develops into the panoramic situation of seeing or feeling the whole ground, the open ground. This open situation has no hint of limitation, of imposed solemnity. And if you do try to treat life as a "serious business," if you try to impose solemnity upon life as though everything is a big deal, then it is funny. Why such a big deal?

A person might attempt to meditate in a 100 percent or 200 percent correct posture. Big Deal. Funny. Or on the other hand, a person might try to develop a sense of humor, trying always to make fun of things, to find humor in every corner, every crack. That in itself is a very serious game, which is equally funny. If you build up physical tension to the point where you are clenching your teeth, biting your tongue, then suddenly something will tickle you because you have been building too much; it is too absurd to go to such extremes. That extreme intensity itself becomes humor, automatically.

There is the Tibetan story of a certain monk who renounced his samsaric, confused life and decided to go live in a cave in order to meditate all the time. Prior to this he had been thinking continually of pain and suffering. His name was Ngonagpa of Langru, the Black-Faced One of Langru, because he never smiled at all but saw everything in life in terms of pain. He remained in retreat for many years, very solemn and deadly honest, until one day he looked at the shrine and saw that someone had presented a big lump of turquoise as a gift to him. As he viewed the gift, he saw a mouse creep in and try to drag away the piece of turquoise. The mouse could not do it, so it went back to its hole and called another mouse. They both tried to drag away this big lump of turquoise but could not do it. So they squeaked together and called eight more mice who came and finally managed to drag the whole lump back into their hole. Then for the first time Ngonagpa of Langru began to laugh and smile. And that was his first introduction to openness, a sudden flash of enlightenment.

So a sense of humor is not merely a matter of trying to tell jokes or make puns, trying to be funny in a deliberate fashion. It involves seeing the basic irony of the juxtaposition of extremes, so that one is not caught taking them seriously, so that one does not seriously play their game of hope and fear. This is why the experience of the spiritual path is so significant, why the practice of meditation is the most insignificant experience of all. It is insignificant because you place no value judgment on it. Once you are absorbed into that insignificant situation of openness without involvement in value judgment, then you begin to see all the games going on around you. Someone is trying to be stern and spiritually solemn, trying to be a good person. Such a person might take it seriously if someone offended him, might want to fight. If you work in accordance with the basic insignificance of what is, then you begin to see the humor in this kind of solemnity, in people making such a big deal about things.

Q: Most of the arguments I've heard for doing the good thing and the right thing say: First accumulate merit, be good, give up evil; then later on it will be even easier to give up the "good hang-ups." What do you make of this approach?

A: If we look at it from the point of view of a sense of humor, the idea of "giving up" seems to be too literal and naive. If you are attempting to be good and give up everything, ironically it is not giving up at all; it is taking on more things. That is the funny part of it. Someone might think himself able to abandon the big load he is carrying but the absence of the load, the giving up, is heavier, hundreds of times heavier than what the person has left behind. It is easy to give something up but the by-product of such renunciation could consist of some very heavy virtue. Each time you meet someone you will be thinking or will actually say, "I have given up this and that." "Giving up" can become heavier and heavier, as though you were carrying a big bag of germs on your back. Finally it might become a big fungus that you are carrying, growing faster and faster. At some stage a person begins to become completely unbearable because he has given up so many things.

For that matter, if we treat the practice of meditation as a serious matter, a matter of consequence, then it will become embarrassing and heavy, overwhelming. We will not even be able to think about it. It would be as though a person had eaten an extremely heavy meal. He is just about to get sick and he will begin to think, "I wish I were hungry. At least that would feel light. But now I have all the food in my stomach and I am just about to be sick. I wish I had never eaten." One cannot take spirituality so seriously. It is self-defeating, counter to the true meaning of "giving up."

Q: Is a sense of tragedy then something that an enlightened person has overcome?

A: You do not necessarily have to be enlightened to give up tragedy. If you are involved with the intensity of crescendo situations, with the intensity of tragedy, then you might begin to see the humor of these situations as well. As in music, when we hear the crescendo building, suddenly if the music stops, we begin to hear the silence as part of the music. It is not an extraordinary experience at all: it is very ordinary, very mundane. That is why I said it is one of the most insignificant experiences of all, because we do not attach our value judgments to it. The experience is hardly there. Of course if we employ the basic twist of ego, we could go on and say that because the experience is hardly there, because it is so insignificant, therefore it is one of the most valuable and extraordinary experiences of all. This would just be a conceptualized way of trying to prove that what you are involved in is a big deal. It is *not* a big deal.

Q: Is sense of humor related in any way to the experience of instant enlightenment, satori?

A: Certainly. There is the story of a person who died laughing. He was a simple village person who asked a teacher the color of Amitabha which traditionally, iconographically, is red. Somehow, by mistake, he thought the teacher said Amitabha's color was the color of ash in a fire. And this influenced his whole meditation practice; because when he practiced visualizing Amitabha, it was a gray Amitabha.

Finally the man was dying. As he lay on his deathbed he wanted to make sure, so he asked another teacher the color of Amitabha. The teacher said that Amitabha's color was red and the man suddenly burst into laughter: "Well, I used to think him the color of ash, and now you tell me he is red." He burst into laughter and died laughing. So it is a question of overcoming some kind of seriousness.

There are many stories of people who were actually able to see the awakened state by breaking into laughter—seeing the contrast, the irony of polar situations. For instance there was the hermit whose devotee lived several miles away in a village. This devotee supported the hermit, supplying him with food and the other necessities of life. Most of the time the devotee sent his wife or daughter or son to bring the hermit his supplies; but one day the hermit heard that the donor himself was coming to see him. The hermit thought, "I must impress him, I must clean and polish the shrine objects and make the shrine very neat and my room extremely tidy." So he cleaned and rearranged everything until his shrine looked very impressive with bowls of water and butter lamps burning brightly. And when he had finished, he sat down and began to admire the room and look around. Everything looked very neat, somehow unreal, and he saw that his shrine appeared unreal as well. Suddenly, to his surprise he realized that he was being a hypocrite. Then he went into the kitchen and got handfuls of ashes and threw them at the shrine until his room was a complete mess. When his patron came, he was extremely impressed by the natural quality of the room, by its not being tidy. The hermit could not hold himself together. He burst into laughter and said, "I tried to tidy myself and my room, but then I thought perhaps I should show it to you this way." And so they both, patron and hermit, burst into laugher. That was a great moment of awakening for both of them.

Q: In each lecture you describe some seemingly inescapable situation in which we are all trapped, in which we have already become enmeshed. I just wonder if you ever mean to imply that there is a way out?

A: You see, the whole point is that if we are speaking of a way out all the time, then we are dealing in fantasy, the dream of escape, salvation, enlightenment. We need to be practical. We must examine what is here, now, our neurotic mind. Once we are completely familiar with the negative aspects of the state of our being, then we know the "way out" automatically. But if we talk about how beautiful and joyous our attainment of the goal will be, then we become extremely sincere and romantic; and this approach becomes an obstacle.

One must be practical. It is like visiting your physician because you are ill. If a doctor is going to treat you, then he must first know what is wrong with you. It is not a question of what could be right with you;

that is not relevant. If you tell the doctor what is wrong with you, then that is the way out of your illness. That is why the Buddha taught the four noble truths, his first teaching. One must begin with the realization of pain, duhkha, suffering. Then having realized duhkha, one goes on to the origin of suffering and the path leading out of suffering and liberation. The Buddha did not begin by teaching the beauty of the enlightenment experience.

Q: Following the usual patterns of evaluation and judgment, I find myself thinking that the errors and obstacles which you describe in later lectures are somehow more advanced than those described in the earlier lectures. Is this correct?

A: That is true. Even after one has stepped onto the path, as in the case of bodhisattvas, once you have begun to awaken there could be a tendency to analyze your awakened state. This involves looking at oneself, analyzing and evaluating, and continues until there is a sharp blow which is called the vajra-like samadhi. This is the last samadhi state of meditation. The attainment of enlightenment is called "vajra-like" because it does not stand for any nonsense; it just cuts right through all our games. In the story of the Buddha's life we hear of the temptations of Mara, which are extremely subtle. The first temptation is fear of physical destruction. The last is the seduction by the daughters of Mara. This seduction, the seduction of spiritual materialism, is extremely powerful because it is the seduction of thinking that "I" have achieved something. If we think we have achieved something, that we have "made it," then we have been seduced by Mara's daughters, the seduction of spiritual materialism.

The portrait of samsara.
DRAWING BY GLEN EDDY.

The Development of Ego

As we are going to examine the Buddhist path from beginning to end, from the beginner's mind to the enlightened one, I think it would be best to start with something very concrete and realistic, the field we are going to cultivate. It would be foolish to study more advanced subjects before we are familiar with the starting point, the nature of ego. We have a saying in Tibet that, before the head has been cooked properly, grabbing the tongue is of no use. Any spiritual practice needs this basic understanding of the starting point, the material with which we are working.

If we do not know the material with which we are working, then our study is useless; speculations about the goal become mere fantasy. These speculations may take the form of advanced ideas and descriptions of spiritual experiences, but they only exploit the weaker aspects of human nature, our expectations and desires to see and hear something colorful, something extraordinary. If we begin our study with these dreams of extraordinary, "enlightening," and dramatic experiences, then we will build up our expectations and preconceptions so that later, when we are actually working on the path, our minds will be occupied largely with what *will be* rather than with what *is*. It is destructive and not fair to people to play on their weaknesses, their expectations and dreams, rather than to present the realistic starting point of what they are.

It is necessary, therefore, to start on what we are and why we are searching. Generally, all religious traditions deal with this material, speaking variously of alayavijnana or original sin or the fall of man or the basis of ego. Most religions refer to this material in a somewhat pejorative way, but I do not think it is such a shocking or terrible thing. We do not have to be ashamed of what we are. As sentient beings we have wonderful backgrounds. These backgrounds may not be particularly enlightened or peaceful or intelligent. Nevertheless, we have soil good enough to cultivate; we can plant anything in it. Therefore, in dealing with this subject we are not condemning or attempting to eliminate our ego-psychology; we are purely acknowledging it, seeing it as it is. In fact, the understanding of ego is the foundation of Buddhism. So let us look at how ego develops.

Fundamentally there is just open space, the *basic ground*, what we really are. Our most fundamental state of mind, before the creation of ego, is such that there is basic openness, basic freedom, a spacious quality; and we have now and have always had this openness. Take, for example, our everyday lives and thought patterns. When we see an object, in the first instant there is a sudden perception which has no logic or conceptualization to it at all; we just perceive the thing in the open ground. Then immediately we panic and begin to rush about trying to add something to it, either trying to find a name for it or trying to find pigeonholes in which we could locate and categorize it. Gradually things develop from there.

This development does not take the shape of a solid entity. Rather, this development is illusory, the mistaken belief in a "self" or "ego." Confused mind is inclined to view itself as a solid, ongoing thing, but it is only a collection of tendencies, events. In Buddhist terminology this collection is referred to as the five skandhas or five heaps. So perhaps we could go through the whole development of the five skandhas.

The beginning point is that there is open space, belonging to no one. There is always primordial intelligence connected with the space and openness. *Vidya,* which means "intelligence" in Sanskrit—precision, sharpness, sharpness with space, sharpness with room in which to put things, exchange things. It is like a spacious hall where there is room to dance about, where there is no danger of knocking things over or tripping over things, for there is completely open space. We *are* this space, we are *one* with it, with vidya, intelligence, and openness.

But if we are this all the time, where did the confusion come from, where has the space gone, what has happened? Nothing has happened, as a matter of fact. We just became too active in that space. Because it is spacious, it brings inspiration to dance about; but our dance became a bit too active, we began to spin more than was necessary to express the space. At this point we became *self*-conscious, conscious that "I" am dancing in the space.

At such a point, space is no longer space as such. It becomes solid. Instead of being one with the space, we feel solid space as a separate entity, as tangible. This is the first experience of duality—space and I, I am dancing in this space, and this spaciousness is a solid, separate thing. Duality means "space and I," rather than being completely one with the space. This is the birth of "form," of "other."

Then a kind of blackout occurs, in the sense that we forget what we were doing. There is a sudden halt, a pause; and we turn around and "discover" solid space, as though we had never before done anything at all, as though we were not the creators of all that solidity. There is a gap. Having already created solidified space, then we are overwhelmed by it and begin to become lost in it. There is a blackout and then, suddenly, an awakening.

When we awaken, we refuse to see the space as openness, refuse to see its smooth and ventilating quality. We completely ignore it, which is called avidya. A means "negation," *vidya* means "intelligence," so it is "un-intelligence." Because this extreme intelligence has been transformed into the perception of solid space, because this intelligence with a sharp and precise and flowing luminous quality has become static, therefore it is called avidya, "ignorance." We deliberately ignore. We are not satisfied just to dance in the space but we want to have a partner, and so we choose the space as our partner. If you choose space as your partner in the dance, then of course you want it to dance with you. In order to possess it as a partner, you have to solidify it and ignore its flowing, open quality. This is avidya, ignorance, ignoring the intelligence. It is the culmination of the first skandha, the creation of ignorance-form.

In fact, this skandha, the skandha of ignorance-form, has three different aspects or stages which we could examine through the use of another metaphor. Suppose in the beginning there is an open plain without any mountains or trees, completely open land, a simple desert without any particular characteristics. That is how we are, what we are. We are very simple and basic. And yet there is a sun shining, a moon shining, and there will be lights and colors, the texture of the desert. There will be some feeling of the energy which plays between heaven and earth. This goes on and on.

Then, strangely, there is suddenly someone to notice all this. It is as if one of the grains of sand had stuck its neck out and begun to look around. We are that grain of sand, coming to the conclusion of our separateness. This is the "birth of ignorance" in its first stage, a kind of chemical reaction. Duality has begun.

The second stage of ignorance-form is called "the ignorance born within." Having noticed that one is separate, then there is the feeling that one has always been so. It is an awkwardness, the instinct toward self-consciousness. It is also one's excuse for remaining separate, an individual grain of sand. It is an aggressive type of ignorance, though not exactly aggressive in the sense of anger; it has not developed as far as that. Rather it is aggression in the sense that one feels awkward, unbalanced, and so one tries to secure one's ground, create a shelter for oneself. It is the attitude that one is a confused and separate individual, and that is all there is to it. One has identified oneself as separate from the basic landscape of space and openness.

The third type of ignorance is "self-observing ignorance," watching oneself. There is a sense of seeing oneself as an external object, which leads to the first notion of "other." One is beginning to have a relationship with a so-called "external" world. This is why these three stages of ignorance constitute the skandha of form-ignorance; one is beginning to create the world of forms.

When we speak of "ignorance" we do not mean stupidity at all. In a sense, ignorance is very intelligent, but it is a completely two-way intelligence. That is to say, one purely reacts to one's projections rather than just seeing what is. There is no situation of "letting be" at all, because one is ignoring what one is all the time. That is the basic definition of ignorance.

The next development is the setting up of a defense mechanism to protect our ignorance. This defense mechanism is feeling, the second skandha. Since we have already ignored open space, we would like next to feel the qualities of solid space in order to bring complete fulfillment to the grasping quality we are developing. Of course space does not mean just bare space, for it contains color and energy. There are tremendous, magnificent displays of color and energy, beautiful and picturesque. But we have ignored them altogether. Instead there is just a solidified version of that color; and the color becomes captured color, and the energy becomes captured energy, because we have solidified the

THE DEVELOPMENT OF EGO

whole space and turned it into "other." So we begin to reach out and feel the qualities of "other." By doing this we reassure ourselves that we exist. "If I can feel that out there, then I must be here."

Whenever anything happens, one reaches out to feel whether the situation is seductive or threatening or neutral. Whenever there is a sudden separation, a feeling of not knowing the relationship of "that" to "this," we tend to feel for our ground. This is the extremely efficient feeling mechanism that we begin to set up, the second skandha.

The next mechanism to further establish ego is the third skandha, perception-impulse. We begin to be fascinated by our own creation, the static colors and the static energies. We want to relate to them, and so we begin gradually to explore our creation.

In order to explore efficiently there must be a kind of switchboard system, a controller of the feeling mechanism. Feeling transmits its information to the central switchboard, which is the act of perception. According to that information, we make judgments, we react. Whether we should react for or against or indifferently is automatically determined by this bureaucracy of feeling and perception. If we feel the situation and find it threatening, then we will push it away from us. If we find it seductive, then we will draw it to us. If we find it neutral, we will be indifferent. These are the three types of impulse: hatred, desire, and stupidity. Thus perception refers to receiving information from the outside world and impulse refers to our response to that information.

The next development is the fourth skandha, concept. Perception-impulse is an automatic reaction to intuitive feeling. However, this kind of automatic reaction is not really enough of a defense to protect one's ignorance and guarantee one's security. In order to really protect and deceive oneself completely, properly, one needs intellect, the ability to name and categorize things. Thus we label things and events as being "good," "bad," "beautiful," "ugly," and so on, according to which impulse we find appropriate to them.

So the structure of ego is gradually becoming heavier and heavier, stronger and stronger. Up to this point, ego's development has been purely an action and reaction process; but from now on ego gradually develops beyond the ape instinct and become more sophisticated. We begin to experience intellectual speculation, confirming or interpreting ourselves, putting ourselves into certain logical, interpretive situations. The basic nature of intellect is quite logical. Obviously there will be the tendency to work for a positive condition: to confirm our experience, to interpret weakness into strength, to fabricate a logic of security, to confirm our ignorance.

In a sense, it might be said that the primordial intelligence is operating all the time, but it is being employed by the dualistic fixation, ignorance. In the beginning stages of the development of ego this intelligence operates as the intuitive sharpness of feeling. Later it operates in the form of intellect. Actually it seems that there is no such thing as the ego at all; there is no such thing as "I am." It is an accumulation of a lot of stuff. It is a "brilliant work of art," a product of the intellect which says, "Let's give it a name, let's call it something, let's call it 'I am'," which is very clever. "I" is the product of intellect, the label which unifies into one whole the disorganized and scattered development of ego.

The last stage of the development of ego is the fifth skandha, consciousness. At this level an amalgamation takes place: the intuitive intelligence of the second skandha, the energy of the third, and the intellectualization of the fourth combine to produce thoughts and emotions. Thus at the level of the fifth skandha we find the six realms as well as the uncontrollable and illogical patterns of discursive thought.

This is the complete picture of ego. It is in this state that all of us have arrived at our study of Buddhist psychology and meditation.

In Buddhist literature there is a metaphor commonly used to describe this whole process, the creation and development of ego. It speaks of a monkey locked in an empty house, a house with five windows representing the five senses. This monkey is inquisitive, poking its head out of each window and jumping up and down, up and down, restlessly. He is a captive monkey in an empty house. It is a solid house, rather than the jungle in which the monkey leaped and swung, rather than the trees in which he could hear the wind moving and the rustling of the leaves and branches. All these things have become completely solidified. In fact, the jungle itself has become his solid house, his prison. Instead of perching in a tree, this inquisitive monkey has been walled in by a solid world, as if a flowing thing, a dramatic and beautiful waterfall, had suddenly been frozen. This frozen house, made of frozen colors and energies, is completely still. This seems to be the point where time begins as past, future, and present. The flux of things becomes solid tangible time, a solid idea of time.

The inquisitive monkey awakens from his blackout, but he does not awaken completely. He awakens to find himself trapped inside of a solid, claustrophobic house with just five windows. He becomes bored, as though captured in a zoo behind iron bars, and he tries to explore the bars by climbing up and down. That he has been captured is not particularly important; but the idea of capture is magnified a thousand times because of his fascination with it. If one is fascinated, the sense of claustrophobia becomes more and more vivid, more and more acute, because one begins to explore one's imprisonment. In fact fascination is part of the reason he remains imprisoned. He is captured by his fascination. Of course at the beginning there was the sudden blackout which confirmed his belief in a solid world. But now having taken solidity for granted, he is trapped by his involvement with it.

Of course this inquisitive monkey does not explore all the time. He begins to become agitated, begins to feel that something is very repetitive and uninteresting, and he begins to become neurotic. Hungry for entertainment, he tries to feel and appreciate the texture of the wall, attempting to make sure that this seeming solidity is really solid. Then, assured that the space is solid, the monkey begins to relate to it by grasping it, repelling it, or ignoring it. If he attempts to grasp the space in order to possess it as his own experience, his own discovery, his own understanding, this is desire. Or, if the space seems a prison to him so that he tries to kick and batter his way out, fighting harder and harder, then this is hatred. Hatred is not just the mentality of destruction alone; but it is even more a feeling of defensiveness, defending oneself against claustrophobia. The monkey does not necessarily feel that there is an opponent or enemy approaching; he simply wants to escape his prison.

Finally the monkey might try to ignore that he is imprisoned or that there is something seductive in his environment. He plays deaf and dumb and so is indifferent and slothful in relation to what is happening around him. This is stupidity.

To go back a bit, you might say that the monkey is born into his house as he awakens from the blackout. He does not know how he arrived in this prison, so he assumes he has always been there, forgetting that he himself solidified the space into walls. Then he feels the texture of the walls, which is the second skandha, feeling. After that, he relates to the house in terms of desire, hatred, and stupidity, the third skandha, perception-impulse. Then, having developed these three ways of relating to his house, the monkey begins to label and categorize it: "This is a window. This corner is pleasant. That wall frightens me and is bad." He develops a conceptual framework with which to label and categorize and evaluate his house, his world, according to whether he desires, hates, or feels indifferent to it. This is the fourth skandha, concept.

The monkey's development through the fourth skandha has been fairly logical and predictable. But the pattern of development begins to break down as he enters the fifth skandha, consciousness. The thought pattern becomes irregular and unpredictable and the monkey begins to hallucinate, to dream.

When we speak of "hallucination" or "dream," it means that we attach values to things and events which they do not necessarily have. We have definite opinions about the way things are and should be. This is projection: we project our version of things onto what is there. Thus we become completely immersed in a world of our own creation, a world of conflicting values and opinions. Hallucination, in this sense, is a misinterpretation of things and events, reading into the phenomenal world meanings which it does not have.

This is what the monkey begins to experience at the level of the fifth skandha. Having tried to get out and having failed, he feels dejected, helpless, and so he begins to go completely insane. Because he is so tired of struggling, it is very tempting for him to relax and let his mind wander and hallucinate. This is the creation of the six lokas or six realms. There is a great deal of discussion in the Buddhist tradition about hell beings, people in heaven, the human world, the animal realm, and other psychological states of being. These are the different kinds of projections, the dream worlds we create for ourselves.

Having struggled and failed to escape, having experienced claustrophobia and pain, this monkey begins to wish for something good, something beautiful and seductive. So the first realm he begins to hallucinate is the deva loka, the god realm, "heaven," a place filled with beautiful, splendid things. The monkey dreams of strolling out of his house, walking in luxuriant fields, eating ripe fruit, sitting and swinging in the trees, living a life of freedom and ease.

Then he also begins to hallucinate the asura realm, or the realm of the jealous gods. Having experienced the dream of heaven, the monkey wants to defend and maintain his great bliss and happiness. He suffers from paranoia, worrying that others may try to take his treasures from him, and so he begins to feel jealousy. He is proud of himself, has enjoyed his creation of the god realm, and this has led him into jealousy of the asura realm.

Then he also perceives the earthbound quality of these experiences. Instead of simply alternating between jealousy and pride, he begins to feel comfortable, at home in the "human world," the "earthy world." It is the world of just leading a regular life, doing things ordinarily, in a mundane fashion. This is the human realm.

But then the monkey also senses that something is a bit dull, something is not quite flowing. This is because, as he progresses from the realm of the gods to the realm of the jealous gods to the realm of human beings and his hallucinations become more and more solid, then this whole development begins to feel rather heavy and stupid. At this point he is born into the animal realm. He would rather crawl or moo or bark than enjoy the pleasure of pride or envy. This is the simplicity of the animals.

Then the process is intensified, and the monkey starts to experience a desperate feeling of starvation, because he really does not want to descend to any lower realms. He would like to return to the pleasure realms of the gods; so he begins to feel hunger and thirst, a tremendous feeling of nostalgia for what he remembers once having had. This is the realm of the hungry ghosts or *preta* realm.

Then there is a sudden losing of faith and the monkey begins to doubt himself and his world, begins to react violently. All this is a terrible nightmare. He realizes that such a nightmare could not be true and he begins to hate himself for creating all this horror. This is the dream of the hell realm, the last of the six realms.

Throughout the entire development of the six realms the monkey has experienced discursive thoughts, ideas, fantasies, and whole thought patterns. Up to the level of the fifth skandha his process of psychological evolution has been very regular and predictable. From the first skandha each successive development arose in a systematic pattern, like an overlay of tiles on a roof. But now the monkey's state of mind becomes very distorted and disturbed, as suddenly this mental jigsaw puzzle erupts and his thought patterns become irregular and unpredictable. This seems to be our state of mind as we come to the teachings and the practice of meditation. This is the place from which we must start our practice.

I think that it is very important to discuss the basis of the path—ego, our confusion—before we speak of liberation and freedom. If I were only to discuss the experience of liberation, that would be very dangerous. This is why we begin by considering the development of ego. It is a kind of psychological portrait of our mental states. I am afraid this has not been an especially beautiful talk, but we have to face the facts. That seems to be the process of working on the path.

Q: Could you say something more about what you mean by the "blackout?"

A: It is nothing particularly profound. It is just that at the level of the first skandha we have worked very hard on trying to solidify space. We have worked so hard and with such speed that intelligence suddenly collapses. This could be said to be a kind of reverse satori, reverse enlightenment experience, the experience of ignorance. You suddenly go into a trance, because you have worked so hard. This is something which you have actually *achieved*, a masterpiece, all this solidity. And having achieved it completely, then suddenly you are overwhelmed by it. It is a meditation of its kind, a sort of reverse samadhi.

Q: Do you think that people have to be aware of death in order actually to be alive?

A: I don't think you have to be particularly aware of death, in the sense of analyzing it, but you just have to see what you are. Often we tend to look for the positive side, the beauty of spirituality, and ignore ourselves as we are. This is the greatest danger. If we are engaged in self-analysis, our spiritual practice is trying to find some ultimate analysis, an ultimate self-deception. Ego's intelligence is tremendously talented. It can distort anything. If one seizes on the ideas of spirituality or self-analysis or transcendence of ego, immediately ego takes hold of them and translates them into self-deception.

Q: When the monkey starts to hallucinate, is it something he has known before? Where does hallucination come from?

A: It is a kind of instinct, a secondary instinct, the ape instinct that we all have. If there is pain, then one will hallucinate pleasure, by contrast. There is the urge to defend oneself, establish one's territory.

Q: Equipped only with the level of consciousness we now have, are we not doomed to fight and struggle hopelessly at this level, unless we can get back to the space you have been describing?

A: Of course we are going to fight all the time, there is no end. We could go on talking forever about the succession of struggles we will endure. There is no other answer at all, except just as you said, trying to find the primordial space again. Otherwise we are stuck in the psychological attitude of *this* as opposed to *that,* which is an obstacle. We are always fighting an opponent. There is never a moment when we give up fighting. The problem is duality, warfare in terms of I and my opponent.

The practice of meditation is a completely different way of working. One has to change one's whole attitude and way of conducting life. One has to change all one's policies, so to speak. This could be very painful. Suddenly one begins to realize, "If I do not fight, how am I going to deal with my enemies? It is all very well for me not to fight, but what about them? They are still going to be there." That is the interesting point.

Q: To see the wall and recognize that you are there and not go further—it seems like a very dangerous position.

A: That is precisely it; it isn't dangerous. It might be painful at the time to realize that the wall is solid and that you are trapped inside it, but that is the interesting point.

Q: But weren't you just saying that it is instinctive to want to return to the other state, the open space?

A: Of course, but this monkey will not let himself just *be* anymore. He continually fights, or else he is involved in hallucinations. He never stops, never allows himself to actually feel anything properly. That is the problem. That is why simply stopping, just allowing a gap, is the first step in the practice of meditation.

Q: Say you have a barrier, an inhibition, and you are very aware of it. Should the inhibition just disappear through your awareness of it?

A: The whole point is that we must not attempt to figure out how we are going to escape our dilemma, but for now we must think about all these claustrophobic rooms that we are in. This is the first step to learning. We have to actually identify ourselves and feel ourselves properly. This will provide us with inspiration for further study. We had better not speak of getting free yet.

Q: Would you say that these claustrophobic rooms were intellectual fabrications?

A: The intensity of the primordial intelligence triggers us off all the time. All these activities of the monkey are, therefore, not to be regarded as something we should escape but as something which is a product of primordial intelligence. The more we try to struggle, the more we will discover that the walls really are solid. The more energy we put into struggle, by that much will we strengthen the walls, because the walls need our attention to solidify them. Whenever we pay more attention to the walls, we begin to feel the hopelessness of escape.

Q: What does the monkey perceive when he looks out of the five windows of the house?
A: Well, he perceives the east, west, south, and north.

Q: How do they look to him?
A: A square world.

Q: What about outside the house?
A: Well, a square world, because he sees through windows.

Q: He doesn't see anything in the distance?
A: He could, but it is also a square picture, because it is like hanging a picture on the wall, isn't it?

Q: What happens to the monkey when he takes a little LSD or peyote?
A: He has already taken it.

The Six Realms

W HEN WE LEFT the monkey, he was in the hell realm, trying to
kick and claw and push his way through the walls of his house.
The monkey's experiences in the hell realm are quite terrifying and horrific. He finds himself walking through gigantic fields of red-hot iron, or
being chained and marked with black lines and cut apart, or roasting
in hot iron cubicles, or boiling in large cauldrons. These and the other
hallucinations of hell are generated from an environment of claustrophobia and aggression. There is a feeling of being trapped in a small space
with no air to breathe and no room in which to move about. Trapped as
he is, the monkey not only tries to destroy the walls of his claustrophobic
prison; he even attempts to kill himself in order to escape his excruciating and continuous pain. But he cannot really kill himself, and his suicide
attempts only intensify his torture. The more the monkey struggles to
destroy or control the walls, the more solid and oppressive they become,
until at some point the intensity of the monkey's aggression wears out a
bit and, instead of battling with the walls, he stops relating to them, stops
communicating with them. He becomes paralyzed, frozen, remaining
enveloped in pain without struggling to escape it. Here he experiences
the various tortures involving freezing and dwelling in harsh, barren,
desolate areas.

However, eventually the monkey begins to become exhausted from
his struggle. The intensity of the hell realm begins to diminish, the monkey begins to relax, and suddenly he sees the possibility of a more open,
spacious way to be. He hungers for this new state, and this is the realm
of the hungry ghost or preta loka: the feeling of impoverishment and
hunger for relief. In the hell realm he had been too busy struggling to

even have time to consider the possibility of relief. Now he experiences great hunger for more pleasurable, spacious conditions and fantasizes numerous ways to satisfy his hunger. He may imagine that he sees far away from him some open space, but when he approaches it, he finds a vast terrifying desert. Or he may see in the distance a huge fruit tree, but as he goes closer to it, he discovers that it is barren or that someone is guarding it. Or the monkey may fly to a seemingly lush and fertile valley, only to find it filled with poisonous insects and the repelling smells of rotting vegetation. In each of his fantasies he glimpses the possibility of satisfaction, reaches out for it, and is quickly disappointed. Each time he seems about to achieve pleasure, he is rudely awakened from his idyllic dream; but his hunger is so demanding that he is not daunted and so continues to constantly churn out fantasies of future satisfaction. The pain of disappointment involves the monkey in a love-hate relationship with his dreams. He is fascinated by them, but the disappointment is so painful that he is repelled by them as well.

The torture of the hungry ghost realm is not so much the pain of not finding what he wants; rather it is the insatiable hunger itself which causes pain. Probably if the monkey found large quantities of food, he would not touch it at all; or else he would eat everything and then desire more. This is because, fundamentally, the monkey is fascinated with *being* hungry rather than with *satisfying* his hunger. The quick frustration of his attempts to satisfy his hunger enables him to be hungry again. So the pain and hunger of the preta loka, as with the aggression of the hell realm and the preoccupations of the other realms, provide the monkey with something exciting to occupy himself, something solid to relate to, something to make him feel secure that he exists as a real person. He is afraid to give up this security and entertainment, afraid to venture out into the unknown world of open space. He would rather stay in his familiar prison, no matter how painful and oppressive it might be.

However, as the monkey is repeatedly frustrated in his attempts to fulfill his fantasies, he begins to become somewhat resentful and at the same time resigned. He begins to give up the intensity of hunger and relax further into a set series of habitual responses to the world. He ignores other ways of dealing with life experiences, relies on the same set of responses, and in this way limits his world: a dog tries to smell everything with which it comes into contact; a cat takes no interest in television. This is the animal realm, the realm of stupidity. The monkey blinds himself to what is around him and refuses to explore new territory, clinging to familiar goals and familiar irritations. He is intoxicated with his safe, self-contained, familiar world and so fixes his attention on familiar goals and pursues them with unswerving and stubborn determination. Thus the animal realm is symbolized by the pig. A pig just eats whatever comes in front of its nose. It does not look right or left; it just goes right through, just does it. It does not matter to the pig if it has to swim through a tremendous mud pool or face other obstacles; it just plows through and eats whatever appears in front of it.

But eventually the monkey begins to realize that he can pick and choose his pleasures and pains. He begins to become somewhat more intelligent, discriminating between pleasurable and painful experiences in an effort to maximize pleasure and minimize pain. This is the human realm, the realm of discriminating passion. Here the monkey stops to consider what it is that he is reaching for. He becomes more discriminating, considers alternatives, thinks more, and therefore hopes and fears more. This is the human realm, the realm of passion and intellect. The monkey becomes more intelligent. He does not simply grasp; he explores, feels textures, compares things. If he decides that he wants something, he tries to grasp it, draw it to him, and possess it. For example, if the monkey were to want a beautiful silk material, he would go to different shops and feel the texture of their materials to see if any one of them was exactly what he wanted. When he came to the material which precisely fit his preconception, or the nearest thing to it, he would feel it and say, "Ah, that's right. Isn't it beautiful? I think it's worth buying." Then he would pay for it and take it home and show it to his friends and ask them to feel it and appreciate the texture of his beautiful material. In the human realm the monkey is always thinking about how to possess pleasurable things: "Maybe I should buy a teddy bear to take to bed— something lovable, cuddly, soft, warm, and hairy."

But the monkey discovers that, although he is intelligent and can manipulate his world to achieve some pleasure, still he cannot hold on to pleasure nor can he always get what he wants. He is plagued by illness, old age, death—by frustrations and problems of all kinds. Pain is the constant companion of his pleasures.

So he begins, quite logically, to deduce the possibility of heaven, the complete elimination of pain and achievement of pleasure. His version of heaven may be the acquisition of extreme wealth or power or fame—

whatever it is he would like his world to be, and he becomes preoccupied with achievement and competition. This is the asura realm, the
realm of the jealous gods. The monkey dreams of ideal states that are
superior to the pleasures and pains of the human realm and is always
trying to achieve these states, always trying to be better than anyone
else. In his constant struggle to achieve perfection of some sort, the
monkey becomes obsessed with measuring his progress, with comparing
himself to others. Through developing increased control of his thoughts
and emotions and therefore greater concentration, he is able to manipulate his world more successfully than in the human realm. But his preoccupation with always being best, with always being master of a situation,
makes him insecure and anxious. He must always struggle to control his
territory, overcoming all threats to his achievements. He is always fighting for mastery of his world.

The ambition to gain victory and the fear of losing a battle provide a
sense of being alive as well as cause irritation. The monkey constantly
loses sight of his ultimate goal, but is still driven on by his ambition to
be better. He is obsessed with competition and achievement. He seeks
out pleasurable, appealing situations that seem beyond his reach and
tries to draw them into his territory. When it is too difficult to achieve
his goals, he may shy away from the struggle and condemn himself for
not disciplining himself, for not working harder. So the monkey is
caught in a world of unfulfilled ideals, self-condemnation and fear of
failure.

Eventually the monkey may achieve his goal—become a millionaire,
a leader of a country, a famous artist. At first, upon achieving his goal,
he will still feel somewhat insecure; but sooner or later he begins to realize that he has made it, that he is there, that he is in heaven. Then he
begins to relax, to appreciate and dwell upon his achievements, shielding
out undesirable things. It is an hypnotic-like state, natural concentration.
This blissful and proud state is the deva loka or realm of the gods. Figuratively, the bodies of the gods are made out of light. They do not have
to bother with earthbound concerns. If they want to make love, just
glancing and smiling at each other satisfies them. If they want to eat,
they just direct their minds toward beautiful sights which feed them. It
is the utopian world which human beings expect it to be. Everything
happens easily, naturally, automatically. Whatever the monkey hears is
musical, whatever he sees is colorful, whatever he feels is pleasant. He

has achieved a kind of self-hypnosis, a natural state of concentration which blocks out of his mind everything he might find irritating or undesirable.

Then the monkey discovers that he can go beyond the sensual pleasures and beauties of the god realm and enter into the *dhyana* or concentration states of the realm of the formless gods, which is the ultimate refinement of the six realms. He realizes that he can achieve purely mental pleasure, the most subtle and durable of all, that he is able to maintain his sense of a solid self continuously by expanding the walls of his prison to seemingly include the whole cosmos, thereby conquering change and death. First he dwells upon the idea of limitless space. He watches limitless space; he is here and limitless space is there and he watches it. He imposes his preconception on the world, creates limitless space, and feeds himself with this experience. Then the next stage is concentration upon the idea of limitless consciousness. Here one does not dwell on limitless space alone, but one also dwells upon the intelligence which perceives that limitless space as well. So ego watches limitless space and consciousness from its central headquarters. The empire of ego is completely extended, even the central authority cannot imagine how far its territory extends. Ego becomes a huge, gigantic beast.

Ego has extended itself so far that it begins to lose track of the boundary of its territory. Wherever it tries to define its boundary, it seems to exclude part of its territory. Finally, it concludes that there is no way of defining its boundaries. The size of its empire cannot be conceived or imagined. Since it includes everything, it cannot be defined as this or that. So the ego dwells on the idea of not this and not that, the idea that it cannot conceive or imagine itself. But finally even this state of mind is surpassed when the ego realizes that the idea that it is inconceivable and unimaginable is in itself a conception. So the ego dwells on the idea of *not* not this, and *not* not that. This idea of the impossibility of asserting anything is something which ego feeds on, takes pride in, identifies with, and therefore uses to maintain its continuity. This is the highest level of concentration and achievement that confused, samsaric mind can attain.

The monkey has managed to reach the ultimate level of achievement; but he has not transcended the dualistic logic upon which achievement depends. The walls of the monkey's house are still solid, still have the quality of "other" in a subtle sense. The monkey may have achieved a temporary harmony and peace and bliss through a seeming union with his projections; but the whole thing is subtly fixed, a closed world. He has become as solid as the walls, has achieved the state of egohood. He is still preoccupied with securing and enhancing himself, still caught up in fixed ideas and concepts about the world and himself, still taking the fantasies of the fifth skandha seriously. Since his state of consciousness is based on concentration, on dwelling upon other, he must continually check and maintain his achievement. "What a relief to be here in the realm of the gods. I finally made it. I have really got it now. But wait a minute . . . have I really made it? Ah, there it is. Yes, I've made it. *I* have made it." The monkey thinks that he has achieved nirvana, but actually he has achieved only a temporary state of egohood.

Sooner or later the absorption wears out and the monkey begins to panic. He feels threatened, confused, vulnerable and plunges into the realm of the jealous gods. But the anxiety and envy of the realm of the jealous gods is overpowering and the monkey becomes preoccupied with figuring out what has gone wrong. So he returns to the human realm. But the human realm is very painful as well: the continual effort to figure out what is happening, what has gone wrong, just increases the pain and confusion. So the monkey escapes the hesitation and critical perspective of the human intellect and plunges into the animal realm where he just plods along, ignoring what is around him, playing deaf and dumb to messages that might challenge the security of following narrow, familiar ways. But messages from the environment break through and a hunger for something more develops. Nostalgia for the god realm becomes very strong and the intensity of the struggle to go back to it increases. The monkey fantasizes enjoying the pleasures of the god realm. But the satisfaction derived from the fantasy of fulfilling his hunger is brief and he quickly finds himself hungry again. The hunger goes on and on, until finally he is overwhelmed by the frustration of his recurring hunger and plunges into a still more intense struggle to fulfill his desires. The monkey's aggression is so intense that the environment around him responds with equal aggression and an atmosphere of heat and claustrophobia develops. The monkey finds himself back in hell. He has managed to make a full circle from hell to heaven and back again. This perpetual cycle of struggle, achievement, disillusionment, and pain is the circle of samsara, the karmic chain reaction of dualistic fixation.

How can the monkey get out of this seemingly endless, self-contained cycle of imprisonment? It is in the human realm that the possibility of breaking the karmic chain, or the circle of samsara, arises. The intellect of the human realm and the possibility of discriminating action allows room to question the whole process of struggle. There is a possibility for the monkey to question the obsession of relating to something, of getting something, to question the solidity of the worlds that he experiences. To do this, the monkey needs to develop panoramic awareness and transcendental knowledge. Panoramic awareness allows the monkey to see the space in which the struggle occurs so that he can begin to see its ironical and humorous quality. Instead of simply struggling, he begins to experience the struggle and see its futility. He laughs through the hallucinations. He discovers that when he does not fight the walls, they are not repulsive and hard but are actually warm, soft, and penetrable. He finds that he does not have to leap from the five windows or break down the walls or even dwell upon them; he can step through them anywhere. That is why compassion, or karuna, is described as "soft and noble heart." It is a communication process that is soft, open, and warm.

The clarity and precision of transcendental knowledge allows the monkey to see the walls in a different way. He begins to realize that the world was never outside of himself, that it was his own dualistic attitude, the separation of "I" and "other," that created the problem. He begins to understand that he himself is making the walls solid, that he is imprisoning himself through his ambition. And so he begins to realize that to be free of his prison he must give up his ambition to escape and accept the walls as they are.

Q: What if you never really felt that you had to struggle—you have never reached the point of wanting to get out of the house? Perhaps you are a bit afraid of what is outside the walls, so you use them as protection.

A: Somehow, if you are able to establish friendly terms with the walls, then there are no more walls, as such. Much as you would like to have the walls for protection, the walls will not be there anymore. It is very paradoxical that, the more you dislike the wall, the stronger and thicker the wall becomes, and the more you make friends with the wall, the more the wall disappears.

Q: I wonder if pain and pleasure are on the same footing as this intellectual discrimination between good and bad or right and wrong. Is this discrimination due to a subjective attitude?

A: I think pleasure and pain are born in the same kind of background. Generally people regard pain as bad and pleasure as good, so much so that pleasure is regarded as joy and spiritual bliss, and is connected with heaven, while pain is associated with hell. So if one is able to see the absurdity and irony of trying to achieve pleasure by rejecting pain, fearing extreme pain and so striving toward pleasure, it is all very funny. There is some lacking of a sense of humor in people's attitudes toward pleasure and pain.

Q: You stated earlier that we hallucinate the phenomenal world and want to break out of it. I understand the Buddhist teaching to say that the phenomenal world is simply the manifestation of emptiness, so what would there be to break out of?

A: The point is that in the perception of ego the phenomenal world is very real, overwhelming, solid. It may in fact be hallucinatory, but as far as the monkey is concerned the hallucination is quite real and solid. From his confused point of view even thought becomes very solid and tangible. It is not good enough to say that these hallucinations do not exist because form is emptiness and emptiness is form. Try telling that to a neurotic monkey. As far as he is concerned, form exists as solid and heavy form. It is real to him because he is so obsessed with it that he does not allow any space to see otherwise. He is too busy continuously trying to reinforce his own existence. He never allows a gap. Thus there is no room for inspiration, no room to see other aspects, different angles of the situation. From the monkey's point of view the confusion is *real*. When you have a nightmare, at that moment it is real, terribly frightening. On the other hand, when you look back at the experience, it seems merely to have been a dream. You cannot use two different kinds of logic simultaneously. You have to see the confused aspect completely in order to see through it, to see the absurdity of it.

The Four Noble Truths

HAVING PAINTED a colorful picture of the monkey with his many qualities—inquisitive, passionate, aggressive, and so on—we could at this point examine the details of how he might deal with his predicament.

One comes to an understanding and transcendence of ego by using meditation to work backward through the five skandhas. And the last development of the fifth skandha is the neurotic and irregular thought patterns which constantly flit across the mind. Many different kinds of thoughts develop along with the monkey's hallucinating of the six realms: discursive thoughts, grasshopper-like thoughts, display-like thoughts, filmshow-like thoughts, etc. It is from this point of confusion that we must start; and in order to clarify the confusion it would be helpful to examine the ideas of the four noble truths which constitute the first turning of the "wheel of dharma" by the Buddha.

The four noble truths are the truth of suffering, the truth of the origin of suffering, the truth of the goal, and the truth of the path. We start with the truth of suffering, which means that we must begin with the monkey's confusion and insanity.

We must begin to see the actuality of *duhkha,* a Sanskrit word which means "suffering," "dissatisfaction," or "pain." Dissatisfaction occurs because the mind spins around in such a way that there seems to be no beginning and no end to its motion. Thought processes continue on and on: thoughts of the past, thoughts of the future, thoughts of the present moment. This creates irritation. Thoughts are prompted by and are also identical with dissatisfaction, duhkha, the constantly repeated feeling that something is lacking, incomplete in our lives. Somehow,

Shakyamuni Buddha in earth-witness mudra, with disciples
Shariputra and Mahamaudgalyayana.
DRAWING BY GLEN EDDY.

something is not quite right, not quite enough. So we are always trying to fill the gap, to make things right, to find that extra bit of pleasure or security. The continuing action of struggle and preoccupation is very irritating and painful. Eventually, one begins to become irritated by just being "me."

So to understand the truth of duhkha is actually to understand mind's neurosis. We are driven here and there with so much energy. Whether we eat, sleep, work, play, whatever we do, life contains duhkha, dissatisfaction, pain. If we enjoy pleasure, we are afraid to lose it; we strive for more and more pleasure or try to contain it. If we suffer in pain, we want to escape it. We experience dissatisfaction all the time. All activities contain dissatisfaction or pain, continuously.

Somehow we pattern life in a way that never allows us enough time to actually taste its flavor. There is continual busyness, continual searching for the next moment, a continual grasping quality to life. That is duhkha, the first noble truth. Understanding and confronting suffering is the first step.

Having become acutely aware of our dissatisfaction, we begin to search for a reason for it, for the source of the dissatisfaction. By examining our thoughts and actions we discover that we are continually struggling to maintain and enhance ourselves. We realize that this struggle is the root of suffering. So we seek an understanding of the process of struggle: that is, of how ego develops and operates. This is the second noble truth, the truth of the origin of suffering.

As we discussed in the chapters dealing with spiritual materialism, many people make the mistake of thinking that, since ego is the root of suffering, the goal of spirituality must be to conquer and destroy ego. They struggle to eliminate ego's heavy hand but, as we discovered earlier, that struggle is merely another expression of ego. We go around and around, trying to improve ourselves through struggle, until we realize that the ambition to improve ourselves is itself the problem. Insights come only when there are gaps in our struggle, only when we stop trying to rid ourselves of thought, when we cease siding with pious, good thoughts against bad, impure thoughts, only when we allow ourselves simply to see the nature of thought.

We begin to realize that there is a sane, awake quality within us. In fact this quality manifests itself only in the absence of struggle. So we discover the third noble truth, the truth of the goal: that is, nonstriving.

We need only drop the effort to secure and solidify ourselves and the awakened state is present. But we soon realize that just "letting go" is only possible for short periods. We need some discipline to bring us to "letting be." We must walk a spiritual path. Ego must wear itself out like an old shoe, journeying from suffering to liberation.

So let us examine the spiritual path, the practice of meditation, the fourth noble truth. Meditation practice is not an attempt to enter into a trancelike state of mind nor is it an attempt to become preoccupied with a particular object. There has developed, both in India and Tibet, a so-called system of meditation which might be called "concentration." That is to say that this practice of meditation is based on focusing the mind on a particular point so as to be better able to control the mind and concentrate. In such practice the student chooses an object to look at, think about, or visualize and then focuses his entire attention upon it. In so doing, he tends to develop by force a certain kind of mental calm. I call this kind of practice "mental gymnastics" because it does not attempt to deal with the totality of any given life-situation. It is based entirely on *this* or *that*, subject and object, rather than transcending the dualistic view of life.

The practice of samadhi on the other hand does not involve concentration. This is very important to realize. Concentration practices are largely ego-reinforcing, although not purposely intended as such. Still, concentration is practiced with a particular aim and object in mind, so we tend to become centralized in the "heart." We set out to concentrate upon a flower, stone, or flame, and we gaze fixedly at the object, but mentally we are going into the heart as much as possible. We are trying to intensify the solid aspect of form, the qualities of stability and stillness. In the long run such a practice could be dangerous. Depending upon the intensity of the meditator's willpower, we might become introverted in a way which is too solemn, fixed, and rigid. This sort of practice is not conducive to openness and energy nor to a sense of humor. It is too heavy and could easily become dogmatic, in the sense that those who become involved in such practices think in terms of imposing discipline upon themselves. We think it necessary to be very serious and solemn. This produces a competitive attitude in our thinking—the more we can render our minds captive, the more successful we are—which is a rather dogmatic, authoritarian approach. This way of thinking, always focused on the future, is habitual with ego: "I would like to see such and such results. I have an idealized theory or dream which I would like to put into effect." We tend to live in the future, our view of life colored by the expectation of achieving an ideal goal. Because of this expectation we miss the precision and openness and intelligence of the present. We are fascinated, blinded, and overwhelmed by the idealized goal.

The competitive quality of ego can readily be seen in the materialistic world in which we live. If you want to become a millionaire, you first try to become a millionaire *psychologically*. You start by having an image of yourself as a millionaire and then work very hard toward that goal. You push yourself in that direction, regardless of whether or not you are able to achieve it. This approach creates a kind of blindfold, rendering you insensitive to the present moment because you are living too much in the future. One could take the same mistaken approach to the practice of meditation.

Inasmuch as real meditation practice is a way to step out of ego, the first point is not to focus yourself too much upon the future attainment of the awakened state of mind. The whole practice of meditation is essentially based upon the situation of this present moment, here and now, and means working with this situation, this present state of mind. Any meditation practice concerned with transcending ego is focused in the present moment. For this reason it is a very effective way to live. If you are completely aware of your present state of being and the situation around you, you cannot miss a thing. We may use various meditation techniques to facilitate this kind of awareness, but these techniques are simply a way of stepping out of ego. Technique is like a toy given to a child. When the child grows up, the toy is discarded. In the meantime technique is necessary in order to develop patience and to refrain from dreaming about the "spiritual experience." One's whole practice should be based on the relationship between you and nowness.

You do not have to push yourself into the practice of meditation but just let be. If you practice in this way, a feeling of space and ventilation automatically comes, the expression of the buddha nature or basic intelligence that is working its way through confusion. Then you begin to find the understanding of the "truth of the path," the fourth noble truth, simplicity, such as the awareness of walking. First you become aware of standing, then you are aware that your right leg is lifting, swinging, touching, pressing; then the left leg is lifting, swinging, touching, pressing. There are many, many details of action involved in the simplicity and sharpness of being in this very moment, here, now.

And it is the same with the practice of the awareness of breathing. You become aware of the breath coming into your nostrils, going out, and finally dissolving into the atmosphere. It is a very gradual and detailed process and acute precision is involved with its simplicity. If an act is simple, then you begin to realize its precision. One begins to realize that whatever we do in everyday life is beautiful and meaningful.

If you pour a cup of tea, you are aware of extending your arm and touching your hand to the teapot, lifting it and pouring the water. Finally the water touches your teacup and fills it, and you stop pouring and put the teapot down precisely, as in the Japanese tea ceremony. You become aware that each precise movement has dignity. We have long forgotten that activities can be simple and precise. Every act of our lives can contain simplicity and precision and can thus have tremendous beauty and dignity.

The process of communication can be beautiful, if we see it in terms of simplicity and precision. Every pause made in the process of speaking becomes a kind of punctuation. Speak, allow space, speak, allow space. It does not have to be a formal and solemn occasion necessarily, but it is beautiful that you are not rushing, that you are not talking at tremendous speed, raucously. We do not have to churn out information and then stop suddenly with a feeling of letdown in order to get a response from the other person. We could do things in a dignified and proper way. Just allow space. Space is as important in communicating to another person as talking. You do not have to overload the other person with words and ideas and smiles all at once. You can allow space, smile, say something, and then allow a gap, and then talk, and then space, punctuation. Imagine if we wrote letters without any punctuation. The communication would be very chaotic. You do not have to be self-conscious and rigid about allowing space; just feel the natural flow of it.

This practice of seeing the precision of situations at every moment, through such methods as the awareness of walking, is called shamatha (Pali *samatha*) meditation. Shamatha meditation is associated with the hinayana path or the "lesser vehicle," the disciplined or narrow path. *Shamatha* means "peacefulness." There is a story concerning the Buddha which relates how he taught a village woman to develop such mindfulness in the act of drawing water from a well. He taught her to be aware of the precise movement of her hands and arms as she drew up the water. Such practice is the attempt to see the nowness quality in action, which is why it is known as shamatha, the development of peace. When you see the nowness of the very moment, there is no room for anything but openness and peace.

Q: Could you say something more about allowing gaps to appear? I understand what you mean, but I do not understand how they come about, how someone allows a gap. How does one "let be?"

A: Actually this question leads into the next topic, the discussion of the bodhisattva path, the mahayana path of compassion and freedom, the wide path. However, to answer the question from the hinayana point of view of simplicity, one should be completely satisfied with whatever situation arises and not look for entertainment from an external source. Generally, when we speak, we do not simply want to communicate to the other person, but we want a response as well. We want to be fed by the other person, which is a very egocentric way of communicating. We have to give up this desire to be fed, and then the gap automatically comes. We cannot produce the gap through effort.

Q: You said we have to prepare ourselves to enter the path. We cannot rush into it. We have to pause. Could you speak a bit more about this preparation?

A: In the beginning we have the feeling that the spiritual search is something very beautiful, something that will answer all our questions. We must go beyond this kind of hope and expectation. We might expect our teacher to solve all our problems, relieve all our doubts. But when we confront our teacher, he does not actually answer every question. He leaves many things for us to work out ourselves, which is a tremendous letdown and disappointment for us.

We have many expectations, especially if we seek a spiritual path and involve ourselves with spiritual materialism. We have the expectation that spirituality will bring us happiness and comfort, wisdom and salvation. This literal, egocentric way of regarding spirituality must be turned completely upside down. Finally, if we give up all hope of attaining any sort of enlightenment, then at that moment the path begins to open. It is like the situation of waiting for someone to arrive. You are about to give up all hope that he will ever come, you have begun to think that the notion of his arrival was simply a fantasy on your part, that he was never coming in the first place. The moment you give up hope, the person turns up. The spiritual path works in this way. It is a matter of wearing out all expectation. Patience is necessary. You do not have to push yourself too energetically into the path but just wait, just allow some space, do not be too busy trying to understand "reality." It is necessary first to see the motivation for our spiritual search. Ambition is unnecessary if we are going to start our path open-mindedly, with a mind that transcends both "good" and "bad."

A tremendous hunger for knowledge develops when we begin to realize the origin of duhkha. There will be a tremendous push to get beyond it. If we push ourselves too much, then the path of spirituality becomes instead the path of pain, confusion, and samsara, because we are very busy trying to save ourselves. We are too keen to learn something, too busy attending to our ambition to progress on the path rather than letting ourselves be and examining the whole process before we start. It is necessary not to rush onto the spiritual path but to prepare ourselves properly and thoroughly. Just wait. Wait and examine the whole process of the "spiritual search." Allow some gap.

The main point is that we have this basic intelligence that shines through our confusion. Consider the original analogy of the monkey. He wanted to get out of his house and so became very busy trying to escape, examining the walls and windows, climbing up and down. The tremendous energy that drives the monkey is the primeval intelligence which pushes us outward. This intelligence is not like a seed which you must nurture. It is like the sun that shines through gaps in the clouds. When we allow a gap, then spontaneous, intuitive understanding of how to proceed on the path suddenly, automatically comes to us. This was the experience of the Buddha. After he had studied numerous yogic disciplines under many Hindu masters, he realized that he could not achieve a completely awakened state simply by trying to apply these techniques. So he stopped and decided to work on himself as he already was. That is the basic instinct which is pushing its way through. It is very necessary to acknowledge this basic instinct. It tells us that we are not condemned people, that we are not fundamentally bad or lacking.

Q: How does one deal with practical life situations while trying to be simple and experience space?

A: You see, in order to experience open space one also must experience the solidity of earth, of form. They are interdependent. Often we romanticize open space and then we fall into traps. As long as we do not romanticize open space as a wondrous place but rather relate that space to earth, then we will avoid these traps. Space cannot be experienced without the outline of the earth to define it. If we are going to paint a picture of open space, we must express it in terms of the earth's horizon. So it is necessary to bring oneself back to the problems of everyday life, the kitchen-sink problems. That is why the simplicity and precision of everyday activities is very important. If you perceive open space, you should bring yourself back to your old, familiar, claustrophobic life situations and look into them more closely, examine them, absorb yourself into them, until the absurdity of their solidity strikes you and you can see their spaciousness as well.

Q: How does one relate to the impatience that accompanies the waiting period?

A: Impatience means that you do not have a complete understanding of the process. If you see the completeness of each action, then you will not be impatient any more.

Q: I experience calm thoughts as well as neurotic thoughts. Are these calm thoughts something I should cultivate?

A: In the practice of meditation all thoughts are the same: pious thoughts, very beautiful thoughts, religious thoughts, calm thoughts— they are all still thoughts. You do not try to cultivate calm thoughts and suppress so-called neurotic thoughts. This is an interesting point. When we speak of treading the path of the dharma, which is the fourth noble truth, it does not mean that we become religious, calm, good. Trying to be calm, trying to be good, is also an aspect of striving, of neuroticism. Religiously inclined thoughts are the watcher, the judge, and confused, worldly thoughts are the actor, the doer. For instance if you meditate, you might experience ordinary domestic thoughts and at the same time there is a watcher saying, "You shouldn't do this, you shouldn't do that, but you should come back to meditation." These pious thoughts are still thoughts and should not be cultivated.

Q: Could you say something more about using pauses as well as speech to communicate, and how this process relates to ego?

A: Usually, when we communicate with another person, we are driven by a kind of neurotic speed. We must begin to allow some spontaneity to penetrate this speed so that we do not push ourselves onto the person with whom we are communicating, do not impose ourselves, do not overload the other person. In particular, when we speak of something in which we are very interested, we do not just talk but we leap at the other person. Spontaneity is always there, but it is clouded over by thought. Whenever there is a gap in the cloudbank of thought, it shines through. Reach out and acknowledge that first openness and through that opening the basic intelligence will begin to function.

Q: Many people are aware of the truth of suffering but do not move on to the second step, awareness of the origin of suffering. Why is that?

A: I think that it is largely a matter of paranoia. We want to escape. We want to run away from pain rather than regard it as a source of inspiration. We feel the suffering to be bad enough, so why investigate it further? Some people who suffer a great deal and realize that they cannot escape their suffering really begin to understand it. But most people are too busy attempting to rid themselves of irritation, too busy seeking distractions from themselves to look into the material they already have. It is too embarrassing to look into it. This is the attitude of paranoia: if you look too closely, you will find something fearful. But in order to be a completely inspired person like Gautama Buddha, you have to be very open-minded and intelligent, an inquisitive person. You have to want to explore everything, even though it may be ugly, painful, or repulsive. This kind of scientific-mindedness is very important.

Q: In the awakened mind, where does motivation come in?

A: Inspired motivation comes from something beyond thought, something beyond the conceptualized ideas of "good" and "bad," "desirable" and "undesirable." Beyond thought there is a kind of intelligence which is our basic nature, our background, an intuitive primordial intelligence, a feeling of space, a creative open way of dealing with situations. This kind of motivation is not intellectual: it is intuitive, precise.

Q: Can one work on one's mind by controlling the physical situation?

A: Whatever you do with the situations of life, there is always a communication going on between mind and matter. But one cannot rely upon the gadgetry of matter alone; you cannot get around the problems of mind by manipulating things external to it. We see so many people in our society trying to do just this. People put on robes and renounce the world and lead very austere lives, renouncing every common habit of human behavior. But eventually they will have to deal with their confused minds. Confusion originates in mind, so one has to start directly with mind rather than attempting to go around it. If one is trying to get around mental confusion by manipulating the physical world, then I do not think it will work.

In the dance of life, matter reflects mind and mind reacts to matter. There is a continual exchange. If one is holding a lump of rock, one should feel the solid earth qualities of rock. One has to learn how to communicate with the rocklike quality. If one is holding a flower, then the particular shape and color of the petals connect to our psychology as well. We cannot completely ignore the symbolism of the external world.

However, in the beginning as we attempt to confront our own neuroses, we must be very direct and not think that we can evade the problems of mind by playing with matter. For instance, if a person is psychologically unbalanced, completely confused, like the monkey we have been discussing, and if we dress him in the robes of the Buddha or sit him in a meditation posture, his mind will still spin around in the same way. But later on, when he learns to settle himself down and becomes a simple monkey, then there might be a certain effectiveness in taking him into a quiet place or retreat.

Q: When I see the ugliness in myself, I do not know how to accept it. I try to avoid it or change it rather than accept it.

A: Well, you do not have to hide it. You do not have to change it. Investigate it further. When you see the ugliness in yourself, that is just a preconception. You see it as ugliness, which is still connected with the ideas of "good" and "bad." But you have to transcend even those words, "good" and "bad." You have to get beyond words and conceptualized ideas and just get into what you are, deeper and deeper. The first glimpse is not quite enough: you have to examine the details without judging, without using words and concepts. Opening to oneself fully is opening to the world.

The three principal bodhisattvas: Avalokiteshvara, Manjushri, and Vajrapani. They represent the aspects of the enlightened state: compassion, knowledge, and power.

DRAWING BY GLEN EDDY.

The Bodhisattva Path

WE HAVE DISCUSSED the hinayana meditation practice of simplicity and precision. By allowing a gap, space in which things may be as they are, we begin to appreciate the clear simplicity and precision of our lives. This is the beginning of meditation practice. We begin to penetrate the fifth skandha, cutting through the busyness and speed of discursive thought, the cloud of "gossip" that fills our minds. The next step is to work with emotions.

Discursive thought might be compared to the blood circulation which constantly feeds the muscles of our system, the emotions. Thoughts link and sustain the emotions so that, as we go about our daily lives, we experience an ongoing flow of mental gossip punctuated by more colorful and intense bursts of emotion. The thoughts and emotions express our basic attitudes toward and ways of relating to the world and form an environment, a fantasy realm in which we live. These "environments" are the six realms, and although one particular realm may typify the psychology of a particular individual, still that person will constantly experience the emotions connected with the other realms as well.

In order to work with these realms we must begin to view situations in a more panoramic way, which is vipashyana (Pali *vipassana*) meditation. We must become aware not only of the precise details of an activity, but also of the situation as a whole. Vipashyana involves awareness of space, the atmosphere in which precision occurs. If we see the precise details of our activity, this awareness also creates a certain space. Being aware of a situation on a small scale also brings awareness on a larger scale. Out of this develops panoramic awareness, mahavipashyana (Pali *mahavipassana*) meditation: that is, awareness of the overall pattern rather than the focusing of attention upon details. We begin to see the pattern of our fantasies rather than being immersed in them. We discover that we need not struggle with our projections, that the wall that separates us from them is our own creation. The insight into the insubstantial nature of ego is prajna, transcendental knowledge. As we glimpse prajna we relax, realizing that we no longer have to maintain the existence of ego. We can afford to be open and generous. Seeing another way of dealing with our projections brings intense joy. This is the first spiritual level of attainment of the bodhisattva, the first *bhumi*. We enter the bodhisattva path, the mahayana path, the open way, the path of warmth and openness.

In mahavipashyana meditation there is a vast expanse of space between us and objects. We are aware of the space between the situation and ourselves and anything can happen in that space. Nothing is happening here or there in terms of relationship or battle. In other words, we are not imposing our conceptualized ideas, names, and categories on experience, but we feel the openness of space in every situation. In this way awareness becomes very precise and all-encompassing.

Mahavipashyana meditation means allowing things to be as they are. We begin to realize that this needs no effort on our part because things *are* as they are. We do not have to look at them in that way: they *are* that way. And so we begin to really appreciate openness and space, that we have space in which to move about, that we do not have to try to be aware because we already are aware. So the mahayana path is the open way, the wide path. It involves the open-minded willingness to allow oneself to be awake, to allow one's instinct to spring out.

Previously we discussed allowing space in order to communicate, but that kind of practice is very deliberate and self-conscious. When we practice mahavipashyana meditation, we do not simply watch ourselves communicate, deliberately allowing a gap, deliberately waiting; but we communicate and then just space out, so to speak. Let be and not care anymore; don't possess the letting be as belonging to you, as your creation. Open, let be, and *disown*. Then the spontaneity of the awakened state springs out.

The mahayana scriptures speak of those who are completely ready to open, those who are just about ready to open, and those who have the potential to open. Those who have the potential are intellectual people who are interested in the subject but who do not allow enough room for this instinct to spring out. Those who are almost ready are quite open-minded, but they are watching themselves more than necessary. Those who are completely ready to open have heard the secret word, the password of tathagata: someone has already done it, somebody has already crossed over, it is the open path, it is possible, it is the tathagata path. Therefore, disregarding how or when or why, simply open. It is a beautiful thing, it has already happened to someone else, why not to you? Why do you discriminate between "me" and the rest of the tathagatas?

Tathagata means "those who have experienced the *tathata*," which is, "as it is": those who have experienced "as it is." In other words, the idea of tathagata is a way of inspiration, a starting point; it tells us that other people have already made it, that others have already experienced it. This instinct has already inspired someone, the instinct of "awake," of openness, of coolness in the sense of intelligence.

The path of the bodhisattva is for those who are brave and convinced of the powerful reality of the tathagata nature which exists within themselves. Those actually awakened by such an idea as tathagata are on the bodhisattva path, the path of the brave warrior who trusts in his potential to complete the journey, who trusts in the buddha nature. The word *bodhisattva* means "he who is brave enough to walk on the path of the bodhi." *Bodhi* means "awake," "the awakened state." This is not to say that the bodhisattva must already be fully awake; but he is willing to walk the path of the awakened ones.

This path consists of six transcendental activities which take place spontaneously. They are: transcendental generosity, discipline, patience, energy, meditation, and knowledge. These virtues are called "the six paramitas," because *param* means "other side" or "shore," "other side of the river," and *ita* means "arrived." *Paramita* means "arriving at the other side or shore," which indicates that the activities of the bodhisattva must have the vision, the understanding which transcends the centralized notions of ego. The bodhisattva is not trying to be good or kind, but he is spontaneously compassionate.

GENEROSITY

Transcendental generosity is generally misunderstood in the study of the Buddhist scriptures as meaning being kind to someone who is lower than you. Someone has this pain and suffering and you are in a superior position and can save them—which is a very simple-minded way of looking down upon someone. But in the case of the bodhisattva, generosity is not so callous. It is something very strong and powerful; it is communication.

Communication must transcend irritation, otherwise it will be like trying to make a comfortable bed in a briar patch. The penetrating qualities of external color, energy, and light will come toward us, penetrating our attempts to communicate like a thorn pricking our skin. We will wish to subdue this intense irritation and our communication will be blocked.

Communication must be radiation and receiving and exchange. Whenever irritation is involved, then we are not able to see properly and fully and clearly the spacious quality of that which is coming toward us, that which is presenting itself as communication. The external world is immediately rejected by our irritation which says, "No, no, this irritates me, go away." Such an attitude is the complete opposite of transcendental generosity.

So the bodhisattva must experience the complete communication of generosity, transcending irritation and self-defensiveness. Otherwise, when thorns threaten to prick us, we feel that we are being attacked, that we must defend ourselves. We run away from the tremendous opportunity for communication that has been given to us, and we have not been brave enough even to look to the other shore of the river. We are looking back and trying to run away.

Generosity is a willingness to give, to open without philosophical or pious or religious motives, just simply doing what is required at any moment in any situation, not being afraid to receive anything. Opening could take place in the middle of a highway. We are not afraid that smog and dust or people's hatreds and passions will overwhelm us; we simply open, completely surrender, give. This means that we do not judge, do not evaluate. If we attempt to judge or evaluate our experience, if we try to decide to what extent we should open, to what extent we should remain closed, then openness will have no meaning at all and the idea of paramita, of transcendental generosity, will be in vain. Our action will not transcend anything, will cease to be the act of a bodhisattva.

The whole implication of the idea of transcendence is that we see through the limited notions, the limited conceptions, the warfare mentality of *this* as opposed to *that*. Generally, when we look at an object, we do not allow ourselves to see it properly. Automatically we see our version of the object instead of actually seeing that object as it is. Then we are quite satisfied, because we have manufactured our own version of the thing within ourselves. Then we comment on it, we judge, we take or reject; but there is no real communication going on at all.

So transcendental generosity is giving whatever you have. Your action must be completely open, completely naked. It is not for you to make judgments; it is for the recipients to make the gesture of receiving. If the recipients are not ready for your generosity, they will not receive it. If they are ready for it, they will come and take it. This is the selfless action of the bodhisattva. He is not self-conscious: "Am I making any mistakes?" "Am I being careful?" "To whom should I open?" He never takes sides. The bodhisattva will, figuratively, just lie like a corpse. Let people look at you and examine you. You are at their disposal. Such noble action, such complete action, action that does not contain any hypocrisy, any philosophical or religious judgment at all. That is why it is transcendental. That is why it is paramita. It is beautiful.

DISCIPLINE

And if we proceed further and examine the paramita of "morality" or "discipline," the shila paramita, we find that the same principles apply. That is, shila or discipline is not a matter of binding oneself to a fixed set of laws or patterns. For if a bodhisattva is completely selfless, a completely open person, then he will act according to openness, will not have to follow rules; he will simply fall into patterns. It is impossible for the bodhisattva to destroy or harm other people, because he embodies transcendental generosity. He has opened himself completely and so does not discriminate between *this* and *that*. He just acts in accordance with what *is*. From another person's point of view—if someone were observing the bodhisattva—he always appears to act correctly, always seems to do the right thing at the right time. But if we were to try to imitate him, it would be impossible to do so, because his mind is so precise, so accurate that he never makes mistakes. He never runs into unexpected problems, never creates chaos in a destructive way. He just falls into patterns. Even if life seems to be chaotic, he just falls in,

CUTTING THROUGH SPIRITUAL MATERIALISM

participates in the chaos and somehow things sort themselves out. The bodhisattva is able to cross the river, so to speak, without falling into its turbulence.

If we are completely open, not watching ourselves at all, but being completely open and communicating with situations as they are, then action is pure, absolute, superior. However, if we attempt to achieve pure conduct through effort, our action will be clumsy. However pure it may be, still there will be clumsiness and rigidity involved. In the case of the bodhisattva his whole action is flowing, there is no rigidity at all. Everything just fits into place, as if someone had taken years and years to figure out the whole situation. The bodhisattva does not act in a pre-meditated way; he just communicates. He starts from the generosity of openness and falls into the pattern of the situation. It is an often-used metaphor that the bodhisattva's conduct is like the walk of an elephant. Elephants do not hurry; they just walk slowly and surely through the jungle, one step after another. They just sail right along. They never fall nor do they make mistakes. Each step they take is solid and definite.

PATIENCE

The next act of the bodhisattva is patience. Actually you cannot really divide the six activities of the bodhisattva into strictly separate practices. One leads into and embodies the next. So in the case of the paramita of patience, this action is not a matter of trying to control oneself, trying to become a hard worker, trying to be an extremely forebearing person, disregarding one's physical or mental weakness, going on and on and on until one completely drops dead. But patience also involves skillful means, as with discipline and generosity.

Transcendental patience never expects anything. Not expecting anything, we do not get impatient. However, generally in our lives we ex-pect a lot, we push ourselves, and this kind of action is very much based on impulse. We find something exciting and beautiful and we push our-selves very hard toward it, and sooner or later we are pushed back. The more we push forward, the more we will be pushed back, because im-pulse is such a strong driving force without wisdom. The action of im-pulse is like that of a person running without eyes to see, like that of a blind man trying to reach his destination. But the action of the bodhisattva never provokes a reaction. The bodhisattva can accommodate himself to any situation because he never desires or is fascinated by anything. The force behind transcendental patience is not driven by premature impulse nor by anything else of that nature. It is very slow and sure and continuous, like the walk of an elephant.

Patience also feels space. It never fears new situations, because nothing can surprise the bodhisattva—nothing. Whatever comes—be it destructive, chaotic, creative, welcoming, or inviting—the bodhisattva is never disturbed, never shocked, because he is aware of the space between the situation and himself. Once one is aware of the space between the situation and oneself, then anything can happen in that space. Whatever occurs does so in the midst of space. Nothing takes place "here" or "there" in terms of relationship or battle. Therefore transcendental patience means that we have a flowing relationship with the world, that we do not fight anything.

ENERGY

And then we could go to the next stage, the paramita of energy, virya, which is the kind of energy that immediately leads us into situations so that we never miss a chance, never miss an opportunity. In other words, it is joy, joyous energy, as Shantideva points out in his *Bodhisattva-charyavatara*. This energy is joy, rather than the kind of energy with which we work hard because we feel we must. It is joyous energy because we are completely interested in the creative patterns of our lives. One's whole life is opened by generosity, activated by morality, strengthened by patience, and now one arrives at the next stage, that of joy. One never sees situations as uninteresting or stagnant at all, because the bodhisattva's view of life is extremely open-minded, intensely interested. He never evaluates; though that does not mean that he becomes a complete blank. It does not mean that he is absorbed into a "higher consciousness," the "highest state of samadhi," so that he cannot differentiate day from night or breakfast from lunch. It does not mean he becomes vague or woolly-minded. Rather, he actually sees verbalized and conceptualized values as they are, and then he sees beyond concept and evaluation. He sees the sameness of these little distinctions that we make. He sees situations from a panoramic point of view and therefore takes a great deal of interest in life as it is. So the bodhisattva does not strive at all; he just lives.

He takes a vow when he enters the bodhisattva path that he will not attain enlightenment until he has helped all sentient beings to attain the awakened state of mind or buddhahood before him. Beginning with such a noble act of giving, of opening, of sacrifice, he continues to follow this path, taking tremendous interest in everyday situations, never tiring of working with life. This is virya, working hard with joy. There is tremendous energy in realizing that we have given up trying to become the Buddha, that now we have the time to really live life, that we have gone beyond neurotic speed.

Interestingly, although the bodhisattva has taken a vow not to attain enlightenment, because he is so precise and accurate, he never wastes one second. He always lives life thoroughly and fully, and the result is that, before he realizes where he is, he has attained enlightenment. But his unwillingness to attain enlightenment continues, strangely enough, even after he has reached buddhahood. Then compassion and wisdom really burst out, reinforcing his energy and conviction. If we never tire of situations, our energy is joyous. If we are completely open, fully awake to life, there is never a dull moment. This is virya.

MEDITATION

The next paramita is dhyana or meditation. There are two types of dhyana. The first is that of the bodhisattva, where because of his compassionate energy, he experiences continual panoramic awareness. *Dhyana* literally means "awareness," being in a state of "awake." But this does not only mean the practice of meditation in a formal sense. The bodhisattva never seeks a trance state, bliss, or absorption. He is simply awake to life situations as they are. He is particularly aware of the continuity of meditation with generosity, morality, patience, and energy. There is a continual feeling of "awake."

The other type of dhyana is the concentration practice of the realm of the gods. The main difference between that type of meditation and the meditation of the bodhisattva is that the bodhisattva does not dwell upon anything, although he deals with actual physical life situations. He does not set up a central authority in his meditation, does not watch himself acting or meditating, so that his action is always meditation and his meditation is always action.

KNOWLEDGE

The next paramita is prajna or "knowledge." Prajna is traditionally symbolized by a sharp, two-edged sword which cuts through all confusion. Even if the bodhisattva has perfected the other five paramitas, lacking prajna the other actions are incomplete. It is said in the sutras that the five paramitas are like five rivers flowing into the ocean of prajna. It also says in the sutras that the chakravartin or universal emperor goes to war at the head of four different armies. Without the emperor to lead them, the armies have no direction. In other words, prajna is the intelligence, the basic pattern into which all these other virtues lead and dissolve. It is that which cuts through the conceptualized versions of bodhisattva action—generosity, discipline, and all the rest. The bodhisattva might perform his actions methodically and properly, but without knowledge, without the sword that cuts through doubt and hesitation his action is not really transcendental at all. Thus prajna is intelligence, the all-seeing eye, the opposite of the ego's watching itself doing everything.

The bodhisattva transmutes the watcher or ego into discriminating knowledge, prajna paramita. *Pra* means "super," *jna* means "knowing": superknowledge, complete, accurate knowledge which sees everything. Consciousness fixed on "this" and "that" has been cut through, which produces the twofold knowledge, the prajna of knowing and the prajna of seeing.

The prajna of knowing deals with the emotions. It is the cutting through of conflicting emotions—the attitudes that one has toward oneself—thereby revealing what one is. The prajna of seeing is the transcendence of primitive preconceptions of the world. It is seeing situations as they are. Therefore the prajna of seeing allows for dealing with situations in as balanced a way as possible. Prajna completely cuts through any kind of awareness which has the slightest inclination toward separating "that" and "this." This is the reason why the blade is two-edged. It does not just cut in *this* direction, but in *that* one as well. The bodhisattva no longer experiences the irritating quality that comes from distinguishing between *this* and *that*. He just sails through situations without needing to check back. So all the six paramitas are interdependent.

Q: Would you define meditation as simply paying attention to what you're doing, as being mindful?

A: Dhyana, the fifth paramita, is just being aware, being mindful. But dhyana or any of the other paramitas cannot exist independently without transcendental knowledge, prajna. Prajna throws the practice of awareness into a completely different light, transforms it into something more than simple concentration, the one-pointed practice of keeping the mind focused on a particular object or thing. With prajna, meditation becomes awareness of the whole environment of the particular situation you are in. It also results in precision and openness as well, so that you are aware of every moment, every step, every movement you make. And this precision, this simplicity expands into an overall awareness of the entire situation. So meditation is not a matter of dwelling upon one thing, but it means being awake to the whole situation, as well as experiencing the simplicity of events. Meditation is not merely awareness practice alone, because if you only practice awareness, then you do not develop the intuitive insight necessary to expand your practice. Then you have to shift awareness from one subject to another.

Developing prajna is like learning to walk. You might have to begin by developing awareness of just one thing and then develop awareness of two things, and then three, four, five, six, and so on. But finally, if you are to walk properly, you must learn to expand your awareness to include the entire situation you are in so that there is one awareness of everything in the same situation. In order to do this it is necessary not to dwell on anything; then you are aware of everything.

Q: If you have conflicts with other people, making it difficult to relate to them, what do you do?

A: Well, if your desire to communicate, which is generosity, is strong, then you have to apply prajna, knowledge, to discover why you are unable to communicate. Perhaps your communication is only one-directional. Perhaps you are unwilling for communication to come from the other direction as well. Perhaps you have a great desire to communicate and put all your energy into your communication. This is a very intense approach, overwhelming for the person to whom you are communicating. They have no room to communicate back to you. You do this with all good intentions, of course, but we have to be careful to see the whole situation, rather than just being keen to throw something at the other person. We must learn to see from the other person's point of view as well. Essentially, we have to provide some kind of space and openness. The urge to convert the other person into our way of thinking is quite difficult to resist; we often experience it. But we must be careful that our communication doesn't become too heavy–handed. And the only way to do this is by learning how to provide space and openness.

Q: What makes us give up desire?
A: The discovery of the truth, the hard fact that you cannot become a bodhisattva unless you give up wanting to become anything. It is not a matter of playing games with yourself. You simply have to surrender. You have to really open and give up. Once you have had some glimpse of what it would be like to surrender, then there is inspiration to go beyond that, to go further. Once you have experienced a tiny glimpse of the awakened state of mind, just a fraction-of-a-second glimpse, there is tremendous desire and effort to proceed on the path. And then one also realizes that in order to go further one must give up altogether the idea of going. The bodhisattva path is divided into ten stages and five paths. At the end of the last path, at the tenth stage, you have a sudden glimpse that you are about to give birth to the awakened state of mind, that you are just about to click into it, when something pulls you back. Then you realize that the only thing holding you back is that you have to give up trying. That is the vajra-like samadhi, the death of desire.

Q: In normal life, not caring is associated with boredom. If, as with the bodhisattva, one doesn't care, then will one be a vegetable?
A: Not caring does not mean becoming a stone or jellyfish; there is still energy. But from the point of view of a person who cares, if we experience desire or anger but do not act them out and instead try to keep ourselves cool, if we do not put our energy into action, we feel let down, cheated, stifled. This is a one-sided view of energy.

Energy does not at all manifest itself purely in terms of being destructive or possessive. There are further energies which are not at all connected with love or hate. These are the energies of precision, of clarity, of seeing through situations. There are energies of intelligence which arise continuously and which we do not allow ourselves to experience properly. We always regard energy in terms of being destructive or possessive. There is something more than that. There is never a dull moment if you are actually in touch with reality as it is. The spark of energy arises all the time which transcends ignorance and the simple-minded one-directional way.

Q: But how does one know how and where to direct the energy?
A: Because you see situations very clearly, much more clearly than you did before, because you see them as they really are, you know how and where to direct the energy. Previously you imposed your version of reality onto life, rather than seeing things as they are. So when this kind of veil is removed, you see the situation as it is. Then you can communicate with it properly and fully. You do not have to force yourself to do anything at all. There is a continual exchange, a continual dance. It is similar to the sun shining and plants growing. The sun has no desire to create the vegetation; plants simply react to sunlight and the situation develops naturally.

Q: Spontaneously?
A: Spontaneously. Therefore it is accurate, as in the case of causing vegetables to grow; it is very scientific, right on the point. So your actions become exceedingly accurate because they are spontaneous.

Q: Do situations ever call for aggressive action?
A: I don't think so, because aggressive action is generally connected with defending oneself. If the situation has the quality of nowness, of precision, it never gets out of hand. Then there is no need to control it, to defend oneself.

Q: I'm thinking of Christ chasing the money lenders out of the temple.
A: I would not say that was aggressive action; that was truthful action, which is very beautiful. It occurred because he saw the precision of the situation without watching himself or trying to be heroic. We need action like that.

Q: How do we make the transition between a calm, passive state of mind that lets everything in and a more active, discriminating state of mind?
A: I think the point is to look at it in a completely different way. In

fact I do not think our version of everyday life is as precise and accurate and sharp as we generally think it is. Actually we are completely confused, because we don't do one thing at a time. We do one thing and our mind is occupied with a hundred other things, which is being terribly vague. We should approach everyday life in a wholly different manner. That is, we should allow the birth of an intuitive insight which really sees things as they are. The insight at the beginning might be rather vague, only a glimpse of what is, a very small glimmer compared with the darkness of the confusion. But as this kind of intelligence becomes more active and penetrating, the vagueness begins to be pushed aside and dissolves.

Q: Doesn't seeing things as they are require an understanding of the subject, the perceiver, as well as of the object?

A: Yes, that is an interesting point. Somehow you have to be right in no-man's-land in order to see things as they are. Seeing things as they are requires a leap, and one can only take this so-called leap without leaping from anywhere. If you see from somewhere, you will be conscious of the distance and conscious of the seer as well. So you can only see things as they are in the midst of nowhere. Like one cannot taste one's own tongue. Think about it.

Q: You speak of only being able to see things as they are from the midst of nowhere. Yet the Buddhist scriptures talk of crossing to the other shore of the river. Could you clarify this?

A: It is something of a paradox, like the idea of leaping from nowhere. Certainly the Buddhist scriptures speak of crossing to the other shore of the river. But you only arrive at the other shore when you finally realize that there is no other shore. In other words, we make a journey to the "promised land," the other shore, and we have arrived when we realize that we were there all along. It is very paradoxical.

Prajnaparamita, the Mother of all the Buddhas, the Ground of all Dharmas.
DRAWING BY GLEN EDDY.

Shunyata

CUTTING THROUGH OUR conceptualized versions of the world with the sword of prajna, we discover shunyata—nothingness, emptiness, voidness, the absence of duality and conceptualization. The best known of the Buddha's teachings on this subject are presented in the *Prajnaparamita-hridaya*, also called *Heart Sutra;* but interestingly in this sutra the Buddha hardly speaks a word at all. At the end of the discourse he merely says, "Well said, well said," and smiles. He created a situation in which the teaching of shunyata was set forth by others, rather than himself being the actual spokesman. He did not impose his communication but created the situation in which teaching could occur, in which his disciples were inspired to discover and experience shunyata. There are twelve styles of presenting the dharma and this is one of them.

This sutra tells of Avalokiteshvara, the bodhisattva who represents compassion and skillful means, and Shariputra, the great arhat who represents prajna, knowledge. There are certain differences between the Tibetan and Japanese translations and the Sanskrit original, but all versions make the point that Avalokiteshvara was compelled to awaken to shunyata by the overwhelming force of prajna. Then Avalokiteshvara spoke with Shariputra, who represents the scientific-minded person or precise knowledge. The teachings of the Buddha were put under Shariputra's microscope, which is to say that these teachings were not accepted on blind faith but were examined, practiced, tried, and proved.

Avalokiteshvara said: "O Shariputra, form is empty, emptiness is form; form is no other than emptiness, emptiness is no other than form." We need not go into the details of their discourse, but we can examine this statement about form and emptiness, which is the main point of the sutra. And so we should be very clear and precise about the meaning of the term "form."

Form is that which *is* before we project our concepts onto it. It is the original state of "what is here," the colorful, vivid, impressive, dramatic, aesthetic qualities that exist in every situation. Form could be a maple leaf falling from a tree and landing on a mountain river; it could be full moonlight, a gutter in the street, or a garbage pile. These things are "what is," and they are all in one sense the same; they are all forms, they are all objects, they are just what is. Evaluations regarding them are only created later in our minds. If we really look at these things as they are, they are just forms.

So form is empty. But empty of what? Form is empty of our preconceptions, empty of our judgments. If we do not evaluate and categorize the maple leaf falling and landing on the stream as opposed to the garbage heap in New York, then they are *there*, what *is*. They are empty of preconception. They are precisely what they are, of course! Garbage is garbage, a maple leaf is a maple leaf, "what is" is "what is." Form is empty if we see it in the absence of our own personal interpretations of it.

But emptiness is also form. That is a very outrageous remark. We thought we had managed to sort everything out, we thought we had managed to see that everything is the "same" if we take out our preconceptions. That made a beautiful picture: everything bad and everything good that we see are both good. Fine. Very smooth. But the next point is that emptiness is also form, so we have to reexamine. The emptiness of the maple leaf is also form; it is not really empty. The emptiness of the garbage heap is also form. To try to see these things as empty is also to clothe them in concept. Form comes back. It was too easy, taking away all concept, to conclude that everything simply is what is. That could be an escape, another way of comforting ourselves. We have to actually *feel* things as they are, the qualities of the garbage heap*ness* and the qualities of the maple leaf*ness*, the *isness* of things. We have to feel them properly, not just trying to put a veil of emptiness over them. That does not help at all. We have to see the "isness" of what is there, the raw and rugged qualities of things precisely as they are. This is a very accurate way of seeing the world. So first we wipe away all our heavy preconceptions, and then we even wipe away the subtleties of such words as "empty," leaving us nowhere, completely with what is.

Finally we come to the conclusion that form is just form and empti-ness is just emptiness, which has been described in the sutra as seeing that form is no other than emptiness, emptiness is no other than form; they are indivisible. We see that looking for beauty or philosophical meaning to life is merely a way of justifying ourselves, saying that things are not so bad as we think. Things *are* as bad as we think! Form is form, emptiness is emptiness, things are just what they are and we do not have to try to see them in the light of some sort of profundity. Finally we come down to earth, we see things as they are. This does not mean having an inspired mystical vision with archangels, cherubs, and sweet music playing. But things are seen as they *are*, in their *own* qualities. So shunyata in this case is the complete absence of concepts or filters of any kind, the absence even of the "form is empty" and the "emptiness is form" conceptualization. It is a question of seeing the world in a direct way without desiring "higher" consciousness or significance or profun-dity. It is just directly perceiving things literally, as they are in their own right.

We might ask how we could apply this teaching to everyday life. There is a story that when the Buddha gave his first discourse on shun-yata, some of the arhats had heart attacks and died from the impact of the teaching. In sitting meditation these arhats had experienced absorp-tion in space, but they were still dwelling upon space. Inasmuch as they were still dwelling upon something, there was still an experience and an experiencer. The shunyata principle involves not dwelling upon any-thing, not distinguishing between this and that, being suspended no-where.

If we see things as they are, then we do not have to interpret or ana-lyze them further; we do not need to try to understand things by impos-ing spiritual experience or philosophical ideas upon them. As a famous Zen master said: "When I eat, I eat; when I sleep, I sleep." Just do what you do, completely, fully. To do so is to be a rishi, an honest, truthful person, a straightforward person who never distinguishes between this and that. He does things literally, directly, as they are. He eats whenever he wants to eat; he sleeps whenever he wants to sleep. Sometimes the Buddha is described as the Maharishi, the Great Rishi who was not trying to be truthful but simply was true in his open state.

The interpretation of shunyata which we have been discussing is the view of the Madhyamaka or "Middle Way" philosophical school founded by Nagarjuna. It is a description of an experiential reality which can never be accurately described because words simply are not the experience. Words or concepts only *point* to partial aspects of experience. In fact, it is dubious that one can even speak of "experiencing" reality, since this would imply a separation between the experiencer and the experience. And finally, it is questionable whether one can even speak of "reality" because this would imply the existence of some objective knower outside and separate from it, as though reality were a nameable thing with set limits and boundaries. Thus the Madhyamaka simply speaks of the tathata, "as it is." Nagarjuna much preferred to approach truth by taking the arguments of other philosophical schools on their own terms and logically reducing them ad absurdum, rather than by himself offering any definitions of reality.

There are several other major philosophical approaches to the problems of truth and reality which preceded and influenced the development of the Madhyamaka school. These lines of thought find their expression not only in the earlier Buddhist philosophical schools but also in the approaches of theistic Hinduism, Vedantism, Islam, Christianity, and most other religious and philosophical traditions. From the point of view of the Madhyamaka school, these other approaches can be grouped together into three categories: the eternalists, the nihilists, and the atomists. The madhyamikas viewed the first two of these approaches as being false, and the third as being only partially true.

The first and most obvious of these three "misconceptions of the nature of reality" is eternalism, an approach which is often that of the more naive versions of theism. Eternalistic doctrines view phenomena as containing some sort of eternal essence. Things are born and die, yet they contain an essence which does not perish. The quality of eternal existence must adhere to some *thing*, so the holders of this doctrine usually subscribe to belief in God, a soul, an atman, an ineffable self. Thus the believer asserts that something does exist as solid, ongoing, and eternal. It is reassuring to have something solid to hang on to, to dwell upon, a fixed way of understanding the world and one's relationship to it.

However, eventually the believer in eternalistic doctrines may become disillusioned with a God he has never met, a soul or essence he cannot find. Which brings us to the next and somewhat more sophisticated misconception of reality: nihilism. This view holds that everything is generated out of nothingness, mystery. Sometimes this approach appears as both theistic and atheistic assertions that the Godhead is unknowable. The sun shines, throws light upon the earth, helps life to grow, provides heat and light. But we can find no origin to life; there is no logical starting point from which the universe began. Life and the world are merely the dance of maya, illusion. Things are simply generated spontaneously out of nowhere. So nothingness seems important in this approach: an unknowable reality somehow beyond apparent phenomena. The universe takes place mysteriously; there is no real explanation at all. Possibly a nihilist would say that the human mind cannot comprehend such mystery. Thus, in this view of reality, mystery is treated as a *thing*. The idea that there is no answer is relied upon and dwelled upon as the answer.

The nihilistic approach evokes the psychological attitude of fatalism. You understand logically that if you do something, things happen in reaction to it. You see a continuity of cause and effect, a chain reaction over which you have no control. This chain reactive process springs from the mystery of "nothingness." Therefore, if you murder someone, it was your karma to murder and was inevitable, foreordained. For that matter if you do a good deed, it has nothing to do with whether or not you are awake. Everything springs from this mysterious "nothingness" which is the nihilistic approach to reality. It is a very naive view: one leaves everything to mystery. Whenever we are not quite certain of things which are beyond the scope of our conceptualized ideas, then we begin to panic. We are afraid of our own uncertainty and we attempt to fill the gap with something else. The something else is usually a philosophical belief—in this case, the belief in mystery. We very eagerly, very hungrily search for nothingness, surveying every dark corner in our attempts to find it. But we find only the crumbs. We find nothing more than that. It is very mysterious. As long as we continue to look for a conceptual answer there will always be areas of mystery, which mystery is itself another concept.

Whether we are eternalists or nihilists or atomists, we constantly assume that there is a "mystery," something which we do not know: the meaning of life, the origin of the universe, the key to happiness. We struggle after this mystery, trying to become a person who knows or possesses it, naming it "God," the "soul," "atman," "Brahman," "shunyata," and so on. Certainly this is not the Madhyamaka approach to reality, though the early hinayana schools of Buddhism to some extent fell into this trap, which is why their approach is considered only a partial truth.

The hinayana approach to reality sees impermanence as the great mystery: that which is born must change and die. However, one cannot see impermanence itself but only its manifestation in form. Thus the hinayanists describe the universe in terms of atoms existing in space and moments existing in time. As such, they are atomistic pluralists. The hinayana equivalent of shunyata is the understanding of the transitory and insubstantial nature of form, so hinayana meditation practice is twofold: contemplation of the many aspects of impermanence—the processes of birth, growth, decay, and death, and their elaborations; and mindfulness practice which sees the impermanence of mental events. The arhat views mental events and material objects and begins to see them as momentary and atomistic happenings. Thus he discovers that there is no permanent substance or solid thing as such. This approach errs in conceptualizing the existence of entities relative to each other, the existence of "this" relative to "that."

We can see the three elements of eternalism, nihilism, and atomistic pluralism in different combinations in almost all the major philosophies and religions of the world. From the Madhyamaka point of view, these three misconceptions of reality are virtually inescapable as long as one searches for an answer to an assumed question, as long as one seeks to probe the so-called "mystery" of life. Belief in anything is simply a way of labeling the mystery. Yogachara, a mahayana philosophical school, attempted to eliminate this mystery by finding a union of mystery and the phenomenal world.

The main thrust of the Yogachara school is epistemological. For this school the mystery is intelligence, that which knows. The Yogacharins solved the mystery by positing the indivisible union of intelligence and phenomena. Thus there is no *individual* knower; rather everything is "self-known." There is only " one mind," which the Yogacharins called "self-luminous cognition," and both thoughts and emotions and people and trees are aspects of it. Thus this school is also referred to in the traditional literature as the *chitta-matra* or "mind-only" school.

The Yogachara school was the first school of Buddhist thought to transcend the division between the knower and the known. Thus its adherents explain confusion and suffering as springing from the mistaken belief in an individual knower. If a person believes that he knows the world, then the one mind appears to be split, though actually its clear surface is only muddied. The confused person feels that he has thoughts about and reactions to external phenomena and so is caught in a constant action and reaction situation. The enlightened person realizes that thoughts and emotions on the one hand, and the so-called external world on the other, are *both* the "play of the mind." Thus the enlightened person is not caught in the dualism of subject and object, internal and external, knower and known, I and other. Everything is *self*-known.

However, Nagarjuna contested the Yogacharin "mind-only" proposition and, in fact, questioned the very existence of "mind" altogether. He studied the twelve volumes of the *Prajnaparamita* scriptures, which came out of the second turning of the wheel of doctrine by the Buddha, the teaching of the middle portion of his life. Nagarjuna's conclusions are summed up in the principle of "nondwelling," the main principle of the Madhyamaka school. He said that any philosophical view could be refuted, that one must not dwell upon any answer or description of reality, whether extreme or moderate, including the notion of "one mind." Even to say that nondwelling is the answer is delusory, for one must not dwell upon nondwelling. Nagarjuna's way was one of non-philosophy, which was not simply another philosophy at all. He said, "The wise should not dwell in the middle either."

Madhyamaka philosophy is a critical view of the Yogacharin theory that everything is an aspect of mind. The Madhyamaka argument runs: "In order to say that mind exists or that everything is the play of the one mind, there must be someone watching mind, the knower of mind who vouches for its existence." Thus the whole of Yogachara is necessarily a theory on the part of this watcher. But according to the Yogacharins' own philosophy of self-luminous cognition, subjective thoughts *about* an object are delusive, there being no subject or object but only the one mind of which the watcher is a part. Therefore, it is impossible to state that one mind exists. Like the physical eye, self-luminous cognition cannot see itself, just as a razor cannot cut itself. By the Yogacharins' own admission, there is no one to know that the one mind exists.

Then what can we say about mind or reality? Since there is no one to perceive a mind or reality, the notion of existence in terms of "things" and "form" is delusory; there is no reality, no perceiver of reality, and no thoughts derived from perception of reality. Once we have taken away this preconception of the existence of mind and reality, then situations emerge clearly, as they are. There is no one to watch, no one to know anything. Reality just *is*, and this is what is meant by the term *shunyata*. Through this insight the watcher which separates us from the world is removed.

How then does belief in an "I" and the whole neurotic process begin? Roughly, according to the madhyamikas, whenever a perception of form occurs, there is an immediate reaction of fascination and uncertainty on the part of an implied perceiver of the form. This reaction is almost instantaneous. It takes only a fraction of a fraction of a second. And as soon as we have established recognition of what the thing is, our next response is to give it a name. With the name of course comes concept. We tend to conceptualize the object, which means that at this point we are no longer able to perceive things as they actually are. We have created a kind of padding, a filter or veil between ourselves and the object. This is what prevents the maintenance of continual awareness both during and after meditation practice. This veil removes us from panoramic awareness and the presence of the meditative state, because again and again we are unable to see things as they are. We feel compelled to name, to translate, to think discursively, and this activity takes us further away from direct and accurate perception. So shunyata is not merely awareness of what we are and how we are in relation to such and such an object, but rather it is clarity which transcends conceptual padding and unnecessary confusions. One is no longer fascinated by the object nor involved as a subject. It is freedom from *this* and *that*. What remains is open space, the absence of the this-and-that dichotomy. This is what is meant by the Middle Way or Madhyamaka.

The experience of shunyata cannot be developed without first having worked through the narrow path of discipline and technique. Technique is necessary to start with, but it is also necessary at some stage for the technique to fall away. From the ultimate point of view the whole process of learning and practice is quite unnecessary. We could perceive the absence of ego at a single glance. But we would not accept such a simple truth. In other words, we have to learn in order to unlearn. The whole process is that of undoing the ego. We start by learning to deal with neurotic thoughts and emotions. Then false concepts are removed through the understanding of emptiness, of openness. This is the experience of shunyata. *Shunyata* in Sanskrit means literally "void" or "emptiness," that is to say, "space," the absence of all conceptualized attitudes.

Thus Nagarjuna says in his *Commentary on Madhyamaka:* "Just as the sun dispels darkness, the perfect sage has conquered the false habits of mind. He does not see the mind or thought derived from the mind."

The *Heart Sutra* ends with "the great spell" or mantra. It says in the Tibetan version: "Therefore the mantra of transcendent knowledge, the mantra of deep insight, the unsurpassed mantra, the unequalled mantra, the mantra which calms all suffering, should be known as truth, for there is no deception." The potency of this mantra comes not from some imagined mystical or magical power of the words but from their meaning. It is interesting that after discussing shunyata—form is empty, emptiness is form, form is no other than emptiness, emptiness is identical with form and so on—the sutra goes on the discuss mantra. At the beginning it speaks in terms of the meditative state, and finally it speaks of mantra or words. This is because in the beginning we must develop a confidence in our understanding, clearing out all preconceptions; nihilism, eternalism, all beliefs have to be cut through, transcended. And when a person is completely exposed, fully unclothed, fully unmasked, completely naked, completely opened—at that very moment he sees the power of the word. When the basic, absolute, ultimate hypocrisy has been unmasked, then one really begins to see the jewel shining in its brightness: the energetic, living quality of openness, the living quality of surrender, the living quality of renunciation.

Renunciation in this instance is not just throwing away but, having thrown everything away, we begin to feel the living quality of peace. And this particular peace is not feeble peace, feeble openness, but it has a strong character, an invincible quality, an unshakable quality, because it admits no gaps of hypocrisy. It is complete peace in all directions, so that not even a speck of a dark corner exists for doubt and hypocrisy. Complete openness is complete victory because we do not fear, we do not try to defend ourselves at all. Therefore this is a great mantra. One would have thought that instead of saying OM GATE GATE PARAGATE PARASAMGATE BODHI SVAHA, this mantra would say something about shunyata—OM SHUNYATA MAHASHUNYATA or something of the sort. Instead it says, GATE GATE—"gone, gone, gone beyond, completely gone." This is much stronger than saying "shunyata," because the word *shunyata* might imply a philosophical interpretation. Instead of formulating something philosophical, this mantra exposes that which lies beyond philosophy. Therefore it is GATE GATE—"gone, given up, got rid of, opened." The first GATE is "rid of the veil of conflicting emotions." The second GATE represents the veil of primitive beliefs about reality. That is, the first GATE represents the idea that "form is empty," and the second GATE refers to "emptiness is form." Then the next word of the mantra is PARAGATE— "gone beyond, completely exposed." Now form is form—PARAGATE— and it is not only that form is form but emptiness is emptiness, PARASAMGATE—"completely gone beyond." BODHI. BODHI here means "completely awake." The meaning is "given up, completely unmasked, naked, completely open." SVAHA is a traditional ending for mantras which means, "So be it." "Gone, gone, gone beyond, completely exposed, awake, so be it."

Q: How does desire lead to birth?

A: Each time there is a desire there is another birth. You plant want-ingness, wanting to do something, wanting to grasp something. Then that desire to grasp also invites something further. Birth here means the birth of further confusion, further dissatisfaction, further wanting. For example, if you have a great desire for money and you manage to get a lot of it, then you also want to buy something with that money. One thing leads to the next, a chain reaction, so that desire becomes a kind of network. You want something, want to draw something into you, continually.

The experience of shunyata, seeing precisely and clearly what is, somehow cuts through this network, this spider's web, because the spi-der's web is woven in the space of desire, the space of wanting. And when the space of shunyata replaces it, so to speak, the whole conceptu-alized formulation of desire is completely eliminated, as though you had arrived on another planet with different air, or a place without oxygen at all. So shunyata provides a new atmosphere, a new environment, which will not support clinging or grasping. Therefore the experience of shunyata also makes impossible the planting of the seed of karma, which is why it is said that shunyata is that which gives birth to all the buddhas, all the awakened ones. "Awakened" means not being involved in the chain reactions and complications of the karmic process.

Q: Why is it that so many of us have such a strong tendency to not see things as they really are?

A: I think largely because we are afraid that we will see it.

Q: Why are we afraid of seeing it?

A: We want an umbilical cord attached to the ego through which we can feed all the time.

Q: Can this understanding of "emptiness is form" be attained through the practice of meditation techniques or must it come to us spontaneously?

A: The perception of shunyata is not achieved through the practice of mental gymnastics; it is a matter of actually *seeing* it. It could be perceived in sitting meditation or it could be seen in life situations. There is no set pattern to producing it. In the case of Naropa, the great Indian yogi, he perceived shunyata when his master took off his sandal and slapped him on the cheek. That very moment he saw it. It depends upon the individual situation.

Q: Then it is not something you go looking for?

A: If one is really keen, really devoted to finding it, completely devoted to understanding, it, then one has to give up looking for it.

Q: I have some difficulty reconciling the concept of shunyata with what is going on right now.

A: When you have a shunyata experience, it does not mean that you cease to perceive, cease to live on Earth. You still live on the Earth, but you see more precisely what is here. We believe that we know things as they are. But we only see our version which is not quite complete. There is much more to learn about the true subtleties of life. The things we see are a very crude version of what is. Having an experience of shunyata does not mean that the whole world completely dissolves into space, but that you begin to notice the space so that the world is somewhat less crowded. For example, if we are going to communicate to someone, we might prepare ourselves to say such and such to calm him down or explain things to him. But then he comes out with so many complications of his own, he churns out so much himself, that before you know where you are, you are completely confused by him. You share his confusion rather than having the clarity you prepared at the beginning. You have been completely absorbed into his confusion. So shunyata means seeing through confusion. You keep precision and clarity all the time.

Q: And with this experience, you are still alive in this world?

A: Yes, of course! You see, enlightenment does not mean dying. Otherwise, enlightenment would be a kind of suicide, which is ridiculous. That is the nihilistic approach, attempting to escape from the world.

Q: Is an enlightened person omniscient?

A: I am afraid this is a mistaken conclusion drawn from the Yogacharin one mind theory, a theory which has also appeared in other religious and philosophical traditions. The idea is that an enlightened person has become the one mind and so knows everything that ever was, is, or could be. You always get this kind of wild speculation when people involve themselves with "mystery," the unknowable. But I am afraid that there really is no such thing as the one mind.

Q: How is one to begin to see what is?

A: By not beginning, by giving up the idea of a beginning. If you try to affirm a particular territory—my experience—then you are not going to see shunyata. You have to give up the idea of territory altogether. Which can be done, it is not impossible. It is not just philosophical speculation. One can give up the idea of territory, one *can* not begin.

Q: Is part of not beginning to try for so long that one gives up from exhaustion? Can one give up before one has tried? Is there any shortcut? Must the monkey go through the whole process of banging himself against the walls and hallucinating?

A: I think we must. Sudden enlightenment comes only with exhaustion. Its suddenness does not necessarily mean that there is a shortcut. In some cases, people might experience a sudden flash of enlightenment, but if they do not work their way through, their habitual thought patterns will resume and their minds will become overcrowded again. One must make the journey because, as you said, at the point where you begin to be disappointed you get it.

Q: This seems to lead back to the hinayana path of discipline. Is that correct?

A: Yes, meditation is hard work, manual work, so to speak.

Q: Having begun, it seems that there is something to do.

A: There is something to do, but at the same time whatever you are doing is only related to the moment rather than being related to achieving some goal in the future, which brings us back to the practice of meditation. Meditation is not a matter of beginning to set foot on the path; it is realizing that you are already on the path—fully being in the nowness of this very moment—now, now, now. You do not actually begin because you have never really left the path.

Q: You described enlightened people as being free from the karmic chain. I would like to know what you meant by that, because it seems to me that they create a new karmic chain.

A: The work *karma* means "creation" or "action"—chain reaction. For example, by looking toward the future we plant a seed in the present. In the case of enlightened people, they do not plan for the future because they have no desire to provide security for themselves. They do not need to know the pattern of the future anymore. They have conquered the preconception of "future." They are fully in the now. The now has the potential of the future in it, as well as that of the past. Enlightened people have completely mastered the restless and paranoid activities of mind. They are completely, fully in the moment; therefore they are free from sowing further seeds of karma. When the future comes they do not see it as a result of their good deeds in the past; they see it as present all the time. So they do not create any further chain reactions.

Q: Is the "awake quality" different from just being in the now?

A: Yes. Enlightenment is being *awake* in the nowness. For instance, animals live in the present and, for that matter, an infant child lives in the present; but that is quite different from being awake or enlightened.

Q: I do not quite understand what you mean by animals and babies living in the present. What is the difference between living in the present in that form and being an enlightened person?

A: I think it is a question of the difference between dwelling upon something and really being in the nowness in terms of "awake." In the case of an infant or animal, it is being in the nowness but it is dwelling upon the nowness. They get some kind of feedback from it by dwelling upon it, although they may not notice it consciously. In the case of an enlightened being, he is not dwelling upon the idea—"I am an enlightened being"—because he has completely transcended the idea of "I am."

He is just fully being. The subject-object division has been completely transcended.

Q: If the enlightened being is without ego and feels the sorrows and the sadness of those around him but does not feel his own necessarily, then would you call his willingness to help them get over their difficulties "desire"?

A: I don't think so. Desire comes in when you want to see someone happy. When that person is happy, then you feel happy because the activities you have engaged in to make him happy are, in a sense, done for yourself rather than for the other person. You would like to see him happy. An enlightened being has no such attitude. Whenever someone requires his help, he just gives it; there is no self-gratification or self-congratulation involved.

Q: Why did you name your center here Karma Dzong?

A: Karma means "action" as well as "buddha activity," and dzong is the Tibetan word for "fortress." Situations just present themselves rather than being deliberately premeditated. They are perpetually developing, happening quite spontaneously. Also there seems to be a tremendous amount of energy at the center, which also could be said of karma. It is energy which is not being misled by anyone, energy which is in the fortress. What is happening definitely had to happen. It takes the shape of spontaneous karmic relationships rather than of missionary work or the conversion of people into Budddhists.

Q: How would you relate samadhi and nirvana to the concept of shunyata?

A: There is a problem here with words. It is not a matter of differences; it is a matter of different emphases. Samadhi is complete involvement and nirvana is freedom and both are connected with shunyata. When we experience shunyata, we are completely involved, without the subject-object division of duality. We are also free from confusion.

Prajna and Compassion

IN DISCUSSING SHUNYATA, we found that we impose our preconceptions, our ideas, our version of things onto phenomena instead of seeing things as they are. Once we are able to see through our veil of preconception, we realize that it is an unnecessary and confused way of attaching handles to experiences without considering whether the handles fit or not. In other words, preconceptions are a form of security. when we see something, immediately we name it and place it in a category. But form is empty; it does not need our categorizations to express its full nature, to be what it is. Form is *in itself* empty of preconception.

But, emptiness is form. This means that at this level of understanding we place too much value on seeing form naked of preconceptions. We would like to experience this kind of insight, as though seeing form as empty were a state we could force our minds to achieve. We search for emptiness so that it too becomes a thing, a form, instead of true emptiness. It is a problem of too much ambition.

Thus, the next stage is for us to give up our ambition to see form as empty. At this point form really emerges from behind the veil of our preconceptions. Form is form, naked form without any philosophical implication behind it. And emptiness is emptiness; there is nothing to hang on to. We have discovered the experience of nonduality.

Nevertheless, having realized that form is form and emptiness is emptiness, we still appreciate our insight into nonduality. There is still a sense of the knower, the experiencer of the insight. There is an awareness that something has been removed, something is absent. Subtly, we dwell on nonduality. Here we enter into a transitional phase between the mahayana path and tantra in which prajna is a continuous experience and compassion is no longer deliberate. But there is still some self-con-sciousness, some sense of perceiving our own prajna and compassion, some sense of checking and appreciating our actions.

As we discussed in the talk on bodhisattva action, prajna is a very clear, precise, and intelligent state of being. It has a sharp quality, the ability to penetrate and reveal situations. Compassion is the open atmo-sphere in which prajna sees. It is an open awareness of situations which triggers action informed by the eye of prajna. Compassion is very pow-erful, but it must be directed by the intelligence of prajna, just as intelli-gence needs the atmosphere of the basic openness of compassion. The two must come simultaneously.

Compassion contains fundamental fearlessness, fearlessness without hesitation. This fearlessness is marked by tremendous generosity, in con-trast to the fearlessness of exerting one's power over others. This "gen-erous fearlessness" is the fundamental nature of compassion and transcends the animal instinct of ego. Ego would like to establish its ter-ritory, whereas compassion is completely open and welcoming. It is a gesture of generosity which excludes no one.

Compassion begins to play a part in the practice of meditation when you experience not only calm and peace, but also warmth. There is a great feeling of warmth which gives rise to an attitude of openness and welcoming. When this feeling arises, there is no longer any anxiety or fear that external agents will act as obstacles to your practice of meditation.

This instinctive warmth, which is developed in meditation practice, also extends into the postmeditation experience of awareness. With this kind of true awareness you cannot divorce yourself from your activity. To do so would be impossible. If you try to concentrate upon your ac-tion—making a cup of tea or any daily-life activity—and at the same time try to be aware, you are living in a dream state. As one of the great Tibetan teachers said, "Trying to combine awareness and action in an unskillful way is like trying to mix oil and water." True awareness must be open rather than cautious or protective. It is open-mindedness, expe-riencing the open space within a situation. You may be working, but awareness could also operate within the context of your work, which then would be the practice of compassion and meditation.

Generally awareness is absent in our lives; we are completely ab-sorbed in whatever we are doing and we forget the rest of the environ-ment, we seal it off. But the positive force of compassion and prajna is open and intelligent, sharp and penetrating, giving us a panoramic view of life which reveals not only specific actions and events but their whole environments as well. This creates the right situation for communication with other people. In dealing with other people, we must not only be aware of what they are saying, but we must also be open to the whole tone of their being. A person's actual words and smile represent only a small fraction of his communication. What is equally important is the quality of his presence, the way he presents himself to us. This communicates much more than words alone.

When a person is both wise and compassionate, his actions are very skillful and radiate enormous energy. This skillful action is referred to as *upaya*, "skillful means." Here *skillful* does not mean devious or diplomatic. Upaya just happens in response to a situation. If a person is totally open, his response to life will be very direct, perhaps even outrageous from a conventional point of view, because "skillful means" does not allow any nonsense. It reveals and deals with situations as they are: it is extremely skillful and precise energy. If the coverings and masks we wear were suddenly to be torn away by this energy, it would be extremely painful. It would be embarrassing because we would find ourselves with nothing on, naked. At such a moment this kind of openness and directness, the outrageously blunt nature of prajna and compassion, might seem extremely cold and impersonal.

To the conventional way of thinking, compassion simply means being kind and warm. This sort of compassion is described in the scriptures as "grandmother's love." You would expect the practitioner of this type of compassion to be extremely kind and gentle; he would not harm a flea. If you need another mask, another blanket to warm yourself, he will provide it. But true compassion is ruthless, from ego's point of view, because it does not consider ego's drive to maintain itself. It is "crazy wisdom." It is totally wise, but it is crazy as well, because it does not relate to ego's literal and simple-minded attempts to secure its own comfort.

The logical voice of ego advises us to be kind to other people, to be good boys and girls and lead innocent little lives. We work at our regular jobs and rent a cozy room or apartment for ourselves; we would like to continue in this way, but suddenly something happens which tears us out of our secure little nest. Either we become extremely depressed or something outrageously painful occurs. We begin to wonder why heaven has been so unkind. "Why should God punish me? I have been a good person, I have never hurt a soul." But there is something more to life than that.

What are we trying to secure? Why are we so concerned to protect ourselves? The sudden energy of ruthless compassion severs us from our comforts and securities. If we were never to experience this kind of shock, we would not be able to grow. We have to be jarred out of our regular, repetitive, and comfortable lifestyles. The point of meditation is not merely to be an honest or good person in the conventional sense, trying only to maintain our security. We must begin to become compassionate and wise in the fundamental sense, open and relating to the world as it is.

Q: Could you discuss the basic difference between love and compassion and in what relation they stand to each other?

A: Love and compassion are vague terms; we can interpret them in different ways. Generally in our lives we take a grasping approach, trying to attach ourselves to different situations in order to achieve security. Perhaps we regard someone as our baby, or, on the other hand, we might like to regard ourselves as helpless infants and leap into someone's lap. This lap might belong to an individual, an organization, a community, a teacher, any parental figure. So-called "love" relationships usually take one of these two patterns. Either we are being fed by someone or we are feeding others. These are false, distorted kinds of love or compassion. The urge to commitment—that we would like to "belong," be someone's child, or that we would like them to be our child—is seemingly powerful. An individual or organization or institution or anything could become our infant; we would nurse it, feed it milk, encourage its growth. Or else the organization is the great mother by which we are continuously fed. Without our "mother" we cannot exist, cannot survive. These two patterns apply to any life energy which has the potential to entertain us. This energy might be as simple as a casual friendship or an exciting activity we would like to undertake, and it might be as complicated as marriage or our choice of career. Either we would like to control the excitement or we would like to become a part of it.

However, there is another kind of love and compassion, a third way. Just be what you are. You do not reduce yourself to the level of an infant nor do you demand that another person leap into your lap. You simply be what you are in the world, in life. If you can be what you are, external situations will become as they are, automatically. Then you can communicate directly and accurately, not indulging in any kind of nonsense, any kind of emotional or philosophical or psychological interpretation. This third way is a balanced way of openness and communication which automatically allows tremendous space, room for creative development, space in which to dance and exchange.

Compassion means that we do not play the game of hypocrisy or self-deception. For instance, if we want something from someone and we say, "I love you," often we are hoping that we will be able to lure them into our territory, over to our side. This kind of proselytizing love is extremely limited. "You should love me, even if you hate me, because I am filled with love, am high on love, am completely intoxicated!" What does it mean? Simply that the other person should march into your territory because you say that you love him, that you are not going to harm him. It is very fishy. Any intelligent person is not going to be seduced by such a ploy. "If you really love me as I am, why do you want me to enter your territory? Why this issue of territory and demands at all? What do you want from me? How do I know, if I do march into your 'loving' territory, that you aren't going to dominate me, that you won't create a claustrophobic situation with your heavy demands for love?" As long as there is territory involved with a person's love, other people will be suspicious of his "loving" and "compassionate" attitude. How do we make sure, if a feast is prepared for us, that the food is not dosed with poison? Does this openness come from a centralized person, or is it total openness?

The fundamental characteristic of true compassion is pure and fearless openness without territorial limitations. There is no need to be loving and kind to one's neighbors, no need to speak pleasantly to people and put on a pretty smile. This little game does not apply. In fact it is embarrassing. Real openness exists on a much larger scale, a revolutionarily large and open scale, a universal scale. Compassion means for you to be as adult as you are, while still maintaining a childlike quality. In the Buddhist teachings they symbol for compassion, as I have already said, is one moon shining in the sky while its image is reflected in one hundred bowls of water. The moon does not demand, "If you open to me, I will do you a favor and shine on you." The moon just shines. The point is not to want to benefit anyone or make them happy. There is no audience involved, no "me" and "them." It is a matter of an open gift, complete generosity without the relative notions of giving and receiving. That is the basic openness of compassion: opening without demand. Simply be what you are, be the master of the situation. If you will just "be," then life flows around and through you. This will lead you into working and communicating with someone, which of course demands tremendous warmth and openness. If you can afford to be what you are, then you do not need the "insurance policy" of trying to be a good person, a pious person, a compassionate person.

Q: This ruthless compassion sounds cruel.

A: The conventional approach to love is like that of a father who is extremely naive and would like to help his children satisfy all their desires. He might give them everything: money, drink, weapons, food, anything to make them happy. However, there might be another kind of father who would not merely try to make his children happy, but who would work for their fundamental health.

Q: Why would a truly compassionate person have any concern with giving anything?

A: It is not exactly giving but opening, relating to other people. It is a matter of acknowledging the existence of other people as they are, rather than relating to people in terms of a fixed and preconceived idea of comfort or discomfort.

Q: Isn't there a considerable danger of self-deception involved with the idea of ruthless compassion? A person might think he is being ruthlessly compassionate, when in fact he is only releasing his aggressions.

A: Definitely, yes. It is because it is such a dangerous idea that I have waited until now to present it, after we have discussed spiritual materialism and the Buddhist path in general and have laid a foundation of intellectual understanding. At the stage of which I am speaking, if a student is to actually practice ruthless compassion, he must have already gone through a tremendous amount of work: meditation, study, cutting through, discovering self-deception and sense of humor, and so on. After a person has experienced this process, made this long and difficult journey, then the next discovery is that of compassion and prajna. Until a person has studied and meditated a great deal, it would be extremely dangerous for him to try to practice ruthless compassion. ·

Q: Perhaps a person can grow into a certain kind of openness, compassion with regard to other people. But then he finds that even this compassion is still limited, still a pattern. Do we always rely on our openness to carry us through? Is there any way to make sure we are not fooling ourselves?

A: That is very simple. If we fool ourselves at the beginning, there will be some kind of agreement that we automatically make with ourselves. Surely everyone has experienced this. For instance, if we are speaking to someone and exaggerating our story, before we even open our mouths we will say to ourselves, "I know I am exaggerating, but I would like to convince this person." We play this little game all the time. So it is a question of really getting down to the nitty-gritty of being honest and fully open with ourselves. Openness to other people is not the issue. The more we open to ourselves, completely and fully, then that much more openness radiates to others. We really know when we are fooling ourselves, but we try to play deaf and dumb to our own self-deception.

Vajradhara and consort. The personification of Shakyamuni Buddha teaching tantra.
Symbol of the Absolute in its polarity aspect.
DRAWING BY GLEN EDDY.

Tantra

AFTER THE BODHISATTVA has cut through fixed concepts with the sword of prajna, he comes to the understanding that "form is form, emptiness is emptiness." At this point he is able to deal with situations with tremendous clarity and skill. As he journeys still further along the bodhisattva path, prajna and compassion deepen and he experiences greater awareness of intelligence and space and greater awareness of peace. Peace in this sense is indestructible, tremendously powerful. We cannot be truly peaceful unless we have the invincible quality of peace within us; a feeble or temporary peacefulness could always be disturbed. If we try to be kind and peaceful in a naive way, encountering a different or unexpected situation might interfere with our awareness of peace because that peace has no strength in it, has no character. So peace must be stable, deep-rooted, and solid. It must have the quality of earth. If we have power in ego's sense, we tend to exert that power and use it as our tool to undermine others. But as bodhisattvas we do not use power to undermine people; we simply remain peaceful.

Finally we reach the tenth and last stage of the bodhisattva path: the death of shunyata and the birth into "luminosity." Shunyata as an experience falls away, exposing the luminous quality of form. Prajna transforms into jnana or "wisdom." But wisdom is still experienced as an external discovery. The powerful jolt of the vajra-like samadhi is necessary to bring the bodhisattva into the state of *being* wisdom rather than *knowing* wisdom. This is the moment of bodhi or "awake," the entrance into tantra. In the awakened state the colorful, luminous qualities of the energies become still more vivid.

If we see a red flower, we not only see it in the absence of ego's complexity, in the absence of preconceived names and forms, but we also see the brilliance of that flower. If the filter of confusion between us and the flower is suddenly removed, automatically the air becomes quite clear and vision is very precise and vivid.

While the basic teaching of mahayana buddhism is concerned with developing prajna, transcendental knowledge, the basic teaching of tantra is connected with working with energy. Energy is described in the *Kriyayoga Tantra* of Vajramala as "that which abides in the heart of all beings, self-existing simplicity, that which sustains wisdom. This indestructible essence is the energy of great joy; it is all-pervasive, like space. This is the dharma body of nondwelling." According to this tantra, "This energy is the sustainer of the primordial intelligence which perceives the phenomenal world. This energy gives impetus to both the enlightened and the confused states of mind. It is indestructible in the sense of being constantly ongoing. It is the driving force of emotion and thought in the confused state, and of compassion and wisdom in the enlightened state."

In order to work with this energy the yogi must begin with the surrendering process and then work on the shunyata principle of seeing beyond conceptualization. He must penetrate through confusion, seeing that "form is form and emptiness is empty," until finally he even cuts through dwelling upon the shunyata experience and begins to see the luminosity of form, the vivid, precise, colorful aspect of things. At this point whatever is experienced in everyday life through sense perception is a naked experience, because it is direct. There is no veil between him and "that." If a yogi works with energy without having gone through the shunyata experience, then it may be dangerous and destructive. For example, the practice of some physical yoga exercises which stimulate one's energy could awaken the energies of passion, hatred, pride, and other emotions to the extent that one would not know how to express them. The scriptures describe a yogi who is completely intoxicated with his energy as being like a drunken elephant who runs rampant without considering where he is going.

Tantric teaching surpasses the "looking beyond" bias of the transcendental attitude that "form is form." When we speak of transcendence in the mahayana tradition, we mean transcendence of ego. In the tantric tradition we do not speak of going beyond ego at all: it is too dualistic an attitude. Tantra is much more precise than that. It is not a question of "getting *there*" or "being *there*"; the tantric tradition speaks of being *here*. It speaks of transmutation and the analogy of alchemistic practice is used a great deal. For example, the existence of lead is not rejected but lead is transmuted into gold. You do not have to change its metallic quality at all; you must simply transmute it.

Tantra is synonymous with dharma, the path, The function of tantric practice is to transmute ego, enabling the primordial intelligence to shine through. The word *tantra* means "continuity." It is like the thread which strings beads together. The thread is the path. The beads are the working basis of tantric practice: that is, the five skandas or the five constituents of ego as well as the primordial potential of the Buddha within oneself, the primordial intelligence.

Tantric wisdom brings nirvana into samsara. This may sound rather shocking. Before reaching the level of tantra, you try to abandon samsara and strive to achieve nirvana. But eventually you must realize the futility of striving and then become completely one with nirvana. In order to really capture the energy of nirvana and become one with it you need a partnership with the ordinary world. Therefore the term "ordinary wisdom," *thamal gyi shepa,* is used a great deal in the tantric tradition. It is the completely ordinary version of "form is form, emptiness is empty"; it is what is. One cannot reject the physical existence of the world as being something bad and associated with samsara. You can only understand the essence of nirvana by looking into the essence of samsara. Thus the path involves something more than simply going beyond duality, something more than mere nondualistic understanding. You are able to see the "nondualisticness," so to speak, the "isness" quality of nonduality. You see beyond the negation aspect of shunyata, the negation of duality. Therefore, the term *shunyata* is not used very much in tantra. In tantric tradition *tathata,* "what is," is used, rather than shunyata or "emptiness." The word *ösel* (Tibetan) or *prabhasvara* (Sanskrit), which means "luminosity," is also used a lot rather than *shunyata*. You find this reference to the tantric tradition in the Buddha's last turning of the wheel of dharma: instead of saying, "Form is empty, emptiness is form," and so on, he says that form is luminous. Luminosity or prabhasvara is connected with mahasukha, the "great joy" or "bliss," the full realization that "emptiness is emptiness." It is not empty simply because form is also form.

The dynamic quality of energy is not expressed enough in the doctrine of shunyata because the whole discovery of shunyata derives its meaning relative to samsaric mind. Shunyata offers an *alternative* to samsara and so the teaching of shunyata is directed toward the samsaric mentality. Even if this teaching goes beyond saying that "form is empty and emptiness is form" to say that "emptiness is no other than form" and "form is no other than emptiness," still it does not go so far as to say that form has this energy and emptiness has this energy. In the vajrayana or tantric teaching the principle of energy plays a very important part.

The teaching must connect with the day-to-day lives of its practitioners. We are confronted with the thoughts, emotions, and energies of our relationships with other people and the world. How are we going to relate our understanding of shunyata to everyday events unless we recognize the energy aspect of life? If we cannot dance with life's energies, we will not be able to use our experience of shunyata to unite samsara and nirvana. Tantra teaches not to suppress or destroy energy but to transmute it; in other words, go with the pattern of energy. When we find balance going with the energy, we begin to get acquainted with it. We begin to find the right path with the right direction. This does not mean that a person has to become a drunken elephant, a wild yogi in the pejorative sense.

A perfect example of going with energy, of the positive wild yogi quality, was the actual transmission of enlightenment from Tilopa to Naropa. Tilopa removed his sandal and slapped Naropa in the face. He used the situation of the moment, Naropa's energy of curiosity and seeking, transmuting it into the awakened state. Naropa had tremendous energy and intelligence, but his energy was not related to Tilopa's understanding, to his openness of mind, which was another kind of energy. In order to penetrate this barrier a sudden jolt was needed, a shock which was not artificial. It is like a crooked building which is just about to fall down but is straightened suddenly, accidentally, by an earthquake. Natural circumstances are used to restore the original state of openness. When one goes with the pattern of energy, then experience becomes very creative. The energy of wisdom and compassion is continually operating in a precise and accurate way.

As the yogi becomes more sensitive to the patterns and qualities of energy, he sees more clearly the meaning or symbolism in life experiences. The first half of tantric practice, the lower tantra, is called mahamudra, which means "great symbol." Symbol, in this sense, is not a "sign" representing some philosophical or religious principle; it is the demonstration of the living qualities of what is. For instance, in the direct perception of a flower, the perception of naked insight, unclothed and unmasked, the color of the flower conveys a message over and beyond the simple perception of color. There is great meaning in this color, which is communicated in a powerful, almost overwhelming way. Conceptualized mind is not involved in the perception and so we are able to see with great precision, as though a veil had been removed from before our eyes.

Or if we hold a piece of rock in our hands with that clarity of perception which is the direct contact of naked insight, we not only feel the solidity of that one rock, but we also begin to perceive the spiritual implications of it; we experience it as an absolute expression of the solidity and majesty of earth. In fact we could be holding Mount Everest in our hands, as far as the recognition of fundamental solidity is concerned. That small rock represents every aspect of solidness. I do not mean this in the physical sense alone; but I am speaking of solidity in the spiritual sense, the solidity of peace and energy, indestructible energy. The yogi feels the solidity and forbearance of earth—whatever you plant or bury in it, the earth never reacts against it. In this rock he is aware of the enlightened wisdom of equanimity as well as the samsaric quality of ego-pride which wants to build a high pyramid or monument to its own existence. Every situation we encounter has this vivid connection with our state of being. It is interesting to note that in the tantric iconography a number of symbolic figures are shown holding a mountain in one hand, which represents exactly what we have been discussing: solid peace, solid compassion, solid wisdom which cannot be influenced by the frivolity of ego.

Every texture we perceive has some spiritual implication automatically, and we begin to realize the tremendous energy contained within this discovery and understanding. The meditator develops new depths of insight through direct communication with the reality of the phenomenal world. He is able to see not only the absence of complexity, the absence of duality, but the *stoneness* of stone and the *waterness* of water. He sees things precisely as they are, not merely in the physical sense, but with awareness of their spiritual significance. Everything he sees is an expression of spiritual discovery. There is a vast understanding of symbolism and a vast understanding of energy. Whatever the situation, he no longer has to force results. Life flows around him. This is the basic mandala principle. The mandala is generally depicted as a circle which revolves around a center, which signifies that everything around you becomes part of your awareness, the whole sphere expressing the vivid reality of life. The only way to experience things truly, fully, and properly is through the practice of meditation, creating a direct link with nature, with life, with all situations. When we speak of being highly developed spiritually, this does not mean that we float in the air. In fact, the higher we go, the more we come down to earth.

It is important to remember that the practice of meditation begins with the penetration of the neurotic thought pattern which is the fringe of ego. As we proceed further, we see through not only the complexity of the thought processes but also the heavy "meaningfulness" of concepts expressed in names and theories. Then at last we create some space between *this* and *that*, which liberates us tremendously. Having created space, we then go on to the vajrayana practice of creating a direct link with life experience. These three steps are, in essence, the three yanas: the hinayana, the vehicle of method; the mahayana, the vehicle of shunyata or space; and the vajrayana or tantra, the vehicle of direct energy.

In the tantric tradition energy is categorized in five basic qualities or buddha families: vajra, ratna, padma, karma, and buddha. Each buddha family has an emotion associated with it which is transmuted into a particular "wisdom" or aspect of the awakened state of mind. The buddha families are also associated with colors, elements, landscapes, directions, seasons, with any aspect of the phenomenal world.

Vajra is associated with anger, which is transmuted into mirrorlike wisdom. We sense something beyond the cloudy, possessive, and aggressive qualities of anger and this intuitive insight enables us to automatically transmute the essence of anger into precision and openness, rather than deliberately changing it.

Vajra is also associated with the element of water. Cloudy, turbulent water symbolizes the defensive and aggressive nature of anger while clear water suggests the sharp, precise, clear reflectiveness of mirrorlike wisdom.

Vajra is the color white. Anger is the very blunt and direct experience of defending oneself; therefore it is like a sheet of white paper, very flat and opaque. But it also has the potential of luminosity, of the brilliance of reflection which is mirrorlike wisdom.

Vajra is connected with the east, the dawn, winter. It is a winter morning, crystal clear, icicles sharp and glittering. The landscape is not empty or desolate but is full of all sorts of thought-provoking sharpness. There are many things to intrigue the observer. For example, the ground, trees, plants all have their own way of freezing. Different trees have different ways of carrying snow and different ways of relating to temperature.

Vajra deals with objects in terms of their textures and their relations to each other. Everything is analyzed in its own terms. The intelligence of vajra never leaves any unexplored areas or hidden corners. It is like water flowing over a flat surface, completely covering the surface but remaining transparent.

Ratna is associated with pride and earth—solidity, mountains, hills, pyramids, buildings. "I am completely secure. I am what I am." It is a very proud way of looking at oneself. This means that one is afraid to loosen up, is continually piling up defenses, building a fortress. Equally, ratna is the wisdom of equanimity, which is all-pervading. Whether you construct buildings out of earth or whether you simply leave the earth as it is, it is the same thing. The earth remains as it is. You do not feel defeated or threatened at all. If you are a proud person, you feel yourself constantly challenged by the possibility of failure and defeat. In the enlightened mind the anxiety of maintaining oneself is transmuted into equanimity. There is still awareness of the solidity and stability of earth but there is no fear of losing it. Everything is open, safe, and dignified; there is nothing to fear.

Ratna is related to the south and autumn, fertility, richness in the sense of continual generosity. When fruit is ripe, it automatically falls to the ground, asking to be eaten up. Ratna has this kind of giving away quality. It is luscious and open with the quality of midmorning. It is yellow, connected with the sun's rays. Where vajra is associated with crystal, ratna is gold, amber, saffron. It has a sense of depth, real earthiness rather than texture, whereas vajra is purely texture, a crispy quality rather than fundamental depth. Ratna is so ripe and earthy, it is like a gigantic tree which falls to the ground and begins to rot and grow mushrooms all over it and is enriched by the weeds growing around it. It is a log in which animals might nest. Its color begins to turn to yellow and its bark to peel off, revealing an interior which is very rich and very solid. If you were to attempt to remove this log in order to use it as part of a garden arrangement, it would be impossible because it would crumble and fall apart. It would be too heavy to carry anyway.

Padma is connected with passion, a grasping quality, a desire to possess. In the background of passion there is the instinct toward union, wanting to be completely one with something. But passion has an hysterical quality, a neurotic quality which ignores the real state of being united and instead wants to possess in order to *become* united. Passion defeats its own purpose automatically. In the case of discriminating awareness, which is the wisdom aspect of passion, one sees the quality of "this" and "that" precisely and sharply. In other words, communication takes place. If you are going to communicate with someone, you must respect the existence of the other person as well as your process of communication. Discriminating awareness wisdom recognizes the fact of union, which is quite different from dualistically separating "that" from "this" in order to maintain oneself. The consuming quality of burning fire, desire, is transmuted into the wisdom of binding together through communication. You may be completely caught up with possessiveness in a spiritual or material sense. You may want something more than you can have. You may be so fascinated by the exotic qualities of the thing you want that you are blind to the world around you. You are completely wrapped up in desire, which produces an automatic sort of stupidity and ignorance. This ignorance in desire is transcended in discriminating awareness wisdom.

Padma is linked with the west and the color red. Red stands out from any other color, is very provocative, draws you toward it. It is also connected with the element of fire. In the confused state fire does not discriminate among the things that it grasps, burns, and destroys. In the awake state the heat of passion is transmuted into the warmth of compassion.

Padma is related to early spring. The harshness of winter is just about to soften with the promise of summer. Ice begins to melt, snowflakes become soggy. Padma is very much connected with facade; it has no feeling of solidity or texture; it is purely concerned with colors, the glamorous qualities, sunset. The visual quality of the surface is more important than its being. So padma is involved with art rather than science or practicality.

Padma is a reasonable location, a place where wildflowers grow, a perfect place to have animals roaming about, such as a highland plateau. It is a place of meadows scattered with gentle rocks suitable for young animals to play among.

Karma is associated with the emotion of jealousy, envy, and the element of wind. However, the terms "jealousy" and "envy" are not powerful and precise enough to describe the quality of karma. "Absolute paranoia" probably is a good phrase. You feel that you are not going to achieve any of your goals. You become irritated by the accomplishments of other people. You feel left behind and cannot bear to see others surpass you. This fear, this distrust of oneself, is connected with the element of wind. Wind never blows in all directions but it blows in one direction at a time. This is the one-way view of paranoia or envy.

Karma is connected with the wisdom of all-accomplishing action. The quality of paranoia falls away but the qualities of energy, keenness to action, and openness remain. In other words, the active aspect of wind is retained so that one's activity touches everything in its path. One's action is appropriate because it does not involve self-conscious panic or paranoia anymore. It sees the possibilities inherent in situations and automatically takes the appropriate course. It fulfills the purpose.

Karma suggests summer in the north. It is the efficiency of karma which connects it with this season, for it is a summer in which all things are active, growing, fulfilling their function. Millions of interconnected actions take place: living things grow, plants, insects, animals. There are thunderstorms and hailstorms. There is the sense that you are never left to enjoy the summer because something is always moving in order to maintain itself. It is a bit like late spring, but it is more fertile because it sees that all things are fulfilled at the right moment. The color of karma is the green of vegetables and grasses, of growing energy. Whereas the karma of summer is still competing, trying to give birth, the ratna of autumn has tremendous confidence; everything has been accomplished. The mood of karma is after sunset, dusk, late day and early night.

Buddha is associated with dullness and has an all-pervading quality because it contains and goes with all the rest of the emotions. The active factor in this dullness is the action of ignoring. Ignoring does not want to see. It just ignores and overcrowds itself. You are completely relaxed, completely careless. You would rather maintain your stupor than search or struggle for anything, and a slothful, stupid quality is brought to all the other emotions.

The wisdom connected with buddha is that of all-encompassing space. The all-pervading quality of dullness is kept as the foundation, but the flicker of doubt and sloth in this dullness is transformed into wisdom. This wisdom contains tremendous energy and intelligence which run right through all the other elements, colors, and emotions, which activate all the rest of the five wisdoms.

Buddha is the foundation or the "basic ground." It is the environment or oxygen which makes it possible for the other principles to function. It has a sedate, solid quality. Ratna is very solid and earthy as well, but it is not as earthy as buddha which is dull-earthy, uninteresting-earthy. Buddha is somewhat desolate, too spacious. It is a campsite where only the stones from campfires are left. The place has a sense of having been inhabited for a long time, but at present no one is there. The inhabitants were not killed or forced to move violently; they simply left. The mood is like that of the caves where American Indians used to live. They have a feeling of the past, but at the same time there are no outstanding characteristics. The tone is very dull, quite possibly in the plains, very flat. Buddha is connected with the color blue, the cool, spacious quality of sky.

Q: How do the pictures of buddhas, yidams, wrathful gods, and other symbols fit into the Tibetan spiritual path?

A: There is a great deal of misunderstanding regarding Tibetan iconography. Perhaps we should quickly go through the structure of iconography and symbolism in tantra. There is what is called "the iconography of the guru," which is connected with the pattern of the path, with the fact that, before you start to receive any teaching, you must surrender willingly, must open yourself. In order to surrender you somehow must identify yourself completely with the fullness and richness of life. At this point surrendering is not emptying in the sense of shunyata emptiness, which is a more advanced experience. But in the early stages of the path surrender means becoming an empty vessel. It also means identification with the fullness, with the richness of the teaching. So symbolically the gurus of the lineage wear highly ornamented robes, hats, and scepters and have other ornaments which they hold in their hands.

Then there is the iconography of the yidams which is connected with tantric practice. Yidams are the different aspects of the five buddha principles of energy. They are depicted as male herukas or female dakinis and can be either wrathful or peaceful. The wrathful aspect is associated with transmutation by force, leaping into wisdom, and choiceless transmutation. It is the act of cutting through, associated with crazy wisdom. Peaceful yidams are associated with transmutation by "process"; that is, confusion is pacified and gradually worn out.

The yidams wear the costumes of rakshasas, who in Indian mythology are vampires connected with Rudra, King of the Maras, the evil ones. The symbolism involved is that, when ignorance, symbolized by Rudra, has created its empire, then wisdom appears and destroys the empire and takes the costumes of its emperor and his retinue. The yi-dams' costumes symbolize that they have transmuted ego into wisdom. The five-skulled crowns they wear represent the five emotions which have been transmuted into the five wisdoms. These emotions are not thrown away but are worn as ornaments. Furthermore, the trident or *trishula* which the yidams carry is ornamented with three heads: a fresh head, a dry shrunken head, and a skeleton head. The fresh head represents hot passion. The dry one represents cold anger and toughness, like tough meat. The skeleton head represents stupidity. The trishula is an ornament which symbolizes transcendence of these three impulses. In addition the trident has three points which represent the three basic principles of being: shunyata, energy, and the quality of manifestation. These are the three "bodies" of the Buddha, the three kayas: dharmakaya, sambhogakaya and nirmanakaya. All the ornaments worn by the yidams—the bone ornaments, snakes, and others—are associated with different aspects of the path. For example, they wear a garland of fifty-one skulls which represents transcendence of the fifty-one types of thought patterns discussed in the hinayana doctrine of abhidharma.

In tantric practice one identifies with a yidam of a particular buddha family corresponding to one's nature. For instance, if a yidam is associated with the ratna family, then he will be yellow in color and have symbolism characteristic of ratna. The types of mandalas given to you by your teacher depend upon the family to which you belong, whether you belong to the passionate family or the family of pride, or whether you have the quality of air or water in you. Generally one can feel that certain people have the quality of earth and solidness, and certain people have the quality of air, rushing here and there, and other people have the quality of warmth and a presence connected with fire. The mandalas are given to you so that you can identify yourself with your particular emotions which have the potential of transmuting into wisdom. Sometimes you practice the visualization of these yidams. However, when you begin working with them, you do not visualize them immediately. You begin with an awareness of shunyata and then develop the feeling of the presence of that image or form. Then you recite a mantra which has an association with this particular feeling. In order to weaken the strength of ego, one somehow must establish a link between the imaginary presence and the watcher of oneself, the ego. The mantra is the link. After the practice of mantra, you dissolve the image or the form into a certain color of light appropriate to the specific yidam. Finally you end your visualization with, again, an awareness of shunyata. The whole idea is that these yidams must not be regarded as external gods who will save you, but they are expressions of your true nature. You identify yourself with the attributes and colors of particular yidams and feel the sound that comes from the mantra so that finally you begin to realize that your true nature is invincible. You become completely one with the yidam.

In *maha ati,* the highest tantra, the sense of identification falls away and one merges into one's true nature. Only the energies and colors remain. Previously you saw through forms and images and sounds, saw their empty quality. Now you see the forms, images, and sounds in their true quality. It is the idea of returning to samsara which is expressed in the Zen tradition by the ox-herding pictures: you have no man and no ox, and then at the end, you have return to the world.

Thirdly, there is the iconography of the "protective divinities." In the practice of identifying yourself with a particular yidam you have to develop an awareness which throws you back to your true nature from your confused nature. You need sudden shocks, reminders all the time, an awake quality. This awareness is represented by the protective divinities which are shown in wrathful form. It is a sudden jerk which reminds you. It is a wrathful awareness because it involves leaping. This leap needs a certain kind of energy to cut through confusion. You have to actually take the initiative to leap without any hesitation from the boundary of confusion into openness. You must really destroy hesitation. You must destroy all obstacles you meet on the path. Therefore this divinity is called protective. "Protection" does not mean securing your safety, but it signifies a reference point, a guideline which reminds you, keeps you in your place, in the open. For instance, there is a *mahakala* protective divinity called Six-Armed Mahakala who is black in color and stands on Ganesha, the elephant-headed god who here symbolizes subconscious thoughts. This subconscious gossip is an aspect of slothfulness that automatically distracts you from being aware and invites you back to being fascinated by your thoughts and emotions. It especially plays upon the survey nature of your thoughts—intellectual, domestic, emotional thoughts, whatever they may be. The mahakala brings you back to openness. The intent of the symbolism is that the mahakala overpowers subconscious gossip by standing on it. The mahakala represents the leap into penetrating awareness.

Generally, all Buddhist tantric iconography is included in these three categories: the guru, the yidams, and the protective divinities. The iconography of the guru expresses the richness of the lineage. The yidams allow you to identify with your particular nature. Then there are the protective divinities to act as reminders to you. The yidams and the protective divinities are generally shown in varying intensities of wrath, depending upon the intensity of awareness needed in order for you to see your true nature.

The wrathful yidams are always associated with what is known in tantric terms as *vajra anger,* the anger which has the tathata quality; in other words, it is anger without hatred, a dynamic energy. This particular energy, whatever wisdom it may belong to, is invincible. It is completely indestructible, imperturbable, because it is not created but is discovered as an original quality. It is, therefore, not subject to birth and death. It is always depicted as angry, wrathful, and warriorlike.

Q: How does transmutation take place?

A: Transmutation takes place with the understanding of shunyata and then the sudden discovery of energy. You realize that you no longer have to abandon anything. You begin to see the underlying qualities of wisdom in your life situation, which means that there is a kind of leap. If you are highly involved in one emotion such as anger, then by having a sudden glimpse of openness, which is shunyata, you begin to see that you do not have to suppress your energy. You do not have to keep calm and suppress the energy of anger, but you can transform your aggression into dynamic energy. It is a question of how open you are, how much you are really willing to do it. If there is less fascination and satisfaction with the explosion and release of your energy, then there is more likelihood of transmuting it. Once we become involved with the fascination and satisfaction of energy, then we are unable to transmute it. You do not have to completely change yourself, but you can use part of your energy in an awakened state.

Q: What is the difference between jnana and prajna?

A: One cannot regard wisdom as an external experience. That is the difference between wisdom and knowledge, jnana and prajna. Prajna is knowledge in terms of relativity, and jnana is wisdom beyond any kind of relativity. You are completely one with wisdom; you do not regard it as something educational or something experiential.

Q: How do you transmute emotion? How do you deal with it?

A: Well, that is a very personal question rather than an intellectual one. The whole point is that we have not actually experienced our emotions, although we think we have. We have only experienced emotions in terms of me and my anger, me and my desire. This "me" is a kind of central governing structure. The emotions play the part of messengers, bureaucrats, and soldiers. Instead of experiencing emotions as being separate from you, your rather unruly employees so to speak, you must actually feel the texture and real living quality of the emotions. Expressing or acting out hatred or desire on the physical level is another way of trying to escape from your emotions, just as you do when you try to repress them. If one actually feels the living quality, the texture of the emotions as they are in their naked state, then this experience also contains ultimate truth. And automatically one begins to see the simultaneously ironical and profound aspects of the emotions, as they are. Then the process of transmutation, that is, transmuting the emotions into wisdom, takes place automatically. But, as I have said, it is a personal question; we really have to do it. Until we actually do it, no words can describe it. We have to be brave enough to actually encounter our emotions, work with them in a real sense, feel their texture, the real quality of the emotions as they are. We would discover that emotion actually does not exist as it appears, but it contains much wisdom and open space. The problem is that we never experience emotions properly. We think that fighting and killing express anger, but these are another kind of escape, a way of releasing rather than actually experiencing emotion as it is. The basic nature of the emotions has not been felt properly.

Q: When emotions are transmuted, that doesn't mean they disappear, does it?

A: Not necessarily, but they are transmuted into other forms of energy. If we are trying to be good or peaceful, trying to suppress or subdue our emotions, that is the basic twist of ego in operation. We are being aggressive toward our emotions, trying forcefully to achieve peace or goodness. Once we cease being aggressive toward our emotions, cease trying to change them, once we experience them properly, then transmutation may take place. The irritating quality of the emotions is transmuted once you experience them as they are. Transmutation does not mean that the energy quality of the emotions is eliminated; in fact it is transformed into wisdom, which is very much needed.

Q: What about sexual tantra? Is that the process of transmuting sexual energy into something else?

A: It is the same thing. When the grasping quality of passion or desire is transformed into open communication, a dance, then the relationship of two people begins to develop creatively rather than being stagnating or being irritating to them.

Q: Does this principle of transmutation apply to sattvic and rajasic and tamasic energy as described in the Hindu tradition? You don't want to take tamasic energy and turn it into rajasic, but you take it and use it.

A: That's right, yes. It is very practical, actually. Generally we tend to prepare too much. We say, "Once I make a lot of money, then I will go somewhere to study and meditate and become a priest," or whatever it is we would like to become. But we never do it on the spot. We always speak in terms of, "Once I do something, then . . ." We always plan too much. We want to change our lives rather than use our lives, the present moment, as part of the practice, and this hesitation on our part creates a lot of setbacks in our spiritual practice. Most of us have romantic ideas— "I'm bad now but one day, when I change, I'll be good."

Q: Is the principle of transmutation expressed in art?

A: Yes. As we all know, similar combinations of colors and patterns have been created by different people from different cultures at different times. Spontaneous, expressive art automatically has a universal quality. That is why you do not have to go *beyond* anything. If you see fully and directly, then *that* speaks, *that* brings some understanding. Choosing a green light for go in traffic and a red light for stop, for danger, suggests some kind of universality in the effect of color.

Q: What about dance and theater?

A: It is the same thing. The trouble is, if you become too self-conscious in creating a work of art, then it ceases to be a work of art. When masters of art are completely absorbed in their work, they produce masterpieces, not because they are aware of their teachers, but because they become completely absorbed in the work. They do not question, they just do it. They produce the right thing quite accidentally.

Q: How is the fear or paranoia that interferes with spontaneity transmuted into action?

A: There are no special tricks involved in overcoming this and over-coming that in order to achieve a certain state of being. It is a question of leaping. When a person actually understands that he is in a state of paranoia, then that implies an underlying deep subconscious understanding of the other side, some feeling of the other aspect of it in his mind. Then he has to really take the leap. How to take the leap is very difficult to explain in words; one simply has to do it. It is rather like suddenly being pushed overboard into a river and discovering that you can swim; you just swim across the river. However, if you were to go back to the river and attempt to practice, you probably would not be able to swim at all. It is a question of spontaneity, of using the current intelligence. One cannot explain taking the leap in words; it is beyond words. But it is something that you will be able to do if you really are willing to do it, if you put yourself in the situation to leap and somehow surrender.

Q: If you are frightened and have a strong reaction to the fear, you are aware of the reaction but don't want to get lost in it, you want to remain conscious. How do you do it?
A: It is a question of first acknowledging that such energy is there, which is the energy to leap, as well. In other words, instead of running away from fear, one must become completely involved in it and begin to feel the rough and rugged quality of the emotion.

Q: Become a warrior?
A: Yes. At the beginning one might be satisfied with seeing the absur-dity of the emotion, which would disperse it. But this is still not enough to effect the transmutation principle of vajrayana. One must see the "form is form" quality of the emotions. Once you are able to look at the emo-tions properly, from the point of view of "form is form, emotion is emo-tion," without your preconceptions attached, once you see the naked quality of the emotions as they are, then you are ready to leap. It does not need much effort. You are already delivered to the leap, so to speak. This does not mean of course that, if you are angry, you go out and commit murder.

Q: In other words, see the emotion as it is instead of involving your-self in a scattered, penetrating reaction to a situation.
A: Yes. You see, we do not actually see emotion properly, although we are completely filled with it. If we follow our emotions and escape them by doing something, that is not experiencing them properly. We

try to escape or repress our emotions because we cannot bear to be in such a state. But the vajrayana speaks of looking properly, directly at the emotion and feeling it, its naked quality. You do not actually have to transmute. In fact, you see the already transmuted quality in the emotions: "form is form." It is very subtle and quite dangerous to just throw about.

Q: How does Milarepa's life fit into the pattern of tantra? He does not seem to practice transmutation, but rather, renunciation.

A: Of course, in his lifestyle Milarepa is a classic example of the yogi-renunciate tradition. But usually, when we think of a renunciant, we think of someone who is trying to escape the "evil" of the "worldly" life. This is not the case with Milarepa at all. He was not trying to suppress his "evil" inclinations by meditating alone in the wilderness. He did not lock himself into retreat. He was not trying to punish himself. His asceticism was simply an expression of his character, just as each of our lifestyles is an expression of who we are, determined by our psychologies and past histories. Milarepa wanted to be simple and he led a very simple life.

Certainly there is a tendency on the part of people following a religious path to become otherworldly for awhile, and Milarepa was no exception. But people can do this in the middle of a city. Wealthy people can spend a great deal of money going on a religious "trip." But sooner or later, if a person is going to really connect with the teachings, there must be a return to the world. When Milarepa was meditating in retreat, living very austerely, some hunters appeared by chance and gave him some fresh venison. He ate it and his meditation improved immediately. And later on, when he was hesitating to come down to the cities, some villagers appeared at his cave asking for teachings. He was continually being drawn out of isolation by the seemingly accidental play of life situations, which one could say is the play of the guru, the universality of guru, which always presents itself to us naturally. We may be sitting in meditation in our New York apartment, feeling very "high" and euphoric, very "spiritual." But then we get up and walk into the streets and someone steps on our toe and we have to deal with that. It brings us down to earth, back to the world.

Milarepa was tremendously involved with the process of transmutation of energies and emotions. In fact, when we read *The Hundred Thousand Songs of Milarepa*, the whole first part of the book is dealing with Milarepa's experience of this process. In "The Tale of Red Rock Jewel Valley" Milarepa had only recently left Marpa to go off and meditate alone. This might be called his "adolescent stage," because he was still involved with reliance upon a personal guru. Marpa was still his "daddy." Having opened and surrendered to Marpa, Milarepa still had to learn to transmute the emotions. He was still clinging to the notions of "good" and "bad," and so the world was still appearing to him in the guise of gods and demons.

In "The Tale of Red Rock Jewel Valley," when Milarepa went back into his cave after having a comforting vision of Marpa, he was confronted with a gang of demons. He tried every way he could think of to get rid of them, all kinds of tactics. He threatened them, cajoled them, he even preached the dharma to them. But they would not leave until he ceased regarding them as "bad" and opened to them, saw them as they were. This was the beginning of Milarepa's period of learning how to subjugate the demons, which is the same thing as transmuting the emotions. It is with our emotions that we create demons and gods: those things which we don't want in our lives and world are the demons; those things which we would draw to us are the gods and goddesses. The rest is just scenery.

By being willing to accept the demons and gods and goddesses as they are, Milarepa transmuted them. They became dakinis, or the energies of life. The whole first part of *The Hundred Thousand Songs* deals with Milarepa's mastery of transmutation, his growing ability to open to the world as it is, until he finally conquered all the demons in the chapter "The Goddess Tserinma's Attack." In this chapter thousands of demons assemble to terrify and attack Milarepa while he is meditating, but he preaches to them, is open and accepting, willing to offer them his whole being, and they are subjugated. At one point five demonesses, beginning to realize that they cannot frighten Milarepa, sing to him.

> *If the thought of demons*
> *Never rises in your mind,*
> *You need not fear the demon hosts around you.*
> *It is most important to tame your mind within . . .*[1]

> *On the steep path of fear and hope*
> *They lie in ambush . . .*[2]

---

1. Garma C. C. Chang, *The Hundred Thousand Songs of Milarepa* (New York, 1962), p. 306.
2. Ibid., p. 307.

And later Milarepa himself says, "Insofar as the Ultimate, or the true nature of being is concerned, there are neither Buddhas nor demons. He who frees himself from fear and hope, evil and virtue, will realize the insubstantial and groundless nature of confusion. Samsara will then appear to be the Mahamudra itself. . . ."[3]

The rest of *The Hundred Thousand Songs* deals with Milarepa's development as a teacher and his relationships with his students. Toward the end of his life he had completely perfected the transmutation process to the point where he could be called the vidyadhara, or "holder of the crazy wisdom." No longer could he be swayed by the winds of hope and fear. The gods and goddesses and demons, his passions and their external projections, had been completely subjugated and transformed. Now his life was a continual dance with the dakinis.

Finally Milarepa reached the "old dog" stage, his highest attainment. People could tread on him, use him as a road, as earth; he would always be there. He transcended his own individual existence so that, as we read his last teachings, there is a sense of the universality of Milarepa, the example of enlightenment.

---

3. Ibid., p. 308.

THE MYTH OF FREEDOM AND THE WAY OF MEDITATION

Edited by JOHN BAKER
and MARVIN CASPER

*This book is dedicated to Dorje Trolö,
the Crazy Wisdom form of Padmasambhava,
the father and protector of all beings.*

Foreword

I N 1972 I was teaching at an alternative school in New Mexico. I intro-duced my class of eight- to twelve-year-olds to a book called *Born in Tibet* and we all fell in love with it. When we learned that the author, Chögyam Trungpa Rinpoche, was living in Boulder, Colorado, the children wrote a letter asking if they could meet him. Rinpoche replied that in fact he was soon coming to teach at the nearby Lama Foundation. To our delight, we were invited to visit him there. When we arrived, one of Rinpoche's students met with us briefly. He told the children that Chögyam Trungpa was happy that we had come, but that he wanted the children to know that he was just an ordinary person, nothing special. With plenty of questions and handmade gifts, the children approached him, and they had a wonderful encounter. Three hours later, they returned home. As for me, I guess you could say that I never left. That is when I became the student of this ordinary extraordinary man.

When *The Myth of Freedom* was published a few years later, I read it over and over. It is a profound distillation of Buddhist truths expressed in the accessible style of a master adept at translating them into the language of his audience. I was extremely eager to digest what he was saying. Over the years, this book has continued to be an endless source of benefit to me and many others in our understanding and teaching Buddhism in North America. I think I have now read it at least twenty times, and each time I find something new. Its power lies in how directly it addresses the extremely unhabitual process of dissolving the barriers we put up between ourselves and the rest of the world.

When I took to heart the teachings presented here, a curious change slowly began to take place. I became far more open to the pain of myself and others; far more open to laughing and crying; far more able to love and accept and see my interconnectedness with all beings. As the years go by, I gradually become more and more at home in this world with its inevitable ups and downs.

It is in this spirit that I invite you to read the teachings presented here. If you too bring them into your life and put them into practice, I have no doubt that you will make a similar journey.

As my root teacher, the Vidyadhara Chögyam Trungpa Rinpoche vividly demonstrated this path to me, he also supported and encouraged me in following it. I feel glad that I can now encourage you and those who come after you to do the same. Thanks to the teachings of Chögyam Trungpa Rinpoche, ordinary people like you and me can do something extraordinary: we can learn to benefit all beings, including ourselves.

PEMA CHÖDRÖN

Editors' Preface

THE MYTH OF FREEDOM is based on lectures given by Chögyam Trungpa Rinpoche in various parts of the United States between 1971 and 1973. The enormous interest in Trungpa's previous book, *Cutting Through Spiritual Materialism*, has inspired us to present another set of his lectures in book form. *The Myth of Freedom* can be viewed as a companion volume to *Cutting Through* or as an independent introduction to the Buddhist psychology and meditative practice of Tibet.

The book is flanked in the front by an original poem by Chögyam Trungpa which describes the stages of the spiritual path and in back by Trungpa's translation of a classic text, Tilopa's instructions on mahamudra meditation to his disciple Naropa. The text seemed particularly appropriate since Tilopa was the father of Trungpa's eleven-hundred-year-old Kagyü lineage.

Page 186: His Holiness the sixteenth Gyalwang Karmapa, Rangjung Rikpe Dorje (1923–1981). The Gyalwang Karmapa is the supreme head of the Kagyü order of Tibetan Buddhism. He is the embodiment of the power and compassion of Buddhist tantra. He was a friend and inspiration to the author.

ENTHRONEMENT

ONE

Parents are very kind,
But I am too young to appreciate it.
The highland mountains and valleys are beautiful,
But having never seen the lowlands, I am stupid.

TWO

Having striven for mind's nourishment,
Sharpening the spearhead of intellect,
I discovered permanent parents
Whom I can never forget.

THREE

Having no one to influence my outlook,
I display my primordial nature
And adopt the style of a youthful prince.
This is due to the only father guru.

FOUR

I am busy working for others.
Prajna, penetrating all obstacles,
Has made the prince old and wise,
Fearing no one.

FIVE

Dancing in space,
Clad in clouds,
Eating the sun and holding the moon,
The stars are my retinue.

SIX

The naked child is beautiful and dignified.
The red flower blooms in the sky.
It is ironic to see the formless dancer,
Dancing to the trumpet without a trumpeter.

SEVEN

At the palace of red ruby,
Listening to the utterance of the seed syllable,
It is joyful to watch the dance of illusion,
The seductive maidens of phenomena.

EIGHT

The warrior without a sword,
Riding on a rainbow,
Hears the limitless laughter of transcendent joy.
The poisonous snake becomes amrita.

NINE

Drinking fire, wearing water,
Holding the mace of the wind,
Breathing earth,
I am the lord of the three worlds.

January 22, 1973

ONE

The Myth of Freedom

FANTASY AND REALITY

IF WE ARE TO plant the complete Buddhist teachings in American soil we must first understand the fundamental principles of Buddhism and work through its basic meditation practices. Many people respond to Buddhism as if it were a new cult which might save them, which might enable them to deal with the world in the manner of picking flowers in a beautiful garden. But if we wish to pick flowers from a tree, we must first cultivate the roots and trunk, which means that we must work with our fears, frustrations, disappointments, and irritations, the painful aspects of life.

People complain that Buddhism is an extremely gloomy religion because it emphasizes suffering and misery. Usually religions speak of beauty, song, ecstasy, bliss. But according to Buddha, we must begin by seeing the experience of life as it is. We must see the truth of suffering, the reality of dissatisfaction. We cannot ignore it and attempt to examine only the glorious, pleasurable aspects of life. If one searches for a promised land, a Treasure Island, then the search only leads to more pain. We cannot reach such islands, we cannot attain enlightenment in such a manner. So all sects and schools of Buddhism agree that we must begin by facing the reality of our living situations. We cannot begin by dreaming. That would be only a temporary escape; real escape is impossible.

In Buddhism, we express our willingness to be realistic through the practice of meditation. Meditation is not a matter of trying to achieve ecstasy, spiritual bliss, or tranquillity, nor is it attempting to become a better person. It is simply the creation of a space in which we are able to expose and undo our neurotic games, our self–deceptions, our hidden fears and hopes. We provide space through the simple discipline of doing nothing. Actually, doing nothing is very difficult. At first, we must begin by approximating doing nothing, and gradually our practice will develop. So meditation is a way of churning out the neuroses of mind and using them as part of our practice. Like manure, we do not throw our neuroses away, but we spread them on our garden; they become part of our richness.

In meditation practice, we neither hold the mind very tightly nor let it go completely. If we try to control the mind, then its energy will rebound back on us. If we let the mind go completely, then it will become very wild and chaotic. So we let the mind go, but at the same time there is some discipline involved. The techniques used in the Buddhist tradition are extremely simple. Awareness of bodily movement, breath, and one's physical situation are techniques common to all traditions. The basic practice is to be present, right here. The goal is also the technique. Precisely being in this moment, neither suppressing nor wildly letting go, but being precisely aware of what you are. Breath, like bodily existence, is a neutral process which has no "spiritual" connotations. We simply become mindful of its natural functioning. This is called shamatha practice. With this practice we begin to tread the hinayana, or narrow, path. This is not to say that the hinayana approach is simplistic or narrow-minded. Rather, because the mind is so complicated, so exotic, craving all sorts of entertainment constantly, the only way to deal with it is to channel it into a disciplined path without sidetracks. The hinayana is a vehicle which does not speed, one which is right on the point, a vehicle which does not get sidetracked. We have no opportunity to run away; we are right here and cannot step out. It is a vehicle without a reverse gear. And the simplicity of narrowness also brings an open attitude toward life situations, because we realize that there is no escape of any kind and give in to being right on the spot.

So we acknowledge what we are rather than try to hide from our problems and irritations. Meditation should not help you forget your commitment at the office. In fact, in the practice of sitting meditation you relate to your daily life all the time. Meditation practice brings our neuroses to the surface rather than hiding them at the bottom of our minds. It enables us to relate to our lives as something workable. I think people have the idea that, if only they could get away from the hustle and bustle of life, then they could really get into some sort of contemplative practice up in the mountains or at the seashore. But escaping the mundanity of our lives is to neglect the food, the actual nourishment which exists between two layers of bread. When you order a sandwich, you do not order two layers of bread. You have something in the middle which is chunky, eatable, delicious, and the bread comes along with it.

Then becoming more clearly aware of emotions and life situations and the space in which they occur might open us to a still more panoramic awareness. A compassionate attitude, a warmth, develops at this point. It is an attitude of fundamental acceptance of oneself while still retaining critical intelligence. We appreciate the joyful aspect of life along with the painful aspect. Relating to emotions ceases to be a big deal. Emotions are as they are, neither suppressed nor indulged but simply acknowledged. So the precise awareness of details leads into an openness to the complex totality of situations. Like a great river that runs down toward the ocean, the narrowness of discipline leads into the openness of panoramic awareness. Meditation is not purely sitting alone in a particular posture attending to simple processes, but is also an openness to the environment in which these processes take place. The environment becomes a reminder to us, continually giving us messages, teachings, insights.

So before we indulge in any exotic techniques, playing with energies, playing with sense perceptions, playing with visions in terms of religious symbolism, we must sort out our minds fundamentally. We must begin our practice by walking the narrow path of simplicity, the hinayana path, before we can walk upon the open highway of compassionate action, the mahayana path. And only after our highway journey is well on its way need we concern ourselves about how to dance in the fields—the vajrayana, or tantric, teachings. The simplicity of the hinayana is the foundation for appreciating the splendor of the mahayana and the tremendous color of tantra. So before we relate with heaven we must relate to earth and work on our basic neuroses. The whole approach of Buddhism is to develop transcendental common sense, seeing things as they are, without magnifying what is or dreaming about what we would like to be.

DISAPPOINTMENT

As long as we follow a spiritual approach promising salvation, miracles, liberation, then we are bound by the "golden chain of spirituality." Such a chain might be beautiful to wear, with its inlaid jewels and intricate carvings, but nevertheless, it imprisons us. People think they can wear the golden chain for decoration without being imprisoned by it, but they are deceiving themselves. As long as one's approach to spirituality is based upon enriching ego, then it is spiritual materialism, a suicidal process rather than a creative one.

All the promises we have heard are pure seduction. We expect the teachings to solve all our problems; we expect to be provided with magical means to deal with our depressions, our aggressions, our sexual hangups. But to our surprise we begin to realize that this is not going to happen. It is very disappointing to realize that we must work on ourselves and our suffering rather than depend upon a savior or the magical power of yogic techniques. It is disappointing to realize that we have to give up our expectations rather than build on the basis of our preconceptions.

We must allow ourselves to be disappointed, which means the surrendering of me-ness, my achievement. We would like to watch ourselves attain enlightenment, watch our disciples celebrating, worshiping, throwing flowers at us, with miracles and earthquakes occurring and gods and angels singing and so forth. This never happens. The attainment of enlightenment from ego's point of view is extreme death, the death of self, the death of me and mine, the death of the watcher. It is the ultimate and final disappointment. Treading the spiritual path is painful. It is a constant unmasking, peeling off of layer after layer of masks. It involves insult after insult.

Such a series of disappointments inspires us to give up ambition. We fall down and down and down, until we touch the ground, until we relate with the basic sanity of earth. We become the lowest of the low, the smallest of the small, a grain of sand, perfectly simple, no expectations. When we are grounded, there is no room for dreaming or frivolous impulse, so our practice at last becomes workable. We begin to learn how to make a proper cup of tea, how to walk straight without tripping. Our whole approach to life becomes more simple and direct, and any teachings we might hear or books we might read become workable. They become confirmations, encouragements to work as a grain of sand, as we are, without expectations, without dreams.

We have heard so many promises, have listened to so many alluring descriptions of exotic places of all kinds, have seen so many dreams, but from the point of view of a grain of sand, we could not care less. We are just a speck of dust in the midst of the universe. At the same time our situation is very spacious, very beautiful and workable. In fact, it is very inviting, inspiring. If you are a grain of sand, the rest of the universe, all the space, all the room is yours, because you obstruct nothing, overcrowd nothing, possess nothing. There is tremendous openness. You are the emperor of the universe because you are a grain of sand. The world is very simple and at the same time very dignified and open, because your inspiration is based upon disappointment, which is without the ambition of the ego.

SUFFERING

We begin our spiritual journey by asking questions, by doubting our deceptions. There is continual uncertainty as to what is real and unreal, what is happiness and what is misery. We experience this moment by moment and year by year as our lives unfold. We keep on asking questions and eventually the questions turn sour and begin to rot. They turn into pain. Pain increases as the questions become more solid and the answers more elusive.

As we grow older, in one way or another we begin to ask, "What is the meaning of life?" We might say, "What isn't the meaning of life? Everything is life." But that is too cute, too clever, and the question still remains. We could say that the meaning of life is to exist. Again, exist for what? What are we trying to achieve by leading our lives? Some people say that the meaning of life is to put our effort and energy toward higher goals: commuting between the earth and moon or becoming enlightened, becoming a great professor, great scientist, great mystic, to improve the world, clean up the earth's pollution. Maybe that is the meaning of life—that we are supposed to work hard and achieve something. We should discover wisdom and share it with others. Or we should create a better political order, reinforcing democracy so that all men are equal and everyone has a right to do whatever he wants within the limits of mutual responsibility. Perhaps we should raise the level of our civilization to the highest point so that our world becomes a fantastic place, a seat of wisdom, of enlightenment, of learning and the highest technological developments. There should be plenty to eat, pleasant houses, amiable company. We should become sophisticated, rich, and happy, without quarrels, war, or poverty, with tremendously powerful intellects that know all the answers, the scientific explanations of how the jellyfish began and how the cosmos operates.

I am not mocking this mentality, not at all, but have we considered the significance of death? The counterpart of life is death. Have we considered that? The very message of death is painful. If you were to ask your fifteen-year-old child to write his will, people would regard that as being completely absurd. No one would do that. We refuse to acknowledge death, but our highest ideals, our speculations on the meaning of life, the highest forms of civilization—all are impractical if we do not consider the process of birth, suffering, and death.

From moment to moment, birth, suffering, and death take place. Birth is opening into a new situation. Immediately after birth, there is the sense of refreshment, freshness, like watching the sun rise in the early morning. The birds begin to wake up and sing their songs, the air is fresh, we begin to see the hazy silhouettes of the trees and mountains. As the sun rises, the world becomes clearer and more defined. We watch the sun become redder and redder, finally turning into white light, bright sunshine. One would prefer to hold on to the dawn and sunrise, to keep the sun from rising completely, to hold on to the glowing promise. We would prefer to do this, but we cannot. No one has ever achieved it. We struggle to maintain the new situation, but finally we cannot hold on to anything and we are dead. When we die, there is a gap between the death and the next birth; but still that gap is filled with all kinds of subconscious gossip, questions as to what we should do, and we latch on to a new situation and are born again. We repeat this process again and again and again.

From this point of view, when you give birth to a child, if you really want to cling to life, you should not cut the umbilical cord as he is born. But you must. Birth is an expression of the separateness between mother and child. Either you are going to witness your child's death or the child is going to witness your death. Perhaps this is a very grim way of looking at life, but still it is true. Every move we make is an expression of birth, suffering, and death.

There are three categories of suffering or pain in the Buddhist tradition: all-pervading pain, the pain of alternation, and the pain of pain. All-pervading pain is the general pain of dissatisfaction, separation, and loneliness. We are alone, we are lonely people, we cannot regenerate our umbilical cord, we cannot say of our birth that "it was a rehearsal." It has already happened. So pain is inevitable as long as there is the presence of discontinuity and insecurity.

All-pervading pain is general frustration resulting from aggression. Whether you are polite or blunt, a seemingly happy or unhappy person, is irrelevant. As long as we try to hold on to our existence, we become a bundle of tense muscles protecting ourselves. This creates discomfort. We tend to feel that our existence is slightly inconvenient. Even if we are self-contained and have plenty of money, food, shelter, companionship, still there is this little thing in our being which is in the way. Something is protruding from which we constantly have to shield and hide ourselves. We have to be watchful in case we goof up, but we are uncertain as to what we are going to goof up. There is a sort of universal understanding that there is something we must keep secret, something we should not goof up, something unnameable. It is not logical, but there is still some sort of threat.

So fundamentally, no matter how happy we may be, we are still careful and angry. We do not really want to be exposed, we do not really want to encounter this thing, whatever it is. Of course we could attempt to rationalize this feeling saying, "I didn't get enough sleep last night so I feel funny today and don't want to do difficult work—I might goof up." But such self-justifications are not valid. The concern over goofing up involves being angry as well as hiding. We are angry at the unnameable private parts that we do not want exposed. "If only I could get rid of this thing, then I would be relieved, I would feel free."

This fundamental pain takes innumerable forms—the pain of losing a friend, the pain of having to attack an enemy, the pain of making money, the pain of wanting credentials, the pain of washing dishes, the pain of duty, the pain of feeling that someone is watching over your shoulder, the pain of thinking that we haven't been efficient or successful, the pain of relationships of all kinds.

In addition to all-pervading pain, there is the pain of alternation, which is realizing that you are carrying a burden. Sometimes you begin to feel that the burden has disappeared because you feel free, that you do not have to keep up with yourself anymore. But the sense of alternation between pain and its absence, between sanity and insanity, again and again, is itself painful. Shouldering the burden again is very painful.

And then there is the pain of pain, which is the third type. You are already insecure, feeling uncertain about your territory. On top of that you worry about your condition and develop an ulcer. While rushing to the doctor to treat the ulcer you stub your toe. Resisting pain only increases its intensity. The three types of pain quickly follow one another in life, they pervade life. First you feel fundamental pain, and then the pain of alternation, from pain to its absence and back again; and then you have the pain of pain, the pain of all those life situations you do not want.

You decide to take a vacation in Paris, planning to have a good time, but something goes wrong. Your longtime French friend had an accident. He is in the hospital and his family is very upset, unable to provide you with the hospitality you had expected. Instead you have to stay in a hotel, which you cannot afford, as your money is running out. You decide to change your money on the black market and you get swindled. And your supposed friend, who had an accident and is in the hospital, suddenly starts to dislike you, begins to regard you as a nuisance. You want to return home, but you can't. All flights are canceled because of bad weather. You are really desperate. Every hour, every second is important to you. You are pacing up and down in the airport and your visa is running out. You have to get out of the country soon. And explaining to the officials is very difficult because you do not speak French.

Such situations occur all the time. We are speeding, trying to get rid of our pain, and we find more pain by doing so. Pain is very real. We cannot pretend that we are all happy and secure. Pain is our constant companion. It goes on and on—all-pervading pain, the pain of alternation, and the pain of pain. If we are seeking eternity or happiness or security, then the experience of life is one of pain, duhkha, suffering.

EGOLESSNESS

The effort to secure our happiness, to maintain ourselves in relation to something else, is the process of ego. But this effort is futile because there are continual gaps in our seemingly solid world, continual cycles of death and rebirth, constant change. The sense of continuity and solidity of self is an illusion. There is really no such thing as ego, soul, or atman. It is a succession of confusions that create ego. The process which is ego actually consists of a flicker of confusion, a flicker of aggression, a flicker of grasping—all of which exist only in the moment. Since we cannot hold on to the present moment, we cannot hold on to me and mine and make them solid things.

The experience of oneself relating to other things is actually a momentary discrimination, a fleeting thought. If we generate these fleeting thoughts fast enough, we can create the illusion of continuity and solidity. It is like watching a movie, the individual film frames are played so quickly that they generate the illusion of continual movement. So we build up an idea, a preconception, that self and other are solid and continuous. And once we have this idea, we manipulate our thoughts to confirm it, and are afraid of any contrary evidence. It is this fear of exposure, this denial of impermanence, that imprisons us. It is only by acknowledging impermanence that there is the chance to die and the space to be reborn and the possibility of appreciating life as a creative process.

There are two stages to understanding egolessness. In the first stage we perceive that ego does not exist as a solid entity, that it is impermanent, constantly changing, that it was our concepts that made it seem solid. So we conclude that ego does not exist. But we still have formulated a subtle concept of egolessness. There is still a watcher of the egolessness, a watcher to identify with it and maintain his existence. The second stage is seeing through this subtle concept and dropping the watcher. So true egolessness is the absence of the concept of egolessness. In the first stage there is a sense of someone perceiving egolessness. In the second, even the perceiver does not exist. In the first, we perceive that there is no fixed entity because everything is relative to something else. In the second stage there is the understanding that the notion of relativity needs a watcher to perceive it, to confirm it, which introduces another relative notion, the watcher and the watched.

To say that egolessness does exist because things are constantly changing is quite feeble, since we still hold on to change as something solid. Egolessness is not simply the idea that, since there is discontinuity, therefore there is nothing to hang on to. True egolessness involves the nonexistence of the discontinuity as well. We cannot hang on to the idea of discontinuity either. In fact, discontinuity really does not operate. Our perception of discontinuity is the product of insecurity; it is concept. So too is any idea about the oneness behind or within phenomena.

The idea of egolessness has often been used to obscure the reality of birth, suffering, and death. The problem is that, once we have a notion of egolessness and a notion of pain, birth, and death, then we can easily entertain or justify ourselves by saying that pain does not exist because there is no ego to experience it, that birth and death do not exist because there is no one to witness them. This is just cheap escapism. The philosophy of shunyata has often been distorted by the presentation of the idea that: "There is no one to suffer, so who cares? If you suffer, it must be your illusion." This is pure opinion, speculation. We can read about it, we can think about it, but when we actually suffer, can we remain indifferent? Of course not; suffering is stronger than our petty opinions. A true understanding of egolessness cuts through opinion. The absence of a notion of egolessness allows us to fully experience pain, birth, and death because then there are no philosophical paddings.

The whole idea is that we must drop all reference points, all concepts of what is or what should be. Then it is possible to experience the uniqueness and vividness of phenomena directly. There is tremendous room to experience things, to allow experience to occur and pass away. Movement happens within vast space. Whatever happens, pleasure and pain, birth and death and so forth, are not interfered with but are experienced in their fullest flavor. Whether they are sweet or sour, they are experienced completely, without philosophical overlays or emotional attitudes to make things seem lovable or presentable.

We are never trapped in life, because there are constant opportunities for creativity, challenges for improvisation. Ironically, by seeing clearly and acknowledging our egolessness, we may discover that suffering contains bliss, impermanence contains continuity or eternity, and egolessness contains the earth quality of solid being. But this transcendental bliss, continuity, and beingness is not based on fantasies, ideas, or fears.

TWO

Styles of Imprisonment

COSMIC JOKE

IN ORDER TO CUT through the ambition of ego, we must understand
how we set up me and my territory, how we use our projections as
credentials to prove our existence. The source of the effort to confirm
our solidity is an uncertainty as to whether or not we exist. Driven by
this uncertainty, we seek to prove our own existence by finding a reference point outside ourselves, something with which to have a relationship, something solid to feel separate from. But the whole enterprise is
questionable if we really look back and back and back. Perhaps we have
perpetrated a gigantic hoax?

The hoax is the sense of the solidity of I and other. This dualistic
fixation comes from nothingness. In the beginning there is open space,
zero, self-contained, without relationship. But in order to confirm zero-
ness, we must create one to prove that zero exists. But even that is not
enough; we might get stuck with just one and zero. So we begin to ad-
vance, venture out and out. We create two to confirm one's existence,
and then we go out again and confirm two by three, three by four, and
so on. We set up a background, a foundation from which we can go on
and on to infinity. This is what is called samsara, the continuous vicious
cycle of confirmation of existence. One confirmation needs another confirmation needs another . . .

The attempt to confirm our solidity is very painful. Constantly we
find ourselves suddenly slipping off the edge of a floor which had

appeared to extend endlessly. Then we must attempt to save ourselves from death by immediately building an extension to the floor in order to make it appear endless again. We think we are safe on our seemingly solid floor, but then we slip off again and have to build another extension. We do not realize that the whole process is unnecessary, that we do not need a floor to stand on, that we have been building all these floors on the ground level. There was never any danger of falling or need for support. In fact, our occupation of extending the floor to secure our ground is a big joke, the biggest joke of all, a cosmic joke. But we may not find it funny: it may sound like a serious double cross.

To understand more precisely the process of confirming the solidity of I and other, that is, the development of ego, it is helpful to be familiar with the five skandhas, a set of Buddhist concepts which describe ego as a five-step process.

The first step or skandha, the birth of ego, is called "form" or basic ignorance. We ignore the open, fluid, intelligent quality of space. When a gap or space occurs in our experience of mind, when there is a sudden glimpse of awareness, openness, absence of self, then a suspicion arises: "Suppose I find that there is no solid me? That possibility scares me. I don't want to go into that." That abstract paranoia, the discomfort that something may be wrong, is the source of karmic chain reactions. It is the fear of ultimate confusion and despair. The fear of the absence of self, of the egoless state, is a constant threat to us. "Suppose it is true, what then? I am afraid to look." We want to maintain some solidity but the only material available with which to work is space, the absence of ego, so we try to solidify or freeze that experience of space. Ignorance in this case is not stupidity, but it is a kind of stubbornness. Suddenly we are bewildered by the discovery of selflessness and do not want to accept it; we want to hold on to something.

Then the next step is the attempt to find a way of occupying ourselves, diverting our attention from our aloneness. The karmic chain reaction begins. Karma is dependent upon the relativity of this and that—my existence and my projections—and karma is continually reborn as we continually try to busy ourselves. In other words, there is a fear of not being confirmed by our projections. One must constantly try to prove that one does exist by feeling one's projections as a solid thing. Feeling the solidity of something seemingly outside you reassures you that you are a solid entity as well. This is the second skandha, "feeling."

In the third stage, ego develops three strategies or impulses with which to relate to its projections: indifference, passion, and aggression. These impulses are guided by perception. Perception, in this case, is the self-conscious feeling that you must officially report back to central headquarters what is happening in any given moment. Then you can manipulate each situation by organizing another strategy.

In the strategy of indifference, we numb any sensitive areas that we want to avoid, that we think might hurt us. We put on a suit of armor. The second strategy is passion—trying to grasp things and eat them up. It is a magnetizing process. Usually we do not grasp if we feel rich enough. But whenever there is a feeling of poverty, hunger, impotence, then we reach out, we extend our tentacles and attempt to hold on to something. Aggression, the third strategy, is also based upon the experience of poverty, the feeling that you cannot survive and therefore must ward off anything that threatens your property or food. Moreover, the more aware you are of the possibilities of being threatened, the more desperate your reaction becomes. You try to run faster and faster in order to find a way of feeding or defending yourself. This speeding about is a form of aggression. Aggression, passion, indifference are part of the third skandha, "perception/impulse."

Ignorance, feeling, impulse, and perception—all are instinctive processes. We operate a radar system which senses our territory. Yet we cannot establish ego properly without intellect, without the ability to conceptualize and name. By now we have an enormously rich collection of things going on inside us. Since we have so many things happening, we begin to categorize them, putting them into certain pigeonholes, naming them. We make it official, so to speak. So "intellect" or "concept" is the next stage of ego, the fourth skandha, but even this is not quite enough. We need a very active and efficient mechanism to keep the instinctive and intellectual processes of ego coordinated. That is the last development of ego, the fifth skandha, "consciousness."

Consciousness consists of emotions and irregular thought patterns, all of which taken together form the different fantasy worlds with which we occupy ourselves. These fantasy worlds are referred to in the scriptures as the "six realms." The emotions are the highlights of ego, the generals of ego's army; subconscious thought, daydreams, and other thoughts connect one highlight to another. So thoughts form ego's army and are constantly in motion, constantly busy. Our thoughts are neurotic in the sense that they are irregular, changing direction all the time and overlapping one another. We continually jump from one thought to the next, from spiritual thoughts to sexual fantasies to money matters to domestic thoughts and so on. The whole development of the five skandhas—ignorance/form, feeling, impulse/perception, concept, and consciousness—is an attempt in our part to shield ourselves from the truth of our insubstantiality.

The practice of meditation is to see the transparency of this shield. But we cannot immediately start dealing with the basic ignorance itself; that would be like trying to push a wall down all at once. If we want to take this wall down, we must take it down brick by brick; we start with immediately available material, a stepping-stone. So the practice of meditation starts with the emotions and thoughts, particularly with the thought process.

SELF-ABSORPTION

The six realms, the different styles of samsaric occupation, are referred to as realms, in the sense that we dwell within a particular version of reality. We are fascinated with maintaining familiar surroundings, familiar desires and longings, so as not to give in to a spacious state of mind. We cling to our habitual patterns because confusion provides a tremendously familiar ground to sink into as well as a way of occupying ourselves. We are afraid to give up this security and entertainment, afraid to step into open space, into a meditative state of mind. The prospect of the awakened state is very irritating because we are uncertain how to handle it, so we prefer to run back to our prison rather than release ourselves from it. Confusion and suffering become an occupation, often quite secure and delightful.

The six realms are: the realm of the gods, the realm of the jealous gods, the human realm, the animal realm, the realm of the hungry ghosts, and the hell realm, The realms are predominantly emotional attitudes toward ourselves and our surroundings, emotional attitudes colored and reinforced by conceptual explanations and rationalizations. As human beings we may, during the course of a day, experience the emotions of all the realms, from the pride of the god realm to the hatred and paranoia of the hell realm. Nonetheless, a person's psychology is usually firmly rooted in one realm. This realm provides us with a style of confusion, a way of entertaining and occupying ourselves so as not to have to face our fundamental uncertainty, our ultimate fear that we may not exist.

The fundamental occupation of the god realm is mental fixation, a meditative absorption of sorts, which is based upon ego, upon the spiritually materialistic approach. In such meditation practice the meditator maintains himself by dwelling upon something. The particular topic of meditation, no matter how seemingly profound, is experienced as a solid body rather than as transparent. This practice of meditation begins with a tremendous amount of preparation or "self-development." Actually the aim of such practice is not so much to create the solidity of a place to dwell as it is to create the self-consciousness of the dweller. There is tremendous self-consciousness, which of course reaffirms the meditator's existence.

You do not very dramatic results from such practice, if you are successful at it. One might experience inspiring visions or sounds, seemingly profound mental states, physical bliss and mental bliss. All sorts of "altered states of consciousness" could be experienced or manufactured through the efforts of self-conscious mind. But these experiences are imitations, plastic flowers, man-made, manufactured, prefabricated.

We could dwell on a technique as well—repetition of a mantra or visualization. One is not completely absorbed into the visualization or mantra, but instead *you* are visualizing, *you* are repeating the mantra. Such practice, based upon "me," that "I am doing this," is once again the development of self-consciousness.

The realm of the gods is realized through tremendous struggle, is manufactured out of hope and fear. The fear of failure and the hope of gain builds up and up and up to a crescendo. One moment you think you are going to make it and the next moment you think you are going to fail. Alternation between these extremes produces enormous tension. Success and failure mean so much to us—"This is the end of me," or "This is my achievement of ultimate pleasure."

Finally we become so excited that we begin to lose the reference points of our hope and fear. We lose track of where we are and what we were doing. And then there is a sudden flash in which pain and pleasure become completely one and the meditative state of dwelling on the ego dawns upon us. Such a breakthrough, such a tremendous achievement.

And then pleasure begins to saturate our system, psychologically and physically. We no longer have to care about hope or fear. And quite possibly we might believe this to be the permanent achievement of enlightenment or union with God. At that moment everything we see appears to be beautiful, loving, even the most grotesque situations of life seem heavenly. Anything that is unpleasant or aggressive seems beautiful because we have achieved oneness with ego. In other words, ego lost track of its intelligence. This is the absolute, ultimate achievement of bewilderment, the depths of ignorance—extremely powerful. It is a kind of spiritual atomic bomb, self-destructive in terms of compassion, in terms of communication, in terms of stepping out of the bondage of ego. The whole approach in the realm of the gods is stepping in and in and in, churning out more and more chains with which to bind oneself. The more we develop our practice, the more bondage we create. The scriptures cite the analogy of the silkworm which binds itself with its own silk thread until it finally suffocates itself.

Actually we have only been discussing one of two aspects of the realm of the gods, the self-destructive perversion of spirituality into materialism. However, the god realm's version of materialism can also be applied to so-called worldly concerns in the search for extreme mental and physical pleasure, the attempt to dwell on seductive goals of all kinds: health, wealth, beauty, fame, virtue, whatever. The approach is always pleasure-oriented, in the sense of maintenance of ego. What characterizes the realm of the gods is the losing track of hope and fear. And this might be achieved in terms of sensual concerns as well as in terms of spirituality. In both cases, in order to achieve such extraordinary happiness, we must lose track of who is searching and what is the goal. If our ambition expresses itself in terms of worldly pursuits, at first we search for happiness, but then we begin to enjoy the struggle toward happiness as well and we begin to relax into our struggle. Halfway to achieving absolute pleasure and comfort we begin to give in and make the best of our situation. The struggle becomes an adventure and then a vacation or holiday. We are still on our adventurous journey to the actual ultimate goal, but at the same time we consider every step along the way a vacation, a holiday.

So the realm of the gods is not particularly painful, in itself. The pain comes from the eventual disillusionment. You think you have achieved a continually blissful state, spiritual or worldly; you are dwelling on that.

But suddenly something shakes you and you realize that what you have achieved is not going to last forever. Your bliss becomes shaky and more irregular, and the thought of maintenance begins to reappear in your mind as you try to push yourself back into your blissful state. But the karmic situation brings you all kinds of irritations and at some stage you begin to lose faith in the continuity of the blissful state. A sudden violence arises, the feeling that you have been cheated, that you cannot stay in this realm of the gods forever. So when the karmic situation shakes you and provides extraordinary situations for you to relate with, the whole process becomes profoundly disappointing. You condemn yourself or the person who put you into the god realm or what brought you out of it. You develop anger and disappointment because you think you have been cheated. You switch into another style of relating to the world, another realm. This is what is called samsara, which literally means "continual circle," "whirlpool," the ocean of confusion which spins around again and again and again, without end.

PARANOIA

The dominant characteristic of the next realm, the jealous god or asura realm, is paranoia. If you are trying to help someone who has an asura mentality, they interpret your action as an attempt to oppress them or infiltrate their territory. But if you decide not to help them, they interpret that as a selfish act: you are seeking comfort for yourself. If you present both alternatives to them, then they think you are playing games with them. The asura mentality is quite intelligent: it sees all the hidden corners. You think that you are communicating with an asura face-to-face, but in actual fact he is looking at you from behind your back. This intense paranoia is combined with an extreme efficiency and accuracy which inspires a defensive form of pride. The asura mentality is associated with wind, speeding about, trying to achieve everything on the spot, avoiding all possibilities of being attacked. It is trying constantly to attain something higher and greater. To do so one must watch out for every possible pitfall. There is no time to prepare, to get ready to put your action into practice. You just act without preparation. A false kind of spontaneity, a sense of freedom to act develops.

The asura mentality is preoccupied with comparison. In the constant struggle to maintain security and achieve greater things, you need points of reference, landmarks to plot your movement, to fix your opponent, to measure your progress. You regard life situations as games, in the sense of there being an opponent and yourself. You are constantly dealing with them and me, me and my friends, me and myself. All corners are regarded as being suspicious or threatening, therefore one must look into them and be careful of them. But one is not careful in the sense of hiding or camouflaging oneself. You are very direct and willing to come out in the open and fight if there is a problem or if there is a plot or a seeming plot against you. You just come out and fight face-to-face, trying to expose the plot. At the same time that one is going out in the open and facing the situation, one is distrustful of the messages that you receive from the situation, so you ignore them. You refuse to accept anything, refuse to learn anything that is presented by outsiders, because everyone is regarded as the enemy.

PASSION

Passion is the major occupation in the human realm. Passion in this sense is an intelligent kind of grasping in which the logical reasoning mind is always geared toward the creation of happiness. There is an acute sense of the separateness of pleasurable objects from the experiencer resulting in a sense of loss, poverty, often accompanied by nostalgia. You feel that only pleasurable objects can bring you comfort and happiness, but you feel inadequate, not strong or magnetic enough for the objects of pleasure to be drawn naturally into your territory. Nevertheless, you try actively to draw them in. This often leads to a critical attitude toward other people. You want to magnetize the best qualities, the most pleasurable, most sophisticated, most civilized situations.

This kind of magnetizing is different from that of the asura realm, which is not as selective and intelligent. The human realm by comparison involves a high degree of selectivity and fussiness. There is an acute sense of having your own ideology and your own style, of rejecting things not your style. You must have the right balance in everything. You criticize and condemn people who do not meet your standards. Or else you might be impressed by someone who embodies your style or is superior to you at achieving it, someone who is very intelligent and has very refined taste, who leads a pleasurable life and has the things you would like to have. It might be an historical figure or a mythological figure or one of your contemporaries who has greatly impressed you. He is very accomplished and you would like to possess his qualities. It is not simply a matter of being jealous of another person; you want to draw that person into your territory. It is an ambitious kind of jealousy in that you want to equal the other person.

The essence of the human realm is the endeavor to achieve some high ideal. Often those who find themselves in this realm will have visions of Christ or Buddha or Krishna or Muhammad or other historical figures who have tremendous meaning for them because of their achievements. These great personages have magnetized everything that one could possibly think of—fame, power, wisdom. If they wanted to become rich they could do so because of their enormous influence over other people. You would like to be like them—not necessarily better than but at least equal to them. Often people have visions in which they identify themselves with great politicians, statesmen, poets, painters, musicians, scientists, and so forth. There is an heroic attitude, the attempt to create monuments, the biggest, greatest, historical monument. This heroic approach is based on fascination with what you lack. When you hear of someone who possesses remarkable qualities, you regard them as significant beings and yourself as insignificant. This continual comparing and selecting generates a never-ending procession of desires.

The human mentality places a strong emphasis on knowledge, learning, and education, on collecting all kinds of information and wisdom. The intellect is most active in the human realm. There is so much going on in your mind as a result of having collected so many things and having planned so many projects. The epitome of the human realm is to be stuck in a huge traffic jam of discursive thought. You are so busy thinking that you cannot learn anything at all. The constant churning out of ideas, plans, hallucinations, and dreams is a quite different mentality from that of the god realm. There you are completely absorbed in a blissful state, a kind of self-stuck sense of satisfaction. In the jealous god realm you are completely drunk on competitiveness; there is less possibility of thought happening because your experiences are so strong that they overpower you, hypnotize you. In the case of the human realm there are more thoughts happening. The intellectual or logical mind becomes much more powerful so that one is completely overwhelmed by the possibilities of magnetizing new situations. Thus one tries to grasp new ideas, new strategies, relevant case histories, quotations from books, significant incidents that have occurred in one's life, and so on, and one's mind becomes completely full of thought. The things that have been recorded in the subconscious play back continually, much more so than in the other realms.

So it is a very intellectual realm, very busy and very disturbing. The human mentality has less pride than the mentalities of the other realms. In the other realms you find some occupation to hang on to and derive satisfaction from, whereas in the human realm there is no such satisfaction. There is a constant searching, constant looking for new situations or attempts to improve given situations. It is the least enjoyable state of mind because suffering is not regarded as an occupation nor as a way of challenging oneself; rather it is a constant reminder of ambitions created out of suffering.

STUPIDITY

The descriptions of the different realms are related to subtle but distinct differences in the ways individuals handle themselves in daily life—how they walk, talk, write letters, the way they read, eat, sleep, and so on. Everyone tends to develop a style which is peculiar to them. If we hear a tape recording of our voice or see a videotape or movie of ourselves, we are often shocked to see our style as someone else sees it. It feels extremely alien. Usually we find other people's point of view irritating or embarrassing.

Blindness to our style, to how others see us, is most acute in the animal realm. I am not speaking of literally being reborn as an animal but of the animal quality of mind, a mentality which stubbornly pushes forward toward predetermined goals. The animal mentality is very serious. It even makes humor into a serious occupation. Self-consciously trying to create a friendly environment, a person will crack jokes or try to be funny, intimate, or clever, However, animals do not really smile or laugh; they just behave. They may play, but it is unusual for animals to actually laugh. They might make friendly noises or gestures, but the subtleties of a sense of humor are absent. The animal mentality looks directly ahead, as if wearing blinders. It never looks to the right or left but very sincerely goes straight ahead, trying to reach the next available situation, continually trying to adjust situations to make them conform to its expectations.

The animal realm is associated with stupidity: that is, preferring to play deaf and dumb, preferring to follow the rules of available games rather than redefine them. Of course, you might try to manipulate your perception of any given game, but you are really just following along, just following your instinct. You have some hidden or secret wish that you would like to put into effect, so when you come to obstacles, to irritations, you just push forward, regardless of whether or not you may hurt someone or destroy something of value. You just go out and pursue whatever is available and if something else comes up, you take advantage of that as well and pursue it.

The ignorance or stupidity of the animal realm comes from a deadly honest and serious mentality which is quite different from the bewilderment of the basic ignorance of the first skandha. In animal ignorance you have a certain style of relating to yourself and refuse to see that style from other points of view. You completely ignore such possibilities. If somebody attacks you or challenges your clumsiness, your unskilled way of handling a situation, you find a way of justifying yourself, find a rationale to keep your self-respect. You are not concerned with being truthful as long as your deception can be maintained in front of others. You are proud that you are clever enough to lie successfully. If you are attacked, challenged, criticized, you automatically find an answer. Such stupidity can be very clever. It is ignorance or stupidity in the sense that you do not see the environment around you, but you see only your goal and only the means to achieve that goal, and you invent all kinds of excuses to prove that you are doing the right thing.

The animal mentality is extremely stubborn, but this stubbornness can be sophisticated as well and quite skillful and ingenious, but without a sense of humor. The ultimate sense of humor is a free way of relating with life situations in their full absurdity. It is seeing things clearly, including self-deception, without blinders, without barriers, without excuses. It is being open and seeing with panoramic vision rather than trying to relieve tension. As long as humor is used as a way to relieve tension or self-consciousness or pressure, then it is the humor of the animal realm, which is actually extremely serious. It is a way of looking for a crutch. So the essence of the animal style is to try to fulfill your desires with extreme honesty, sincerity, and seriousness. Traditionally, this direct and mean way of relating with the world is symbolized by the pig. The pig does not look to the right or left but just sniffs along, consuming whatever comes in front of its nose; it goes on and on and on, without any sense of discrimination—a very sincere pig.

Whether we are dealing with simple domestic tasks or highly sophisticated intellectual projects, we can have an animal style. It does not matter whether the pig eats expensive sweets or garbage. What is important is *how* he eats. The extreme animal mentality is trapped in a continual, self-contained, self-justifying round of activity. You are not able to related with the messages given to you by your environment. You do not see yourself mirrored by others. You may be dealing with very intellectual matters, but the style is animal since there is no sense of humor, no way of surrendering or opening. There is a constant demand to move on from one thing to the next, regardless of failures or obstacles. It is like being a tank that rolls along, crushing everything in its path. It does not matter if you run over people or crash through buildings—you just roll along.

POVERTY

In the preta or hungry ghost realm one is preoccupied with the process of expanding, becoming rich, consuming. Fundamentally, you feel poor. You are unable to keep up the pretense of being what you would like to be. Whatever you have is used as proof of the validity of your pride, but it is never enough, there is always some sense of inadequacy.

The poverty mentality is traditionally symbolized by a hungry ghost who has a tiny mouth, the size of the eye of a needle, a thin neck and throat, skinny arms and legs, and a gigantic belly. His mouth and neck are too small to let enough food pass through them to fill his immense belly, so he is always hungry. And the struggle to satisfy his hunger is very painful since it is so hard to swallow what he eats. Food, of course, symbolizes anything you may want—friendship, wealth, clothes, sex, power, whatever.

Anything that appears in your life you regard as something to consume. If you see a beautiful autumn leaf falling, you regard it as your prey. You take it home or photograph it or paint a picture of it or write in your memoirs how beautiful it was. If you buy a bottle of Coke, it is exciting to hear the rattlings of the paper bag as you unpack it. The sound of the Coke spilling out of the bottle gives a delightful sense of thirst. Then you self-consciously taste it and swallow it. You have finally managed to consume it—such an achievement. It was fantastic; you brought the dream into reality. But after a while you become restless again and look for something else to consume.

You are constantly hungering for new entertainment—spiritual, intellectual, sensual, and so on. Intellectually you may feel inadequate and decide to pull up your socks by studying and listening to juicy, thoughtful answers, profound, mystical words. You consume one idea after another, trying to record them, trying to make them solid and real. Whenever you feel hunger, you open your notebook or scrapbook or a book of satisfying ideas. When you experience boredom or insomnia or depression, you open your books, read your notes and clippings and ponder over them, draw comfort from them. But this becomes repetitive at some point. You would like to re-meet your teachers or find new ones. And another journey to the restaurant or the supermarket or the delicatessen is not a bad idea. But sometimes you are prevented from taking the trip. You may not have enough money, your child gets sick, your parents are dying, you have business to attend to, and so on. You realize that when more obstacles come up, then that much more hunger arises in you. And the more you want, the more you realize what you cannot get, which is painful.

It is painful to be suspended in unfulfilled desire, continually searching for satisfaction. But even if you achieve your goal then there is the frustration of becoming stuffed, so full that one is insensitive to further stimuli. You try to hold on to your possession, to dwell on it, but after a while you become heavy and dumb, unable to appreciate anything. You wish you could be hungry again so you could fill yourself up again. Whether you satisfy a desire or suspend yourself in desire and continue to struggle, in either case you are inviting frustration.

ANGER

The hell realm is pervaded by aggression. This aggression is based on such a perpetual condition of hatred that one begins to lose track of whom you are building your aggression toward as well as who is being aggressive toward you. There is a continual uncertainty and confusion. You have built up a whole environment of aggression to such a point that finally, even if you were to feel slightly cooler about your own anger and aggression, the environment around you would throw more aggression at you. It is like walking in hot weather; you might feel physically cooler for a while, but hot air is coming at you constantly so you cannot keep yourself cool for long.

The aggression of the hell realm does not seem to be your aggression, but it seems to permeate the whole space around you. There is a feeling of extreme stuffiness and claustrophobia. There is no space in which to breathe, no space in which to act, and life becomes overwhelming. The aggression is so intense that, if you were to kill someone to satisfy your aggression, you would achieve only a small degree of satisfaction. The aggression still lingers around you. Even if you were to try to kill yourself, you would find that the killer remains; so you would not have managed to murder yourself completely. There is a constant environment of aggression in which one never knows who is killing whom. It is like trying to eat yourself from the inside out. Having eaten yourself, the eater remains, and he must be eaten as well, and so on and so on. Each time the crocodile bites his own tail, he is nourished by it; the more he eats, the more he grows. There is no end to it.

You cannot really eliminate pain through aggression. The more you kill, the more you strengthen the killer who will create new things to be killed. The aggression grows until finally there is no space: the whole environment has been solidified. There are not even gaps in which to look back or do a double take. The whole space has become completely filled with aggression. It is outrageous. There is no opportunity to create a watcher to testify to your destruction, no one to give you a report. But at the same time the aggression grows. The more you destroy, the more you create.

Traditionally aggression is symbolized by the sky and earth radiating red fire. The earth turns into a red hot iron and space becomes an environment of flame and fire. There is no space to breathe any cool air or feel coldness. Whatever you see around you is hot, intense, extremely claustrophobic. The more you try to destroy your enemies or win over your opponents, the more you generate resistance, counteraggression bouncing back at you.

In the hell realm we throw out flames and radiations which are continually coming back to us. There is no room at all in which to experience any spaciousness or openness. Rather there is a constant effort, which can be very cunning, to close up all the space. The hell realm can only be created through your relationships with the outside world, whereas in the jealous god realm your own psychological hang-ups could be the material for creating the asura mentality. In the hell realm there is a constant situation of relationship; you are trying to play games with something and the attempt bounces back on you, constantly recreating extremely claustrophobic situations; so that finally there is no room in which to communicate at all.

At that point the only way to communicate is by trying to recreate your anger. You thought you had managed to win a war of one-upmanship, but finally you did not get a response from the other person; you one-upped him right out of existence. So you are faced only with your own aggression coming back at you and it manages to fill up all the space. One is left lonely once more, without excitement, so you seek another way of playing the game, again and again and again. You do not play for enjoyment, but because you do not feel protected nor secure enough. If you have no way to secure yourself, you feel bleak and cold, so you must rekindle the fire. In order to rekindle the fire you have to fight constantly to maintain yourself. One cannot help playing the game; one just finds oneself playing it, all the time.

Milarepa with Vajrayogini above his head. Milarepa, one of the founding fathers of the Kagyü lineage, is renowned for having attained enlightenment in one lifetime. His life serves as an example of the approach of the yogi in Tibetan Buddhism, combining asceticism with devotion. Thus his followers are known as Kagyüpas, the practicing lineage. Above his head is Vajrayogini, who represents the feminine aspect of one's innate nature and the clarity gained from discriminating awareness. The Vajrayogini principle plays an important role in the Kagyü tradition.

DRAWING BY GLEN EDDY.

THREE

Sitting Meditation

THE FOOL

Having understood about ego and neurosis, knowing the situation with which we are confronted, what do we do now? We have to relate with our mental gossip and our emotions simply and directly, without philosophy. We have to use the existing material, which is ego's hang-ups and credentials and deceptions, as a starting point. Then we begin to realize that in order to do this we must actually use some kind of feeble credentials. Token credentials are necessary. Without them we cannot begin. So we practice meditation using simple techniques; the breath is our feeble credential. It is ironic: we were studying buddha-dharma without credentials and now we find ourselves doing something fishy. We are doing the same thing we were criticizing. We feel uncomfortable and embarrassed about the whole thing. Is this another way to charlatanism, another egohood? Is this the same game? Is this teaching trying to make great fun of me, make me look stupid? We are very suspicious. That is fine. It is a sign that our intelligence is sharper. It is a good way to begin, but, nevertheless, finally, we have to do something. We must humble ourselves and acknowledge that despite our intellectual sophistication, our actual awareness of mind is primitive. We are on the kindergarten level, we do not know how to count to ten. So by sitting and meditating we acknowledge that we are fools, which is an extraordinarily powerful and necessary measure. We begin as fools. We sit and meditate. Once we begin to realize that we are actually one hundred percent fools for doing such a thing, then we begin to see how the techniques function as a crutch. We do not hang on to our crutch or regard it as having important mystical meaning. It is simply a tool which we use as long as we need it and then put aside.

We must be willing to be completely ordinary people, which means accepting ourselves as we are without trying to become greater, purer, more spiritual, more insightful. If we can accept our imperfections as they are, quite ordinarily, then we can use them as part of the path. But if we try to get rid of our imperfections, then they will be enemies, obstacles on the road to our "self-improvement." And the same is true for the breath. If we can see it as it is, without trying to use it to improve ourselves, then it becomes a part of the path because we are no longer using it as the tool of our personal ambition.

SIMPLICITY

Meditation practice is based on dropping dualistic fixation, dropping the struggle of good against bad. The attitude you bring to spirituality should be natural, ordinary, without ambition. Even if you are building good karma, you are still sowing further seeds of karma. So the point is to transcend the karmic process altogether. Transcend both good and bad karma.

There are many references in the tantric literature to mahasukha, the great joy, but the reason it is referred to as the great joy is because it transcends both hope and fear, pain and pleasure. Joy here is not pleasurable in the ordinary sense, but it is an ultimate and fundamental sense of freedom, a sense of humor, the ability to see the ironical aspect of the game of ego, the playing of polarities. If one is able to see ego from an aerial point of view, then one is able to see its humorous quality. Therefore the attitude one brings to meditation practice should be very simple, not based upon trying to collect pleasure or avoid pain. Rather meditation is a natural process, working on the material of pain and pleasure as the path.

You do not try to use meditation techniques—prayer, mantra, visualization, rituals, breathing techniques—to create pleasure or to confirm your existence. You do not try to separate yourself from the technique, but you try to become the technique so that there is a sense of nonduality. Technique is a way of imitating the style of nonduality. In the beginning a person uses technique as a kind of game because he is still imagining that he is meditating. But the techniques—physical feeling, sensations, and breathing, for instance—are very earthy and tend to ground a person. And the proper attitude toward technique is not to regard it as magical, a miracle or profound ceremony of some kind, but just see it as a simple process, extremely simple. The simpler the technique, the less the danger of sidetracks because you are not feeding yourself with all sorts of fascinating, seductive hopes and fears.

In the beginning the practice of meditation is just dealing with the basic neurosis of mind, the confused relationship between yourself and projections, your relationship to thoughts. When a person is able to see the simplicity of the technique without any special attitude toward it, then he is able to relate himself with his thought pattern as well. He begins to see thoughts as simple phenomena, no matter whether they are pious thoughts or evil thoughts, domestic thoughts, whatever they may be. One does not relate to them as belonging to a particular category, as being good or bad; just see them as simple thoughts. When you relate to thoughts obsessively, then you are actually feeding them because thoughts need your attention to survive. Once you begin to pay attention to them and categorize them, then they become very powerful. You are feeding them energy because you have not seen them as simple phenomena. If one tries to quiet them down, that is another way of feeding them. So meditation in the beginning is not an attempt to achieve happiness, nor is it the attempt to achieve mental calm or peace, though they could be by-products of meditation. Meditation should not be regarded as a vacation from irritation.

In fact, a person always finds when he begins to practice meditation that all sorts of problems are brought out. Any hidden aspects of your personality are brought out into the open, for the simple reason that for the first time you are allowing yourself to see your state of mind as it is. For the first time you are not evaluating your thoughts.

One begins to appreciate more and more the beauty of simplicity. You actually do things for the first time *completely*. Just breathing or walking or whatever the technique may be, you just start doing it and working along with it very simply. Complications become transparent complications rather than solidified ones. So the first step in dealing with ego is to begin with a very simple way of dealing with thoughts. Not dealing with them in the sense of quieting them down, but just see their transparent quality.

Sitting meditation needs to be combined with an awareness practice in everyday life. In awareness practice you begin to feel the aftereffects of sitting meditation. Your simple relationship with breathing and your simple relationship with thoughts continues. And every situation of life becomes a simple relationship—a simple relationship with the kitchen sink, a simple relationship with your car, a simple relationship with your father, mother, children. Of course this is not to say that a person suddenly is transformed into a saint. Familiar irritations are still there of course, but they are simple irritations, transparent irritations.

Little domestic things may not seem to be important or meaningful, but dealing with them in a very simple way is extremely valuable and helpful. If a person is able to perceive the simplicity as it is, then meditation becomes twenty-four-hour-a-day work. One begins to experience a tremendous sense of space because one does not have to watch oneself in a very heavy-handed way. Rather you are the recipient of the situation. Of course you may still comment upon and watch this process, but when you sit in meditation you just are; you do not use the breath or any other techniques. You are getting into the grip of something. Finally you do not need a translator anymore, a watcher anymore. Then the language is understood properly.

MINDFULNESS AND AWARENESS

Meditation is working with our speed, our restlessness, our constant busyness. Meditation provides space or ground in which restlessness might function, might have room to be restless, might relax by being restless. If we do not interfere with restlessness, then restlessness becomes part of the space. We do not control or attack the desire to catch our next tail.

Meditation practice is not a matter of trying to produce a hypnotic state of mind or create a sense of restfulness. Trying to achieve a restful state of mind reflects a mentality of poverty. Seeking a restful state of mind, one is on guard against restlessness. There is a constant sense of paranoia and limitation. We feel a need to be on guard against the sudden fits of passion or aggression which might take us over, make us lose control. This guarding process limits the scope of the mind by not accepting whatever comes.

Instead, meditation should reflect a mentality of richness in the sense of using everything that occurs in the state of mind. Thus, if we provide enough room for restlessness so that it might function within the space, then the energy ceases to be restless because it can trust itself fundamentally. Meditation is giving a huge, luscious meadow to a restless cow. The cow might be restless for a while in its huge meadow, but at some stage, because there is so much space, the restlessness becomes irrelevant. So the cow eats and eats and eats and relaxes and falls asleep.

Acknowledging restlessness, identifying with it, requires mindfulness, whereas providing a luscious meadow, a big space for the restless cow requires awareness. So mindfulness and awareness always complement each other. Mindfulness is the process of relating with individual situations directly, precisely, definitely. You communicate or connect with problematic situations or irritating situations in a simple way. There is ignorance, there is restlessness, there is passion, there is aggression. They need not be praised or condemned. They are just regarded as fits. They are conditioned situations, but they could be seen accurately and precisely by the unconditioned mindfulness. Mindfulness is like a microscope; it is neither an offensive nor a defensive weapon in relation to the germs we observe through it. The function of the microscope is just to clearly present what is there. Mindfulness need not refer to the past or the future; it is fully in the now. At the same time it is an active mind involved in dualistic perceptions, for it is necessary in the beginning to use that kind of discriminating judgment.

Awareness is seeing the discovery of mindfulness. We do not have to dispose of or keep the contents of mind. The precision of mindfulness could be left as it is because it has its own environment, its own space. We do not have to make decisions to throw it away or keep it as a treasure. Thus awareness is another step toward choicelessness in situations. The Sanskrit word for awareness is *smriti*, which means "recognition," "recollection." Recollection not in the sense of remembering the past but in the sense of recognizing the product of mindfulness. The mindfulness provides some ground, some room for recognition of aggression, passion, and so on. Mindfulness provides the topic or the terms or the words, and awareness is the grammar which goes around and correctly locates the terms. Having experienced the precision of mindfulness, we might ask the question of ourselves, "What should I do with that? What can I do next?" And awareness reassures us that we do not really have to do anything with it but can leave it in its own natural place. It is like discovering a beautiful flower in the jungle; shall we pick the flower and bring it home or shall we let the flower stay in the jungle? Awareness says leave the flower in the jungle, since it is the natural place for that plant to grow. So awareness is the willingness not to cling to the discoveries of mindfulness, and mindfulness is just precision; things are what they are. Mindfulness is the vanguard of awareness. We flash on a situation and then diffuse that one-pointedness into awareness.

So mindfulness and awareness work together to bring acceptance of living situations as they are. We need not regard life as worth boycotting or indulging in. Life situations are the food of awareness and mindfulness; we cannot meditate without the depressions and excitement that go on in life. We wear out the shoe of samsara by walking on it through the practice of meditation. The combination of mindfulness and awareness maintains the journey, so meditation practice or spiritual development depends upon samsara. From the aerial point of view, we could say that there need not be samsara or nirvana, that making the journey is useless. But since we are on the ground, making the journey is extraordinarily useful.

BOREDOM

We must use the human body as an analogy to describe the development of ego. In this analogy, the fundamental dualism, feeling, impulse, and concepts are like the bones of the body. Emotions are like the muscles of the body and subconscious gossip and all the little mental activities are the circulatory system which feeds and sustains the muscles. So in order to have a completely functioning body we need to have a muscle system and a circulatory system and bones to support them.

We begin meditation practice by dealing with thoughts, the fringe of ego. The practice of meditation is an undoing process. If you want to dissect and examine the body of ego, you start by cutting a slit in the skin and then you cut through the arteries. So the practitioner who is not involved with credentials begins with an operation. Credentials are an illness and you need an operation to remove them. With your sickness you are trying to prove that you exist. "I am sick, therefore I am real, I feel pain." So the operation is to eliminate the notion of being an important person simply because you are sick. Of course you can attract all kinds of attention if you declare that you are sick. Then you can phone your relatives and friends and tell them that you are sick and they will come and help you.

That is a very wretched way of proving your existence. That is precisely what the credentials do. They prove that you are sick so that you can have attention from your friends. We have to operate on this person to eliminate the credential sickness. But if we give this person an anesthetic, he will not realize how much he has to give up. So we should not use anesthetics at all. It should be like natural childbirth. The mother sees her child being born, how it comes out of her body, how it enters into the outside world. Giving birth to buddhadharma without credentials should be the same; you should see the whole process. You are taken straight to the operating room. Now, in the operating theater, the first step of the operation is to make a little slit in the area of complaint with an extraordinarily sharp surgical knife, the sword of Manjushri, the sword of compassion and wisdom. Just a little slit is made, which is not as painful as we expected.

Sitting and meditation is the little slit in your artery. You may have been told that sitting meditation is extremely boring and difficult to accomplish. But you do not find it all that difficult. In fact it seems quite easy. You just sit. The artery, which is the subconscious gossip in your mind, is cut through by using certain techniques—either working on breathing or walking or whatever. It is a very humble gesture on your part—just sit and cut through your thoughts, just welcome your breathing going out and in, just natural breathing, no special breathing, just sit and develop the watchfulness of your breathing. It is not concentrating on breathing. Concentration involves something to grasp, something to hold on to. You are "here" trying to concentrate on something "there." Rather than concentration we practice mindfulness. We see what is happening there rather than developing concentration, which is goal-oriented. Anything connected with goals involves a journey toward somewhere from somewhere. In mindfulness practice there is no goal, no journey; you are just mindful of what is happening there.

There is no promise of love and light or visions of any kind—no angels, no devils. Nothing happens: it is absolutely boring. Sometimes you feel silly. One often asks the question, "Who is kidding whom? Am I on to something or not?" You are not on to something. Traveling the path means you get off everything, there is no place to perch. Sit and feel your breath, be with it. Then you begin to realize that actually the slitting of the artery did not take place when you were introduced to the practice. The actual slitting takes place when you begin to feel the boredom of the practice—real boredom. "I'm supposed to get something out of Buddhism and meditation. I'm supposed to attain different levels of realization. I haven't. I'm bored stiff." Even your watcher is unsympathetic to you, begins to mock you. Boredom is important because boredom is anti-credential. Credentials are entertaining, always bringing you something new, something lively, something fantastic, all kinds of solutions. When you take away the idea of credentials, then there is boredom.

We had a film workshop in Colorado in which we discussed whether it was important to entertain people or make a good film. And what I said was that perhaps the audience might be bored with what we have to present, but we must raise the intelligence, the standards of the audience, up to the level of what we are presenting, rather than trying to constantly match their expectations, their desire for entertainment. Once you begin to try to satisfy the audience's desire for entertainment, you constantly bend down and bend down and bend down, until the whole thing becomes absurd. If a filmmaker presents his own ideas with dignity, his work might be ill-received in the beginning but possibly well-received once people begin to catch up to it. The film might raise the audience's level of sophistication.

Similarly, boredom is important in meditation practice; it increases the psychological sophistication of the practitioners. They begin to appreciate boredom and they develop their sophistication until the boredom begins to become cool boredom, like a mountain river. It flows and flows and flows, methodically and repetitiously, but it is very cooling, very refreshing. Mountains never get tired of being mountains and waterfalls never get tired of being waterfalls. Because of their patience we begin to appreciate them. There is something in that. I don't want to sound especially romantic about the whole thing, I am trying to paint a black picture, but I slipped a bit. It is a good feeling to be bored, constantly sitting and sitting. First gong, second gong, third gong, more gongs yet to come. Sit, sit, sit, sit. Cut through the artery until the boredom becomes extraordinarily powerful. We have to work hard at it.

At this point we cannot really study the vajrayana or, for that matter, even the mahayana. We are not up to it because we have not actually made a relationship with boredom yet. To begin with we have to relate with the hinayana. If we are to save ourselves from spiritual materialism and from buddhadharma with credentials, if we are to become the dharma without credentials, the introduction of boredom and repetitiousness is extremely important. Without it we have no hope. It is true—no hope.

There are definite styles of boredom. The Zen tradition in Japan creates a definite style of boredom in its monasteries. Sit, cook, eat. Sit zazen and do your walking meditation and so on. But to an American novice who goes to Japan or takes part in traditional Japanese practice in this country, the message of boredom is not communicated properly. Instead, if I may say so, it turns into a militant appreciation of rigidity, or an aesthetic appreciation of simplicity, rather than actually being bored, which is strange. Actually it was not designed to be that way. To the Japanese, Zen practice is an ordinary Japanese life situation in which you just do your daily work and sit a lot of zazen. But Americans appreciate the little details—how you use your bowl and how you eat consciously in zazen posture. This is only supposed to create a feeling of boredom, but to American students it is a work of art. Cleaning your bowl, washing it out, folding your white napkin and so forth, becomes living theater. The black cushion is supposed to suggest no color, complete boredom. But for Americans it inspires a mentality of militant blackness, straightforwardness.

The tradition is trying to bring out boredom, which is a necessary aspect of the narrow path of discipline, but instead the practice turns out to be an archeological, sociological survey of interesting things to do, something you could tell your friends about: "Last year I spent the whole fall sitting in a Zen monastery for six months. I watched autumn turn into winter and I did my zazen practice and everything was so precise and beautiful. I learned how to sit and I even learned how to walk and eat. It was a wonderful experience and I did not get bored at all."

You tell your friends, "Go, it's great fun," and you collect another credential. The attempt to destroy credentials creates another credential. The first point in destroying ego's game is the strict discipline of sitting meditation practice. No intellectual speculation, no philosophizing. Just sit and do it. That is the first strategy in developing buddhadharma without credentials.

THE WAY OF THE BUDDHA

Boredom has many aspects: there is the sense that nothing is happening, that something might happen, or even that what we would like to happen might replace that which is not happening. Or, one might appreciate boredom as a delight. The practice of meditation could be described as relating with cool boredom, refreshing boredom, boredom like a mountain stream. It refreshes because we do not have to do anything or expect anything. But there must be some sense of discipline if we are to get beyond the frivolity of trying to replace boredom. That is why we work with the breath as our practice of meditation. Simply relating with the breath is very monotonous and unadventurous—we do not discover that the third eye is opening or that chakras are unfolding. It is like a stone-carved Buddha sitting in the desert. Nothing, absolutely nothing, happens.

As we realize that nothing is happening, strangely we begin to realize that something dignified is happening. There is no room for frivolity, no room for speed. We just breathe and are there. There is something very satisfying and wholesome about it. It is as though we had eaten a good meal and were satisfied with it, in contrast to eating and trying to satisfy oneself. It is a very simple-minded approach to sanity.

It is recorded that the Buddha was given many Hindu meditation practices. He scorched himself in fires. He related with the energy of tantra by visualizing all kinds of things. He saw a neurological light by pressing his eyeballs and he heard a neurological buzz of supposedly yogic sound by pressing his ears. He went through all of this himself and realized that these phenomena were gimmicks rather than real samadhi or meditation. Maybe the Buddha was a dumb yoga student without any imagination. However, we follow his dumbness, his example as the enlightened one, the samyaksambuddha, the completely enlightened one.

As the Buddha's approach to the practice of meditation evolved, he realized that gimmicks are merely neurotic affectations. He decided to look for what is simple, what is actually there, to discover the relationship between mind and body, his relationship with the kusha grass mat on which he sat and the bodhi tree above his head. He looked into his relationships with everything very simply and directly. It was not especially exciting—there were no flashes of anything—but it was reassuring. At the dawn of his enlightenment someone asked the Buddha, "What are your credentials? How do we know that you are enlightened?" He touched his hand to the ground. "This solid earth is my witness. This solid earth, this same earth, is my witness." Sane and solid and definite, no imaginings, no concepts, no emotions, no frivolity, but being basically what is: this is the awakened state. And this is the example we follow in our meditation practice.

As far as Buddha was concerned, at that point it was not the message but the implications that were more important. And, as followers of Buddha, we have this approach, which is the idea of *vipashyana*, literally meaning "insight." Insight is relating not only with what you see but also with the implications of it, the totality of the space and objects around it. Breath is the object of meditation, but the environment around the breath is also part of the meditative situation.

The Buddha then turned the wheel of the dharma, expounding the four noble truths: pain, the origin of pain, the goal, and the path. All this was inspired by his discovery that there is tremendous space in which the universality of inspiration is happening. There is pain, but there is also the environment around the origin of pain. The whole thing becomes more expansive, more open. He wasn't such a bad yoga student after all. Quite possibly he was not good at hatha yoga, but he saw the environment around hatha yoga and pranayama.

The Buddha's demonstrations of basic sanity were spontaneous. He did not preach or teach in the ordinary sense but, as he unfolded, the energy of compassion and the endless resources of generosity developed within him and people began to find this out. That kind of activity of the Buddha is the vipashyana practice that we are attempting. It is realizing that space contains matter, that matter makes no demands on space, and that space makes no demands on matter. It is a reciprocal and open situation. Everything is based on compassion and openness. Compassion is not particularly emotional in the sense that you feel bad that someone is suffering, that you are better than others and that you have to help them. Compassion is that total openness in which the Buddha had no ground, no sense of territory. So much so, that he was hardly an individual. He was just a grain of sand living in the vast desert. Through his insignificance he became the "world enlightened one," because there was no battle involved. The dharma he taught was passionless, without aggression. Passion is grasping, holding on to your territory.

So our practice of meditation, if we follow the Buddha's way, is the practice of passionlessness or nonaggression. It is dealing with the possessiveness of aggression: "This is my spiritual trip and I don't want you to interfere with it. Get out of my territory." Spirituality, or the vipashyana perspective, is a panoramic situation in which you can come and go freely and your relationship with the world is open. It is the ultimate nonviolence.

FOUR

Working with the Emotions

THE DUALISTIC BARRIER

As we have discussed, boredom is very important in the practice of sitting meditation; there is no other way to reach the depths of meditation practice except through boredom. But at the same time, we must look further at the desire for credentials. Even experiencing boredom or relating with boredom could itself be another game, another way of creating a sense of comfort, a sense of security in the practice of meditation. Something else must be dealt with in addition to experiencing boredom, and this something else is the daily living situation involving love and hate, depression and so forth, the subtle but fundamental emotions.

Although we may be able to accomplish smoothly the vipashyana practice of relating with the breathing, still we cannot ignore this large area of potential and unexpected disturbances. You may finish an ideal sitting meditation period in which you experienced boredom, and then you go out into the living room and decide to make a call to your friend and realize that you haven't paid your telephone bill and the telephone is disconnected. And you get outraged: "But that's not my fault, my wife misplaced the bill," or "They have no right to do this," or whatever.

Little things like that happen all the time. If we experience such situations, then we begin to realize that our practice is credential-oriented, that there is a belief in some kind of basic harmony. The problems of everyday life are a way of destroying our credentials, our comfort and

Four-Armed Mahakala.

security, and they present us with an opportunity to relate with our emotions.

Although we may be able to see the simplicity of the discursive thought process, still there are very strong emotions with which it is extremely difficult and quite challenging to work. In working with the emotions we are dealing not only with the fifth skandha, "consciousness," but also with the fourth skandha, "concept," "intellect." The emotions are composed of energy, which can be likened to water, and a dualistic thought process, which could be likened to pigment or paint. When energy and thought are mixed together they become the vivid and colorful emotions. Concept gives the energy a particular location, a sense of relationship, which makes the emotions vivid and strong. Fundamentally, the reason why emotions are discomforting, painful, frustrating, is because our relationship to the emotions is not quite clear.

At the level of the fifth skandha the structure of ego has become so efficient that there is a conflict between the administration of ego and the central ignorance itself. It is as if the king's minister had become more powerful than the king himself. This seems to be the point where emotions become painful, because you are not quite certain what your relationship to your emotions is. There is tremendous conflict, a feeling that you are being overpowered by your emotions, that you are losing your basic identity, you center of command.

So the pain of emotion comes from this conflict; the relationship is always ambivalent. However, if a person is actually able to relate fully and thoroughly with the emotions, then they cease to become an external problem. One is able to make very close contact with the emotions and the war between your emotions and yourself; you and your projections, you and the world outside, becomes transparent. This involves removing the dualistic barriers set up by concepts, which is the experience of shunyata, the absence of relative concepts, emptiness.

Actually, we do not see things completely as they are. Generally we perceive something, and then we look. Looking in this case is the act of imposing names and associations on things. Seeing things means accepting what they are, but looking means unnecessary effort to make sure that you are safe, that nothing is going to confuse you in your relationship to the world. So we create our security by putting things into categories, naming them, by using relative terms to identify their interrelationships, how they fit together. And this security brings temporary happiness and comfort.

This very crude way of finding landmarks in terms of our projections is very childish, and one has to repeat the same game again and again. There is no attempt to deal with projections as exciting and fluid situations at all; instead the world is seen as being absolutely solid and stiff. Everything is frozen movement, frozen space, solidified. We see the world as having an extremely hard facade, a metallic or plastic quality. We see the colors as they are, but somehow they are plastic colors rather than rainbow colors. And this solid quality is the dualistic barrier that we have been talking about. Which is not to say that a person should not feel the texture of a stone or a brick as solid. The physical situation of solidity has no relation to psychological solidity. We are dealing here with mental solidity—harshness, a metallic quality. Actually, it is extremely interesting that we see only our own solid version of the world. So perception is very much individualized, centralized on self-consciousness.

It is impossible immediately to experience shunyata—that is, absence of concept, absence of the dualistic barrier. We must start with a simple practice in the beginning, and then we begin to perceive the transparent quality of thoughts and emotions. Then we must also try to step beyond the relational situation of transparency—that is, the sense of "you" seeing the transparency of thoughts and emotions. In other words, the thought process and the emotions are transparent and they are taking place in the midst of nowhere, in space. That spacious quality, when everything operates and occurs in space, is the positive space of skillful means, of working with everyday life situations. In fact, the creativity and the positive aspect of the emotions and life situations can only be seen through experiencing the space rather than the product. If a person's relationship to space is developed properly, perceived properly, then there is no hesitation at all.

We are speaking here of becoming *one* with the emotions. This is different from and in contrast to the usual approach of suppressing them or acting them out. If we are suppressing our emotions, it is extremely dangerous because we are regarding them as something terrible, shameful, which means that our relationship to our emotions is not really open. Once we try to suppress them, sooner or later they are going to step out and explode.

There is another possibility. If you do not suppress your emotions, then you really allow yourself to come out and be carried away by them. This way of dealing with the emotions also comes from a kind of panic; your relationship with your emotions has not been properly reconciled. This is another way of escaping from the actual emotion, another kind of release, a false release. It is a confusion of mind and matter, thinking that the physical act of practicing emotions, of putting them into effect, supposedly will cure the emotions, relieve their irritation. But generally it reinforces them, and the emotions become more powerful. The relationship between the emotions and mind is not quite clear here.

So the intelligent way of working with emotions is to try to relate with their basic substance, the abstract quality of the emotions, so to speak. The basic "isness" quality of the emotions, the fundamental nature of the emotions, is just energy. And if one is able to relate with energy, then the energies have no conflict with you. They become a natural process. So trying to suppress or getting carried away by the emotions become irrelevant once a person is completely able to see their basic characteristic, the emotions as they are, which is shunyata. The barrier, the wall between you and your projections, the hysterical and paranoid aspect of your relationship to your projections, has been removed—not exactly removed, but seen through. When there is no panic involved in dealing with the emotions, then you can deal with them completely, properly. Then you are like someone who is completely skilled in his profession, who does not panic, but just does his work completely, thoroughly.

We have been discussing how to deal with consciousness, the last stage of the development of ego, and we have also dealt with the prior stage of concept. When we speak of "dealing" with them, it is not a question of eliminating them completely but of really seeing them and transmuting their confused qualities into transcendental qualities. We still use the energies of thought, the energies of the emotions, and the energies of concept. Generally, when the idea of ego is presented, the immediate reaction on the part of the audience is to regard it as a villain, an enemy. You feel you must destroy this ego, this me, which is a masochistic and suicidal approach. People tend to think this way because, usually when we speak of spirituality, we tend to think that we are fighting the bad; we are good, spirituality is the ultimate good, the epitome of good, and the other side is bad. But true spirituality is not a battle; it is the ultimate practice of nonviolence. We are not regarding any part of us as being a villain, an enemy, but we are trying to use everything as a part of the natural process of life. As soon as a notion of polarity between good and bad develops, then we are caught in spiritual materialism, which is working to achieve happiness in a simple-minded sense, on the way to egohood. So the dualistic wall is not something we have to destroy or eliminate or exorcise. But having seen the emotions as they are, we have more material with which to work creatively. This makes it quite clear that the notion of samsara is dependent upon the notion of nirvana, and the notion of nirvana is dependent upon the notion of samsara; they are interdependent. If there were no confusion, there would be no wisdom.

LION'S ROAR

The "lion's roar" is the fearless proclamation that any state of mind, including the emotions, is a workable situation, a reminder in the practice of meditation. We realize that chaotic situations must not be rejected. Nor must we regard them as regressive, as a return to confusion. We must respect whatever happens to our state of mind. Chaos should be regarded as extremely good news.

There are several stages in relating with the emotions: the stages of seeing, hearing, smelling, touching, and transmuting. In the case of seeing the emotions, we have a general awareness that the emotions have their own space, their own development. We accept them as part of the pattern of mind, without question, without reference back to the scriptures, without help from credentials, but we directly acknowledge that they are so, that these things are happening. And then hearing involves experiencing the pulsation of such energy, the energy upsurge as it comes toward you. Smelling is appreciating that the energy is somewhat workable, as when you smell food and the smell becomes an appetizer, whetting your appetite before you eat. It smells like a good meal, it smells delicious, although you have not eaten it yet. It is somewhat workable. Touching is a feeling the nitty-gritty of the whole thing, that you can touch and relate with it, that your emotions are not particularly destructive or crazy but just an upsurge of energy, whatever form they take—aggressive, passive, or grasping. Transmutation is not a matter of rejecting the basic qualities of the emotions. Rather, as in the alchemical practice of changing lead into gold, you do not reject the basic qualities of the material, but you change its appearance and substance somewhat. So you experience emotional upheaval as it is but still work with it, become one with it. The usual problem is that, when emotions arise, we feel that we are being challenged by them, that they will overwhelm our self-existence or the credentials of our existence. However, if we become the embodiment of hatred or passion, then we do not have any personal credentials any more. Usually that is why we react against the emotions, because we feel we might be taken over by them, that we might freak out, lose our heads. We are afraid that aggression or depression will become so overwhelming that we will lose our ability to function normally, that we will forget how to brush our teeth, how to dial a telephone.

There is a fear that emotion might become too much, that we might fall into it and lose our dignity, our role as human beings. Transmutation involves going through such fear. Let yourself be in the emotion, go through it, give in to it, experience it. You begin to go toward the emotion, rather than just experiencing the emotion coming toward you. A relationship, a dance, begins to develop. Then the most powerful energies become absolutely workable rather than taking you over, because there is nothing to take over if you are not putting up any resistance. Whenever there is no resistance, a sense of rhythm occurs. The music and the dance take place at the same time. That is the lion's roar. Whatever occurs in the samsaric mind is regarded as the path; everything is workable. It is a fearless proclamation—the lion's roar. As long as we create "patches" to cover what we regard as unworkable situations—metaphysical, philosophical, religious patches—then our action is not the lion's roar. It is a coward's scream—very pathetic.

Usually, whenever we feel that we cannot work with something, automatically we look back and try to find some external resource, some patch to conceal our insufficiency. Our concern is to save face, avoid being embarrassed, avoid being challenged by our emotions. How might we put another patch on top of another patch in order to get out of this situation? We could burden ourselves with millions upon millions of patches, one on top of the other. If the first one is too delicate, then the second may be stronger, so we end up creating a suit of patches, a suit of armor. But here we have some problems. The joints in our armor begin to squeak and there are holes in the armor where the joints are. It is difficult to put patches on the joints, because we still want to move, still want to dance, but we do not want to squeak. We want to have joints in order to move. So unless one is completely mummified, which is death, being a corpse, there is no way to completely protect oneself. For a living human being patchwork is an absolutely impractical idea.

So the buddhadharma without credentials is, from this point of view, the same thing as the lion's roar. We do not need patches any more. We could transmute the substance of the emotions, which is an extremely powerful act. Indian Ashokan art depicts the lion's roar with four lions looking in the four directions, which symbolizes the idea of having no back. Every direction is a front, symbolizing all-pervading awareness. The fearlessness covers all directions. Once you begin to radiate your fearlessness, it is all-pervading, radiated in all directions. In the traditional iconography certain Buddhas are represented as having a thousand faces or a million faces, looking in all directions in panoramic awareness. Since they look everywhere, there is nothing to defend.

The lion's roar is fearlessness in the sense that every situation in life is workable. Nothing is rejected as bad or grasped as good. But everything we experience in our life situations, any type of emotion, is workable. We can see quite clearly that trying to apply the reference point of credentials is useless. We have to really work into the situation completely and thoroughly. If we are extremely interested in eating food, really hungry, there is not time to read the menu because we want to eat. We really want to relate with food. So forget about the menu. It is an immediate interest, a direct relationship.

The basic point of the lion's roar is that, if we are able to deal with emotions directly, able to relate with them as workable, then there is no need for external aid or explanations. It is a self-maintained situation. Any help from outsiders becomes credentials. So self-existing help develops. At that point, one does not need to avoid the credential problem any more, because there is no room for speculation or rationalization. Everything becomes obvious and immediate, workable. And there is no chance or time or space to speculate on how to become a charlatan, how to con other people, because the situation is so immediate. So the idea of charlatanism does not appear at all, because there is no room for the idea of a game.

WORKING WITH NEGATIVITY

We all experience negativity—the basic aggression of wanting things to be different than they are. We cling, we defend, we attack, and throughout there is a sense of one's own wretchedness, and so we blame the world for our pain. This is negativity. We experience it as terribly unpleasant, foul-smelling, something we want to get rid of. But if we look into it more deeply, it has a very juicy smell and is very alive. Negativity is not bad per se, but something living and precise, connected with reality.

Negativity breeds tension, friction, gossip, discontentment, but it is also very accurate, deliberate, and profound. Unfortunately, the heavy-handed interpretations and judgments we lay on these experiences obscure this fact. These interpretations and judgments are negative negativity, watching ourselves being negative and then deciding that the negativity is justified in being there. The negativity seems good-natured, with all sorts of good qualities in it, so we pat its back, guard it, and justify it. Or if we are blamed or attacked by others, we interpret their negativity as being good for us. In either case the watcher, by commenting, interpreting, and judging, is camouflaging and hardening the basic negativity.

Negative negativity refers to the philosophies and rationales we use to justify avoiding our own pain. We would like to pretend that these "evil" and "foul-smelling" aspects of ourselves and our world are not really there, or that they should not be there, or even that they *should* be there. So negative negativity is usually self-justifying, self-contained. It allows nothing to pierce its protective shell—a self-righteous way of trying to pretend that things are what we would like them to be instead of what they are.

This secondary, commenting kind of intelligence of double negativity is very cautious and cowardly as well as frivolous and emotional. It inhibits identification with the energy and intelligence of basic negativity. So let's forget about justifying ourselves, trying to prove to ourselves how good we are.

The basic honesty and simplicity of negativity can be creative in community as well as in personal relationships. Basic negativity is very revealing, sharp, and accurate. If we leave it as basic negativity rather than overlaying it with conceptualizations, then we see the nature of its intelligence. Negativity breeds a great deal of energy, which clearly seen becomes intelligence. When we leave the energies as they are with their natural qualities, they are living rather than conceptualized. They strengthen our everyday lives.

The conceptualized negativity, the negative negativity, must be cut through. It deserves to be murdered on the spot with the sharp blow of basic intelligence—prajnaparamita. That is what prajna is for: to cut through intelligence when it changes into intellectual speculation or is based upon a belief of some kind. Beliefs are reinforced endlessly by other beliefs and dogmas, theological or moral or practical or businesslike. That kind of intelligence should be killed on the spot, "uncompassionately." This is when compassion should not be idiot compassion. This intellectual energy should be shot, killed, squashed, razed to dust on the spot with one blow. That one blow of basic intelligence is direct compassion. The way to do this does not evolve out of intellectualizing or trying to find a way to justify yourself; but it just comes as the conclusion of basic intelligence and from a feeling of the texture of the situation.

For instance, if you walk on the snow or ice, you feel the texture of it the minute you put your foot down. You feel whether or not your shoe is going to grip. It is the feeling of texture, the richness of texture that we are talking about. If it is negative negativity, then there will be certain ways to squash or murder it. Somehow the energy to do this comes from the basic negativity itself, rather than from some special technique or ability for assassination. There is a time to be philosophical and a time to be soft. There is also a time to be "uncompassionate" and ruthless in dealing with these frivolous situations.

Frivolousness refers to the extra and unnecessary mental and physical acts with which we keep ourselves busy in order not to see what actually is happening in a situation. Whenever there is a frivolous emotional situation and concept growing out of it, then this ground should be completely extinguished with a direct blow—that is, by seeing directly what is not right and wholesome. This is what is called the sword of Manjushri, which cuts the root of dualistic conceptualization with one blow. Here a person should really be "uncompassionate" and illogical. The real objective is just to squash the frivolousness, the unwillingness to see things as they actually are, which appears rational. Frivolousness does not really get a chance to feel the whole ground. It is preoccupied with reacting to your projections as they bounce back at you. True spontaneity feels the texture of the situation because it is less involved with self-consciousness, the attempt to secure oneself in a given situation.

It is obvious that, when you are really squashing frivolousness, you should feel pain, because there is a certain attraction toward the occupation of being frivolous. By squashing it you are completely taking away the occupation. You begin to feel that you have nothing to hold on to any more, which is rather frightening as well as painful. What do you do then, after you have extinguished everything? Then you must not live on your heroism, on having achieved something, but just dance with the continuing process of energy that has been liberated by this destruction.

The tantric tradition of Buddhism describes four actions or karma-yogas. The first is the action of "pacifying" a situation if it is not right. Pacifying is trying to feel the ground very softly. You feel the situation further and further, not just pacifying superficially, but expressing the whole, feeling it altogether. Then you expand your luscious, dignified, and rich quality throughout. This is "enriching," the second karma. If that does not work, then "magnetizing" is the third karma. You bring the elements of the situation together. Having felt them out by pacifying and enriching them, you bring them together. If that is unsuccessful, then there is the action of "destroying" or extinguishing, the fourth karma.

These four karmas are very pertinent to the process of dealing with negativity and so-called problems. First pacify, then enrich, then magnetize, and if that does not work, finally extinguish, destroy altogether. This last is necessary only when the negative negativity uses a strong pseudo-logic or a pseudo-philosophical attitude or conceptualization. It is necessary when there is a notion of some kind which brings a whole succession of other notions, like the layers of an onion, or when one is using logic and ways of justifying oneself so that situations become very heavy and very solid. We know this heaviness is taking place, but simultaneously we play tricks on ourselves, feeling that we enjoy the heaviness of this logic, feeling that we need to have some occupation. When we begin to play this kind of game, there is no room. Out! It is said in the tantric tradition that, if you do not destroy when necessary, you are breaking the vow of compassion which actually commits you to destroying frivolousness. Therefore, keeping to the path does not necessarily mean only trying to be good and not offending anyone; it does not mean that, if someone obstructs our path, we should try to be polite to them and say "please" and "thank you." That does not work, that is not the point. If anyone gets abruptly in our path, we just push them out because their intrusion was frivolous. The path of dharma is not a good, sane, passive, and "compassionate" path at all. It is a path on which no one should walk blindly. If they do—out! They should be awakened by being excluded.

At the very advanced levels of practice we can go through the negative negativity and turn it into the original negativity so that we have a very powerful negative force that is pure and unself-conscious. That is, once having squashed this negative negativity altogether, having gone through the operation without anesthesia, then we re-invite the negativity for the sake of energy. But this could be tricky.

If the pure energy of negativity is involved with any form of ground, then it is always regarded as the property of the secondary, logical energy of negative negativity. This is because of our fascination to relive the basic negativity, to re-create the comfort and occupation of basic negativity. So there should not be any reliving of the occupation at all. Occupations should be completely cleared away. Then the energy which destroys the reliving of occupation turns out to be logical energy transmuted into crazy wisdom—conceptual ideas, let loose. That is to say, there are no more conceptual ideas, but only energy run wild. Originally there were conceptual ideas and then they were cut through altogether, so that you no longer regarded light and dark as light and dark; it becomes the nondualistic state.

Then negativity simply becomes food, pure strength. You no longer relate to negativity as being good or bad, but you continually use the energy which comes out of it as a source of life so that you are never really defeated in a situation. Crazy wisdom cannot be defeated. If someone attacks or if someone praises, crazy wisdom will feed on either equally. As far as crazy wisdom is concerned, both praise and blame are the same thing because there is always some energy occurring . . . a really terrifying thought.

Crazy wisdom could become satanic but somehow it doesn't. Those who fear crazy wisdom destroy themselves. The negative destruction they throw at it bounces back at them, for crazy wisdom has no notion of good or bad or destruction or creation at all. Crazy wisdom cannot exist without communication, without a situation with which to work: whatever needs to be destroyed, it destroys; whatever needs to be cared for, it cares for. Hostility destroys itself and openness also opens itself. It depends on the situation. Some people may learn from destruction and some people may learn from creation. That is what the wrathful and peaceful deities, the mahakalas and the buddhas, symbolize.

The four arms of the mahakala (in the thangka which accompanies this chapter) represent the four karmas. The whole structure of the image is based on energy and complete compassion devoid of idiot compassion. In this particular thangka, the left arm represents pacifying. It holds a skull cup of amrita, the intoxicating nectar of the gods which is a means of pacification. Another arm holds a hooked knife which symbolizes enriching, extending your influence over others, feeling the texture of the ground and the richness. The hooked knife is also regarded as the scepter of the gods. The third arm, on the right, holds a sword which is the tool for gathering energies together. The sword need not strike, but just through its being waved around energies come together. The fourth arm holds the three-pronged spear which symbolizes destruction. You do not have to destroy three times, but with one thrust of this spear you make three wounds, the ultimate destruction of ignorance, passion, and aggression simultaneously.

The mahakala sits on the corpses of demons, which represents the paralysis of ego. This is very interesting and relates to what we have already discussed. You must not make an impulsive move into any situation. Let the situation come, then look at it, chew it properly, digest it, sit on it. The sudden move is unhealthy, impulsive, and frivolous rather than spontaneous.

Spontaneity sees situations as they are. You see, there is a difference between spontaneity and frivolousness, a very thin line dividing them. Whenever there is an impulse to do something, you should not just do it; you should work with the impulse. If you are working with it, then you will not act frivolously; you want really to see it and taste it properly, devoid of frivolousness. Frivolousness means reacting according to reflex. You throw something and when it bounces back you react. Spontaneity is when you throw something and watch it and work with the energy when it bounces back at you. Frivolousness involves too much anxiety. Once you are emotionally worked up, then too much anxiety is put into your action. But when you are spontaneous, there is less anxiety and you just deal with situations as they are. You do not simply react,

THE MYTH OF FREEDOM

but you work with the quality and structure of the reaction. You feel the texture of the situation rather than just acting impulsively.

The mahakala is surrounded by flames representing the tremendous unceasing energy of anger without hatred, the energy of compassion. The skull crown symbolizes the negativities or emotions which are not destroyed or abandoned or condemned for being "bad." Rather they are used by the mahakala for his ornaments and crown.

FIVE

Meditation in Action

WORK

WHEN YOU SEE ordinary situations with extraordinary insight it is like discovering a jewel in rubbish. If work becomes part of your spiritual practice, then your regular, daily problems cease to be only problems and become a source of inspiration. Nothing is rejected as ordinary and nothing is taken as being particularly sacred, but all the substance and material available in life-situations is used.

However, work can also be an escape from creativity. Either you work frantically, filling in all the spaces and not allowing any spontaneity to develop or else you are lazy, regarding work as something to revolt against, which indicates a fear of creativity. Instead of letting the creative process be, you follow your next preconception, fearing a spacious state of mind. Whenever a person feels depressed or is afraid or the situation is not going smoothly, immediately he begins polishing a table or weeding the garden, trying to distract himself. He does not want to deal with the underlying problem so he seeks a kind of pleasure of the moment. He is frightened of the space, of any empty corner. Whenever there is an empty wall, he puts up another picture or hanging. And the more crowded his walls are, the more comfortable he feels.

True work is acting practically, relating to the earth directly. You could be working in the garden, in the house, washing dishes, or doing whatever demands your attention. If you do not feel the relationship between earth and yourself, then the situation is going to turn chaotic.

241

If you do not feel that every step, every situation reflects your state of mind, and therefore has spiritual significance, then the pattern of your life becomes full of problems, and you begin to wonder where these problems come from. They seem to spring from nowhere because you refuse to see the subtlety of life. Somehow, you cannot cheat, you cannot pretend to pour a cup of tea beautifully, you cannot act it. You must actually feel it, feel the earth and your relationship to it.

The Japanese tea ceremony is a good example of action that is in contact with earth. It begins by deliberately collecting the bowl, the napkin, the brush, the tea, and the boiling water. Tea is served and the guests drink deliberately, with a feeling of dealing with things properly. The ceremony also includes how to clean the bowls, how to put them away, how to finish properly. Clearing away is as important as starting.

It is extremely important to work, as long as you are not using work as an escape, as a way of ignoring the basic existence of a problem, particularly if you are interested in spiritual development. Work is one of the most subtle ways of acquiring discipline. You should not look down on someone who works in a factory or produces materialistic things. You learn a tremendous amount from such people. I think that many of our attitudinal problems about work come from a pseudo-sophistication of the analytic mind. You do not want to involve yourself physically at all. You want only to work intellectually or mentally.

This is a spiritual problem. Usually people interested in spiritual development think in terms of the importance of mind, that mysterious, high, and deep thing that we have decided to learn about. But strangely enough the profound and the transcendental are to be found in the factory. It may not fill you with bliss to look at it, it may not sound as good as the spiritual experiences that we have read about, but somehow reality is to be found there, in the way in which we relate with everyday problems. If we relate to them in a simple, earthy way, we will work in a more balanced manner, and things will be dealt with properly. If we are able to simplify ourselves to that extent, then we will be able to see the neurotic aspect of mind much more clearly. The whole pattern of thought, the internal game that goes on, becomes much less of a game. It becomes a very practical way of thinking in situations.

Awareness in work is very important. It could be the same sort of awareness one has in sitting meditation, the leap of experiencing the openness of space. This depends very much upon feeling the earth and the space together. You cannot feel earth unless you feel space. The more you feel space, the more you feel the earth. The feeling of space between you and objects becomes a natural product of awareness, of openness, of peace and lightness. And the way to practice is not to concentrate upon things nor to try to be aware of yourself and the job at the same time, but you should have a general feeling of acknowledging this openness as you are working. Then you begin to feel that there is more room in which to do things, more room in which to work. It is a question of acknowledging the existence of the openness of a continual meditative state. You don't have to try to hold on to it or try to bring it about deliberately, but just acknowledge that vast energy of openness with a fraction-of-a-second flash to it. After acknowledging, then almost deliberately ignore its existence and continue your work. The openness will continue and you will begin to develop the actual feeling of the things with which you are working. The awareness that we are speaking of is not so much a question of constant awareness as of an object of mind, but it is a matter of becoming one with awareness, becoming one with open space. This means becoming one with the actual things with which you are dealing as well. So meditation becomes very easy; it is no longer an attempt to split yourself into different sections and different degrees of awareness, the watcher and the doer. You begin to have a real relationship with external objects and their beauty.

LOVE

There is a vast store of energy which is not centered, which is not ego's energy at all. It is this energy which is the centerless dance of phenomena, the universe interpenetrating and making love to itself. It has two characteristics: a fire quality of warmth and a tendency to flow in a particular pattern, in the same way in which fire contains a spark as well as the air which directs the spark. And this energy is always ongoing, whether or not it is seen through the confused filter of ego. It cannot be destroyed or interrupted at all. It is like the ever-burning sun. It consumes everything to the point where it allows no room for doubt or manipulation.

But when this heat is filtered through ego, it becomes stagnant, because we ignore the basic ground, refuse to see the vast space in which this energy occurs. Then the energy cannot flow freely in the open space shared with the object of passion. Instead it is solidified, narrowed, and directed by the central headquarters of ego to move outward in order to draw the object of passion into its territory. This captive energy extends out to its object and then returns to be programmed again. We extend our tentacles and try to fix our relationship. This attempt to cling to the situation makes the communication process superficial. We just touch another person's surface and get stuck there, never experiencing their whole being. We are blinded by our clinging. The object of passion, instead of being bathed in the intense warmth of free passion feels oppressed by the stifling heat of neurotic passion.

Free passion is radiation without a radiator, a fluid, pervasive warmth that flows effortlessly. It is not destructive because it is a balanced state of being and highly intelligent. Self-consciousness inhibits this intelligent, balanced state of being. By opening, by dropping our self-conscious grasping, we see not only the surface of an object, but we see the whole way through. We appreciate not in terms of sensational qualities alone, but we see in terms of whole qualities, which are pure gold. We are not overwhelmed by the exterior, but seeing the exterior simultaneously puts us through to the interior. So we reach the heart of the situation and, if this is a meeting of two people, the relationship is very inspiring because we do not see the other person purely in terms of physical attraction or habitual patterns, we see the inside as well as the outside.

This whole-way-through communication might produce a problem. Suppose you see right through someone and that person does not want you to see right through and becomes horrified with you and runs away. Then what to do? You have made your communication completely and thoroughly. If that person runs away from you, that is his way of communicating with you. You would not investigate further. If you did pursue and chase him, then sooner or later you would become a demon from that person's point of view. You see right through his body and he has juicy fat and meat that you would like to eat up, so you seem like a vampire to him. And the more you try to pursue the other person, the more you fail. Perhaps you looked through too sharply with your desire, perhaps you were too penetrating. Possessing beautiful keen eyes, penetrating passion and intelligence, you abused your talent, played with it. It is quite natural with people, if they possess some particular power or gifted energy, to abuse that quality, to misuse it by trying to penetrate every corner. Something quite obviously is lacking in such an approach—a sense of humor. If you try to push things too far, it means you do not feel the area properly; you only feel your relationship to the area. What is wrong is that you do not see all sides of the situation and therefore miss the humorous and ironical aspect.

Sometimes people run away from you because they want to play a game with you. They do not want a straight, honest, and serious involvement with you, they want to play. But if they have a sense of humor and you do not, you become demonic. This is where lalita, the dance, comes in. You dance with reality, dance with apparent phenomena. When you want something very badly you do not extend your eye and hand automatically; you just admire. Instead of impulsively making a move from your side, you allow a move from the other side, which is learning to dance with the situation. You do not have to create the whole situation; you just watch it, work with it, and learn to dance with it. So then it does not become your creation, but rather a mutual dance. No one is self-conscious, because it is a mutual experience.

When there is a fundamental openness in a relationship, being faithful, in the sense of real trust, happens automatically; it is a natural situation. Because the communication is so real and so beautiful and flowing, you cannot communicate in the same way with someone else, so automatically you are drawn together. But if any doubt presents itself, if you begin to feel threatened by some abstract possibility, although your communication is going beautifully at the time, then you are sowing the seed of paranoia and regarding the communication purely as ego entertainment.

If you sow a seed of doubt, it may make you rigid and terrified, afraid of losing the communication which is so good and real. And at some stage you will begin to be bewildered as to whether the communication is loving or aggressive. This bewilderment brings a certain loss of distance, and in this way neurosis begins. Once you lose the right perspective, the right distance in the communication process, then love becomes hate. The natural thing with hatred, just as with love, is that you want to make physical communication with the person; that is, you want to kill or injure them. In any relationship in which the ego is involved, a love relationship or any other, there is always the danger of turning against your partner. As long as there is the notion of threat or insecurity of any kind, then a love relationship could turn into its opposite.

WORKING WITH PEOPLE

The idea of helping each other is more subtle than we might think. Generally, when we try to help other people, we make a nuisance of ourselves, make demands upon them. The reason we make a nuisance of ourselves to other people is that we cannot stand ourselves. We want to burst out into something, to make it known that we are desperate. So we extend ourselves and step out into someone else's territory without permission. We want to make a big deal of ourselves, no matter if the other person wants to accept us or not. We do not really want to expose our basic character, but we want to dominate the situation around us. We march straight through into another person's territory, disregarding the proper conditions for entering it. There might be signs saying, "Keep off the grass, no trespassing." But each time we see these signs, they make us more aggressive, more revolutionary. We just push ourselves into the other person's territory, like a tank going through a wall. We are not only committing vandalism to someone else's territory, but we are disrupting our own territory as well—it is inward vandalism too. It is being a nuisance to ourselves as well as to others.

Most people hate being in this situation. They do not want to feel that they are making a nuisance of themselves. On the other hand, one does not have to adopt a cool facade and a genteel manner and do everything correctly and be polite and considerate. True consideration is not diplomacy, putting on a facade of smiles or polite conversation. It is something more than that. It requires much energy and intelligence. It requires opening up our territory rather than marching into someone else's. It requires not playing magnetizing or repelling games, not surrounding our territory with electric wire or magnets. Then there is a faint possibility that we could be of some use to someone else. But we still should be tentative about helping others. We have glimpsed the first step in genuinely helping others, but it takes a lot of time to pick up the thing, put it in our mouth, chew it, taste it, and swallow it. It takes a long time to take our fences down. The first step is to learn to love ourselves, make friends with ourselves, not torture ourselves any more. And the second step is to communicate to people, to establish a relationship and gradually help them. It takes a long time and a long process of disciplined patience.

If we learn to not make a nuisance of ourselves and then to open ourselves to other people, then we are ready for the third stage—selfless help. Usually when we help someone, we are looking for something in return. We might say to our children, "I want you to be happy, therefore I'm putting all my energy into you," which implies that, "I want you to be happy because I want you to provide me with entertainment; bring me happiness, because I want to be happy." In the third stage of selfless help, true compassion, we do not do things because it gives us pleasure but because things need to be done. Our response is selfless, noncentralized. It is not for them or for me. It is environmental generosity.

But we cannot just go out and try to practice this kind of compassion. First we must learn how not to make a nuisance of ourselves. If we can make friends with ourselves, if we are willing to be what we are, without hating parts of ourselves and trying to hide them, then we can begin to open to others. And if we can begin to open without always having to protect ourselves, then perhaps we can begin to really help others.

THE EIGHTFOLD PATH

There seem to be so many sidetracks in relating to our life situations, sidetracks of all kinds by which we are seduced: "Food, gas, and lodging, next exit." We are always promised something if we turn right at the next exit as we travel down our highway. There are so many colorful advertisements. We never want to be just where and what we are; we always want to be somewhere else. We can always turn right at the next exit, even though we really know we are stuck on our highway anyway, that we really have no choice about it. Where we are is embarrassing, and so we would like to hear somebody say that there is an alternative whereby we do not have to be ashamed of ourselves: "I'll provide a mask, just put it on." Then you can get off at that exit and you are "saved" by pretending to be what you are not. You think people see you as a different person, the one wearing the mask of what you would like to be.

Buddhism promises nothing. It teaches us to be what we are where we are, constantly, and it teaches us to relate to our living situations accordingly. That seems to be the way to proceed on our highway without being distracted by the sidetracks and exits of all kinds. The signs say: "Tibetan Village, next exit"; "Japanese Village, next exit"; "Nirvana, next exit"; "Enlightenment, next exit—instant one"; "Disneyland, next exit." If you turn right, everything is going to be okay. You get what you are promised. But after having gone to Disneyland or having taken part in the Nirvana Festival, then you have to think about how you are going to get back to your car, how you are going to get home. This means you have to get back on the highway once more. It is unavoidable. I am afraid that this portrays our basic situation, the process in which we are constantly involved.

I am sorry not to be presenting any glamorous and beautiful promises. Wisdom happens to be a domestic affair. Buddha saw the world as it is and that was his enlightenment. *Buddha* means "awake," being awake, completely awake—that seems to be his message to us. He offered us a path to being awake, a path with eight points, and he called it "the eightfold path."

The first point the Buddha made has to do with "right view." Wrong view is a matter of conceptualization. Someone is walking toward us—suddenly we freeze. Not only do we freeze ourselves, but we also freeze the space in which the person is walking toward us. We call him "friend" who is walking through this space or "enemy." Thus the person is automatically walking through a frozen situation of fixed ideas—"this is that" or "this is not that." This is what Buddha called "wrong view." It is a conceptualized view which is imperfect because we do not see the situation as it is. There is the possibility, on the other hand, of not freezing that space. The person could walk into a lubricated situation of myself and that person as we are. Such a lubricated situation can exist and can create open space.

Of course, openness could be appropriated as a philosophical concept as well, but the philosophy need not necessarily be fixed. The situation could be seen without the idea of lubrication as such, without any fixed idea. In other words, the philosophical attitude could be just to see the situation as it is. "That person walking toward me is not a friend, therefore he is not an enemy either. He is just a person approaching me. I don't have to prejudge him at all." That is what is called "right view."

The next aspect of the eightfold path is called "right intention." Ordinary intention is based upon the process we have just described. Having conceptually fixed the person, now you are ready either to grasp or attack him. Automatically there is an apparatus functioning to provide either a waterbed or a shotgun for that person. That is the intention. It is a thought process which relates thinking to acting. When you encounter a situation, you think; and thinking inclines toward acting. In your constant alertness to relate the situation to your security, the intention is worked between two jaws. The emotional element, concerned with pleasure or pain, expansion or withdrawal, is one jaw; the heavy, physical aspect of the situation is the other. Situations keep you chewing your intention constantly, like gristle. Intention always has the quality of either invitation or attack.

But according to Buddha there is also "right intention." In order to see what this is, we first must understand what Buddha meant by "right." He did not mean to say right as opposed to wrong at all. He said "right" meaning "what is," being right without a concept of what is right. "Right" translates the Sanskrit *samyak,* which means "complete." Completeness needs no relative help, no support through comparison; it is self-sufficient. Samyak means seeing life as it is without crutches, straightforwardly. In a bar one says, "I would like a straight drink." Not diluted with club soda or water; you just have it straight. That is samyak. No dilutions, no concoctions—just a straight drink. Buddha realized that life could be potent and delicious, positive and creative, and he realized that you do not need any concoctions with which to mix it. Life is a straight drink—hot pleasure, hot pain, straightforward, one hundred percent.

So right intention means not being inclined toward anything other than what is. You are not involved in the idea that life *could be* beautiful or *could be* painful, and you are not being careful about life. According to Buddha, life *is* pain, life *is* pleasure. That is the samyak quality of it—so precise and direct: straight life without any concoctions. There is no need at all to reduce life situations or intensify them. Pleasure as it is, pain as it is—these are the absolute qualities of Buddha's approach to intention.

The third aspect of the eightfold path is "right speech." In Sanskrit the word for speech is *vac,* which means "utterance," "word," or *logos.* It implies perfect communication, communication which says, "It is so," rather than, "I think it is so." "Fire is hot," rather than, "I think fire is hot." Fire *is* hot, automatically—the direct approach. Such communication is true speech, in Sanskrit *satya,* which means "being true." It is dark outside at this time. Nobody would disagree with that. Nobody would have to say, "I think it is dark outside," or, "You must believe it is dark outside." You would just say, "It is dark outside." It is just the simple minimum of words we could use. It is true.

The fourth aspect of the eightfold path is "right morality" or "right discipline." If there is no one to impose discipline and no one to impose discipline on, then there is no need for discipline in the ordinary sense at all. This leads to the understanding of right discipline, complete discipline, which does not exist relative to ego. Ordinary discipline exists only at the level of relative decisions. If there is a tree, there must be branches; however, if there is no tree, there are no such things as branches. Likewise, if there is no ego, a whole range of projections becomes unnecessary. Right discipline is that kind of giving-up process; it brings us into complete simplicity.

We are all familiar with the samsaric kind of discipline which is aimed at self-improvement. We give up all kinds of things in order to make ourselves "better," which provides us with tremendous reassurance that we can *do* something with our lives. Such forms of discipline are just unnecessarily complicating your life rather than trying to simplify and live the life of a rishi.

Rishi is a Sanskrit word which refers to the person who constantly leads a straightforward life. The Tibetan word for "rishi" is *trangsong (drang sron). Trang* means "direct," *song* means "upright." The term refers to one who leads a direct and upright life by not introducing new complications into his life situation. This is a permanent discipline, the ultimate discipline. We simplify life rather than get involved with new gadgets or finding new concoctions with which to mix it.

The fifth point is "right livelihood." According to Buddha, right livelihood simply means making money by working, earning dollars, pounds, francs, pesos. To buy food and pay rent you need money. This is not a cruel imposition on us. It is a natural situation. We need not be embarrassed by dealing with money nor resent having to work. The more energy you put out, the more you get in. Earning money involves you in so many related situations that it permeates your whole life. Avoiding work usually is related to avoiding other aspects of life as well.

People who reject the materialism of American society and set themselves apart from it are unwilling to face themselves. They would like to comfort themselves with the notion that they are leading philosophically virtuous lives, rather than realizing that they are unwilling to work with the world as it is. We cannot expect to be helped by divine beings. If we adopt doctrines which lead us to expect blessings, then we will not be open to the real possibilities in situations. Buddha believed in cause and effect. For example, you get angry at your friend and decide to cut off the relationship. You have a hot argument with him and walk out of the room and slam the door. You catch your finger in the door. Painful, isn't it? That is cause and effect. You realize there is some warning there. You have overlooked karmic necessity. It happens all the time. This is what we run into when we violate right livelihood.

The sixth point is "right effort." The Sanskrit, *samyagvyayama*, means energy, endurance, exertion. This is the same as the bodhisattva's principle of energy. There is no need to be continually just pushing along, drudging along. If you are awake and open in living situations, it is possible for them and you to be creative, beautiful, humorous, and delightful. This natural openness is right effort, as opposed to any old effort. Right effort is seeing a situation precisely as it is at that very moment, being present fully, with delight, with a grin. There are occasions when we know we are present, but we do not really want to commit ourselves, but right effort involves full participation.

For right effort to take place we need gaps in our discursive or visionary gossip, room to stop and be present. Usually, someone is whispering some kind of seduction, some gossip behind our back; "It's all very well to meditate, but how about going to the movies? Meditating is nice, but how about getting together with our friends? How about that? Shall we read that book? Maybe we should go to sleep. Shall we go buy that thing we want? Shall we? Shall we? Shall we?" Discursive thoughts constantly happening, numerous suggestions constantly being supplied—effort has no room to take place. Or maybe it is not discursive thoughts at all. Sometimes it is a continual vision of possibilities: "My enemy is coming and I'm hitting him—I want war." Or, "My friend is coming, I'm hugging him, welcoming him to my house, giving him hospitality." It goes on all the time. "I have a desire to eat lambchops—no, leg of lamb, steak, lemon ice cream. My friend and I could go out to the shop and get some ice cream and bring it home and have a nice conversation over ice cream. We could go to that Mexican restaurant and get tacos 'to go' and bring them back home. We'll dip them in the sauce and eat together and have a nice philosophical discussion as we eat. Nice to do that with candlelight and soft music." We are constantly dreaming of infinite possibilities for all kinds of entertainment. There is no room to stop, no room to start providing space. Providing space: effort, noneffort and effort, noneffort—it's very choppy in a sense, very precise, knowing how to release the discursive or visionary gossip. Right effort—it's beautiful.

The next one is "right mindfulness." Right mindfulness does not simply mean being aware; it is like creating a work of art. There is more spaciousness in right mindfulness than in right effort. If you are drinking a cup of tea, you are aware of the whole environment as well as the cup of tea. You can therefore trust what you are doing, you are not threatened by anything. You have room to dance in the space, and this makes it a creative situation. The space is open to you.

The eighth aspect of the eightfold path is "right samadhi," right absorption. Samadhi has the sense of being as it is, which means relating with the space of a situation. This pertains to one's living situation as well as to sitting meditation. Right absorption is being completely involved, thoroughly and fully, in a nondualistic way. In sitting meditation the technique and you are one; in life situations the phenomenal world is also part of you. Therefore you do not have to meditate as such, as though you were a person distinct from the act of meditating and the object of meditation. If you are one with the living situation as it is, your meditation just automatically happens.

The Open Way

THE BODHISATTVA VOW

BEFORE WE COMMIT ourselves to walking the bodhisattva path, we must first walk the hinayana or narrow path. This path begins formally with the student taking refuge in the buddha, the dharma, and the sangha—that is, in the lineage of teachers, the teachings, and the community of fellow pilgrims. We expose our neurosis to our teacher, accept the teachings as the path, and humbly share our confusion with our fellow sentient beings. Symbolically, we leave our homeland, our property and our friends. We give up the familiar ground that supports our ego, admit the helplessness of ego to control its world and secure itself. We give up our clingings to superiority and self-preservation. But taking refuge does not mean becoming dependent upon our teacher or the community or the scriptures. It means giving up searching for a home, becoming a refugee, a lonely person who must depend upon himself. A teacher or fellow traveler or the scriptures might show us where we are on a map and where we might go from there, but we have to make the journey ourselves. Fundamentally, no one can help us. If we seek to relieve our loneliness, we will be distracted from the path. Instead, we must make a relationship with loneliness until it becomes aloneness.

In the hinayana the emphasis is on acknowledging our confusion. In the mahayana we acknowledge that we are a buddha, an awakened one, and act accordingly, even though all kinds of doubts and problems might

Longchenpa (Klong chen rab byams pa) with Shri Simha above his head. Longchenpa was a great teacher of the Nyingma lineage of Tibetan Buddhism. He is known for systematizing the oral teachings of this lineage. Shri Simha was an Indian master of the highest teachings of tantra. He was a teacher of Padmasambhava, who brought the buddhadharma to Tibet.

<small>DRAWING BY GLEN EDDY.</small>

arise. In the scriptures, taking the bodhisattva vow and walking on the bodhisattva path is described as being the act of awakening bodhi or "basic intelligence." Becoming "awake" involves seeing our confusion more clearly. We can hardly face the embarrassment of seeing our hidden hopes and fears, our frivolousness and neurosis. It is such an overcrowded world. And yet it is a very rich display. The basic idea is that, if we are going to relate with the sun, we must also relate with the clouds that obscure the sun. So the bodhisattva relates positively to both the naked sun and the clouds hiding it. But at first the clouds, the confusion, which hide the sun are more prominent. When we try to disentangle ourselves, the first thing we experience is entanglement.

The stepping-stone, the starting point in becoming awake, in joining the family of buddhas, is the taking of the bodhisattva vow. Traditionally, this vow is taken in the presence of a spiritual teacher and images of the buddhas and the scriptures in order to symbolize the presence of the lineage, the family of Buddha. One vows that from today until the attainment of enlightenment I devote my life to work with sentient beings and renounce my own attainment of enlightenment. Actually we cannot attain enlightenment until we give up the notion of "me" personally attaining it. As long as the enlightenment drama has a central character, "me," who has certain attributes, there is no hope of attaining enlightenment because it is nobody's project; it is an extraordinarily strenuous project but nobody is pushing it. Nobody is supervising it or appreciating its unfolding. We cannot pour our being from our dirty old vessel into a new clean one. If we examine our old vessel, we discover that it is not a solid thing at all. And such a realization of egolessness can only come through the practice of meditation, relating with discursive thoughts and gradually working back through the five skandhas. When meditation becomes an habitual way of relating with daily life, a person can take the bodhisattva vow. At that point discipline has become ingrown rather than enforced. It is like becoming involved in an interesting project upon which we automatically spend a great deal of time and effort. No one needs to encourage or threaten us; we just find ourselves intuitively doing it. Identifying with buddha nature is working with our intuition, with our ingrown discipline.

The bodhisattva vow acknowledges confusion and chaos—aggression, passion, frustration, frivolousness—as part of the path. The path is like a busy, broad highway, complete with roadblocks, accidents, construction work, and police. It is quite terrifying. Nevertheless it is majestic, it is the great path. "From today onward until the attainment of enlightenment I am willing to live with my chaos and confusion as well as with that of all other sentient beings. I am willing to share our mutual confusion." So no one is playing a one-upmanship game. The bodhisattva is a very humble pilgrim who works in the soil of samsara to dig out the jewel embedded in it.

HEROISM

The bodhisattva path is a heroic path. In the countries in which it developed—Tibet, China, Japan, Mongolia—the people are rugged, hard-working and earthy. The style of practice of the mahayana reflects the heroic qualities of these people—the Japanese samurai tradition, the industriousness of the Chinese peasant, the Tibetan struggle with barren, forbidding land. However, in America the ruggedly heroic approach to practice of these peoples is often translated and distorted into a rigid militantism, a robotlike regimentation. The original approach involved the delight of feeling oneself invincible, of having nothing to lose, of being completely convinced of your aloneness. Sometimes, of course, beginning bodhisattvas have second thoughts about such a daring decision to abandon enlightenment and throw themselves to the mercy of sentient beings and work with them, taking delight and pride in compassionate action. They become frightened. This hesitation is described metaphorically in the sutras as standing in the doorway of your house, having one foot out in the street and the other foot inside the house. That moment is the test of whether you go beyond the hesitation and step out into the no-man's-land of the street or decide to step back into your familiar home ground, of whether you are willing to work for the benefit of all sentient beings or wish to indulge yourself in the arhat mentality of self-enlightenment.

The preparation for the bodhisattva path is the unification of body and mind: the body works for the mind and the mind works for the body. The hinayana shamatha and vipashyana practices make the mind precise, tranquil, and smooth in the positive sense—precisely being there, rather than dreaming or sleeping or hazily perceiving. We can make a cup of tea properly, cook sunny-side-up properly, serve food properly, because the body and mind are synchronized.

Then we are ready to leap on to the bodhisattva path, to open to the joy of working with sentient beings, including oneself. The bodhisattva makes friends with himself as well as with others. There are no mysterious, dark corners left of which to be suspicious; no surprises can occur to destroy the bodhisattva's spiritual intelligence, his dignity and heroism. This is the first step, the first bhumi* or spiritual level.

The word *bhumi* in Sanskrit, or the word *sa* in Tibetan, means "earth" or "level" or "ground," the ground where you can relate with yourself and others. There is no mystification, no confusion; it is obviously solid earth. In other words, it is the equivalent of the basic sanity, fundamentally being *there*. Since the bodhissattva knows his body and his mind and how to relate with the two, the whole process becomes "skillful means" because of such transcendental security. Which is more like being *in* security rather than being secured, rather than watching yourself to make sure everything is okay. That fundamental security comes from realizing that you have broken through something. You reflect back and realize that you used to be extraordinarily paranoid and neurotic, watching each step you made, thinking you might lose your sanity, that situations were always threatening in some way. Now you are free of all those fears and preconceptions. You discover that you have something to give rather than having to demand from others, having to grasp all the time. For the first time, you are a rich person, you contain basic sanity. You have something to offer, you are able to work with your fellow sentient beings, you do not have to reassure yourself anymore. Reassurance implies a mentality of poverty—you are checking yourself, "Do I have it? How could I do it?" But the bodhisattva's delight in his richness is based upon experience rather than theory or wishful thinking. It is *so*, directly, fundamentally. He is fundamentally rich and so can delight in generosity.

Thus the bodhisattva at the level of the first bhumi develops generosity. He is not acting generously in order to get something in return, but he is just being generous and warm. If you are acting kindly to someone in the conventional sense, it has the connotation of looking down upon someone lower, less fortunate than you. "I am rich and you need help because you are not like me." The bodhisattva's generosity need not be gentle and soothing; it could be very violent or sharp because he gives you what you need rather than what will please you superficially. He

---

*A chart of the ten bhumis and their corresponding paramitas in Tibetan, Sanskrit, and English is given in the Appendix.

does not expect anything in return at all. He can be generous physically, giving food, wealth, clothes, and shelter, or spiritually, giving food for the mind, restoring your mental health. The best kind of generosity according to the scriptures is that of working with another person's state of mind. But the bodhisattva does not go beyond his own understanding; he regards himself as a student rather than as a teacher. Nor does he try to seduce the object of his generosity. He is aware not only of "me and them" but also of the space that both the giver and the receiver are sharing. The perception of the shared space is the operation of the sharp intelligence of prajna.

The joyous generosity of the first bhumi is accompanied by prajna, transcendental knowledge. This knowledge is the result of vipashyana practice, the basic training you inherited from your hinayana practice. Opening to the joyous richness of the first bhumi automatically brings transcendental knowledge as well. Prajna is often translated as "wisdom," but it is preferable to translate it as "transcendental knowledge" and to use the word wisdom to refer to jnana, the meditative state at the level of trantra which is more advanced than prajna.

At the level of the first bhumi, prajna involves cutting through, dissolving the boundary between meditation and nonmeditation. The sense of someone being there, someone being "aware" does not occur. The bodhisattva might still practice his discipline of sitting meditation, but he begins to find it irrelevant in some sense; it is just a disciplinary act. In actual fact his arising from meditation and participating in daily life does not change his mental state at all. His acts of generosity go on all the time. In other words, the bodhisattva already has the sharpness, the intelligence of the awakened state of mind. That is why his generosity becomes dana paramita. *Dana* means "generosity," *para* means "other," *mita* means "shore." It is generosity that transcends, that goes to the other shore. You go beyond the river of samsara, the river of confusion, the continual chain reaction pattern of karma in which each flow initiates the next flow like an electric current in which each spark of electricity is independent but initiates the next.

Prajna is transcendence, cutting through the volitional chain reaction of karma. But the act of cutting through the karmic chain might itself generate some chain reaction, because you are cutting something and acknowledging the cutting through. It becomes very subtle. Until the bodhisattva reaches the tenth bhumi he cannot completely cut the chain of karmic bondage because he is acknowledging the very act of cutting through. Prajna is knowledge in the sense that you still regard the dharma or the knowledge as external to yourself; there is still confirmation of the experience, one still experiences cutting through as an event that gives you information, an event from which you learn. The bodhisattva must go through ten stages of development to cut through the watcher, the acknowledger. The rejoicing process of the first bhumi is celebrating getting away from samsara rather than getting beyond it, so the bodhisattva still carries elements of samsara with him constantly.

The first bhumi is described in the scriptures as a state in which you have drunk half a cup of tea and still have half left. You have selected the tea, brewed it, tasted it, and begun to drink it, but you still have not drunk the whole cup of tea. You are stuck, though not in the sense of being trapped, but you still have to work through the drinking of the other half of the cup, which takes ten steps to complete. Then you must clean your cup and put it back where it belongs.

THE SANITY OF EARTH

The second bhumi is called the "spotless" bhumi, and it involves the shila paramita of "morality" or "discipline." The purity of the bodhisattva referred to by the shila paramita is based upon making friends with oneself, loving oneself. You are not a nuisance to yourself anymore; you are good company, an inspiration to yourself. You do not have to control yourself so as to avoid temptations or follow rules or laws. You find temptations less relevant and guidelines less necessary, because you naturally follow the appropriate patterns. There is no need to try to be pure, to painfully discipline yourself to be pure, to apply detergent to your natural condition. The spotlessness or purity of the second bhumi is realized when you acknowledge your natural purity.

It is like feeling naturally at home in a clean, orderly place. You do not have to fit yourself into it; if you try to fit yourself in, you become rigid and create chaos. So the morality of the bodhisattva is a natural process. Unskillful action becomes irrelevant. The bodhisattva delights in working with people rather than regarding compassionate action as a duty. He has no dogma about how he should act or how other people should be. He does not try to reform or transform anyone because they do not fit his model. If people are determined to convert others into their mold, then they are attempting to reassure themselves by using the convert to relieve their doubt. The bodhisattva is not concerned with conversion; he respects others' lifestyles, speaks their language, and allows them to evolve according to their nature rather than making them into a replica of himself. It requires tremendous discipline to avoid converting people. The bodhisattva will experience strong impulses to tell people how things ought to be. But instead of acting on these impulses, the bodhisattva regards them as mature to work through, an expression of his insecurity. He no longer needs that kind of reinforcement.

One type of discipline known as the "gathering of virtue" is connected with relating to physical things. Because the bodhisattva has been well trained in shamatha and vipashyana meditation, he does not relate to a cup of tea by knocking it over. He picks it up, drinks it, and puts it down properly. There is no frivolousness involved. The *Bodhicharyavatara* notes that, when the bodhisattva decides to relax and sit on the ground, he does not make doodles with the dust on the ground. He does not need to entertain himself restlessly. He is just sitting there. Making doodles would seem an effort to him. I hope you do not take it too seriously, that if you make doodles you are not a potential bodhisattva. The idea is that, if you are respectful of your environment, you will take care of it, not treat it frivolously. As a cameraman respects his cameras or a professor his books, so the bodhisattva respects the earth. Frivolousness is arduous to him. There is an "old dog" quality, a "sitting bull" quality; he is just being there, precisely, properly. Making an additional move is frivolous. Of course he may be very active as well as peaceful, but he would not give in to a sudden outburst of energy; his action is deliberate and sane, deliberate in the sense of not being impulsive.

The bodhisattva's discipline is to relate to earth properly, to relate to his senses and mind properly. He is not concerned with psychic phenomena or other worlds. Ignoring earth to chase after psychic phenomena is like the play of children trying to find gold at the end of a rainbow. We do not have to concern ourselves with the cosmic world, the world of gods, psychic powers, angels, and devils. To do so may be to lose track of the physical world in which we live, and this results in madness. The test of the bodhisattva's sanity is how directly he relates to earth. Anything else is a sidetrack.

PATIENCE

Before we discuss the third bhumi, I would like to point out that the ten stages of the bodhisattva's path toward enlightenment should be regarded as landmarks, points of reference on a map, rather than as events to be celebrated, such as birthdays or graduations. There are no medals for achievement along the bodhisattva path. Each stage, even enlightenment itself, is like the different stages in the growth of a tree. The first bhumi is an extremely spectacular experience, a sudden explosion of joy, realizing that you could be generous, you could open, but beyond that the other bhumis are less spectacular. One bhumi develops to a peak point, and then gradually the next bhumi suggests itself and you cross the border very gently and arrive at the beginning of the next bhumi. It is frivolous to ask what bhumi you are in or to develop courses aimed at achieving the various levels. It is a very gentle, very gradual process.

Patience, the paramita connected with the third bhumi, is particularly related with the idea that the bodhisattva does not desire to be a buddha but would rather work with sentient beings to save them from their confusion. Patience also implies heroism in the sense of having nothing to lose. The meditation practice connected with patience is working with territory. There is no territory that is yours or that is others'; everyone is in no-man's land. Not seeking enlightenment for ego's personal benefit, you have no need for territory so your space becomes a public park, a common ground, no-man's-land. No-man's-land is free ground, not subject to the laws of any government. You are free to do anything there, no one can make any demands upon you, so you can afford to wait, to be patient. Because there are no obligations you are free from time, not in the sense of being oblivious to what time it might be, but in the sense of not being compulsively driven by obligations to keep within time limits.

Patience does not mean forbearance in the sense of enduring pain, allowing someone to torture you at his leisure. The bodhisattva would strike down his torturer and defend himself, which is commonsense sanity. In fact the bodhisattva's blow would be more powerful because it would not be impulsive or frivolous. The bodhisattva has great power because nothing can shake him; his action is calm, deliberate, and persevering. Since there is space between himself and others, he does not feel threatened, but he is very careful. He scans the whole environment for things which need to be dealt with. Both patience and intelligent caution are operating in no-man's-land. So the bodhisattva can spring out like a tiger and claw you, bit you, crush you. He is not inhibited by conventional morality or idiot compassion. He is not afraid to subjugate what needs to be subjugated, to destroy what needs to be destroyed, and to welcome that which needs to be welcomed.

The conventional notion of patience is to be very kind and wait and hold your temper, repressing your restlessness. If we are waiting for someone, we smoke cigarettes, read, pace back and forth to keep ourselves cool. When they say, "I'm sorry I'm late," we say, "Don't mention it. I've been enjoying myself, looking at the scenery, talking to strangers. Let's get to our business, I'm glad you're here." Although we pretend that we are not concerned about the time, actually we are compulsively caught up in living by the clock so our denial of concern and the hiding of our anger is hypocritical. The bodhisattva, on the other hand, free from the compulsive concern with time, can just sit patiently without feeling that he is "waiting" for something else to happen. Although there is a sense of timelessness in the bodhisattva's action, this does not mean that he does everything so slowly that his action is inefficient. In fact, he is very efficient because his action is direct and persevering. Nothing sidetracks him, nothing scares him. He does not complain in the conventional sense, but he does point out discrepancies in organization or in the neurosis of workers. He does not complain about them, but he just relates to them as facts, as things that need correction. This sounds like a good strategy for a businessman to adopt, but unless a person has surrendered to the whole process of treading the path, it is not possible to be patient in this way.

TRADITION

Virya, the paramita of the fourth bhumi, is taking delight in and working hard with whatever working base or material we are presented with—our state or mind, our traditions, our society. It is not taking sides for or against our traditions or our state of mind, but it is taking delight in them and then working with them. It is not enough to reject superficially the different aspects of the world around us. It is too simple-minded just to abandon traditional morality as being old-fashioned, like an old clothing

style, and then substitute a swinging morality, an up-to-date, "mod" morality. Many of the young reject tradition altogether, even the smell of
it. They see no truth in it at all. "I'm unhappy, neurotic because of
them—my parents, my teachers, the media, the politicians, the psychiatrists, the capitalists, the clergymen, the computers, the scientists." We
denounce the government, the schools, the churches, the synagogues,
the hospitals. But there is some uncertainty in this stance. Perhaps there
could be some truth in what the establishment says, in the way it does
things? "Well, if there is, I'll pick only what is meaningful to me and
reject the rest. I'll interpret tradition my way." We want to justify our
existence as a good person, a little Christ or Buddha. This self-conscious
attempt to define our identity or style is another form of spiritual materialism. We get a kick out of a certain style and self-justification from certain ideas that clothe our rebellion in glamorous imagery.

The bodhisattva, on the other hand, firmly roots himself in the traditions of his society but does not feel obligated to follow them. He is not
afraid to take a new step, but the reason he is stepping out of the tradition is because he knows it so well. His inspiration to step out comes
from that tradition. First we must step into the tradition, must understand it fully, its wise and its foolish aspects, why people are hypnotized
by its dogmas; we must understand what wisdom, if any, lies behind the
dogma. Then we can step out of it sanely.

The traditional approach to being a good person is to eliminate all
color, all spectacle. You camouflage yourself and blend into the social
landscape; you become white. White is associated with purity, cleanli-
ness, gentleness, presentableness. But to be an extraordinarily good citizen you need to add color to the basic white. To improve society you
need some color to contrast with the white.

So the bodhisattva is not bound by white, by law, by convention, or
by traditional morality, but neither does he kill someone on the spot
because he feels some faint aggression toward him, nor does he make
love to a woman on the street because he feels passion toward her. The
conventional approach is to hesitate out of fear of embarrassment or a
sense of impropriety or vice. "I shouldn't do it, it's wrong." There is a
faint suggestion and the rejection of the suggestion, which is depressing.
"I wish I could, but society or my conscience does not permit me." But
perhaps there is something more to our hesitation, perhaps it is our basic
sanity that keeps us from acting impulsively.

Sanity lies somewhere between the inhibitions of conventional morality and the looseness of extreme impulse, but the area in-between is very fuzzy. The bodhisattva delights in the play between hesitation and extreme impulsiveness—it is beautiful to look at—so delight in itself is the approach of sanity. Delight is to open our eyes to the totality of the situation rather than siding with this or that point of view. The bodhisattva does not side with rejecting convention, mocking everything out of sheer frustration, trying to get the world to acknowledge him. Nor does he side with blind dogma, holding back out of fear, trying to mold the world to conform to rigid ideas and rules. The bodhisattva takes delight in polarities but does not side with any extreme. He accepts what is there as the message and explores it further and further, and the conflict between polarities becomes his inspiration. In order to be a communist you must have a model of what not to be, which means you must understand capitalism, so capitalism is your inspiration.

The bodhisattva's inspiration is the war between the awakened mentality and the samsaric mentality: the samsaric mentality is the inspiration for the awakened mentality. We need not change ourselves, need not negate what we are. We can use what we are as inspiration. So virya, the fourth bhumi, is taking delight in and working hard with whatever working base we have—our neurosis, our sanity, our culture, our society. We do not make sectarian distinctions or assert our superiority, but we take delight in what is and then work with it.

Zen and Prajna

The paramita of the fifth bhumi is panoramic awareness. This meditative state has been called dhyana in the Indian tradition, ch'an in the Chinese tradition, and zen in the Japanese tradition. They all mean a state of total involvement, without center or fringe. If there is a center and a fringe, then our state of mind ceases to be one of total involvement because we have to keep track of both ends; a sense of polarity is always present.

So dhyana or zen is awareness without a watcher. In the superficial sense, when we speak of awareness, we mean egocentric watching, knowing what we are doing, knowing where we are supposed to be and how we handle the situation, which is quite a complicated process. We have to keep track of ourselves and our situation, keep track of how we are handling it and how the situation is affected by our action. There are so many things to manage at one time that we fear losing control, so we have to be extraordinarily alert and careful. Trying to be totally aware in this way is very difficult and complicated.

Awareness in the sense of zen is much simpler. The Tibetan word for it is *samten (bsam gtan): sam* means "awareness," *ten* means "making stable." So samten means "stable awareness," sane awareness rather than neurotic awareness, awareness in the sense that there are very few things to keep track of because everything has been simplified into one situation. If there is simplicity and spaciousness, then the bodhisattva actions, the paramitas, generosity, patience, energy, discipline, and so on, are seen to be distinct processes. And if these processes take place in a very open situation, then there is no conflict between generosity and patience and the rest; they can be combined together to complement each other.

The spaciousness of dhyana or "panoramic awareness" inspires the further development of prajna, which is the sharp, precise, biting aspect of space, like crisp, cold winter air: clear, cool, and precise. Until the sixth bhumi, the maturation of prajna, the bodhisattva's actions reflect subtle attitudes. The bodhisattva does not have enough clarity and "awakeness" to see through them. Prajna cuts through the pieties of the bodhisattva's approach—being extraordinarily compassionate, being smooth and skillful, able to handle any situation, the syrupy, honeylike quality of the bodhisattva, being sweet and kind and gentle and at the same time slippery. Prajna cuts through any subtle attitude, any sense of virtue or manipulation, any sense of fixed concepts.

As the cutting through process of prajna develops, the next stage, the seventh bhumi, also begins to unfold—upaya or "skillful means," the perfect application of method. In the earlier bhumis the bodhisattva's actions—generosity, patience, and so forth—were skillful, but there was an element of piety, some sense of gratification, of acknowledging that one's practice has fulfilled its function. So there is a very faint but fundamental expectation in the first six bhumis. Of course, the sense of "this and that" is not as heavy and clumsy as with those who are not bodhisattvas, but at the same time, the bodhisattva's neuroses are also spiritually materialistic. They are very gentle, very slippery and difficult to catch because they contain nonduality as well as falsehood. It tends to get very complicated at this level; the more perfect you become, the subtler your imperfection. So the development of "skillful means" signifies fully stepping out of spiritual materialism. Skillful means involves using the cutting through method of prajna as well as developing a sense of the absence of "me" and "that." In other words, there is less sense of journey, less sense of a reference or checking point. You are completely tuned into what is happening on a larger scale.

Developing upaya is not so much a matter of overcoming something as it is a matter of gaining extra confidence, total confidence without a reference point. Just fully being skillful involves total lack of inhibition. We are not afraid to be. We are not afraid to live. We must accept ourselves as being warriors. If we acknowledge ourselves as warriors, then there is a way in, because a warrior dares to *be*, like a tiger in the jungle.

THE APPROACH TO ENLIGHTENMENT

The paramita of the eighth bhumi is *monlam (smon lam)* in Tibetan or *pranidhana* in Sanskrit, which literally means "wishful thinking" or "best wishes." *Monlam* means inspiration, a vision of how future developments might occur. It does not refer to wishful thinking in the ordinary sense of speculation as to what might plausibly happen in the future. This inspiration or greater vision refers to future in the sense of the pregnant aspect of the present, the present possibilities for the future. It is a very realistic approach, relating to the present as a stepping-stone that contains the potential of the future.

The inspiration of the eighth bhumi is derived from relating to what is, what we are. We are inspired to walk on the broad, complete mahayana path, to deal with the world on a larger scale, a cosmic scale. The present state of being contains past and future as well.

The bodhisattva at this stage is extraordinarily confident but not in a self-centered way. His point of reference is not himself but the totality of sentient beings, so he loses track of "this" and "that." Perhaps he and all sentient beings are one and the same, so he gives up keeping track of who is who, what is what, not with blind faith or through confusion, but realistically, because there is no point in carving out territories. The future situation is there, the present situation is here, because it is so.

The paramita of the ninth bhumi is *bala* in Sanskrit or *top (stobs)* in Tibetan, which means "power." Power in this sense is a further expression of the confidence of skillful means. Skillful means is the confidence to step up to the edge of a cliff and power is the confidence to leap. It seems to be a very daring decision, but since there is no reference point, it is an extraordinarily ordinary situation; you simply do it. In a sense, it is much easier than self-consciously making a cup of tea.

At the beginning of the bodhisattva path there is the tremendous joy of realizing that we have all kinds of richness and skill, that we are a total human being. Beyond that level the journey is not self-conscious, but still the unself-consciousness becomes another kind of self-consciousness. We are still using reference points, in a transcendental way of course, but we are nevertheless confirming our experience. And then, beyond the seventh bhumi, we begin to break through this barrier by experiencing complete skillful means. Finally we do not have to make a reference, we do not have to make a journey at all. Our path becomes an evolutionary process in which further power begins to develop, complete power, enlightened power. Which leads into the tenth bhumi, dharma-megha or dharma cloud, the development of the paramita of yeshe (Tibetan *ye shes*), or wisdom (Sanskrit *jnana*).

Wisdom is nonidentification with the teaching, nonidentification with the path, nonidentification with the technique. The bodhisattva doesn't identify with the path any longer because he has *become* the path. He *is* the path. He has worked on himself, trod on himself, until he has become the path and the chariot as well as the occupant of the chariot, all at the same time. He is vision, energy, skillful means, generosity, knowledge, panoramic awareness. It is unspeakably powerful, and yet at the same time the bodhisattva is powerless when he is in the tenth bhumi, because he is completely programmed by the Buddha's way. This might sound paradoxical, but it is so.

There is a story of a king in India whose court soothsayers told him that within seven days there would be a rain whose water would produce madness. The king collected and stored enormous amounts of fresh water, so that when the rain of madness fell, all of his subjects went mad except himself. But after a while he realized that he could not communicate with his subjects because they took the mad world to be real and could smoothly function in the world created by their mutual madness. So finally the king decided to abandon his supply of fresh water and drink the water of madness. It is a rather disappointing way of expressing the realization of enlightenment, but it is a very powerful statement. When we decide to drink the water of madness, then we have no reference point. So from that point of view, total enlightenment is total madness. But there is still a king and his subjects and they must run the world together. Running the world becomes an expression of sanity because there is no reference point against which to fight. There is something logical about the whole bodhisattva process but something extraordinarily illogical about it as well.

SEVEN

Devotion

SURRENDERING

AT FIRST, DEVOTION is inspired by a sense of inadequacy. We begin to realize that we are not up to coping with life or that we are confused about it. Even the little lighthouses we might have in the midst of our darkness seem quite vulnerable. So devotion in the hinayana stage comes from a sense of poverty. We take refuge in the buddha, dharma, and sangha because we feel trapped in the problems of life. We have failed to make a comfortable nest. We want to change our claustrophobic and painful world.

You might say that certain people approach the path from more positive inspirations. They might have had a dream or a vision or an insight that inspired them to search more deeply. Possibly they had money to fly to India or the charm and courage to hitchhike there. Then they had all sorts of exotic and exciting experiences. Someone stuck in New York City might consider it a rich and heroic journey. But fundamentally such people still have the mentality of poverty. Although their initial inspiration may have been expansive, still they are uncertain about how to relate to the teachings. They feel that the teachings are too precious, too rich for them to digest. They doubt whether they can master a spiritual discipline. The more inadequate they feel, the more devoted they become. Fundamentally, such devotion involves valuing the object of devotion. The poorer you feel, the richer the guru seems by contrast. As the seeming gap between what he has and what you have grows, your

Vajradhara. The Buddha manifests himself as Vajradhara to expound the teachings of tantra. He is also the supreme buddha expressing the whole of existence as unborn and unoriginated. The tantric practitioner's personal teacher is identified with Vajradhara. He is the source of several important lineages of Buddhism in Tibet.
DRAWING BY GLEN EDDY.

devotion grows as well. You are more willing to give something to your guru.

But what do you want in return? That is the problem. "I want to be saved from pain, my misery, my problems. I would like to be saved so that I might be happy. I want to feel glorious, fantastic, good, creative. I want to be like my guru. I want to incorporate his admirable qualities into my personality. I want to enrich my ego. I want to get some new information into my system so that I might handle myself better." But this is like asking for a transplant of some kind. "Maybe the Heart of the Great Wisdom could be transplanted into my chest. Perhaps I could exchange my brain." Before we wholeheartedly give ourselves to serving a guru we should be very suspicious of why we are doing it. What are we looking for, really?

You may approach a spiritual friend and declare your intention to surrender to him. "I am dedicated to your cause, which I love very much. I love you and your teachings. Where do I sign my name? Is there a dotted line that I could sign on?" But the spiritual friend has none—no dotted line. You feel uncomfortable. "If it is an organization, why don't they have a place for me to sign my name, some way to acknowledge that I have joined them? They have discipline, morality, a philosophy but no place for me to sign my name." "As far as this organization is concerned, we do not care what your name is. Your commitment is more important than putting down your name." You might feel disturbed that you will not get some form of credentials. "Sorry, we don't need your name or address or telephone number. Just come and practice."

This is the starting point of devotion—trusting a situation in which you do not have an ID card, in which there is no room for credits or acknowledgment. Just give in. Why do we have to know who gave in? The giver needs no name, no credentials. Everybody jumps into a gigantic cauldron. It does not matter how or when you jump into it, but sooner or later you must. The water is boiling, the fire is kept going. You become part of a huge stew. The starting point of devotion is to dismantle your credentials. You need discoloring, depersonalizing of your individuality. The purpose of surrender is to make everyone gray—no white, no blue—pure gray. The teaching demands that everyone be thrown into the big cauldron of soup. You cannot stick your neck out and say, "I'm an onion, therefore I should be more smelly." "Get down, you're just another vegetable." "I'm a carrot, isn't my orange color noticeable?"

271

"No, you are still orange only because we haven't boiled you long enough."

At this point you might say to yourself, "He's warning me to be very suspicious of how I approach the spiritual path, but what about questioning him? How do I know that what he is saying is true?" You don't. There is no insurance policy. In fact, there is much reason to be highly suspicious of me. You never met Buddha. You have only read books that others have written about what he said. Assuming that Buddha knew what was true, which of course is itself open to question, we do not know whether his message was transmitted correctly and completely from generation to generation. Perhaps someone misunderstood and twisted it. And the message we receive is subtly but fundamentally wrong. How do we know that what we are hearing is actually trustworthy? Perhaps we are wasting our time or being misled. Perhaps we are involved in a fraud. There is no answer to such doubts, no authority that can be trusted. Ultimately, we can trust only in our own basic intelligence.

Since you are at least considering the possibility of trusting what I am saying, I will go on to suggest certain guidelines for determining whether your relationship with a teacher is genuine. Your first impulse might be to look for a one hundred percent enlightened being, someone who is recognized by the authorities, who is famous, who seems to have helped people we know. The trouble with that approach is that it is very difficult to understand what qualities an enlightened being would have. We have preconceptions as to what they are, but do they correspond to reality? Selecting a spiritual friend should be based upon our personal experience of communication with this person, rather than upon whether or not the person fits our preconceptions. Proper transmission requires intimate friendship, direct contact with the spiritual friend. If we see the guru as someone who possesses higher, superior knowledge, who is greater than us, who is extremely compassionate to actually pay attention to us, then transmission is blocked. If we feel that we are a miserable little person who is being given a golden cup, then we are overwhelmed by the gift, we do not know what to do with it. Our gift becomes a burden because our relationship is awkward and heavy.

In the case of genuine friendship between teacher and student there is direct and total communication which is called "the meeting of the two minds." The teacher opens and you open; both of you are in the same space. In order for you to make friends with a teacher in a complete sense, he has to know what you are and how you are. Revealing that is surrendering. If your movements are clumsy or if your hands are dirty when you shake hands, you should not be ashamed of it. Just present yourself as you are. Surrendering is presenting a complete psychological portrait of yourself to your friend, including all your negative, neurotic traits. The point of meeting with the teacher is not to impress him so that he will give you something, but the point is just to present what you are. It is similar to a physician-patient relationship. You must tell your doctor what is wrong with you, what symptoms you have. If you tell him all your symptoms, then he can help you as much as possible. Whereas if you try to hide your illness, try to impress him with how healthy you are, how little attention you need, then naturally you are not going to receive much help. So to begin with devotion means to be what you are, to share yourself with a spiritual friend.

SPIRITUAL FRIEND

In the hinayana Buddhist approach to devotion you are confused and need to relate to a model of sanity, to a sensible human being who, because of his disciplined practice and study, sees the world clearly. It is as if you are flipping in and out of hallucinations, so you seek out someone who can distinguish for you what is real and what is illusion. In that sense the person you seek must be like a parent educating a child. But he is the kind of parent who is open to communicate with you. And like a parent, he seems to be an ordinary human being who grew up experiencing difficulties, who shares your concerns and your common physical needs. The hinayanists view Buddha as an ordinary human being, a son of man who through great perseverance attained enlightenment but who still had a body and could still share our common human experience.

In contrast to the hinayana view of the teacher as a parental figure, the mahayanists view the teacher as a spiritual friend—*kalyanamitra* in Sanskrit—which literally means "spiritual friend" or "companion in the virtue." Virtue, as it is used here, is inherent richness, rich soil fertilized by the rotting manure of neurosis. You have tremendous potential, you are ripe, you smell like one-hundred-percent ripe blue cheese, which can be smelled miles away. Devotion is the acknowledging of that potential by both the teacher and the student. The student is like an adolescent who obviously has great potential talents but who does not know the ways of the world. He needs a master to teach him what to do, how to develop his talent. He is always making mistakes due to his inexperience and needs close supervision. At the mahayana level the spiritual friend seems to possess much more power and understanding than you. He has mastered all kinds of disciplines and techniques and knows how to handle situations extraordinarily well. He is like a highly skilled physician who can prescribe the right remedies for your frequent spiritual illnesses, your continual blundering.

At the mahayana level you are not as bothered by trying to make sure your world is real: "At last I've found solid ground, a solid footing. I have discovered the meaning of reality." We begin to relax and feel comfortable. We have found out what is edible. But how do we eat? Do we eat everything at once, without discrimination? We could get a stomach upset if we combine our foods improperly. We have to open ourselves to the suggestions of the spiritual friend at this point; he begins to mind our business a great deal. At first he may be kind and gentle with us, but nevertheless there is no privacy from him; every corner is being watched. The more we try to hide, the more our disguises are penetrated. It is not necessarily because the teacher is extremely awake or a mind reader. Rather our paranoia about impressing him or hiding from him makes our neurosis more transparent. The covering itself is transparent. The teacher acts as a mirror, which we find irritating and discomforting. It may seem at that point that the teacher is not trying to help you at all but is deliberately being provocative, even sadistic. But such overwhelming openness is real friendship.

This friendship involves a youthful and challenging relationship in which the spiritual friend is your lover. Conventionally, a lover means someone who relates with your physical passion and makes love to you and acknowledges you in that way. Another type of lover admires you generally. He would not necessarily make love to you physically, but would acknowledge or understand your beauty, your flair, your glamorousness. In the case of the spiritual friend, he is your lover in the sense that he wants to communicate with your grotesqueness as well as your beauty. Such communication is very dangerous and painful. We are unclear how to relate to it.

Such a spiritual friend is outrageously unreasonable simply because he minds your business so relentlessly. He is concerned about how you say hello, how you handle yourself coming into the room, and so on. You want him to get out of your territory, he is too much. "Don't play games with me when I'm weak and vulnerable." Even if you see him when you feel strong, then you usually want him to recognize your strength, which is another vulnerability. You are looking for feedback in either case. He seems invulnerable and you feel threatened. He is like a beautifully built train coming toward you on solid tracks; there is no way to stop him. Or he is like an antique sword with a razor-sharp edge about to strike you. The heavy-handedness of the spiritual friend is both appreciated and highly irritating. His style is extremely forceful but so together, so right that you cannot challenge it. That is devotion. You admire his style so much, but you feel terrified by it. It is beautiful but it is going to crush you, cut you to pieces. Devotion in this case involves so much sharpness that you cannot even plead for mercy by claiming to be a wretched, nice little person who is devoted and prostrates to his teacher all the time and kisses his feet. Conmanship is ineffective in such a situation. The whole thing is very heavy-handed. The real function of a spiritual friend is to insult you.

The Great Warrior

As you advanced to the mahayana path, the spiritual friend was like a physician. At first your relationship was sympathetic, friendly, predictable. When you visited your friend he would always sit in the same chair and you would always be served the same kind of tea. The spiritual friend would do everything precisely and everything had to be done for him precisely; if you were imprecise he would caution you. Or you might have a friend who did all kinds of crazy things, but that style was also predictable. You might even expect that he would challenge you if you acted too predictably. In either case, you were afraid of the guru changing his style, of becoming truly unpredictable. You preferred to maintain the smooth, beautiful, peaceful style of communication. You were very comfortable and could trust the situation, devote yourself wholeheartedly to it, absorb yourself in it, as though you were watching a railroad train whose wheels go round and round, chug, chug, always predictable. You knew when the train would reach the station. You knew when it would leave again—chug, chug, chug—always predictable. You hoped that your friend would always be kind and noble with you.

But at some point this kind of relationship becomes stagnant; it is too indulgent and must be cut through. Your spiritual friend will sit in your chair and serve you beer instead of tea. You are confused, you feel as if the carpet had been pulled from under your feet. The regularity and predictableness of your relationship has been challenged. That is how the spiritual friend turns into a crazy-wisdom guru. He acts unexpectedly and the atmosphere of tranquillity is disturbed, which is very painful. The physician becomes wild, which is terrifying. We do not want to trust a wild doctor or surgeon. But we must. We have been nursed by our parents and treated by our physician and now we must become an adult, a real grown-up person ready to face the world. We have to become an apprentice warrior. Devotion, at this point, involves being extraordinarily accommodating to the darts that the spiritual friend throws at you.

You have to learn to believe in the mysteries or mystical aspect of the art of war. In the vajrayana, war is not regarded as a struggle to gain victory. War is regarded as an occupation. The guru is the archetypical warrior who has knowledge of war and peace. He is a great warrior who is familiar with the mysteries of the world, with the mystical aspect of the world. He knows how the world functions, how situations occur, and how situations can fool you. Devotion to the guru develops with the realization of the tremendous difficulty of finding your way in the midst of this warfare. You need to learn from a master warrior. Warfare demands fundamental bravery in handling situations, a willingness to fight with situations and a willingness to believe in the mysteriousness of life.

The guru has fantastic skill in developing you and destroying you at the same time, because the guru can communicate with the real world, which in turn can communicate to you either positively or negatively. That is one of the mysteries. People refer to it as magic or miracle, but I do not think we have a true understanding of it. The popular idea of magic is the dream of the comic books—Clark Kent transforming himself into Superman. But a guru will not turn you upside down or suspend you in the air. Nor does he have a mystical power to watch you being old and infantile at the same time. Nor does he have the power to turn you into a reptile to confess your sins to him and then, having confessed, turn you back into a human. People would like to have such power, of course. It would be a tremendous thrill. "I wish I had the power to turn this person into a bug so that I could step on him." We have been reading too many comic books. Mystical power can only be expressed through an extraordinarily direct relationship with what is happening, with reality. Without a sense of compassion nothing can take place. We cannot conquer the world if we desire victory over something. We must have the sense of our relatedness with the world. Otherwise, our relationship with the world is imaginary, based upon false devotion to the guru.

One must make a very direct and personal relationship with the guru. You might give twenty million dollars to your spiritual friend whom you love dearly, but that is not enough. You must give your ego to him. The guru must receive your juice, your vital fluid. It is not enough to give him your feathers or hair or nails. You have to surrender the real core of you, the juicy part. Even if you give everything you have—your car, your clothes, your property, your money, your contact lenses, your false teeth—it is not enough. How about giving yourself, you who possess all these things? You still hang out. It is very clumsy. Particularly in the vajrayana, teachers expect you to give yourself—it is not enough to strip off your skin and flesh and pull your bones apart and your heart out. What do you have left to give then? That is the best gift of all.

We might feel proud that we gave one of our fingers to our guru: "I cut off my ear as a gift to him," or "I cut my nose as an expression of devotion to him. I hope he will take it and regard it as a sign of how serious I am about the whole thing. And I hope he will value it because it means so much to me." To the crazy wisdom guru such sacrifice is insignificant. Vajrayana surrender is much more painful and powerful and intimate. It is a problem of total communication; if you hold anything back, your relationship will be false, incomplete, and both you and your guru will know it.

COMMITMENT

The crazy wisdom guru has tremendous power—the power of transformation, the power of development, and also the power of deadly rejection which could destroy you. It is said that the guru should be regarded as being like fire: if you get too close to him you get burned; if you stay too distant you receive no warmth. You have to keep a reasonable distance. Getting too close means that you would like to obtain some kind of acknowledgment that your neuroses are a valid and serious matter, that they should be included as part of the bargain of the spiritual unification of guru and student. But such a bargain cannot be made because your guru will not sign his name on the dotted line.

Unfortunately, we usually think that devotion is very safe, pleasant, and a harmonious relationship to enter into, almost like getting married. But in the devotional relationship there is more doubt as to whether it will continue. You wish you could keep it a secret in case it does not work out. There is still a great deal of mystery concerning the teachings and the teacher. In relating with your wife or husband there is less mysteriousness. You know each other's backgrounds and have learned each other's habits and you begin to suspect possible boredom. But in the case of the teachings you do not suspect boredom but you do suspect tremendous possibilities of failure and danger. Whenever this distrust arises, you surrender more, you trust more blindly, and you commit your energy more to the unknown. In spite of being unknown it is secure, absolutely safe, since you are on the side of goodness or God. You are willing to fight his enemies—vice, the devil, whatever. You are linked with goodness. "If I devote myself enough, my teacher will accept me and then he will free me." That is a big problem.

We do not realize that the wrath of the goodness is tremendously powerful. It could strike us at any time. We could be hit by any little deception, which to you is only a way of speaking, but in actual fact it seems to be much more than that. You might bend the income tax laws or plead your way out of a fine for a traffic violation, but it is not so easy with spirituality. It is a much more subtle, very acute, very immediate, very sensitive situation. When minds tune into subtle situations, then the consequences become subtle as well. The usual expectation is that when we tune our minds into a subtle situation, we get subtle pleasure out of it and can ignore the subtle pain. But both pleasurable and painful messages are equally potent.

What I am trying to say is that devotion to a teacher involves tremendous consequences. Reading this in itself can be dangerous. You are surrendering yourself, acknowledging that you have some kind of commitment. And if you go so far as to regard yourself as a student of spirituality, then you are not only siding with the goodness of the teaching but you are also embedding yourself into the soil of the teaching. Each time you fold your hands and bow, each time the teacher acknowledges your commitment, each time you light candles or incense at a shrine or sit in a meditation hall, you are rooting yourself more deeply. It is like planting a tree. Each time you water the plant, the roots grow further into the ground. Devotion is usually regarded as inconsequential. You bow and you get what you want. If you do not get it, you can walk away without any difficulty. Not so. Each bow creates a stronger umbilical cord. You become more deeply rooted in the teaching and more deeply rooted in the debt you have to repay to all sentient beings. It is extraordinarily demanding. Not realizing this is comparable to saying, "I'm doing the landlord a favor by moving into his property and signing a lease. I am doing him a favor so that he can make money from me." But you do not realize the consequence, that you are committed to pay rent as long as the lease is in effect. It is ordinary common logic.

Even if you try to pull yourself out of the relationship, some link will remain; you cannot completely undo your past. You cannot really leave without being touched. It is a terrible trap in that sense, an extraordinarily haunting thing. So realize what you are doing.

The Universality of Guru

Discipline goes hand in hand with devotion. They are both important to each other. We could say that discipline and devotion are like the two wings of a bird. Without both of them together there is no way to relate to the spiritual friend, teacher, or warrior. And without a spiritual friend there is no way to realize the teachings. And without the teachings there is no way of developing basic sanity. And without basic sanity there is no journey, no movement, there is no creative energy.

One of the problems of spiritual searching is that we tend to feel that we can help ourselves purely by reading a lot and practicing by ourselves, not associating ourselves with a particular lineage. Without a teacher to surrender to, without an object of devotion, we cannot free ourselves from spiritual materialism.

It is important first to develop a sense of devotion that allows us to be disowned by our ego. Devotion is a process of unlearning. If there is no devotion, no surrendering, we cannot unlearn. Of course we could say that sometimes even having a spiritual friend might generate further spiritual materialism as well. But it depends on the qualities of the friend and the communication of the student, whether a link is properly made or not. It is possible that a spiritual friend who is highly evolved could meet an embryonically highly evolved person and not form a proper link. Their chemistry together must produce a spark.

Each of the approaches to devotion that we have talked about has its place. We cannot begin immediately with the vajrayana devotional approach. It would be suicidal. It would be like an infant trying to imitate a grown-up. The various styles of devotion are not just progressive stages of development. They are also different aspects of each stage of development. One minute you might need a parental figure, another minute you feel sick and need a physician, another minute you might need warriorlike encouragement.

Nevertheless, we must start with the hinayana version of devotion which contains elements of the sympathy of the mahayana approach and the bravery of the vajrayana approach. But the external acts are predominantly hinayanist. Each stage along the path has its dominant themes. The hinayana approach to devotion is predominantly a simple relationship with your spiritual friend, a human relationship. The spiritual friend is not regarded as a god, saint, or angel, but he is regarded as a human being who has gone through tremendous discipline and learning. We can identify with this person because we can communicate with him. He is not a Martian who is pretending to be an earthman, but he is a son of man who grew up in this world and experienced all kinds of difficulties and was able to relate with the teaching and accomplish tremendous things. We can relate with this person without fantasizing all kinds of mysteries.

The hinayanist approach is very matter of fact: you are relating to another human being who happens to be accomplished. And the mahayanist approach is that this person is so highly accomplished that he is extraordinarily in tune with the events of everyday life. He has a perfectly constant awareness so that he does not miss a point. And he has developed exceedingly powerful compassion to live through your negativities. Your trying to walk on the spiritual path may be a big joke to your spiritual friend. You may act as an absolutely confused and absurd person. Nevertheless this person never gives up hope for you. He accepts you and goes through the irritations that you create. He is tremendously patient with you. You do something wrong and he instructs you how to correct it. But then you slip up or distort the instruction; you create further mistakes. You back to your spiritual friend and he says, "Fine, we can still work together, but now try this project," and you try again. You start with tremendous energy and confidence that you can do it. Several days later you get tired of the whole thing. You find something else with which to entertain yourself. The spiritual friend might ask you to do an intensive meditation practice without reading books, but you find that a book jumps into your lap and you cannot help reading it. It seems to be a part of the teaching as well. And you go back to the spiritual friend and say, "I followed your instructions but this book jumped into my lap and I could not help reading it." The spiritual friend then says, "That's fine. Did you learn anything from it? If you did, take the book and keep reading, find out what the book has to say in depth." And you go back and try to read the book, but you tire of reading. It's springtime. The flowers and trees and nature are so glamorous that you cannot help putting the book aside and taking a nice walk, enjoying the beauty of nature and the "meditative" state of being in nature. Following discipline is very difficult and you constantly create sidetracks by not realizing that you are sidetracking. The problem is not that you disobey your spiritual friend. In fact, the problem is that you are too serious; you find your sidetracks by being very serious. So it requires tremendous patience for your spiritual friend to work with you despite your slipping in and out of disciplines, despite your frivolousness.

A bodhisattva is like a crocodile: once you land in its mouth it never lets you go. If you were to want to leave your spiritual friend in order to live a free life away from such involvement, he would say, "That's great, do as you wish, go ahead and leave." By approving your leaving he removes the object of your rebellion, so instead of going away you come closer. It is a reciprocal situation: the guru's devotion to the student is intense and therefore the student's devotion begins to awaken, even if he is stupid and thick and burdened with all kinds of problems. The teacher's devotion to the student is compassion and the devotion of the student to the teacher is discipline. So compassion and discipline begin to meet together at some point.

And then we come to the vajrayana type of devotion in which you have given up fascination. You have identified with the path and the phenomenal world becomes an expression of the guru. There is a sense of devotion to the phenomenal world. You finally identify with the teachings and occasionally you act as a spokesman for them. Even to your own subconscious mind you act as their spokesman. If we are able to reach this level, then any events which occur in life have messages in them, have teachings in them. Teachings are everywhere. This is not a simple-minded notion of magic in the sense of gadgetry or trickery, but it is an astounding situation which you could interpret as magic. There is cause and effect involved. The events of your life act as a spokesman constantly and you cannot get away from this guru; in fact you do not want to because you identify with it. Thus the teachings become less claustrophobic, which enables you to discover the magical quality of life situations as a teaching.

Generally, devotion is regarded as coming from the heart rather than the head. But tantric devotion involves the head as well as the heart. For instance, the *Tibetan Book of the Dead* uses the symbolism of the peaceful deities coming out of your heart and the wrathful deities coming from your head. The vajrayana approach is a head approach—head plus heart together. The hinayana and mahayana approaches to devotion come from the heart. The tantric approach to life is intellectual in some sense because you begin to read the implications behind things. You begin to see messages that wake you up. But at the same time that intellect is not based upon speculation but is felt wholeheartedly, with one-hundred-percent heart. So we could say that the tantric approach to the messages of the all-pervading guru is to begin with intellect, which is transmuted into vajra intellect, and that begins to ignite the intuition of the heart at the same time.

This is the ideal fundamental union of prajna and shunyata, the union of eyes and heart together. Everyday events become self-existing teachings. Even the notion of trust does not apply any more. You might ask, "Who is doing this trusting?" Nobody! Trust itself is trusting itself. The mandala of self-existing energy does not have to be maintained by anything at all; it maintains itself. Space does not have a fringe or a center. Each corner of space is center as well as fringe. That is the all-pervading devotion in which the devotee is not separate from the object of devotion.

But before we indulge too much in such exciting and mystical language, we have to start very simply by giving, opening, displaying our ego, making a gift of our ego to our spiritual friend. If we are unable to do this, then the path never begins because there is nobody to walk on it. The teaching exists but the practitioner must acknowledge the teaching, must embody it.

EIGHT

Tantra

ALONENESS

THE SPIRITUAL PATH is not fun—better not begin it. If you must begin, then go all the way, because if you begin and quit, the unfinished business you have left behind begins to haunt you all the time. The path, as Suzuki Roshi mentions in *Zen Mind, Beginner's Mind*, is like getting on to a train that you cannot get off; you ride it on and on and on. The mahayana scriptures compare the bodhisattva vow of acceptance of the path to planting a tree. So stepping on the path involves you in continual growth, which may be tremendously painful since you sometimes try to step off the path. You do not really want to get into it fully; it is too close to the heart. And you are not able to trust in the heart. Your experiences become too penetrating, too naked, too obvious. Then you try to escape, but your avoidance creates pain which in turn inspires you to continue on the path. So your setbacks and suffering are part of the creative process of the path.

The continuity of the path is expressed in the ideas of ground tantra, path tantra, and fruition tantra. Ground tantra is acknowledging the potential that exists within you, that you are part of buddha nature, otherwise you would not be able to appreciate the teachings. And it acknowledges your starting point, your confusion and pain. Your suffering is truth; it is intelligent. The path tantra involves developing an attitude of richness and generosity. Confusion and pain are viewed as sources of inspiration, a rich resource. Furthermore, you acknowledge that you are intelligent and courageous, that you are able to be funda-

Mandala of the five buddha-wisdoms. These are the basic attributes of how enlightened mind perceives and manifests in the phenomenal world through the manner of the five wisdoms: wisdom of all-encompassing space, mirrorlike wisdom, wisdom of equanimity, discriminating-awareness wisdom, and wisdom of accomplishing all actions.
DRAWING BY GLEN EDDY.

mentally alone. You are willing to have an operation without the use of anesthetics, constantly unfolding, unmasking, opening on and on and on. You are willing to be a lonely person, a desolate person, are willing to give up the company of your shadow, your twenty-four-hour-a-day commentator who follows you constantly, the watcher.

In the Tibetan tradition the watcher is called *dzinba ('dzin pa)*, which means "fixation" or "holding." If we give up the watcher, then we have nothing left for which to survive, nothing left for which to continue. We give up hope of holding on to something. That is a very big step toward true asceticism. You have to give up the questioner and the answer—that is, discursive mind, the checking mechanism that tells you whether you are doing well or not doing well. "I am this, I am that." "Am I doing all right, am I meditating correctly, am I studying well, am I getting somewhere?" If we give all this up, then how do we know if we are advancing in spiritual practice? Quite possibly there is no such thing as spiritual practice except stepping out of self-deception, stopping our struggle to get hold of spiritual states. Just give that up. Other than that there is no spirituality. It is a very desolate situation. It is like living among snow-capped peaks with clouds wrapped around them and the sun and moon starkly shining over them. Below, tall alpine trees are swayed by strong, howling winds and beneath them is a thundering waterfall. From our point of view, we may appreciate this desolation if we are an occasional tourist who photographs it or a mountain climber trying to climb to the mountain top. But we do not really want to live in those desolate places. It's no fun. It is terrifying, terrible.

But it is possible to make friends with the desolation and appreciate its beauty. Great sages like Milarepa relate to the desolation as their bride. They marry themselves to desolation, to the fundamental psychological aloneness. They do not need physical or psychological entertainment. Aloneness becomes their companion, their spiritual consort, part of their being. Wherever they go they are alone, whatever they do they are alone. Whether they relate socially with friends or meditate alone or perform ceremonies together or meditate together, aloneness is there all the time. That aloneness is freedom, fundamental freedom. The aloneness is described as the marriage of shunyata and wisdom in which your perception of aloneness suggests the needlessness of dualistic occupation. It is also described as the marriage of shunyata and compassion in which aloneness inspires compassionate action in living situations. Such a discovery reveals the possibility of cutting through the karmic chain reactions that recreate ego-oriented situations, because that aloneness or the space of desolation does not entertain you, does not feed you anymore. Ultimate asceticism becomes part of your basic nature. We discover how samsaric occupations feed and entertain us. Once we see samsaric occu-

THE MYTH OF FREEDOM

pations as games, then that in itself is the absence of dualistic fixation, nirvana. Searching for nirvana becomes redundant at that point.

So at the beginning of the path we accept our basic qualities, which is ground tantra, and then we tread the path, which could be hot or cold, pleasurable or painful. In fruition tantra, which is beyond what we have discussed, we discover our basic nature. The whole process of the spiritual path, from the Buddhist point of view, is an organic one of natural growth: acknowledging the ground as it is, acknowledging the chaos of the path, acknowledging the colorful aspect of the fruition. The whole process is an endless odyssey. Having attained realization, one does not stop at that point, but one continues on, endlessly expressing buddha activity.

MANDALA

We found that in the mahayana or bodhisattva path there is still some kind of effort involved, not necessarily the effort of the heavy-handed ego, but there is still some kind of self-conscious notion that "I am practicing this, I am putting my effort into this." You know exactly what to do, there is no hesitation, action happens very naturally, but some solid quality of ego is still present in a faint way. At that stage a person's experience of shunyata meditation is very powerful, but still there is a need to relate to the universe more directly. This requires a leap rather than a disciplined effort, a generosity in the sense of willingness to open yourself to the phenomenal world, rather than merely being involved with a strategy of how to relate with it. Strategy becomes irrelevant and the actual perception of energy becomes more important.

One must transcend the ego's strategies—aggression, passion, and ignorance—and become completely one with those energies. We do not try to remove or destroy them, but we transmute their basic nature. This is the approach of the vajrayana, the tantric or yogic path. The word *yoga* means "union," complete identification, not only with the techniques of meditation and skillful, compassionate communication, but also with the energies that exist within the universe.

The word *tantra* means "continuity." The continuity of development along the path and the continuity of life experience becomes clearer and clearer. Every insight becomes a confirmation. The symbolism inherent in what we perceive becomes naturally relevant rather than being another fascinating or interesting imposition from outside, as though it were something we had never known about before. Visual symbolism, the sound symbolism of mantra, and the mental symbolism of feeling, of energy, all become relevant. Discovering a new way of looking at experience does not become a strain or too potent; it is a natural process. Complete union with the energy of the universe and seeing the relationships of things to each other as well as the vividness of things as they are is the mandala principle.

Mandala is a Sanskrit word that means "society," "group," "association." It implies that everything is centered around something. In the case of the tantric version of mandala, everything is centered around centerless space in which there is no watcher or perceiver. Because there is no watcher or perceiver, the fringe becomes extremely vivid. The mandala principle expresses the experience of seeing the relatedness of all phenomena, that there is a continual cycle of one experience leading to the next. The patterns of phenomena become clear because there is no partiality in one's perspective. All corners are visible, awareness is all-pervading.

The mandala principle of complete identification with aggression, passion, and ignorance is realized by practice of the father tantra, the mother tantra, and the union tantra. The father tantra is associated with aggression or repelling. By transmuting aggression, one experiences an energy that contains tremendous force. No confusion can enter into it; confusion is automatically repelled. It is called "vajra anger" since it is the diamondlike aspect of energy. Mother tantra is associated with seduction or magnetizing which is inspired by discriminating wisdom. Every texture of the universe or life is seen as containing a beauty of its own. Nothing is rejected and nothing is accepted but whatever you perceive has its own individual qualities. Because there is no rejection or acceptance, therefore the individual qualities of things become more obvious and it is easier to relate with them. Therefore discriminating wisdom appreciates the richness of every aspect of life. It inspires dancing with phenomena. This magnetizing is a sane version of passion. With ordinary passion we try to grasp one particular highlight of a situation and ignore the rest of the area in which that highlight is located. It is as if we try to catch a fish with a hook but are oblivious to the ocean in which the fish swims. Magnetizing in the case of mother tantra is welcoming every situation but with discriminating wisdom. Everything is seen precisely as it is, and thus there is no conflict. It does not bring indigestion. Union tantra involves transmuting ignorance into all-pervading space. In ordinary ignorance we try to maintain our individuality by ignoring our environment. But in the union tantra there is no maintenance of individuality. It is perception of the whole background of space, which is the opposite of the frozen space of ignorance.

To transmute aggression, passion, and ignorance one must be able to communicate with energy directly and completely, without strategizing. Someone who is involved with a completely open attitude to the universe does not have to try to work these things out intellectually or even intuitively by effort, but the orders of the universe are obvious to him. Whatever he perceives speaks to him. Often it is said in the scriptures that all sight is the visual mandala, all sound is the mantra mandala, all thought is chitta mandala, and the essence of consciousness is space. A person who perceives these mandalas does not see deities dancing around with strange mantras echoing, nor does he see space with all sorts of psychic flashes occurring in his mind. Such notions are a kindergarten view of heaven. If we literally see colors and shapes and hear mantras echoing in space and take note of them, we are actually confirming our ego. Quite likely we could get tired of hearing them and seeing them. Sooner or later we would want to run away from them, they would become too much, too constant. One might prefer to go to hell rather than remain in heaven. Hell might seem more exciting, more rugged.

In the ultimate experience of mandala the simple colors and shapes are metaphors. Of course if you see very vivid passion, you could paint a picture of it with all sorts of flames and ornaments. It is very interesting that tantric practitioners in India created an iconographic structure with divinities clothed in classical Indian royal costumes with turbans and crowns and jewels and rainbow-colored clothing. While in China, the tantric practitioners depicted deities wearing Chinese imperial dress, long brocade robes with big sleeves; they are seen with big moustaches and holding Chinese scepters. One might ask which depiction is more accurate. The Indians would say, "Ours is more accurate because we perceive it that way, we imagined it that way," and the Chinese would claim the same. We could say that both are accurate, and both are also inaccurate.

On the whole, understanding the vividness of the energy of the universe in terms of symbolism, in terms of patterns, colors, and shapes, is not a matter of imagination or hallucination for the real tantric practitioner. It is real. It is similar to a person hearing music that is very moving to him and feeling that he could almost carve statues out of it, that he could almost hold it, handle it. Sound becomes almost a solid object, almost a color or a shape. If a person is able to see the energies of the universe as they are, then shapes and colors and patterns suggest themselves; symbolism happens. That is the meaning of *mahamudra,* which means "great symbol." The whole world is symbol—not symbol in the sense of a sign representing something other than itself, but symbol in the sense of the highlights of the vivid qualities of things as they are.

Mahamudra Upadesa

Oral Instructions on Mahamudra Given by Sri Tilopa to Naropa at the Banks of the Ganges River

Translated from the Sanskrit into Tibetan by Chökyi Lodrö (Chos kyi bLo gros), Marpa the Translator

Homage to the Coemergent Wisdom![1]

Mahamudra cannot be shown;
But for you who are devoted to the guru, who have
    mastered the ascetic practices
And are forbearant in suffering, intelligent Naropa,
Take this to heart, my fortunate student.

Kye-ho![2]

Look at the nature of the world,
Impermanent like a mirage or dream;
Even the mirage or dream does not exist.
Therefore, develop renunciation and abandon worldly
    activities.

Renounce servants and kin, causes of passion and
    aggression.
Meditate alone in the forest, in retreats, in solitary places.
Remain in the state of nonmeditation.
If you attain nonattainment, then you have attained
    mahamudra.

The dharma[3] of samsara is petty, causing passion and
    aggression.
The things we have created have no substance; therefore,
    seek the substance of the ultimate.
The dharma of mind cannot see the meaning of
    transcendent mind.
The dharma of action cannot discover the meaning of
    nonaction.

If you would attain the realization of transcendent mind and
    nonaction,
Then cut the root of mind and let consciousness remain
    naked.
Let the polluted waters of mental activities clear.
Do not seek to stop projections, but let them come to rest
    of themselves.
If there is no rejecting or accepting, then you are liberated
    in the mahamudra.

When trees grow leaves and branches,
If you cut the roots, the many leaves and branches wither.
Likewise, if you cut the root of mind,
The various mental activities will subside.

The darkness that has collected in thousands of kalpas[4]
One torch will dispel.
Likewise, one moment's experience of luminous mind
Will dissolve the veil of karmic impurities.

Men of lesser intelligence who cannot grasp this,
Concentrate your awareness and focus on the breath.
Through different eye-gazes and concentration practices,
Discipline your mind until it rests naturally.

If you perceive space,
The fixed ideas of center and boundary dissolve.
Likewise, if mind perceives mind,
All mental activities will cease, you will remain in a state of
    nonthought,
And you will realize the supreme bodhichitta.[5]

Vapors arising from the earth become clouds and then
    vanish into the sky;
It is not known where the clouds go when they have
    dissolved.
Likewise, the waves of thoughts derived from mind
Dissolve when mind perceives mind.

Space has neither color nor shape;
It is changeless, it is not tinged by black or white.
Likewise, luminous mind has neither color nor shape;
It is not tinged by black or white, virtue or vice.

The sun's pure and brilliant essence
Cannot be dimmed by the darkness that endures for a
    thousand kalpas.
Likewise, the luminous essence of mind
Cannot be dimmed by the long kalpas of samsara.

Though it may be said that space is empty,
Space cannot be described.
Likewise, though it may be said that mind is luminous,
Naming it does not prove that it exists.
Space is completely without locality.
Likewise, mahamudra mind dwells nowhere.

Without change, rest loose in the primordial state;
There is no doubt that your bonds will loosen.
The essence of mind is like space;
Therefore, there is nothing which it does not encompass.

Let the movements of the body ease into genuineness,
Cease your idle chatter, let your speech become an echo,
Have no mind, but see the dharma of the leap.

The body, like a hollow bamboo, has no substance.
Mind is like the essence of space, having no place for
    thoughts.
Rest loose your mind; neither hold it nor permit it to
    wander.
If mind has no aim, it is mahamudra.
Accomplishing this is the attainment of supreme
    enlightenment.

The nature of mind is luminous, without object of
    perception.

You will discover the path of Buddha when there is no path
    of meditation.
By meditating on nonmeditation you will attain the
    supreme bodhi.[6]

This is the king of views—it transcends fixing and holding.[7]
This is the king of meditations—without wandering mind.
This is the king of actions—without effort.
When there is no hope and fear, you have realized the goal.

The unborn alaya[8] is without habits and veils.
Rest mind in the unborn essence; make no distinctions
    between meditation and postmeditation.
When projections exhaust the dharma of mind,
One attains the king of views, free from all limitations.

Boundless and deep is the supreme king of meditations.
Effortless self-existence is the supreme king of actions.
Hopeless self-existence is the supreme king of the fruition.

In the beginning mind is like a turbulent river.
In the middle it is like the River Ganges, flowing slowly.
In the end it is like the confluence of all rivers, like the
    meeting of son and mother.

The followers of tantra, the *Prajnaparamita,*
The Vinaya,[9] the sutras, and other religions—
All these, by their texts and philosophical dogmas,
Will not see the luminous mahamudra.

Having no mind, without desires,
Self-quieted, self-existing,
It is like a wave of water.
Luminosity is veiled only by the rising of desire.

The real vow of samaya[10] is broken by thinking in terms of
    precepts.
If you neither dwell, perceive, nor stray from the ultimate,
Then you are the holy practitioner, the torch which
    illumines darkness.

If you are without desire, if you do not dwell in extremes,
You will see the dharmas of all the teachings.

If you strive in this endeavor, you will free yourself from
    samsaric imprisonment.
If you meditate in this way, you will burn the veil of karmic
    impurities.
Therefore, you are known as "The Torch of the Doctrine."

Even ignorant people who are not devoted to this teaching
Could be saved by you from constantly drowning in the
    river of samsara.

It is a pity that beings endure such suffering in the lower
    realms.
Those who would free themselves from suffering should
    seek a wise guru.
Being possessed by the adhishthana,[11] one's mind will be
    freed.

If you seek a karmamudra,[12] then the wisdom of the union
    of joy and emptiness will arise.
The union of skillful means and knowledge brings blessings.
Bring it down and give rise to the mandala.
Deliver it to the places and distribute it throughout the
    body.

If there is no desire involved, then the union of joy and
    emptiness will arise.
Gain long life, without white hairs, and you will wax like
    the moon.
Become radiant, and your strength will be perfect.
Having speedily achieved the relative siddhis,[13] one should
    seek the absolute siddhis.
May this pointed instruction in mahamudra remain in the
    hearts of fortunate beings.

Notes to Mahamudra Upadesa

1. *Coemergent wisdom:* the primordial wisdom, born simultaneously with ignorance, just as nirvana and samsara must come simultaneously into being.

2. *Kye-ho!:* Hark! or Listen!

3. *Dharma:* here taken as law, pattern, path.

4. *Kalpas:* eons.

5. *Bodhichitta:* awakened mind.

6. *Bodhi:* the awakened state.

7. *Fixing and holding*—fixing: believing in the existence of a projector; holding: holding on to projections.

8. *Unborn alaya:* The dharmadhatu, the primordial state beyond being and nonbeing.

9. *Vinaya:* the scriptures containing the hinayana rules of discipline.

10. *Samaya:* the tantric vows of discipline.

11. *Adhishthana:* blessings, the atmosphere created by the guru.

12. *Karmamudra:* one's consort in the practice of the third abhisheka, the third initiation.

13. *Siddhis:* miraculous powers.

Ekajati with Samantabhadra above her head. Ekajati is a protectress of the dharma and a guide to the masters of tantric teachings. She is a destroyer of those who pervert the true meaning of the dharma. Samantabhadra is the primordial buddha who represents the final state of wakefulness.

DRAWING BY GLEN EDDY.

APPENDIX

The Ten Bhumis and Their Corresponding Paramitas

T HIS ORGANIZATION of the ten bhumis and the ten paramitas is taken from the *Dasabhumikasutra*.

Tibetan Pronunciation	Tibetan Spelling	Sanskrit	English
sa	sa	bhumi	stage
pharoltu chinpa	pha rol tu phyin pa	paramita	transcendental activity

THE TEN BHUMIS

1. raptu gawa	rab tu dga' ba	pramudita	very joyful
2. trima mepa	dri ma med pa	vimala	stainless
3. o jepa	'od byed pa	prabhakari	luminous
4. o trowa	'od 'phro ba	archismati	radiant
5. shintu jang kawa	shin tu sbyang dka' ba	sudurjaya	difficult to conquer
6. ngontu gyurpa	mngon du gyur pa	abhimukhi	face to face
7. ringtu songwa	ring du song ba	durangama	far going
8. mi yowa	mi g.yo ba	achala	immovable
9. legpe lotro	legs pa'i blo gros	sadhumati	having good intellect
10. chokyi trin	chos kyi sprin	dharmamegha	cloud of dharma

The Ten Paramitas

1. jinpa	sbyin pa	dana	generosity
2. tsültrim	tshul khrims	shila	discipline
3. sopa	bzod pa	kshanti	patience
4. tsöndrü	brtson 'grus	virya	exertion
5. samten	bsam gtan	dhyana	meditation
6. sherab	shes rab	prajna	knowledge
7. thap	thabs	upaya	skillful means
8. monlam	smon lam	pranidhana	vision
9. top	stobs	bala	power
10. yeshe	ye shes	jnana	wisdom

THE HEART OF THE BUDDHA

Edited by
JUDITH L. LIEF

Acknowledgments

I WOULD LIKE TO thank the many people who worked on the development of the articles included in this book. Especially I would like to thank my fellow members of the Vajradhatu Editorial Office, who over the years have taken primary responsibility for the editing and production of Trungpa Rinpoche's written work, including: Sherab Chödzin Kohn, Carolyn Rose Gimian, and Sarah Coleman. Each of these editors trained directly with Trungpa Rinpoche in how best to convey his spoken teachings in written form, and in the appropriate forms and levels of editing for different occasions and audiences. The articles collected in *The Heart of the Buddha* exhibit the resulting variety of editorial styles. Sherab Chödzin Kohn, who was the first Vajradhatu editor-in-chief, was the original editor for several of the articles included in this collection. He also edited *Garuda* magazine, where many of these articles were first published. Carolyn Gimian worked closely with Trungpa Rinpoche as my successor to the Vajradhatu editorial post and did the original editorial work on the "Sacred Outlook" article. She also did a careful reading of the book and gave much advice on the manuscript in its entirety. Sarah Coleman worked with Vajradhatu Editorial Office for many years, during which time she worked on a number of the articles in this collection.

The original production of the articles included in this collection involved the work of countless volunteers who carried out such tasks as tape recording, transcribing, typing, and manuscript checking. I would like to thank all of them for their donations of time and effort.

I would like to thank Mrs. Diana Mukpo for her kind permission to work with this material.

Most especially, I would like to thank the Venerable Chögyam Trungpa for his tireless efforts in leading students on the path of awakening.

JUDITH L. LIEF
Editor

Editor's Foreword

THE HEART OF THE BUDDHA is a collection of fifteen previously published articles by the Venerable Chögyam Trungpa Rinpoche. In choosing the particular articles to be included, the intent was to introduce the reader to as complete a range of Rinpoche's teachings as possible. For that reason, both introductory essays and more technical or scholarly presentations have been included. Some articles were written for particular publications or for distribution among his students. Others were derived from seminars and talks he gave over his teaching career; as such, they embody the living quality of oral transmission and the importance of discussion and dialogue between student and teacher.

In his many seminars, Trungpa Rinpoche was careful always to balance the role of practice and of study. Students attending such seminars always spent time in formal meditation practice as well as in studying the Buddha's teachings through lectures, reading, and discussion groups. In that way, they could test their understanding through the mechanism of their own experience, so that refinement of intellectual understanding could be accompanied by a deepening of insight.

PERSONAL JOURNEY

At the heart of the Buddhist path is the practice of meditation. The development of mindfulness and awareness is an essential foundation for both understanding ourselves and working with others. It is a common preconception that the spiritual journey takes us away from ourselves, to some higher or more peaceful existence. In this context, meditation practice is seen as a kind of drug, or as a way of removing ourselves from the harsh realities of life. However, throughout his teachings, Trungpa Rinpoche stressed that meditation practice is not an escape but a way to "begin at the beginning."

In beginning the path, we need to be willing to confront ourselves directly, without either wishful thinking or harsh judgmentalism. Through the practice of meditation, we are constantly brought back to working with what is, rather than with what might be; we are constantly brought back to "square one." So at the heart of the very personal journey of meditation practice is the willingness simply to be who we are. It is a process of acceptance rather than one of manipulation.

While each student's journey is a solitary one, it is through the meeting of student and teacher that the spiritual path is awakened. The teacher-student relationship is of central importance in the Buddhist tradition. Devotion is the key to unlocking the power of the tradition. However, this concept is quite subtle, and we must be careful to distinguish genuine devotion from the naive approach of blind faith.

STAGES ON THE PATH

According to the Tibetan system, an individual student's journey has three main stages: hinayana, mahayana, and vajrayana. (In this context, these terms are simply descriptive of stages of the path and should not be confused with their more common usage as names for historical schools of Buddhist thought.) These three stages work together in a very powerful way. The hinayana marks the beginning stage, in which one explores the workings of one's own mind and emotions and begins to settle the mind through the practice of meditation. This allows one to lessen one's sense of struggle and to begin to make friends with oneself. In the second stage, mahayana, this friendliness begins to extend outward. There is a great appreciation for the phenomenal world as well as an understanding of the depth of suffering of fellow sentient beings. This gives rise to compassion and the intent to work for the benefit of others. The third stage, or vajrayana, is one of not holding back but of extending fearlessly to any situation that arises. There is a willingness to relate directly to the wisdom and power of one's mind and emotions, as evoked in visualization practice and tantric ritual.

While these may be viewed as three stages, they must all work together in a balanced way if the journey is to be successful. That is, each stage expands upon and enriches the previous stage, reawakening its insight in a broader context. So each serves to complement and enrich the others.

WORKING WITH OTHERS

The insights gained through the formal practice of meditation can be applied to the variety of circumstances we encounter in our day-to-day lives. So daily life is not rejected, or viewed as simply a distraction to our "spiritual" practice. Instead, by joining practice and ordinary life, the entirety of our experience is seen as valuable and, in fact, sacred.

Although classically trained in the ancient tradition of Tibetan Buddhism, Trungpa Rinpoche was immensely interested in the workings of modern society and in the social implications of the Buddhist teachings. Therefore he gave considerable attention in his talks and seminars to such issues as education, health care, the raising of children, the nature of relationships, and the conduct of business.

It is hoped that this collection of essays will give the reader a sense of the richness and variety of Trungpa Rinpoche's teachings and of their relevance in day-to-day life.

Part One

PERSONAL JOURNEY

ONE

What Is the Heart of the Buddha?

"Fundamentally speaking, ladies and gentlemen, here is the really good news, if we may call it that: We are intrinsically buddha and we are intrinsically good. Without exception and without the need for analytical studies, we can say that we automatically have buddha within us. That is known as buddha nature, or bodhichitta, the heart of the buddha."

IN BUDDHISM, THERE are three codes of discipline, known as shila, samadhi, and prajna. Shila is discipline or conduct, a certain meditative way of behaving. Samadhi is the practice of mindfulness/awareness: the totality of your state of mind can be experienced without distraction. And prajna, or discriminating awareness, is the state of clarity in which you are able to distinguish different states of mind; you are no longer excited or depressed by particular states of mind. These three disciplines bring us to the next stage—of finally transcending the deception of ego, which is the experience of egolessness.

Egohood is the state of mind in which you are either repelled by or attracted to the phenomenal world. What you would like to see depends on your mentality, on what you think is desirable in order to maintain your "I am-ness," your "me-ness." We are talking about transcending "I am-ness," "me-ness," which is called egolessness.

Egolessness doesn't mean that you are going to be completely

Based on a talk from "Conquering Ego's Deception," Cape Breton, 1981.

dissolved into nothingness. In Western literature, Buddhism is often accused of saying this, especially in early Victorian Christian literature, as well as in various high school courses on Buddhism. They say Buddhists believe in nothingness, which is certainly not the case.

Egolessness means less "maniac-ness," in some sense—free from being an egomaniac. Egomania has several levels of subtlety. Ordinarily people think of an egomaniac as an obvious maniac, but if we study enough and look enough, we will see that there are subtleties of egomania. The dictators of the world could be seen as egomaniacal people, obviously, because they perform their functions in that way. But more ordinary people also function in that way, including ourselves in some sense. We would like to possess our world, and so we act in such a way that whatever we see around us is completely in order, according to our desire to maintain the security of "me," "myself"—which is egohood.

Inspired by means of shila, samadhi, and prajna—discipline, meditation, and discriminating awareness—we have freedom from egomaniac-ness, freedom from egohood. Beyond that, seeing through our own egomaniac-ness, we give birth to, or awaken, our innate greater existence, which is known as bodhichitta in Sanskrit.

Bodhi, which is related to *buddha*, literally means "awake." *Buddha* is a noun; *bodhi* is an epithet or an adjective for awakened ones, or for those who are in the process of awakening. *Chitta* is a Sanskrit word meaning "heart" or, occasionally, "essence." So bodhichitta is the essence of the buddha, the essence of the awakened ones.

We cannot give birth to the essence of the awakened ones unless we train, to begin with, in meditation practice: the shamatha discipline of mindfulness and the vipashyana discipline of awareness. Beyond that, it is necessary to fulfill the three disciplines of shila, samadhi, and prajna. That is, we know what to do and what not to do.

When we practice shila, samadhi, and prajna, we begin to be aware of the buddha in us. It is not that those principles *produce* buddhalike awareness particularly; we have that essence in us already. But shila, samadhi, and prajna bring us into the actual realization of who we are, what we are, finally.

According to the Buddhist tradition, we don't get *new* wisdom, nor does any foreign element come into our state of mind at all. Rather, it is a question of waking up and shedding our covers. We have those goodies in us already; we only have to uncover them.

The logic here is, if we have to transplant foreign goodie-ness into our system, it does not belong to us; it remains foreign. Because it is not part of us, it is likely to cease to exist at some point. Sooner or later, our basic nature is bound to reject that foreign transplant in our system. (Maybe this logic doesn't apply to heart transplants. These days they say if you have a foreign heart transplanted in you, you might live; you might survive.)

But here we are talking about awakening what we haven't already awakened. It is as if we have been kept in captivity and haven't been able to exercise our faculties properly; our activities have been controlled by circumstances. Giving birth to bodhichitta in one's heart, buddha in one's heart, brings extra freedom. That is the notion of *freedom* in Buddhism, altogether. Of course, when we talk about freedom, we are not talking about overthrowing the head of the state or anything like that: we are talking about freedom from the constriction of our own capabilities.

It is as if we were extraordinary children, possessing all sorts of genius, and we were being undermined by the society around us, which was dying to make us normal people. Whenever we would show any mark of genius, our parents would get embarrassed. They would try to put the lid on our pot, saying, "Charles, don't say those things. Just be like an ordinary person." That is what actually happens to us, with or without our parents.

I don't particularly want to blame our parents alone; we have also been doing this to ourselves. When we see something extraordinary, we are afraid to say so; we are afraid to express ourselves or to relate to such situations. So we put lids on ourselves—on our potential, our capabilities. But in Buddhism we are liberated from that kind of conventionality.

According to Buddhist terminology, *conventionality* refers to belief in habitual patterns. Conventional realities are synonymous with habitual patterns; and the authors of habitual patterns are ignorance and desire. Ignorance and desire go against shila discipline; they go against samadhi mindfulness, because they prevent us from keeping our minds on the point; and they go against prajna, because they develop dullness rather than discriminating sharpness.

Fundamentally speaking, ladies and gentlemen, here is the really good news, if we may call it that: We are intrinsically buddha and we are intrinsically good. Without exception, and without the need for analytical studies, we can say that we automatically have buddha within us. That is known as buddha nature, or bodhichitta, the heart of the buddha.

We might ask ourselves, "What is the heart of the buddha like? Does it think the way we do? Does it want to have fish and chips or is it just a pious heart that does nothing but religious things alone? Would that heart be the most holy heart of all, from a Christian point of view?" The answer is no. That heart is not necessarily pious.

The heart of the buddha is a very open heart. That heart would like to explore the phenomenal world; it is open to relating with others. That heart contains tremendous strength and confidence in itself, which is called fearlessness. That heart is also extremely inquisitive, which at this point is synonymous with prajna. It is expansive and sees in all directions. And that heart contains certain basic qualities, which we could call our true *basic genes*—our buddha-genes. We all possess those particular buddha-genes. Isn't it strange to say that the mind has genes? But it turns out to be true.

These buddha-genes have two characteristics. First, they are able to see through, as well as not be afraid of, the reality of the phenomenal world. We might come up with obstacles and difficulties of all kinds, but those particular genes are not afraid to deal with them. We just shed the coverings of such possibilities as we go along. Second, these genes also contain gentleness; they are ever so loving, which goes beyond just being kind. They are extremely tender and capable of reflecting themselves, even to those who don't want to relate with them. And they are absolutely free from any form of aggression. They are so soft and kind.

The buddha-genes are also full of a sense of humor and delight, which is referred to as *great joy*. When you are able to experience that such genes exist within you, you begin to feel cheerful and smile and have a sense of humor.

There are two different kinds of humor. One kind of humor comes from not taking the world seriously: you come up with all sorts of jokes about other people's problems. The other kind is a general sense of joy. Nothing is regarded as downgrading; everything is uplifted, constantly. Here we are talking about the second kind of humor.

From the practitioner's point of view, we have all sorts of disciplines to awaken our enlightened genes. The main discipline is known as exchanging oneself for other. That is to say, we completely identify with others' pain; and we project out, or give away, pleasure altogether. In that way, we begin to see through, and actually expose, the clumsiness of how we hold on to ourselves.

Let us have a short discussion.

Student: Rinpoche, I was wondering about the second characteristic of the buddha-genes. Is this tender loving quality present all the time or just at certain moments?

Trungpa Rinpoche: That's an interesting question. Can I ask you a question back? Does a fire have the potential of blazing when it's at the level of a spark? What would you say?

S: I guess it depends on the circumstances.

TR: What kind of circumstances would they be?

S: Well, if you were in a garage with gas fumes, or if you were out in an open field—

TR: Sure, sure. But, intrinsically speaking, in itself does it have that potential?

S: I will agree that it could blaze up.

TR: It could blaze up and blow up our garage, right? I am talking about exactly the same thing. In itself, the buddha-gene is capable of the whole thing.

Student: Sir, what is the difference between meditation-in-action and sitting meditation? I have the impression that when I am working on a sculpture in my studio, lots of insight is given to me. That seems as important to me as straight sitting. Is there anything wrong with that?

Trungpa Rinpoche: Well, it's an interesting point, you see. We were just talking about fire. Somebody first has to make the fire; then it blazes. In the same way, you might have the intuition that you don't have to do sitting practice. You might feel you have the experience of that already, which I don't doubt. Probably a lot of people do. Nonetheless, we do need some kind of field training. We have to know how to relate with reality, and we also have to know how to develop discipline. If we sit and practice shamatha-vipashyana meditation, probably nothing will happen for a long period of time. And the idea isn't that anything *should* happen to us. We are just silent.

At the end of the letter you sent me, you signed off *paix,* "peace." Real peace is nonaction; that is the source of all action. We have to learn how to be a rock in order to be a tree or a flower or wind or lightning

313

or a typhoon. We have to be still, then we go beyond that. Therefore sitting practice is very important.

We are not particularly training ourselves to destroy or conquer the world. We are trying to relate to the world in the same way that we relate to the birth of our first child or, for that matter, to our own orgasm—which happens, I hope, when we make love. Anything active that happens has some relationship to that very stillness. That stillness is not vacant or deadly; it is full of energy, automatically.

So that is the difference between postmeditation and meditation itself. Meditation prepares us for action, and sometimes action prepares us for nonaction. It is like breathing in and out: when you breathe out, it's action; but in order to breathe out you have to breathe in again. It goes on that way. So it is important to have a very strict discipline of being still and solid. Out of that comes a lot of energy and a lot of wisdom. Meditation and postmeditation are equally valid in our lives—just as breathing in and breathing out are both important.

S: Merci beaucoup.

Student: Rinpoche, could you say a little bit about vipashyana mediation? You mentioned it in your talk, but I'm not really sure what it is.

Trungpa Rinpoche: Vipashyana is a Sanskrit word which literally means "seeing clearly." In Tibetan we use the word *lhakthong. Lhak* means "superior" and *thong* means "seeing." So *lhakthong* means "clear seeing," "superior seeing."

Vipashyana begins once we have developed substantial shamatha discipline of being precise and mindful, on the spot, all the time. In shamatha, sound, smell, feeling, thought process, and everything else are looked at, but with such precision that they are nothing other than stillness. They don't produce further bubbles, or further percolation, of any kind at all.

You might say, "Ah, I thought of my father telling me no." At that moment, both your father and the idea of him saying "No, don't do that" are divided into now, now, now, all the time. Everything is chopped into that level of precision, into a grain of sand. That is shamatha.

Usually, memory is predominant in everything you experience. If you are sitting in a meditation hall and the smell of food comes from the kitchen, you think about what kind of dinner they are cooking for you. Or else, you feel the ache in your buttocks and back and you want to shift around. Shamatha means that everything is simply looked at. It is sliced up, but not aggressively; it is just looked at—look, look, look.

Through shamatha you are capable of looking at these experiences as individual entities, without referring to the past and without thinking about where they are going, or what they are going to do to you. Everything is without beginning and without end, just on the spot. If you think of onion soup and how you would like to go out and *get* onion soup, it is only on the level of thought. So you chop your thoughts—now, now, now.

Out of that comes vipashyana. On the level of vipashyana, you chop thoughts because of your training in shamatha, but at the same time you bring them along. The world is a panoramic view, but at the same time things really don't hang together the way they ordinarily used to.

Things are made out of pieces of simple realities, primitive realities. Even if you smell onions for a long time—for half an hour—those smells are chopped into pieces: you smell them, then you don't smell them, you smell them, then you don't smell them. Otherwise, if there were no gap, you couldn't smell at all.

Experiences are not continuous at the ego level. We think they are all together, in cahoots, but it doesn't really happen that way. Everything is made out of dots. When experiences are chopped into small pieces, some realization of the unity of the display could come out of that. That is vipashyana.

You begin to feel good when, for instance, you touch a rock, because you feel that the rock is not a continuous rock, but the rock of the moment. When you hold your fan, it is the fan of the moment; when you blink, your blink is of the moment; when you meet your friends, they are friends of the moment. Nothing is expected and nothing is demanded any more. Everything is seen clearly.

Clear seeing: that is the definition of vipashyana, which is the result of shamatha. Things could be seen as a great display, as a Disney world, or whatever you want to call it. You realize that things are not all that together. But because they are not together, they are fantastically colorful. The more you see the mark of discontinuity, the more you see things as colorful. In order to see color you have to take a rest; then you see color again. So you see, you rest, and then you see brilliance again. That is the precision of how to perceive the phenomenal world.

Student: Rinpoche, you said to an earlier questioner that you hoped he would have pleasure experiencing his orgasm. In my experience, I have some confusion about whether pleasure is pleasurable. Since I haven't gotten over aggression and passion, how can I relate to things at all—if pleasure isn't pleasurable and pain isn't particularly painful, and I'm still caught in that way?

Trungpa Rinpoche: Well, the point is that there is no such thing as pleasure per se. In other words, different people experience so-called pleasure entirely differently, depending on their state of mind, where they are coming from, and how they are going to proceed after the pleasure. Pleasure is not a solid thing.

Sometimes people get very angry and discouraged when they go back to a restaurant where they had great pleasure before, and they find that the food is lousy and the service is not so good. So they complain to the manager.

One doesn't get the expected services or expected situations *any* time. I am not the same Trungpa you saw a few days ago. I am a fresh, new Trungpa—right now! And I will always be that way. I will be dead and gone tonight, and right now, this very moment, I am dying and being born. So the next time I give a talk, I will be entirely different.

You can't rely on one particular reference point. In some sense that is extraordinarily fresh and feels good, but on the other hand it may be sad, because you want to hang onto the past, constantly. Until there's enough familiarity with the mentality of shamatha and vipashyana, you won't understand this. And that practice of shamatha/vipashyana goes on, up to the level of vajrayana discipline, as well.

When you see a fantastic display, it is chopped into little pieces. This allows you to breathe, because there's a gap between the pieces; therefore you begin to appreciate those pieces altogether. I don't think I can say it more vividly than that. You actually have to do it. "Seeing is believing," as they say in the English language.

S: Thank you very much.

TR: You're more than welcome.

Student: Sir, earlier tonight you were talking about how we put a lid on ourselves, and how it is the nature of one's heart to be inquisitive. And yet within Buddhism there is a notion of ethics. There are certain ways to do things and certain ways not to do things.

In my own personal experience, when I feel inquisitive sometimes I flash back on Buddhist ethics, as a reference point for whether I am doing the proper thing. But I sometimes wonder how much I should stick to the scriptures and how much I should just go ahead and be inquisitive. My question is, how does one know when to put a lid on oneself and when to go forward?

Trungpa Rinpoche: It's purely up to you. That is to say, you have to have enough training, or at least understanding of the momentariness of your mind. Your mind doesn't continue, therefore you appreciate the world. Then you can go on to explore further.

There is no particular dogma that goes with that; there's no particular guideline either, apart from having erect posture and imitating the Buddha. You can do that. You will never be referred to as being presumptuous.

S: So, I should just keep on practicing.

TR: Keep on practicing, yes.

TWO

Intellect and Intuition

"The transition from knowledge to wisdom is not simply one of first acquiring knowledge and then suddenly becoming wise. The definition of wisdom is that one intuitively knows everything already; it is independent of amassing information. But we do not seem to know how to make this transition from intellect to wisdom. There seems to be a very big gap between them, and we are uncertain as to how to handle it, how to become both a scholar and a yogi. We seem to need a mediator. That mediator is compassion, or warmth: knowledge is transformed into wisdom by means of compassion."

THERE SEEM TO BE two distinct approaches to the spiritual path: the intellectual and the intuitive. In the intellectual tradition, spiritual development is viewed as a sharpening of intellectual precision, primarily through the study of theology. Whereas in the intuitive or mystical tradition, spiritual development is viewed as a deepening of awareness or devotion through practices such as meditation. However, neither the intellectual nor the intuitive approach is complete without the other. These two approaches are not in opposition to one another. Rather they are two channels which combine to form the spiritual path.

Let us examine the intellectual and intuitive traditions in more detail. In the West, the intellectual tradition has for a long time been predomi-

---

Opening talk, 1973 Vajradhatu Seminary, Teton Village, Wyoming.

nant. And in some Buddhist countries the emphasis on scholasticism has grown so strong that Buddhist scholars have completely lost touch with the meditative tradition. Buddhists who emphasize the scholarly side of the teaching frequently feel that it is dangerous to begin meditating until they have mastered the theory. So they begin the spiritual path by studying very intensely and becoming extremely learned. But then, when they have discovered everything intellectually and completely mastered the theories of Buddhism, they feel they no longer need to meditate because they have all the answers already. Adherents of this approach view the Buddha as a superscholar and enlightenment as being totally informed.

Adherents of the intuitive tradition, on the other hand, regard study and analysis as obstacles to spiritual development. Seeing the irrelevance of acquiring knowledge disconnected from personal experience, they tend to react by rejecting the intellectual approach altogether. Instead they stress the practice of meditation as the only way to develop insight. From their viewpoint, in order to attain enlightenment one does not need to know anything at all. The Buddha is regarded as the perfect meditator; and the more beautifully one can sit and meditate, the closer one is to enlightenment.

By focusing on only one aspect of experience, each of these approaches to spirituality remains only partial. The contemplative traditions of Buddhism, such as the Tibetan and Zen traditions, while emphasizing meditation practice very strongly, see study as something which should go alongside it. It is felt that a student cannot rely on meditation practice alone without sharpening his intelligence. The idea is that one first needs some grounding in meditation practice. Then one can begin to work with the intellectual aspect of the tradition. In this way study becomes a confirmation of experience rather than simply the acquisition of banks of irrelevant information. Rather than becoming a stupid meditator or an absent-minded intellectual, the student can become an intelligent yogi—a scholar and a practitioner at the same time.

The notion of enlightenment transcends the limitations of both the contemplative and the scholarly traditions. As a description of human wholeness, it expresses the flavor of the Buddhist approach to spirituality. The dawn of enlightenment could be described as a form of absorption. But that does not mean it is a trancelike state in which one loses contact with the world around one. It is a sense of totality and a sense of openness which does not seem to have any beginning or end. Such a state of being is known as vajra-like samadhi. The notion of *vajra* is that of psychological indestructibility. Because that quality of sanity does not have any gaps or faults, because it is thoroughly united with its own faculties, it cannot be destroyed. And samadhi refers to the stillness of intelligence, which is self-existing rather than constantly speeding along trying to find a conclusion to everything. Vajra-like samadhi is a three-fold process consisting of prajna, which is the highest form of intellect; karuna, which is the highest form of compassion; and jnana, which is the highest form of wisdom.

Prajna, or intellect, is completely intuitive as well as intellectually precise. The working of prajna is such that when we pay proper attention to persons or situations, they automatically give us answers or understanding. So we do not have to analyze or to cultivate our intelligence anymore. That quality of intelligence seems to be all-pervasive—but at the same time it is to the point. It is sharp, precise, and direct, but not in the limited manner of a chisel or a thumbtack.

Karuna, or compassion, is another attribute of the process of samadhi. *Karuna* is usually translated as "compassion." However, the word *compassion* is filled with connotations in English which have nothing to do with karuna. So it is important to clarify what is meant by enlightened compassion and how it differs from our usual notion of compassion. Usually we think of a compassionate person as someone who is kind and gentle and who never loses his temper. Such a person is always willing to forgive our mistakes and to comfort us. But enlightened compassion is not quite as simple-minded as that notion of a kindly, well-meaning soul.

An analogy often used in the Buddhist tradition is that true compassion is like a fish and prajna is like water. That is, intellect and compassion are dependent on one another; but at the same time, each has its own life and its own functions. Compassion is a state of calmness; it also involves intelligence and enormous vitality. Without intelligence and skillfulness, compassion can degenerate into a bungling sort of charity. For instance, if we give food to someone who is extremely hungry, he will temporarily recover from his hunger. But he gets hungry every day. And if we keep giving food to that person, eventually he will learn that whenever he is hungry he can get food from us. At that point we have succeeded in turning that person into a jellyfish who is unwilling to explore the possibility of getting food for himself. Such an approach is, in fact, uncompassionate compassion, or compassion without skillful means. It is known as idiot compassion.

True compassion is spacious and wise as well as resourceful. In this type of compassion we do not just blindly launch into a project but we look into situations dispassionately. There is a sense of priorities as to which situations should be handled immediately and which are worth putting off. This type of compassion could be called intelligent love or intelligent affection. We know how to express our affection so that it does not destroy a person but instead helps him to develop. It is more like a dance than a hug. And the music behind it is that of prajna, or intellect.

So the stage is set by the dance of compassion and the music of prajna. And the setting in which this dance takes place is known as jnana, or wisdom, which is the whole perspective, the entire panorama.

Let us examine in greater detail how these three qualities of enlightenment—knowledge, compassion, and wisdom—are interrelated. We begin with prajna, or knowledge: we need to know where we are; we have to explore our environment, our particular location in time and space. So knowledge comes first, and wisdom comes later. Once we have knowledge as to where we are, then we can become wise because we do not have to struggle with our bearings. We do not have to fight for our position. So, in a sense, wisdom is an expression of nonviolence: we do not have to fight for it because we are already wise.

The transition from knowledge to wisdom is not simply one of first acquiring knowledge and then suddenly becoming wise. The definition of wisdom is that one intuitively knows everything already; it is independent of amassing information. But we do not seem to know how to make this transition from intellect to wisdom. There seems to be a very big gap between them, and we are uncertain as to how to handle it, how to become both a scholar and a yogi. We seem to need a mediator. That mediator is compassion, or warmth: knowledge is transformed into wisdom by means of compassion.

We may begin by collecting all kinds of information, trying to become great scholars or walking books. In fact, prajna is a very scholarly process in which we acquire enormous amounts of information and logic. At this level we can handle our experience logically, even mathematically. But how do we make that knowledge part of ourselves rather than purely an assortment of lists of information?

When we develop prajna in its fullest sense, psychologically and spiritually, then we may begin to develop a sense of friendliness or warmth not only toward ourselves but also toward the world. This does not mean boosting our egos—patting ourselves on the back for all the Ph.D.'s we have earned. Instead, friendliness is a kind of fascination for our collection of ideas and knowledge; we have become fascinated by the world and extremely curious as to what it is all about. For instance, in the West great scientists like Einstein have been known to become rather eccentric. They seem to transcend ordinary logic and to become extremely individualistic. As they become absorbed by their knowledge, or prajna, they begin to develop a quality of softness or eccentricity. That eccentricity seems to be the area of compassion, in which there is room to journey back and forth between being wise and being knowledgeable. In this state of mind, there is no gap between intellect and intuition. Instead, there is simply a further development of energy, which is called compassion.

As the energy of compassion develops, we begin to celebrate what we have discovered. We begin to like the knowledge we have acquired. We have seen the way things work, and now we begin to take that understanding personally. We would like to share it with everyone. There is an enormous celebration taking place. We do not need to prove our ideas to anybody, and we do not feel that we are under attack. There is a sense of joy in being part of this knowledge, and that sense of joy, which triggers the transition from knowledge to wisdom, is compassion, or unconditional love.

It seems to take a long time for us to get to the point of being wise, where we no longer need external reinforcement or encouragement—or, in fact, any external reference point at all. Such wisdom is extremely inventive; rather than needing to study each detail of a particular area, we simply sense the whole area intuitively and very precisely. We are very much in tune with things. That is why the Buddha is known as the Omniscient One. It is not because he was a great scholar who read all the books and therefore had all the information, but because he had an accurate general sense of everything. At the level of wisdom, or jnana, all the conceptual master plans of the world or the universe have been seen through, so facts and figures do not play a particularly important part.

As individuals on the spiritual path, we experience more and more glimpses of this enlightened state. To give a somewhat negative analogy, if we develop a terminal illness, at first we may feel an attack of sickness just once a month. But as we go on, our sickness becomes worse and the attacks become more frequent, maybe once a day. Then the attacks of sickness come every day—in fact, several times a day. And finally we face death because the attacks of sickness are constant; the sickness has become overwhelming. The death of ego, or the development of enlightenment, happens in the same way. We do not consciously have to create the experience of enlightenment—it just happens. It comes to us as our life situation evolves.

THREE

The Four Foundations of Mindfulness

"As far as meditation practice is concerned, in meditation we work on this thing, rather than on trying to sort out the problem from the outside. We work on the projector rather than the projection. We turn inward, instead of trying to sort out external problems of A, B, and C. We work on the creator of duality rather than the creation. That is beginning at the beginning."

FOR THE FOLLOWER of the buddhadharma, the teachings of Buddhism, there is a need for great emphasis on the practice of meditation. One must see the straightforward logic that mind is the cause of confusion and that by transcending confusion one attains the enlightened state. This can only take place through the practice of meditation. The Buddha himself experienced this, by working on his own mind; and what he learned has been handed down to us.

Mindfulness is a basic approach to the spiritual journey that is common to all traditions of Buddhism. But before we begin to look closely at that approach, we should have some idea of what is meant by spirituality itself. Some say that spirituality is a way of attaining a better kind of happiness, transcendental happiness. Others see it as a benevolent way to develop power over others. Still others say the point of spirituality is to acquire magical powers so we can change our bad world into a good world or purify the world through miracles. It seems that all of these

---

Remarks on meditation practice, 1973 Vajradhatu Seminary.

points of view are irrelevant to the Buddhist approach. According to the buddhadharma, spirituality means relating with the working basis of one's existence, which is one's state of mind.

There is a problem with one's basic life, one's basic being. This problem is that we are involved in a continual struggle to survive, to maintain our position. We are continually trying to grasp onto some solid image of ourselves. And then we have to defend that particular fixed conception. So there is warfare, there is confusion, and there is passion and aggression; there are all kinds of conflicts. From the Buddhist point of view, the development of true spirituality is cutting through our basic fixation, that clinging, that stronghold of something-or-other, which is known as ego.

In order to do that we have to find out what ego is. What is this all about? Who are we? We have to look into our already existing state of mind. And we have to understand what practical step we can take to do that. We are not involved here in a metaphysical discussion about the purpose of life and the meaning of spirituality on an abstract level. We are looking at this question from the point of view of a working situation. We need to find some simple thing we can do in order to embark on the spiritual path.

People have difficulty beginning a spiritual practice because they put a lot of energy into looking for the best and easiest way to get into it. We might have to change our attitude and give up looking for the best or the easiest way. Actually, there is no choice. Whatever approach we take, we will have to deal with what we are already. We have to look at who we are. According to the Buddhist tradition, the working basis of the path and the energy involved in the path is the mind—one's own mind, which is working in us all the time.

Spirituality is based on mind. In Buddhism, mind is what distinguishes sentient beings from rocks or trees or bodies of water. That which possesses discriminating awareness, that which possesses a sense of duality—which grasps or rejects something external—that is mind. Fundamentally, it is that which can associate with an "other"—with any "something" that is perceived as different from the perceiver. That is the definition of mind. The traditional Tibetan phrase defining mind means precisely that: "That which can think of the other, the projection, is mind."

So by mind we mean something very specific. It is not just something very vague and creepy inside our heads or hearts, something that just happens as part of the way the wind blows and the grass grows. Rather, it is something very concrete. It contains perception—perception that is very uncomplicated, very basic, very precise. Mind develops its particular nature as that perception begins to linger on something other than oneself. Mind makes the fact of perceiving something else stand for the existence of oneself. That is the mental trick that constitutes mind. In fact, it should be the opposite. Since the perception starts from oneself, the logic should be: "I exist, therefore the other exists." But somehow the hypocrisy of mind is developed to such an extent that mind lingers on the other as a way of getting the feedback that it itself exists, which is a fundamentally erroneous belief. It is the fact that the existence of self is questionable that motivates the trick of duality.

This mind is our working basis for the practice of meditation and the development of awareness. But mind is something more than the process of confirming self by the dualistic lingering on the other. Mind also includes what are known as *emotions,* which are the highlights of mental states. Mind cannot exist without emotions. Daydreaming and discursive thoughts are not enough. Those alone would be too boring. The dualistic trick would wear too thin. So we tend to create waves of emotion which go up and down: passion, aggression, ignorance, pride—all kinds of emotions. In the beginning we create them deliberately, as a game of trying to prove to ourselves that we exist. But eventually the game becomes a hassle; it becomes more than a game and forces us to challenge ourselves more than we intended. It is like a hunter who, for the sport of practicing his shooting, decides to shoot one leg of a deer at a time. But the deer runs very fast, and it appears it might get away altogether. This becomes a total challenge to the hunter, who rushes after the deer, now trying to kill it completely, to shoot it in the heart. So the hunter has been challenged and feels defeated by his own game.

Emotions are like that. They are not a requirement for survival; they are a game we developed that went wrong at some point—it went sour. In the face of this predicament we feel terribly frustrated and absolutely helpless. Such frustration causes some people to fortify their relationship to the "other" by creating a god or other projections, such as saviors, gurus, and mahatmas. We create all kinds of projections as henchmen, hitmen, to enable us to redominate our territory. The implicit sense is that if we pay homage to such great beings, they will function as our helpers, as the guarantors of our ground.

So we have created a world that is bittersweet. Things are amusing but, at the same time, not so amusing. Sometimes things seem terribly funny but, on the other hand, terribly sad. Life has the quality of a game of ours that has trapped us. The setup of mind has created the whole thing. We might complain about the government or the economy of the country or the prime rate of interest, but those factors are secondary. The original process at the root of the problems is the competitiveness of seeing oneself only as a reflection of the other. Problematic situations arise automatically as expressions of that. They are our own production, our own neat work. And that is what is called mind.

According to the Buddhist tradition, there are eight types of consciousness and fifty-two types of conceptions and all kinds of other aspects of mind, about which we do not have to go into detail. All these aspects are based largely on the primeval dualistic approach. There are the spiritual aspects and the psychological aspects and all sorts of other aspects. All are bound up in the realm of duality, which is ego.

As far as meditation practice is concerned, in meditation we work on *this* thing, rather than on trying to sort out the problem from the outside. We work on the projector rather than the projection. We turn inward, instead of trying to sort out external problems of A, B, and C. We work on the creator of duality rather than the creation. That is beginning at the beginning.

According to the Buddhist tradition, there are three main aspects of mind, which in Tibetan are called sem, rikpa, and yi. The basic mind, the simple capacity for duality we have already described, is sem. Rikpa literally means "intelligence" or "brightness." In colloquial Tibetan, if you say that somebody has rikpa, it means he is a clever, sharp fellow. This sharpness of rikpa is a kind of side function that develops from the basic mind; it is a kind of lawyer's mentality that everybody develops. Rikpa looks at a problem from various angles and analyzes the possibilities of different ways of approaching it. It looks at a problem in every possible way—inside out and outside in.

The third aspect, yi, is traditionally classified as the sixth sense consciousness. The first five sense consciousnesses are sight, smell, taste, hearing, and touch, and the sixth is yi. Yi is mental sensitivity. It is associated with the heart and is a kind of balancing factor that acts as a switchboard in relation to the other five sense consciousnesses. When you see a sight and hear a sound at the same time, the sight and sound are synchronized by the sixth sense to constitute aspects of a single event. Yi does a kind of automatic synchronization, or automatic computerization, of the whole process of sense experience. You can see, smell, hear, taste, and feel all at the same time, and all of those inputs are coherently workable. They make sense to you because of yi.

So yi is a sort of central-headquarters switchboard which coordinates experience into a coherent whole. In some sense it is the most important of all the three aspects of mind. It is not as intelligent in the sense of manipulation as sem. Sem has something of a political attitude toward one's relationship with the world; it is somewhat strategy oriented. The sixth sense is more domestic in function. It just tries to maintain the coordination of experience so that all information comes through efficiently and there is no problem of being out of communication with anything that is going on. On the other hand, rikpa, which is the intelligence—the research worker, as it were—in this administration of mind, takes an overall view of one's whole situation. It surveys the relationship between mind and the sixth sense and tries to search out all the possibilities of where things are going wrong, where things might go wrong, where things have gone wrong, how things could be put right. This research worker does not have the power actually to take action on the level of external relations. It is more like an adviser to the State Department.

These three principles of sem, rikpa, and yi are the most important for us to be aware of at this point. Many other aspects of mind are described in the traditional literature, but these three will suffice for our present understanding.

We should consider this understanding not so much as something that we have been told and therefore we should believe in. The experience described here can actually be felt personally. It can be worked on, related to. A certain part of our experience is organized by basic mind, a certain part by the sixth sense, and a certain part by intelligence. In order to understand the basic functions of mindfulness-awareness practice, I think it is very important for us to understand and realize these complexities of mind.

A gigantic world of mind exists to which we are almost totally unexposed. This whole world—this tent and this microphone, this light, this grass, the very pair of spectacles that we are wearing—is made by mind.

Minds made this up, put these things together. Every bolt and nut was put in by somebody-or-other's mind. This whole world is mind's world, the product of mind. This is needless to say; I am sure everybody knows this. But we might remind ourselves of it so that we realize that meditation is not an exclusive activity that involves forgetting this world and getting into something else. By meditating, we are dealing with the very mind that devised our eyeglasses and put the lenses in the rims, and the very mind that put up this tent. Our coming here is the product of our minds. Each of us has different mental manifestations, which permit others to identify us and say, "This guy is named so-and-so, this girl is named so-and-so." We can be identified as individuals because we have different mental approaches, which also shape the expressions of our physical features. Our physical characteristics are part of our mental activity as well. So this is a living world, mind's world. Realizing this, working with mind is no longer a remote or mysterious thing to do. It is no longer dealing with something that is hidden or somewhere else. Mind is right here. Mind is hanging out in the world. It is an open secret.

The method for beginning to relate directly with mind, which was taught by Lord Buddha and which has been in use for the past twenty-five hundred years, is the practice of mindfulness. There are four aspects to this practice, traditionally known as the four foundations of mindfulness.

MINDFULNESS OF BODY

Mindfulness of body, the first foundation of mindfulness, is connected with the need for a sense of being, a sense of groundedness.

To begin with, there is some problem about what we understand by *body*. We sit on chairs or on the ground; we eat; we sleep; we wear clothes. But the body we relate with in going through these activities is questionable. According to the tradition, the body we think we have is what is known as psychosomatic body. It is largely based on projections and concepts of body. This psychosomatic body contrasts with the enlightened person's sense of body, which might be called "body-body." This sense of body is free from conceptualizations. It is just simple and straightforward. There is a direct relationship with the earth. As for us, we do not actually have a relationship with the earth. We have some relationship with body, but it is very uncertain and erratic. We flicker back and forth between body and something else—fantasies, ideas. That seems to be our basic situation.

Even though the psychosomatic body is constituted by projections of body, it can be quite solid in terms of those projections. We have expectations concerning the existence of this body, therefore we have to refuel it, entertain it, wash it. Through this psychosomatic body we are able to experience a sense of being. For instance, as you listen to this talk, you feel that you are sitting on the ground. Your buttocks are resting on the earth; therefore you can extend your legs and lean back a little so you have less strain on your body. All of this affects your sense of being. You have some sense of relaxation as opposed to how it would be if you were standing—standing on your feet, standing on your toes, or standing on your palms. The posture that you are adopting at the moment seems to be an agreeable one; in fact it is one of the most congenial postures that one could ever think of. So being in this posture, you can relax and listen—you can listen to something other than the demands of your body.

Sitting down now, you feel somewhat settled. On the other hand, if the ground were very damp, you would not feel so settled. Then you would begin to perch on the ground, like a bird on a branch. This would be another matter altogether. If you are intensely concerned with some event about to happen or if you are worried about some encounter you are about to have—for example, if you are being interviewed for a job by some executive—you don't really sit on your chair, you perch on it. Perching happens when some demand is being made on you and you feel less of your body and more of your tension and nervousness. It involves a very different sense of body and of being than if you are just sitting, as you are doing now.

Right now you are sitting on the ground, and you are so completely sitting down that you have been able to shift gears and turn on your tape recorders, or even start taking notes, and you do not regard that as doing two things at once. You sit there, you have totally flopped, so to speak, and, having done that, you can turn to your other perceptions—listening, looking, and so on.

But your sitting here at this point is not actually very much a matter of your body per se sitting on the ground; it is far more a matter of your psychosomatic body sitting on the ground. Sitting on the ground as you are—all facing in one direction, toward the speaker; being underneath the roof of the tent; being attracted to the light that is focused on the

stage—all gives you a particular idea; it creates a certain style of participation, which is the condition of your psychosomatic body. You are
somewhat involved in sitting per se, but at the same time you are not.
Mind is doing it; concept is doing it. Your mind is shaping the situation
in accordance with your body. Your mind is sitting on the ground. Your
mind is taking notes. Your mind is wearing glasses. Your mind has such-
and-such a hairdo; your mind is wearing such-and-such clothes. Everyone is creating a world according to the body situation, but largely out
of contact with it. That is the psychosomatic process.

Mindfulness of body brings this all-pervasive mind-imitating-body activity into the practice of meditation. The practice of meditation has to
take into account that mind continually shapes itself into body*like* attitudes. Consequently, since the time of Buddha, sitting meditation has
been recommended and practiced, and it has proved to be the best way
of dealing with this situation. The basic technique that goes with sitting
meditation is working with the breath. You identify with the breath, particularly with the out-breath. The in-breath is just a gap, a space. During
the in-breath you just wait. So you breathe out and then you dissolve
and then there is a gap. Breathe out . . . dissolve . . . gap. An openness,
an expansion, can take place constantly that way.

Mindfulness plays a very important role in this technique. In this case,
mindfulness means that when you sit and meditate, you actually do sit.
You actually do sit as far as the psychosomatic body is concerned. You
feel the ground, body, breath, temperature. You don't try specifically to
watch and keep track of what is going on. You don't try to formalize
the sitting situation and make it into some special activity that you are
performing. You just sit. And then you begin to feel that there is some
sense of groundedness. This is not particularly a product of being deliberate, but it is more the force of the actual fact of being there. So you
sit. And you sit. And you breathe. And you sit and you breathe. Sometimes you think, but still you are thinking sitting thoughts. The psychosomatic body is sitting, so your thoughts have a flat bottom.

Mindfulness of body is connected with the earth. It is an openness
that has a base, a foundation. A quality of expansive awareness develops
through mindfulness of body—a sense of being settled and of therefore
being able to afford to open out.

Going along with this mindfulness requires a great deal of trust. Probably the beginning meditator will not be able simply to rest there, but

331

will feel the need for a change. I remember someone who had just finished a retreat telling me how she had sat and felt her body and felt grounded. But then she had thought immediately how she should be doing something else. And she went on to tell me how the right book had "just jumped" into her lap, and she had started to read. At that point one doesn't have a solid base anymore. One's mind is beginning to grow little wings. Mindfulness of body has to do with trying to remain human, rather than becoming an animal or fly or etheric being. It means just trying to remain a human being, an ordinary human being.

The basic starting point for this is solidness, groundedness. When you sit, you actually sit. Even your floating thoughts begin to sit on their own bottoms. There are no particular problems. You have a sense of solidness and groundedness, and, at the same time, a sense of being.

Without this particular foundation of mindfulness, the rest of your meditation practice could be very airy-fairy—vacillating back and forth, trying this and trying that. You could be constantly tiptoeing on the surface of the universe, not actually getting a foothold anywhere. You could become an eternal hitchhiker. So with this first technique you develop some basic solidness. In mindfulness of body, there is a sense of finding some home ground.

MINDFULNESS OF LIFE

The application of mindfulness has to be precise. If we cling to our practice, we create stagnation. Therefore, in our application of the techniques of mindfulness, we must be aware of the fundamental tendency to cling, to survive. We come to this in the second foundation of mindfulness, which is mindfulness of life, or survival. Since we are dealing with the context of meditation, we encounter this tendency in the form of clinging to the meditative state. We experience the meditative state and it is momentarily tangible, but in that same moment it is also dissolving. Going along with this process means developing a sense of letting go of awareness as well as of contacting it. This basic technique of the second foundation of mindfulness could be described as touch-and-go: you are there—present, mindful—and then you let go.

A common misunderstanding is that the meditative state of mind has to be captured and then nursed and cherished. That is definitely the wrong approach. If you try to domesticate your mind through meditation—try to possess it by holding on to the meditative state—the clear result will be regression on the path, with a loss of freshness and spontaneity. If you try to hold on without lapse all the time, then maintaining your awareness will begin to become a domestic hassle. It will become like painfully going through housework. There will be an underlying sense of resentment, and the practice of meditation will become confusing. You will begin to develop a love-hate relationship toward your practice, in which your concept of it seems good, but, at the same time, the demand this rigid concept makes on you is too painful.

So the technique of the mindfulness of life is based on touch-and-go. You focus your attention on the object of awareness, but then, in the same moment, you disown that awareness and go on. What is needed here is some sense of confidence—confidence that you do not have to securely own your mind, but that you can tune into its process spontaneously.

Mindfulness of life relates to the clinging tendency not only in connection with the meditative state, but, even more importantly, in connection with the level of raw anxiety about survival that manifests in us constantly, second by second, minute by minute. You breathe for survival; you lead your life for survival. The feeling is constantly present that you are trying to protect yourself from death. For the practical purposes of the second foundation, instead of regarding this survival mentality as something negative, instead of relating to it as ego-clinging as is done in the abstract philosophical overview of Buddhism, this particular practice switches logic around. In the second foundation, the survival struggle is regarded as a stepping-stone in the practice of meditation. Whenever you have the sense of the survival instinct functioning, that can be transmuted into a sense of being, a sense of having already survived. Mindfulness becomes a basic acknowledgment of existing. This does not have the flavor of "Thank God, I have survived." Instead, it is more objective, impartial: "I am alive, I am here, so be it."

We may undertake the practice of meditation with a sense of purity or austerity. We somehow feel that by meditating we are doing the right thing, and we feel like good boys or good girls. Not only are we doing the right thing, but we are also getting away from the ugly world. We are becoming pure; we are renouncing the world and becoming like the yogis of the past. We don't actually live and meditate in a cave, but we can regard the corner of the room that we have arranged for meditation as a cave. We can close our eyes and feel that we are meditating in a cave in the mountains. That kind of imagination makes us feel rather good. It feels fitting; it feels clean and secure.

This strong tendency is an attempt to isolate the practice of meditation from one's actual living situation. We build up all kinds of extraneous concepts and images about it. It is satisfying to regard meditation as austere and above life. But mindfulness of life steers us in just the opposite direction. The approach of mindfulness of life is that if you are meditating in a room, you are meditating in a room. You don't regard the room as a cave. If you are breathing, you are breathing, rather than convincing yourself you are a motionless rock. You keep your eyes open and simply let yourself be where you are. There are no imaginations involved with this approach. You just go through with your situation as it is. If your meditation place is in a rich setting, just be in the midst of it. If it is in a simple setting, just be in the midst of that. You are not trying to get away from here to somewhere else. You are tuning in simply and directly to your process of life. This practice is the essence of here and now.

In this way, meditation becomes an actual part of life, rather than just a practice or exercise. It becomes inseparable from the instinct to live that accompanies all one's existence. That instinct to live can be seen as containing awareness, meditation, mindfulness. It constantly tunes us in to what is happening. So the life force that keeps us alive and that manifests itself continually in our stream of consciousness itself becomes the practice of mindfulness. Such mindfulness brings clarity, skill, and intelligence. Experience is brought from the framework of intense psychosomatic confusion into that of the real body, because we are simply tuning into what is *already* happening, instead of projecting anything further.

Since mindfulness is part of one's stream of consciousness, the practice of meditation cannot be regarded as something alien, as an emulation of some picturesque yogi who has a fixation on meditating all the time. Seen from the point of view of mindfulness of life, meditation is the total experience of any living being who has the instinct to survive. Therefore meditating—developing mindfulness—should not be regarded as a minority-group activity or as some specialized, eccentric pursuit. It is a worldwide approach that relates to all experience: it is tuning in to life.

We do not tune in as part of trying to live further. We do not approach mindfulness as a further elaboration of the survival instinct. Rather we just see the sense of survival as it is taking place in us already. You are here; you are living; let it be that way—that is mindfulness. Your heart pulsates and you breathe. All kinds of things are happening in you at once. Let mindfulness work with that, let that be mindfulness, let every beat of your heart, every breath, be mindfulness itself. You do not have to breathe specially; your breath *is* an expression of mindfulness. If you approach meditation in this way, it becomes very personal and very direct.

Having such an outlook and such a relationship with the practice of meditation brings enormous strength, enormous energy and power. But this only comes if one's relationship to the present situation is accurate. Otherwise there is no strength because we are apart from the energy of that situation. The accuracy of mindfulness, on the other hand, brings not only strength, but a sense of dignity and delight. This is simply because we are doing something that is applicable that very moment. And we are doing it without any implications or motives. It is direct and right on the point.

But again it is necessary to say, once you have that experience of the presence of life, don't hang onto it. Just touch and go. Touch that presence of life being lived, then go. You do not have to ignore it. "Go" does not mean that we have to turn our backs on the experience and shut ourselves off from it; it means just being in it without further analysis and without further reinforcement. Holding on to life, or trying to reassure oneself that it is so, has the sense of death rather than life. It is only because we have that sense of death that we want to make sure that we are alive. We would like to have an insurance policy. But if we feel that we *are* alive, that is good enough. We do not have to make sure that we actually do breathe, that we actually can be seen. We do not have to check to be sure we have a shadow. Just living is enough. If we don't stop to reassure ourselves, living becomes very clear-cut, very alive, and very precise.

So mindfulness here does not mean pushing oneself toward something or hanging on to something. It means allowing oneself to be there in the very moment of what is happening in one's living process and then letting go.

MINDFULNESS OF EFFORT

The next foundation of mindfulness is mindfulness of effort. The idea of *effort* is apparently problematical. Effort would seem to be at odds with the sense of being that arises from mindfulness of body. Also, pushing of any kind does not have an obvious place in the touch-and-go technique of the mindfulness of life. In either case, deliberate, heavy-handed effort would seem to endanger the open precision of the process of mindfulness. Still we cannot expect proper mindfulness to develop without some kind of exertion on our part. Effort is necessary. But the Buddhist notion of right effort is quite different from conventional definitions of effort.

One kind of conventional effort is oriented purely toward the achievement of a result: there is a sense of struggle and pushing, which is egged on by the sense of a goal. Such effort picks up momentum and begins to thrive on its own speed, like the run of a roadrunner. Another approach to effort is fraught with a sense of tremendous meaningfulness: there is no sense of uplift or inspiration in the work. Instead there is a strong feeling of being dutiful. One just slogs along, slowly and surely, trying to chew through obligations in the manner of a worm in a tree. A worm just chews through whatever comes in front of its mouth; the channel that its belly passes through is its total space.

Neither of these kinds of effort has a sense of openness or precision. The traditional Buddhist analogy for right effort is the walk of an elephant or tortoise. The elephant moves along surely, unstoppably, with great dignity. Like the worm, it is not excitable, but unlike the worm, it has a panoramic view of the ground it is treading on. Though it is serious and slow, because of the elephant's ability to survey the ground there is a sense of playfulness and intelligence in its movement.

In the case of meditation, trying to develop an inspiration that is based on wanting to forget one's pain and on trying to make one's practice thrive on a sense of continual accomplishment is quite immature. On the other hand, too much solemnity and dutifulness creates a lifeless and narrow outlook and a stale psychological environment. The style of right effort, as taught by the Buddha, is serious but not *too* serious. It takes advantage of the natural flow of instinct to bring the wandering mind constantly back to the mindfulness of breathing.

The crucial point in the bringing-back process is that it is not necessary to go through deliberate stages: first preparing to do it, then getting a hold on one's attention, then finally dragging it back to the breathing as if we were trying to drag a naughty child back from doing something terrible. It is not a question of forcing the mind back to some particular object, but of bringing it back down from the dream world into reality. We are breathing, we are sitting. That is what we are doing, and we should be doing it completely, fully, wholeheartedly.

There is a kind of technique, or trick, here that is extremely effective and useful, not only for sitting meditation, but also in daily life, or meditation-in-action. The way of coming back is through what we might call the *abstract watcher*. This watcher is just simple self-consciousness, without aim or goal. When we encounter anything, the first flash that takes place is the bare sense of duality, of separateness. On that basis, we begin to evaluate, pick and choose, make decisions, execute our will. The abstract watcher is just the basic sense of separateness—the plain cognition of being there before any of the rest develops. Instead of condemning this self-consciousness as dualistic, we take advantage of this tendency in our psychological system and use it as the basis of the mindfulness of effort. The experience is just a sudden flash of the watcher's being there. At that point we don't think, "I must get back to the breath" or "I must try and get away from these thoughts." We don't have to entertain a deliberate and logical movement of mind that repeats to itself the purpose of sitting practice. There is just suddenly a general sense that something is happening here and now, and we are brought back. Abruptly, immediately, without a name, without the application of any kind of concept, we have a quick glimpse of changing the tone. That is the core of the mindfulness of effort practice.

One of the reasons that ordinary effort becomes so dreary and stagnant is that our intention always develops a verbalization. Subconsciously, we actually verbalize: "I must go and help so-and-so because it is half-past one" or "This is a good thing for me to do; it is good for me to perform this duty." Any kind of sense of duty we might have is always verbalized, though the speed of conceptual mind is so great that we may not even notice the verbalization. Still, the contents of the verbalization are clearly felt. This verbalization pins the effort to a fixed frame of reference, which makes it extremely tiresome. In contrast, the abstract effort we are talking about flashes in a fraction of a second, without any name or any idea with it. It is just a jerk, a sudden change of course which does not define its destination. The rest of the effort is just like an elephant's walk—going slowly, step by step, observing the situation around us.

You could call this abstract self-consciousness *leap* if you like, or *jerk,* or *sudden reminder;* or you could call it *amazement.* Sometimes it could also be also felt as panic, unconditioned panic, because of the change of course—something comes to us and changes our whole course. If we work with this sudden jerk, and do so with no effort in the effort, then effort becomes self-existing. It stands on its own two feet, so to speak, rather than needing another effort to trigger it off. If the latter were the case, effort would have to be deliberately manufactured, which would run counter to the whole sense of meditation. Once you have had that sudden instant of mindfulness, the idea is not to try to maintain it. You should not hold on to it or try to cultivate it. Don't entertain the messenger. Don't nurse the reminder. Get back to meditation. Get into the message.

This kind of effort is extremely important. The sudden flash is a key to all Buddhist meditation, from the level of basic mindfulness to the highest levels of tantra. Such mindfulness of effort could definitely be considered the most important aspect of mindfulness practice. Mindfulness of body creates the general setting; it brings meditation into the psychosomatic setup of one's life. Mindfulness of life makes meditation practice personal and intimate. Mindfulness of effort makes meditation workable: it connects the foundations of mindfulness to the path, to the spiritual journey. It is like the wheel of a chariot, which makes the connection between the chariot and the road, or like the oar of a boat. Mindfulness of effort actualizes the practice; it makes it move, proceed.

But we have a problem here. Mindfulness of effort cannot be deliberately manufactured; on the other hand, it is not enough just to hope that a flash will come to us and we will be reminded. We cannot just leave it up to "that thing" to happen to us. We have to set some kind of general alarm system, so to speak, or prepare a general atmosphere. There must be a background of discipline which sets the tone of the sitting practice. Effort is important on this level also; it is the sense of not having the faintest indulgence toward any form of entertainment. We have to give something up. Unless we give up our reservations about taking the practice seriously, it is virtually impossible to have that kind of instantaneous effort dawn on us. So it is extremely important to have respect for the practice, a sense of appreciation, and a willingness to work hard.

Once we do have a sense of commitment to relating with things as they actually are, we have opened the way to the flash that reminds us: *that, that, that.* "That what?" does not apply any more. Just *that,* which triggers an entirely new state of consciousness and brings us back automatically to mindfulness of breathing or a general sense of being.

We work hard at not being diverted into entertainment. Still, in some sense, we can enjoy the very boring situation of the practice of sitting meditation. We can actually appreciate not having lavish resources of entertainment available. Because of having already included our boredom and ennui, we have nothing to run away from and we feel completely secure and grounded.

This basic sense of appreciation is another aspect of the background that makes it possible for the spontaneous flash of the reminder to occur more easily. This is said to be like falling in love. When we are in love with someone, because our whole attitude is open toward that person somehow or other we get a sudden flash of that person—not as a name or as a concept of what the person looks like; those are afterthoughts. We get an abstract flash of our lover as *that.* A flash of *that* comes into our mind first. Then we might ponder on that flash, elaborate on it, enjoy our daydreams about it. But all this happens afterward. The flash is primal.

Openness always brings that kind of result. A traditional analogy is that of the hunter. The hunter does not have to think of a stag or a mountain goat or a bear or any specific animal; he is looking for *that.* When he walks and hears some sound, or senses some subtle possibility, he does not think of what animal he is going to find; just a feeling of *that* comes up. Anybody in any kind of complete involvement—on the level of the hunter, the lover, or the meditator—has the kind of openness that brings about sudden flashes. It is an almost magical sensation of thatness, without a name, without concept, without idea. This is the instant of effort, concentrated effort, and awareness follows after that. Having disowned that sudden experience, awareness very slowly comes and settles back to the earthy reality of just being there.

MINDFULNESS OF MIND

Often mindfulness is referred to as watchfulness. But that should not give the impression that mindfulness means watching something happening. Mindfulness means *being* watchful, rather than watching some *thing*. This implies a process of intelligent alertness, rather than the mechanical business of simply observing what happens. Particularly the fourth foundation—mindfulness of mind—has qualities of an aroused intelligence operating. The intelligence of the fourth foundation is a sense of light-handedness. If you open the windows and doors of a room the right amount, you can maintain the interior feeling of roomness and, at the same time, have freshness from outside. Mindfulness of mind brings that same kind of intelligent balance.

Without mind and its conflicts, we could not meditate or develop balance, or develop anything at all for that matter. Therefore, conflicts that arise from mind are regarded as a necessary part of the process of mindfulness. But at the same time, those conflicts have to be controlled enough so that we can come back to our mindfulness of breathing. A balance has to be maintained. There has to be a certain discipline so that we are neither totally lost in daydream nor missing the freshness and openness that come from not holding our attention too tightly. This balance is a state of wakefulness, mindfulness.

People with different temperaments bring different approaches to the practice of meditation. Some people are extremely orthodox, in fact dictatorial, with themselves. Others are extraordinarily loose; they just hang out, so to speak, in the meditation posture and let everything happen. Other people struggle back and forth between those two extremes, not knowing exactly what to do. How one approaches the sitting situation will depend on one's moods and the type of person one is, obviously. But always a certain sense of accuracy is required, and a certain sense of freedom is required.

Mindfulness of mind means being with one's mind. When you sit and meditate, you are there: you are being with your body, with your sense of life or survival, with your sense of effort, and at the same time, you are being with your mind. You are being there. Mindfulness of mind suggests a sense of presence and a sense of accuracy in terms of being there. You are there, therefore you can't miss yourself. If you are not there, then you might miss yourself. But that also would be a double take: if you realize you are not there, that means you are there. That brings you back to where you are—back to square one.

The whole process is very simple, actually. Unfortunately, explaining the simplicity takes a lot of vocabulary, a lot of grammar. However, it is a very simple matter. And that matter concerns you and your world. Nothing else. It does not particularly concern enlightenment, and it does not particularly concern metaphysical comprehension. In fact, this simple matter does not particularly concern the next minute, or the minute before this one. It only concerns the very small area where we are now.

Really we operate on a very small basis. We think we are great, broadly significant, and that we cover a whole large area. We see ourselves as having a history and a future, and here we are in our big-deal present. But if we look at ourselves clearly in this very moment, we see we are just grains of sand—just little people concerned only with this little dot which is called *nowness*.

We can only operate on one dot at a time, and mindfulness of mind approaches our experience in that way. We are there, and we approach ourselves on the very simple basis of *that*. *That* does not particularly have many dimensions, many perspectives; it is just a simple thing. Relating directly to this little dot of nowness is the right understanding of austerity. And if we work on this basis, it is possible to begin to see the truth of the matter, so to speak—to begin to see what nowness really means.

This experience is very revealing in that it is very personal. It is not personal in the sense of petty and mean. The idea is that this experience is *your* experience. You might be tempted to share it with somebody else, but then it becomes their experience, rather than what you wished for: your/their experience, jumbled together. You can never achieve that. People have different experiences of reality, which cannot be jumbled together. Invaders and dictators of all kinds have tried to make others have their experience, to make a big concoction of minds controlled by one person. But that is impossible. Everyone who has tried to make that kind of spiritual pizza has failed. So you have to accept that your experience is personal. The personal experience of nowness is very much there and very obviously there. You cannot even throw it away!

In sitting practice, or in the awareness practice of everyday life, for that matter, you are not trying to solve a wide array of problems. You are looking at one situation that is very limited. It is so limited that there is not even room to be claustrophobic. If it is not there, it is not there. You missed it. If it is there, it is there. That is the pinpoint of mindfulness of mind, that simplicity of total up-to-dateness, total directness. Mind functions singly. Once. And once. One thing at a time. The practice of mindfulness of mind is to be there with that one-shot perception, constantly. You get a complete picture from which nothing is missing: that is happening, now that is happening, now that is happening. There is no escape. Even if you focus yourself on escaping, that is also a one-shot movement of which you could be mindful. You can be mindful of your escape—of your sexual fantasy or your aggression fantasy.

Things always happen one at a time, in a direct, simple movement of mind. Therefore, in the technique of mindfulness of mind, it is tradition-ally recommended that you be aware of each single-shot perception of mind as thinking: "I am thinking I hear a sound." "I am thinking I smell a scent." "I am thinking I feel hot." "I am thinking I feel cold." Each one of these is a total approach to experience—very precise, very direct, one single movement of mind. Things always happen in that direct way.

Often we tend to think that we are very clever and we can get away from that direct nature of things. We feel we can get around that choice-less simplicity by approaching something from the back door—or from above, from the loft. We feel that we can prove ourselves to be ex-tremely intelligent and resourceful that way. We are cunning and shifty. But somehow it does not work. When we think we are approaching something from the back door, we do not understand that it is an illusion that there is *something else* to approach. At that moment there is only the back-doorness. That one-shot back-doorness is the totality of what is. We *are* the back door. If we are approaching from the loft, you, me, every-body, all of us are up there. The whole thing is up there, rather than there being something else for us to go down and invade and control. There isn't anything else at all. It is a one-shot deal. That one-shot reality is all there is. Obviously we can make up an illusion. We can imagine that we are conquering the universe by multiplying ourselves into hun-dreds of aspects and personalities: the conquering and the conquered. But that is like the dream state of someone who is actually asleep. There is only the one shot; everything happens only once. There is just *that*. Therefore mindfulness of mind is applicable.

So meditation practice has to be approached in a very simple and very basic way. That seems to be the only way that it will apply to our experience of what we actually are. That way, we do not get into the illusion that we can function as a hundred people at once. When we lose the simplicity we begin to be concerned about ourselves: "While I'm doing this, such-and-such is going to happen. What shall I do?" Thinking that more than *that* is happening, we get involved in hope and fear in relation to all kinds of things that are not actually happening. Really it does not work that way. While we are doing *that*, we are doing that. If something else happens, we are doing something else. But two things cannot happen at once; it is impossible. It is easy to *imagine* that two things are happening at once, because our journey back and forth between the two may be very speedy. But even then we are doing only one thing at a time.

The idea of mindfulness of mind is to slow down the fickleness of jumping back and forth. We have to realize that we are not extraordinary mental acrobats. We are not all that well trained. And even an extraordinarily well-trained mind could not manage that many things at once—not even two. But because things are very simple and direct, we can focus on, be aware and mindful of, one thing at a time. That one-pointedness, that bare attention, seems to be the basic point.

It is necessary to take that logic all the way and realize that even to apply bare attention to what we are doing is impossible. If we try, we have two personalities: one personality is the bare attention; the other personality is doing things. Real bare attention is being there all at once. We do not apply bare attention *to* what we are doing; we are not mindful *of* what we are doing. That is impossible. Mindfulness is the act as well as the experience, happening at the same time. Obviously, we could have a somewhat dualistic attitude at the beginning, before we get into real mindfulness, that we are willing to be mindful, willing to surrender, willing to discipline ourselves. But then we do the thing; we just do it. It is like the famous Zen saying "When I eat, I eat; when I sleep, I sleep." You just do it, with absolutely no implication behind what you are doing, not even of mindfulness.

When we begin to feel implications of mindfulness, we are beginning to split ourselves. Then we are faced with our resistance, and hundreds of other things seemingly begin to attack us, to bother us. Trying to be mindful by deliberately looking at oneself involves too much watcher. Then we have lost the one-shot simplicity. Perhaps we could have a discussion.

Student: I don't understand how sem works.

Trungpa Rinpoche: Sem is basic mind. But instead of using the word *mind* as a noun, it might be more helpful to think of it as a verb, as in "minding one's business." Sem is an active process, because you cannot have mind without an object of mind. Mind and its object are one process. Mind only functions in relation to a reference point. In other words, you cannot see anything in the dark. The function of sight is to see something that is not darkness—to see an object, in the light. In the same way, the function of mind is to have a reference point, a relative reference point which survives the mind, the minding process. That is happening right now, actually, everywhere.

Student: I was wondering if you could speak a little more about how mind, or "minding," creates the world. Are you talking about creating in the sense that if we are not mindful of the world the world does not exist? I feel you're saying something else besides that.

Trungpa Rinpoche: Well, mind is very simple perception: it can only survive on "other." Otherwise it starves to death.

S: You mean the mind can only exist on things outside of itself?

TR: That is right. But there is also the possibility that mind can go too far in that direction. Mind cannot exist without the projection of a relative reference point; on the other hand, mind also cannot exist if it is too crowded with projections. That way it also loses its reference point. So mind has to maintain a certain balance. To begin with, mind looks for a way to secure its survival. It looks for a mate, a friend; it creates the world. But when it begins to get too crowded—too many connections, too much world—it rejects its projections; it creates a little niche somewhere and fights tooth and nail to maintain it in order to survive. Sometimes mind loses the game. It becomes psychotic, completely mad. You "lose your mind," as we say: you cannot even function on an ordinary logical level. Such psychosis results from either of the two extremes: you are completely overcrowded by the whole projection of the world or, on the other hand, you lack anything for mind to work with. So mind can only exist in the neurosis of relative reference, not in psychosis. When it reaches the psychotic level, mind ceases to function as mind. It becomes something else, something poisonous.

Student: According to that model, how would meditation practice affect the relationship between mind and the world it's doing battle with?

Trungpa Rinpoche: The purpose of meditation practice is to try to save oneself from psychosis.

S: But you still maintain the world? You still maintain the neurotic state, basically?

TR: Not that necessarily, either. There is an alternative mind that does not need the neurotic world. This is where the idea of enlightenment comes in. Enlightened mind can go further and further, beyond questions of relative reference. It does not have to keep up with this world. It reaches a point where it does not have to sharpen itself on this neurotic world any more. There is another level of experience which still has a reference point, but it is a reference point without demand, a reference point that does not need further reference points. That is called nonduality. This does not mean to say that you dissolve into the world or the world becomes you. It's not a question of oneness but rather a question of zeroness.

Student: Rinpoche, how does the notion of mind that you've talked about relate to the notion of ego and the strategies of maintaining ego?

Trungpa Rinpoche: Mind as we have been talking about it *is* ego. Ego can survive only in relation to a reference point, not by itself. But I am trying to make the whole thing quite simple and relate it directly to the practice of meditation. If we think practicing meditation is concerned with working with ego, that sounds like too big a deal. Whereas if we just work with mind, that is an actual, real thing to us. In order to wake up in the morning you have to know it is morning—there is light outside and you have awakened. Those simple things are a perfect example of basic ego. Ego survives and thrives on reference point. So sem is ego, yes.

Student: You talked about mind relating to externals only. What do you consider it when the mind is functioning in pure intellection or imagination, creating its own object, so to speak?

Trungpa Rinpoche: That is external.

S: But there could be nothing out there. You could be in a darkened cell imagining that you are hearing a symphony, for example; it exists only in your mind.

TR: Sure. That is outside. That seems to be the point. Maybe you are not really talking to me now. Maybe you are in a dark room and you are talking to your version of me. Somehow the physical visual situation is not that important a factor. Any mental object, mental content, is regarded as an external thing.

Student: In regard to the technique of breathing, is there any particular reason why we identify with the out-breath rather than the in-breath?

Trungpa Rinpoche: That's a question of openness. You have to create some kind of gap, some area where there is less strain. Once you breathe out, you're sure to breathe in again, so there's room for relief of some kind. Nothing needs watching there.

Also, out-breathing is an expression of stepping out of your centralized system. Out-breathing has nothing to do with centralizing in your body, where usually everything is psychosomatically bottled up. Instead, by identifying with the out-breath you are sharing, you are giving something out.

Student: When you were talking about "flat-bottomed" ideas, you said that the flat bottom is what provides an openness, or a space, as opposed to having wings on your mind—flying thoughts or whatever. What makes the panic arise that made the retreatant you spoke of turn to her book, and that makes us run away from that sense of groundedness?

Trungpa Rinpoche: A lot of fear comes when things are too clearly defined. The situation becomes overwhelmingly sharp and direct and accurate, so that you would rather interpret it than simply acknowledge it. It is like when you say something very plain and direct to someone and you find him saying, "In other words, you are saying blah, blah, blah, blah, blah." Instead of relating directly to what has been said, he has a tendency to try to keep his twist. That seems to be a problem of shyness, of being shy of the bluntness of reality, of the "formness," the "thingness" that exists in our world and that nobody wants to face. Facing that is the highest form of sanity and enlightened vision. That seems to be the basic point of certain descriptions in the *Tibetan Book of the Dead*, where it describes a bright light coming toward you that you shy away from; you are frightened of it. Then there is a dull, seductive light coming from one of the six realms of neurotic existence, and you are attracted to that instead. You prefer the shadow to the reality. That is the kind of problem that exists. Often the reality is so blunt and outrageous and overwhelming that you feel facing it would be like sitting on a razor blade.

Student: You spoke of experiencing the body. There are a lot of techniques and practices for feeling the body, where you focus attention on a physical sensation, tension, or whatever you feel when you attempt to feel the physical body. I'm wondering what relation that kind of practice has to the practice with the breath that you described. Are those techniques a different thing, or would they reinforce the practice with the breath?

Trungpa Rinpoche: Your breath *is* your physical body from the point of view of this approach. There are all kinds of sensations that you experience along with the breath: pains, aches, itches, pleasurable feelings, and so on. You experience all those things along with the breath. Breath is the theme, and the other things go along with it. So the idea of the breathing technique is simply to be very precise about what you are experiencing. You relate to those sensations as they come up, along with your breath, without imagining that you are experiencing your body. Those experiences are not at all your body's experiences. That is impossible. Actually, you are in no way in a position to experience your body. Those experiences are just thoughts: "I'm thinking I'm in pain." It is the thought of pain, the thought of itch, and so forth.

S: So you are saying that the breathing technique is in a way a saner attitude than believing, "Now I'll feel my body" and making a project out of that?

TR: The breathing technique is a literal one, a direct one. It faces what is actually the case rather than just trying to turn out some result.

Student: Before, you were saying that when we are sitting here and taking notes, or focusing on the speaker and relaxing, we have a psychosomatic notion of body. And *psychosomatic,* the way I understand it, is sort of an imagined thing, or something that has to do with one's mind, with how the mind is affecting the body. Like when we say someone has a psychosomatic disease, it means their mind is having some effect on their body. How is that related to the fact that we're sitting here relaxing and listening to a speaker? How is that a psychosomatic sense of body?

Trungpa Rinpoche: The point is that whatever we do in our lives, we don't actually just do it; we are affected by mind. Maybe the body, the

347

true body, is being pressured by the psychosomatic speed of the mind. You might say that there is a possibility that you are sitting here now properly, in a nonpsychosomatic way. But still, the whole situation of sitting here was brought together, the whole incident was moved into place, by a psychosomatic driving force. So your sitting here was set up by the psychosomatic system, basically. If you have some kind of psychosomatic convulsion and you throw up—you actually do throw up stuff, which is not psychosomatic stuff but body stuff—it is nevertheless manifested in psychosomatic style. Its being thrown up was instigated by a psychosomatic process. That is the kind of situation we are in. Fundamentally our whole world is psychosomatic from that point of view. The whole process of living is composed of psychosomatic hangups. The desire to listen to the teachings comes from beginning to be aware of one's hang-ups. Since we have begun to be aware of our hang-ups we would like to create this further hang-up to clear up the existing hang-ups.

S: Instead of relating directly?

TR: Well, one never does that until one has some kind of flash of something on the level of enlightenment. Until that point everything one does is always by innuendo.

S: So any kind of disease or anything that's affecting you is psychosomatic?

TR: It is not only disease that is psychosomatic. Your process of health is psychosomatic, already. Actually, disease is sort of an extra thing, like yeast growing on top of your back.

Student: Rinpoche, with regard to touch-and-go, if a fantasy arises, to what point do you allow that fantasy to develop before you let go of it?

Trungpa Rinpoche: Once it arises, that is already "touch." Then let it be as it is. Then it goes. There is a peak point there. First, there is creation of the fantasy; then it reaches maturity; then it is beyond its prime; and then it slowly vanishes or tries to turn into something else.

S: Sometimes a fantasy will turn into a whole emotional plot which seems to get more and more complex.

TR: That is beating a dead horse. You just let it come, let it play out its impetus or energy, then just let it go. You have to taste it, then let it go. Having tasted it, it is not recommended to manipulate it any further.

S: When you speak of touch-and-go, evidently meditating, sitting practice, is the "touch." Do you mean that there are also times when it's inappropriate to be mindful in this manner? That in everyday life we should just let mindfulness go?

TR: I think there is some misunderstanding there. "Touch" and "go" always come together. It is like whenever there is a one, there is a zero. The number series, starting with one, implies zero. Numbers do not make sense if there is no such thing as zero. "Touch" has no meaning without "go." They are simultaneous. That simultaneity is mindfulness, which during both formal sitting practice and the postmeditation experience of everyday life.

Student: Previously you mentioned the retreatant who had the feeling of sitting on a razor blade when things became very clear, very distinct. Could you relate that experience to the sense of delight in the mindfulness of life?

Trungpa Rinpoche: It is the same experience, actually. Whenever there is a threat of death, that also brings a sense of life. It is like taking a pill because you fear that otherwise you might die. The pill is associated with the threat of death, but you take it with the attitude that it will enable you to live. Facing the moment clearly is like taking that pill: there is a fear of death and a love of life simultaneously.

Student: How does mindfulness of life inform ethical behavior, ethical action?

Trungpa Rinpoche: Things are done without mindfulness in the samsaric world; we thrive on that. Consequently, almost everything we do is somewhat disjointed: somehow things don't click, they don't fit; there is something illogical about our whole approach. We might be very reasonable, good people; still, behind the facade we are somewhat off. There is fundamental neurosis taking place all the time on our part, which in turn creates pain for other people as well as ourselves. People get hurt by that, and their reactions create more of the same. That is what we call the neurotic world, or samsara. Nobody is actually having a good time. Even ostensibly good times are somewhat pushed. And the undercurrent of frustration from sensing that creates further indulgence.

Mindfulness of life is an entirely different approach, in which life is treated as precious, which is to say, mindfully. Things are seen in their own right rather than as aspects of the vicious cycle of neurosis. Everything is jointed rather than disjointed. One's state of mind becomes coherent, so there is a basic workability concerning how to conduct one's life, in a general sense. One begins to become literate in reading the style of the world, the pattern of the world. That is just the starting point; it is by no means the final stage. It is just the beginning of seeing how to read the world.

Student: I really cannot imagine what experience would be like without all kinds of imagination and projections. I can't get a sense of what it would be like to participate in the world just as it is, just as things are occurring and coming up.

Trungpa Rinpoche: Are you interested in finding out?

S: I guess so.

TR: Well, it is very hard to do. The reason it is hard is that you are doing it. It is like looking for a lost horse. In order to look for it, you need to ride your lost horse. On the other hand, maybe you are riding on your lost horse, but still you are looking for it. It is something like that. It's one of those.

You see, there is really no such thing as ultimate reality. If there was such a thing, for that reason alone that could not be it. That is the problem. So you are back to square one. And the only thing, it seems, that you can do is to practice. That is good enough.

Student: In connection with the flash of waking up, in mindfulness of effort, I still don't clearly understand where you are supposed to come back from and what you are supposed to come back to.

Trungpa Rinpoche: Once that flash happens, you do not have to find out and appreciate where you came from. That is what I mean by, "Don't entertain the messenger." You also do not need an idea of where you are going. After the flash, your awareness is like a snowflake released from the clouds. It is going to settle down to the ground anyway. You have no choice.

Student: Sometimes being mindful of the exhalation seems to become too deliberate. It seems too much that the watcher is doing it from above, rather than the breathing and the mindfulness being simultaneous.

Trungpa Rinpoche: The touch-and-go approach is applicable here. You touch the exhalation and then disown the awareness even of that. If you are trying to have bare attention constantly, then you have a problem of being very rigid and dragging yourself along. So you touch with the breath and go with the breath. That way there is a sense of freshness, a change of air. It is like a pulsation, or like listening to a musical beat. If you are trying to keep with one beat you miss another. But if you touch and go you begin to hear the rhythm; and then you hear the entirety of the music, too. Another example is eating food: when you eat food you don't taste it constantly, just now and then. It is the same way with any experience. We hover around our interest. Always we just touch the highlights of our interest. So the touch-and-go style of mindfulness practice is borrowed from the basic style of mind. If you go along with that, then there is no problem at all.

Student: I somewhat understand how mindfulness of mind is a one-shot movement. But then if effort comes in, that no longer seems simultaneous or spontaneous.

Trungpa Rinpoche: Effort comes in off and on—at the beginning, during, and at the end. For instance, you are holding that microphone because you had an interest in asking a question. Now while you are listening to the answer, you have forgotten that you are holding the microphone, but that original effort is still hanging over. You are still holding it, not dropping it. So a lot of journeys back and forth take place with one's effort, rather than its being maintained constantly. Therefore you do not have to strain and push constantly. If you do, there is no practice, no meditation; the whole thing just becomes a big deal of effort. Shifting, alternating constantly, creates the space of meditation. If you are one hundred percent effortful, you blow the whole thing. There is nothing left but a tense lump of muscle sitting in the middle of a field. This happens all the time in life situations. It is like trying to knead dough. If you knead too hard you won't have any dough left in your hand—you will just be pushing your hand against the board. But if you have the feeling that the purpose of kneading hard is to work with the dough, then you have some compromises taking place, some intelligence coming into play. Without that, effort alone just kills.

Student: Without exercising some kind of incredible deliberateness, my entire meditation practice seems to be fantasy. There seems to be hardly any time that I am relating with my breath. I am basically just

sitting there daydreaming or else very deliberately, heavy-handedly trying to relate with my breath.

Trungpa Rinpoche: Well, go and sit.

S: What should I do when I sit?

TR: Sit.

S: That's all? What about working with my breath?

TR: Sit. Go ahead and sit. Just go ahead and do it.

FOUR

Devotion

"The devotional relationship between student and master becomes a living analogy for the student's relationship to life in general. Over a period of time this relationship works through many layers of inauthentic communication, based on ever more subtle deceptions of ego. The result for the student can be a totally clear and unencumbered relationship to his or her world."

DEVOTION, IN THE conventional sense, is a feeling of trust. The object of devotion, whether a person or an idea, is felt to be trustworthy and definite, more solid and real than oneself. In comparison, the devotee feels himself to be somewhat uncertain, not solid or full enough. He feels he lacks something, and this is the reason for his devotion toward somebody or something else. He feels inadequate standing on his own two feet, so he turns elsewhere for advice, security, or warmth. This type of devotion can be directed toward any number of ideas, or it can be directed toward our parents, our school teachers, our spiritual teacher, our bank manager, our wife or husband—toward whomever seems to have achieved life's goal in the conventional sense, which perhaps means anyone who has accumulated a lot of experience or information.

In general, the character of devotion seems to depend on the manner in which we relate the quality of trust or sanity within ourselves to

Based on "The True Meaning of Devotion," Barnet, Vermont, 1973.

353

THE HEART OF THE BUDDHA

something outside us. In the tradition of Buddhism, devotion to a teacher or master plays an extremely important role. Although, like conventional devotion, it may in the beginning be based on a sense of inadequacy and a wish to flee that inadequacy rather than to face and work with it, it goes far beyond that point. The devotional relationship between student and master becomes a living analogy for the student's relationship to life in general. Over a period of time this relationship works through many layers of inauthentic communication, based on ever more subtle deceptions of ego. The result for the student can be a totally clear and unencumbered relationship to his or her world. What makes the student persist in this long, difficult, and often extremely painful voyage of discovery is his or her devotion to the teacher—the conviction that the teacher indeed embodies the truth of his teaching. Throughout its various levels of development, devotion can be seen as having two aspects: admiration and absence of arrogance.

Admiration may be construed as hero worship. We look up to people who have a great deal of talent and dignity. We may idolize such people, hoping to make them part of us, to incorporate them into our territory. We hope in this way to participate in their greatness.

On the other hand, seeing talented people and their fine creations may make us jealous and depressed. We could feel we are too stupid and incompetent to compete with such tremendous discipline and talent. We might find ourselves actually resentful toward someone who is beautiful or polished. We may even experience their existence and their accomplishments as a hurt. Fine accomplishments or works of beauty may be such a threat that something in us would almost like to destroy them, to burn down all the art museums. At the very least we would like to insult those people who are more talented than we are. This is hero hatred, which is another version of hero worship.

A third possibility is that we may feel a really immense distance between the great and talented people and ourselves. We may feel that their accomplishments are splendid, but that they have nothing to do with us because they are so far above us. This attitude permits us to avoid being pained by a comparison with such accomplished people. With this attitude, we seal ourselves off completely.

The hidden assumption of this approach, whether in the form of adoration, hatred, or aloofness, is that there are heroes and there are incompetents, and we are among the incompetents. A separation is maintained.

In relating to a spiritual teacher, admiration is usually expressed in one of those three neurotic styles. In the case of seductive admiration, we want to consume the teacher completely so that he or she becomes part of us; in that case, we obliterate the actual features of the relationship under a thick layer of honey. In the repelling style of admiration, we are so overcome by awe and fear that, although we cannot help still being involved with the teacher, we keep the teacher in such a lofty niche that the possibility of direct appreciation is completely closed off. No matter what our style, it is usual to try to strategize our devotion so that the guru is not a threat.

A combination of these styles was visible in the fad that developed in the early part of this decade, when gurus were related to as popular idols or good luck charms. Young people completely covered their walls with pictures of spiritual superstars: gurus from India and Japan, American Indians, Eskimos, Tibetans—pinups of all kinds. In this way they could consider themselves on the good side of all sorts of great beings or great concepts. By relating to teachers as icons, they could express their admiration safely, without any danger of uncomfortable feedback.

Real admiration is much more direct than these contrived attitudes, and therefore it is more dangerous. Real admiration is based on a sense of courage and tremendous dignity. When we admire someone in a real way, we are not competing with that person or trying to win him over, but we are sharing his immense vision. The relationship can be a great celebration, because we do not approach it with a personal investment in any strategy or cause. In such admiration, our role is simply to devote ourselves completely, just to travel along without expecting anything in return for our admiration.

True admiration has clarity and bite. It is like breathing mountain air in winter, which is so cold and clear that we are afraid that it may freeze our lungs. Between breaths we may want to run into the cabin and throw a blanket over our heads lest we catch cold—but in true admiration we do not do that. Although the mountain air is threateningly clear as well as fantastically invigorating, we just breathe, without trying either to protect ourselves or to trap the air and take it with us. Like the mountains we are simply a part of that briskness: that is proper admiration or sharing.

The second quality of devotion is absence of arrogance. The arrogant approach is to be so passionately involved with our teacher that we become devotional chauvinists and cease to see the rest of the world properly. In fact, we become passionately involved with our own arrogance. We indulge our "devotion" by collecting information, techniques, stories, little words of wisdom—all to confirm our chauvinistic view. It actually reaches a point that the teacher upon whom our arrogance is based himself becomes a threat. The absurdity is that we even end up wanting to use our collection of ammunition against our teacher when he begins giving our "devotion" a hard time.

If our devotion is without arrogance there is not this resentment toward the world or the guru. Absence of such arrogance is absolutely necessary. When courting a teacher, students frequently make a sort of detailed application, listing all their insights and spiritual credentials. That is too arrogant; it is phony, out of the question altogether. It is fine to offer our particular skills or neuroses to the guru as a gift or an opening gesture. But if we begin to dress up our neuroses as virtues, like a person writing a resumé, that is unacceptable. Devotion without arrogance demands that we stop clinging to our particular case history, that we relate to the teacher and to the world in a naked and direct way, without hiding behind credentials.

Buddhism has three levels of development: hinayana; mahayana; and vajrayana, or tantra. Initially, at the hinayana level, devotion is very definite and very direct. The formula of devotion is what is known as taking refuge. One takes refuge in the Buddha as an example; in the dharma, or teaching, as a way of life; and in the sangha, or fellowship of practitioners, as companionship.

At this level the inspiration for devotion arises from a sense of being trapped in the whirlpool of samsara—of being filled with pain, dissatisfaction, and neurosis. Not only are we in that state, but there is the further frustration that however much we try to get out of that state, our too-speedy, too-desperate attempts only make our situation more hopeless. The traditional analogy for this is that of an elephant who feels very hot in the tropical sun and, wanting to bathe in some cool water, jumps into a mud hole. The more he moves around the more he sinks. At the beginning it seems very pleasurable, but when two-thirds of his body has sunk into the mud he begins to panic. He struggles more and more to get out, but it is too late.

Like the elephant, we try to rescue ourselves from our frustration, but the more we try to pull ourselves out the more we sink in. We feel completely helpless. It sometimes reaches the point of feeling that we have made a complete mess out of our lives. What are we to do if we do not get what we want? What are we to do when we have already gotten what we wanted? Even if we have had some success, what are we to do when things still go on after that? We are always back at square one. Our master plan has cheated us. There seems to be no alternative to frustration and confusion. It is this situation that is the inspiration to take refuge. At some point, instead of merely trying to struggle within ourselves, we feel that perhaps we ought to look around and try to find someone to rescue us. Taking refuge in the Buddha as an example means identifying with a person who was able in one lifetime to attain enlightenment and save himself. Since somebody has already done it, perhaps we could do the same thing.

Since we are in an emergency situation, the first thing we learn is that our struggle to pull ourselves out of samsara has to be given up. Being engaged in a struggle may give us some sense of security, in that at least we feel we are doing something. But that struggle has become useless and irrelevant: it only makes things worse. However, the pain we have experienced in our struggle cannot be forgotten. We have to work with it. Rather than struggling to escape pain, we have to make it our path. It then becomes a rich resource for learning. Relating to our pain in this manner is taking refuge in the dharma.

The sangha is composed of the people who follow such a path. We respect those who have undertaken the journey—those who have been able to get out of the mud—as well as our companions, who are working like ourselves. It is not a matter of leaning on others to avoid facing our loneliness. Rather, by taking refuge in the sangha, we acknowledge our aloneness, which in turn becomes an inspiration to others.

The hinayana approach to devotion is not directed toward attaining a sense of emotional security. It is purely a response to an emergency. If we have been hurt in a car accident, we need an ambulance to take us to the hospital. When such an emergency arises, the hypothetical comforts of a successful journey are remote. The only thing we need is for the ambulance to come and fetch us. It is very alarming; we are completely stuck. So devotion in the hinayana is based on the desire to be rescued from the hopeless and chaotic situation in which we seem to dwell continually.

It should be clear at this point that those who become involved with the teaching in this way are quite different from spiritual shoppers who have the luxury of drifting from one involvement to another. For those who are really engaged in working on themselves, there is no time to shop around. They are simply concerned with getting some basic treatment. They have no time for philosophizing or analysis: they are stuck. Help is desperately needed because the pain is so intense.

Psychologically, there seems to be a basic difference in honesty between the hinayana practitioner, who acknowledges the urgent need for a rescuer, and the dilettante spiritual shopper. Spiritual shoppers might acknowledge that there is a problem, but they feel the problem can be patched over until they can get service to their liking. Spiritual shopping is a naive and simplistic version of the fantastic project of spiritual materialism—a project which simply creates and perpetuates suffering in its attempt to achieve egohood. Spiritual shoppers are looking for entertainment from spiritual teachings. In such an approach devotion is nonexistent. Of course, if such shoppers visit a store where the salesman has a tremendous personality and his merchandise is also fantastically good, they might momentarily feel overwhelming trust of some kind. But their basic attitude is not desperate enough. Their desperation has been concealed or patched over, so they make no real connection with the teaching. However, their patchwork is bound to fall apart, and in the midst of that chaos they will have no choice but to come to terms with their desperation. That is the point of emergency out of which the rudiments of genuine devotion arise. Desperation becomes very straightforward.

But what happens after we already have been treated for our pain—when our basic problems have been dealt with and we can afford to relax a little bit? Although our initial symptoms have been cured, our particular medical service may now appear not to be totally ideal, and we may begin to look for a better one. We can once again afford the luxury of shopping for the last word in spirituality, and devotion may be forgotten. We may even begin to develop a sense of resentment toward our teacher, feeling that he has interfered in our business and undermined our dignity. Once we have regained our strength—or hypocrisy—we tend to forget the kindness and generosity of the rescuer, and the compassionate acts he performed. Now that we are no longer stupid, unworthy persons looking for a rescuer, we may feel resentful of having been seen in that abject position. At that point, there is a need for eye-level communication, for a friend rather than a teacher. But how do we bridge the gap between the notion of a rescuer and that of a spiritual friend?

On the hinayana level our condition was similar to that of a patient in an emergency room. There was no point then in being personally introduced to the physician or in trying to be polite. However, when we have recovered from our operation, there is the possibility that the person who performed the operation may take a further interest in us because he has learned a great deal about us during the course of our treatment. He also happens to like us tremendously. But there is the difficulty that as we recover we may resent his interest. We do not want to be intimidated by having our case history recalled.

At that point it is very hard to make a connection, but it is absolutely necessary. It is not like ordinary medical practice in which the doctor can transfer our case to someone else. The person we ran into in the emergency room has to carry on with us until real, fundamental, basic sanity has developed.

Now the notion of surrendering is very important. The greatest gift we can make is to open and expose ourselves. We have to show our physician our secret ailments. Still, the physician keeps calm and quiet and goes on liking us, however repulsive our secret ailments may be. So our relationship with the physician is ongoing.

So the second stage of devotion, on the level of mahayana, comes from discovering our teacher as a spiritual friend, or kalyanamitra in Sanskrit. The guru becomes a friend with whom we can communicate completely in the sense of communication between equals. But at the same time this particular friend is rather heavy-handed: he minds our business.

On the mahayana level, devotion is based on the feeling that we are, up to a point, worthy persons capable of receiving the teachings. Our inspiration, insights, pain, and neuroses all constitute us as good vessels. Our neuroses and pain are not regarded as bad, nor, for that matter, are our virtues regarded as good. Both are just the substance of the vessel. There is an overall sense of trust—a sense of warmth and compassion toward ourselves in that all our aspects can be included in the relationship with the spiritual friend. And devotion to the spiritual friend is complementary to that development of trust in ourselves: devotion at this point is no longer directed toward an external object alone. This attitude of nonaggression toward oneself and others is central to the bodhisattva path, which is at the heart of mahayana Buddhism.

Aggression manifests toward others as pride and toward oneself as depression. If we get fixated in either of these extremes we become unsuitable vessels for the teachings. The arrogant student is like a container turned upside down; he is completely unreceptive to anything coming from outside himself. And the depressed student is like a container with holes in it; since he feels nothing will help he does not heed anything. It is not that before forming a relationship with a spiritual friend we have to become ideal vessels. That would be impossible. But if we have an occasional glimpse of that attitude of nonaggression—a positive attitude toward ourselves, without arrogance or pride—then that creates the possibility of our spiritual friend communicating with us directly.

The first obstacle to devotion at this point is negativity toward ourselves; we judge ourselves too harshly. The usual response to depression, to feeling unworthy of the teachings, is to try to change completely, by making a one hundred percent improvement. We set up a kind of totalitarian regime with the aim of making ourselves into perfect individuals without any faults whatsoever. Whenever we begin to notice our faults peeking through, our automatic reaction is to feel that our journey is being delayed and our perfection challenged. So we try to prune ourselves. We are willing to impose all sorts of discipline on ourselves, punishing our bodies and our minds. We inflict pain on ourselves through stringent rules of all kinds. We may go so far as to seek some magical cure for our shortcomings, since in moments of clarity we realize we cannot handle ourselves. This totalitarian approach seems to be falling once more into the pitfall of spiritual materialism, of trying to make oneself perfect.

The second obstacle to devotion is a further form of arrogance. The student may have received some glimpse of the teachings, and some preliminary sanity may have already developed in him; but then he starts taking liberties. He has too much trust in his own home-brewed potion, too much trust in do-it-yourself projects: "I have developed myself to this level, and I have achieved a lot of the things that I wanted to achieve. I'm sure that I don't have to go through the embarrassment of regarding someone as my spiritual friend any more. I can study the appropriate books and learn how to brew the spiritual medicines myself."

It is true than in some sense Buddhism can be described as a do-it-yourself process. The Buddha himself said, "Work out your own salvation with diligence." So it seems clear that, to a certain extent, salvation is up to us and we cannot really get help from outside. There is no magical gimmick that will solve our problems for us without pain. But while there is no possibility that such external magic or divine powers will save us, a spiritual friend is still necessary. Such a friend might only tell us that doing it ourselves is the only way, but we have to have someone to encourage us to do that and to show us that it can be done. Our friend has done it himself, and his predecessors in his spiritual lineage have done it as well. We have to have this proof that the spiritual path is not a gigantic hoax but a real thing, and that there *is* someone who can pass on the message, the understanding, the techniques. And it is necessary that this friend be a human being, not an abstract figure that can be manipulated by our wishful thinking; he is someone who shares the human condition with us and who works with us on that level. He must have a direct and very concrete understanding of us personally in order for there to be a proper connection. Without that, we are unable to receive any real teachings, any real benefit.

In relating to the spiritual friend, at the same time that we trust ourselves and consider ourselves worthy vessels, there should also be some sense of hopelessness. At this point hopelessness does not mean despair, but simply a loss of interest in manufacturing further expectations. Ordinarily, we live in our world of expectations, which we embellish constantly. Hopelessness means being willing to live nakedly in the moment, without the reference point of our expectations. Expecting good fortune or bad fortune is like believing in fortune cookies: it is just entertaining ourselves with expectations. Chaos might arise or development and creativity might arise—either situation is possible—but in communicating with a spiritual friend we are not looking ahead; we are directly involved in the very moment. The spiritual friend does not exist as a dream of the future, like an arranged marriage that is yet to be consummated. The spiritual friend is right there in front of us—six inches away. He is right there. Whatever image we present to such a friend is immediately reflected back to us. That is why the spiritual friend is referred to as heavy-handed: he minds our business. He has no shyness of himself or us. Just being right there, he minds our business totally.

We cannot tread the path of mahayana without a spiritual friend— absolutely not—because we have to receive the good news of the bodhisattva's wide-open path. The spiritual friend both is and conveys that good news. He makes it possible to know the teachings and the practice as real, rather than purely as a myth to accept on the basis of blind faith. We have a tendency to look for miracles and magic as solutions to our problems. One reason for this is that we do not believe what we have been told concerning the hard facts of spirituality, and we actually regard the whole thing as a fable. We are so bored with living on this earth, we would like to go to the moon or to Mars, or to explore other solar systems. We do not want to believe that dealing with our situation happens right here; this place seems to be too small, too unexciting, too polluted and unclean. But the spiritual friend does not offer us any magical solution, any escape from our boredom. He relates to us on a very mundane level, right here on earth. While he does not perform miracles or magic, we see that he belongs to a lineage of generations and generations of teachers who have achieved complete openness. He provides proof of the teachings by acting as an example.

In this sense the spiritual friend is like a good baker in a lineage of bakers. The earliest bakers passed on their secrets for making good bread, from generation to generation. The present baker also bakes good bread and feeds it to us. The loaf he gives us to sample was not preserved through the generations as an antique; it is not a museum piece. This loaf has been baked fresh and is now hot, wholesome, and nourishing. It is an example of what freshness can be. The knowledge that has been handed down to us through the spiritual lineage has the same qualities. We can make an immediate connection with the spiritual friend and understand that in the past, generations of teachers and students also experienced such a fresh and direct relationship.

The spiritual friend has real, living teachings, and we can relate with him thoroughly and completely. If we are simple and straightforward with him, neither condemning nor aggrandizing ourselves, then instead of blind faith, we begin to develop real devotion. We are convinced that something is happening—something that could make life completely workable—but at the same time we are not expecting anything extraordinary. So the relationship with the spiritual friend is very ordinary; it is communication on the level of our day-to-day living situation.

Our relationship with a spiritual friend tends to become even more demanding and much more energy consuming as we develop on the path. From the standpoint of fundamental devotion the sense of friendship is simply an appetizer. The true meaning of devotion manifests on the vajrayana level alone.

At the hinayana level our devotion was conditioned by our sense of desperation, and at the mahayana level it was conditioned by our loneliness. Only at the vajrayana level is there unconditioned devotion. At this level the relationship between student and teacher is very dangerous—but also extremely powerful. Finally, at this level, it could be described as a magical relationship.

When we reach the third stage of the Buddhist path—the vajrayana, or the stage of tantra—devotion brings with it an increased sense of its appropriate expression through action, particularly through what is known as surrendering, or offering. Such surrendering takes a great deal of effort and energy. Before discussing the vajrayana, we need to understand this notion of surrendering.

Usually we do not give merely for the sake of giving. We may give because we want to get rid of something, in which case it is like throwing it into a garbage pail. Or we may give at required times, such as at Christmas or on birthdays. Sometimes we give to express our appreciation to someone who has given us something, such as love, education, or support. Or we may use a gift to try to win somebody over. But we never seem to give in the absence of some purpose or scheme. We do not just give things—just like that.

Even at the mahayana level, generosity has a scheme to it, in that it is regarded as an act of letting go and has the purpose of learning the generosity that does not expect anything in return. Only at the vajrayana level does even that kind of scheme disappear and the total simplicity of just giving become possible. That type of giving may not seem to be very practical. From an ordinary business point of view, it is like throwing money down the drain; we could go so far as to say that it is insane to do such a thing. In this type of generosity we are not giving to prove how wealthy we are, or how visionary, but we are just giving everything—body, speech, and mind. In other words, we are giving the giver, so there ceases even to be a gift. It is just letting go.

Naturally, we would always like to watch the receiver of the gift appreciating what has been received. If we give our whole being and somebody thanks us for it, then we have not actually given it completely; we have gotten it back. We thrive on such confirmation. We do not want to just give, not knowing whether or not we will have ourselves with us any more. That is a terrible thought: if we give completely and hold nothing back we cannot even watch the process of giving; we cannot take part in that ritual. Losing ourselves is such a terrible idea that we would not even like to give up our anger or passion, because even such neuroses produce some kind of security. They may be painful, but they still serve to make the statement, "I do exist."

We might say that just giving is asking too much; it definitely is. That is why it is important. Giving without concept is what makes room for the awakened state to be experienced. This cannot take place as a business deal. We cannot possess the dharma and deposit it in the bank. When we actually receive the teachings properly, there is nobody home to receive anything; there is no one to reap a profit. The teachings simply become a part of us, part of our basic being. The dharma cannot be owned as property or adornment.

The approach of ego at this level is to collect initiations and teachers as ornaments: "I received millions of ordinations and trillions of initiations. I am completely soaked in blessings." That is the most decadent way of relating to the teachings, the most blatant form of spiritual materialism. In that approach we use the teaching and the teachers as part of ego's conspiracy to adorn itself, and thus we fall deeper and deeper asleep rather than opening up to anything. We become beggarly mystical egomaniacs.

Such attempts to strategize giving or to use the teachings for personal gain have to be given up completely at the vajrayana level. There is no longer room for the conditioned devotion of the hinayana and mahayana. At this level total generosity, or surrendering, is required; otherwise the meeting of minds between the teacher and student through which transmission takes place is impossible.

In vajrayana Buddhism the process of surrendering is catalyzed through what are known as the four preliminary practices: one hundred thousand prostrations; one hundred thousand repetitions of the refuge formula; one hundred thousand repetitions of a purifying mantra; and one hundred thousand symbolic offerings of one's body, speech, and mind and the whole universe to the guru. It should be noted that we cannot embark immediately on the vajrayana approach without first going through the hinayana and mahayana. Without that preparation, these preliminary practices tend to be ineffectual, because we do not actually give up anything through them. We merely go through the motions of surrendering, performing the gymnastics of a hundred thousand prostrations and playing with our spiritual gadgets. So unless we have started from the beginning with the disciplined meditation practice of the hinayana and the expansiveness and openness of the mahayana, we are unable to receive real empowerment and real transmission through the vajrayana tradition.

We initially related to the teacher as our rescuer; later he became a spiritual friend who engaged us in very intense communication. Now, in the vajrayana, the guru, or vajra master, begins to demand this further surrendering. At first we feel we have already done our giving away and trusting, and that we do not have anything more to surrender. We have already paid our dues and therefore we are worthy of the vajrayana teachings. At the beginning of the path we were in bad shape, and we surrendered ourselves to the physician in the emergency room; later, when we began to recover, we felt lonely and sought companionship. Now we feel we have already done everything we wanted to do: we have thrown everything overboard and surrendered our egos. But there is still something that needs to be surrendered, which is our collection of pride in the pain that we have already gone through. We have surrendered, but in the process of surrendering we have collected credentials, which are an obstacle. We have become respectable surrenderers who have carefully donated a certain chunk of their body, speech, mind, and energy. But something more is needed: complete surrender, complete humiliation, so to speak. And such devotion is possible only with the aid of a real friend.

In the beginning of the vajrayana one takes what is known as the samaya vow. A samaya vow is a bond that one establishes with one's teacher—a bond between oneself, one's teacher, and the teacher's lineage. To create a samaya bond it is not enough just to get up and do it. If we wanted to get married we could run off and have a quick ceremony before a justice of the peace, without having our parents' acknowledgment or even a good wedding feast, but the meaning and purpose of the marriage would be lost because there was no big deal. We just wanted to glue ourselves to somebody else. In the case of the samaya vow, a real marriage takes place between oneself, one's teacher, and the lineage. That is why there is a tremendous need for surrendering and opening. It is absolutely necessary because of the demand that that marriage makes on us.

As soon as the student drinks the water of the samaya oath the water turns into the elixir of life, or amrita, which sustains the student's conviction and remains in his heart. But the surrendering process can also have deathly consequences. If the student has any trace of doubt or confusion or deceit, the water turns into molten iron and destroys him, carrying him to what is known as vajra hell. So samaya is a very heavy commitment. It is extremely potent and powerful. I personally feel that introducing the vajrayana outright, in a country whose citizens have no idea of how dangerous a step it is, is taking advantage of people's weakness. Collecting hundreds of thousands of candidates for vajra hell seems to be uncompassionate, even if there are all kinds of gadgets and excitement for them along the way.

In order to prepare suitable tantric students, we must start with all sorts of warnings. Such warnings are absolutely necessary. There is a traditional story about Indian merchants who sailed out onto the ocean to collect pearls. One merchant who had a large ship gathered together a number of people who wanted to go along on the venture. Attached to the ship were four anchors. When it came time to sail each day he would cut away one anchor with a warning: "Are you sure you want to go through with this?" Only on the fourth day did he set sail. Similarly, in order to launch vajrayana in America, we must give repeated warnings about the dangers of tantric practice. Of course, if we get out on the ocean and collect beautiful pearls, it will be a fantastic thing, an extraordinary situation. But suppose we are unable to do that; suppose the participants are just blindly latching on to the big businessman who owns the ship? That would be disastrous, so there must be constant warnings.

In tantra, the guru is regarded as absolutely essential. He is the central figure for all the teachings. Without the guru we cannot transmute the water of the oath into elixir. To relate to the guru we need a tremendous amount of openness and surrendering—real surrendering, not surrendering with an ulterior motive, like that of the shopper who butters up the salesman because he wants his merchandise.

At first, this surrendering involves the body; we surrender the feeling that our body is a cozy nest—that if we go mad at least we will have something to relate to, which is our body. When we surrender our body to the guru we are surrendering our primal reference point. One's body becomes the possession of the lineage; it is not ours anymore. I am not talking here of becoming hysterical and losing sense consciousness; I mean that, surrendering one's body, psychologically one's dear life is turned over to somebody else. We do not have our dear life to hold on to any more. At the second stage of tantra, speech, which is the emotional level, is also surrendered. Our emotional security is no longer regarded as necessary or relevant. That need also is surrendered to the teachings and to the lineage as represented by the guru. The third stage involves the mind, the registering mechanism that exists in one's state of consciousness. The mind is also surrendered, so that we no longer have our logical intellectual games to cling to.

Finally everything is surrendered: body, speech, and mind. However, this does not mean that we become zombies or jellyfish. Such surrendering is a continual process rather than a one-shot suicidal affair, and the uncompromising intelligence that has emerged through our surrendering remains active and, through the surrendering process, becomes progressively more free.

Such a surrendering process and the demands that the tantric lineage make on the student might be described as outrageous, unlawful, or criminal. From the viewpoint of maintaining ego's kingdom, it is criminal. It is the final and ultimate way to uproot this thing that we try so hard to hold on to. It is absolutely terrible, even deathly. But such surrendering is a necessary part of opening.

At this point it could be said that we worship the guru—but not as a purely chauvinistic person to whom we have to surrender. That is the wrong frame of reference completely. He is not a dharma chauvinist: there is no chauvinism involved. Rather, the guru is a spokesman, ambassador, executioner, and policeman of openness, and he is a donor with tremendous wealth to give us. The guru is also in some way like a mirage of a lake in the desert. When we feel very thirsty in the desert we may think we see a lake or a brook, but really there is no brook or lake at all. In the same way, by holding out the fulfillment of our desires, the guru tantalizes us and inspires us to walk further into the desert of egolessness.

It seems that the important thing is the level of our own commitment—the extent to which we are willing to be embarrassed and humiliated through acknowledging our chaos, our confusion, our desire and grasping. We cannot work with these fixations if we do not acknowledge them and accept their existence. The more we accept them, the more we are able to let go of them. To that extent the guru is able to relate to us as the spokesman and ambassador of enlightenment.

The vajra master is like a master samurai instructing a novice. He trains us and encourages us to leap and take chances. He teaches us to cut through our hesitations. The appropriate way for us to relate to him is with simple, naked trust, without hope and fear. Our actual experiences of such trust may be momentary, but it is necessary at least to develop the right intellectual attitude toward trusting. Even though we may be unable to open completely, at least through understanding on the intellectual level we have the willingness to open, which is very important.

In fact, intellect plays a very important part in the process of opening. What we are referring to as intellect here is quite different from the ordinary notion of intellect as a faculty of philosophical speculation. Intellect in this case is clear seeing, real precision. Often when that precision arises fleetingly we try to sustain or recapture it, but it just fades away. It is necessary to work with that glimpse of precision, because it is what enables us to see the need for openness, but we must do so without trying to capture it. When such a glimpse of precision arises, we should disown it rather than trying to hang on to it or recreate it. Then at some point we start to develop confidence in ourselves; we develop confidence that such intellect is ours rather than a foreign element that we are introducing into our systems. It was not given to us from the outside, but was awakened within us. It will arise spontaneously, without being manipulated into place. That kind of awakening, that glimpse of intellectual understanding, is of great importance.

In many cases a glimpse of openness and precision brings unexpected fear. There may be a sense of being lost or exposed, a sense of vulnerability. That is simply a sign that ego is losing its grip on its territory; it is not a fundamental threat. The concept of threat only makes sense in relation to ego. If we have something to lose we feel threatened, and what we have to lose is our dear life, our ego. But if we have nothing to lose we cannot be threatened. The feeling of threat is a great stepping-stone, for it is the working basis for development. In fact, the student of tantra should be in a constant state of panic. Only then is his or her situation regarded as worthwhile. Such a state of panic serves two purposes: it overcomes the student's smugness and complacency, and it sharpens his clarity.

It has been said by the Tibetan master Pema Karpo and other great teachers that studying tantra is like riding on a razor. Finding we are on a razor's edge, we do not know whether we should try to slide down or try to freeze and stay put. If we only knew how to slide down a razor we might do it as easily as a child slides down a banister. If we knew the nature of the blade we could do so. But if we do not know the nature of the blade and are just trying to prove ourselves, we might find ourselves sliced in half.

As I have said, warnings that alert the student to his actual situation are very important. The more warnings that are made about tantra, the more the student benefits. When the tantric master does not give enough warnings the student becomes a bad tantra student because he is not riding on the edge of a razor.

When students first hear about vajrayana, they may find it very fascinating. There are all kinds of exciting stories and possibilities, which become extremely seductive and appealing. Since the tantric approach is supposedly the quick path, students might think they should stop wasting time; they might feel they should get their money's worth and become enlightened as quickly as possible. Not only are they impatient but they are also cowardly: they do not want to have any pain or difficulties. Such students are not willing to open and expose themselves. They are not willing to face the successive panics that we are talking about. Actually, the panic is the source of openness, the source of questioning; it is the source of opening one's heart.

Usually when we panic we take a gasp of air, and that creates enormous freshness. That is what the tantric tradition is supposed to do. So if we are good tantric students we open ourselves each moment: we panic a thousand times a day, a hundred and eight times an hour. We are open constantly; we panic constantly. Thus the tantric approach to the world means refreshing our contact, reopening ourselves constantly so that we are able to perceive our cosmos properly and thoroughly. That sounds great, enormously promising, but there is a catch. Once we are in a position to be fascinated by the world, this naked world without a filter or screen, we too are naked. We are relating to the world without even any skin to protect our bodies. Experience becomes so intimate and so personal that it actually burns us or freezes us directly. We may become extremely sensitive and jumpy. It is possible that as we panic more, we may react more intensely. Experience becomes so direct and magical that it gives a direct shock. It is not like sitting back in a theater seat and being entertained by the fabulous world happening on the screen. It does not work that way. Instead it works mutually: to the extent that the naked world is uncovered, we too must be willing to expose ourselves.

Therefore tantra is very dangerous. It is electric. In addition to the naked electricity of ourselves and our world there is the vajra master, the teacher who introduces the possibilities of the true world to us. The teacher has the same electricity; the teacher is also naked. Traditionally he holds in his hand the symbol of a thunderbolt, which is called a *dorje*, or *vajra*. With this vajra, if we and the cosmos are not connecting, the teacher can reignite the shock.

In this sense, the teacher has a lot of power, but not power *over* us in the manner of an egomaniac. As always, the teacher is a spokesperson of reality; he introduces us to our world. So the vajra master becomes extremely powerful and somewhat dangerous at this point. But he does not use this power simply to play tricks on us whenever he sees a weak point; he conducts his movements in a disciplined manner, according to the tradition. He touches us, he smells us, he looks at us, and he listens to our heartbeat. These processes are known as abhishekas.

Abhisheka is a Sanskrit word which literally means "anointment." We are bathed in holy water that is created by the master and the mandala around the master. Abhishekas are popularly known as "initiations," but that is actually a weak translation. The notion of abhisheka is different from a tribal initiation or rite of passage where we are accepted as a member of the tribe if we pass certain kinds of tests. It is entirely different. Our teacher's empowering us and our receiving the power depends both on our capability and the teacher's capability. The term *empowerment* is more appropriate than *initiation* because there is no tribe into which to be initiated. In other words, abhisheka does not mean being accepted into a closed circle; rather we are introduced into the universe. We cannot say the universe is a big tribe or that it is a big ego. It is just open space. The teacher empowers us so that we can enter our enlarged universe.

The teacher is the only embodiment of power in this transmission of energy. Without the teacher we cannot experience this properly, fully. And the only way to relate to such a teacher is through devotion. Devotion proceeds through various stages of unmasking until we reach the point of seeing the world directly and simply, without imposing our fabrications. This is called basic sanity. Devotion is a way of bringing us down to earth and of enabling us to develop this basic sanity through the challenges constantly presented by our relationship to our master.

We have to start out very simply. We have to give; we have to open up and display our ego; we have to present our ego as a gift to our spiritual friend. If we are unable to do that, then the path never begins because there is no working basis; there is nobody to walk on it.

Part Two

STAGES ON THE PATH

FIVE

Taking Refuge

"Becoming a refugee is acknowledging that we are groundless, and it is acknowledging that there is really no need for home, or ground. Taking refuge is an expression of freedom, because as refugees we are no longer bounded by the need for security. We are suspended in a no-man's-land in which the only thing to do is to relate with the teachings and with ourselves."

BECOMING A REFUGEE

In the Buddhist tradition, the purpose of taking refuge is to awaken from confusion and associate oneself with wakefulness. Taking refuge is a matter of commitment and acceptance and, at the same time, of openness and freedom. By taking the refuge vow we commit ourselves to freedom.

There is a general tendency to be involved in all kinds of fascinations and delusions, and nothing very much ever takes root in one's basic being. Everything in one's life experience, concerning spirituality or anything else, is purely a matter of shopping. Our lives consist of problems of pain, problems of pleasure, problems of points of view—problems about all kinds of alternatives—which make our existence complicated. We have allegiance to "that" and allegiance to "this." There are hun-

Taken from selected Refuge Vow ceremonies, 1973–1978.

dreds and millions of choices involved in our lives—particularly in regard to our sense of discipline, our ethics, and our spiritual path. People are very confused in this chaotic world about what is really the right thing to do. There are all kinds of rationales, taken from all kinds of traditions and philosophies. We may try to combine all of them together; sometimes they conflict, sometimes they work together harmoniously. But we are constantly shopping, and that is actually the basic problem.

It is not so much that there is something wrong with the traditions that exist around us; the difficulty is more our own personal conflict arising from wanting to have and to be the best. When we take refuge we give up some sense of seeing ourselves as the good citizen or as the hero of a success story. We might have to give up our past; we might have to give up our potential future. By taking this particular vow, we end our shopping in the spiritual supermarket. We decide to stick to a particular brand for the rest of our lives. We choose to stick to a particular staple diet and flourish on it.

When we take refuge we commit ourselves to the Buddhist path. This is not only a simple but also an extremely economical approach. Henceforth we will be on the particular path that was strategized, designed, and well thought out twenty-five hundred years ago by the Buddha and the followers of his teaching. There is already a pattern and a tradition; there is already a discipline. We no longer have to run after that person or this person. We no longer have to compare our lifestyle with anybody else's. Once we take this step, we have no alternatives; there is no longer the entertainment of indulging in so-called freedom. We take a definite vow to enter a discipline of choicelessness—which saves us a lot of money, a lot of energy, and lots and lots of superfluous thinking.

Perhaps this approach may seem repressive, but it is really based on a sympathetic attitude toward our situation. To work on ourselves is really only possible when there are no sidetracks, no exits. Usually we tend to look for solutions from something new, something outside: a change in society or politics, a new diet, a new theory. Or else we are always finding new things to blame our problems on, such as relationships, society, what have you. Working on oneself, without such exits or sidetracks, is the Buddhist path. We begin with the hinayana approach—the narrow path of simplicity and boredom.

By taking refuge, in some sense we become homeless refugees. Taking refuge does not mean saying that we are helpless and then handing all our problems over to somebody or something else. There will be no refugee rations, nor all kinds of security and dedicated help. The point of becoming a refugee is to give up our attachment to basic security. We have to give up our sense of home ground, which is illusory anyway. We might have a sense of home ground as where we were born and the way we look, but we don't actually have any home, fundamentally speaking. There is actually no solid basis of security in one's life. And because we don't have any home ground, we are lost souls, so to speak. Basically we are completely lost and confused and, in some sense, pathetic.

These are the particular problems that provide the reference point from which we build the sense of becoming a Buddhist. Relating to being lost and confused, we are more open. We begin to see that in seeking security we can't grasp on to anything; everything continually washes out and becomes shaky, constantly, all the time. And that is what is called life.

So becoming a refugee is acknowledging that we are homeless and groundless, and it is acknowledging that there is really no need for home, or ground. Taking refuge is an expression of freedom, because as refugees we are no longer bounded by the need for security. We are suspended in a no-man's-land in which the only thing to do is to relate with the teachings and with ourselves.

The refuge ceremony represents a final decision. Acknowledging that the only real working basis is oneself and that there is no way around that, one takes refuge in the Buddha as an example, in the dharma as the path, and in the sangha as companionship. Nevertheless, it is a total commitment to oneself. The ceremony cuts the line that connects the ship to the anchor; it marks the beginning of an odyssey of loneliness. Still, it also includes the inspiration of the preceptor—in this case myself—and his lineage. The participation of the preceptor is a kind of guarantee that you will not be getting back into the question of security as such, that you will continue to acknowledge your aloneness and work on yourself without leaning on anyone. Finally you become a real person, standing on your own feet. At that point, everything starts with you.

This particular journey is like that of the first settlers. We have come to no-man's-land and have not been provided with anything at all. Here we are, and we have to make everything with our own bare hands. We are, in our own way, pioneers: each is a historical person on his own journey. It is an individual pioneership of building spiritual ground. Everything has to be made and produced by us. Nobody is going to throw us little chocolate chips or console us with goodies. So we have to learn how to milk the cows. In fact, we have to find the cows first—they might be wild animals at this point—and we have to tame them, put them into a corral, milk them, and nurse their young. We have to learn how to make a sword: we have to melt the stone and make iron out of it. We have to make everything. We came here barefoot and naked, and we even have to make our own clothes—our own shoes and hats, whatever we need. This is the starting point, right here at this point. It is necessary to make this beginning.

If we adopt a prefabricated religion that tells us exactly the best way to do everything, it is as though that religion provides a complete home with wall-to-wall carpeting. We get completely spoiled. We don't have to put out any effort or energy, so our dedication and devotion have no fiber. We wind up complaining because we didn't get the deluxe toilet tissue that we used to get. So at this point, rather than walking into a nicely prepared hotel or luxurious house, we are starting from the primitive level. We have to figure out how we are going to build our city and how we are going to relate with our comrades who are doing the same thing.

We have to work with the sense of sacredness and richness and the magical aspect of our experience. And this has to be done on the level of our everyday existence, which is a personal level, an extremely personal level. There are no scapegoats. When you take refuge you become responsible to yourself as a follower of the dharma. You are isolating yourself from the rest of your world in the sense that the world is not going to help you any more; it is no longer regarded as a source of salvation. It is just a mirage, maya. It might mock you, play music for you, and dance for you, but nevertheless the path and the inspiration of the path are up to *you*. You have to do it. And the meaning of taking refuge is that you are *going* to do it. You commit yourself as a refugee to yourself, no longer thinking that some divine principle that exists in the holy law or holy scriptures is going to save you. It is very personal. You experience a sense of loneliness, aloneness—a sense that there is no savior, no help.

But at the same time there is a sense of belonging: you belong to a tradition of loneliness where people work together.

You might say: "I have been this way for a long time. Why does there have to be a ceremony?" The ceremony is important because then there will be a particular time and a date on which your commitment takes place. There will be one particular fraction of a second after which you are committed to yourself, and you will know that very precisely and clearly. It is the same as celebrating the New Year: when the clock strikes twelve, we finally say "Happy New Year." There is that particular moment. So we make sure that there are no fuzzy edges to your memory or commitment. You are a slippery fish, and you have to be provided with some kind of net. The net is the situation of taking refuge that you are caught in; and the fisherman, the person who fishes you out of the water, is the preceptor. At that point the fish has no choice but to surrender to the fisherman. Without the ceremony, somehow it doesn't work; the whole thing is left too much to your imagination and your slippery subjectifying process.

When you become a refugee, a follower of the Buddha's teaching, you get onto a train that is without reverse and without brakes. The train comes along and pulls up to a certain station at a certain time. You get onto the train, then the whistle toots and off you go.

So the refuge ceremony is a landmark of becoming a Buddhist, a nontheist. You no longer have to make sacrifices in somebody else's name, trying to get yourself saved or to earn redemption. You no longer have to push yourself overboard so that you will be smiled at by that guy who watches us, the old man with the beard. As far as Buddhists are concerned, the sky is blue and the grass is green—in the summer, of course. As far as Buddhists are concerned, human beings are very important and they have never been condemned—except by their own confusion, which is understandable. If nobody shows you a path, any kind of path, you're going to be confused. That is not your fault. But now you are being shown the path and you are beginning to work with a particular teacher. And at this point nobody is confused. You are what you are, the teachings are what they are, and I am what I am—a preceptor to ordain you as Buddhist persons. This is a very joyous situation as far as I am concerned: we are going to work together from the beginning to the end.

Taking refuge in the Buddha as an example, taking refuge in the

379

dharma as the path, and taking refuge in the sangha as companionship is very clean-cut, very definite, very precise, and very clear. People have done this for the past twenty-five hundred years of the Buddhist tradition. By taking refuge you receive that particular heritage into your own system; you join that particular wisdom that has existed for twenty-five hundred years without interruption and without corruption. It is very direct and very simple.

Taking Refuge in the Buddha

You take refuge in the Buddha not as a savior—not with the feeling that you have found something to make you secure—but as an example, as someone you can emulate. He is an example of an ordinary human being who saw through the deceptions of life, both on the ordinary and spiritual levels. The Buddha found the awakened state of mind by relating with the situations that existed around him: the confusion, chaos, and insanity. He was able to look at those situations very clearly and precisely. He disciplined himself by working on his own mind, which was the source of all the chaos and confusion. Instead of becoming an anarchist and blaming society, he worked on himself and he attained what is known as bodhi, or enlightenment. The final and ultimate breakthrough took place, and he was able to teach and work with sentient beings without any inhibition.

The example of the Buddha's life is applicable because he started out in basically the same kind of life that we lead, with the same confusion. But he renounced that life in order to find the truth. He went through a lot of religious "trips." He tried to work with the theistic world of the Hinduism of the time, and he realized there were a lot of problems with that. Then, instead of looking for an outside solution, he began working on himself. He began pulling up his own socks, so to speak, and he became a buddha. Until he did that, he was just a wishy-washy spiritual tripper. So taking refuge in the Buddha as an example is realizing that our case history is in fact completely comparable with his, and then deciding that we are going to follow his example and do what he did.

By taking refuge you begin to realize that you can actually compete with the Buddha. You can do that. Twenty-five hundred years ago one person, who also had to deal with his daily living situation, managed to awaken himself and experience the pain of life. He was able to work through that and work along with it and finally attain buddhahood, enlightenment. That person was called Gautama, the chief of the Shakya tribe. He was a prince who had all kinds of luxury and security and who felt alienated from his basic state of sanity. So he decided to question the whole thing. He escaped from his kingdom, and he practiced meditation in the jungles and the woods. The only friends or spiritual teachers he could find were all spiritual materialists: they were using meditation to fortify ego. He tried all kinds of physical gimmicks—holding his breath, turning upside down, sitting in the middle of a campfire—and he found them all futile. Then he began to rouse himself, to make his own liberation by himself. So he won enlightenment single-handedly. He was such a smart person that he was able to get out of the psychological materialism of trying to shore up ego through ideas, and out of spiritual materialism as well. He was able to win a victory over both kinds of materialism. Henceforth he was known as the Buddha, the Awakened One.

We can do that as well. Thousands of people in the Buddha's tradition have done so. We have psychological materialism and spiritual materialism happening constantly in our lives, so we have the same material to work on. There is no doubt that we have plenty of that kind of food for our minds.

One of the big steps in the Buddha's development was his realization that there is no reason we should believe in or expect anything greater than the basic inspiration that exists in us already. This is a nontheistic tradition: the Buddha gave up relying on any kind of divine principle that would descend on him and solve his problems. So taking refuge in the Buddha in no way means regarding him as a god. He was simply a person who practiced, worked, studied, and experienced things personally. With that in mind, taking refuge in the Buddha amounts to renouncing misconceptions about divine existence. Since we possess what is known as buddha nature, enlightened intelligence, we don't have to borrow somebody else's glory. We are not all that helpless. We have our own resources already. A hierarchy of divine principles is irrelevant. It is very much up to us. Our individuality has produced our own world. The whole situation is very personal.

TAKING REFUGE IN THE DHARMA

Then we take refuge in the *teachings* of the Buddha, the dharma. We take refuge in the dharma as path. In this way we find that everything in our life situation is a constant process of learning and discovery. We do not regard some things as secular and some things as sacred, but everything is regarded as *truth*—which is the definition of dharma. Dharma is also *passionlessness,* which in this case means not grasping, holding on, or trying to possess—it means nonaggression.

Usually, the basic thread that runs through our experience is our desire to have a purely goal-oriented process: everything, we feel, should be done in relation to our ambition, our competitiveness, our one-upmanship. That is what usually drives us to become greater professors, greater mechanics, greater carpenters, greater poets. Dharma— passionlessness—cuts through this small, goal-oriented vision, so that everything becomes purely a learning process. This permits us to relate with our lives fully and properly. So, taking refuge in the dharma as path, we develop the sense that it is worthwhile to walk on this earth. Nothing is regarded as just a waste of time; nothing is seen as a punishment or as a cause of resentment and complaint.

This aspect of taking refuge is particularly applicable in America, where it is quite fashionable to blame everything on others and to feel that all kinds of elements in one's relationships or surroundings are unhealthy or polluted. We react with resentment. But once we begin to do that, there is no way. The world becomes divided into two sections: sacred and profane, or that which is good and proper and that which is regarded as a bad job or a necessary evil. Taking refuge in the dharma, taking a passionless approach, means that all of life is regarded as a fertile situation and a learning situation, always. Whatever occurs—pain or pleasure, good or bad, justice or injustice—is part of the learning process. So there is nothing to blame; everything is the path, everything is dharma.

That passionless quality of dharma is an expression of nirvana— freedom, or openness. And once we have that approach, then any spiritual practice we might go through becomes a part of the learning situation, rather than merely ritualistic or spiritual, or a matter of religious obligation. The whole process becomes integral and natural.

We have always tried to make sense out of the looseness and unsatisfactoriness of life by trying to make things secure and trying to freeze that washed-out quality into some definite story line. But now we can no longer make very much sense out of it. Things constantly change, constantly move, constantly become something else. So now we begin to work with the basic premise that that flow, or fluctuation of ups and downs, in our lives can be seen as a mirror reflection, or as waves in the ocean. Things come close to us and we can almost hold on to them, but then they disappear. Things seem as if they are just about to make sense; then suddenly there is immense confusion and what was about to make sense seems quite remote, a million miles away. We are constantly trying to grasp something, and we lose it just as we think we have our fingertips on it. This is the source of frustration, suffering—or duhkha, as the Buddha called it. Duhkha is the first noble truth. Recognizing that, we begin to make sense out of nothing, so to speak. Transitoriness begins to become more meaningful than trying to freeze truth into a solid lump. That realization—understanding the fluctuation that goes on and working with it—is the meaning of taking refuge in the dharma.

This approach involves a quality of directness and absence of deception—or we might even say absence of politeness. It means that we actually face the facts of life directly, personally. We do not have to come up with any padding of politeness or ordinary cheapness, but we actually experience life. And it is very ordinary life: pain is pain and pleasure is pleasure. We don't have to use another word or innuendo. Pain and pleasure and confusion—everything takes place very nakedly. We are simply ordinary. But nakedness and absence of politeness don't necessarily mean being completely savage. We are naked just in going without the padding that we usually provide ourselves with. With our friends, with our relatives, in everything that goes on, we can afford to be very simple and direct and personal.

In that way all the things that go on in life—economic, domestic, and spiritual—are no longer regarded as belonging in separate compartments, but everything is combined into one situation. That is what it means to follow the path of the dharma. Neither hot, intense moments of complete claustrophobia nor cool, noncaring moments are regarded as either extraordinarily good or extraordinarily terrible. Those are just the fashions of life that we are involved in. It is a natural process taking place constantly. Taking refuge in the dharma means relating to everything that happens, from the splinter in your little finger to your granddad's committing suicide in your name, from the littlest to the biggest, as part of that natural process. There are all sorts of shapes of journeys taking place constantly. And all of them are just a trick; they are just interesting facets of life.

But still you can't just say, "Let's leave it alone. Let's just watch everything and become great poets." Oh no. You can't just write poems about it, play music about it, or dance to it. You have to get into all those facets of life completely. And getting into them is the meaning of *path*—they become the path. That is accompanied by the practice of meditation, which actually makes the whole thing very clear and precise. The clearer our minds become, the more real and vivid become all the little things that are promising and threatening: the hopes and fears, the pains and pleasures.

The dharma is traditionally divided into two aspects. The first is *what has been told,* which means the holy scriptures, the books of the teachings which have been written from the time of the Buddha until the present. Those sacred books, which have been handed down from generation to generation, contain the truth of *what has been experienced,* which is the second aspect of the dharma. Throughout the Buddhist lineage, individuals have experienced reality and truth within the teachings, and this can also be experienced by you. It is a discovery within your own life that happens both with your teacher and by yourself. It happens particularly through your experience of meditation, both in formal sitting practice and in meditation-in-action.

Taking refuge in the dharma means that the experiences that go through your life, pain and pleasure alike, are also sacred teachings. The teachings are not sacred because they were discovered in space or because they came from the sky and were given by divine principles. But the teachings were discovered in the heart, in human hearts—in buddha nature. For example the Buddhist canon, the Tripitaka, is based on *somebody's* experience. It is all *somebody's* discourse. The one hundred and eight volumes of sutras are spoken words—communications from one human being to another. The Buddha, who was fully awakened, was communicating with other human beings who were not awakened, were half-awakened, or were in a somewhat-awakened state. The truth has never come from the sky; it has always come from the human condition. The four noble truths of the Buddha describe the human experience of pain, the origin of pain, the possibilities of salvation, and the possibilities of the path. These are very literal truths; they are the direct truth, rather than something that was manufactured upstairs.

So in taking refuge in the dharma, the books of the teachings are not regarded as mystical writings that were created by the clouds and the sun meeting together and engraving script on a tablet. These books were written with ink and pen on pieces of paper. The memories of the seminars, talks, and discourses that Lord Buddha gave were recorded simply as a description of what an awakened man said, how an awakened person conducted himself in the living situation. So taking refuge in the dharma has nothing to do with unearthly influence; it has nothing to do with Martians, and it has nothing to do with Jehovah either—but it definitely has something to do with sanity. Taking refuge in the dharma means that human beings' experience can be heightened so much that, extraordinarily, we can actually awaken ourselves within ourselves.

Once again, whatever goes on in our minds is a learning situation: the love and hate relationships that evolve around us, the sense of misfortune, the sense of being lucky, the sense of defeat, the sense of arrogance and egohood, the sense of patriotism, the sense of smartness, the sense of being special, and the sense of confusion—all are included in our particular basic situation. That *is* the path. It is the only way; it is the only thing that we can work on. We cannot just milk the cow of the guru all the time, whenever we are hungry or thirsty. But we can experience our lifestyle and our process of development according to the dharma of what has been told. Then we become in tune with the dharma of what has been experienced at the same time, as the followers of the dharma have done in the past—which is very powerful and very meaningful for all of us.

TAKING REFUGE IN THE SANGHA

Having taken refuge in the Buddha as an example and the dharma as path, then we take refuge in the sangha as companionship. That means that we have a lot of friends, fellow refugees, who are also confused, and who are working with the same guidelines as we are. Everybody is simultaneously struggling with their own discipline. As the members of the sangha experience a sense of dignity, and their sense of taking refuge in the Buddha, dharma, and sangha begins to evolve, they are able to act as a reminder and to provide feedback for each other. Your friends in the sangha provide a continual reference point which creates a continual learning process. They act as mirror reflections to remind you or warn you in living situations. That is the kind of companionship that is meant by *sangha*. We are all in the same boat; we share a sense of trust and a sense of larger-scale, organic friendship.

At the same time, you have to stand on your own two feet. A sense of individuality and a sense of comradeship are both involved. You are working together and helping each other, but you are not helping so much that you become addicted to each other's help. If you lean on somebody in a weak moment of your life, the person you lean on may seem strong, but he will also begin to catch your weakness. If he falls down, you will fall down too. If the principle were just to lean on one another, we could have thousands of people all leaning on each other, but then if one person fell down, everybody would fall down. The whole thing would collapse, like an old dilapidated building, and there would be great chaos. It would be a suicidal process, with thousands all collapsing at the same time—which would be very messy, very dusty.

So taking refuge in the sangha means being willing to work with your fellow students—your brothers and sisters in the dharma—while being independent at the same time. That's a very important point here, actually, in terms of taking the refuge vow. Nobody imposes his or her heavy notions on the rest of the sangha. If one particular person tries to act as a catalyst or spokesman for the whole sangha, that is regarded as frivolous. If someone is extremely timid, credulous, and dependent, that is also regarded as frivolous. Instead, each member of the sangha is an individual who is on the path in a different way from all the others. It is because of that that you get constant feedback of all kinds: negative and positive, encouraging and discouraging. These very rich resources become available to you when you take refuge in the sangha, the fellowship of students. It is as though yeast is put into a batch of hundreds of grains of barley. Each grain begins to fill up with yeast, until finally there is a huge, beautiful, gigantic vat of beer. Everything is yeasted completely; each one of the grains has become powerful individually—so the whole thing becomes a real world.

The sangha is the community of people who have the perfect right to cut through your trips and feed you with their wisdom, as well as the perfect right to demonstrate their own neurosis and be seen through by you. The companionship within the sangha is a kind of clean friendship—without expectation, without demand, but at the same time, fulfilling.

The sangha is a source of learning as much as the spiritual friend or teacher. So there is a need for some trust in the sangha. But we have to make a very definite point here: we are speaking of the *organized* sangha, which is the sangha of practitioners who actually sit together, practice together, and also work on themselves. Without that sangha, we have no reference point; we are thrown back into the big samsaric soup, and we have no idea who or what we are. We are lost.

So we no longer regard ourselves as lone wolves who have such a good thing going on the side that we don't have to relate with anybody at all, whether the organization, the sitting practice, or the sangha at large. At the same time we must not simply go along with the crowd. Either extreme is too secure. The idea is one of constantly opening, giving up completely. There is a lot of need for giving up.

Joining the particular club of lonely people who call themselves the sangha is a very heroic thing to do. Conventionally, you don't join anything unless all the ground is secured. Normally you pay a certain amount of money to join a particular club, and that gives you the kind of service that makes you feel good and secure. But at this point it is a very impersonal approach; in a strange way it is also very personal. You are willing to work with your loneliness in a group. The sangha is made up of thousands of people who are alone together, working together with their own loneliness, their own aloneness. Together they make an orchestra; you are able to dance with its music, and that is a very personal experience. You begin to join that particular energy, which allows individuality and spontaneity as well as nonaggression.

The sense of trust and frankness in the sangha frightens a lot of people; nevertheless, genuine communication takes place. Also, the level of sophistication of the sangha naturally becomes heightened. We cannot regard the sangha as an in-group situation, like a cheap, greasy spoon household of brown rice eaters. At this level the sangha is an immaculate household, with immaculate relationships, in which experiences with each other occur personally. The real sangha is made up of dedicated people who are actually working on themselves. They haven't developed any fantastic tricks, magic, extraordinary philosophy, or anything like that. From that point of view, such companionship might seem

THE HEART OF THE BUDDHA

somewhat boring, too ordinary. Nevertheless, it is very real. Quite possibly, you might occasionally seek out extraordinary friends and pursuits, but somehow those pursuits turn out to be purely plastic, part of a dream world, so that you return to the real sangha, the real people who actually care about themselves, care about you as a friend, and relate with the whole situation completely, without any areas shielded through a consensus of weakness.

Having taken the refuge vow, there are three types of change that take place: change of attitude, change of mark, and change of name.

CHANGE OF ATTITUDE

Change of attitude involves developing a sense of sympathy toward oneself, and therefore toward the world. One's attitude changes to that of nonaggression and passionlessness. Aggression refers to a general sense of uptightness and unfriendliness—of regarding the world as an object to do battle with. And in passion, one is trying to win something over, engaging in continual one-upmanship. In either case one has a constant battle going on with the world—that is to say, with oneself.

When you change your attitude you develop an awareness that allows you to be friendly with yourself and thus with the rest of sentient beings. There is some sense of gentleness. This is connected with commitment to the practice of meditation, which creates an openness to your own ups and downs, and a willingness to go along with them and work on them. You develop such a thorough relationship with the teachings that they become part of you. The three jewels—the Buddha, the dharma, and the sangha—become a part of your existence and you thrive on that, you work with that, you live on that. You do not become a religious person as such, but you become gentle, soft, and very amiable and workable. You don't create defense mechanisms all the time.

As a Buddhist, you are less greedy. If your breakfast isn't cooked just the way you want it, you give in and eat the crummy breakfast you don't like. There is a sense that you can give an inch in your demands—just a little inch, a fraction of a second. So trying to give in, which is the change of attitude, is very important. Usually we don't want to give in: "I want to have my own way. I want complete, one hundred percent hospitality; and if I don't get it, I'm going to fight for my rights," and so forth. This is problematic and anti-Buddhist in some sense.

Another aspect of the change of attitude is that when you become a full-fledged Buddhist you feel that your life is workable in any situation. You don't feel alienated from your problems, and you don't try to put yourself in some kind of special spiritual orbit. You can be very gentle and friendly to yourself and other people and relate with the world—which seems to be the basic point of the Buddhist teachings. But you don't have to conduct yourself with the superficial smile and gleaming, honey-smeared attitude of "love and light." This is a genuine experience: you enter the tradition of the nonaggressive state of mind, and you are capable of conducting yourself in that way without artifice.

Nonaggression in this context also means refraining from taking life; you refrain from the personal rejection of animals, enemies, human beings, or whatever. People sometimes take pride in killing flies; in that kind of little situation they become involved in some kind of "gotcha!" mentality. That's a very savage kind of behavior. Becoming a follower of the dharma means becoming more sophisticated in the fundamental sense. You begin to pay attention to the details of your daily life situation, which become more important, and in fact sacred.

Such an attitude cannot be made up. It only comes from lots of meditation practice; that seems to be the only way. The sitting practice of meditation seems to produce gentleness and compassion naturally.

Change of Mark

Change of mark is closely related to change of attitude. Once you begin to behave with nonaggression, you begin to show signs of the sanity that is already in you. You don't actually have to try to prove anything to your relatives, your parents, your friends. The words don't count; the people around you can simply and actually appreciate the development of gentleness and reasonableness taking place in you. It is not that you are trying to be polite and understanding in the cheap sense, but you are trying to be polite and understanding beyond consideration of your own personal comfort. So some sense of gentleness and sympathy takes place, and that is the mark of being Buddhist. You begin to turn into a different breed of man. You become a gentle, considerate person who is open and brave at the same time.

You are not suddenly going to become a glowing, happy, easygoing, enlightened person, obviously. But the whole idea is that it is possible, if one's sitting practice and discipline are taking place, that one's personality could change from that painful, serious, deep-down level of neurosis into something open, sharp, profound, and delightful. This is not particularly a salesman's pitch—that change has been happening to students throughout the whole of our experience in this country.

CHANGE OF NAME

Traditionally, in Tibet and other Buddhist countries, the parents would give their child a nickname that was used during childhood. Then, when the child took the refuge vow, they would be given a Buddhist name. The nickname would be phased out, or maybe just used occasionally among one's close circle of relatives, and the Buddhist name would then be assumed. In this setting, that situation may be somewhat sticky, so I like to leave it up to each person whether or not they want to use their refuge name. The point is that when you are called by your Buddhist name, you should assume that particular attitude of gentleness. Your name should act as a reminder rather than as something that provides further identification for your ego or that is just purely a handle.

The meaning behind the name is connected with some kind of inspiration that you might develop. It is not necessarily a flattering name, nor is it condescending—but it is some kind of message. Your Buddhist name represents an encouragement for some kind of development in your personality which is connected with the practice of meditation—some sense of your individual style in approaching the dharma.

THE REFUGE VOW CEREMONY

The main part of the refuge vow ceremony involves offering three prostrations, then repeating the refuge formula three times: "I take refuge in the Buddha, I take refuge in the dharma, I take refuge in the sangha." I should explain the purpose of prostrations. There are all kinds of self-made spiritual journeys that we might be able to take, but what is important and necessary is to surrender our ego trips. Such surrender makes us much more self-made and much more closely and personally related with reality. So the idea of the prostrations is to surrender your personal clingings of all kinds so that you can begin to tune in to this particular path.

When you prostrate you hold your palms together successively at the level of your forehead, your throat, and your heart, which represents surrendering your body, speech, and mind to the Buddha, dharma, and sangha without expecting anything in return. Prostrating on the ground is very significant; it means surrendering finally. You are making a *real* commitment; you are willing to give in completely to the choiceless sanity of the earth and become a refugee in no-man's-land. The past, present, and future lineage holders are represented by this earth. You may get pissed off at this earth; you may feel very good about this earth; you may feel very unconcerned about this earth—but still the earth remains here, and it remains solid. Bowing yourself down on this earth is surrendering yourself to this basic sanity.

You do the three prostrations to the shrine, which represents our heritage. More explicitly, it represents the lineage of those who transmit awakened mind, which exists in the past, present, and future. You are also prostrating to the preceptor, who is the inheritor of this lineage. The method used in the past is no longer a myth, but is real and living. You have a living Buddhist in front of you.

Kneeling and repeating the refuge formula three times is the actual refuge-taking. It has three aspects: acknowledging oneself, acknowledging one's need for protection, and acknowledging the other. When you say, "I take refuge," you are requesting to be accepted as a refugee. And when you say, "in the Buddha, dharma, sangha," you are acknowledging the other, which is the example, the path, and the sense of community. In this situation you have to be very deliberate, precisely aware of all the processes you are going through.

You repeat the refuge formula three times. The first time is preparing the ground; the second time you are going further; and the third time you have actually gone completely.

The discipline of taking refuge is something more than a doctrinal or ritual thing: you are being physically infected with commitment to the buddhadharma; Buddhism is transmitted into your system. Something in the lineage which is very physical, almost at the level of chemistry, enters your heart as your commitment to openness takes place. The third time you say "I take refuge in the sangha," the preceptor snaps his fingers. That is the moment of real transmission. At that moment the sperm, so to speak, enters your system and you become part of the lineage. From that moment onward, you are a follower of the practicing lineage of the Kagyü. At that particular point, the energy, the power, and the blessing of basic sanity that has existed in the lineage for twenty-five hundred years, in an unbroken tradition and discipline from the time of Buddha, enters your system, and you finally become a full-fledged follower of buddhadharma. You are a living future buddha at that point.

The Bodhisattva Vow

"Taking the bodhisattva vow has tremendous power for the very reason that it is not something we do just for the pleasure of ego. It is beyond oneself. Taking the vow is like planting the seed of a fast-growing tree, whereas something done for the benefit of ego is like sowing a grain of sand. Planting such a seed as the bodhisattva vow undermines ego and leads to a tremendous expansion of perspective. Such heroism, or bigness of mind, fills all of space completely, utterly, absolutely."

THE BODHISATTVA VOW is the commitment to put others before oneself. It is a statement of willingness to give up one's own well-being, even one's own enlightenment, for the sake of others. And a bodhisattva is simply a person who lives in the spirit of that vow, perfecting the qualities known as the six paramitas—generosity, discipline, patience, exertion, meditation, and transcendental knowledge—in his effort to liberate beings.

Taking the bodhisattva vow implies that instead of holding on to our individual territory and defending it tooth and nail we become open to the world that we are living in. It means we are willing to take on greater responsibility, immense responsibility. In fact it means taking a big chance. But taking such a chance is not false heroism or personal eccentricity. It is a chance that has been taken in the past by millions of bodhi-

---

Taken from selected Bodhisattva Vow ceremonies, 1973–1978.

sattvas, enlightened ones, and great teachers. So a tradition of responsibility and openness has been handed down from generation to generation; and now we too are participating in the sanity and dignity of this tradition.

There is an unbroken lineage of bodhisattvas, springing from the great bodhisattvas Avalokiteshvara, Vajrapani, and Manjushri. It is unbroken because no one in that lineage, through generations and centuries, has indulged himself in self-preservation. Instead these bodhisattvas have constantly tried to work for the benefit of all sentient beings. This heritage of friendship has continued unbroken up to the present day, not as a myth but as a living inspiration.

The sanity of this tradition is very powerful. What we are doing in taking the bodhisattva vow is magnificent and glorious. It is such a wholehearted and full tradition that those who have not joined it might feel somewhat wretched by comparison. They might be envious of such richness. But joining this tradition also makes tremendous demands on us. We no longer are intent on creating comfort for ourselves; we work with others. This implies working with *our* other as well as the *other* other. *Our* other is our projections and our sense of privacy and longing to make things comfortable for ourselves. The *other* other is the phenomenal world outside, which is filled with screaming kids, dirty dishes, confused spiritual practitioners, and assorted sentient beings.

So taking the bodhisattva vow is a real commitment based on the realization of the suffering and confusion of oneself and others. The only way to break the chain reaction of confusion and pain and to work our way outward into the awakened state of mind is to take responsibility ourselves. If we do not deal with this situation of confusion, if we do not do something about it ourselves, nothing will ever happen. We cannot count on others to do it for us. It is our responsibility, and we have the tremendous power to change the course of the world's karma. So in taking the bodhisattva vow, we are acknowledging that we are not going to be instigators of further chaos and misery in the world, but we are going to be liberators, bodhisattvas, inspired to work on ourselves as well as with other people.

There is tremendous inspiration in having decided to work with others. We no longer try to build up our own grandiosity. We simply try to become human beings who are genuinely able to help others; that is, we develop precisely that quality of selflessness which is generally lacking in our world. Following the example of Gautama Buddha, who gave up his kingdom to dedicate his time to working with sentient beings, we are finally becoming useful to society.

We each might have discovered some little truth (such as the truth about poetry or the truth about photography or the truth about amoebas) which can be of help to others. But we tend to use such a truth simply to build up our own credentials. Working with our little truths, little by little, is a cowardly approach. In contrast, the work of a bodhisattva is without credentials. We could be beaten, kicked, or just unappreciated, but we remain kind and willing to work with others. It is a totally noncredit situation. It is truly genuine and very powerful.

Taking this mahayana approach of benevolence means giving up privacy and developing a sense of greater vision. Rather than focusing on our own little projects, we expand our vision immensely to embrace working with the rest of the world, the rest of the galaxies, the rest of the universes.

Putting such a broad vision into practice requires that we relate to situations very clearly and perfectly. In order to drop our self-centeredness, which both limits our view and clouds our actions, it is necessary for us to develop a sense of compassion. Traditionally this is done by first developing compassion toward oneself, then toward someone very close to us, and finally toward all sentient beings, including our enemies. Ultimately we regard all sentient beings with as much emotional involvement as if they were our own mothers. We may not require such a traditional approach at this point, but we can develop some sense of ongoing openness and gentleness. The point is that somebody has to make the first move.

Usually we are in a stalemate with our world: "Is he going to say he is sorry to me first, or am I going to apologize to him first?" But in becoming a bodhisattva we break that barrier: we do not wait for the other person to make the first move; we have decided to do it ourselves. People have a lot of problems and they suffer a great deal, obviously. And we have only half a grain of sand's worth of awareness of the suffering happening in this country alone, let alone in the rest of the world. Millions of people in the world are suffering because of their lack of generosity, discipline, patience, exertion, meditation, and transcendental knowledge. The point of making the first move by taking the bodhisattva vow is not to convert people to our particular view, necessarily;

the idea is that we should contribute something to the world simply by our own way of relating, by our own gentleness.

In taking the bodhisattva vow, we acknowledge that the world around us is workable. From the bodhisattva's point of view it is not a hard-core, incorrigible world. It can be worked with within the inspiration of the buddhadharma, following the example of Lord Buddha and the great bodhisattvas. We can join their campaign to work with sentient beings properly, fully, and thoroughly—without grasping, without confusion, and without aggression. Such a campaign is a natural development of the practice of meditation because meditation brings a growing sense of egolessness.

By taking the bodhisattva vow, we open ourselves to many demands. If we are asked for help, we should not refuse; if we are invited to be someone's guest, we should not refuse; if we are invited to be a parent, we should not refuse. In other words, we have to have some kind of interest in taking care of people, some appreciation of the phenomenal world and its occupants. It is not an easy matter. It requires that we not be completely tired and put off by people's heavy-handed neurosis, ego-dirt, ego-puke, or ego-diarrhea; instead we are appreciative and willing to clean up for them. It is a sense of softness whereby we allow situations to take place in spite of little inconveniences; we allow situations to bother us, to overcrowd us.

Taking the bodhisattva vow means that we are inspired to put the teachings of Buddhism into practice in our everyday lives. In doing so we are mature enough not to hold anything back. Our talents are not rejected but are utilized as part of the learning process, part of the practice. A bodhisattva may teach the dharma in the form of intellectual understanding, artistic understanding, or even business understanding. So in committing ourselves to the bodhisattva path, we are resuming our talents in an enlightened way, not being threatened or confused by them. Earlier our talents may have been "trips," part of the texture of our confusion, but now we are bringing them back to life. Now they can blossom with the help of the teaching, the teacher, and our practice. This does not mean that we completely perfect our whole situation on the spot. There will still be confusion taking place, of course! But at the same time there is also a glimpse of openness and unlimited potentiality.

It is necessary at this point to take a leap in terms of trusting ourselves. We can actually correct any aggression or lack of compassion—

anything anti-bodhisattva-like—as it happens; we can recognize our own neurosis and work with it rather than trying to cover it up or throw it out. In this way one's neurotic thought pattern, or "trip," slowly dissolves. Whenever we work with our neurosis in such a direct way, it becomes compassionate action.

The usual human instinct is to feed ourselves first and only make friends with others if they can feed us. This could be called "ape instinct." But in the case of the bodhisattva vow, we are talking about a kind of superhuman instinct which is much deeper and more full than that. Inspired by this instinct, we are willing to feel empty and deprived and confused. But something comes out of our willingness to feel that way, which is that we can help somebody else at the same time. So there is room for our confusion and chaos and ego-centeredness: they become stepping-stones. Even the irritations that occur in the practice of the bodhisattva path become a way of confirming our commitment.

By taking the bodhisattva vow, we actually present ourselves as the property of sentient beings: depending on the situation, we are willing to be a highway, a boat, a floor, or a house. We allow other sentient beings to use us in whatever way they choose. As the earth sustains the atmosphere and outer space accommodates the stars, galaxies, and all the rest, we are willing to carry the burdens of the world. We are inspired by the physical example of the universe. We offer ourselves as wind, fire, air, earth, and water—all the elements.

But it is necessary and very important to avoid idiot compassion. If one handles fire wrongly, he gets burned; if one rides a horse badly, he gets thrown. There is a sense of earthy reality. Working with the world requires some kind of practical intelligence. We cannot just be "love-and-light" bodhisattvas. If we do not work intelligently with sentient beings, quite possibly our help will become addictive rather than beneficial. People will become addicted to our help in the same way they become addicted to sleeping pills. By trying to get more and more help they will become weaker and weaker. So for the benefit of sentient beings, we need to open ourselves with an attitude of fearlessness. Because of people's natural tendency toward indulgence, sometimes it is best for us to be direct and cutting. The bodhisattva's approach is to help others to help themselves. It is analogous to the elements: earth, water, air, and fire always reject us when we try to use them in a manner that is beyond what is suitable, but at the same time, they offer themselves generously to be worked with and used properly.

One of the obstacles to bodhisattva discipline is an absence of humor; we could take the whole thing too seriously. Approaching the benevolence of a bodhisattva in a militant fashion doesn't quite work. Beginners are often overly concerned with their own practice and their own development, approaching mahayana in a very hinayana style. But that serious militancy is quite different from the lightheartedness and joy of the bodhisattva path. In the beginning you may have to fake being open and joyous. But you should at least attempt to be open, cheerful, and, at the same time, brave. This requires that you continuously take some sort of leap. You may leap like a flea, a grasshopper, a frog, or finally, like a bird, but some sort of leap is always taking place on the bodhisattva path.

There is a tremendous sense of celebration and joy in finally being able to join the family of the buddhas. At last we have decided to claim our inheritance, which is enlightenment. From the perspective of doubt, whatever enlightened quality exists in us may seem small-scale. But from the perspective of actuality, a fully developed enlightened being exists in us already. Enlightenment is no longer a myth: it does exist, it is workable, and we are associated with it thoroughly and fully. So we have no doubts as to whether we are on the path or not. It is obvious that we have made a commitment and that we are going to develop this ambitious project of becoming a buddha.

Taking the bodhisattva vow is an expression of settling down and making ourselves at home in this world. We are not concerned that somebody is going to attack us or destroy us. We are constantly exposing ourselves for the benefit of sentient beings. In fact, we are even giving up our ambition to attain enlightenment in favor of relieving the suffering and difficulties of people. Nevertheless, helplessly, we attain enlightenment anyway. Bodhisattvas and great tathagatas in the past have taken this step, and we too can do so. It is simply up to us whether we are going to accept this richness or reject it and settle for a poverty-stricken mentality.

TRANSPLANTING BODHICHITTA

The bodhisattva vow is a leap in which we begin to let go of our egocentric approach to spiritual development. In the absolute sense, the bodhisattva vow is the complete transplantation of bodhichitta, awakened mind, into our hearts—a complete binding of ourselves with the gentleness and compassion of our inherent wakefulness. But we do not become complete bodhisattvas at once; we simply put ourselves forward as candidates for bodhisattvahood. Because of this we speak of relative and absolute bodhichitta. Relative bodhichitta is like having the intention to take a journey and buying a ticket; absolute bodhichitta is like actually being a traveler. In the same way, we buy our ticket first and fly later.

The ceremony of taking the bodhisattva vow is also an acknowledgment of our potential for enlightenment. It inspires us to recognize that we have bodhichitta in us already. So in taking the bodhisattva vow we are expanding our vision infinitely, beyond this little square world of ours. In a sense, it is like a heart transplant. We are replacing our old heart, which is oriented toward ego and self-aggrandizement, with a new heart characterized by compassion and a larger vision.

The quality that makes this transplant possible is our own gentleness. So in a sense this new heart has been present all along. It is simply rediscovered within the old heart, as in peeling an onion. That discovery of bodhichitta is extremely powerful. Since we have basic generosity and compassion within ourselves, we do not have to borrow from anybody else. Based on that inherent quality of wakefulness, we can act directly, on the spot.

Often our sense of vulnerability, our feeling that we need to protect ourselves, acts as an obstacle to any sense of warmth. But on the bodhisattva path we take chances, extending ourselves without reservation for the sake of others. And it is the discovery of our own wakefulness, or bodhichitta, that creates the trust that allows us to take such chances. Such wakefulness, once acknowledged, develops constantly and cannot be destroyed. As long as such warmth and sympathy exist within us we are like food for flies; opportunities for expressing our warmth come upon us like swarms of flies. It is as though we magnetically attract such situations to ourselves. And this is our chance not to reject them but to work with them.

When we begin to give up personal territory, automatically there is some sense of awakeness, or gap in conceptualization, in our hearts. We begin to develop friendliness toward the world. At that point we can no longer blame society or the weather or the mosquitoes for anything. We have to take personal responsibility, blaming not the world but ourselves, rightly or wrongly. It is our duty to do so. There is no point in creating endless cosmic court cases as to who is right and who is wrong. Nobody wins, and such cases will only escalate into cosmic battles, a third world war. So somebody has to begin somewhere: the person taking the bodhisattva vow has to make the first move. Otherwise there is no beginning of generosity and no end of chaos and aggression. In fact, on the bodhisattva path, such nonaggression becomes one's total view of the world.

GIVING UP PRIVACY

We cannot have personal pleasure once we launch onto the bodhisattva path. We cannot reserve a little area just for ourselves. Usually keeping something back for ourselves is very important. But in this case there is no personal privilege or pleasure. Of course we would still like to have a little corner to ourselves; we would like to shut the door and play a little music or read a novel or *Time* magazine or perhaps study Buddhism. But those days are gone. From the time we take the bodhisattva vow, there is no privacy. In fact a personal reference point of any kind is needless at this point. We have been sold to sentient beings, merchandised. Sentient beings can plow on us, shit on us, sow seeds on our back—use us like the earth. And it is very, very dangerous and irritating to no longer have any privacy.

It is interesting that we could be totally public persons, twenty-four hours a day. Even when we fall asleep we could still be doing something—we are completely dedicated. With such a commitment, we no longer ask for vacations. If we ask for a vacation, or a break from that public world, it is a little fishy: we are still trying to preserve the little corner that we personally control, which is one of our biggest problems. In taking the bodhisattva vow, we are finally giving up privacy at the crude level, but we are also giving up privacy within ourselves. Our minds are usually somewhat schizophrenic: one aspect would like to keep itself hidden from the other aspects. But we are giving that up as well. So in whatever a bodhisattva does there is no privacy, no secrecy. In other words, we are not leading double lives any more; we are leading a single life dedicated to practice as well as to helping other beings. That does not mean that we become miniature gurus or masters controlling other people. Instead of being big currents in the ocean, we may be just little drops. If we become too ambitious, we may become too egotistical. So we should watch ourselves. Sitting meditation provides immense help in this regard. It shows us that we can simply be completely open and awake, realizing that the world we live in is not our personal world but a shared one.

REFUGEES AND BODHISATTVAS

Entering the bodhisattva path is very demanding—much more demanding than being a refugee. When we took the refuge vow, we committed ourselves to the path. We were inspired by the buddhadharma, and we knew that we were not going to cop out. Because we developed some understanding of our basic nature, we became strong, disciplined people, no longer nuisances to the rest of society. But, at the same time, the path of individual salvation, or individual commitment, was not completely fulfilling. Something was missing: we had not yet worked with other people, other sentient beings. Having taken the refuge vow, strong messages began to come to us that our commitment to sentient beings had not yet been fulfilled. Our whole approach seemed to become an ingrown toenail: we were eating ourselves up rather than expanding and working with others.

Having prepared the ground with the refuge vow, having given up everything, we begin to be inspired to relate with the world. We have put our own situation in order. If we had not already developed some compassion and openness toward ourselves, we could make no headway at all. But having done that, we are still not completely free. In order to develop further, we need to be energized; we need to take another leap of some kind, which is the bodhisattva vow. But this does not mean we are already bodhisattvas. In fact, we are barely ready to take the vow. But since we have responsibilities to the world, we can no longer sit back and sulk about our own negativities and upheavals. At the same time that such things are happening with ourselves, we have to go out and work with other people. We may have a wound on our foot, but we can still try to support somebody else. That is the style of the bodhisattva path: our own inconvenience is not considered all that important. At the bodhisattva level, not only are we travelers on the path but we are also spokesmen for the enlightened attitude, which means giving up self-indulgence altogether.

BODHISATTVA ACTIVITY

The bodhisattva's way of relating to others is expressed in the phrase "inviting all sentient beings as one's guests." By treating someone as a guest we view our relationship with him as important. We offer our guests specially cooked food with special hospitality. There is also a sense that our relationship to our guest is impermanent; our guest is going to leave. Therefore there is constant appreciation and a sense that this is a very opportune time. So the life of a bodhisattva is one of seeing every-one as one's guest, constantly. And that notion of inviting all sentient beings as guests is the starting point of compassion.

Compassion is the heart of the practice of meditation-in-action, or bodhisattva activity. It happens as a sudden glimpse—simultaneous awareness and warmth. Looking at it fully, it is a threefold process: a sense of warmth in oneself, a sense of seeing through confusion, and a sense of openness. But this whole process happens very abruptly. There is no time to analyze. There is no time to walk out or to hold on. There is not even time to refer back, to note that "I am doing this."

A bodhisattva's activity is both energetic and gentle. We have enough power to exert our energy, but at the same time there is the gentleness to change our decisions to suit the situation. Such gentle, energetic activ-ity is based on knowledge: we are aware of the situation around us, but we are also aware of our version of the situation—what we want to do. Every aspect is seen clearly.

Having taken the bodhisattva vow, we may feel somewhat hesitant to act on our inspiration. Looked at generally, the situations we find our-selves in seem illogical and confusing. But once we look at our everyday life in the definite way of ongoing practice, our actions can become much more clear-cut: when there is a pull toward ego we can cut through that tendency; when there is hesitation about going beyond our egocentric perspective we can let go. Our hesitation may be that we are afraid we may not make the right decision, that we don't know what to do. But we can push ourselves into the situation so that the proper direc-tion comes about naturally. We may be slightly fearful of the conse-quences of our action, somewhat tentative in our approach. But at the same time there is confidence, the inspiration to deal with things prop-erly. That combined mentality of confidence and tentativeness com-prises skillful action.

In a sense, taking the bodhisattva vow is a tremendous pretense. We are uncertain that we are able to tread on the bodhisattva path, but we still decide to do it. That leap is necessary in developing basic confidence. The situations we encounter in our everyday lives are both solid and workable. We don't have to shy away from them, nor do we have to exaggerate them by rolling in like a tank. We work with each situation simply and directly, as it happens.

This kind of bodhisattva activity is traditionally described in terms of the six paramitas, or transcendental virtues: generosity, discipline, patience, exertion, meditation, and transcendental knowledge.

The paramita of generosity is particularly connected with the notion of sharing knowledge, or teaching. In fact, everybody who takes the bodhisattva vow is regarded as a potential teacher. If out of paranoia, embarrassment, or a sense that we want to possess our knowledge we refuse to teach, we are abandoning sentient beings. Even if we feel we are not up to becoming teachers, we should be prepared to become apprentice teachers. We should be willing to share what we know with others. At the same time, we have to control ourselves to the extent that we do not share something we do *not* know.

In the bodhisattva ceremony, we express our generosity by making an offering to the three jewels: the Buddha, the dharma, and the sangha. Fundamentally, we are offering our own ego: we are offering our sense of sanity to the Buddha, our keen perception of the nature of the path to the dharma, and our sense of companionship to the sangha.

A traditional way of developing generosity is to offer our food to someone else. Even if we are hungry, we hold our plate of food in our hands and give it away mentally before eating. At that very moment of giving something away, we are actually beginning to practice the paramitas. By giving away something personal and significant in our lives, we are helping to clarify our attachments and to overcome the habitual pattern of spiritual materialism. And in fact, we are also abandoning the attainment of enlightenment at that point.

The paramita of discipline, or morality, is based on a sense of trust in oneself. In contrast, traditional morality is often based on a lack of trust and a fear of one's own aggressive impulses. When we have such little confidence in our own intelligence and wakefulness, so-called immoral persons pose a tremendous threat to us. For instance, when we reject a murderer as an immoral person it might be because of our fear that we might murder somebody as well. Or we might even be afraid to hold a gun, which represents death and killing, thinking that we might shoot ourselves on the spot. In other words, we do not trust ourselves or our own generosity. That obsession with our own inadequacies is one of the biggest obstacles on the bodhisattva path. If we feel we are inadequate bodhisattvas, we do not make good bodhisattvas at all. In fact, that obsession with a moralistic, guilt-ridden approach is a form of being trapped in the hinayana perspective. It is an attempt to confirm one's ego. The sense of trust in oneself allows the bodhisattva to work skillfully with whatever is happening, to the point of being willing to commit immorality out of compassion for sentient beings. This is obviously quite delicate, but it fundamentally involves trying to work with people in an intelligent way.

Bodhisattva discipline arises from a sense of trust in oneself, but it also involves arousing trust in others. There is a sense of heroism, of raising the banner of sanity and proclaiming an open way. If we are too mousy or small, we do not know who we are or with whom we are communicating. There is still a feeling of territoriality, of keeping things to ourselves. And since we base our trust on some feeling of being special, we are afraid of arousing the confidence of those around us. We do not want to destroy our own petty base of power. In contrast, the bodhisattva path is expansive—a great vision of openness in which there is tremendous room to work with people without one-upsmanship or impatience. Since our vision is not dependent on maintaining ego, we cannot be threatened. We have nothing to lose, so we can actually give an inch in our relations with people.

The paramita of patience is the willingness to work with our own emotions through the practice of meditation. This in turn allows us to begin to work peacefully with others. Usually we don't want to work with aggressive people because we feel they will not give us an easy time. They are a threat to our unbodhisattvalike mentality of looking for pleasure and security. And when we encounter somebody who wrongs us, we harbor tremendous resentment and refuse to forgive him. Our tendency is always to view such aggressive people, rather than our attitude of holding back, as the problem. But the paramita of patience requires that we stop the ego-centered approach of always blaming others. Quite simply, the practice of patience means not returning threats, anger, attacks, or insults. But this does not mean being purely passive.

Instead we use the other person's energy, as in judo. Since we have related to our own aggression through the practice of meditation, we are not threatened by the other person's aggression, nor do we need to respond impulsively or aggressively. Our response is self-defensive in the sense that we do not return such a person's threat, and at the same time, we prevent further aggression by allowing the other person's own energy to undercut itself.

The paramita of exertion involves being willing to work hard for the sake of others. Tremendous energy comes from overcoming the emotional complications and conceptual frivolity of one's mind, which usually provides an excuse for avoiding bodhisattva activity. We no longer indulge our laziness and self-centeredness by dwelling on the familiarity and snugness of our own emotional complications. The bodhisattva is inspired to overcome such laziness by developing simplicity. Such simplicity arises from a perspective of spaciousness in which we do not need to manipulate our emotions in any way or to get rid of them by acting them out; instead we can deal directly with them as they arise. In this way emotions are no longer obstacles but a source of further energy.

In addition to our emotions, our minds also have a conceptualizing quality, which seems to be a combination of panic and logical reasoning. We are constantly insecure, and therefore we are constantly trying to reassure ourselves. Our minds have the ability to produce hundreds of answers, hundreds of reasons to assure ourselves that what we are doing is right. And when we teach, we impose this conceptualizing chatter on others. In order to justify ourselves in such a situation, we talk a lot, trying to con our students. The bodhisattva is able to see this tremendously complicated structure of ongoing self-confirming chatter. Having overcome the laziness of emotional indulgence through simplicity, the bodhisattva is also able to see through the conceptual superstructure arising out of the emotions. To the bodhisattva, neither the emotions nor conceptual mind is seen as an obstacle. In fact, nothing is regarded as an obstacle, and nothing is regarded as evil or bad. Everything is simply part of the landscape of the bodhisattva's journey. So the bodhisattva sees his or her life as one continuous venture—the perpetual discovery of new understanding. And since his notion of path is not restricted in any way, there is the development of tremendous energy and a willingness to work very hard. So the paramita of exertion is not a project; it is the natural and spontaneous expression of the vastness of the bodhisattva's vision.

In practicing the paramita of meditation, we relate to meditation as a natural process; it is neither an obstacle nor a particular virtue. If we become impatient with constant thought-chattering in our meditation practice, we may avoid meditating. We had been expecting a comfortably rewarding situation, so we are unwilling to work with the irritations that constantly come up—we can't be bothered. On the other hand, we might get very attached to how good a meditator we are. Any kind of blissful experience we regard as some form of divine grace, as proof that what we are doing makes sense. We feel we can meditate better and more than anybody else. In this case, we view our meditation practice as a contest for the championship. But whether we try to avoid sitting practice or become attached to it as some sort of self-confirmation, we are still avoiding the paramita of meditation, which is a willingness to work unceasingly with our own neurosis and speed.

The paramita of transcendental knowledge is a quality of interest in the teachings that is nondogmatic and not based on furthering the development of ego. From the point of view of transcendental knowledge, any gesture based on developing ego or taking the easy way out is heretical. Such heresy is not a question of theism or atheism, but of preaching the language of ego, even if it is done in the name of buddhadharma. Even while practicing the mahayana, we may still be looking for a self as our basic being: "There's still some hope, I can develop tremendous muscles. I can develop tremendous lungs. I can show you that I can control my mind even though I believe in the mahayana tradition." But that double-agent approach is extremely stupid and unworkable.

It is possible for us to become so attached to the mahayana perspective that we renounce and disparage hinayana. But without the discipline of hinayana there is no basis for the development of mahayana. On the other hand, we may become very dogmatic and attached solely to hinayana. This seems to be an expression of our cowardice: we are not willing to step onto the wide-open path of mahayana. In contrast to these dogmatic extremes, the paramita of transcendental knowledge has a perky quality of interest in the intellectual logic of all three yanas: hinayana, mahayana, and vajrayana. This interest and curiosity is not purely intellectual but is based on the practice of meditation.

Basically, the idea of bodhisattva activity is to have good manners. In spite of our own irritation we should be able to extend our hospitality to others. This is quite different from hypocritical hospitality. Rather, it is an expression of enlightenment; it is a working state of mind in which we extend hospitality beyond our irritations.

It is perhaps most important in working with others that we do not develop idiot compassion, which means always trying to be kind. Since this superficial kindness lacks courage and intelligence, it does more harm than good. It is as though a doctor, out of apparent kindness, refuses to treat his patient because the treatment might be painful, or as though a mother cannot bear the discomfort of disciplining her child. Unlike idiot compassion, real compassion is not based on a simple-minded avoidance of pain. Real compassion is uncompromising in its allegiance to basic sanity. People who distort the path—that is, people who are working against the development of basic sanity—should be cut through on the spot if need be. That is extremely important. There is no room for idiot compassion. We should try to cut through as much self-deception as possible in order to teach others as well as ourselves. So the final cop-out of a bodhisattva is when, having already achieved everything else, he is unable to go beyond idiot compassion.

Taking the bodhisattva vow has tremendous power for the very reason that it is not something we do just for the pleasure of ego. It is beyond oneself. Taking the vow is like planting the seed of a fast-growing tree, whereas something done for the benefit of ego is like sowing a grain of sand. Planting such a seed as the bodhisattva vow undermines ego and leads to a tremendous expansion of perspective. Such heroism, or bigness of mind, fills all of space completely, utterly, absolutely. Within such a vast perspective, nothing is claustrophobic and nothing is intimidating. There is only the vast idea of unceasingly helping all sentient beings, as limitless as space, along the path to enlightenment.

THE BODHISATTVA VOW CEREMONY

Taking the bodhisattva vow is a public statement of your intention to embark on the bodhisattva path. Simply acknowledging that intention to yourself is not enough. You have to be brave enough to say it in front of others. In so doing, you are taking a big chance, but you are going to go ahead with it anyway.

To begin the ceremony, you request the teacher to give the bodhisattva vow and to accept you into the family of the Buddha by saying: "May the teacher be gracious to me. Just as the former tathagatas, arhats, samyaksambuddhas, exalted ones, and bodhisattvas living at the level of the great bhumis developed an attitude directed toward unsurpassable, perfect great enlightenment, so also I request the teacher to help me in developing such an attitude." The teacher responds by instructing you, as his disciple, to renounce samsara and to develop compassion for sentient beings, desire for enlightenment, devotion to the three jewels, and respect for the teacher. He reminds you to deepen the feeling of compassion and to plant it firmly in your heart, since "sentient beings are as limitless as celestial space and as long as there are sentient beings they will be affected by conflicting emotions, which will cause them to do evil, for which in turn they will suffer."

This ceremony is magical: the bodhisattvas of the past, present, and future are present, watching you. At this point you prostrate three times to these people, as well as to your own conscience. In doing these three prostrations, you bind yourself to the earth and reacknowledge your basic state of homelessness.

You then begin the actual vow by saying: "From now on, until I have become the very quintessence of enlightenment, I will develop an attitude directed toward unsurpassable, perfect great enlightenment so that the beings who have not crossed over may do so, who have not yet been delivered may be so, who have not yet found relief may find it, and who have not yet passed into nirvana may do so."

The discipline at this point in the ceremony is to identify with the elements, which nurture all sentient beings. You are becoming mother earth; therefore, you will have to accommodate all sorts of pokings and proddings and dumping of garbage—but in fact you are delighted by the whole thing. At this point you read a passage from the *Bodhicharyavatara* by Shantideva that expresses this process quite beautifully: "As earth and other elements, together with space, eternally provide sustenance in many ways for the countless sentient beings, so may I become sustenance in every way for sentient beings to the limits of space until all have attained nirvana."

Now that you have given yourself to others, you are not going to be resentful. Sometimes after a guest has arrived and you are offering him your hospitality, you may have a sense of regretting that you ever invited him. Or you may remember that as a child you sometimes found your parents' hospitality very claustrophobic and annoying: "I wish Daddy wouldn't invite those strangers over. I like my privacy." But from the point of view of a bodhisattva, your parents' example is fantastic. You are committing yourself to that kind of hospitality, and you are willing to admit people into your space. In doing so you are following the example of former bodhisattvas who also committed themselves to basic generosity, intelligence, and enlightenment. So with that in mind, you repeat: "As the sugatas of old gave birth to the bodhichitta and progressively established themselves in the discipline of a bodhisattva, so I too, for the benefit of beings, shall give birth to the bodhichitta and progressively train myself in that discipline."

Next, you offer a gift as an expression of generosity and further commitment. Even if the gift is a corpse, you are going to present whatever you have as a real gesture of committing yourself to bodhichitta. In giving something about which you care very much, too much—whatever it may be—you are offering your sense of attachment, your basic attitude of clinging.

The presentation of a gift is equivalent to the moment in the refuge vow when the preceptor snaps his fingers. But the reason you don't have the abstract energies of the lineage or of basic Buddhism coming into your system in this case is that the bodhisattva vow is more on the emotional level. Taking refuge is related to the ordinary, moralistic level: your commitment is that you are not going to be unfaithful. The bodhisattva vow is much more subtle: you don't really have a specific moment in which bodhichitta enters into you. But in some way or other, when you give your gift and you are inspired to let go of your clinging and self-centeredness, at that moment you really become a child of the Buddha, a bodhisattva. At that point, whether you like it or not, you take on a heavy burden—which is happily unavoidable. You cannot undo it. In the case of hinayana, you can give up your vow, but you cannot give up your bodhisattva vow, even after lives and lives. You cannot give it up because the discipline of mahayana is not based on physical existence but on conscience, in the very ordinary sense.

Having offered your gift, you can appreciate what you have done. Realizing that you have not made a mistake you say: "At this moment my birth has become fruitful, I have realized my human life. Today I am born into the family of the Buddha. Now I am a child of the Buddha."

The next passage you recite gives all kinds of examples of how you can be helpful to society and to the world—how you can live with yourself and with other sentient beings: "From now on I will forthrightly perform the actions befitting to my family. I will act so as not to degrade the faultlessness and discipline of my family. Just as with a blind man finding a jewel in a heap of dust, thus, somehow, bodhichitta has been born in me. This is the supreme amrita which destroys death, the inexhaustible treasure which removes the world's poverty; it is the supreme medicine which cures the world's sickness, the tree which provides rest for beings weary of wandering on the paths of existence; it is the universal bridge on which all travelers may pass over the lower realms, the rising moon of mind which dispels the torment of the kleshas; it is the great sun which puts an end to the obscurity of ignorance, the pure butter which comes of churning the milk of holy dharma. For travelers wandering on the paths of existence seeking happiness from objects of enjoyment, it is supreme bliss near at hand, the great feast which satisfies sentient beings."

Now you are ready to receive your bodhisattva name. The name you receive symbolizes generosity in working with others. It is not a further means of building up your territory or identity, but an expression of non-ego. You are no longer yours, but you belong to others. Bodhisattva names are more powerful than refuge names because there is more need of being reminded to work with others than of being reminded to work on yourself. Your bodhisattva name is an expression of your subtle style: somebody could insult you by using it; somebody could encourage you by using it. It expresses a more sensitive area than the refuge name, which is extremely useful. In other words, your bodhisattva name acts as a password; it is a very accurate guideline to your particular style of basic openness in working with all sentient beings. Both your potentialities and your basic attributes are expressed in your bodhisattva name, which should be recalled whenever a critical situation comes up. Instead of looking to a savior, you should remember your name as a reminder of the solidness of your involvement on the bodhisattva path. It is a token that you have made a link with your buddha nature, tathagata-garbha: you have dug a well and found fresh water which you can use continuously. Your bodhisattva name represents your commitment to basic sanity, your willingness to devote your life to all sentient beings. Therefore it is very powerful and important.

Without any doubt, having taken the bodhisattva vow, you should celebrate. Taking the vow is a landmark, not just a casual thing. It is something extraordinary, something historic. Keeping that in mind, you invite everyone to share your joy that you finally have become a worker for all sentient beings, by saying: "Today, witnessed by all the protectors, I have welcomed the sentient beings and sugatas. Devas and asuras rejoice!"

That ends the bodhisattva vow ceremony. It is a simple ceremony that presents you with the extreme challenge of committing yourself to people without consideration for your own comfort. And the key to meeting such a challenge is fearlessness. By taking the vow you therefore enter the fearless world of the warrior.

Sacred Outlook:
The Practice of Vajrayogini

"Experiencing the vajra mind of Vajrayogini is so deep and vast that if thoughts arise, they do not become highlights: they are small fish in a huge ocean of space."

THE VAJRAYANA, the tantric teaching of the Buddha, contains tremendous magic and power. Its magic lies in its ability to transform confusion and neurosis into awakened mind and to reveal the everyday world as a sacred realm. Its power is that of unerring insight into the true nature of phenomena and of seeing through ego and its deceptions.

According to the tantric tradition, the vajrayana is regarded as the complete teaching of the Buddha: it is the path of complete discipline, complete surrender, and complete liberation. It is important to realize, however, that the vajrayana is firmly grounded in the basic teachings of the sutrayana, the teachings of egolessness and compassion.

Frequently, the exceptional strength and efficacy of the vajrayana are misunderstood as a promise of instant enlightenment. But one cannot become enlightened overnight; in fact, it is highly deceptive and even dangerous to think in such a way. Without exception, the Buddhist teachings point to the erroneous belief in a self, or ego, as the cause of suffering and the obstacle to liberation. All of the great teachers of the

---

Written to accompany a 1983 exhibit of Himalayan Buddhist art.

past practiced the preliminary meditative disciplines diligently before becoming students of the vajrayana. Without this basic training in the practice of meditation, there is no ground from which to work with the vajrayana at all.

The Vajrayogini principle, as it has been experienced, understood, and transmitted by the gurus of the Karma Kagyü lineage of Tibet, to which I belong, is part of the vajrayana tradition. I feel very honored to have the opportunity to explain the Vajrayogini principle and the shrine connected with Vajrayogini practice. At the same time, I have a responsibility to the lineage, as well as to the reader, to introduce Vajrayogini properly.

EGOLESSNESS AND COMPASSION

A brief discussion of fundamental Buddhism as well as of the mahayana path is necessary here so that it will be clearly understood that Vajrayogini is not to be perceived as an external deity or force. This is sometimes rather difficult for Westerners to understand because of the Judeo-Christian belief in God. Buddhism is a nontheistic religion; there is no belief in an external savior. Nontheism is synonymous with the realization of egolessness, which is first discovered through the practices of shamatha and vipashyana meditation.

In shamatha meditation, we work with breath and posture as expressions of our state of being. By assuming a dignified and upright posture and identifying with the outgoing breath, we begin to make friends with ourselves in a fundamental sense. When thoughts arise, they are not treated as enemies, but they are included in the practice and labeled simply as "thinking." *Shamatha* in Sanskrit, or *shi-ne* in Tibetan, means "dwelling in a state of peace." Through shamatha practice one begins to see the simplicity of one's original state of mind and to see how confusion, speed, and aggression are generated by ignoring the peacefulness of one's being. This is the first experience of egolessness, in which one realizes the transparency of fixed ideas about oneself and the illusoriness of what one thinks of as "I" or "me."

With further practice, we begin to lose the reference point of self-consciousness, and we experience the environment of practice and the world without bringing everything back to the narrow viewpoint of "me." We begin to be interested in "that," rather than purely being interested in "this." The development of perception that is penetrating and precise without reference to oneself is called *vipashyana* in Sanskrit and *lhakthong* in Tibetan, which means "clear seeing." The technique of vipashyana does not differ from shamatha; rather, vipashyana grows out of the continued application of shamatha practice. The clear seeing, or insight, of vipashyana sees that there is no more of a solid existence in phenomena than there is in oneself, so that we begin to realize the egolessness of "other." We also begin to see that suffering in the world is caused by clinging to erroneous conceptions about self and phenomena. We perceive that philosophical, psychological, and religious ideas of eternity and external liberation are myths created by ego-mind. So, in vipashyana practice, egolessness is the recognition of fundamental aloneness, the nontheistic realization that we cannot look for help outside of ourselves.

Altogether, the ground of Buddhist practice is called the path of "individual liberation," which is *pratimoksha* in Sanskrit and *so sor tharpa* in Tibetan. By practicing the disciplines of shamatha and vipashyana, both in meditation and throughout one's life, we can actually liberate ourselves from personal confusion and neurosis and free ourselves from causing harm to ourselves and others. We become inspired to commit ourselves fully to this path by taking refuge in the Buddha (as the example of a human being who attained enlightenment by renouncing external help and working with his own mind), in the dharma (the teachings of egolessness that can be heard and experienced), and in the sangha (the community of practitioners who follow the path of the Buddha by practicing as he did). We realize that in this spinning world of confused existence we have had the rare good fortune to encounter the true path of liberation.

The mahayana, or "great vehicle," goes beyond the inspiration of individual liberation. On the whole, the mahayana approach is basically one of working for the benefit of others with whatever the world presents; therefore, it is an endless journey. As we embark on this journey without destination, our preconceptions begin to fall away. This experience of non-reference point, which initially could be just a momentary flash in one's mind, is the first glimpse of shunyata. Shunya means "empty," and *ta* makes it "empti*ness*." According to tradition, shunyata is empty of "I" and empty of "other"; it is absolutely empty. This experience of emptiness is realizing that there is no "I" as actor, no action, and no "other" to be acted upon.

Shunyata is not the nihilistic idea of nothingness, or voidness. It is the complete absence of grasping and fixation—the complete egolessness of subject and object. It is therefore the absence of separation between self and other.

The experience of shunyata provides tremendous room and tremendous vision. There is room because we see that there is no obstacle to going out, to expanding. And there is vision because there is no separation between oneself and one's experience. We can perceive things clearly, as they are, without filters of any kind. This unbiased perception is called prajna, or "discriminating awareness." Prajna is the sharpness of the perception of shunyata and the knowledge that comes from that perception.

In fact, *prajna* literally means "superior knowledge" or "best knowledge." The highest knowledge that one can have is the knowledge of egoless insight, which begins as the experience of vipashyana and matures in the mahayana into prajna. The discriminating awareness of prajna sees that "I" and "other" are not separate and, therefore, that the enlightenment of oneself and the enlightenment of others cannot be separated.

In this way, the perception of shunyata makes us altogether more wakeful and compassionate. We feel immense interest in others and immense caring for others, whose suffering is not different from our own. This is the beginning of the mahayana practice of exchanging oneself for others.

The notion of exchange means giving whatever assistance is needed; we extend our kindness, sanity, and love to other people. In exchange, we are willing to take on others' pain, confusion, and hypocrisy. We are willing to take the blame for any problems that might come up—not because we wish to be martyrs, but because we feel that there is an infinite reservoir of goodness and sanity to share. At the mahayana level, egolessness is expanded into the path of selfless action, which goes completely beyond ego-clinging. It is this surrendering of ego, which we shall discuss later, that makes it possible to enter the vajrayana path.

VAJRA NATURE AND THE YIDAM PRINCIPLE

When we let go of grasping and fixation completely, we are able to rest in the intrinsic goodness of our minds, and we regard whatever discursive thoughts that arise—passion, aggression, delusion, or any conflicting emotions—as merely ripples in the pond of mind. Out of that, we begin to realize that there is a greater vision beyond grasping and fixation. That vision is very firm and definite. It is not definite in the style of ego, but it is like the sun, which shines all the time. When we fly in an airplane above the clouds, we realize that the sun is always shining even when it is cloudy and rainy below. In the same way, when we cease to hold on to our identity, our ego, we begin to see that the nonexistence of ego is a powerful, real, and indestructible state of being. We realize that, like the sun, it is a continuous situation which does not wax or wane.

This state of being is called vajra nature. *Vajra*, or *dorje* in Tibetan, means "indestructible," or "having the qualities of a diamond." Vajra nature is the tough, immovable quality of egolessness, which is the basis for the vajrayana path. The term *vajrayana* itself means "vehicle of indestructibility"—the "vajra vehicle." The vajrayana is also called the tantrayana, or "tantric vehicle." *Tantra*, or *gyü* in Tibetan, means "continuity" or "thread." Vajra nature is the continuity of egolessness, or wakefulness, which, like the sun, is brilliant and all-pervasive.

The deities of the vajrayana are embodiments of vajra nature. In particular, the deities called yidams are important for the practice of vajrayana. The best translation of *yidam* that I have found is "personal deity." Actually, *yidam* is a shortened form of the phrase *yi kyi tamtsik*, which means "sacred bondage of one's mind." *Yi* means "mind," *kyi* means "of," and *tamtsik* means "sacred word" or "sacred bondage." *Tamtsik,* which in Sanskrit is *samaya,* will become important in a later discussion of the sacred commitments of the vajrayana. *Mind* here refers to vajra nature, the basic sanity and wakefulness of one's being, freed from ego-clinging. The yidam is the manifestation of this enlightened mind; it is the yidam who connects or binds the practitioner to the enlightened sanity within himself. So, according to the tantric understanding, the yidam is a nontheistic deity who embodies one's innate vajra nature, rather than any form of external help.

There are many thousands of tantric deities, but in the Karma Kagyü lineage, Vajrayogini is a particularly important yidam. When a student has completed the preliminary vajrayana practices, called the ngöndro, he receives abhisheka, or empowerment, to begin yidam practice, in which he identifies with a personal deity as the embodiment of his innate wakefulness, or vajra nature. In the Karma Kagyü tradition, Vajrayogini is the first yidam given to a student. In order to understand the Vajrayo-gini principle in any depth, a discussion of the stages of vajrayana prac-tice through which a student is introduced to the yidam is necessary.

DEVOTION

In the Buddhist tradition, relating to a teacher is not hero worship; the teacher is appreciated as an example of living dharma. When entering the Buddhist path, the practitioner respects the teacher as a wise man or elder. The teacher in the mahayana is called the kalyanamitra, or "spiri-tual friend"—he is a friend in the sense that he is willing to share one's life completely and to walk with one on the path. He is truly an example of the mahayana practice of exchanging oneself for others.

At the vajrayana level, we begin with faith in the teachings and the teacher, because we have already experienced the truth and the work-ability of the teachings for ourselves. Then, with the discovery of vajra nature, faith begins to develop into devotion, which is *mögü* in Tibetan. *Mö* means "longing," and *gü* means "respect." We develop tremendous respect for the teacher and a longing for what he can impart because we see that he is the embodiment of vajra nature, the embodiment of wakeful mind. At this level, the teacher becomes the guru. He is the vajra master—the one who has mastered vajra truth, indestructible truth, and who can transmit that vajra power to others. However, the vajrayana can be extremely destructive if we are not properly prepared to receive these teachings. Therefore, in order to practice the vajrayana, we must have a relationship with a vajra master, who completely un-derstands the practitioner and the practice and who knows how to bring the two together.

One's relationship with the vajra master involves surrendering one-self to the teacher as the final expression of egolessness. This allows the practitioner to develop fully the threefold vajra nature: vajra body, vajra speech, and vajra mind. The maturation of devotion into complete sur-rendering is called *lote lingkyur* in Tibetan. *Lote* means "trust," *ling* means "completely," and *kyur* means "abandoning" or "letting go." So *lote ling-kyur* means "to trust completely and let go"—to abandon one's ego completely. Without such surrender, there is no way to give up the last vestiges of ego; nor could the teacher introduce the yidam, the essence of egolessness. In fact, without such devotion to the teacher, one might attempt to use the vajrayana teachings to rebuild the fortress of ego.

NGÖNDRO

In order to develop proper devotion and surrender, a student of the vajrayana begins with the practice of ngöndro, the foundation practices that are preliminary to receiving abhisheka. *Ngön* means "before," and *dro* means "going." In the Karma Kagyü lineage, there are five practices that make up ngöndro: prostrations, the recitation of the refuge vow, the Vajrasattva mantra practice, the mandala offering, and the practice of guru yoga. These are called the extraordinary foundations.

Ngöndro is the means of connecting oneself with the wisdom of the guru and the guru's lineage. In prostrations, as the starting point, one is humbling oneself and expressing one's gratitude for the example of the vajra master and the lineage forefathers. One visualizes the gurus of the lineage, including one's own guru, in the form of the primordial buddha. Over the course of many practice sessions, the practitioner prostrates to the lineage 108,000 times while reciting the refuge vow 108,000 times. In that way, one reaffirms one's commitment to the basic path of discipline and renunciation and, at the same time, expresses surrender to the vajrayana teachings and the vajra master. Through prostrations, one catches one's first glimpse of the lineage.

Mantra practice leads to a closer experience of the lineage wisdom. It allows one to work directly with obstacles and psychological obscurations and to realize that defilements are temporary and can be overcome. The deity Vajrasattva—literally, "vajra being"—is visualized as a youthful white prince who is both the essence of vajra wisdom and the wisdom body of one's guru. In contrast, the practitioner's own body is visualized as being filled with impurities of all kinds: physical, mental, and emotional. While reciting the mantra of Vajrasattva 108,000 times, one visualizes that one's body is slowly cleansed of these impurities by the action of Vajrasattva. By the end of a practice period, one visualizes oneself as possessing the same pure nature as Vajrasattva. The point of mantra practice, therefore, is to recognize one's inherent purity.

In mandala practice, one gives oneself and one's world as an offering to the lineage. The student offers 108,000 mandalas made from heaps of saffron-scented rice mixed with jewels and other precious substances. While constructing the mandala, one visualizes the world and everything in it—all its wealth and beauty and one's myriad sense perceptions—as an offering to the gurus and buddhas, who are visualized before one. The practitioner's sense of pure being should also be included in the offering and given up; this is called "giving up the giver." When one gives up so completely, there is no one left to watch what is being given, and no one to appreciate how generous one is being. The more one surrenders in this way, the more richness one develops. There is never a problem of running out of things to offer. One's human life is in itself an immensely rich situation to offer to the lineage.

Having completed the mandala offerings one then practices guru yoga, which is like actually meeting the guru face-to-face for the first time. Guru yoga is the first opportunity to receive the adhishthana, or blessings, of the guru's wisdom.

In guru yoga, the practitioner begins to realize the nondual nature of devotion: there is no separation between the lineage and oneself and, in fact, the vajra being of the guru is a reflection of one's own innate nature. In this way, the practice of ngöndro, culminating in guru yoga, helps to overcome theistic notions about the teacher or about the vajrayana itself. One realizes that the lineage is not an entity outside of oneself: one is not worshiping the teacher or his ancestors as gods. Rather, one is connecting with vajra sanity, which is so powerful because of its nonexistence—its utter egolessness.

SACRED OUTLOOK

When we begin to mix our minds with the energy of the lineage, we are not doing so in order to protect ourselves from the world. In fact, devotion brings us closer to our experience, to our world. As a result of the practice of ngöndro, we feel a greater sense of warmth and gentleness in ourselves. Because of that, we can relax and take a fresh look at the phenomenal world. We find that life can be an easy, natural process. Because there is no need to struggle, we start to experience goodness everywhere: we experience a tremendous sense of freedom and sacredness in everything.

When we experience this self-existing sacredness, we realize that the only way to abide continuously in this state of freedom is to enter completely into the guru's world, because such freedom is the blessing of the guru. It was the guru who presented the practice that led to the experience of freedom, and it is the guru who manifests the epitome of this freedom. In fact, we begin to see that the self-existing sacredness of the world is simultaneously an expression of the guru. This experience is known as sacred outlook, or tag nang in Tibetan. *Tag nang* literally means "pure perception." The idea of purity here refers to an absence of imprisonment. Sacred outlook means perceiving the world and oneself as intrinsically good and unconditionally free.

THE FIVE BUDDHA FAMILIES

Having developed sacred outlook, it is possible to take a further step into the vajra world. When we experience the self-existing sacredness of reality, the vajrayana iconography begins to make sense; it makes sense to picture the world as a sacred realm, as a mandala of enlightened mind. From the viewpoint of sacred outlook, the phenomenal world is seen in terms of five styles of energy: buddha, vajra, padma, ratna, and karma. Oneself and the people one meets, the seasons, the elements—all aspects of the phenomenal world—are made up of one or more of these styles, or buddha families. In tantric iconography, the buddha families make up a mandala with buddha in the center, and vajra, ratna, padma, and karma at the four cardinal points.

One or more of the buddha families can be used to describe a person's intrinsic perspective or stance in the world. Each buddha family principle can have either a neurotic or an enlightened expression. The particular neurosis associated with a buddha family is transmuted into its wisdom, or enlightened, form by the taming process of shamatha-vipashyana meditation, by training in compassion in the mahayana, and, particularly, by the development of sacred outlook in the vajrayana. In their enlightened expression, the buddha families are manifestations of vajra freedom.

The basic quality of buddha energy is spaciousness. The confused manifestation of this spacious quality is ignorance, which in this case involves avoiding vivid or unpleasant experience. When buddha energy is transmuted, it becomes the wisdom of all-encompassing space. Buddha is associated with the color white and is symbolized by a wheel, which represents this all-encompassing, open nature.

Vajra, which is in the east of the mandala,* is represented by the color blue. The symbol of vajra is a vajra scepter, or dorje, whose five prongs pierce the neurosis of ego-mind. The vajra scepter is like a thunderbolt—electric and powerful. Vajra energy is precise and direct. It is the ability to view situations from all possible perspectives and to accurately perceive the details of experience and the larger frameworks in which things take place. The neurotic expressions of vajra energy are aggression and intellectual fixation. When the intellectual accuracy of vajra is transmuted into its enlightened form, it becomes mirrorlike wisdom. Vajra is associated with the element of water. Its neurotic expression, anger, is like clouded, turbulent water; its wisdom aspect is like the clear reflection of a still pond.

The ratna family, in the south, is represented by the color yellow. The symbol of the ratna family is a jewel, expressing richness. Ratna energy is like autumn, when fruits and grains are ripe and farmers celebrate the harvest. Ratna is associated with the element of earth, which expresses its solidity and fertility. The neurotic style of ratna is envy or hunger—wanting everything and trying to engulf everything. Its enlightened expression is the wisdom of equanimity, because ratna accommodates all experiences and brings out their innate richness. When it is freed from hunger, ratna becomes an expression of powerful expansiveness.

In the west is the padma family, which is associated with the color red. The symbol of padma is a lotus, a beautiful, delicate flower which blooms in the mud. Padma is the basic energy of passion, or seduction. Its neurotic aspect is grasping or clinging, which is the confused expression of passion. When passion is freed from fixation on the object of its desire, it becomes discriminating-awareness wisdom—the appreciation of every aspect and detail of experience. Padma is associated with the element of fire. In the confused state passion, like fire, does not distinguish among the things it grasps, burns, and destroys. In its enlightened expression, the heat of passion becomes the warmth of compassion.

Karma, in the north of the mandala, is associated with the color

---

*In a traditional mandala, east is at the bottom, south is to the left, west is at the top, and north is to the right.

green. Its symbol, a sword, represents cutting through hesitation and confusion and accomplishing one's goals accurately and thoroughly. Karma is the wisdom of all-accomplishing action in its enlightened manifestation. The neurotic expression of karma energy is resentment and excessive speed. Karma neurosis would like to create a uniform world and resents any sloppiness or inefficiency. When karma is freed from neurosis, it becomes accurate and energetic without resentment or pettiness. Karma is associated with the element of wind, which represents this forceful and energetic quality of action.

Perceiving the energies of the buddha families in people and in situations, we see that confusion is workable and can be transformed into an expression of sacred outlook. The student must reach this understanding before the teacher can introduce the tantric deities, or yidams. Every yidam "belongs" to a buddha family and is "ruler" of the wisdom aspect of that family. The buddha family principles provide a link between ordinary samsaric experience and the brilliance and loftiness of the yidams' world. By understanding the buddha family principles, we can appreciate the tantric deities as embodiments of the energies of sacred world and identify ourselves with that sacredness. With that understanding we can receive abhisheka, or empowerment; we are ready to be introduced to Vajrayogini.

ABHISHEKA

By receiving the abhisheka of Vajrayogini, the student enters the mandala of Vajrayogini. Through this process, Vajrayogini becomes one's yidam—the embodiment of one's basic being or basic state of mind. *Abhisheka,* which is Sanskrit, literally means "anointment." The Tibetan *wangkur* means "empowerment." The principle of empowerment is that there is a meeting of the minds of the student and vajra master, which is the product of devotion. Because the student is able to open fully to the teacher, the teacher is able to communicate directly the power and wakefulness of the vajrayana through the formal ceremony of abhisheka. In reviewing the history of the Vajrayogini transmission in the Karma Kagyü lineage, the directness of this communication becomes apparent.

VAJRAYOGINI'S SYMBOLIC MEANING

Iconographical Aspect	Symbolic of
a. Hooked Knife	a. Cutting neurotic tendencies. Also the weapon of nonthought.
b. Skull cup filled with amrita	b. Prajna and intoxication of extreme beliefs.
c. Staff (khatvanga)	c. Skillful means. The staff is eight-sided, representing the eightfold Aryan Path taught by the Buddha.
1. Scarf	1. The two folds of the scarf represent the inseparability of mahayana and vajrayana.
2. Three skulls	2. The trikaya principle: the top head is a skull representing dharmakaya: the middle head is of a putrefying corpse representing sambhogakaya; the bottom head is a freshly severed head representing nirmanakaya.
d. Sow's head (usually shown over the right ear)	d. Vajra ignorance or nonthought.
e. Hair streaming upward	e. The wrath of passion. (When Vajrayogini's hair hangs loosely on her shoulders it is a symbol of compassion. Here the emphasis is more on her wrathful aspect.)
f. Crown of five skulls	f. The wisdoms of the five buddha families.
g. Three eyes	g. Knower of the past, present, and future. Also Vajrayogini's omniscient vision.
h. Wrathful expression, clenching her fangs and biting the lower lip	h. Enraged against the maras.
i. Necklace of freshly severed heads	i. The 51 samskaras, completely liberated in nonthought.
j. One face	j. All dharmas are of one flavor in dharmakaya.
k. Bone ornaments: headdress, earrings, necklace, girdle, anklets and bracelets	k. Perfection of the 5 paramitas of generosity, discipline, patience, exertion, meditation.
l. Two arms	l. Unity of upaya and prajna.
m. Left leg bent and right leg extended	m. Not dwelling in extremes of samsara or nirvana.
n. Corpse seat	n. Death of ego.
o. Sun and moon: disk seats (only the sun is shown)	o. Sun: wisdom Moon: compassion.

Iconographical Aspect	Symbolic of
p. Lotus seat	p. Spontaneous birth of enlightenment.
q. Vajrayogini's form: red and blazing with rays of light	q. Enraged against the hordes of maras and very wrathful. Also prajnaparamita.
Not shown:	
r. Necklace of red flowers	r. Total nonattachment.

THE VAJRAYOGINI SADHANA IN THE KARMA KAGYÜ LINEAGE

The abhisheka of Vajrayogini is an ancient ceremony which is part of the *Vajrayogini Sadhana,* the manual and liturgy of Vajrayogini practice. There are many sadhanas of Vajrayogini, including those according to Saraha, Nagarjuna, Luyipa, Jalandhara, and Shavari. In the Karma Kagyü tradition, one practices the sadhana of Vajrayogini according to the Indian siddha Tilopa, the forefather of the Kagyü lineage.

According to spiritual biographies, after studying the basic Buddhist teachings for many years, Tilopa (998–1069 C.E.) traveled to Uddiyana, the home of the dakinis, or female yidams, to seek vajrayana transmission. He gained entrance to the palace of the dakinis and received direct instruction there from Vajrayogini herself, who manifested to him as the great queen of the dakinis. It may be rather perplexing to speak of encountering Vajrayogini in anthropomorphic form, when she is discussed throughout this article as the essence of egolessness. However, this account of Tilopa's meeting is the traditional story of his encounter with the direct energy and power of Vajrayogini.

Naropa (1016–1100), who received the oral transmission of the Vajrayogini practice from Tilopa, was a great scholar at Nalanda University. Following a visit from a dakini who appeared to him as an ugly old hag, he realized that he had not grasped the inner meaning of the teachings, and he set out to find his guru. After encountering many obstacles, Naropa found Tilopa dressed in beggar's rags, eating fish heads by the side of a lake. In spite of this external appearance, Naropa at once recognized his guru. He remained with him for many years and underwent numerous trials before receiving final empowerment as the holder of his lineage.

From Naropa, the oral tradition of the Vajrayogini practice passed to

Vajrayogini: The Sovereign of Desire.

Marpa (1012–1097), the first Tibetan holder of the lineage. Marpa made three journeys from Tibet to India to receive instruction from Naropa. It is said that, during his third visit to India, Marpa met Vajrayogini in the form of a young maiden. With a crystal hooked knife she slashed open her belly, and Marpa saw in her belly the mandala of Vajrayogini surrounded by a spinning mantra wheel. At that moment, he had a realization of Vajrayogini as the Coemergent Mother, a principle that will be discussed later. This realization was included in the oral transmission of Vajrayogini, which has been passed down to the present day.

Marpa gave the oral instructions for the Vajrayogini practice to the renowned yogin Milarepa (1040–1123); he in turn transmitted them to Gampopa (1079–1153), a great scholar and practitioner who established the monastic order of the Kagyü. Chief among Gampopa's many disciples were the founders of the "four great and eight lesser schools" of the Kagyü tradition. The Karma Kagyü, one of the four great schools, was founded by Tüsum Khyenpa (1110–1193), the first Karmapa and a foremost disciple of Gampopa. Since that time, the Karma Kagyü lineage has been headed by a succession of Karmapas, numbering sixteen in all. Tüsum Khyenpa handed down the oral transmission of the *Vajrayogini Sadhana* to Drogön Rechenpa (1088–1158); from him it was passed to Pomdrakpa, who transmitted it to the second Karmapa, Karma Pakshi (1206–1283). Karma Pakshi passed the Vajrayogini transmission to Ugyenpa (1230–1309), who gave it to Rangjung Dorje (1284–1339), the third Karmapa. It was Rangjung Dorje, the third Karmapa, who composed the written form of the sadhana of Vajrayogini according to Tilopa and the oral instructions of Marpa, which is still practiced today. It is this sadhana that is the basis for this discussion of the Vajrayogini principle.

The first Trungpa was a student of the siddha, Trung Mase (fifteenth century), who was a close disciple of the fifth Karmapa, Teshin Shekpa (1384–1415). When Naropa transmitted the teachings of Vajrayogini to Marpa, he told him that these teachings should be kept as a transmission from one teacher to one student for thirteen generations, and then they could be propagated to others. This transmission is called chig gyü, the "single lineage" or "single thread" transmission. Because of this, the Kagyü lineage is frequently called the "hearing lineage." Trung Mase received the complete teachings on Vajrayogini, Chakrasamvara, and the Four-Armed Mahakala, and these became a special transmission that he was to hold. Since Trung Mase belonged to the thirteenth generation, he became the first guru to transmit this particular lineage of mahamudra teachings to more than a single dharma successor, and in fact he taught it widely. The first Trungpa, Künga Gyaltsen, was one of Trung Mase's disciples who received this transmission. As the eleventh Trungpa Tulku, I received the Vajrayogini transmission from Rölpa Dorje, the regent abbot of Surmang and one of my main tutors.

Since 1970, when I arrived in America, I have been working to plant the buddhadharma, and particularly the vajrayana teachings, in American soil. Beginning in 1977 and every year since then, those of my students who have completed the preliminary vajrayana practices, as well as extensive training in the basic meditative disciplines, have received the abhisheka of Vajrayogini. As of 1980 there are more than three hundred Vajrayogini sadhakas (practitioners of the sadhana) in our community, and there are also many Western students studying with other Tibetan teachers and practicing various vajrayana sadhanas. So the Vajrayogini abhisheka and sadhana are not purely part of Tibetan history; they have a place in the history of Buddhism in America as well.

The Ceremony of Abhisheka

The abhisheka of Vajrayogini belongs to the highest of the four orders of tantra: anuttaratantra. *Anuttara* means "highest," "unsurpassed," or "unequaled." Anuttaratantra can be subdivided into three parts: mother, father, and nondual. The Karma Kagyü lineage particularly emphasizes the teachings of the mother tantra, to which Vajrayogini belongs.

Mother tantra stresses devotion as the starting point for vajrayana practice. Therefore, the key point in receiving the abhisheka is to have one-pointed devotion to the teacher. By receiving abhisheka, one is introduced to the freedom of the vajra world. In the abhisheka, the vajra master manifests as the essence of this freedom, which is the essence of Vajrayogini. He therefore represents the yidam as well as the teacher in human form. Thus, when one receives abhisheka, it is essential to understand that the yidam and the guru are not separate.

In the tradition of anuttaratantra, the student receives a fourfold abhisheka. The entire ceremony is called an abhisheka, and each of the four parts is also called an abhisheka, because each is a particular empowerment. The four abhishekas are all connected with experiencing the phenomenal world as a sacred mandala.

Before receiving the first abhisheka, the student reaffirms the refuge and bodhisattva vows. At this point the attitude of the student must be one of loving-kindness for all beings, with a sincere desire to benefit others. The student then takes a vow called the samaya vow, which binds the teacher, the student, and the yidam together. As part of this oath, the student vows that he or she will not reveal his or her vajrayana experience to others who are not included in the mandala of Vajrayogini. The student then drinks what is known as the samaya oath water from a conch shell on the shrine, to seal this vow. It is said that if the student violates this oath the water will become molten iron: it will burn the student from within and he will die on the spot. On the other hand, if the student keeps his vow and discipline, the oath water will act to propagate the student's sanity and experience of the glory, brilliance, and dignity of the vajra world. The notion of samaya will be discussed in greater detail after the discussions of the abhisheka itself.

After taking the samaya oath, the student receives the first abhisheka, the abhisheka of the vase (kalasha abhisheka), also known as the water abhisheka. Symbolically, the abhisheka of the vase is the coronation of the student as a prince or princess—a would-be king or queen of the mandala. It signifies the student's graduation from the ordinary world into the world of continuity, the tantric world.

The abhisheka of the vase has five parts, each of which is also called an abhisheka. In the first part, which is also called the abhisheka of the vase, the student is given water to drink from a vase on the shrine, called the tsobum. The tsobum is the principal abhisheka vase and is used to empower the student. The text of the abhisheka says:

> Just as when the Buddha was born
> The devas bathed him,
> Just so with pure, divine water
> We are empowered.

Receiving the water from the tsobum in the first abhisheka of the vase symbolizes psychological cleansing as well as empowerment. Before ascending the throne, the young prince or princess must bathe and put on fresh clothes. The five abhishekas of the vase are connected with the five buddha families. The first abhisheka of the vase is connected with the vajra family; the student is presented with a five-pointed vajra scepter, symbolizing his ability to transmute aggression into mirrorlike wisdom.

In the second abhisheka of the vase, the crown abhisheka, the student is presented with a crown inlaid with five jewels representing the wisdom of the five buddha families. He is symbolically crowned as a confident and accomplished student worthy of taking his place in the mandala of Vajrayogini. The crown abhisheka is connected with the ratna family; the student is also presented with a jewel, the symbol of the ratna wisdom of equanimity. There is a sense of being enriched, a feeling of openness and generosity, and a sense of confidence that one is able to overcome any sense of threat or poverty.

In the third abhisheka of the vase, the abhisheka of the vajra, the student is presented with a nine-pronged vajra scepter, or dorje. The vajra is the symbol of indestructibility and of complete skillfulness in working with the phenomenal world. So, in receiving the vajra the student is presented with the means to overcome obstacles and to propagate vajra sanity. The abhisheka of the vajra is related to the padma family: although the vajra is both a powerful scepter and a deadly weapon, its power comes from generating and extending compassion, warmth, and generosity. The student is also presented with a lotus, the symbol of the padma family, signifying the ability to transmute the grasping quality of desire into discriminating-awareness wisdom.

The abhisheka of the ghanta, or bell, is the fourth abhisheka of the vase. Presenting the student with the ghanta signifies that he is not only concerned with personal realization but is also willing to proclaim the teachings for the benefit of others. The piercing sound of the ghanta signifies that the vajra proclamation of truth is unobstructed. The abhisheka of the ghanta is connected with the karma family. The student is presented with a sword, the symbol of the karma family, signifying the wisdom of all-accomplishing action which conquers neurotic speed and jealousy.

The final abhisheka of the vase is the abhisheka of name. In this abhisheka, the vajra master rings a ghanta with a vajra attached to it above the student's head. When the bell rings, the student is given a tantric name, which is a secret name. This name is not publicized like an ordinary name, but when the practitioner needs to use his power to wake someone up, he says his own vajra name, his secret name, as a reminder of vajra nature. The giving of the secret name signifies the final act in the coronation of the tantric prince or princess. Because of merit accumulated through practice and devotion to the teacher, the student deserves to change his or her name from a common name to that of a would-be king or queen, a potential master of the mandala; the student is acknowledged as a future tathagata.

The abhisheka of name is connected with the buddha family. There is a sense of complete spaciousness and openness that comes when one takes one's place in the vajra mandala. Having been coronated, the student is presented with a hooked knife, which Vajrayogini holds in her right hand. At this point, the student is introduced to the chief deity of the mandala and to her buddhalike quality, which is the wisdom of all-encompassing space. Although Vajrayogini is red in color, symbolizing her feminine quality of warmth and passion, her basic quality is definitely that of the buddha family.

Having received the complete abhisheka of the vase, there is a sense of significant psychological progress and psychological change in the student. At that point, the vajra master is able to confer the remaining three abhishekas. We cannot go into too much detail about these aspects of the ceremony. But in brief, the second abhisheka is known as the secret abhisheka (guhya abhisheka). By drinking amrita—a mixture of liquor and other substances—from the skull cup on the shrine, the mind of the student merges with the mind of the teacher and the mind of the yidam, so that the boundary between confusion and wakefulness begins to dissolve. In the third abhisheka, the prajna-jnana abhisheka, or abhisheka of knowledge and wisdom, the student begins to experience joy, mahasukha—a uniting with the world. This is sometimes called the union of bliss and emptiness, which signifies greater openness and greater vision taking place.

The fourth abhisheka (chaturtha abhisheka) is known as the abhisheka of suchness. The student experiences that he or she does not have to dwell on the past, present, or future; he could just wake himself up on the spot. The student's mind is opened into the ultimate notion of sacred outlook, in which there is nobody to "flash" sacred outlook. There is just a sense of the doer and the doing dissolving into one, which is a sense of basic shock: the possibilities of conventional mind are dissolving into nothing.

Samaya

The principle of samaya, or sacred bondage, becomes extremely important once we have taken abhisheka. The definition of yidam as the "sacred bondage of one's mind" was discussed earlier. When we receive empowerment to practice the sadhana of Vajrayogini, we take on that samaya, or bondage. We bind ourselves to indestructible wakefulness, committing ourselves fully to maintaining sacred outlook throughout our lives. This is done by identifying oneself completely with the vajra sanity of the teacher and of Vajrayogini. One is inseparably bound together with the teacher and the yidam; and, at this point, one's very being and one's sanity depend on keeping up this commitment.

This is not to say that if a student has one "bad" thought or trace of confusion he will be rejected or destroyed. There is still a sense of journey and path that takes place once one has received abhisheka. In fact, it is said that samaya is nearly impossible to keep: it is like a mirror in that, no matter how thoroughly it is polished, it always collects dust and must be polished again. In taking abhisheka, one is taught to experience sacred outlook on the spot, which *is* samaya. When obstacles or difficulties arise, they become reminders of sacred outlook rather than purely hindrances. This is called the samaya of experiencing everything as sacred in vajra nature, which has three categories: the samaya of body, or mudra; the samaya of speech, or mantra; the samaya of mind, or vajra.

The samaya of body involves always regarding one's basic phenomenal situation as an expression of sacredness. We do not doubt the sacredness of our world. The samaya of speech involves also regarding any occurrence—anything that comes up in our experience—as sacred. This could be either an internal or an external occurrence, so that any subconscious gossip or emotional upheaval is included here. The samaya of mind is connected with the indestructible wakefulness of the vajra mandala—in this case the mandala of Vajrayogini. Even the hint or the possibility of neurosis is unable to enter into one's state of being because the whole world is seen as part of the mandala of sacredness that one has entered.

It is interesting that abhisheka brings both a greater sense of freedom and a greater sense of bondage. The more we develop a sense of openness, of letting go and shedding ego, the more we develop a commitment to the world of sanity. So taking abhisheka and beginning yidam

THE HEART OF THE BUDDHA

practice is a very serious step. In fact, we should be somewhat frightened of it and, at the same time, we could appreciate it as the most precious opportunity to realize our human birth.

COEMERGENT WISDOM

Fundamentally, the magic of the vajrayana tradition is the ability to transform confusion into wisdom on the spot. From the point of view of vajrayana, real magic, or *siddhi* in Sanskrit, is the ability to work with and tame one's mind. This is completely different from the usual notion of magic as a supernatural power over the universe. As mentioned in the previous discussion of the samayas of body, speech, and mind, any potential confusion and neurosis becomes an opportunity to experience sacred outlook. At the beginning of the path of meditation, we work to tame our minds and subdue the forces of confusion. In the mahayana, we see the emptiness of self and phenomena; out of that, we rouse compassion for beings who do not realize the emptiness, and therefore the freedom, of their nature. In the vajrayana, we could actually bring together confusion and enlightenment on one spot, and thereby completely overcome the dualism of samsara and nirvana.

The simultaneous experience of confusion and sanity, or being asleep and awake, is the realization of coemergent wisdom. Any occurrence in one's state of mind—any thought, feeling, or emotion—is both black and white; it is both a statement of confusion and a message of enlightened mind. Confusion is seen so clearly that this clarity itself *is* sacred outlook. Vajrayogini is called "the Coemergent Mother." In fact, the sadhana of Vajrayogini according to Tilopa is entitled *The Sadhana of the Glorious Coemergent Mother Vajrayogini*. By practicing the sadhana and by identifying ourselves with the body, speech, and mind of the yidam, we become able to experience the coemergent boundary between confusion and wakefulness. Then we can use confusion itself as a stepping-stone for realizing further sanity and further wisdom.

VISUALIZATION

A practitioner's connection to, and understanding of, the iconography come about through the visualization practice of Vajrayogini. There are two stages of visualization practice: utpattikrama (*kyerim* in Tibetan) and sampannakrama (*dzogrim* in Tibetan). *Utpattikrama* literally means "developing stage," and *sampannakrama* means "fulfillment stage." Utpattikrama is the process of visualizing the yidam, in this case, Vajrayogini. In the self-visualization, the practitioner visualizes himself as the yidam. The visualization arises from shunyata, or emptiness, as do all tantric visualizations. The text amplifies this concept:

> All the dharmas comprising grasping and fixation become empty. From within emptiness . . . arises the triangular source of dharmas . . . On that is the nature of my consciousness . . . Like a fish leaping from water, I arise in the body of Jetsun Vajrayogini.

So the process of visualizing oneself as the yidam comes first from the experience of emptiness and egolessness. Out of that arises the source of dharmas, the abstract form of coemergence; and on that, the practitioner visualizes himself as the yidam. The visualization, therefore, is essentially empty as well. The practice of visualization is identifying oneself with the yidam, realizing the deity as the nonmanifested, or empty, manifestation of basic enlightened nature. The form of the yidam, including her clothing, ornaments, and stance, represents aspects of the enlightened state of mind. So when one visualizes oneself as a blazing, youthful red lady decked with bone ornaments, one is not particularly trying to conjure up an exotic costume as the latest fashion, but one is identifying oneself with Vajrayogini as the embodiment of wisdom and compassion.

The visualization of oneself as Vajrayogini is called the samayasattva: the "sacred bondage of one's being." The samayasattva is basically the expression of the samayas of body, speech, and mind. It expresses one's commitment to the teacher and the teachings and one's trust in one's fundamental state of mind.

Having visualized the samayasattvas of basic being, one invites what is known as jnanasattva. The jnanasattva is another level of being or experience. Jnana is a state of wakefulness or openness, whereas samaya is an experience of bondage, of being solidly grounded in one's experience. *Jnana* literally means "wisdom" or, more accurately, "being wise." One invites this state of wisdom, this level of wakefulness, into one's own imperfect visualization, so that the visualization comes alive with a feeling of openness and humor.

At the conclusion of the visualization practice, the visualization is dissolved back into the emptiness and one meditates, or rests, in that nondual state of mind. This is the sampannakrama, or fulfillment, stage. It is said in the tantric texts that the proper understanding of visualization practice is that the utpattikrama and sampannakrama stages are not fundamentally different; that is, in this case, the sampannakrama experience of emptiness-emptiness and the utpattikrama experience of form-emptiness should not be seen as two things, but as one expression of the world of the Coemergent Mother.

Sampannakrama meditation is similar to the practice of shamatha-vipashyana; in fact, without prior training in these meditation practices, it is impossible to practice sampannakrama. Sampannakrama is an expression of vastness. Experiencing the vajra mind of Vajrayogini is so deep and vast that if thoughts arise, they do not become highlights: they are small fish in a huge ocean of space.

THE VAJRAYOGINI PRINCIPLE AND ITS ICONOGRAPHY

An examination of the meaning of the following praise to Vajrayogini from the sadhana may help us to understand the Vajrayogini principle in relation to the iconography of Vajrayogini. The praise begins:

> Bhagavati Vajrayogini,
> Personification of vajra emptiness,
> Blazing with the kalpa-ending fire, uttering
>   the terrifying sound of HUM—
> We prostrate to Vajra-chandali.

Bhagavati means "blessed one." This stanza refers first to Vajrayogini as the anthropomorphic form of shunyata, the "personification of vajra emptiness." It then praises her fiery quality of passion and cosmic lust. In the iconography, Vajrayogini's body is red and blazes with rays of light, which is described here as "blazing with the kalpa-ending fire." This is her padma family quality, which transmutes neurotic passion into all-consuming compassion. *Kalpa* means "a historical era." The "kalpa-ending fire" in Indian mythology is an explosion of the sun, which burns up the solar system and brings an end to the kalpa. Vajrayogini's passion is so bright and so consuming that it is likened to that fire. The "terrifying sound of HUM" expresses the wrath of her passion, which is terrifying to ego. Chandali (*tummo* in Tibetan) is the yogic heat, cosmic heat, in yogic practice, which is again the Vajrayogini principle of passion arising free from habitual tendencies. Such passion is immensely powerful; it radiates its warmth in all directions. It simultaneously nurtures the welfare of beings and blazes to destroy the neurotic tendencies of ego. The praise continues:

> Your sow's face manifesting nonthought, the unchanging
>   dharmakaya,
> You benefit beings with wrathful mercy;
> Accomplishing their welfare; with horrific accoutrements.
> We prostrate to you who benefit beings in nonthought.

Nonthought is an important aspect of the Vajrayogini principle. It is the experience of mind totally freed from the habitual chatter of ego, freed from the grasping and fixation that give rise to neurotic thought patterns. Until the aggression and wildness of mind are tamed through meditation practice, there is no possibility of experiencing the nonthought possibilities in one's mind.

Vajrayogini is often depicted with a sow's head over her right ear. When she wears this ornament, she is referred to as Vajravarahi, "Vajra Sow." The sow traditionally represents ignorance or stupidity. In this case, the sow's head symbolizes the transmutation of ignorance, or delusion, into the vajra ignorance, which is nonthought or complete spaciousness of mind.

This stanza equates nonthought with dharmakaya, which, roughly translated, is the primordial mind of buddha. The practice of the Vajrayogini Sadhana is very much connected with realizing this primordial non–reference point. The purpose of the sadhana practice is not so much to cut immediate thoughts as it is to cut the habitual tendencies that are the root of discursive thought.

The "horrific accoutrements" referred to in the stanza are the necklace of freshly severed heads that Vajrayogini wears. It says in the sadhana that she wears this necklace because "the fifty-one samskaras are completely purified." *Samskara* means "formation," which refers to concepts. Vajrayogini's necklace of heads signifies that all habitual concepts are purified or destroyed in nonthought.

The praise continues:

> Terrifying heroine who annihilates the unsuitable,
> With three eyes, clenched fangs, the absolute trikaya,
> Your terrifying cry cuts off the kleshas.
> We prostrate to you who subjugate and conquer the maras.

Vajrayogini is frequently called the conqueror of the maras, which are the forces of worldly confusion. In the stories of the Buddha's en-lightenment, Mara, "the Evil One," sends his daughters, the four maras, to tempt Shakyamuni and his armies to attack him. Vanquishing them, Shakyamuni becomes the Buddha, "the Awakened One." Thus, the basic idea of Vajrayogini as the conqueror of the maras is the conquest of ego. From ego's point of view, Vajrayogini is "terrifying" because her wake-fulness is so piercing and uncompromising. At another point the sadhana says: "Grimacing wrathfully to subdue the four maras, she clenches her fangs and bites her lower lip." This further explains the stanza's refer-ence to Vajrayogini's fierceness.

The reference to Vajrayogini's three eyes means that nothing escapes the vision of Vajrayogini; therefore, ego has nowhere to hide. The sa-dhana also says: "Because she is the knower of the past, present, and future, she rolls her three furious bloodshot eyes."

The notion that Vajrayogini is "the absolute trikaya" is that her wis-dom and skillful means manifest on all levels of body and mind: the dharmakaya level of absolute, primordial mind; the sambhogakaya level of energy, emotions, and symbols; and the nirmanakaya level of mani-fested form, or body. The trikaya also refers to the levels of body, speech, and mind in one's practice, which are the levels of physical body, the emotions and concepts, and the basic spaciousness of mind. Vajrayo-gini joins all of those levels together, and again she leaves no place for the maras to hide.

The stanza also says that her terrifying cry "cuts off the kleshas." Kleshas, or obscurations, refer to conflicting emotions, neurotic emo-tion. The five kleshas are passion, aggression, delusion, jealousy, and pride, all of which are subjugated by the Vajrayogini principle.

The next stanza reads:

> Naked, with loosed hair, of faultless and terrifying form;
> Beyond the vice of the kleshas, benefiting sentient beings;
> You lead beings from the six realms with your hook of
>   mercy.
> We prostrate to you who accomplish Buddha activity.

Vajrayogini is naked because she is completely untouched by the neurosis of the kleshas; therefore she has no armor of ego to clothe her. Because of this, she is able to "do benefit for sentient beings," to extend absolute compassion to them. The reference to her loosed hair signifies her compassion for beings. The "hook of mercy" refers to Vajrayogini's hooked knife, with which she lifts beings out of the suffering of the six realms, or samsara, into the vajra world. Therefore, she completely accomplishes action that is free from karmic defilement—buddha activity, or action that is completely awake.

The next stanza reads:

> Dwelling in the charnel ground, subjugating Rudra and his
>   wife,
> Wrathful, fearsome, uttering the sound of PHAT,
> You benefit beings with the mercy of your skill.
> We prostrate to the wrathful one who subjugates the maras.

The "charnel ground" refers to the basic space in which birth and death, confusion and wakefulness arise—the ground of coemergence. Vajrayogini is not an ethereal principle; she dwells in the heart of samsaric chaos, which is also the heart of wisdom. "Rudra and his wife" refers to ego and its embellishments, which Vajrayogini subjugates utterly. She is "the terrifying heroine who annihilates the unsuitable"; therefore, "she is wrathful and fearsome and utters the sound of PHAT," a syllable associated with subjugation, destruction of ego-clinging, and the proclamation of vajra truth. At the same time, she is skilled and merciful. Combining these qualities, she is, again, the subjugator of the maras.

The next verse reads:

> You have realized ultimate dharmata and abandoned death.
> On a seat of a corpse, sun, moon, and lotus,

Your wrathful form is beautified with all the ornaments.
We prostrate to you who have perfected all good qualities.

The lotus, sun disk, and moon disk are the customary seats for both
buddhas and yidams in tantric iconography. The lotus is a symbol of
purity, and it also signifies the birth of enlightenment amidst the world
of confused existence. The sun symbolizes jnana, or wisdom, while the
moon is a symbol of bodhichitta, or compassion. The fact that Vajrayogini also stands on a corpse signifies that she is a semiwrathful deity.
There are peaceful, semiwrathful, and wrathful yidams in tantric iconography. The peaceful deities represent the energy of pacifying and taming
while semiwrathful and wrathful yidams work more directly and forcefully with passion, aggression, and delusion—conquering and trampling
them on the spot.

The figure of the corpse symbolizes the death of ego and shows that
Vajrayogini has "abandoned death." "Ultimate dharmata" in the stanza
is a reference to Vajrayogini's stance. In an earlier section of the sadhana,
it says: "Since she does not dwell in the extremes of samsara or nirvana,
she stands on a seat of a lotus, corpse, and sun disk, with her left leg bent
and her right leg raised in dancing posture." The idea of ultimate dharmata is transcending the dualism, or extremes, of samsara and nirvana
by realizing coemergent wisdom: seeing how confusion and enlightenment arise simultaneously. *Dharmata* means "the state of dharma." It
is complete realization of the dharma, which is seeing the "isness" or
"suchness" of reality.

This stanza also refers to the ornaments that beautify Vajrayogini's
wrathful form: her bone headdress, her bone earrings, her necklace, her
girdle, and her anklets and bracelets. These present her perfection of
generosity, discipline, patience, exertion, and meditation—five of the six
paramitas, or transcendent actions of the mahayana. The perfection of
the sixth paramita, prajna, is not represented as an ornament because the
being of Vajrayogini is itself the epitome of prajna. Thus she is called
Prajnaparamita. Prajna as the perception of shunyata was mentioned
earlier. At the level of prajnaparamita, prajna is complete, nondual realization which cuts through any clinging to either existence or nonexistence. Prajnaparamita is also called "the Mother of All the Buddhas": all
the buddhas of the past, present, and future are born from this stainless
good knowledge which shows the nature of phenomena as shunyata. In
an earlier section of the sadhana, Vajrayogini is praised as Prajnaparamita:

Prajnaparamita, inexpressible by speech or thought,
Unborn, unceasing, with a nature like sky,
Only experienced by discriminating awareness wisdom,
Mother of the victorious ones of the three times, we praise
    you and prostrate.

The next stanza reads:

Holding a hooked knife, skull cup, and khatvanga in your
    hands,
Possessing the light of wisdom, cutting off the kleshas.
As the spontaneous trikaya, you cut off the three poisons.
We prostrate to you who benefit beings.

The second line—"Possessing the light of wisdom, cutting off the
kleshas"—further emphasizes the Vajrayogini principle as Prajnaparamita, the essence of discriminating-awareness wisdom.

The hooked knife has been discussed as Vajrayogini's "hook of
mercy." It is also a weapon that is used to slice through the deceptions
of ego. It is a symbol of the power and cutting quality of nonthought. In
her left hand Vajrayogini holds a skull cup, or kapala, filled with amrita,
representing the principle of intoxicating extreme beliefs. The kapala
filled with amrita is also a symbol of wisdom. The khatvanga is the staff
that Vajrayogini holds up against her shoulder. It represents her skillful
means. The staff is also the secret symbol of Vajrayogini's union with
her consort, Chakrasamvara, who is the essence of skillful means.

On the khatvanga are three heads representing the trikaya principle
mentioned in this stanza. The reference to Vajrayogini as the spontaneous trikaya means that the brilliance of her wisdom applies equally to all
levels of experience. Because of the universality of her wisdom, she utterly cuts off the three poisons: passion, aggression, and delusion. In
doing so, she benefits beings.

The next stanza reads:

Self-born great bliss, O Vajrayogini,
Unchanging wisdom vajra of dharmakaya,
Nonthought, unconditioned wisdom, absolute
    dharmadhatu—
We prostrate to your pure, nondual form.

Again, this stanza praises Vajrayogini as the essence of wisdom, which is the primordial "wisdom vajra of dharmakaya" and the even more primordial "unconditioned wisdom" of "absolute dharmadhatu"; this wisdom is completely nondual. Beyond that, this stanza brings together the Vajrayogini principle of wisdom with the principle of the great bliss, mahasukha, which is self-born, that is, self-existing rather than created or manufactured by conceptual mind.

Mahasukha is an actual experience of bliss—a physical, psychological, total experience of joy that comes from being completely without discursive thoughts, completely in the realm of nonthought. One unites with the nondual, awake state of being. This experience is the fruition of the Vajrayogini practice; it comes only from complete identification with the wisdom mind of the yidam. According to the scriptures, mahasukha and wisdom are indivisible; therefore, the practice of Vajrayogini leads to this experience of the self-born great bliss because she is the essence of wisdom.

In the next stanza of the praise, the third line reads:

Self-born great bliss, you are ultimate mahamudra

This refers to Vajrayogini. Experiencing mahasukha, or the wisdom of bliss and emptiness, is the realization of mahamudra, which is the pinnacle of the tradition of anuttaratantra. *Maha* means "great" and *mudra* means "sign" or "gesture." To experience mahamudra is to realize that the literal truth, the symbolic truth, and the absolute truth are actually one thing, that they take place on one dot, one spot. One experiences reality as the great symbol which stands for itself.

The bliss of mahamudra is not so much great pleasure, but it is the experience of tremendous spaciousness, freedom from imprisonment, which come from seeing through the duality of existence and realizing that the essence of truth, the essence of space, is available on this very spot. The freedom of mahamudra is measureless, unspeakable, fathomless. Such fathomless space and complete freedom produce tremendous joy. This type of joy is not conditioned by even the experience of freedom itself; it is self-born, innate.

CONCLUSION

Some of what has been discussed here may be very difficult to grasp. In fact, it should be that way. If it were possible to experience the vajrayana simply by reading about it, it would cease to exist, because no one would practice it; everyone would simply study the texts. Luckily this does not work. The only way to gain the vajra freedom is to practice buddha-dharma as it was taught by the Buddha and as it has been preserved and passed down for twenty-five hundred years.

I am very happy that it has been possible to discuss the vajrayana and the Vajrayogini tradition so genuinely and thoroughly. But the most important thing that one can ever do for oneself and others is to sit down and unravel the confusion in one's mind. This is a very, very simple thing to do, and because it is so simple, it is also very easy not to see this possibility.

It is my hope that this discussion will provide a glimpse of the vajra-yana world—its grandeur and its sacredness. Sacred possibilities always exist in our lives. The goodness and the gentleness of the world are al-ways there for us to appreciate. This is not a myth; it is actual fact. We could experience Vajrayogini at any time if we have the courage to ac-knowledge our own wakeful nature and the greatness of our heritage as human beings.

> Eternally brilliant, utterly empty,
> Vajra dancer, mother of all,
> I bow to you.
> The essence of all sentient beings lives as Vajrayogini.
> From the milk ocean of her blessing
> Good butter is churned
> Which worthy ones receive as glory.
> May everyone eternally enjoy
> The lotus garden of the Coemergent Mother.

Part Three

WORKING WITH OTHERS

EIGHT

Relationship

"The idea of relationship needs to fall apart. When we realize that life is the expression of death and death is the expression of life, that continuity cannot exist without discontinuity, then there is no longer any need to cling to one and fear the other. There is no longer any ground for the brave or the cowardly. One sees that relationship is the lack of any viewpoint whatsoever."

VIEW BASED ON HOPE FOR ETERNITY

Eternity is one of the notions we cherish as an encouragement in our lives. We feel that since there is eternity there will be eternal communication. Somehow or other there will be an endless continuity to give meaning to things: a spiritual background or an atmosphere of transcendental promise.

We hardly realize how this attitude influences our approach toward relationships. When we become good friends with somebody in high school, we automatically expect the friendship to go on forever. It may be fifteen years since we built a cabin with a friend but now we continue to celebrate our comradeship by going over how skillfully we did the framing, the joints, what nails we used, and so on.

Many relationships are formed on the basis of some common pain or

---

Composed during 1972 retreat in Charlemont, Massachusetts.

some shared task. We tend to make a big deal of this pain or task: we make it the keepsake of the relationship. Or else we meet someone in circumstances of lively common interest where communication flows without obstacles and then we celebrate the smoothness as if fending off a common enemy. Either way, the pain or the smoothness develops a legendary quality in regard to the relationship.

"Good friends" implies forever. You expect that the person you are committed to in that way will pour honey on your grave; otherwise you will feel you have been cheated. You are constantly struggling to keep your eternal friendship beautiful, which becomes an enormous strain on the relationship. Nevertheless, this is the model of relationship presented by theistic traditions, such as Christianity or Hinduism. Having such a relationship is regarded as behaving as God commanded or as coming closer to the example of God's own love, which is eternal.

The idea of eternity has been misunderstood; it has been used to prove the profundity of our relationship, our deathless friendship. We tend to assume that something is going to go on forever, and therefore we venerate it like someone might venerate a piece of rusty fence wire known to have been hanging on a fence at a famous Civil War battle. We venerate it for its eternity rather than for its profundity. Ironically, it actually becomes a profound statement because of the basic truth of impermanence.

In societies influenced—at the sophisticated level at least—by a non-theistic point of view, such as Buddhist or Confucian, relationship is more a matter of manners and integrity than of approaching an eternal divine model. There is less sense of guilt, but there is still a sense of righteousness or of acting justly. In the humanistic context, relationship seems to be based on a model derived from ancient patterns of barter. In the commerce of barter more is involved than just vying for monetary units: something of value has to be given and something of value has to be received in exchange. But this approach is still based on the backdrop of eternity and on the veneration of ancient models of relationship.

VIEW BASED ON FEAR OF DEATH

Distrust and suspicion of eternity arise when we develop a sense of what might go wrong with the relationship—or what might go right for that matter—independent of our will. There is a suggestion of inevitable chaos or death. Fearing the independent, spontaneous development of the relationship we try to ignore our actual emotions and independent will. Brave people do this semiconsciously by developing a sense of mission or dogma in the relationship. Cowardly people manage it as a subconscious twist.

In general the brave strategy is less successful than the cowardly in creating an "ideal" relationship. This dogmatic approach can only succeed by continually making a basically illogical position logically believable to the friend or partner. Then constant maintenance of the magnificent edifice is required. The less brave but more diligent do the whole work without ever confronting the partner on major issues. Instead he or she continually puts off the sense of death onto a thousand small things. The partner forgets to put the cap back on the ketchup bottle, or always squeezes the toothpaste tube at the wrong end. The fault lies in all these little things.

In spite of philosophical and religious beliefs in eternity, there is a sense of the constant threat of death, that ultimately the relationship is doomed. Whether cowardly or brave, we are trapped in that actual situation, making a constant patchwork in order to survive.

BEYOND HOPE AND FEAR

Making a big deal out of relationship is deathly—as when in chopping an onion, we become more conscious of the chopper than the chopping process. Quite possibly we might chop our fingers off. When we begin to realize this, the sense of helplessness is startling. Viewpoint and attitude don't help. They are no more than a shell. The theistic view of naive belief in eternity and the humanistic view of good manners and dignity are both merely conventional games remote from the actuality of the situation. Their adages of relationship, such as "patience is virtue" or "death before dishonor" are not just the products of convention; they are in themselves purely conventional.

The idea of relationship needs to fall apart. When we realize that life is the expression of death and death is the expression of life, that continuity cannot exist without discontinuity, then there is no longer any need to cling to one and fear the other. There is no longer any ground for the brave or the cowardly. One sees that relationship is the lack of any view-point whatsoever.

We might think that such a relationship is only for the spiritually advanced, but actually it is just normal and ordinary. Any conceptual reference point becomes destructive. We actually begin to suspect that the relationship does not exist. But there is no need to worry: that nonexistence continues as a powerful breeding ground of further relationship. Such wariness is still a viewpoint, but it is one that is open to surprises, unlike living in the promise of eternity. It is also unlike complete mistrust, which does not allow the naiveté of relationship to flower. Whereas a covenant of trust breeds further mistrust, wariness of trust can bring enormously warm and genuine relationships.

NINE

Acknowledging Death

"We do not have to conceal the unspeakable; on the other hand, we do not have to push it to the extreme. At the least, we should help a person to have some understanding of the idea of loss—of the possibility of nonexistence and of dissolving into the unknown. The whole point of any relationship is to share some degree of honesty and to explore how far we can go with it. In that way relationships can become extremely powerful and intense, and beautiful."

I N DISCUSSING SICKNESS, whether physical or mental, we should recognize the importance of our sense of survival. We want to survive, and when we talk about healing, we are talking about how to survive. Viewed from another angle, our strategy of survival is the pattern of our reaction to the fact of death.

One's attitude toward death is central to any healing process. Although it is frequently ignored it is always in the background. No one actually wants to face the possibility of death, or even the idea of death. Even a mild sickness points to the possibility of nothingness: we might lose control of our physical or mental situation; we might become lost in midair. Since as healers we are dealing constantly with the fear of loss, we should actually bring that possibility into the picture. Facing it will

---

Based on 1973 seminar, "The Meaning of Death," Barnet, Vermont.

449

not exactly solve the problem, but, to begin with, the problem should at least be faced.

Many people are confused in their attitude toward death and toward dying persons: should we try to conceal the situation or should we talk about it? Sometimes we do not want to talk about what is happening because it seems that to do so would be to suggest that something is basically wrong. Because of such attitudes there is often a loss of spirit on the part of both the patient and the physician. But when we are willing to acknowledge what is really happening, we pick up spirit, or buoyancy. One could even go so far as to say that by such acknowledgment some kind of sanity develops. So I think it is very important to present the possibility to people that they might have to face some kind of loss, some sense of bewilderment. In fact, the vanguard of death is uncertainty and complete bewilderment. It would be much healthier and more helpful to relate directly to this possibility, rather than just ignoring it. The healer should encourage people who are sick to confront their uncertainty. Such open communication will allow a real meeting to take place, an honest relationship.

We do not have to try to conceal the unspeakable; on the other hand, we do not have to push it to the extreme. At the least, we should help a person to have some understanding of the idea of loss—of the possibility of nonexistence and of dissolving into the unknown. The whole point of any relationship is to share some degree of honesty and to explore how far we can go with it. In that way relationships can become extremely powerful and intense, and beautiful. Sometimes we might only be able to get a hint of this intensity; we might only open up to just the bare minimum. Still, even then it is worthwhile. It is a step in the right direction.

In the healer-patient relationship, we are not concerned with trying to change people, particularly. Sickness and health are not black-and-white situations, but are part of an organic process. We are simply working with sickness and the potential of death, rather than relying on any particular doctrine. We are not talking about converting people. Nevertheless, the materials we have to work with are very rich; as we go along we can see the seed changing into a flower. We do not really change people; they simply grow. Encouraging patients to accept death or uncertainty does not mean that they have to face the devil. Instead such acceptance is something positive in people's lives; conquering the final fear of the unknown is very powerful.

Some people talk about healing in a magical sense, as when so-called healers put their hands on a sick person and miraculously heal them; others talk about the physical approach to healing, using drugs, surgery, and so forth. But I think the important point is that any real healing has to come out of some kind of psychological openness. There are constant opportunities for such openness—constant gaps in our conceptual and physical structures. If we begin to breathe out, then we create room for fresh air to rush in. If we do not breathe, there is no way for the fresh air to enter. It is a question of psychological attitude rather than of being taken over by external powers that heal us. Openness seems to be the only key to healing. And openness means we are willing to acknowledge that we are worthy; we have some kind of ground to relate with whatever is happening to us.

The role of the healer is not just to cure the disease; it is to cut through the tendency to see disease as an external threat. By providing companionship and some kind of sympathy, the healer creates a suggestion of health or underlying sanity, which then undermines naive conceptions of disease. The healer deals with the mishandling of the gaps that occur in one's life, with one's losses of spirit.

People tend to feel that their particular sickness is something special, that they are the only person with such an illness. But in fact, their illness is not so special—nor so terrible. It is a question of acknowledging that we are born alone and that we die alone, but that it is still okay. There is nothing particularly terrible or special about it.

Often the whole notion of sickness is taken as a purely mechanical problem: something is wrong with one's machine, one's body. But somehow that is missing the point. It is not the sickness that is the big problem, but the psychological state behind it. We could not have gotten sick in the first place without some kind of loss of interest and attention. Whether we were run down by a car or we caught a cold, there was some gap in which we did not take care of ourselves—an empty moment in which we ceased to relate to things properly. There was no ongoing awareness of our psychological state. So to the extent that we invite it to begin with, all sicknesses—and not just those diseases traditionally considered to be psychosomatic—are psychological. All diseases are instigated by one's state of mind. And even after we have dealt with the disease and the symptoms have disappeared, by pretending that the problem is over we only plant seeds for further neurosis.

THE HEART OF THE BUDDHA

It seems that we generally avoid our psychological responsibility, as though diseases were external events imposing themselves upon us. There is a quality of sleepiness, and of missing the gaps in the seemingly solid structure of our lives. Out of that sense of carelessness comes an immense message. Our bodies demand our attention; our bodies demand that we actually pay attention to what is going on with our lives. Illness brings us down to earth, making things seem much more direct and immediate.

Disease is a direct message to develop a proper attitude of mindfulness: we should be more intelligent about ourselves. Our minds and bodies are both very immediate. You alone know how your body feels. No one else cares; no one else can know but you. So there is a natural wakefulness about what is good for you and what is not. You can respond intelligently to your body by paying attention to your state of mind.

Because of this the practice of meditation may be the only way to really cure ourselves. Although the attempt to use meditation as some sort of cure may seem materialistic, the practice itself soon cuts through any materialistic attitude. Basically, mindfulness is a sense of composure. In meditation we are not accomplishing anything; we are just there, seeing our lives. There is a general sense of watchfulness, and an awareness of the body as an extremely sensitive mechanism which gives us messages constantly. If we have missed all the rest of the opportunities to relate with these messages, we find ourselves sick. Our bodies force us to be mindful on the spot. So it is important not to try to get rid of the sickness but to use it as a message.

We view our desire to get rid of disease as a desire to live. But instead it is often just the opposite: it is an attempt to avoid life. Although we seemingly want to be alive, in fact we simply want to avoid intensity. It is an ironic twist: we actually want to be healed in order to avoid life. So the hope for cure is a big lie; it is the biggest conspiracy of all. In fact, all entertainment—whether it is the movies or various programs for so-called self-growth—lures us into feeling that we are in touch with life, while in fact we are putting ourselves into a further stupor.

The healing relationship is a meeting of two minds: that of the healer and patient, or for that matter, of the spiritual teacher and student. If you and the other person are both open, some kind of dialogue can take place that is not forced. Communication occurs naturally because both are in the same situation. If the patient feels terrible, the healer picks up that sense of the patient's wretchedness: for a moment he feels more or less the same, as if he himself were sick. For a moment the two are not separate and a sense of authenticity takes place. From the patient's point of view, that is precisely what is needed: someone acknowledges his existence and the fact that he needs help very badly. Someone actually sees through his sickness. The healing process can then begin to take place in the patient's state of being, because he realizes that someone has communicated with him completely. There has been a mutual glimpse of common ground. The psychological underpinning of the sickness then begins to come apart, to dissolve. The same thing applies to meetings between a meditation teacher and his or her student. There is a flash of understanding—nothing particularly mystical or "far out," as they say— just very simple, direct communication. The student understands and the teacher understands at the same moment. In this common flash of understanding, knowledge is imparted.

At this point I am not making any distinction between physicians and psychiatrists: whether we are dealing at the psychological or the medical level, the relationship with one's patient has to be exactly the same. The atmosphere of acceptance is extremely simple but very effective. The main point is that the healer and the patient are able to share their sense of pain and suffering—their claustrophobia or fear or physical pain. The healer has to feel herself to be part of that whole setup. It seems that many healers avoid that kind of identification; they do not want to get involved in such an intense experience. Instead they try to play extremely cool and unconcerned, taking a more businesslike approach.

We all speak the same language; we experience a similar type of birth and a similar exposure to death. So there is bound to always be some link, some continuity between you and the other. It is something more than just mechanically saying "Yes, I know; it hurts very badly." Rather than just sympathizing with the patient, it is important to actually feel her pain and share her anxiety. You can then say "Yes, I feel that pain" in a different way. To relate with total openness means that you are completely captured by someone's problem. There may be a sense of not knowing quite how to handle it and just having to do your best, but even such clumsiness is an enormously generous statement. So, complete openness and bewilderment meet at a very fine point.

There is much more involved in the healer-patient relationship than just going by the books and looking up the appropriate medicine. According to Buddhism, the human essence is compassion and wisdom. So you do not have to acquire skillful communication from outside yourself; you have it already. It has nothing to do with mystical experience or any kind of higher spiritual ecstasy; it is just the basic working situation. If you have an interest in something, that is openness. If you have an interest in people's suffering and conflicts, you have that openness constantly. And then you can develop some sense of trust and understanding, so that your openness becomes compassion.

It is possible to work with sixty people a day and have something click with each of them. It requires a sense of complete dedication, and a willingness to stay alert, without trying to achieve a specific goal. If you have a goal, then you are trying to manipulate the interaction and healing cannot take place. You need to understand your patients and encourage them to communicate, but you cannot force them. Only then can the patient, who is feeling a sense of separation, which is also a sense of death, begin to feel that there is hope. At last someone really cares for him, someone really does listen, even if it is only for a few seconds. That allows intense, very genuine communication to take place. Such communication is simple: there is no trick behind it and no complicated tradition to learn. It is not a question of learning *how* to do it, but of just going ahead with it.

Psychiatrists and physicians, as well as their patients, have to come to terms with their sense of anxiety about the possibility of nonexistence. When there is that kind of openness, the healer does not have to solve a person's problem completely. The approach of trying to repair everything has always been a problem in the past; such an approach creates a successive string of cures and deceptions, which seem to go hand in hand. Once the basic fear is acknowledged, continuing with the treatment becomes very easy. The path comes to you: there is no need to try to create the path for yourself. Healing professionals have the advantage of being able to develop themselves by working with the great variety of situations that come to them. There are endless possibilities for developing one's awareness and openness. Of course, it is always easier to look down on your patients and their predicament, thinking how lucky you are that you do not have their diseases. You can feel somewhat superior. But the acknowledgment of your common ground—your common experience of birth, old age, sickness, and death, and the fear that underlies all of those—brings a sense of humility. That is the beginning of t. healing process. The rest seems to follow quite easily and naturally, based on one's inherent wisdom and compassion. This is not a particularly mystical or spiritual process; it is simple, ordinary human experience. The first time you try to approach a person in this way it may seem to be difficult. But you just do it on the spot.

And finally, what do we mean when we say that a patient has been healed? To be healed, ironically, means that a person is no longer embarrassed by life; she is able to face death without resentment or expectation.

TEN

Alcohol as Medicine or Poison

"In the Guhyasamaja *Tantra, the Buddha says, 'That which intoxicates the dualistic mind is the natural antideath potion indeed.' In the Buddhist tantra, alcohol is used to catalyze the fundamental energy of intoxication; this is the energy that transmutes the duality of the apparent world in* advaya—*not two. In this way, form, smell, and sound can be perceived literally, as they are, within the realm of* mahasukha, *or great joy."*

M AN'S NATURAL PURSUIT is to seek comfort and entertain himself with all kinds of sensual pleasures. He wants a secure home, a happy marriage, stimulating friends, delicious foods, fine clothes, and good wine. But morality generally teaches that this kind of indulgence is not good; we should think of our lives in a broader sense. We should think of our brothers and sisters who lack these things; rather than indulging ourselves, we should share generously with them.

Moralistic thinking tends to see alcohol as belonging to the category of excessive self-indulgences; it might even see drinking as a bourgeois activity. On the other hand, those who like drinking draw a sense of well-being from it and feel it enables them to be warmer and more open with their friends and colleagues. But even they often harbor some sense of guilt about drinking; they fear they might be abusing their bodies and feel deficient in self-respect.

Composed during 1972 retreat in Charlemont, Massachusetts.

One type of drinker works hard during the day, doing heavy labor in one or another of the physical trades. Such drinkers like to come home and have a drink after work or raise a glass or two in a hearty gathering at the bar. Then there are the more genteel drinkers—business executives and such—who are often in the habit of creating an atmosphere of conviviality in their business relations by breaking out the bottle. The latter type is more likely to have a hidden sense of guilt about alcohol than his proletarian brother celebrating the end of a day's work. Still, in spite of all doubts, inviting somebody for a drink seems to have more life to it than inviting somebody for a cup of tea.

Other people drink to try to kill boredom, much in the same way as they try by smoking. A housewife who has just finished dusting or the wash might sit down and take a drop while contemplating the decor or leafing through the latest fashion and home-improvement magazines. When the baby cries or the doorbell rings, she might take a hefty shot before facing the situation. The bored office worker might keep a flask in his desk so he can take an occasional nip between visits from the boss or his heavy-handed secretary. He might seek relief from the day's ennui through a lunchtime visit to the bar.

People who take drinking seriously relate to it as a refuge from life's hustle and bustle; they also fear they might be becoming alcoholics. In either psychological situation, there is love and hate in their style of drinking, coupled with a sense of going into the unknown. In some cases, this journey into the unknown might already have produced a clarity which, in the present situation, can only be dealt with by drinking. Otherwise the clarity would be too painful.

One of the problems convinced drinkers might be facing is being hounded by the moralistic approach to drinking, which raises the artificial question: should one drink or not? In the grips of this question, one looks to one's friends for reinforcement. Some of them might join one in drinking quite freely. Others will have definite reservations about when and how to drink. The real drinker feels such people are amateurs, since they have never related wholeheartedly with alcohol. Quite often their reservations are just a matter of social form: just as one knows that the place to park one's car is the parking lot, so one has the sense of the proper point beyond which one shouldn't drink. It is all right to drink heavily at parties or testimonial dinners so long as one drinks with one's wife or husband and drives home carefully.

There seems to be something wrong with an approach to alcohol that is based entirely on morality or social propriety. The scruples implied have solely to do with the external effects of one's drinking. The real effect of alcohol is not considered, but only its impact on the social format. On the other hand, a drinker feels that there is something worthwhile in his drinking aside from the pleasure he or she gets out of it. There are the warmth and openness that seem to come from the relaxation of his usual self-conscious style. Also there is the confidence of being able to communicate his perceptions accurately, which cuts through his usual feeling of inadequacy. Scientists find they are able to solve their problems; philosophers have new insights; and artists find clear perception. The drinker experiences greater clarity because he feels more really what he is; therefore daydreams and fantasies can be temporarily put aside.

It seems that alcohol is a weak poison which is capable of being transmuted into medicine. An old Persian folktale tells how the peacock thrives on poison, which nourishes his system and brightens his plumage.

The word *whiskey* comes from the Gaelic *uisgebeatha*, which means "water of life." The Danes have their aquavit. The Russian potato produces vodka, the "little water." The traditional names imply that alcohol is at the least harmless, probably medicinal. Harmless or medicinal, the power of alcohol has affected social and psychological structures in most parts of the world throughout history. In Indian mysticism, both Hindu and Buddhist, alcohol is called amrita, the potion that is antideath. Birwapa, an Indian siddha, won enlightenment when he drank seven gallons of liquor in one afternoon. Mr. Gurdjieff, a spiritual teacher who taught in Europe, spoke of the virtues of "conscious drinking" and insisted that his students do conscious drinking together. Conscious drinking is a real and obvious demonstration of mind over matter. It allows us to relate to the various stages of intoxication: we experience our expectations, the almost devilish delight when the effect begins to be felt, and the final breakdown into frivolity in which habitual boundaries begin to dissolve.

Nevertheless, alcohol can as easily be a death potion as a medicine. The sense of joviality and heartiness can seduce us to relinquish our awareness. But fortunately there is also a subtle depression that goes with drinking. There is a strong tendency to latch on to the heartiness and ignore the depression; this is the ape instinct. It is a great mistake. If we take alcohol merely as a substance that will cheer us up or loosen us up like a sedative, it becomes exceedingly dangerous. It is the same with alcohol as with anything else in life that we relate to only partially.

There is a great difference between alcohol and other inebriants. In contrast with alcohol, such substances as LSD, marijuana, and opium do not bring simultaneous depression. If depression does occur, it is of a purely conceptual nature. But with alcohol, there are always physical symptoms: weight gain, loss of appetite, increased feeling of solidity (which includes hangovers). There is always the sense that one still has a body. Psychologically, intoxication with alcohol is a process of coming down, rather than, as with the other substances, of going up into space.

Whether alcohol is to be a poison or a medicine depends on one's awareness while drinking. Conscious drinking—remaining aware of one's state of mind—transmutes the effect of alcohol. Here awareness involves a tightening up of one's system as an intelligent defense mechanism. Alcohol becomes destructive when one gives in to the joviality: letting loose permits the poisons to enter one's body. Thus alcohol can be a testing ground. It brings to the surface the latent style of the drinker's neuroses, the style that he is habitually hiding. If his neuroses are strong and habitually deeply hidden, he later forgets what happened when he was drunk or else is extremely embarrassed to remember what he did.

Alcohol's creativity begins when there is a sense of dancing with its effect—when one takes the effects of drink with a sense of humor. For the conscious drinker, or for the yogi, the virtue of alcohol is that it brings one down to ordinary reality, so that one does not dissolve into meditation on nonduality. In this case alcohol acts as a longevity potion. Those who are overly involved with the sense that the world is a mirage, an illusion, have to be brought down out of their meditation into a state of nonmeditation to relate with people. In this state, the sights, sounds, and smells of the world become overwhelmingly poignant with their humor. When the yogi drinks, it is his way of accepting the dualistic world of ordinary appearance. The world demands his attention—his relationship and compassion. He is glad and amused to have this invitation to communicate.

For the yogi, alcohol is fuel for relating with his students and with the world in general, as gasoline allows a motorcar to relate with the road. But naturally the ordinary drinker who tries to compete with or imitate this transcendental style of drinking will turn his alcohol into poison. In the hinayana teaching of Buddhism, it is recorded that the Buddha reproved a monk who so much as tasted a blade of grass soaked in alcohol. It is necessary to understand that here the Buddha was not condemning the effects of alcohol; he was condemning the attraction toward it, the involvement with it as a temptation.

The conception of alcohol as a temptation of the devil is a highly questionable one. Questioning this conception brings uncertainty as to whether alcohol is allied with good or evil. This uncertainty can create in the drinker a sense of intelligence and fearlessness. It brings him to relate to the present moment as it is. Fearless willingness to be intelligent about what is happening in the face of the unknown is the very energy of transmutation that has been described in the tantric tradition of Buddhism. In the *Guhyasamaja Tantra*, the Buddha says, "That which intoxicates the dualistic mind is the natural antideath potion indeed." In the Buddhist tantra, alcohol is used to catalyze the fundamental energy of intoxication; this is the energy that transmutes the duality of the apparent world into advaya—"not two." In this way, form, smell, and sound can be perceived literally, as they are, within the realm of mahasukha, or great joy. The *Chakrasamvara Tantra* says, "By pure pain without pleasure, one cannot be liberated. Pleasure exists within the calyx of the lotus. This must the yogi nourish." This puts a lot of emphasis on pleasure. But the realization of pleasure comes about through openly relating with pain. Alcohol brings an elation that seems to go beyond all limitations; at the same time it brings the depression of knowing one still has a body and that one's neuroses are heavy upon one. Conscious drinkers might have a glimpse of both of these polarities.

In tantric mysticism, the state of intoxication is called the state of nonduality. This should not be understood as an enticement to entertain oneself, but at the same time, a glimpse of the cosmic orgasm of mahasukha is highly possible for the conscious drinker. If one is open enough to surrender the pettiness of attachment to one's personal liberation by accepting the notion of freedom rather than doubting it, one achieves skillful means and wisdom. This is regarded as the highest intoxication.

ELEVEN

Practice and Basic Goodness:
A Talk for Children

"As you are growing up it is a good idea to jazz yourselves up—to feel strong and to take pride in yourselves. You don't have to feel inadequate because you are children trying to reach adulthood. Those struggles are not even necessary. You just have to be. In order to do that, you need to develop an attitude of believing in your basic goodness, and you need to practice meditation."

I WOULD LIKE to talk about how we came to be here and why we are Buddhists. It is very simple and straightforward in some sense: you and your parents and I are all following a particular discipline, a particular tradition, called Buddhism. When you go to your school, which is not a Buddhist school, you might find the atmosphere to be somewhat strange. You might want to do things the way others are doing them; and when you come home, you might want to follow your parents' way. On the other hand, you might feel resistance to your parents.

What Buddhism boils down to is that we try to follow the example of the Buddha, who was an Indian—not an American Indian, but an Indian Indian. The Buddha was a prince who decided to abandon his palace and his kingdom in order to find out what life is all about. He was looking for the meaning of life, the purpose of life. He wanted to know

---

Based on a 1978 seminar for children held in Boulder, Colorado.

who and what he was. So he went and practiced meditation, and he ate very little. He meditated for six years, twenty-four hours a day. And at the end of those six years he discovered something: he realized that people don't have to struggle so much. We don't have to give in so much to our hassles, our pain, our discomfort. The Buddha discovered that there is something in us known as basic goodness. Therefore, we don't have to condemn ourselves for being bad or naughty. The Buddha taught what he had learned to the rest of mankind. What he taught then—twenty-five hundred years ago—is still being taught and practiced. The important point for us to realize is that we are basically good.

Our only problem is that sometimes we don't actually acknowledge that goodness. We don't see it, so we blame somebody else or we blame ourselves. That is a mistake. We don't have to blame others, and we don't have to feel nasty or angry. Fundamental goodness is always with us, always in us. That is why our education is not difficult. If we have fundamental goodness in us, then knowledge is already a part of us. Therefore, going to school and meditation are just ways of acknowledging that basic goodness.

As you are growing up it is a good idea to jazz yourselves up—to feel strong and to take pride in yourselves. You don't have to feel inadequate because you are children trying to reach adulthood. Those struggles are not even necessary. You just have to *be*. In order to do that, you need to develop an attitude of believing in your basic goodness, and you need to practice meditation. Sitting meditation is a living tradition. We know how the Buddha did it, and we know how to do it ourselves. When you sit like the Buddha, you begin to realize something called enlightenment. That is just realizing that there is something very straightforward and very sparkling in you. It is not necessarily "feeling good." It is much better than feeling good: you have a sense of tremendous buoyancy, up-liftedness. You feel healthy and simple and strong.

If you would like to ask questions, please do so.

Student: This is a foolish question, but if the Buddha sat for six years, twenty-four hours a day, how did he eat?

Trungpa Rinpoche: Well, he ate very little. According to history he had one meal in the morning—something like our breakfast. And he slept very little. Mostly he just sat. When his friends came to see him, they didn't recognize him at first, because he was so thin. On the morning of the day he attained enlightenment, he was visited by a lady who gave him rice and milk, which energized him. Then he returned to his sitting practice, so to speak, but he wasn't thin from then on. In paintings of the Buddha, like the one you see on the shrine, there are halos around his head. The halo represents the idea of glowing health and glowing greatness.

Student: Rinpoche, could you recommend how long children should sit?

Trungpa Rinpoche: A daily sitting practice would be very good. Hopefully you can do that. I started sitting when I was nine; I used to sit for about forty-five minutes. But due to the circumstances, I think probably seven minutes would be fine—every day. That is quite long enough. If you can only do it once a week, you should try to sit for half an hour. Your parents could sit with you, or you could do it alone. And the place where you sit should be elegant and comfortable. Do you sit at home?

S: Sometimes.

TR: How often? Once a week?

S: After school.

TR: Well, maybe that is a good model. So you could come home and relax that way.

Student: I get depressed a lot, and I want to know if I should sit more.

Trungpa Rinpoche: Yes, you should sit more. That is the whole idea. Particularly when you feel depressed or when you are too excited, you should sit more, because then you have something to work with. That is what the Buddha did. Before he went for his six-year retreat, he was very depressed; he was very unhappy with his whole life. Because he was so depressed, he had something to work on.

Student: When I sit, I usually get restless.

Trungpa Rinpoche: Well, people do—always. That's all right, but don't give in to your restlessness. Just try to hold your posture and come back to your breath. You see, what you are doing is imitating the Buddha. You should hold your head and shoulders upright, like he did. In that way you feel good. When you begin to feel restless, you begin to hunch your head and shoulders. You become restless like an animal. When you sit upright, you are different from an animal. That posture will cut through your restlessness.

Student: When you led all those people out of Tibet, did you just guess which way to go?

Trungpa Rinpoche: No, I didn't quite guess.

S: But when you got lost, did you guess which way to go?

TR: Well, you have a sense of direction and you have a feeling that India is that way. When you have lost your way, you stop for five minutes and sit. After that, you have much clearer vision and you know where to go. You only lose your way if you are distracted. So, if your mind is clear, you know where India is. Then there is little problem. There are trails that go in that direction, and you just follow them.

S: When you were leading people through the snow in the mountains, did you feel calm all the way?

TR: Well, we had to be calm. Otherwise we would lose our way. And we would lose our strength. We also felt very energized. I never felt any doubt; we just went on. So calmness was very important, as well as some kind of strength. We zeroed in on the idea that we were going to do it, and we did it.

S: So your confidence helped you to be strong enough to go over the mountains?

TR: Yes.

Student: In pictures of the Buddha, you usually see three jewels. I don't know what they mean.

Trungpa Rinpoche: The three jewels represent the idea of Buddha's students opening themselves up and making offerings to him. They represent offering one's body, speech, and mind to the Buddha. You are giving yourself to him and to his teachings. These jewels will supposedly give you more riches, more wealth. By giving to the Buddha whatever is precious to you, you attain patience and richness.

Student: On your trip, did you ever run out of food?

Trungpa Rinpoche: Well, we did—absolutely. Did you read about it in the book? Have you read *Born in Tibet?* You should read it. It's some story. [*Laughter.*] We did run out of food. In the last month or so, we didn't have much to eat. We had to cook our own leather bags. When we got to the lower elevations, we found bamboo and litchis and banana trees. But we passed right by the banana trees; we didn't know they were edible. Nobody had ever seen banana trees before.

S: When you were traveling, did you sit?

TR: Yes, we did. We made a point of doing that. That is how we gained our strength, our energy. Otherwise we would have been destroyed. It was a ten-month journey altogether—very long.

Student: Did any people die on your trip?

Trungpa Rinpoche: Three people died. They were too old to walk. Because our schedule was very tight, we had to walk from morning to evening. Their legs began to hurt and they just collapsed.

Student: Were there any children with you?

Trungpa Rinpoche: Lots of them. It was difficult for mothers with babies, but the older children did fine. Actually, they were the best, because they began to get more and more energized. They gained strength.

Once we were crossing the Chinese highway. We had to time it so that the Chinese soldiers wouldn't see us. Below us was the highway with troops on it. We had to wait on the side of the ridge until dark. We planned to cross all together, in one batch. Just as we were about to cross, a truck went by, and the infants started to cry at the top of their lungs. But the Chinese didn't see us. After we had crossed, somebody swept the road with a broom so that the Chinese wouldn't find our footprints.

Student: How tall were the eight biggest men—the ones who used to lie down and make a path for the others through the snow?

Trungpa Rinpoche: Well, they were not particularly big. They were tough, that's all.

S: Are they still alive?

TR: Yes—although we started with three hundred people, and a lot of them were captured. Only twenty-nine of us escaped.

Student: Are the Chinese and the Tibetan Buddhists still at war, or is the war over? Are they still shooting at each other?

Trungpa Rinpoche: No, not at this point. The Chinese destroyed or exiled most of the Buddhist leaders, so now they have no one left to fight.

Student: Since you were meditating on the trip, you don't feel very rebellious or angry at the Chinese, do you?

Trungpa Rinpoche: Well, not particularly. What happened with the Chinese was like a rainstorm: you can't get angry at it. It was a timely situation. If the Chinese weren't in Tibet, I wouldn't be here.

Student: Why do people look up to Christ? What is it in him that they like?

Trungpa Rinpoche: Well, he was very heroic. And he was inspired, as we know. He sacrificed his life for the sake of other people. Crowds gathered to hear him talk on Sunday morning. He was a gentle person, a good person. There were a lot of other good people apart from Christ. There was Muhammad, for example. Who else?

S: King David.

TR: Yes, and lots of other people who have done similar things.

Student: On your trip, did the Chinese ever try to track you down?

Trungpa Rinpoche: Yes, they certainly did. I think they followed us all the way, but we outsmarted them. They are still supposed to be looking for me, actually. I have a friend who went to the Chinese embassy in London. He saw my photograph there with a price on my head.

Student: What caused the war between the Chinese and the Buddhists?

Trungpa Rinpoche: Well, the communists don't like meditation practice. They think it is a waste of time. They think that people should be working all the time. Meditation produces too much personal strength. The communists want to develop group strength, not personal strength. They do not believe in the basic goodness of the individual; they believe in the basic goodness of the group. That is why it is called communism; that's it in a nutshell.

Well, maybe we should close at this point. Thank you, children, for being so patient and for not being restless. Your patience is quite remarkable. It must be due to your practice of meditation. Please keep sitting, okay? And study Buddhism more, and try to make friends with your parents—if you can. [*Laughter.*] Regard them as friends rather than as relatives. That is a very important point. Thank you.

T W E L V E

Dharma Poetics

"When we talk about poets and poetics altogether, we are talking in terms of expressing ourselves so thoroughly, so precisely, that we don't just mumble our words, mumble our minds, mumble our bodies. Being in the poetic world, we have something to wake up and excite ourselves. There is a sense of gallantry and there is a tremendous, definite attitude of no longer being afraid of threats of any kind. We begin to help ourselves to appreciate our world, which is already beautiful."

IN DISCUSSING POETICS, we are not bound to the theme of written poetry. Poetics also includes one's vision, hearing, and feeling, altogether. So, we are not talking about writing poetry alone; we are talking about a complete, comprehensive realization of the phenomenal world—seeing things as they are. We are talking in terms of the poetic way of eating one's food and drinking one's tea. We could call this approach dharma poetics. Dharma, as you know, is the teachings of the Buddha. Basically, the word *dharma* means "norm," or some form of experiencing reality properly.

We could speak of three stages of poetics. The first is the rejection stage. We reject habitual patterns which are caused by ego-oriented situations, such as the desire to develop aggression, passion, and ignorance. We have to free ourselves from these patterns. For instance, if we do not

---

Based on discussion with Naropa Institute poetics students, 1982.

THE HEART OF THE BUDDHA

wash a piece of cloth completely clean, we will be unable to dye it another color, such as bright red, bright green, or bright blue. The point is that we have to have a sense of purity and giving up before we can put the cloth that we have woven into the various dyes that we would like to use. We first have to wash it thoroughly.

It is similar with our minds and our bodies. We have to go through some sense of purification, natural purification. This process might include letting go of our personal trips, letting go of desires, and letting go of any philosophy that has been taught to us.

In the second stage, we can aspire to the basic meaning of poetics. There are two main kinds of poetics: rejuvenating poetics and growing-old poetics. Between the two, many other kinds of poetics could arise. We could appreciate the sun, the moon, the green grass, the flowers, the brooks, and the mountains. We could appreciate rainstorms; we could appreciate snowfalls; we could appreciate our father and mother. We could appreciate the whole world. Or, for that matter, we could mock them. Mocking is also acceptable—always acceptable. We could mock April's snowfall; we could mock our father or mother treating us badly.

In general, poetics is based on the idea that first we see our universe very clearly, very precisely, and very thoroughly. We are not fooled by anybody. That seems to be the basic notion of poetics here.

I could give you one poem as an example; it is not memorized, but composed on the spot:

> Father's love is good.
> Did I borrow from my mother?
> Nonetheless, I still remain
> chrysanthemum.

Student: You said there are two kinds of poetics: rejuvenating and growing-old. What did you mean by that?

Trungpa Rinpoche: Well, either you have seen enough of the world already, or you're about to see the world as it is growing up. It's like the difference between a good spring and a good autumn.

S: Or a young poet and an old poet?

TR: That's right. Very much so.

S: What is it that the old poet knows that the young poet doesn't?

TR: Well, what you just said is in itself poetry. Ask yourself! You see, the trick is that I'm not going to help you particularly. You have to discover it for yourself.

S: That's helpful. [*Laughter.*]

TR: Being less helpful is more helpful than being helpful.

Student: I feel that there is some beauty in imperfection. If you did wash your cloth completely, and you dyed it a pure color, then your color would be pure, but it would only be one color.

Trungpa Rinpoche: It wouldn't necessarily be only one color. You could dye your cloth lots of colors. And each time you did, a different kind of smile and a different delight would take place. We are not talking about completely totalitarian poetics; we are talking about poetics that can encompass multilateral situations—different types for different people. But at the beginning we have to clean up first. That is always the case. Having cleaned up, then lots of colors can come through. It is like a well-cleaned mirror: many things can be reflected in it.

Now, without delaying too much, I would like to continue to discuss the evolution from purification and a sense of longing for liberation, which we talked about earlier on, and add a third stage.

The three stages that we are discussing are actually connected with a basic sense of joy. Sometimes joy means having one's individual way of not working genuinely with oneself and instead working toward a sense of indulgency. But here joy means *not* indulging oneself. That is the first stage, which we described earlier as purifying oneself and rejecting one's habitual patterns.

In other words, joy means that our perception of the world can be clarified. The best poetic philosophy, in this case, is to have a sense of precision and accuracy in how we see the universe, how we actually perceive the universe, which is the second stage.

When we clarify our perception, we are not fooled by green, yellow, red, blue, pink, or orange. We are not fooled by them, and we are also not fooled by mountains, brooks, flowers, or bees. I leave it up to your imagination to come up with all sorts of things like that. We are not fooled by our father, our mother, our sisters, our brothers, or our lovers, either. All these things could create central themes for poetry, but at the same time, these things could create obstacles; they could create a blindfoldedness.

Perhaps there is more to say about joy here. Joy is something that we see, something that we experience properly, fully, and thoroughly in the universe, in our world. In other words, we do not pull long faces; we begin to appreciate this world that we're living in. This world is a lovely world, a wonderful world. The Judeo-Christian tradition would say it's a gift of God. In the Buddhist tradition it is said to be a result of our karmic magnificence. In any case, joy is always there.

The third stage is that we must be clear and pure in our speech and our minds. When we talk about poets and poetics altogether, we are talking in terms of expressing ourselves so thoroughly, so precisely, that we don't just mumble our words, mumble our minds, mumble our bodies. Being in the poetic world, we have something to wake up and excite in ourselves. There is a sense of gallantry and there is a tremendous, definite attitude of no longer being afraid of threats of any kind. We begin to help ourselves to appreciate our world, which is already beautiful. So, I think that's the point.

Student: You talked about many things in our everyday experience that we shouldn't be fooled by. What did you mean by that?

Trungpa Rinpoche: Well, I think it's a question of simply just being on the dot. We shouldn't let ourselves be used by somebody else as part of their trip—their egomania or philosophy. We should simply remain as what we are. Just on the dot. Philosophy in this case could be anything— religious, sociological, or political. The idea is that we should not let ourselves be subject to any experience, unless we experience it properly, thoroughly, by knowing what we're doing.

S: By knowing that we are laying our philosophy on the mountain or the brooks?

TR: Well, you can praise the mountain, you can praise the sky; you can do those things. But any trips you lay on things, you have to let go of.

S: And then there's joy?

TR: Yes. If you are unhappy—not joyful—then you buy a lot of trips. You still have a long face, but you always buy it when somebody presents some stuff to you. In this case we are saying that once you're joyful and you feel gallantry—you feel who you are and you feel good—then you will automatically know who's trying to fool you and who's trying to help you.

S: How much energy should you expend trying to figure out if someone's fooling you or if you're fooling yourself?

TR: Well, that's very complicated, you know, because sometimes you think you are the other and the other also thinks they are you. So I think the best approach there is to enjoy mountains, rivers, forests, snow, rain, and hailstorms by yourself. You will find some poetic way of saving yourself that way. Actually, I think that's what mountains are for, originally. Brooks are there for you to do that—and trees and jungles as well. So be yourself by yourself. I'm sure you will compose magnificent poetry if you do that.

Allen Ginsberg: I sometimes find it difficult to conceive of enjoying myself when I'm ill or in pain. I wonder what it would be like to be very old and on the road in Jordan with shrapnel and cluster bombs flying around, feeling the end of family, the end of home. I wonder what possibility there would be of writing appreciative poetry under extremely painful situations and conditions, such as old age, sickness, and death.

Trungpa Rinpoche: Well, pain goes with pleasure, always. That's a classic remark. When you feel pain, it is because you feel joyful at the same time. Why do you wear sunglasses, which are black? You wear them because there is lots of light coming toward you. Do you understand the logic? The notion of frustration also goes along with that. You feel a sense of both alternatives, always. When you are in the worst pain, you sometimes feel the best happiness. Have you ever experienced that? We read about that in the stories of Milarepa and Marpa—all the Kagyü lineage poets.

AG: Well, is it the steadiness of mind cultivated by meditation practice that keeps you from total disillusion, depression, and physical pain?

TR: I think there has to be some kind of spark, some kind of explosion of joy, happening in the midst of pain. It usually happens *more* in the midst of pain.

AG: Do you think that's actually happening to people who are under really horrible circumstances, for example in Lebanon?

TR: Yes, I think so. Because there is so much chaos, therefore there is so much tranquillity. Tranquillity is relative to chaos. It's Einstein's philosophy.

Student: Do you feel there's something lacking in American poetry because we don't have a meditative tradition?

Trungpa Rinpoche: Well, I think American poets are getting there, basically speaking. But I must say American poets do need some kind of meditative discipline in order to appreciate the phenomenal world, in order to appreciate that the greenness of green is beautiful, the blueness of the sky is lovely, and the whiteness of the clouds is so fantastic. Maybe poets spend too much time writing poetry. They have to see the vividness of the world.

America is a wonderful place. You have the highest mountains, beautiful lakes, and extraordinary greenery and fruit. You have everything in this country. You should be proud of your country, then you'll see the beauty of America—if you become a poet.

Student: Rinpoche, I've heard the saying that "suffering is the broom that sweeps away the cause of suffering." When you speak about sparks of pleasure in pain, is that the quality you're referring to?

Trungpa Rinpoche: Well said. You must be studying Buddhism! [*Laughter.*] You must be studying vajrayana.

S: It was Situ Rinpoche who said that.

TR: Oh yes, that's good. Thank you very much.

THIRTEEN

Green Energy

*"When we relate to money properly, it is no longer a mere token
of exchange or of abstract energy; it is also a discipline. No longer
hooked by it as a medicine that has become a drug, we can deal
with it in a practical, earthy way as a master deals with his
tools."*

I N DEALING WITH MONEY, we are constantly involved in a kind of
chaos. This results from a break in the relationship between the earth
and oneself. Relating to the earth means knowing when to act practically
and directly; it means actually feeling a kinship with whatever work
is being done. We rarely have this feeling when it comes to money
matters.

Money is basically a very simple thing. But our attitude toward it is
overloaded, full of preconceived ideas that stem from the development
of a self-aggrandizing ego and its manipulative processes. The mere act
of handling money—just pieces of paper—is viewed as a very serious
game. It is almost like building a sand castle and then selling tickets for
admission to it. The difference between playing as a child and playing as
an adult is that in the adult's case, money is involved. Children don't
think about money, whereas adults would like to charge admission to
their solemn construction.

Even when we try to regard money as insignificant—as merely a

---

Originally composed in 1976 for *Harper's* special edition on money.

credential or a token of our creative capacity or our practicality—because money is connected with the energy arising from our preconceptions, it takes on great significance. We may even feel embarrassment about money—it is somewhat too close to the heart. We try to call it something else—"bread" or "bucks"—to relieve that feeling. Or, we choose to think of money as our lifeline, as a source of security: its abstract quality represents some unspeakable aspect of our personality. We may say, for example: "I have gone bankrupt and lost heart"; "I'm a solid citizen with a steady bank account"; "I have so much money that there is no room for simplicity in my life."

The energy money takes on makes a tremendous difference in the process of communication and relationship. If a friend suddenly refuses to pay his check at a restaurant, a feeling of resentment or separation automatically arises in relation to him. If one buys a friend a cup of tea—which is just a cup, hot water, and tea—somehow a factor of meaningfulness gets added.

It seems to me that it is worthwhile to work with the negative aspects of money in order to gain some understanding about ourselves. We must try to discover how to view this embarrassing and potent commodity as a part of ourselves that we cannot ignore. When we relate to money properly, it is no longer a mere token of exchange or of our abstract energy; it is also a discipline. No longer hooked by it as a medicine that has become a drug, we can deal with it in a practical, earthy way, as a master deals with his tools.

FOURTEEN

Manifesting Enlightenment

"If you wait too long, in the Christian tradition, as well as in the Buddhist tradition, nothing happens. For example, the concept of 'Holy Ghost' and the concept of 'first thought, best thought' simply pounce on you, rather than you having to wait for them. This requires a certain sense of bravery: you have to be willing to jump in right away. Whenever there is any inspiration, you just jump in. That is why it is said that 'first thought is best thought.' Just jump in!"

ENLIGHTENMENT IS A RATHER tall subject, and I would like to keep my discussion of it rather simple. The word for enlightenment in Sanskrit is *bodhi*, which means "awake." When the word *bodhi* is made into a noun it becomes *buddha*. Buddha refers to someone who has developed an awake state of being. When we talk about awake here, it has nothing to do with being physically awake as opposed to sleeping. Rather, awake means being basically realized, being able to see the pain of the world and being able to see the way out of the world of suffering.

After the Buddha's attainment of enlightenment, he spent seven weeks contemplating how he could communicate such an experience of wakefulness to others. I suppose we could correlate that with Christ spending such an extensive time in the desert—some people even say Christ went to Tibet, or at least to Kashmir.

Talk given at Naropa Institute's third Conference on Buddhist and Christian Meditation, 1983.

The Buddha discovered and taught that human beings are in fact capable of being woken up. The state of being awake has two main qualities: the first, *karuna* in Sanskrit, is softness, gentleness, which we call "compassion"; the other, *upaya* in Sanskrit, is called "skillful means." The compassion aspect is connected with oneself, and the skillful means aspect is connected with how to deal with others. Compassion and skillful means put together is what is known as egolessness. Non-ego means being free from any kind of bondage, free from any fixed motivation to hold on to one's basic being.

We have a tendency to hold on to concepts and perceptions of all kinds. We must admit that tendency and realize that such situations bind us to the lower realms: the hell realm, the hungry ghost realm, and the animal realm. I suppose in the Christian tradition these realms are connected with the idea of sin. In the Buddhist tradition we don't talk about punishment as such, and the concept of original sin does not exist. Instead, Buddhism speaks about habitual patterns. For example, when a dog sees a person, it wants to bite, it wants to bark; when a flea jumps on your body, it wants to bite; when a human being sees another human being, he wants to kiss, and so forth. That kind of instinctual response is the definition of habitual patterns. When a person gets stuck in habitual patterns, then he exists in the lower realms of his passion, aggression, and delusion.

There are all kinds of habitual tendencies that are connected with holding on to what we are. People get divorced because they think they might find a better mate. People change restaurants because they think they might get cheaper and better food. The habitual patterns of ego work that way. The notion of enlightenment is a sense of freedom from those patterns. And the way to attain that freedom is by means of the sitting practice of meditation.

In sitting practice, we look at our minds, and we maintain good posture. When we combine body and mind that way, we find ourselves emulating the Buddha—the way to *be* properly. Then we begin to develop sympathy toward ourselves rather than just holding on. We begin to develop a sense of softness. We can see this in the way that Buddhists talk softly and walk mindfully.

Beyond sitting meditation itself, we begin to expand our experience of softness and mindfulness to other activities, such as shopping, cooking, cleaning, and any activities that we do. We begin to find that things are workable rather than hassles or problems. We find that life is worth living. And we begin to treat ourselves better; we wear good clothes, eat good food, and constantly smile. We cheer up, and we realize there is something good about life. And we also realize that others can be brought into our society, our world.

We can conduct ourselves mindfully and appreciate the phenomenal world. We can realize that the hassles in our lives are not created by others; rather, we create these hassles for ourselves. Therefore, we can remove them and appreciate our world. I would suggest to everybody: let us be aware of our being, let us celebrate as we experience our lives, and smile at least three times a day. Thank you.

I apologize if this sounds like a sermon. If you would like to ask questions, you are more than welcome.

Question: I am so delighted to be here as a Christian, with your hospitality making it all possible. My heart is full of love of the spirit that makes this possible. We have so much to learn from each other. I have so much to learn. I am told that this meeting at Naropa has been made possible by you because of a meeting that you had with Thomas Merton. If you care to share them, I would be delighted to hear your impressions of that meeting, since we bear the fruits here today.

Trungpa Rinpoche: Thank you. Father Merton's visit to Southeast Asia took place when I was in Calcutta. He was invited by a group that had a philosophy of spiritual shopping, and he was the only person who felt that it was full of confusion. He felt there was a sense of ignorance there, but nonetheless he joined them. We had dinner together, and we talked about spiritual materialism a lot. We drank many gin and tonics. I had the feeling that I was meeting an old friend, a genuine friend.

In fact, we planned to work on a book containing selections from the sacred writings of Christianity and Buddhism. We planned to meet either in Great Britain or in North America. He was the first genuine person I met from the West.

After meeting Father Merton, I visited several monasteries and nunneries in Great Britain, and at some of them I was asked to give talks on meditation, which I did. I was very impressed.

When I was studying at Oxford, I had a tutor who was a Belgian priest, a Jesuit priest, who had studied in Sri Lanka. He knew Sanskrit and he read a lot of the Buddhist sutras and the commentaries that go with them. I was very impressed and moved by the contemplative aspect of Christianity and by the monasteries themselves. Their lifestyles and the way they conducted themselves convinced me that the only way to join the Christian tradition and the Buddhist tradition together would be by bringing together Christian contemplative practice with Buddhist meditative practice.

Question: Sir, Tenshin Anderson Sensei spoke the other day about a still place in the center where the buddhas live—where one experiences the pain of all sentient beings, the suffering of all sentient beings. And he said that from there arise outcroppings, or clouds that begin to form and rise. He said that this is the essence of compassion and skillful means, and that from this arising you can go out into the world and do good for all sentient beings. This made me think about "first thought, best thought." Could you say something about "first thought, best thought," and compassionate action in the world.

Trungpa Rinpoche: I think it is a question of not waiting. If you wait too long, in the Christian tradition, as well as in the Buddhist tradition, nothing happens. For example, the concept of "Holy Ghost" and the concept of "first thought, best thought" simply pounce on you, rather than you having to wait for them. This requires a certain sense of bravery: you have to be willing to jump in right away. Whenever there is any inspiration, you just jump in. That is why it is said that "first thought is best thought." Just jump in!

Question: In relation to that, we have talked about being compulsive in wanting to help, about jumping out too soon and wanting to change someone. If someone is suffering, you want to *stop* that suffering, but that might be compulsive and could just cause more harm. Could you say more about the distinction between true compassionate action and compulsive behavior?

Trungpa Rinpoche: It is a question of sneezing and wiping your nose. You sneeze spontaneously, and after that you wipe your nose.

Q: Thank you very much!

Question: First I would like to say that I thought that was a very nice Christian talk you gave.

Trungpa Rinpoche: Thank you.

Q: But being here and meeting many Christians, I find that they are always very defensive about the idea that Buddhists do not believe in any kind of reality or concept of God. And I try to pacify them by saying that I find in my readings that the Buddhists simply use different words. They capitalize the word *Self,* or they capitalize the word *That,* or they capitalize the word *Suchness.* I assume that has some special significance.

But today I had an interesting experience. I met a person from the Orthodox tradition who became a Buddhist, and that person communicated to me something you once said in his presence, which was that you had a certain affinity with the Orthodox understanding of the reality that the idea of God represents. I would like to hear you say something about that, and how you understand that whole idea.

TR: The Orthodox tradition was actually the saving grace in my life at Oxford because its followers understand the notion of meditation, and they understand that meditation is not just doing *nothing* but also involves radiating one's openness. The contemplative traditions within both Judaism and Christianity, particularly the Jewish Hasidic tradition and also the Orthodox Christian Prayer of the Heart, which I've studied a little bit, seem to be the ground for Eastern and Western philosophy to join together. It is not so much a question of dogma, but it is a question of *heart;* that is where the common ground lies. One of these days I am going to take my students to Mount Athos to see how the Orthodox monks conduct themselves.

Question: I'd be interested in any comments you might have about the practice of deity yoga and how the visualization of deities brings about a change in consciousness.

Trungpa Rinpoche: What kind of consciousness are you talking about?

Q: The change that's produced by the deity yoga, by the practice of the deity yoga, from our normal awareness of the world. The question I'm asking is, where does this lead; what type of consciousness does this produce?

TR: Everybody is a deity here. It is very simple. I think one of the basic points is to realize the ultimate concept of sacredness. *Sacred* in Sanskrit is *adhishthana,* which also means "blessing." Adhishthana gives you open heart and a sense of wakefulness at once. It is taking place right now while we are having a conversation. Got it?

Q: Thank you, sir.

TR: Well, unfortunately, ladies and gentlemen, there is something called time, and we are running out of it, so we might stop here. I would like to thank everybody who took part in this, and especially the organizers of this conference. All of you have been so kind and genuine and good. Hopefully you can return again and contribute more, if you can. That will be a portion of the cake of saving the world. Thank you very much.

APPENDIXES

The Bön Way of Life

THE STUDY OF Bön, the native, pre-Buddhist religion of Tibet, is a vast and largely untreated subject. Unfortunately, accurate information concerning higher spiritual training in Bön is extremely difficult to obtain; materials that are presently available contain only sketchy data, obscured by overlays of popular Buddhism. Moreover, in making inquiries of present-day Bön priests, one finds that they speak a great deal in Buddhist terms, drawing parallels between the highlights of their doctrine and Buddhist teachings.

An investigation of the Bön religion is further complicated by the existence in Tibet of "white Bön," which amounts to a "Bön-ized" Buddhism. "White Bön" is basically an adopted form of Buddhism, but the Buddha is called Shenrap (see below); the Buddhist vajra is replaced by a counterclockwise svastika;* and the bodhisattva is called yungdrung sempa, that is, svastikasattva. Where a text mentions *dharma*, the word *Bön* is substituted. There are Bön equivalent names for all the buddhas and bodhisattvas, and also for the ten stages—or *bhumis* in Sanskrit—of the bodhisattva path. Many contemporary Bön believers are therefore not good sources of information concerning the pure tradition of their religion.

In fact, most of the original Bön texts were eventually destroyed or fell subject to heavy Buddhist editing. In the absence of surviving Bön

---

*The svastika (or *swastika* as it is often pronounced) in Bön represents an unchanging and indestructible quality. In this, it is like the Buddhist vajra, but it differs in that it also connotes richness and plenty. It is often used as a symbol of wealth, appearing as a decoration on an individual's Chuglha bag—a bag containing objects sacred to the god of wealth.

philosophical sources, the cosmological understanding of Bön must be reconstructed from ritual texts that were left intact owing to their assimilation by Buddhism. Nevertheless, some Bön texts have survived, and it is possible to derive the fundamentals of Bön belief from these.

Bön, which in Tibetan means "way of life," is traditionally interpreted in the sense of "basic law." The Tibetan name for Tibet is Bö, which is basically the same word. Moreover, until about the seventh century, Tibet was referred to by its inhabitants as Bön, Bö being adopted only later. This is verified by ancient scrolls found in caves in Afghanistan early in this century, as well as by ancient Khotanese scrolls which tell of taxes paid to "the great king of Bön." Thus the name of the Tibetan religion was, at least archaically, synonymous with the nation itself.

The higher teachings of Bön were transmitted to the Tibetans by the sage Shenrap Miwo. *Shen* means "heavenly"; *rap* means "supreme one"; and *miwo* means "great man." Shenrap lived long before the Buddha. The Shenrap myth refers to the Buddha, the teacher of wisdom; to Gesar, the teacher of war; to the Lord of Taksik, the teacher of the law of wealth; and so forth. All these are considered incarnations of Shenrap. The work of Shenrap still exists in Tibet in the form of some four hundred volumes, but it has undergone heavy Buddhist editing. A few of the books that have not fallen into Buddhist hands give some clue as to how the practitioner should proceed on the path of Bön.

Bön religion is concerned with the creation of the universe in such a way as to consecrate the existence of the country, customs, and habits of the Tibetan people. This is in contrast to the spirituality of Buddhism, which arises in the far more abstract context of psychological evolution.

The spirituality of Bön is founded in a cosmological reality: nine gods created the world, a world in which birth, death, marriage, and sickness all have their place. If the worshiper can attune himself to those gods through various ritualistic ceremonies, and through an understanding of these ceremonies, then he is in a position to fulfill whatever is demanded of him by the cosmic order.

The acquisition of spiritual understanding in Bön is based on the concept of tendrel, which means "cosmic law." This is similar to the Buddhist term *nidana*. Both concepts present the flow of events as a causal enchainment. But whereas the Buddhist concept suggests the matter-of-fact nature of fate, tendrel gives much more the idea of an influenceable agency. According to Bön, anyone who attunes himself, through the appropriate rites and practices, to the movement of the interdependence of events is not in danger of being rejected by it. Understanding this interdependence, he can read its signs. By invoking the name of the supreme Bön deity in the appropriate manner, and also by including repetitions of his own name, he can call the gods to himself as allies and defenders.

The supreme divine principle of Bön is referred to as Yeshen. This supreme deity has the same quality of cosmic totality that is found in most theistic religions. *Ye* means "primordial" or "original"; *shen* means "divine," "heavenly," or "spiritual" but also has an anthropomorphic implication. The impression is of a divine ancestor. *Shen* also has the sense of "friend" or "ally," so a benign quality is added. The ancestor aspect also brings the feeling of the richness of age along with the sense of divinity. Yeshen is seen as passive and peaceful, accommodating the idea of a final peaceful rest for the worshiper.

The energetic aspect of the sphere of the divine is represented by another principle—Se. Se, who is primarily vengeful in character, communicates directly with man. He creates the link between the absolute, divine plane and the relative plane of man. The point is that the practitioner of Bön must acquire the ability to see the Yeshen quality in every life situation. If he is able to do this, guidance for the further application of his practice comes from Se, who points him in the appropriate spiritual direction.

Se is a powerful warrior; the Bön worshiper calls him god (*lha*). The national king of Tibet also used *lha* for his title, partaking as well in the image of powerful warrior. In ancient times, the capital of Tibet was thus named Lhasa (*sa* means "place"), identifying the seat of the king with the seat of the god.

At this point it would perhaps be most useful to give some impression of the methods used for relating with Se and achieving union with Yeshen. Bön, unlike the religious outgrowths of the Aryan culture—especially Hinduism, Buddhism, and Jainism in their quasi-popular forms—gives little heed to the pursuit of salvation through the practice of austerities. Bön philosophy speaks of Yeshen as being reflected in the interplay between heaven and earth. Thus the Bön aspirant seeks magical power through union with the Yeshen nature as manifested in mountains, trees, lakes, and rivers—all of which are impressively present in Tibet. There is a strong orientation toward waterfalls, falling snow, clouds, and mist arising from the deep valleys, since all these are regarded as activities of Yeshen. Belief in the magic of these natural features is paramount.

In attempting to commune with Yeshen, the practitioner must first find the highest peak in the locale. He invokes the name of Yeshen in the lhasang practice, which is a purifying ceremony often performed on auspicious occasions (even by Buddhists) in Tibet.

To prepare for a lhasang, a fire is made of cedar needles. Offerings are made of the "three whites" (curd, milk, and butter); the "three sweets" (brown sugar, crystal sugar, and honey); as well as offerings of tsampa rubbed in butter with popped barley and chalices of barley beer, tea, and milk. Yeshen, Se, and the eight degyes (messengers of Se) are thought to descend from heaven on the smoke of the fire. The cedar is Se's tree, and its wood and smoke are considered ritually pure. The ceremony is intended to bring the divine down into the sphere of human life, as well as to elevate the particular occasion into the sphere of the divine. The burning of the cedar needles is one of the main means of communicating with Yeshen. The devotee becomes absorbed in the smoke of the ritual fire. Certain messages are read from the patterns of the rising smoke; for example, slowly, gently rising white smoke signifies acceptance, while dark smoke that is constantly interrupted by wind signifies obstacles.

There are nine cosmos-creating deities (including Se himself), which figure as part of the Se principle. Only through the mediation of Se, or the other figures who manifest his principle, can the worshiper communicate with Yeshen. There is the sense that, if properly appealed to, Se could approach Yeshen to redispose the ultimate energy of the universe in a way more favorable to the worshiper. The other eight deities are the messengers, or degyes, of Se. The degyes might more accurately be regarded as types, or principles, than as individual beings, since each may have many local manifestations. Each degye also has a retinue of minions, attendants, helpers, and so on who act on its intentions.

The nature of these Bön divinities can be gathered from their associated practices and iconography. A general iconographical feature of Se and the degyes is the per, a kimono-like garment reaching to the ankles with wide, triangular sleeves and a pleat over each hip. The per was the garment of ancient Tibetan royalty. The warlike degyes wear armor beneath the per and helmets pennanted in their particular color. The pennants vary according to the status of the figure. Se wears a white per with crystal armor and helmet. White is associated with divinity; it is pure and contains all the other colors. He rides a white horse with turquoise wings.

The only female degye is Lu, who is associated with water. Bringing rain, she also brings fertility. Thus she is the patron deity of women, especially young maidens. Lakes and sources of springs where shrines have been built are sacred to her. Lu punishes with leprosy, rheumatism, and skin diseases. She can be propitiated with offerings of the three whites and three sweets. Lu is associated with snakes, blue-gray horses, and blue-gray mules. She wears a gown of feathers and seamless water-silk representing mist. She rides a blue horse with white stripes in water designs, and she holds a crystal vase filled with gems.

Tsen is the god of fire. He has the power of instant destruction. He is associated with speed and the accomplishment of actions—especially destructive actions. He does not kill his enemies externally, but, because of the swiftness of his horse and his quickness to anger, he is able to instantly enter his enemy's body through the mouth or anus. Tsen is the patron deity of bandits and warriors. Harms associated with him are heart attack and death by accident. He is offended by making fire in inappropriate places, by roasting meat, or in general, by creating disturbances or disharmony in any particular environment. Offerings to Tsen are goat's blood and goat's meat. He is associated with brown horses and jackals. Tsen wears copper armor beneath his red per and rides a red roan. The general feeling of the image is of blood and fire. His moment par excellence for striking is at sunset. He holds a scimitar and a lasso.

Another degye is Therang, who is thought to be embodied in boulders and ashes as well as in dice. He brings success in games, particularly dice, but also any board games. In ancient warfare, he was thought to guide the trajectories of catapulted boulders. Fever and dizziness are associated with Therang. The appropriate offering to him is popped barley with milk. He is the patron god of children and blacksmiths and is also somewhat associated with rain. Therang rides a goat and wears a goat-skin over his black per. He carries a bellows and a hammer.

Dü is associated with darkness. He brings bad luck unless propitiated with offerings of leftovers. He is connected with crows and black pigs. Dü rides a black horse with a white blaze. He wears iron armor and helmet and a black per. He holds a sword and a spear with a black banner. Fastened to his saddle are a waterbag filled with poison; a long black board with a handle inscribed with his victim's names; and a ball of multicolored thread which has a life of its own and can leap from its place and bind up a victim in an excruciating matter.

Chuglha is the god of wealth. He rewards thrift with prosperity and punishes waste with poverty. He can also bring rheumatism, ulcer, and swelling diseases. He is the patron deity of merchants and of the household and is offered butter and grain. He is associated with the earth, as well as with sheep, yaks, and horses. Chuglha rides a yellow horse or a lion. He wears a golden per over golden armor, and a golden hat with four sides in the stylized form of flower petals. He carries a multicolored, cylinder-shaped victory banner in his right hand and a scroll in the left. He vomits gems.

Nyen is the god of the Tibetan folk culture and the patron of rulers and all patriots. He is associated with the mountains. He is offered cheese, the three whites, the three sweets, and spikelets of grain plants. He is infringed against by chopping down any trees that may be held sacred locally and by digging up sacred ground; he is also offended by the smell of burnt food and by the beams of torches or lamps cast on the tops of hills or mountains consecrated to him. He punishes by magnifying physical weaknesses and causing domestic chaos. The horse and deer (especially the musk deer) are his sacred animals, as well as quadrupeds in general and also birds. His female counterpart is associated with storms and weather. The color of Nyen's armor and per vary locally, but are most often white. He carries a white pennant banner. He also carries either a platter or vase of jewels. The color of his horse also varies with locale.

Za is the god of psychological energy, lightning, hailstorms, and, more recently, electricity. Disturbed, he can addle the senses or cause epileptic fits and madness. He can be offended by interrupting anything continuous—for example, by cutting rope or by ruining paint or ink. He is mollified by offerings of goat's meat and goat's blood. He is the patron of magicians and is associated with dragons. Za rides an angry crocodile. Each of his eighteen faces—he has one for each kind of mythical lightning dragon—is topped by a raven's head that shoots out lightning bolts. He is six-armed and holds a victory banner, a snake lasso, a bag of poisonous water, a bow, and a bundle of arrows. Za has a large mouth in his belly, and his body is covered with eyes.

Drala is the god of war and patron of warlords and warriors. He is somewhat identified with storms and storm clouds. He is offended by the mistreatment of weapons. Drala punishes by humiliation and scandal, insomnia and nightmare, and even by loss of one's *la*, or "soul." He is offered barley beer, tea, and the three whites and three sweets. The white yak, horse, eagle, and raven are sacred to him. Drala rides a horse, usually reddish brown. He wears armor and helmet of lacquered metal and a red per. Eighteen pennants fly from his helmet. He holds a long-hoisted flag with eighteen ribbons flying at its edge and wears a belt which holds a bow and arrows, a lasso, an axe, a spear, a dagger, a sword, and other instruments of war. Drala emanates a tiger from his body, a black bear with a white heart from one of his legs, a jackal from each eye, and a hawk and eagle from his head.

Having given an impression of the divinities and their powers, according to Bön belief, an account of some of the customs and practices relating to the life situations of the Bön believer will give further insight into the world of Bön. According to Bön tradition, when a house is to be built, the site should be chosen by a person known for his wisdom and understanding. There are four main elements to be looked for. The building must be situated so that a mountain of Nyen is in the back, that is, to the west. This mountain is called the lhari, the "mountain of god." This should be a rocky mountain, preferably covered with red lichen, the whole resembling a great red bird. The house is thus protected, like a child in its mother's lap.

There should also be a mountain on the front side, but not so high as the one in back. It should be somewhat chalky in composition, ideally resembling a white tiger. On the right there should be a river running in an open valley, which, by the shape of its course, should resemble a dragon. On the left should be a screen of mountains resembling a tortoise's back. The tops and ridges of this northern range should not be jagged but should present a solid mass, since spaces sharply gapping its silhouette are said to represent the teeth of death. This could bring death to the family. Any decayed or dead trees around the site portend accident and are cut down, if not found to be the haunt of some local god.

The traditional first step in approaching the site is to build a tower, or sekhar, on top of the lhari. The tower is intended as a shrine to Se, the local Nyen, or any other degye that is thought to be powerful in the area. The tower invites their blessing on the site. In the ceremony for consecrating the tower, a wool cord is extended in the four directions.

This acts as a conductor for Se when he descends from heaven. Certain areas around the tower are designated as sacrosanct; no one goes there unless to make an offering.

The follower of Bön considers birth to be extremely sacred. Nevertheless, women were considered impure, since they represent the temptation of passion. Thus, a mother-to-be is required to lie in and remain in the barn until the accomplishment of the birth. Bön also fosters tremendous reverence for the holiness and the wisdom of the old. Thus it is the grandmother who, at the first appearance of the morning star, fetches water from the brook and brings it to the mother and infant. (The morning star is believed to be the star of the forehead, which represents wisdom and learnedness. The Bön notion of the morning star also contains the idea of newness. In the Bön calendar, the change of date takes place when the morning star appears, inviting the dawn.) Once the child is born, it is identified with its family heritage—including its family mountain, family lake, and family tree. It is also assigned a turquoise stone, as the family possesses one for each of its members.

The rite associated with birth is called *lalu*, which means "ransoming the la." The word *la* is similar in meaning to the word "soul." All human beings possess a la; consciousness, or sem; and life, or sok. In the Bön tradition, animals do not possess a la. The la is an entity which is part of one's being but is unintelligent. Therefore it can be stolen, confiscated, or regained, as well as reinforced by spiritual power. It can be magnetized by any form of warmth or invitation. A child's la is born when the child leaves the womb and the umbilicus is cut. Butter and milk are associated with the la because of their white color, which, as already mentioned, represents goodness or divinity. In the lalu ceremony, which is still practiced, an image of a sheep is made from butter, and the infant is washed in milk, to invite the la to stay.

The lalu ceremony is also used to combat sickness. Sickness is thought by Bön believers to be caused directly or indirectly by the degyes or by certain evil forces. It begins through the weakening of a person's vitality. This might be caused by what is called a dön. Döns lurk furtively outside the dominion of Yeshen and have something of a hungry-ghost or thieving-dog quality—timid, but once gaining a hold, not letting go. A dön enters the system of a person who has abused the divine order, or perhaps it enters at a moment of depression or of some other weakness. Once a person is possessed by a dön, there is an opening for a minion of one of the degyes to steal his la. If this happens, then the sok (life) is subject to attack and capture by means of all kinds of sicknesses. If this attack is successful the person dies. In the case of an illness caused by the direct punishment of one of the eight degyes, life can be taken without going through the above stages; a degye can take control of the sok directly. A dön or a minion of a degye takes a la or sok because he can use it to add to his own presence and vitality.

Healing takes different forms, depending on the cause determined for the sickness. In some cases, a ceremony against a dön can be performed. This is done by making an effigy of the sick person and offering it, along with some meat and the hair or clothes of the sick person, to the dön as a replacement. Or, if a highly accomplished priest is available, he may perform a rite to gather all the döns in the area and frighten them off by manifesting as the wrathful Se. If this succeeds, the illness ends. If it fails, the lalu ceremony, mentioned above, is performed.

In this case, the lalu ceremony is performed partly to give a ransom to the confiscator of the la, but in addition to remagnetize the la to the sick person. In order to do this, certain objects are reconsecrated: the person's turquoise stone; his la cup (a cup owned by each individual specifically for this purpose); and the thigh bone of a sheep, inscribed with the person's name and astrological chart, and wrapped with colored threads representing the five elements, with the element of the person's birth year in the center. If this is effective, the illness is cured.

If this process also fails, it is a question of a very serious illness—a matter of life and death. Then an accomplished priest must be summoned. The priest would perform the *to* rite, which invokes the power of Se and calls for the eight degyes. The priest offers them small structures, resembling little houses fashioned out of thread, as dwelling places.

Another still weightier ceremony is called dö. This ceremony is often used by Buddhists in order to invoke the gönpos (or *mahakalas* in Sanskrit)—the protectors. The Bön ceremony invokes the degye thought to be involved in the illness. In this ceremony the degye is offered a new castle, a very elaborate miniature construction called a dö. The intent of the rite is to lure the degye not only out of the sick person but also out of his own dwelling place. Daily offerings are made, and at the end of a certain period there is a special session in which the dö is finally and completely offered to the degye if he will quit the sick person.

491

There are further ceremonies of this nature which can be performed only by priests of the highest accomplishment. In one of these, the priest threatens to destroy the dö if the degye refuses to release the sick person. In a still more dire rite, the priest identifies with Se and thus with the degyes, and, calling them, he imprisons them in certain appropriate sacred objects which he then buries. If the priest fails in the execution of this ceremony, it is considered a catastrophe since the attempt would enrage the degyes and they would take revenge. Quite possibly the priest himself might become sick or die.

Another important Bön practice seems to be the counterclockwise circumambulation of a mountain sacred to Se and the degyes, while performing the lhasang ritual at various points along the way.

As well, we have evidence of some incantations in the ancient Shang-shung language, which there is reason to believe may have been the ancestor of the Tibetan language. These incantations are thought to develop spiritual power, especially when accompanied by certain physical movements in the form of a dance. There were also supposedly some visualizations of Bön deities meant to be combined with the incantation and dance practice, but of these we know nothing. When the practitioner has completed intensive training in these practices he demonstrates his achievement of power by throwing butter sculptures into boiling water and pulling them out again intact, or by licking heated iron.

Many aspects of the Bön religion remain to be described, but unfortunately the task greatly exceeds the scope of this short presentation. Nevertheless we hope that the outlines for an accurate picture of this religion have been sketched and some sense given of its basic nature.

The Vajrayogini Shrine

SOME UNDERSTANDING of coemergent wisdom is necessary in order to appreciate the significance of the Vajrayogini shrine and the ritual objects that are part of it. When we begin to realize the coemergent quality of reality, we recognize that even a simple object, like a vase or a chair or a table, contains the potential power to spark wakefulness. The same is true for any sense perception or any emotion we may experience. We find ourselves in a world of self-existing messages. Because we are able to "read" the messages of the phenomenal world as statements of sacred outlook, we can properly appreciate the shrine of Vajrayogini, for the shrine embodies these self-existing messages and communicates them to others. The shrine is not set up for the worship of an external god or force; rather it is designed to focus the messages of sanity and wakefulness that exist in the world, to bring them down into the experience of the practitioner, and, in some sense, to amplify their brilliance and power.

The vajrayana has sometimes been misinterpreted as a highly symbolic system. For example, we often hear that the vajra scepter *symbolizes* skillful means or that the ghanta *symbolizes* wisdom. When it is said that the vajra is a symbol of skillful means or of indestructibility, that is true; but, in the genuine vajrayana sense, it is not simply that the vajra is used to represent or symbolize skillful means because skillful means is too abstract a concept to be dealt with, or be shown, directly. The vajra scepter *is* skillful means; it actually communicates and transmits skillful action directly if one understands the literalness of the vajrayana. For that reason, the shrine of Vajrayogini and all the implements on the shrine are themselves regarded as sacred objects.

The shrine shown in the illustration is an abhisheka shrine; that is, it includes all of the objects that are used in conferring the abhisheka of Vajrayogini. A simplified version of this shrine would be used for the daily practice of the sadhana.

The mandala of Vajrayogini is placed in the center of the shrine. The mandala is traditionally made of colored sand, or sometimes it is painted. A mandala made of heaps of rice is used if neither a painted mandala nor a sand mandala can be made. The mandala and the objects above it, which will be discussed next, are regarded as a particular power spot, or focus, of the shrine for magnetizing the energy and blessings of Vajrayogini, that is, for magnetizing self-existing wakefulness.

In the center of the painted mandala one finds a symbol for the hooked knife which Vajrayogini holds in her right hand. This means that the principal yidam, Vajrayogini herself, stands at the center of the mandala. In the painted mandala, the hooked knife is situated in the middle of two crossed triangles that represent the two sources of dharmas (chö-jung), which are the palace and the seat of Vajrayogini. The source of dharmas that is Vajrayogini's palace is actually a three-faced pyramid (trihedron), but it is represented in the painted mandala in only two dimensions. The apex of the triangle is an infinitesimal dot that points downward; the mouth of the triangle, in which Vajrayogini stands, is vast and spacious.

The source of dharmas arises out of emptiness and has three characteristics: it is unborn, nondwelling, and unceasing. Essentially it is absolute space with a boundary or frame. This represents the coemergent quality of wisdom and confusion arising from the emptiness of space. The source of dharmas is sometimes referred to as a channel for shunyata or as the cosmic cervix. The source of dharmas is an abstract form of coemergence while Vajrayogini is the iconographic or anthropomorphic form of the Coemergent Mother. The shape of the triangle—pointed at the bottom and wide at the top—signifies that every aspect of space can be accommodated at once—microcosm and macrocosm, the most minute situations as well as the most vast.

It is interesting that, in many theistic traditions, the pyramid is a symbol of reaching upward to unite with the godhead. The pinnacle of a pyramid or the apex of a cathedral reaches high into the clouds above. In this case, the source of dharmas reaches down, so that pleasure, pain, freedom, and imprisonment all meet at the lowest of the low points of

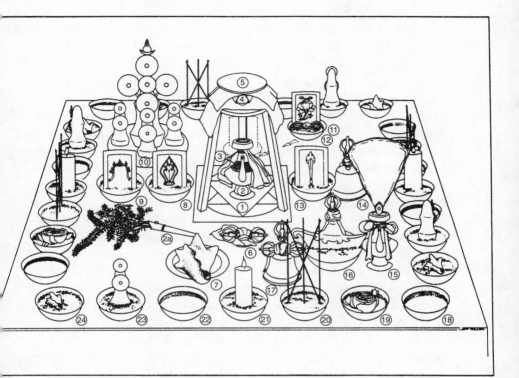

A Traditional Vajrayogini Shrine.

1. Mandala of Vajrayogini
2. Tsobum vase (2a: Top of tosbum vase)
3. Small vajra with five-colored thread
4. Skull cup
5. Mirror mandala
6. Vajra with white ribbon
7. Conch for oath water
8. Jewel tsakali
9. Crown tsakali
10. Phagmo torma
11. Flower tsakali
12. Vajra with red ribbon
13. Sword tsakali
14. Bell with green ribbon
15. Lebum
16. Hooked knife
17. Joined bell and dorje
18–24. Seven traditional offerings (repeated on each of the four sides):
    18. Water
    19. Flowers
    20. Incense
    21. Light
    22. Perfumed water
    23. Food (torma)
    24. Music (symbolized by small conch)

the pyramid. In the nontheistic tradition of Buddhist tantra, the triangle reaches down and down into the ground of reality; when one reaches all the way down to the apex of the triangle, one discovers water in that ground, which is known as compassion and as amrita.

In the four cardinal points of the painted mandala, surrounding the hooked knife in the center, are the symbols of vajra, ratna, padma, and karma. Vajrayogini manifests her basic buddha family quality in the central space of the mandala. However, the energy of Vajrayogini creates a complete mandala that encompasses, or works with, the energies of all of the buddha families. Thus, in the iconography of Vajrayogini, she is surrounded by her retinue: the vajra dakini in the east, the ratna dakini in the south, the padma dakini in the west, and the karma dakini in the north. This is shown in the painted mandala by the symbols of the buddha families in the four cardinal points: the vajra in the east, representing her buddha-vajra quality; the jewel in the south, representing her buddha-ratna quality; the lotus in the west, representing her buddha-padma quality; and the sword in the north, representing her buddha-karma quality. The painted mandala also depicts coils of joy, which symbolize the mahasukha, the great bliss, that Vajrayogini confers.

On top of the mandala on the shrine is placed the chief abhisheka vase, the tsobum. During the first vase abhiseka, as discussed earlier, the practitioners are empowered with water from the tsobum. Above the painted mandala is a tripod on which is placed a skull cup filled with amrita, which is used in conferring the second abhisheka, the secret abhisheka. This transmission dissolves the student's mind into the mind of the teacher and the lineage. In general, amrita is the principle of intoxicating extreme beliefs, based on the belief in ego, and dissolving the boundary between confusion and sanity so that coemergence can be realized.

On the skull cup is placed the mirror mandala of Vajrayogini—a mirror coated with red sindura dust, in which is inscribed the mandala and mantra of Vajrayogini. The mirror shows that the phenomenal world reflects the wakefulness of Vajrayogini and that her mandala is reflected in the experience of the practitioner. This is the same self-existing message that was discussed earlier. The red sindura dust that covers the mirror represents the cosmic lust and passion of the Coemergent Mother. At this level of practice, passion is no longer regarded as a problem. Freed from grasping, it becomes a force of expansion and communication; it is the expression of "self-luminous compassion" as is said in the *Vajrayogini Sadhana*.

Surrounding this arrangement of the painted mandala, the abhisheka vase, the skull cup, and the mirror are objects connected with the five buddha families and used in the transmission of the abhisheka of the vase. Directly in front of the painted mandala, in the east, is placed the five-pointed vajra, the symbol of the vajra family. The symbols of the buddha family—the crossed bell and dorje and the hooked knife—are also placed here, slightly off to one side. In the south (stage right) are placed the crown and the jewel representing the ratna family. In the west (behind the mandala) are placed the nine-pointed vajra and lotus, representing the padma family. In the north (stage left) are the ghanta and the sword, representing the karma family. If the actual objects representing the buddha families are not available, painted cards (tsakali) depicting the objects are placed on the shrine. A second abhisheka vase, the lebum, is placed in the northeast corner of the shrine. The lebum is considered to be the embodiment of the karma dakini. At the beginning of the abhisheka, prior to the abhisheka of the vase, the students drink water from the lebum to purify and cleanse themselves; at various points in the ceremony the vajra master sprinkles the disciples with water from the lebum to signify further purifying and overcoming of psychological obstacles. The conch shell, which holds the oath water of samaya, is placed in the front (east) of the shrine between the vajra family symbols and offering bowls on the edge of the shrine.

In the southern quadrant of the shrine (stage right) are also placed the phagmo tormas, which represent Vajrayogini and her retinue. Torma is a form of bread sculpture made from barley flour, water, alcohol, and other ingredients. The phagmo tormas on the shrine are an important means of making offerings to Vajrayogini, and in doing so, inviting the blessings of the yidam and of the lineage into the environment of practice. The tormas play a central role in the feast offering (ganachakra), a part of the *Vajrayogini Sadhana*. The basic idea of the feast offering is to make an offering of all sense perceptions and experience, transforming what might otherwise be expressions of confusion or indulgence into wakefulness.

On the edges of the shrine box are four sets of offering bowls, seven bowls to a set. The seven offerings are: saffron water, flowers, incense, lamps, food, perfumed water, and musical instruments. The offering of saffron water represents cleansing neurotic tendencies and emotional defilements, or kleshas, of body, speech, and mind. As is said in the sadhana:

> In order to cleanse the klesha tendencies of sentient beings
> We offer this ablution water for body, speech, and mind.

The offering of flowers represents offerings of pleasing sense perceptions:

> Flowers pleasing to the victorious ones of all mandalas
> Superior, well-formed, celestial varieties.

The offering of incense represents discipline:

> The fragrance of discipline is the best supreme incense.

The offering of lamps represents prajna:

> Burning the poisonous kleshas and dispelling the darkness
> of ignorance,
> The brilliance of prajna is a glorious torch.

The offering of perfumed water represents kindness:

> Pure water mixed with perfume and herbal ingredients is
> the bathing water of the victorious ones. . . .
> May kindness, raining continually from cloudbanks of
> wisdom, purify the multitude of foul odors.

The offering of food represents amrita:

> Though the victorious ones have no hunger,
> For the benefit of beings we offer this divine amrita food.

The offering of musical instruments represents the melody of liberation:

> The gong and cymbals are the liberating melody of Brahma.

On the wall behind the shrine or on an adjacent wall is a thangka, or painting, of Vajrayogini. The thangka of Vajrayogini is further tribute to her, and it is also on aid to visualization for the practitioner.

LIST OF SOURCES

CHAPTER 1   What Is the Heart of the Buddha?
Vajradhatu Sun 4, no. 3 (February–March 1981)

CHAPTER 2   Intellect and Intuition
Previously unpublished

CHAPTER 3   The Four Foundations of Mindfulness
Garuda IV (Boulder: Vajradhatu Publications, 1976)

CHAPTER 4   Devotion
Empowerment (Boulder: Vajradhatu Publications, 1976)

CHAPTER 5   Taking Refuge
Garuda V (Boulder: Vajradhatu Publications, 1977)

CHAPTER 6   The Bodhisattva Vow
Garuda V (Boulder: Vajradhatu Publications, 1977)

CHAPTER 7   Sacred Outlook: The Practice of Vajrayogini
"Sacred Outlook: The Vajrayogini Shrine and Practice," in Deborah
   Klimburg-Salter, ed., *The Silk Route and the Diamond Path: Esoteric Bud-
   dhist Art on the Trade Routes of the Trans-Himalayan Region* (Los
   Angeles: UCLA Art Council Press, 1977)

CHAPTER 8   Relationship
Maitreya 5: Relationship (Berkeley: Shambhala Publications, 1974)

CHAPTER 9   Acknowledging Death
Journal of Contemplative Psychotherapy 3 (Boulder: Naropa Institute, 1982).
   First published in *Healing,* ed. Olsen and Fossaghe (New York:
   Human Sciences Press, 1978).

SELECTED WRITINGS

The Wisdom of Tibetan Teachings

BUDDHISM WAS first introduced into Tibet from India in the seventh century when King Songtsen Gampo commissioned the translation of Indian Buddhist sutras into Tibetan and reformed his governmental structure in the light of Buddha's teachings of compassion and nonviolence. King Songtsen Gampo, beleaguered by constant civil strife and disillusioned with the national cult of Bön—which consisted of war rituals, sacrificial ceremonies, and ancestral worship—was inspired by the example of the great Buddhist emperor Ashoka of India.

Several generations later, at a time when Buddhist influence had declined in Tibet, King Trisong Detsen was inspired to follow the example of Songtsen Gampo and invited the great Indian Buddhist teachers Shantarakshita, Padmasambhava, Vimalamitra, and many others to restore and deepen Buddhist practice. Shantarakshita introduced the hinayana and mahayana traditions, while Padmasambhava and Vimalamitra introduced the vajrayana tradition. Thus Tibet inherited the complete Buddhist tradition of India. A follower of the school of Buddhism developed at this time is known as a Nyingmapa. Later the study and practice of this school was revitalized by Longchen Rabjam and other great teachers.

One of the great Indian influences came at the time of Marpa Lotsa, who journeyed to India and returned to Tibet with the oral teachings of the four orders of tantra as well as the hinayana and mahayana teachings. These he received from the renowned Indian siddha Naropa and other great pandits and siddhas. Marpa began the New Translation Era, which restored the pure teachings of the tantra after they had become diluted during a period of social disorder.

Marpa transmitted his teachings to his chief disciple, Milarepa, who became known as "Tibet's Great Yogi." Milarepa in turn transmitted the teachings of the six doctrines of Naropa and other mahamudra transmissions to Gampopa, a Kadam monk in the tradition of Atisha. Gampopa combined the monastic and yogic traditions into what came to be known as the Kagyü or practicing lineage.

The Geluk tradition stems from the lineage of the Kadam teaching founded by Tsongkapa in the fourteenth century. This combines strict monastic discipline with both intellectual understanding of Buddhist philosophy and meditation. The Geluk tradition also embodies the New Translation tantra.

The fourth school of Tibetan Buddhism is Sakya, which follows the mahamudra teachings of the Indian sage Virvapa. Sakya involves monastic discipline, highly developed philosophic thought, and yogic practice.

Following the pattern of all these schools, it is quite clear that the basic principle is to work on the paths of hinayana with its monastic rules, the mahayana practice of the bodhisattva ideal, and the vajrayana practice of Buddhist yoga.

To begin with, the monastic rules of the hinayana order of Sarvastivadin consist of a framework of discipline quite similar to that of the Theravadin order in Burma, Ceylon, and Thailand. As Buddha said, monastic discipline is both teaching and teacher. This enables students to work beyond the inquisitive and fascinated ego and its seductions.

As Tibetan monasticism developed centers for learning and meditation, more opportunities were created for followers to study. Each school was self-contained and its practices were part of the daily lives of its followers. There was practically no emphasis on creating an efficient, hierarchical organization such as one finds in the church of the Catholic tradition, even though some monasteries had as many as 7,700 monks and the smaller monasteries had approximately a hundred members. Each of these monasteries was regarded as an island unto itself—not in the sense of being a fortress or, for that matter, with any attitude of becoming an empire. Nevertheless, there was a natural tendency for the presence of the monasteries to influence the surrounding community.

Within this framework of discipline, the mahayana approach of developing the Buddhist attitude of compassion became important not only for the monks but for the lay followers as well, who found tremendous strength in it for their daily work. Compassion from the Buddhist point of view is without motivation, even without the motivation to become buddha. One simply devotes one's life to the welfare of all sentient beings. Having a goal is part of ego's expression and its struggle to achieve and become continually more self-oriented. As soon as the ambition of ego is used as part of the path, the path itself becomes another tool to benefit ego. Ego in this case consists of the basic neurosis, which automatically sets up a psychological blockage and doesn't allow one to see the primordial deception which creates self-ignoring ignorance. In order to ignore, one has to create a manufactured occupation—"Let's find a place, and name this place. We'll call it *me* or *I* or atman, whatever." Having developed this concept, one has to defend it. This aggressively defending chemical is anger.

Destroying the enemy involves conquering his territory and is regarded as: "It belongs to me." One tends to grasp that territory, and this is passion.

These three constituents of ego—ignorance, aggression, and passion—are not the qualities of an awakened state; there is a constant involvement within the self. Thus it is impossible to see reality as it is. This is not to suggest an attitude of regarding the ego as a villain; rather it is the unwillingness to take part in ego's games, but instead to transmute the energy into compassion.

The mahayana practice of working with life consists of generosity, discipline, patience, energy, concentration, and knowledge. These are known as paramitas, which means "arriving at the other shore." In other words, extraordinary vision as well as its application will lead us to reach beyond ego's shore.

Such egoless application to life brings one to the discovery of reality as it is. The tantric way of life is to live in the vivid world of non-ego where there is no obscurity or confusion. Tantric teaching is the discovery of the mahamudra principle. *Maha* means "great"; *mudra* means "symbol." *Symbol* is used not in the sense of analogy but in the meaning of things as they are. For example, water is water because there are neither conceptualizations nor the hope and fear of the ego imposed upon it. The nakedness of seeing things truly is vivid and colorful, and this is the true sense of *symbol* or *mudra*.

From this experience of seeing things as part of the mandala spectrum of a "divine realm," there are endless iconographical details that are shown in the Tibetan tradition as expressions of mahamudra. A tantric practitioner will visualize and repeat mantras, but the inspiration is more vivid than merely such exotic practices in themselves.

In many cases the Tibetan way of practicing buddhadharma is extremely influenced by the tantra. Tantra is regarded as a self-secret teaching in that, if students are not ready for the experience, it is not comprehensible to them. Most of the ritual ceremonies, such as the use of musical instruments and monastic dance, are examples of this kind of experience. This seems to create a lot of difficulties for foreign visitors, since these highlights are more spectacular than the preparatory training that is required for understanding them. It is impossible to develop a comprehensive understanding of the tradition without going into the background. In other words, mystical experience, in the Buddhist tradition, is not a matter of being mysterious—it is direct comprehension of things as they are.

This direct, ultimately simple understanding is the essence of the Buddhist teachings. Thus, it is said in the scriptures that the path is the goal and the goal is the path.

Transcending Materialism

Night without sun,
Dark without a moon,
Cloudy without stars,
Then the sudden flash of lightning illuminates
As once in a hundred times, Buddha activity sparks
knowledge to the merit of the world.

T HIS QUOTATION FROM Shantideva's work is always applicable to
what happens in the world generally, as it is now to the atmosphere
of the United States at the height of materialism. When we speak of
materialism, it is as a psychological term describing the reign of the three
lords of materialism: the lord of form, the lord of speech, and the lord
of mind.

The lord of form refers to the seductive quality of the apparent psychological comfort which comes from the impersonal, predictable efficiency
of mass production. It is the attitude expressed in the attempt to remove
all irritation from our physical surroundings, trying to reach a total comfort by controlling situations absolutely. It is an antinature attitude of
refusing to see the evolutionary aspect of everything. By a scientific, mechanical approach to things, one manipulates them to shield oneself
from irritation, from the raw and rugged quality of life.

The lord of speech refers to the extension of the technological aspect of
materialism into the realm of philosophy. Thus one sees trust in and
reliance upon sophisticated conceptualized systems, such as the selling
approaches of Madison Avenue or the complicated ideologies of many
nation-states. Temporary and illusory success in manipulating the world

toward the fulfillment of these intellectual systems confirms our trust in them, until we begin to see the world almost completely through the filter of ideology or dogma.

The lord of mind refers to the extension of the materialism of form and speech into the realm of spiritual matters, and it is once again character-ized by the attempt to establish control for the benefit of ego. One can even convince oneself that one is stepping out of ego. One has developed a logical style of rationalizing situations, so much so that this familiar method is applied to the spiritual realm as well. Thus theology is born and one uses yogic practices in the service of ego. ("I want to be 'high' or 'spiritual.'") But the logic of materialism cannot be applied to the realm of spirit.

The process America is going through is not exclusive. It is happening here first, but the rest of the world will go through the cycle, for as we can see, the materialism of form is already rampant.

As Shantideva describes, this surfeit of materialism provokes the un-derlying buddha nature or instinctive intelligence, particularly where the concentration of materialism has the highest energy. And so we see here in America a search for something beyond diagrams or mathematical calculations, a surge toward Eastern religions, tribal structures, dropouts from the system, from school and jobs—even involvement with drugs is a movement in this direction. Many of these alternatives are by no means perfect.

It is not coincidental that the Chinese Communists invaded Tibet and forced the exodus of great teachers at the very time that people in the West had experienced a surfeit of materialism and had begun searching for a spiritual life. One is reminded of the time of Buddha, which was also a time of materialism and social disorganization. The Buddha dropped out of his aristocratic life situation and became an ascetic renun-ciant in search of answers to basic life questions. For seven years he fol-lowed the practices of the Indian Hindu ascetic tradition until, finally, seeing its futility, he renounced it. At this point he began to discover a third way, independently working on his mental processes. Similarly, American youth has found that the continual attempt to solve the prob-lems of life—always trying to remove unpleasant situations and replace them with sophisticated solutions—only further complicates the patterns of our striving. These methods of escaping somehow provoke the same thing again, because we try to put down wall after wall, aggression after aggression, and it is seen very much in terms of a battle. So one seems mainly to exchange one dogma for another.

Then, having built in such an extreme way, questions begin to arise in one's mind, breaking the pattern of speeding and striving. And they are kind of pregnant questions, in that they contain the answers as well. This is the instinct coming out, the instinct of one mind or egolessness rather than the duality of mind and its projections. The simplicity is most apparent by contrast. Once you begin to see this contrast, you begin to step out of the force of psychological materialism. It is seen as competition and ambition, always striving to secure the future, in contrast to the simplicity of nowness, which is down to earth and direct.

The nowness is not just purely the meditative state, but it is seeing things as they are. You have to stop running in order to ask questions, and this cuts the chain reaction of karmic energy, and another kind of motion sets into the wheel of karma from then on.

So therefore, nowness is not a way of seeing the truth; nowness is being true, which helps to unmask the pretense of ego. You begin to examine suffering and pain as it is, the same psychological process as Buddha's discovery of the four noble truths.

In my experience of working with people in this country, it has not been a process of proseletyzing or conversion, but rather people convert themselves through the questioning and arousal of this basic instinct. The great demand creates an interesting and energetic situation where people come to study meditation and bring a new point of view to their lives, or the energy goes in the direction of creating communities on the framework of the dharma (rather than monastic centers) such as Tail of the Tiger in Vermont and Karma Dzong in Colorado.

These situations seem to develop as groups of yogis living together, and, in a sense, both positive and negative experiences are used as part of the path. This pattern encourages independence without dogma.

Many people have already begun their spiritual journey before coming in contact with the teachings, and the learning process is evolutionary rather than purely academic. That is to say, they are working on their already existing psychological states. They start with the hinayana practice of shamatha and vipashyana meditation, and the gradual growth up to yogic teachings seems to be a natural one, rather than straining under the promise of exotic and sudden enlightenment. With the inspiration of a spiritual friend, a certain commitment or discipline develops which acts as skillful means in the process of working with themselves. As their development takes place, the richness of the Buddhist teaching of Tibet is not too potent, because it doesn't present a seductive goal, but rather reaffirms the students' personal experiences, both intuitive and intellectual. Needless to say, the growing comprehension of the play of this whole situation is in itself buddha activity.

Cutting Through

I RECENTLY MADE a lecture tour in California and met quite a few people there. From these encounters and others in the West, it seems that there is, on the whole, a continual fascination with Eastern teachings. People are, in a sense, very honest and generous; that is, they are open to the teachings, but they are also compelled and provoked by them. Somehow confusion sets in because either they are fascinated by the colorful exterior, robes, and rituals; or, being already a part of Western society and having to keep some kind of link with it, they do not know how to relate the teachings to their daily life. Their attempts to make this link between their living in the Western world and the desire for experience beyond reveals something lacking.

This problem relates to a basic underlying pattern in the growth of spiritual movements. It becomes more evident in looking back, for instance, at the development and study of meditation and Buddhist thought in Great Britain and Europe. At the beginning of the nineteenth century, there already was, apparently, a basic dissatisfaction with the established teaching of Christianity. Perhaps familiarity bred contempt, but it seems to have been more than that. At the end of the century many people were involved with such organizations as the Rosicrucians, the Golden Dawn, Aleister Crowley's O.T.O. [Ordo Templi Orientis], and various others, seeking ways out of church doctrine and into the "mysteriousness" which accompanies the teachings. The results were often similar to those of Crowley, who attempted, after having made a crude study of Buddhist thought, to bring it together with the roots of Western civilization. The focus became a mysticism in the sense of the "mysteriousness" found in witchcraft and magic. The organizations arising at this time generally came from the intelligentsia, or people involved with intellect and richness of material comfort, who searched for the patterns in this "mysteriousness," while others merely continued through the established churches.

The establishment of the Theosophical Society attracted many in search of a basic pattern, something more than the ordinary worship of Jesus Christ as a savior. They were looking for the power of mind that exists behind the dogma, but were caught up in the confusion between power of mind and the egocentricity that all these "magical" organizations developed.

Early in the twentieth century this search coincided with certain material problems, a coincidence which occurred in the East as well, for instance with Gandhi's movement in India or in Sun Yat-sen's attempt to revolutionize China. But here the conflict was in a spiritual, a more intellectual realm. The pattern of searching for the "magic" behind dogma continues on and on. It does not provide anything particularly meaningful nor fulfill the object of search. After a while the whole thing is dropped, more or less, and another search begun.

The study of Eastern thought as it has developed in America follows this same pattern. The present availability of Tibetan and Buddhist teachings is mainly due to the Pali Text Society and the work of India's Anagarika Dharmapala, who delivered the message of the Buddha throughout the world. At the same time in Tibet, the monk Gendün Chöphel, an extraordinary and inspired person, rebelled against the pattern of the church structure there; he made a pilgrimage to India and then decided to study Pali in Ceylon. He became a Pali scholar and tried to make some link between modern Western culture and the traditional Tibetan pattern. He translated Pali texts into Tibetan and endeavored to introduce Buddhist thinking that differed from the prevailing ideas. At the same time, Anagarika Dharmapala was working to legalize pilgrimages to Buddhist countries and to restore the inspirational monuments. This whole development was partially Buddhist and partially global. The work of Theosophy in the West was mirrored in the East, a tremendous movement to find new ways of adapting the teachings, a new way of understanding. It is part of the pattern that goes on continuously. And so it seems at this moment that there is this great potential of a search for a new interior and exterior life. If we are particularly searching for an exterior mode, then this pattern will develop as an effort to transplant those religions we are interested in: Hinduism, Buddhism (Zen, Theravadan, or whatever). These patterns may be imitated or followed. Many people have tried to become Tibetan, but it is very clumsy. Others have tried to become Japanese, which is equally as clumsy. Still others have tried to become Burmese, Sinhalese, or Thai as well as Indian, and again it is very clumsy. As we continue to search for images and forms, the pattern continues to be the same. Try to remember our history.

People are inspired by Egyptology; I'm sure many have been. We do not have the oral teachings, but merely study it from the archaeological point of view. We have been given a few clues and would like to follow them on and on. It's a process of working back through the material. In this fascination with externals we could end up back in the Stone Age. We could come to worship the sun and moon; hunt, eat raw meat, and wear skins. It's a great trip. We could just try and be with nature.

Many feel this contact is lacking and often begin to experience a longing for it, reading back into history with nostalgia. But since all this going back to the Stone Age involves searching for more luxury, how are we going to place our minds? It is luxury because people tire of central heating and automatic equipment. Water boils and signals with a whistle, and you don't even have to watch it. But it becomes a child's game to do all this manually and participate in the excitement of watching it happen. But all this is luxury. There is no difference in having this way of life as opposed to that one. It is quite the same. We are searching for some kind of luxury. It seems to follow generally that once we are leading a mechanized life, we feel something is missing.

What is missing? I think we have lost the point. If we look at things with this particular fascination for the exterior alone, we merely want to substitute one thing for another. This is pure materialism. Psychological materialism has gotten into the process in a highly complicated and sophisticated way, going so far as leading the Stone Age life. One can sense possibilities, even in the extreme cases, but they all miss the point. There will still be dropouts in these Stone Age communities, reactionaries and all the rest. This is inevitable as long as we search for comfort, or, more important, the romantic aspect of things. We see this with people who have become completely Japanese or Tibetan. They are completely trained in that way of life. One would live this kind of life with the encouragement, of course, of the Tibetans and Japanese ("What a wonderful transformation they've made; at last they've managed to become like us"). But, then, one would have problems whether one lived as a Tibetan, Japanese, or Indian. So what happens next? Something is fishy; something is lacking. Did we miss the boat somewhere? What is wrong? Having involved myself in becoming completely Tibetan, I can't possibly go back to Western ways; that would be embarrassing! But secretly I would contemplate this, have private conversations with myself about it. "What is wrong? I didn't get some kind of expected utopian civilization as I imagined I would. There is something wrong behind it all." And then I would begin to question my fascination for such a civilization, such a work of art! I used to be able to sit and just gaze at the pure image of the Buddha or certain patterns of the interior decoration. I could really live on and on, spend twenty-four hours a day watching them, but what's gone wrong now? I just can't do that anymore.

It is really a matter of fascination. Nothing is wrong with the design or the inspiration of the work of art, but something is wrong with the fascination. It has gone too far. We haven't checked ourselves in the process of going into it. We've let ourselves be sucked out. We involve ourselves too much. So the situation develops that one has to look back. These philosophies and works of art are beautiful as they are, but we don't have to just plunge into them. We have to realize that we can't change ourselves completely this way. The main thing is to develop a sense of humor on the journey and see the funny side of our involvement. A sense of humor plays a great part in balancing things, sometimes sarcastic, sometimes inspiring. But we certainly can't become Tibetans, Japanese, or Indians, because the very desiring to become so contains the preconceived idea of ambition. The way of life may be extremely attractive to us, but being moved by the wisdom doesn't mean we have to accept the exterior. This exterior is a very difficult thing. Its fascination plays a too important part. If one wants to absorb the teaching, one has to work in a different way.

Although the symbols may contain a certain inspiration, one needn't go through the whole external trip. And what is behind that external trip that seems so embarrassing to look into? Each time there is a little attempt to look into ourselves, it is an embarrassing situation, because it involves the complicated and unfamiliar action of dealing with our own mind. We try to avoid this by involving ourselves more and more with externals. This seems to be the problem, a neurotic pattern, the feeling of embarrassment or hesitation that makes us get lost in outside details.

In any case, one has to face the truth sooner or later. Facing the truth later will be more shocking, more difficult. It will be more disappointing, because you have gone as far as you can, to the point of eating and dressing and behaving as they do, and still something is wrong. It will be very painful and disappointing. So it seems necessary to have a good look before the fascination takes over. The fascination takes us away from looking at ourselves. When there are psychological problems involved, it doesn't work to merely sit and gaze at a work of art and try to get some kind of kick out of it. Many people do just that; all of us do, but it isn't valid. It's a substitution, an escape.

Whenever we are shrouded in a mental depression, we talk to someone, or go to the shrine, or read a book to try to ease the problem, which is a cowardly hesitation. It may seem very easy at the moment, but we are going to get addicted this way. And each time there is a further psychological problem or depression, we are going to escape further and further and at last decide to give up the whole responsibility of our family or business. Suddenly, one completely flips out and decides to give up the whole thing and take the first train or airplane to the nearest place and become a sannyasin or bhikshu or whatever. This is the ultimate hypocrisy, one might say transcendental hypocrisy. So something is wrong there, a hole that we really have to look into. No, we are not supposed to abandon all these uneasy materialistic scenes in Washington or New York, etc. We are supposed to work with it. The world is not built purely for us, but is a mutual effort of ourselves and others. So we have to develop some kind of compassion and openness of love for it.

I know a person who completely abandoned his eight children, wife, home, business, and everything; just completely left like that. After a final blow, he took the first plane east to India. He became a sannyasin and resident of an ashram. I think that is a very selfish act, regarding the world as if it were only for you rather than for everybody. This is the extreme attitude of self-deliverance. We need a great deal of compassion to share pains and problems with others. In order to do this, of course, we have to become willing to offer ourselves to the situation, not make a big scene of it. Not to demand attention for ourselves. We have to learn to dance with the situation, to work with it. This is very important, extremely important. We could be developed spiritually and be working on ourselves continually. Suddenly we run out of inspiration for further development. We don't make any demands or a big scene out of it, which would be a very clumsy kind of skillfulness. If we try to demand inspiration or attention out of something else, an aggressive attitude develops, which is not compassion. Aggression is very involved with trying to secure something within ourselves, or the experience of basic ego.

The ego begins with the fear of not knowing what you are. Then you keep trying to patch up this gap of isolation and separateness. The paranoia is expressed in the clinging quality of feelings, because you are trying to make something out of it. Then impulse develops as an automatic and natural reaction to the feelings, in that it is part of relating self or inside to the outside. This is an automatic tendency, so that there is a continual patching-up in this ego process, and we are constantly involved in it. After this comes consciousness, which is the intelligence that works with our response to the outside world. But since this response to situations involves so much impulse, feeling, and paranoia, walls are set up and we are not able to really work with the response. The ego is based on playing the game of deaf, dumb, and blind. Whenever you don't want to hear anything, you play deaf, when you don't want to see something, you play blind. The ego is very much into this neurotic game, not willing to let anything open. The basic twist is believing you're blind, because you don't want to see. And actually you don't see anything at all, because the insight is not allowed to reach the level of consciousness. There is a fundamental boss operating the switchboard. The whole ego situation is very neurotic, and you have to work to find these structures within yourself. My talking about it may not help at all; it could even be a warning for the ego's sake.

Basically, you have to just look into it with complete honesty and truthfulness. Open to it and look, and you will be able to find the substitutions that are made for the ego's survival, and the ways you go wrong by playing all those games of being other people, clothing yourself with their robes, eating their particular diet, behaving according to their particular notions. To them it may not be a game, but it is to you. And here is an interesting point. One couldn't say Tibetans behave or eat wrongly. Nothing is particularly wrong in their ways; on the other hand it is a game for you because you have another way to compare with it, and this makes you feel superior to your fellow man.

This patterning becomes very important. The whole process that we have been talking about is connected with working honestly with the pattern of ego. These operations on the ego are going to be very painful, without anesthetic, without any shield for self-embarrassment. Then, also, we do not merely want to go back and undo the process of ego with the intellect; we need a precise way of dealing with it. This is the teaching of the nowness of meditation. This means not even trying to humiliate yourself. The nowness of meditation is a precise way of sudden penetration into the heart of the matter. What must be penetrated? It is the idea of the past, the idea of the future, and the conception of achievement in either of these that you need to cut through. You have to forget all these ambitions and hopes, and just open, look directly and thoroughly into the situation of the nowness. It will leave you completely bland, purposeless, open, and speechless, because there is nothing to relate anything to, nothing to secure. Everything is direct, sharp, and precise. This experience is described as the sword of Manjushri, the Bodhisattva of Wisdom. There is the sudden penetration of cutting, one slash of the sword which may take a fraction of a second, but with each stroke the past and future networks are severed completely. It is a very sharp sword.

This is what meditation is. It cuts through the fascination of attaching ourselves to a particularly colorful scene, and cuts through the expectation of a final, ideal, and comfortable way of life, in this case spiritual life, which has confused us. Perhaps we have thought of a spiritual life as a life of being dressed up in some particular fashion and striving to reach some level of perception or another. I have heard people say that English is the language of barbarians and that is why we have to learn Tibetan or Sanskrit. If both languages convey what is, I see no reason to distinguish between them. In fact, what is more inspiring is that we transcend the racial and cultural divisions: as we are, we can penetrate directly into the heart of it. This is the penetration of wisdom cutting through the fascination. Once we are on the spiritual path, there can still be the demons of particular attitudes involved with further fascination. The sword of Manjushri cuts directly through that.

The Tibetan Buddhist Teachings
and Their Application

ACTUALLY, THERE IS no such thing as Tibetan Buddhism. Rather there is the Buddhist tradition as it developed in Tibet, as Tibetans practiced it and applied it to their living situation. Buddhism does not belong to the Tibetans or any other nation. Buddhism belongs to all of us as individuals. That being the case, before we consider the application of the Buddhist teachings, we have to look into who is applying them and with what basic outlook. This background or attitude is, in fact, more important than the application itself.

When we listen to a speaker, for example, we are gathered and expectant. We expect an ideal message or certain edifying ideas from the speaker. Because of our need to satisfy our intellect and emotions and to get some security, we want to hear words of wisdom, and we remold the speaker's words to satisfy that need. We shape them and reshape them, manufacturing fixed and definite impressions from the raw materials of the speaker's words. The result is that we constantly have nothing but ourselves bouncing back on ourselves. That is always a problem. It is very difficult to find both an audience who will sit in no-man's-land and a speaker who speaks from no-man's-land. That kind of attitude is very difficult, extremely hard.

There are many types of Buddhist writings and many styles of Buddhist practice in this country and in the world in general, but the basic principles of Buddhism have not been properly understood or conveyed. The introduction of the Buddhist tradition in this country has been very confused and incomplete. We are fascinated by the glories of the Buddhist tradition, such as the mysticism and magic of the Tibetan vajrayana or tantra. We would like to build a golden roof, but we have not considered how to build a foundation, and when we begin to build our golden roof, we find we have nowhere to put it. That childish approach is quite prevalent. We are hungry for knowledge and want to get results immediately and automatically, but unless we give up that speed and urgency, we are not going to learn anything. The problem seems to be basically one of laziness. We are so lazy that we do not even want to bother eating our food; we would prefer to be satisfied just from reading the menu. And that laziness reaches the extreme when it comes to going further into relating with reality.

ENLIGHTENMENT IS THE
ABSENCE OF PROMISE

The process of learning to wake up takes time and painful measures of all kinds. The learning process is not an easy matter. It is not easy, because we do not want to surrender our basic security. The teachings of Buddhism are not a source of security, such as "the freedom of nirvana" or something of that nature. The teachings do not present another form of security at all, but bring the absence of any kind of security. Enlightenment is the complete absence of any kind of promises. We have to give up the tendency to look for solid, serious, or magical results. We have to give up the tendency to look for solid, serious, or magical results. We have to give up trying to manufacture results through gimmicks. Somehow such neurotic psychological games do not apply.

Nevertheless, there is something extremely positive about our search for understanding, something that we could use as a stepping-stone. That stepping-stone is the chaos in our life, the pain and chaos and dissatisfaction and hunger and thirst. Those dissatisfactions and our search for something better—that psychological pain—is the beginning of the teaching. Unless there is pain and dissatisfaction, there is nowhere at all to begin. That pain is the direct experience of our basic insecurity. Looking for security and failing to find it is a glimpse of egolessness. We perceive possibilities—possibilities of failure, of losing our grip, of not being able to manufacture the ideal pleasurable situation. Such perceptions are extremely positive from the point of view of embarking on the path of buddhadharma.

Everyone begins his journey on the path by experiencing dissatisfaction. Something is missing somewhere, and we are frantically looking for it. But even though we run faster and faster and faster, we do not discover anything at all. There is the constant sense that we are missing the point. So we start to ask questions. We question our whole idea of security and pain and pleasure. We question the validity of spirituality, how efficient, magical, or pleasurable it might be. And all these questions that we ask contain the knowledge that our ego-centered wishes may not be fulfilled in the end. We already have that impression, therefore we ask the questions.

The discovery that comes out of the questioning process is that there is something completely mysterious. At some stage we run out of questions. Something is completely blank, to the point where we cannot even think of questions anymore. We are completely bewildered and we wonder, concerning this questioning process that is going on, who is fooling whom? But if we look and investigate, we find neither the fooler nor the fooling process. When we try to pinpoint anything, it dissolves.

BEWILDERMENT IS THE BASIC GROUND

A basic bewilderment takes place here, and that bewilderment is the ground that we could work on. Such bewilderment is not just passive bewilderment; it contains speed, grasping, and frantically looking for some answers. If we are able to realize and acknowledge all of the basic bewilderment and speed and grasping that we are experiencing—if we are able to relate with it as it is actually happening instead of just imagining something about it, then we are at least getting somewhere. We are starting from somewhere and we are making some kind of contact, intellectually, emotionally.

On the whole, it could be said that the discovery of confusion *is* enlightenment. When we discover confusion, the enlightened state becomes redundant. Discovering the confusion is the most important thing of all. It is facing reality and getting beyond the many kinds of self-deception. Whereas if we are purely searching for something glorious and pleasurable, if we view enlightenment as a promised land or treasure island, then it is just a myth. It just adds further pain. We cannot get to such a treasure island; we cannot get to such a promised land; we cannot actually attain enlightenment. The more we think about enlightenment, the more pain we feel because of the frustration of not getting there, which just creates further confusion.

So the Buddhist tradition tells us, and here all sects and schools concur, that if we are going to begin on the path, we have to begin at the beginning. We cannot begin halfway through and we cannot begin on the dream level. We have to face the reality of our actual living situation.

SIDETRACKED BY SEDUCTIONS

This point is very relevant to what is happening in this country in relation to the spiritual search. We begin to search for something because our life situation does not satisfy us. Physically it might be luxurious, but psychologically something does not satisfy us. Therefore we look for some definite answer. But in the process of looking for this answer, we are sidetracked by all kinds of seductions and we begin to lose track of what we were searching for in the first place. We become involved with exotic practices or techniques, and they become like golden crutches. We become very attracted to the method itself, rather than seeing how it actually functions in our situation. That is because we are looking for an answer that will help us to relate to our pain and our pleasure as an occupation, as entertainment.

At the beginning of such an involvement, because of self-deception and because of strong desire to be satisfied with what we have discovered, these promises tend to be fulfilled—quite simply, quite easily. We tend to get all kinds of immediate results—physical and psychological bliss, visions and messages of all kinds. But as we continue on and on, sooner or later the raw and rugged quality of life begins to poke through; our graspingness and speed begin to catch up with us. Then we set off again to look for another technique that is more efficient or that will last longer. Perhaps we find something better and we go through the same enthusiasm. But then those new efforts being to wear out as well and we have to go on to something else. We could spend millions of years shopping for answers and promises. We have been doing that all along and we are still doing it, hoping that the next discovery will be something new. But I wonder about that.

The practice of meditation is relating with games such as this that we play. Actually, meditation is the only way to relate with neurosis and self-deception. In this case meditation does not mean concentrating on objects or trying to intensify certain psychic faculties or anything of that nature. It is just simply creating a space, a space in which we can unlearn and undo our subconscious gossip, our hidden fears and hidden hopes, and begin to bring them out. Meditation is simply providing space through the discipline of sitting down and doing nothing. Doing nothing is extremely difficult. At the beginning we can only try to do nothing by imitating doing nothing. And then hopefully we can develop gradually from there.

MAKING FRIENDS WITH OURSELVES

So meditation is a way of permitting hang-ups of mind to churn themselves up. These psychological hang-ups are like manure. We do not throw away manure, we use it on our garden. In the same way, we use our hang-ups in our daily living situations. We use them as part of our path, not by rejecting them as a bad thing or by indulging in them, but by simply relating to them as they are. If we try to focus on our neurosis as a practice, that is an escape; and if we try to suppress it, that is also an escape. So the process is to relate with the neurosis as it is, in its true nature, the actual simplicity of it. Then we begin to make some progress, so to speak. As this process of relating to our hang-ups develops, at some point we at last begin to trust ourselves. We begin to develop some kind of faith and trust that what we have and what we are is, after all, not all that bad. It is workable, usable.

MAKING FRIENDS WITH OUR WORLD

And we might have something more in us as well—our world. We also possess that. So we also gradually begin to relate with our world situation, our friends, and so on. And slowly we begin to trust the world as well. We begin to feel that the world is not as bad as we thought—there might be something in it worth learning. But we cannot just go out and love the world. We have to start with ourselves because the world is our world. Running away from ourselves into the world would be like trying to accept the rays of the sun while rejecting the sun itself.

In this sense, therefore, meditation is developing ultimate compassion. It is an inexhaustible resource, because once we are on the path of meditation, every life situation teaches us something. If we go too fast, some incident takes place in our life to slow us down. If we are going too slow, our life begins to push us. Our life situation always contains a message. And that message can be understood, to begin with, if we realize that the resources we have are positive resources. They have nothing to do with destruction or original sin or any pain or misery that we have to reject. So the process of learning spontaneously from our life situation seems to be the starting point.

I am glad we have had an opportunity to begin to study the Buddhism of Tibet. This *is* the Buddhism of Tibet, and the most practical and safest way of looking at it at this point is to consider the beginning. We have to see how to begin, how to use the stepping-stones that exist in our lives as part of the spiritual journey. There may be a lot of people reading this who are extremely advanced. No doubt. But even advanced people have to begin their next stage, so they also could be regarded as beginners. Beginning at the beginning is the most useful approach for all of us, since we are beginning all the time. We cannot re-create the past, we cannot involve ourselves with the future—we have to live in the present. Life constantly begins at the beginning, always fresh. Therefore it has been said, "The dharma is good at the beginning, good in the middle and good at the end."

We could have discussion now if you would like to ask questions.

Question: What is the best way to work on your neurosis? I mean how do you focus on it as a practice?

Rinpoche: Well, if you try to focus on it as a practice, that is an escape; and if you try to suppress it, that is also an escape. So the process is to relate with the neurosis as it is, in its true nature, the actual simplicity of it as it is. Then we begin to make some progress, so to speak. The reason why neurosis is seen as neurosis is that it contains conflict. It is formed out of preconceived ideas and expectations and wishful thinking of all kinds, so actually there is no such thing as a neurosis as a lump entity. What there is are these constituents of "neurosis," grasping and rejecting, and so on. In the process of doing this grasping and rejecting, you are not satisfied with what is happening, and then you begin to distrust your whole process. You think you may be losing your grip, your footing, and you panic—which brings out what is known as "neurosis." But if you are able to see and acknowledge all those little mechanical constituents of neurosis, then it can become a tremendous source of learning. And then the "neurosis" dissolves by itself, works itself out automatically.

Q: What is the purpose or purposes of living our lives?

R: We are always thinking in terms of purpose, aim and object, goal. That seems to be the problem altogether. We might look in another area, that of the purposelessness of life. Perhaps that sounds grim.

People often ask about the meaning of life or the purpose. But if you look for purpose you are defeating its purpose, you are separating yourself from the purpose, segregating yourself from the goal. So our life situations should be the path. The path should be the goal and the goal should be the path. In that sense you could say there is no purpose of any kind. Just live.

Q: When the teacher, meditation teacher, is giving instruction, is there anything more going on than just the meaning of the words?

R: Communication is going on.

Q: But besides the meaning of the words . . .

R: There is the silence between the words. Which enables us to understand the words. The punctuation is the silence. In fact that is probably the most important factor in communication—the generosity of the silence that each person communicates. You are not hurrying to speak, hurrying to overpower the student or control him. The silence that goes between the remarks is also important.

Q: Isn't the idea of enlightenment some kind of goal? Isn't trying to become a buddha the same thing as the golden crutches? Don't you have to throw away the idea of Buddha and the golden crutches and just be?

R: Well, I think more or less you have said it. Trying to become an enlightened person is one point of view, and enlightenment would have to be all points of view. So if you are trying to be an enlightened being or buddha, you are defeating your purpose altogether. You are looking for totality from an inadequate vantage point. Therefore, in the Buddhist tradition there is the bodhisattva vow, which is to give up the idea of attaining enlightenment until all sentient beings have been saved. This is giving up the approach that *I* want to attain enlightenment, that you are at this end and enlightenment is at the other end. This approach automatically makes a polarity; you are already separating yourself from Buddha. So in order to become Buddha you either have to give up the idea of Buddha or give up the idea of you. Both ways are applicable. Both mean the same thing at this point. You could start from either end.

Q: What I meant by giving up the idea of enlightenment is that by giving up the idea of becoming this and becoming that and instead by just being, you are Buddha. What I want to know is whether this takes as long as some schools would like you to believe.

R: That is a question of how much we regard the whole practice as formal, as a big deal. The more we make a big deal out of the practice, the slower the journey is. It is purely up to us. People can attain enlightened understanding in one moment, but for some people it takes eons and eons. It depends on how much we regard the whole practice as ritualistic, ceremonial, as opposed to identifying it with our own basic being. In other words, if there is fundamental trust that we are Buddha actually, not that we might be, but that we are Buddha . . . that kind of positive thinking is necessary. It has nothing to do with arrogance or pride in the conventional sense; but it is the actual truth, the true positive thinking.

Q: How can we be egoless and have self-respect at the same time?

R: Usually the ego does not respect itself. That is common knowledge. It tends to hate itself, so there is no such thing as self-respect as far as ego is concerned. Its whole attitude is terror, fear of losing something; you are missing something all the time. So, you see, egolessness is the only self-respectful attitude we could have.

Q: What do you think of the approach of Western psychology and psychoanalysis to this whole type of subject matter as opposed to the practice of meditation?

R: Well, that is a very broad subject, actually. We cannot make generalizations on the whole thing. Each psychologist and psychiatrist has his or her own understanding, his or her own way of relating with mind. As well as his or her own development. A lot of modern psychologists, psychiatrists, and psychoanalysts do meditation themselves. Therefore their work with their patients can be very enlightened as well.

One of the basic things that can be not so good is if the therapeutic approach is based purely on analysis, based purely on analytical mind, just analysis of the case history as such without any sense of human contact with the patient. Then the whole thing becomes like you are being put under a microscope and examined. That very mechanistic approach is almost the same as saying that you have no hope: because your past is fucked up, therefore you have no hope in the present. Somehow that process becomes very uncompassionate if there is no human connection, no trust in the nowness or the human dignity, so to speak, of the person's neurosis of the time. As far as the patient is concerned, it is worth a great deal of respect. And it is, because the person's basic intelligence must be getting through from somewhere, otherwise he or she would not be having psychological breakdowns.

So, basically, if any compassionate work is being done through Western psychological methods, I think it is very good. I think in general it depends on the psychologist.

Q: The suffering and dissatisfaction you were speaking of seems to be related to our everyday-life situation. Wouldn't the solution be simply to get out of our everyday-life situation and take refuge in spirituality?

R: Well, basically there is no difference between mundane, domestic life and spiritual life. Mundane and domestic life is the spiritual thing. All your pain is psychosomatic pain, whether you have a problem with your kid or you have a problem with your pets or with your landlord. Whatever it is, it is a psychosomatic problem that stems from the fact that *you* are there. *You* are there, therefore the problem exists. If you were not there, the problem would not be there. But one cannot look to the simple solution of committing suicide. That does not solve the problem at all, because you still need a killer to kill yourself. Fundamentally speaking, you cannot destroy yourself completely, because you would like to watch yourself die as well as to make sure that the whole job was done perfectly.

So without you, these problems would not arise; or because of you these problems do exist. Therefore you are a very fertile person for dealing with these particular problems. That is the practice of the path.

Q: I find it very hard to conceive of getting rid of your ego. I think it is necessary in your life situation. You relate with people with your ego. Otherwise they walk all over you. I really think it is necessary.

THE TIBETAN BUDDHIST TEACHINGS AND THEIR APPLICATION

R: Well, you see, on the whole we do not regard ego as a villain at all. Without ego, or without ego's problems, as I have already mentioned, the enlightened state would be redundant. Without samsara, nirvana is redundant. And we use ego as a stepping-stone constantly. It is like wearing out a shoe—we use ego, we tread on it, we work with it. Of course we need ego at the beginning as a stepping-stone. That is very important and we do not want to look at ego as something we should throw away or abandon. In fact, we cannot do that, because that which would begin to throw ego away would also be ego. So the starting point is not abandoning ego as bad, but going along with it and letting it wear itself out.

Q: Do you need a guru? Some say you do and some say you don't.

R: The guru is not regarded as a master or a professor or a big brother. The guru is regarded as a friend with whom you can communicate, with whom you can share experience. Relating with the sanity of such a person is necessary at the beginning; otherwise we can get into all kinds of extravagant fantasies—about how we have received messages and therefore what we are doing is right and so on. If we do not relate with a person who has seen through ego's deceptions, an actual human person, then we can manipulate ourselves into all kinds of self-deceptions.

The process of relating with the guru goes through several stages. At the beginning you find it very difficult to surrender. Then you decide that that person is your friend and you begin to communicate with him. Then at some point you go through a phase of feeling self-conscious; you feel that he just might know what you are thinking and he is watching you all the time. You feel that he acts in some sense like a mirror, that if you present yourself as a confused person, he might let you see how you are confused—and you do not want to receive that message! You do not want to be flushed out. All kinds of such things go on, but at some point you give up that pride of hiding your inadequacy. You begin to communicate as between really good friends. Communication takes place ideally and at some stage becomes extremely comfortable. Now you do not have to do anything for yourself; just go to that friend and he tells you exactly what to do. The whole thing becomes automatic. Very efficient service. At that point usually what happens is that, either physically or psychologically, the guru becomes distant and you are forced to work things out for yourself. Then you begin to relate with your life situation as guru. Everything that comes up in your life is part of the guru. The guru is everywhere. At that point the inner guru begins to wake up.

So we might make that distinction between the spiritual friend, the human person, and the inner aspect which wakes up, which is the guru.

The Three-Yana Principle
in Tibetan Buddhism

T HE TIBETAN APPROACH is unique in that it sees Buddhism in
terms of three yanas, or vehicles. Not just the hinayana, or mahayana or vajrayana, but all three are included in the approach to enlightenment.

Hinayana means "narrow path" and is the beginning stage. One begins by using one's present state of being as the working basis. This is
the intent of Buddha's four noble truths. Our lives are involved with
achievement and pleasure-seeking, which automatically means trying to
correct the existing situation. Therefore there is constant discomfort; we
are constantly in a state of unwillingness to accept things as they are.
Acknowledging this is the realization of the first noble truth. The cause
of this discomfort is grasping, aggression, and lack of recognition. This
is the second noble truth. The third truth is the glimpse that the workings of this plot can be sabotaged. This can be done by treading on the
path of meditation, which is the fourth noble truth. Many different meditation techniques were recommended by Buddha in order to expose the
deceptions of ego, constantly attempting to consolidate its territory.

The hinayana discipline is narrow. It permits no entertainment, but
works on the basic patterns of life. This way it provides a solid foundation for spirituality.

Having developed a certain basic sanity, there is a further need to
share this with the world. *Mahayana* means "open path." It involves a
commitment or vow to work with all sentient beings without heed to
ego's dictatorship. Following the example of the bodhisattvas, one practices the six transcendental actions: generosity, discipline, patience, exertion, meditation, and knowledge. The sense of egolessness then expands.

One breaks through one's primeval sense of identity and becomes the embodiment of clarity and skill.

Vajrayana means "goal is path." The practitioner finds that the goal of enlightenment is the path. Mantras and mudras and visualizations arouse the vividness of the awakened state of mind. The clarity and skill inherited from the mahayana discipline become indestructible power.

The practitioner is able to tread on the spiritual path through the guidance of a competent teacher, who is a holder of wisdom through a lineage of masters. Transmission is possible only through personal contact with a living master.

Cynicism and Warmth

WHAT I'M GOING TO say tonight may be new or old. But disregarding the chronological background, we could look straight ahead in terms of spiritual practice.

It seems necessary in the beginning to develop some sense of an undoing process. This undoing process takes one general pattern, but with different shapes. The first style of undoing is simply unmasking what has been taught, what has been presented to you in terms of indoctrination. You set that aside or turn it off.

But other times, although you would like to set that aside, to turn it off, it won't unstick. It hangs on to you like extremely powerful glue, stuck to you by suction. Then you have to use another means of undoing. You have to go so far as to perform an operation or use some kind of force. For the purpose of unmasking, that measure seems to be absolutely necessary.

So there are two kinds of unmasking. The first unmasking process is extremely easy. You begin to realize that everything in your spiritual practice is repetitious and familiar. It doesn't make sense anymore. You've heard it over and over again. You've read it over and over again, and it doesn't make any sense at all. So you grow tired of it.

But it's not quite enough that you grow tired of hearing the same things over and over again. You have to develop a defensive mechanism so you won't be tempted to listen over and over again—the second time or the third time or the fourth time. The mechanism of preventing yourself from doing the same thing over and over again is cynicism, the cynical attitude.

You have to develop a satirical attitude toward spirituality in general, as well as toward your own particular school of thought. Whatever you have learned, whatever you have studied, is futile because the effect has begun to wear off. The only thing left is a corpse, a mask, purely an image hanging out, which has ceased to have life to it. So the cynical attitude is not only willingness to unmask but willingness to defend yourself from remasking.

The point is that you are defending yourself from spiritual materialism so that you cannot be tricked again. You cannot remask in the same familiar pattern as before. You can't be conned again. So there is a clear perception and understanding of spiritual materialism, as well as having an offensive approach toward it.

The intellectual approach to spirituality is seemingly delightful, sensible, and convincing. The rhetoric of the preacher is beautiful. The beautiful smile of the love-and-lighty person is exceedingly sweet. Often there is a big flicker of thought that goes: "How could I reject this beautiful man, who is actually asking me to accept him and join him? How could I reject such a beautiful thing?

"This man is good, basically. He's spreading the message of goodness and has the invitation of a smile and everything, and he says, 'Join us, we are one.'" But your sense of cynicism triggers off a new sense of humor. At the beginning you see the sense of oneness that he's speaking of, but then you also begin to see that there is a reason why he said, "We are one."

Because he thinks there is a possibility or two, he is denying the twoness of it, and therefore he says, "We are one." All kinds of cynical attitudes develop. And once the sharpness of your cynicism develops, it is extremely uncompassionate and powerful. You cannot miss noticing that seemingly naive goodness is full of holes.

The second part of the unmasking process is more difficult. It's not easy to unmask: you have to use force to unstick, to unglue yourself. The reason why it is so ingrained is that you took it so faithfully, so completely; and something slipped into your system before you knew where you were.

That kind of involvement comes from trusting enormously that such-and-such a spiritually materialistic trip will be able to save you. And you become part of some organization, some ingrown situation, because: "I feel there is truth. The truth came to me. And my total being is part of that truth, I'm completely soaked in that truth, that particular structure of whatever."

You don't realize that you have become a slave of that belief. And that makes it much harder, because there is less room for a sense of humor, since you are so honest and earnest. That whole system, that spiritual organization or philosophy, seeps into your system inside out, outside in. Because that system seems so helpful, unmasking is seen as almost a suicidal process of rejecting your blood system, your bones, your heart, you brain, and everything.

"How could I regard this as spiritual materialism, as just a trip, when the whole thing has become such an integral part of my existence?" Well, you may have made a tremendous relationship with something. Maybe it's true that you have found the path. But at the same time, what is this approach of, "It will be good for me"? What is this falling in love with something?

If you look at the heart of that from a subtle point of view, the basic fact is that you have fallen into a gigantic trap of needing a rescuer, needing a savior. Also, you adopted the message of this particular doctrine to suit your own needs rather than hearing the doctrine as speaking the truth. You are a spokesman for the doctrine for your own sake; therefore you have manufactured the truth of the doctrine.

So it's not so much that the doctrine has converted you, but that you have converted the doctrine into your own ego. Therefore it becomes an integral part of your being. Of course, at the same time there is a sense of separateness, that you are seeking various attainments: happiness, enlightenment, wisdom and so forth.

If you're told: "I think you're on some kind of trip. Why don't you relax the seriousness of it and develop some sense of humor, some cynicism?"—that becomes almost an insult. The obvious answer is, of course, "You don't know what I'm into, and therefore how could you say such a thing? You're tripping, not me. You are just a pure outsider who doesn't know the intensity of this integral feeling." But no matter how much of a layman the other person may be, there is still a grain of truth in his criticism.

At this point, a sense of humor has become a tremendous threat. Taking something lightly seems almost sacrilegious. But nevertheless, that sense of humor is the starting point of the ultimate kind of savior. You could develop an extraordinarily cynical attitude when you begin to realize your own foolishness, then you can begin to turn around and see the whole plot: how you are sucked into this and used, and how all the juice of your energy is taken out. And you see that your conviction and your approach to a savior and liberation are being distorted.

All of this is because the teaching has taken advantage of you, rather than your relating to the teaching as a freeway or highway. And when you begin to realize that, you turn around completely and take the revengeful, cynical approach, extremely super-revengeful. You bounce everything back, and nothing is accepted. Everything is a world of cynicism. When someone says, "This is good for you," even that is questionable.

If you are extremely thirsty, and before you even ask for anything, someone offers you some water, saying: "Would you like some water? I see your thirst."—you are extremely cynical. "Oh, oh, there it goes again." You become extremely unyielding to any kind of help, any kind of forward gesture. You are like a highly paranoid squirrel that is paranoid of the sound of its own chewing of nuts—as if somebody else were doing it.

You see, the psychological development is that at the beginning you are domesticated into this very snug, beautiful, and smelly stable or nest, which is very homey. You're thriving there and appreciating it, when someone tells you how dirty the place is—and you begin to have second thoughts about it.

And when you begin to see that this message makes sense, you begin to react to everything the other way around completely. So then any suggestion, even to sit on a chair or get into any kind of comfortable situation, is also regarded as smelly and dirty. Now, instead of things being snug and cozy, they are very sharp and brittle. Things don't bend, they only chip.

Such a cynical approach is exceedingly powerful and, we could say, somewhat praiseworthy, but nevertheless you are being too harsh on yourself. You become so smart that you even exceed the smartness itself. At that point you begin to bite your own tail. In your cynicism, you are somewhat reliving the past, rather than approaching toward the future.

So that cynicism is a kind of weakness: since you are so defensive and so extremely paranoid toward the rest of the world, you are afraid to create your own world. You may have been criticized by somebody else; in turn you are being critical toward others— you are all the time tiptoeing. It is such a heavy-handed approach.

At that point it is time to develop some element of warmth. That world of cynicism is not the only world, and, as we already know, creating a cozy nest is also not the only world. Other possibilities exist. There could be a world of complete warmth and complete communications, which accommodates the cynical as well as the primitive mind. The world is not necessarily a big joke, but it is also not a big object to attack. So there is another area of newfound land, an entire continent that we haven't looked at, we haven't discovered. We might have found it, but we haven't looked at it. This is the world of mystical experiences. [*Laughter.*]

Mystical experience in this case has nothing to do with astral traveling or conjuring up ritual objects in your hand or turning the ceiling into the floor. Mystical experience in this case is discovering a hidden warmth—the larger version of home, the larger version of new realm. An analogy for that is the pure land that traditional Buddhism talks about: the land of Amitabha, which is the land of the padma family. It is filled with padma-ness, richness. Everything is inviting, drawing in, seductive.

But at the same time, that which makes this seduction different from samsaric seduction is the quality of spaciousness in it. The ordinary sense of seduction automatically suggests that you are trapped in a two-way journey: either you have to be sucked in or you have to reject it. But in this case, in the land of Padmapani or Amitabha, while there are possibilities of seduction everywhere, at the same time there are punctuations of space all over. So at least you can read the whole pattern intelligently.

You might say this is a kind of a new phase. We seem to have gone from extreme cynicism to believing something, developing some kind of devotion, the bhakti approach. At some point the extremely cynical vajra-style approach becomes a process of eating your own body, biting you own tail again and again. You don't get anywhere.

Whenever you feel comfortable, you have one more bite of your tail to make sure you are awake and critical. But in this case you are giving up that continual biting, that continual punishing of yourself. You let the snowflake fall on your head and melt. You do not just brush it off, but you let something relate to you. That does not mean that you have to con it or to go forward and try to grasp it at all. You are simply accepting the existing situation. The idea of bhakti or the devotional approach is the same.

It is not a question of developing faith in someone's mystical power or believing in some person as a savior, a magician. Instead, the idea is that you manufacture the whole world. And since you manufacture the whole world, you don't have to regard it as something bad, just because *you* made it. Why don't you manufacture a world that is okay? Get into your own dream, there is nothing bad about it. You are a manufacturer, you don't have to get imports from foreigners. Live your own production, enjoy your own production.

There is a message coming out of all this. In other words, you can be kind to yourself. In that case, surrendering to a teacher or lineage is not shifting gears into a new approach. The lineage is an example, from this point of view. The lineage is an example of successive people surrendering to themselves and beginning to find the expression of the guru in themselves.

And finally the expression of the guru in themselves turns into universality, naturally and automatically. It is not that you have a guru and then, because he can't give time to you or because he is too busy or distant physically and you can't communicate to him, deciding from sheer frustration to regard the universe as your guru.

There's a different way of looking at things, if you look very closely. The whole approach here is that you have extremely adequate resources within yourself, whether you regard yourself as insane or sane. You have tremendous resources in any case. Whether you take advantage of your insanity or sanity is up to you. Relating with the insanity is extremely powerful, mystical; and at the same time, relating with the sanity is mystical as well.

So the approach here is that in going from extreme cynicism to warmth, finally you are not biting your own tail in order to keep awake. Instead you feel comfortable with your body and falling asleep. Not analyzing what kind of body you have, you are comfortably sleeping: huge tusks, big tail, fat belly, or whatever.

Dome Darshan

I SUPPOSE THE QUESTION which concerns us most is the spiritual search. We're trying to find some means to learn the whatever. That's very well. It's good that we are concerned with something other than purely gaining a physical and economic pleasure. It seems that's a starting point; we have begun to be concerned with the meaning of life, which is something more than the ordinary situation. But still there are all kinds of dangers, so that it is worthwhile to question again and again what our style of spiritual search is. By what method and what means are we trying to get to the realization? It is futile to talk about the nature of realization, at this point anyway. Instead we might discuss our relationship toward the search. The general style of searching for some sense of sanity turns out to be a businesslike approach. We are still collecting more possessions, more information, still involved in a search for happiness, ultimate pleasure of some kind. It's exactly the same as if you are a businessman searching for ultimate pleasure. The spiritual search takes on similar techniques and the same pattern of achievement as a businessman's approach to being successful. So we are in trouble. We know sacrifices can be made to achieve a high spiritual state, but this sacrifice has its root in working toward ultimate pleasure, in a confused way. So we are bound by ego's collecting and ego's approach toward ultimate happiness, goodness.

We never thought of the possibility of approaching it from an entirely new angle. Let us say that there is another way of approaching enlightenment, the spiritual search, some other way than ego's gain, the pattern that we're used to. There's a self-denying tendency that everybody knows of. At least they've read or heard that to gain a higher state of consciousness, to pursue the spiritual quest, you have to lose your selfishness, your egohood. However, that tends to become a strategy, a plot. Ego is pretending to itself it doesn't exist; and then ego says, "Okay, now you got rid of me, now let's both look toward our mutual happiness." So if the approach to deeper spirituality is basically not being concerned with any experiences, then it has to be a funeral, a burial service in which *you* can't take part.

It seems that spiritual searching is a schizophrenic kind of situation. For one thing, you want to get rid of the bad things you have. On the other hand, you love yourself so much that you want to see yourself as being a glorious person. You have never made up your mind in that area. You have a self-existing love-and-hate relationship toward yourself, constantly not knowing which area should be developed and which area should be cut down. You might have vague conceptualized ideas. But you're lacking certain things, you're egotistical; still, a certain aspect of your egomania is lovable. You would like to keep it.

We try all kinds of angles and approaches, all the ways: Buddhism, Christianity, Judaism, psychology. We try to find a way to get around it, so we don't actually have to sacrifice at all. Which particular trip is the safest, the most secure to get into, so that we could identify with it and not have to sacrifice anything, give anything away? Hopefully we won't have to die at all; we will exist eternally. We hope to achieve immortality. So there's a conclusion there again, an angle. Spiritual practice is surrendering, opening, sacrificing, giving something. By doing so we can become immortal. At last we will gain everlasting life; we can go on existing eternally.

Particularly the talk about reincarnation in Eastern religions is exciting to a lot of people. They regard it as the ultimate good news. We could go on after all! We could be ourselves all the time, eternally. Such an approach seems to be utterly simple-minded. We haven't solved the problem of giving, dissolving into nothingness. A lot of people tend to have the conviction that they are the reincarnation of somebody or other, which gives tremendous hope, identifying ourselves with those heroes in the past who have achieved some immortality and become eternal. If we are incarnations of them, then we are going to do the same thing. Such an approach is known as *spiritual materialism*. It's another version of Madison Avenue. On a higher level, of course. I feel that this is a worthwhile thing to know. As far as my work of teaching is concerned, the least I can do is not to encourage spiritual materialism. So these warnings are valid, and necessary.

Giving, opening, sacrificing ego is necessary. It is like performing an operation. It might be painful because finally we realize that we cannot take part in our own burial. Very painful. It's an operation, an organic operation. We lose our grip on the wishful-thinking world of pleasure and goodness. We have to give up trying to associate ourselves with goodness. The experience of our day-to-day living situation consists of dissatisfaction, questioning, pain, depression, aggression, passion. All these are real, and we have to relate with them. Having a relationship with this is maybe extremely difficult. It's an organic operation without any anesthetics. If we really want to get into it, we should be completely prepared to take a chance and get nothing but tremendous disappointment, tremendous hopelessness.

Hope is the source of pain, and hope operates on the level of something other than what there is. We hope, dwelling in the future, that things might turn out right. We do not experience the present, do not face the pain or neurosis as it is. So the only way that is feasible is developing an attitude of hopelessness, something other than future orientation. The present is worth looking at. Whether we are irritated or blissful, the present situation is a point of reference. Often we find the present state of being is not particularly appealing or valuable. Even a state of bliss that happens in the present needs to be maintained, and there's a certain amount of hassle involved with that. So we constantly feel that we have to run, keep going to organizations, to maintain our pleasure, potential pleasure.

The only way to deal with spiritual materialism as such is to develop an ultimately cynical or critical attitude toward the teachings and the teachers and the practices that we're involved with. We shouldn't let ourselves be sucked in, but question twice, thrice, from the point of view, "Is this spiritual materialism to me, or isn't it?" Once we develop that kind of paranoia, which is intelligence, or scientific mind, then we are in a situation of resourcefulness, tremendous wealth. We then have the authority to judge the teachers and the teachings rather than being poverty-stricken, absolutely wretched and helpless. We are so stupid, our only hope is that somebody else might be able to save us. That approach of poverty is blind faith or a materialistic approach. So question all the time, develop a critical attitude.

A critical attitude doesn't necessarily mean that you have to be hateful of yourself. The critical attitude can be accompanied by compassion and warmth. All your polarities are equally valid, whether weakness or strength. Nothing is regarded as irrelevant. Whatever happens in your life, both your neurosis and your enlightened state of being are functioning simultaneously all the time. There's no allegiance toward goodness particularly, or enlightenment. The sense of an enlightened state was developed out of the intensity of the confusion, simultaneously with it, so there's no point in picking and choosing. There's no point in splitting your basic being into several parts and trying to suppress certain parts and cultivating others. That's the attitude of poverty.

Practice in meditation plays an important part in this. The meditation practice is not a way of entering into a manufactured state of tranquillity or equanimity, but a samyak samadhi, the perfect meditation, perfect absorption, as it is called in the Buddhist tradition. It is referred to as perfect because perfection in this case has no allegiance toward samsara or nirvana. That's why it's perfect. Samyak samadhi. So if we don't have allegiance toward samsara or nirvana, then we free ourselves from any of the dogma, any bondage. Some sense of ultimate relaxation begins to occur. All the hidden neurosis which we didn't really want to look at, and didn't really want to experience, begins to come up on the surface. Finally we are exposed. We hoped that we wouldn't have to go through the embarrassment of exposing ourselves; we hoped to have bypassed that particular area and become enlightened. You might just talk about how bad you *used* to be and so on. But *then* it is okay to talk about it because you are already a better person. The practice of meditation is the complete opposite of this. It's not exactly getting a certain state of being at all, artificial being or artificial good vibration. Meditation practice is a way of making friends with ourselves. Whether we are worthy or unworthy, that's not the point. It's developing a friendly attitude to ourselves, accepting the hidden neurosis coming through.

When somebody commits himself to a certain practice and decides to become a spokesman of that particular teaching, then he becomes a total stranger to himself as well as to his old friends. He's very harsh on himself and doesn't relate the same way as he used to. If you are an old friend of his, there's something aggressive about his approach in that he doesn't want to talk about the past. There is a certain black-and-white quality in being completely converted into a new trip, or a trip that you have invented yourself. There's something very sad about that. Such a person is so lonely. He becomes such a stranger to his own friends, parents, relatives, dharma brothers and sisters of the past, having gotten into a new kind of trip. He doesn't even look after himself. Totally miserable.

Now, we can paint a more complete picture of that person by saying that he is into total absorption. He doesn't care about his past or his own loneliness. He has found a new something. But if he has found a new something, why has he become so hostile, become such a stranger? This applies not only to a leader alone, but to individuals, ourselves, as well. When we want to get into something without warmth and compassion, without fundamental softness and fundamental generosity, then the teachings become an act of aggression. "Because the book says so, therefore you should be this way or that way. Because I say so, therefore you should be this way or that way." There's no sense of communication in that. You are a potential egomaniac, if not one already.

So fundamentally one should be cynical and critical as well as making friends with oneself. Being cynical or critical doesn't mean that you have to punish yourself, but you just attack the areas of indulgence of ego. But at the same time you continue the friendship with yourself. That seems to be the general pattern. Meditation plays an important part in this by letting things come to the surface, so you have inexhaustible wealth to work with. So basic sanity and basic richness and basic openness become prominent parts of the path.

Question: The samadhi that you mentioned, you said was just nonattachment to nirvana or samsara? Could you elaborate on that?

Rinpoche: Samadhi is a state of total compassion in which the goal doesn't become the prominent part, but the path becomes the goal in itself. That is, the daily living situation becomes the goal as we go along. It becomes a self-improvised kind of situation.

Q: Would you say that guilt has no survival value?

R: Guilt is a very vague term. It may come from indoctrination into certain fixed philosophical, metaphysical patterns, consisting of shoulds and shouldn'ts. This conceptualized, prefabricated guilt becomes very stuffy, without any fresh air. Or, we might feel guilt in the sense of some general paranoia, having an extremely sensitive antenna, which is okay because that protects us from being frivolous or egomaniacs.

Q: Would you say, then, that the process is one of forgiving yourself and just being yourself?

R: Not even forgiving, you see. Forgiving implies you were wrong, but that now it's okay. Instead, the mistakes or the neuroses becomes adornments, bridges to work with yourself rather than something to forgive yourself for. So then ultimately each mistake, each unskillful action, becomes another brick in your wall, which you can build higher and higher.

Q: I find that the line between spirituality and spiritual materialism is elusive. Would you say a few words about that?

R: Spiritual materialism is using every practice to further your own power and pleasure. True spirituality is relating with the day-to-day living situation rather then hoping for or seeing your dreams coming true. That's a very crude description.

Q: Would you deny hope?

R: Deny? For what purpose?

Q: As part of delusion?

R: Hope is often regarded as a villain, but hope could be regarded as simply unrealistic. You see, any kind of approach to this area has to be scientific rather than just according to some prescription.

Q: What is worth anything?

R: Are you serious? Well, that's saying the same thing. Nothing's worth anything, period. Then you're trying to make everything worth everything. But you still have something, some solid thing to hang on to, the worthlessness, which is the worth.

Q: What is the nature of the cynicism and the self-critical attitude?

R: Well, cynicism is a self-critical attitude in some sense, but it is not self-punishment. A self-critical attitude could be taken as an intelligent measure. Cynicism is knowing that nothing can con you, that everything functions with a relative point of view, relative reference. That seems to be the cynical approach, that the truth hasn't been set forth without a point of reference, rather than taking the negative approach and trying to find a falsehood as such.

Q: Doesn't cynicism destroy faith?

R: Well, that seems to be the source of the faith. If you have ultimate cynicism in an intelligent way, then your faith is founded on very solid ground, because your faith can't be shaken.

Q: I sometimes feel that I have spiritual blocks. . . . What do you suggest I do? There are periods when I feel I'm not making any spiritual progress. My understanding of cynicism is that you could just say, "Well, block from what?"

R: Well, there seems to be a problem of thinking you are supposed to be advancing all the time. You don't have to be constantly on the road, necessarily. In other words, if you have a flat tire, that is also part of the journey. You are getting close to your goal. So I suppose it's a certain ambition that makes you feel that you are not doing anything. There seems to be a hypnotic quality of the ambition and speed, so that you feel you are standing still just because you want to go so fast.

Q: How do you relate the teaching of not having ambition and not having hope and not striving for a goal? How does that relate to teachings which refer to this human lifetime as a unique and special occasion which ought not to be wasted?

R: I don't see any contradiction. In discovering certain means of working with the teachings, the idea of giving up hope becomes a more and more valuable message. You realize this teaching can only be heard in a certain situation. That doesn't mean to say that you have to speed along. In other words, if you have some practice to do like prostrations, it will be better to do it slowly and properly, considering the hopelessness of it, rather than at sixty miles an hour, missing the best point of reference. You have no chance to appreciate the teachings, in that case, and you haven't actually related with the hopelessness either.

Q: If you're doing something that will bring out the neurosis, being in a situation where you have to confront this neurosis, do you feel that's valuable?

R: It's not a question of valuable or not. Relating with the neurosis becomes inescapable. So you have only one choice: choicelessness. So the path is the goal. You don't have much chance to improve otherwise. As you begin to realize this, and that you have to take a leap of some kind in any case, then you do it. You have to be pushed into that kind of understanding, that you have no choice. You are constantly traveling in a vehicle without a reverse, without a brake.

Q: Is saying you have no choice the same as saying you have no will?
R: Not quite. Acknowledging the choicelessness is the will.

Q: When we reach that point, we have no choice but to acknowledge it?
R: Well, if you like.

Q: Could you define egomania?
R: A general definition of egomania, from this point of view, is that you are constantly looking for ultimate security and pleasure. So much so that in the end you become absolutely savage, to the point of self-destructiveness, or of encouraging others to destroy themselves.

Q: To what end would they be destroying themselves?
R: To seek pleasure, to be completely submerged into pleasure, like sinking into honey.

Q: I wonder if your hopelessness is self-destructive?
R: Well, if you really give up hope, completely give up hope, there's no indulgence. Do you see what I mean? Hope is believing in possible pleasure, possible alternatives.

Q: But doesn't pleasure come from hope? Don't we actually get happiness because we hope?
R: Not necessarily, no.

Q: Not necessarily; some have success and others fail, but it's only the hope . . .
R: Well, we don't get a real pleasure out of the hope, but we get the fever out of it. It is only a fever, rather than real happiness, which is identifying with the real treasure, which in tantric tradition is called the mahasukha. We don't get that. We just get a shadow of possible good feeling. We are just getting to the outskirts of pleasure, then we regard that as grace, which is hope.

Q: It is a hope, but I wonder whether the hope is necessary. All the other creatures love life and strive for happiness. I don't see why man should have no hope.

R: Well, man predominantly misuses his power, and even enjoys his hopefulness in the wrong way. Man is the only animal that dwells in the future.

Q: I don't dwell in the future all the time. It's only dwelling in the future somewhat. One has to plan. There is a future. It approaches one all the time.

R: Well, that's the whole point. You don't have to be purely living in the present without a plan, but the plan in the present depends only on the future's aspect within the present situation. You can't plan a future if you don't know what the present situation is. You have to start from now to know how to plan.

Q: Can you find pleasure by living completely within the moment?

R: Well, there's no question of pleasure.

Q: I find myself losing my ego and feeling less myself, and at the same time making decisions and being analytical and knowing myself, like you were saying, being cynical. That's just like having ego. But then, also, I find myself losing my ego and becoming one with everyone and what's outside instead of self. So I'm separating as well as coming together.

R: It seems that everything comes from the problem of analyzing more than necessary. The thing is you can't get cut and dried answers from every move that you make.

Q: Does meditation practice help an individual lose desire?

R: Lose desire? I suppose meditation practice is the only practice by which we can develop. That should also be accompanied by experiencing the daily-living situation as part of the manifestation of the teaching. This is the only process, confronting the chaos and working along with it, improvising each time.

Q: Would you explain the difference between your concept of faith and hope?

R: Faith and hope, did you say? Well, faith is a more realistic attitude than hope is. Hope is a sense of lacking something in the present situation.

We are hopeful about getting better as we go along. Faith is that it's okay in the present situation, and we have some sense of trust in that.

Q: Could you tell me how a person could be more aware of his death?

R: Well, there's a sense of impermanence which happens constantly all the time. I suppose that's the starting point, to realize that you can't hang on to one continuous continuation, that things *do* change constantly, and that you have no permanent security. There's only one eternity, that's the eternity of discontinuity.

Q: In my own spiritual search I find myself wanting to be more aware of my death. I find that I begin to live more if that happens.

R: The idea of physical death, that one day you're going to die, seems to be believing in an eternity of some kind. You're going to die one day, but you're still okay now. It's so dependent.

Q: Is there any way to develop that constant awareness that you are going to die?

R: That doesn't seem to be the point. The point of death is that constant death is happening all the time, that you can't stick to one thing and stay with it all the time.

Q: Do you have any reflections or interpretations of the spiritual currents in North America?

R: I think I have already spoken about that in the talk. Generally what seems to be happening in America is that we involve ourselves in trying to find more happiness. Certainly America's love affair with materialism provides a tremendous opportunity which is unique to this country. Other countries, such as India, for instance, haven't experienced prosperous materialism in its absolute claustrophobia. We begin to realize that after all that isn't the ultimate pleasure. There's a further search, and we put further energy into it. American speed and its neurosis are being put into rediscovering spirituality. That's a very interesting combination, but still it's happening. I would say that America could become the world's leading spiritual center fairly soon, as soon as we get out of spiritual materialism and begin to realize what its consequences are. All the spiritual shopping, spiritual supermarketing, and the ability to buy food from exclusive shops may cost people more money and energy, but it's still worth it.

Q: Would you state the relationship between entertainment and spiritual life? Both in terms of the entertainer who makes the entertainment and those who are entertained, as they relate to spiritual life or spiritual practice.

R: As long as you are entertained, you are fascinated by what's happening rather than relating to what you have experienced, the facts of the scientific approach to life. So you don't have any prajna, or wisdom, knowledge, intelligence. The whole thing becomes an act of very naively going to the theater, forgetting what you've seen outside, and coming back out after having passed several hours. I think that's the spiritual materialism coming through. You could regard the practice as an escape from your boredom; you have nothing else to get into so you might as well get into these good things. Be entertained by them. You keep coming, you become a very successful regular member, but still you have no personal relationship with the teachings. Then if the entertainment stops and the surgery starts without any entertainment, you run away. That seems to be the problem.

Q: Could you say what the nature of boredom is?

R: Boredom could happen in different ways. It may be boredom in the sense that fundamentally, repetitious things are happening constantly. Or, possibly all kinds of things are happening, which help to keep you from boredom. You are looking for a slight challenge, but it is not a complete challenge which you might have to put more energy into. It's just a little leap and doesn't involve any great expenditure of energy. Then there's another type of boredom, which is part of the discipline, such as the meditation practice, which I refer to as cool boredom, refreshing boredom. Boredom is necessary, and you have to work with it. It's constantly very sane and solid, and boring at the same time. But it's refreshing boredom. The discipline then becomes part of one's daily expression of life. Such boredom seems to be absolutely necessary. Cool boredom.

Tower House Discussions I and II

I

Rinpoche: You seem to want constant security—to name things, to make sure, to make your world very solid. You should just acknowledge without giving names. If techniques don't have a name, if they're just functional, that's important. You shouldn't respect them unnecessarily and make them solid, something more than techniques. If you name them they become part of your thoughts. You tend to get tensions all over your body or tightness, drowsiness, all kinds of things begin to come out. Any technique you use should become purely functional.

Student 1: I notice that my technique has a tendency to change. If I'm watching the sensations of my body in vipashyana, sometimes I feel energy moving up and down my spine. Sometimes I resist it and return to what I was told about just feeling the sensations of the body. Sometimes the body has a way of going away, and I'm just watching this sensation of rising and falling, and it's fine, easier to concentrate on. So I let it evolve and watch that. I wonder how much of my own intuition and feeling I can trust and how much I should rely on what I've been told.

R: In the vipashyana practice, the idea of bare attention is not exactly watching but continually getting into it. The difference is that if you watch, then you have direction, you are looking into yourself. It becomes your possession. Whereas if you are just with it, you become the sensation itself. Then you have no direction; the body is neither here nor there. It becomes very impersonal. That's the idea of relating with the sensations and feelings as if they belong to nobody. But they're happening, it feels—but without direction, so you don't generate extra energy. It belongs to nobody; it's just purely the organism maintaining itself. The idea of complete mindfulness, perfect mindfulness, samyak, is being

548

identified with that completely, without even a doer. That seems to be very hard to describe, and that particular thing hasn't been mentioned enough in context with meditation. If energy doesn't belong to anybody, then you can handle it. If energy is chained or labeled, then it plays tricks on you. It becomes the ego's thing then, naturally. It seems to be very subtle.

Student 2: Wouldn't it be dangerous for a beginner, in the sense that just being with whatever comes up is very close to actually being identified with it, in a wrong way, in an egoful way? And the transition might have to be done when you do watch and establish a viewpoint, watching, in order to free yourself, free the ego from yourself.

Rinpoche: Identify means almost a disowning at the same time, rather than getting in it. You don't have to go through a sequence: "Be aware of me and I am therefore aware of my sensations," which is the ego's style usually. The vipashyana practice teaches: Don't go through the sequence, just attend to the feeling. It's very immediate, so for a little while the ego is forgotten somewhat. Because you are so much involved with what's happening with your body, the ego doesn't apply anymore. The only problem with that is if you try to recapture your experience, it becomes the ego's thing. Whatever happens in the meditation practice should not be regarded as either a failure or a success but just happening from moment to moment. Any kind of reference point becomes a problem. If there's nothing laid onto it, then you find that there's no such thing as me, just things happening. But if you begin to analyze it, even if you try to analyze it as the nonexistence of ego, then that exactly becomes the ego's act.

Student 3: Another kind of ploy that the ego has is just barely maintaining itself.

Rinpoche: The point is you don't have to get rid of it. Just understand the subtleties of it, just purely that. In fact you need ego at some point, and you have to find out its fallacies, very simply. Ego seems to be the reference point of enlightenment. Without ego there is no enlightenment.

Student 4: Is that true the other way around? Without enlightenment there is no ego?

R: I don't think so. Well, at some point it's true. If enlightenment becomes a dogma or goal, then when there's no goal there's no dogma, and so no enlightenment—which is being without ego. It depends on your attitude of what is meant by enlightenment.

S3: Sometimes Buddhism seems to be cold, it doesn't work from the heart, from the bhakti. I was talking to Ram Dass, and he felt that many of your students have that attitude.

R: Yes indeed.

S3: I was wondering about that. Is that intrinsic to Buddhism, or maybe there's a reservation about the emotional side in some way?

R: You mean eventually Buddhism might come around to it?

S3: Eventually? It seems that maybe it comes later, or that there's some suspicion in the beginning—something too emotional, feeling too much.

R: The emotional approach is a very familiar one. Since we are all brought up by parents, devotion comes easily, so we don't have to surrender, give away anything. The Buddhist approach at the beginning is from an entirely new angle. It is almost a foreign approach from the point of view of ego. There's no warmth; it's been cut down. Then, having prepared enough ground, the devotional bhakti approach eventually becomes a spacious one without possessiveness. We begin to develop the universality of bhakti, rather than personal longing. This is the real meaning of bhakti. The space which was left by cutting down becomes warmth in itself. As you approach tantra, emotion and bhakti become more prominent, but you can't start right away.

S3: One of the difficulties here at Lama [Foundation], I think, is so many different approaches. Some people prefer much more emotional expression, like dancing, and getting very excited or feeling very good. Other people have different ideas.

R: The bhakti approach is obviously almost tantric, very advanced. The Hindu approach is almost tantric, and Sufism, sort of tantric. It's kind of returning again to the ape instinct, and using that as a transcendental one, which is very advanced. Buddhism warns that it becomes too easy, too much a sedative, so that you are not able to experience any real truth. The truth is purely associated with pleasure, like the mother is associated with milk.

S4: Isn't there in Buddhism, in the primary recognition of suffering in the world, almost a built-in bias which deflects you from the bhakti? The Sufi bhakti may have the same recognition, but the recognition would be that there is joy and celebration of that. I had a very difficult time dealing with those primary realizations of Buddhism, because I felt that they did bias the path that you would then travel. The recognition of suffering, and the recognition of the cause of suffering, and cessation of suffering. All of that seemed a focus which was conscious, deliberate, and intentional, and would take you somewhere. If it didn't completely subdue it, it deflected the ecstatic devotional being which doesn't seem to differentiate between suffering and joy. Is that clear? Do I misunderstand that primary recognition of the nature of the world?

Rinpoche: When Buddhism talks about suffering, it's a larger suffering, it's talking about the area from which both pain and pleasure come. You have to maintain something. You have to maintain pleasure or try to get away from pain. So it refers to the speed rather than the pain.

S4: To the speed?

R: Yes, the speed or unnecessary longing, which brings, fundamentally, discomfort. You have to maintain the world, try to get away from the pain and maintain pleasure. So it's not so much of allegiance toward anything, but acknowledging that there is a fundamental confusion.

Student 5: It seems if you accept the idea of pain as existence, then it seems more possible to accept everything that comes up, depression or anxiety or fear.

S3: The other way is to accept it as a gift from God or something like that. I think it's a way to celebrate.

S5: Even doubt?

S3: I don't know.

S5: I'm not really trying to delineate. What I'm trying to interject is another possibility of accepting suffering, and that is that you're never in the wrong place if you accept suffering as a truth.

S3: I've read somewhere that *dukha* was wrongly translated as pain, and it actually means a split or a fracture or a separation.

R: *Dukha* in ordinary usage means pain. In the Buddhist context it's the fundamental confusion.

S3: Confusion?

R: Yes, it's the duality. The split.

S3: Refusal in some way.

R: Yes, constantly trying to maintain individual existence. Holding on to that which is very hectic, and fundamentally it becomes cosmic worry. You have to keep up with it all the time. It's a kind of awareness which keeps you from opening, because you have something to lose or become vulnerable.

S4: It sounds very very different if you're fundamentally a Christian. You have accepted Christ as having healed the division. The Christian doesn't see the world as confused or divided, that's his fundamental acceptance of Christ, Christ's spirit. It allows him to see the world as healed. It seems very different; because if you see that way, then all of your experiencing of it is very different than if what you see is the fundamental confusion. It's just like if I take my glasses off or put my glasses on. If I put them on, I deal with the world of very distinct entities, clearly defined edges that I walk through and make my way around. If I take my glasses off, I see colors and light continually merging, and I walk through that and I don't have any sense of distinctions, except the memory of what it was like with my glasses on. To me that seems like what we're talking about. You can wear glasses and have sharp, discriminating vision or take them off and because of some accident of physiology or whatever be able to see the fundamental flowing unity.

S3: But what happens if a car comes down the highway?

S4: It depends. I drive with my glasses on, but that's because I accept the responsibility for maintaining that world. I could take my glasses off; I've done it with acid where I no longer accepted the responsibility of the car or killing someone. It just didn't matter and it was fine. Maybe it was just an act of faith. Take your glasses off and do it. I'm not so sure it's any different.

R: Well, I think that there is still some acknowledgment in the Christian way that the fundamental split could possibly happen. You have the choice to have devotion. If you couldn't do it and you're still separated, it comes down to Christ. Then there's you and Christ, which is the same as the original split in Buddhism. Also the sense of clarity and confusion seems to be interdependent. If you develop clarity, that means there is some reference point. You got glasses when you couldn't see. That's why glasses came about.

S4: What couldn't I see? I got glasses because there were certain things I wanted to see or expected to see, a way of seeing that I'd been conditioned to accept.

R: That's the whole point, that there is a kind of secondary truth. Even the discriminating perceptions may be false, fundamentally. Until you see the background where the split was nonexistent. There was a split because there wasn't a split, until you go back and back. Then anything you try to do after the split will become artificial. The tantric term for nonduality is *advaya,* not-two. It's the same as the idea of the third noble truth, the goal, the enlightened state, which is not-two.

When Buddhism talks about the fundamental world of split, that's called the relative world, the world from our point of view. But then there is also the noblest point of view. So fundamentally it's not a split, but a seeming split which is misunderstood; and we are constantly maintaining that misunderstanding as if it were a fact.

S4: And Buddhism leaves open the conclusion. If it's not two, then we know zero; and that's just simply left open?

R: Left open, that's the noblest point of view. If you begin to make it into somebody's point of view, then it becomes two again, and you're not even two yourself.

S3: You mentioned something about the figure/ground. We usually see the figure and not the ground? Before you said something about not seeing the ground?

R: Yes, on the level of the split. There seem to be several types of grounds, like the ground of the planet Earth and the ground of outer space, which are relative things. There is a seemingly relative ground which generally functions, but there is still a basic split. We have a point of reference which is also based on another point of reference as ground. The fundamental ground seems to be where reference doesn't apply anymore, where all the other points of reference come from, that functions simultaneously with secondary ground. It becomes a way to maintain secondary ground. The secondary ground has to have an atmosphere to function within, to survive, which comes from nonground, the basic ground. At that point the realization of confusion doesn't apply anymore.

S3: Is that shunyata?

R: Even shunyata is a slightly directed idea; it's emptiness of something. *Dharmakaya* is also a conditioned word because we have to have a form of dharma. In tantric terms it's vajradhatu, indestructible space, or dharmadhatu; all the names and laws can function within it and not be conditioned by it. It seems that the ground cannot be experienced.

S3: Can it only experience itself?

R: In order to experience that ground, you have to undo old experience. When the old experiences cease to function, are nonexistent, that's the kind of thing it is, because the ground has no allegiance to anything.

S3: There was a Hasidic rabbi here who spoke about the seventh level of God, that God doesn't even know Himself.

R: Because there's no point of reference.

S3: So He manifests to know Himself.

R: Then God and the Devil and others could exist.

S1: Is there a function in meditation of conceptualizing, theorizing, bringing together logical concepts, and seeing how things would be in a place you're not yet perceiving? I might talk about the seventh level and relate it to the sixth, whereas I'm not perceiving it; it's something I'm theorizing. Is there a place in meditation for theory, is there a value in it?

R: There is koan practice in Rinzai Zen, and things like that, where intellect is used in subtly trying to understand something; then finally the intellect short-circuits itself. We could almost say that the function of intellect, in understanding the dharma, is to liberate itself. Finally you begin to realize that speculation does not apply, so you give up hope.

S1: You mean, by practicing speculation you become familiar with it. You go into its nature. You understand its nature and then you can go beyond it?

R: The intellect plays an important part. If you don't use it then, you are missing out on a big area. So use every faculty that there is. Emotion can be used as well; you begin to realize that the goal of emotion becomes itself, which short-circuits emotions.

S1: It seems that sometimes the intellect is used to gather, to collect the information. After a point it starts to become useless because that's all you're doing, just gaining more and more facts. You become an expert in this and that. It seems there's a place where the intellect wants to be used in another way. It wants to be used to perceive right now in a very instantaneous way that hasn't much to do with the future and the past.

R: In the end, when you've made all the discoveries, you begin to realize that there's still a split between you and knowledge, and you look at that. At that point the intellect ceases to function as analytical mind and attains a more intuitive level.

S1: But it is necessary for the intellectual mind to naturally clear itself out and see its own uselessness through practice?

R: Yes, I think so. Otherwise, if you stop doing it, then you have some unfinished business.

II

Rinpoche: The latest development that happened in the Christian Church, particularly among the Catholics, was Teilhard de Chardin, who became an extremely exciting figure in Christendom because he spoke scientific language and at the same time he could conduct prayer. There was a historical moment when Teilhard de Chardin conducted services on the beach with several thousand people taking part in it. He was a scientific person and at the same time he was a Jesuit priest, which seems to be extremely valuable for Christians. Also, the Bishop of Woolwich, Bishop Robinson, wrote a book called *Honest to God* which was tremendously revolutionary. He could still be a bishop in the Anglican Church in England, which was very extraordinary. It seems to make for a very strange kind of reaction, that the church has so much concern for public relations with the scientific world, whereas Buddhists wouldn't pay attention. Bishop Robinson's book from a Buddhist point of view wouldn't be particularly surprising. It would be regarded as just one revolutionary thing—which shows somewhat that Christianity is too self-consciously trying to be accepted in the modern world.

Student 4: What I hear you saying really is that there is something that is knowable. When you talk about using the scientific approach, the underlying assumption is the Buddha as a model for a kind of self-examination process. There is an assumption that there is something knowable; and that in each experiment we move closer to it. In a sense there's a denial of mystery, is that right?

R: Yes, I think so. That's the thing about the mystical approach—the very fact of its being mysterious is because it's knowable, otherwise we couldn't even comprehend such unknowable things at all. If the unknowable is within the realm of knowable, the possibilities have to be proved, examined, worked on, like the scriptures talk about. It should be good gold, beaten, hammered, burned, and then finally it becomes pure gold. That seems to be the ultimate protection from charlatanism. Nobody can con anybody. It has to become real, thorough, and workable. You can save yourself from expending too much energy on purely blind faith. Nothing is a mystery from that point of view. But its knowableness might become a mystery—how much can you know, how much can you understand—and you should give yourself time rather than immediately just being zapped by some understanding, some wisdom. It takes a sequential process. That's why the approach of Buddhism does not begin with tantric practice of visualization or a magical approach, but starts from a lower level, and gradually builds up. Just purely meditating, you simply have to be able to manufacture, create your own herukas. Buddhism is not speaking for itself alone, but is minding the business of other spiritual practices. Spirituality has to be a gradual process; experience of pain to begin with, then experience of the openness and finally realizing the mystical approach to reality in a general sense.

S4: Could we talk without any names, Rinpoche? I mean, not "Buddhism," not "Christianity," or "meditation," but let's go over it a little bit and try to run through what has been said. What's been said is we're here because what else is there to do . . .

R: Sure, that seems to be happening.

S4: And what we're doing is looking at the fact that we're here.

R: Yes, I mean it's very simple. We have to use some more of these phenomena, and mind, and neurosis, or whatever.

S4: If we see things as they are, then there is no more to do. And if we aren't seeing things as they are, then what's to be done?

R: We have to see things as they are!

S4: How?

R: By not trying to see things as they are, but by relying on your ignorance, knowing that you can't see things as they are. Maybe you are seeing things as they are somewhat, because you have some point of reference. Not seeing things as they are, if you are aware of it, means that there are some possibilities that you *might* be seeing things as they are. Reliance on your confusion seems to be the way. The whole thing has to be realistic. Otherwise, what do you do if you have fallen off a construction platform? Is it pure accident or a message?

S4: Depends on what you mean.

R: No, it depends on what it is.

S4: Okay, what is it?

R: Well, if you're drunk and you fall down, you've been drinking too much.

S4: That's the message?

R: And if you are freaked out too much, that's why you fall down—it's very simple.

S4: What if you're not drunk and you fall down?

R: Then maybe you're freaked out. You're not paying attention to what's happening; that's why you fall down.

S4: You really have a lot of faith in cause and effect. It's a very ordered universe that you're talking about in your chaos.

R: Well, sure, chaos is orderly, that's why it's chaotic.

S4: But it has order.

R: Order because there is chaos.

S4: But what you're saying is, if you fall down, there's a reason. You must have a lot of faith.

R: You have to fall down some way, even if it's not an act of faith. How can you fall down?

S4: I don't know. You fell down. That's the only fact that we know. The rest is a kind of speculation. I'm trying to understand the universe that you have created right here.

R: I haven't created it.

S4: Well, somebody has.

R: Sure, naturally, we are here because Steve Durkee has built his cabin here.

S4: Well, then, we have just an infinite chain of causes, and he built his cabin here because . . . So we still haven't gotten to why we're here.

R: We are here because of those things.

S4: You really have a lot of faith.

R: The facts become prominent. If you had a crash running through a traffic light, what do you tell them when you go to court?

S4: The facts. Do you think that's where we are, in a traffic court?

R: All the time. That's why we call it *dharma*, it's the facts. What we're saying is things constantly exist in their *isness*.

S3: What you've been saying is that most of what we're doing is trying to get ourselves out of this particular cause and effect, that we are right here, whether it's by religion or anything else that seems to divert us.

R: We are constantly trying to skip away from the facts of life. That's spiritual materialism; trying to bend the law, sort of a tax dodger.

Student 6: When you gave that analogy of the guy falling off the scaffold, you weren't so much talking about looking for a reason why it happened, but saying that falling off a scaffold is itself a message that you weren't in the moment.

R: Yes, you might try to get rid of the moment; then that alternative is the source of the accident. That's what usually happens. Going through the red light, I might have passed through this car. There's an alternative, that's why we do it. Then we get hit by the choicelessness of it. The nonalternative begins to hit us, punish us.

S6: You're saying that if you're standing on a scaffold and you're thinking about how you'd like to be in Miami Beach instead of working on this building, that's the alternative, the cause of your accident. All Rinpoche is saying is that accidents like that are messages bringing you back to the present moment.

S4: But there is no present moment. If you're falling, you're falling and that's the present moment.

R: That's the problem, that's the reality.

Student 5: You're not supposed to fall off the scaffold.

R: Not only not supposed to, but you don't. You're occupied with some other future or past, that's why you fall.

Student 1: What happens if you're standing on the scaffold and there's another guy on it; then he steps off, pushing it accidentally and you fall—suddenly you're falling.

R: But you share his confusion at the same time, and you're not certain if he's going to do the same thing again. You can't really blame anybody.

S1: No, there's no blame; it's just that I'm questioning about when you are in an apparently causeless situation.

R: Things are never causeless situations.

S1: I can hear you, but I've been in this situation. I was house-painting on a scaffold, and I was just reaching up, painting the eaves of this house. Then suddenly I'm falling because this guy who was working with me—.

R: But you weren't paying attention to your neighbor. You were so concerned with what you were going to do.

S1: Isn't that what I'm supposed to be concerned with?

R: No, you're supposed to be awake in all directions.

S1: You're saying that as I was reaching up—to be aware that he was stepping off the scaffold and that the scaffold only had—

R: Well, you're supposed to be able to tell him, "Don't do that because I'm going to fall off. . . ."

S1: It seems to me that the awareness you're talking about extends to the future.

R: No, no, no, the really present moment, extremely present moment. If your neighbor is being unaware of what you are trying to do, then you should be able to relate with that.

S1: Superhuman awareness.

R: No, it just means a sense of you are where you are at, not that you particularly like laying heavy trips on other people. They can only assimilate your lessons by knowing where you are at. It's very simple. "There's too much draft from your front window; I feel cold." Go and tell him. Sometimes that's the point of view of neurotics and psychotics.

S5: What is the point?

R: That if the person is not aware of the totality and is purely concerned about himself—

S4: Last night you said that there was a war, and who is not your neighbor? Now you described a situation where all that was required was that you be aware of what your neighbor was experiencing so you wouldn't get pushed off the scaffold. So who's not your neighbor, and how does that relate to the war?

R: It depends on how friendly you are with yourself, who's your neighbor, who's your friend. If you're not friendly enough with yourself, then anybody is the enemy. If you're friendly with yourself, then your next-door neighbor is a friend. But if you're very friendly with yourself, then most people become your friends. Schizophrenics can deal with that.

Report from Outside the Closet

H E ROSE FROM his chair. He walked toward the closet. I watched him. He opened the closet door and shut himself in the closet. It was turning five o'clock and he had had his tea, but I'm not sure why he shut himself in the closet. Me or the chair or the atmosphere might have been disturbing to him; but on the other hand it might have been inspiring to him in some way.

There was an occasional sound from the closet. But the closet door seemed functionally all right. It was doing its job. Although the room was dark owing to overcast weather, the inside of the closet must have been still darker.

What would happen next? Maybe he didn't want me to be here to watch him come out of the closet. It might embarrass him. But on the other hand, he might regard this as a victory of some kind which he *wanted* me to witness.

I wonder how *he* would write this story, perhaps approaching it from an entirely different perspective. He might think that *I* would be embarrassed if he came out. On the other hand, he might feel it would be some kind of victory for *me*. Not only that, but he would be able to witness my victory.

I became increasingly impatient. I felt I should do *something*. I reviewed in my mind all sorts of things I might do with regard to his being in the closet. I thought of opening the closet door, quite casually of course, and asking him if he might need something. . . . How could he do this to me, using me in this way, making a fool of me? Then I realized with sudden relief that in fact he was making a fool of *himself*.

As I was lost in these thoughts, abruptly the closet door opened. Still munching his tea biscuits, he came out of the closet and sat down in his chair. Slowly he reached for the teapot and filled his cup. I wasn't quite sure how to relate to him. The tense silence of those few seconds was almost too much. For some reason I felt I had to defend myself. But defend what? I wracked my mind. Trying to be as nonchalant as possible, I decided to address him. I poured myself a cup of tea.

"Well?" I said.

"Well, what?" he said, as though nothing had happened.

Freedom Is a Kind of Gyp

An Interview with Chögyam Trungpa

by Sherman Goldman

East West Journal: First of all, thank you very much for your work and for your coming to America. At the Nalanda Festival, there was a spirit of tolerance between different religions—Tibetan Buddhism, Judaism, Zen, etc.—that seems new. If that openness isn't just "shopping," a sort of spiritual supermarket or fair, if it is really something different, what is it?

Chögyam Trungpa Rinpoche: I suppose there's some sense of inspiration that people are beginning to feel, that they can work in a certain discipline, and there's a conviction that goes with that. In the case of "shopping," there are people sort of without culture, still refusing to stick with a culture. I think that in this case, various people have come from very definite disciplines and traditions and backgrounds, and because of that there is a mutual interest and unity.

EWJ: Your own students seem to show more common sense, good humor, and judgment on their own than many of the other spiritual groups who come to us at the *Journal,* asking for publicity. Does that independent intelligence flow from your teaching of the situation as the guru?

CTR: Anyone want to comment?

First Student: I'd say that having seen Rinpoche's intelligence in action, that sparks my own willingness to deal with things.

Second Student: Ironically, I think it comes from a lot of contact with the guru; that's a challenge to the intelligence.

EWJ: At your lecture last night, someone in the audience asked you about the effects of technology on the future of humanity, and if I remember correctly you said, "What's the problem?" I can understand that, intellectually: if you take the largest view, everything is fine. But there's also the question of compassion. Being macrobiotic, I mean in particular the importance of good food. What is the relationship between the current interest in ecology, social consciousness, and spiritual awareness—if we want to play the full game, rather than taking spirituality as just a way of getting high.

CTR: Well, there's a constant battle which goes on between not paying attention to the details of what goes on in the world and paying too much attention to the world and consequently losing your mind. Finding that line is a problem that goes on all the time.

Ecology, basically, is not a regulation or law; it's just a simple straightforward thing. It becomes a problem only when it becomes a doctrine. So peace marchers may become as warlike as the war people. Where there's an awareness, a general sense of dignity and humor, then there's no room to start behaving frantically, throwing things around, polluting, you know, just grab a hamburger from somewhere, or a piece of junk.

EWJ: The denial that intelligence, or liberation, is within ourselves is a form of dualism that seems characteristic of the Western dogmatic religions rather than many of the Eastern traditions, like Buddhism. What is the origin of than dualistic approach which sees God as something radically other than ourselves?

CTR: I suppose fundamentally the cause is a kind of achievement orientation. Buddhism with it's nontheistic approach is automatically not achievement-oriented, since you don't extend yourself out to a Divine Principle as such. It's not impractical. It doesn't let you become fascinated by the potentialities rather than the way you are.

Dualism is a feeling of separation, so you have to make connection with "that," to make peace with "that," whatever "that" may be. Then you begin to yearn, and consequently there are a lot of things in the way so you have to fight them, destroy them, condemn them, or whatever. It's a sign of ultimate frustration in which you are not really fully as you are.

EWJ: The development of psychological courses like EST seems an indigenous American method for developing awareness. Do you see that as an authentic step toward developing a spiritual path?

CTR: Well, in Buddhism we do have an idea of transcending the ordinary barriers of communication and experience and seeing greater vision, cutting through time and space. But I think when you're talking in these terms, you're talking about an entirely different kind of experience which is just a self-existent thing and can become a gadget. So in the case of ESP, I would say . . .

EWJ: Oh, I'm sorry; I didn't mean ESP—extrasensory perception, psychic guidance and that kind of thing—I said EST—Erhardt Seminar Training, Sensitivity Training.

CTR: Oh, yes; well, that's a good question, but I think the same answer still holds up to this point, so far.

You see, the trick here is that if you put somebody who is in a normal condition who never had an experience as intensive as this . . . people enjoy taking a steam bath, because it's an intense experience, and you feel refreshed afterward. In some sense, it's a similar case: you are locked up in a special place, and you're trained in a very special way with trained people to tell you again and again, and you keep on hearing and at some point your own mental chatter becomes that particular "spiel," so to speak. Obviously, at the end you have immense experience, but somehow I think you've gained something rather than having lost anything. In the Buddhist tradition, in any kind of intense experience, you're supposed to lose something, which is the ego, a fraction of it, or something rather than gain something out of the experience.

EWJ: That's clear. Anyone want to comment?

CTR: Well, Werner Erhardt is an extremely good friend of ours.

EWJ: Speaking of intensity, here's another kind of problem with intensity: Why is it that human beings think they know, or they do know, what's the right thing to do with their lives, and repeatedly they find themselves not doing it?

CTR: That's a good one. Well, I think we have the problem of dogma again. Dogma tells you to do something, and you feel it will be good for you. At the same time, if you don't practice it, you'll be looked down upon as a naughty boy or a naughty girl. Rather than encouragement, there's a critical sense. There's no inspiration but a punishment orientation.

EWJ: What is freedom?

CTR: In one sense, freedom is, I suppose, a kind of gyp. When we feel that we have achieved freedom, we have to maintain freedom; we're stuck with freedom, and we are again crippled. Ultimately freedom does not have to be declared, in the sense that we have no grudge against anything. Freedom does not have to fight for its territory. If there's no center, there's no fringe. Then you're beyond any kind of vulnerability.

EWJ: How would you advise Americans, practically, to begin the practice of sitting meditation?

CTR: We tend to lose a lot of the subtleties that exist in our life, in cooking, or whatever we happen to be doing. I think that sitting meditation basically should not be regarded as a ritual ceremony, but just like your making a cup of tea or whatever. Once that kind of relationship is happening, then sitting meditation becomes real life.

EWJ: Thank you very much.

The Myth of Don Juan

AN INTERVIEW WITH CHÖGYAM TRUNGPA

by KARL RAY

Question: You refer to the Don Juan series of books by Castaneda as the "Myth of Don Juan." Will you explain that?

Rinpoche: I think that in Castaneda's books there is too much of a big deal made out of the "person." It turns out to be more than is necessary. This usually seems to be true of any kind of cult. A personal cult develops in this way and, somehow, reality turns into myth. I'm not saying that Don Juan doesn't exist at all. Maybe he does and maybe he doesn't. Somehow the basis of the whole thing seems to be very simple, and elaboration would seem to be unnecessary. To my way of thinking, the approach is a sort of mixture of native wisdom and native superstition, which, when put together, makes the whole thing seem valid. The point is, who knows that perhaps, fundamentally, what we have here is very profound, may be very profound? But the way that Castaneda makes a big deal out of the whole thing makes the profundity not so fine. So, making a big deal out of something is the beginning of distorting the truth, so to speak. This is usually what happens, as has been seen in past instances. First there is wisdom which is very simple and clear on the folk level, in this case, the Mexican peasantry level. Then it is elaborated, put in books, in printed form, which in itself distorts it a little bit, takes away the feeling of the whole thing. Beyond that, there is reinterpretation of what's been written in the book as well, which goes beyond what was actually said, what it's supposed to be. So I think the whole thing is kind of rape of American wisdom.

Q: Native American wisdom?

R: Yes. Native American wisdom. (*Laughs*) Some people equate this to American tantra. I myself actually thought, at one time, that this might be a good beginning. But somehow, as more of the Don Juan books get published, there is a feeling that . . . a doubt as to the existence of American tantra.

Q: Do you find the teaching, overall, through the four books compatible with a person's spiritual progress—his transformation?

R: In a sense the teaching is compatible, but on the other hand, you can make anything compatible spiritually. Like making a good cup of tea or whatever. Particularly in the first book we have a sort of "myth of the drug." And then slowly that is toned down and sort of fades out. The whole thing becomes a more respectable mysticism, which is a very suspicious kind of switch. There are, you know, a lot of gaps. I think there are a lot of loose ends in the teachings, and these loose ends are made into mystical things. Rather than just simply loose ends, which is quite simple. In some sense they are made to sound more sophisticated than they actually are.

Q: Do you think people who have started on the spiritual path through drugs would not otherwise do so?

R: Well, I think it's a kind of circular thing. Interesting. What usually happens is that a person decides: "Now, I'm going to let go, I've been holding tight, I'm going to bounce with society." A highly evolved society, so to speak. People on drugs, LSD or marijuana or whatever, are a definite kind of people; they are people demonstrating they are going to let go. And if a person has reached such a generous state of letting go, it doesn't particularly have to be drugs. It can be anything, meditation or whatever. But somehow, having an open mind, having taken drugs, and because one has an open mind, one begins to learn to interpret a lot of things beyond their level. Then the whole thing is attributed to the drug effect and not because of their openness. The whole thing sort of snowballs. A lot of people have come to the spiritual path without the drug experience. The effect of the drug does make a person think twice about reality and phenomenological experiences. At the same time, I think that is more of a connotation of taking drugs. I don't particularly attribute it to drugs, so much as to a change in a person's consciousness. Or for that matter, whether the drug experience has any relevancy at all. Usually, what happens to a person is that the drug just heightens their neurosis, which is a very fantastic thing for them to see, their own neurosis operating. But it just heightens. Then they eventually return to a manual way of approaching things. The effect of what people get out of the drug becomes at some point irrelevant to their really following the spiritual path. Drugs are just another fantasy.

Q: Do they skip steps in their development when they take drugs? And if so, do they have to come back again, or can they go on?

R: I think they have to go back, because the only thing the drug experience has done is simply to have started them, showed them how to begin. But the way they have to begin is to go back to pre-drug level of experience: their childhood, their relationship with their parents. So obviously one has to go back and start all over again.

Q: Do people become disappointed with drugs?

R: Yes, more and more. Particularly as they get older and begin to get more experience that begins happening. The whole point is, that in the general spiritual approach one has to work on the disappointments that exist in life, rather than on the glorifications. Glorifications have a lot of loose ends, which are not really real. You know, disappointments sort of bring you back home. You have to face yourself. That's usually the pattern in any case.

Q: What is your opinion on Castaneda's fainting spells? Is this usual when one comes into contact with these profound truths?

R: Well, I don't think so. Of course, you can faint with meeting the samsaric world. You get a shock, obviously. (*Laughter*) I don't think he fainted as often as is described in the book. I think a lot of them are [literary] fabrications.

Q: But one *could* faint?

R: You could faint if you are wholehearted enough. I mean, it's lack of composure.

Q: Lack of composure. It is possible that a person not prepared, not having disciplined himself, would faint?

R: Sure. I think so. Fainting itself is a kind of shock. The kind you have jumping from a hot swimming pool into a cold swimming pool. There is a change, of being lost, change of environment, of losing ground. This obviously takes place. When some guy talks gibberish, half of which you can understand and half you can't, there takes place, obviously, a sort of insecurity. What's more, when someone who is highly Americanized and highly educated, working purely on a mental level, an intellectual level, meets with something very rugged, raw, and of an earthy quality, there is a lot of uncomfortableness; it might go beyond that, and he might faint.

Q: And fear? Does one usually fear a teacher or shaman? Do teachers try to instill it?

R: Well, not as a particular special trick to win the student over to the teacher. In a sense fear could provide some ground for a person, for a student, in order to relate more. The student's snugness has to be changed. So in order to make him more alert, you might have a bucket of cold water above the door. As he opens the door, cold water.

Q: Sort of tension?

R: Yes. In the Buddhist tradition, how to learn, how to listen is to be, first of all, crisp, clear, a winter-morning type of attitude.

Q: As to the teachings themselves, reputed to be those of Don Juan's, are they workable? Can you see a practical application for them?

R: One of the problems is that Don Juan's teachings can be workable on the intellectual level. This is somewhat disappointing. The intellectual world doesn't have to bend down to the Mexican peasantry level; it can be fed in such a way that it gets the best of the two worlds. But it only seems to be true, that without being a peasant, one can know the wisdom of the peasant, as printed in books, and at the same time still be comfortable. I do think what Don Juan has to say is, just sort of, good old-fashioned talk. To be interviewing some native elder who has a lot to say about life and can show us his world and how things operate, is in itself fine, on that level, if left as it is. But when it becomes myth and polished by organized training, anthropological research made out of it, then it becomes a problem. Definitely a problem. Even in Buddhism this has been felt. Especially the Tibetans have particularly felt this same problem. But somehow, fortunately, the people who brought the early messages of Tibetan Buddhism to this country were themselves old-fashioned. Somehow we were saved from that. Now, everybody is beginning to sit [meditate] instead of intellectualizing. If you have been intellectualizing, you must sit. But somehow with this [Castaneda's books] there is no training involved. Just read the book, take marijuana, and everything is happy; you can intellectualize your luminous fibers all over the place and whatever. It's very easy. Somehow the whole thing is too much of a packaged deal. There's got to be something more than that. There's no practical application. I don't think this is the sort of magic that is being presented on the tantric level.

Q: Can this be dangerous?

R: You have the Latin American intelligent person working with his own natives. It is quite dangerous because there is familiarity, and at the same time, there is reeducation, change . . . beyond that native level, instead, on the professorial level. There is a lot of conflict between the two. I suppose you find you have a sensational book, but not a particularly insightful one, to say the least!

Q: Do you think things are just overstated?

R: Yes. Definitely.

Q: Do you see any relationship between the shamanistic teachings that Castaneda says he is reporting in his book and the shamanistic practices of Central Asia?

R: Well, I think there is, if you talk to someone like an old Bön shaman, if there is such a person, who has enough experience about himself, the environment. It is largely based on the environmental situation. I think there are a lot of links. Definitely. Not necessarily only one link. But maybe the same kind of idea, of working with the world, with nature, working with the environment, had spread around the world at the same time. But the interesting point is that, with true spirituality, the shamanistic tradition clearly demands that you must be a native yourself. Because your birth is important, your upbringing is important, the way your babyhood was handled is important. So you have some systems planted in your blood. I guess, in some sense, we can correlate this with Hinduism and Judaism, in some sense, in the original sense. The Taoist, Shintoist, and the grand traditions have the same kind of thing. A particular mountain or valley where you are living is very important for you because that is the place of your birth. And, also, there are local wisdoms existing amongst the trees, the rocks, and the brooks. Everything is impregnated with energy and power . . . magic. You know how to live if you are without connection with the world outside. You can still survive.

Q: Do these shamanistic teachings apply to the contemporary world where there is very little relationship to one's place of birth? Most people's place of birth is in a concrete city and not particularly related to nature. What does the teaching have to say to a contemporary city dweller?

R: Well, not very much. (*Laughter*) Not very much. That is why religions such as Christianity and Buddhism came about. They are not particularly related to nationalism. Christianity came out of Judaism and its shamanistic traditions, and Buddhism came out of Hinduism and its shamanistic traditions. Christ and Buddha both saw that those [traditions] were not going to work forever. In order to step beyond that, there is something more needed than that. So the first message that Buddha left was the four noble truths. The first thing is pain, alienation basically. It is a sort of antishamanistic kind of approach. You are not supposed to feel at home wherever you are. And whenever someone presents you with gefilte fish and matzo balls to see *your* world, to think that some *other* environment exists.

Q: Then Buddhism and Christianity are really in opposition to the shamanistic point of view?

R: Christianity is closest to Buddhism in this respect. It is a matter on one hand of seeing how far one can work with the environment and teach the doctrine of good citizenship purely from conventional truths which exist in a particular locality, a particular province, a particular district, as opposed to seeing how mendicants, who travel from one end of the world to the other, carry out their own thing. These are some of the differences. The evidence we have from Christianity, things like the examples of the desert fathers, who actually dwelled in a completely alien situation and in inhospitable surroundings, is similar to that of the mendicant tradition of the Buddhist monks, who have shaved heads and whose temple is to step into the nearest railroad station, just leave and travel around. It is an entirely different kind of approach.

Foreword to The Jewel Ornament of Liberation

W HEN I WAS ASKED to design the cover for *The Jewel Ornament of Liberation*, I chose the syllable AH because it is the sound representing all-pervading speech as well as the seed syllable of shunyata. I thought it most appropriate for a book born from the energy aspect of a great and dedicated teacher as sGam.po.pa (Gampopa) was.

There have been many attempts made to present the Buddhist teachings of Tibet, and generally there are certain consistent misconceptions, reminiscent of the seven blind men describing the elephant. An example of this is the persistent idea of a lamaist cult with complicated practices leading to magic. This occurs particularly through the isolation and dramatization of certain details out of context: a partial view rather than showing the whole journey in the great vehicle.

The vividness of the book is due not only to sGam.po.pa's philosophical studies as a Kadam monk but also to his years of meditation experiences under Milarepa, in which he managed to achieve the meeting point of meditation and intellectual activity. He exercised great skill in bringing together the Buddhist tantric yoga of Naropa and the hinayana monastic discipline of Sarvastivadin.

The book is particularly good for students of Buddhism because it does not present the complex practices of visualization and other deeply involved symbolic practices, but quite wisely, within the keeping of the tradition, deals first with the neurotic aspect of the samsaric mind. With the understanding of the positive ideas of tathagatagarbha and the good working basis of the human body, the journey becomes a totally creative one. Both his understanding and the development of the realization of impermanence are concerned with training the mind rather than giving practices to the student which lead only to more "insane" mental productions. Unfortunately, the latter occurs all too frequently in the presentation of Tibetan Buddhism to the Western audience.

Throughout the evolutionary development of man searching for the dharma in the West, many people, Buddhist or instinctively Buddhist, have been greatly inspired by this book, and I am sure many more will benefit from it in the future. It is in the flow of karma that this book materialized in 1959 on the very eve of the destruction of the spiritual land of Tibet. Professor Guenther was instrumental in making available the only commentary and guide in English to the bodhisattva tradition of Tibet, Japan, and China. The book remains the classic text of all Buddhists.

I would also like to draw the reader's attention to an occasional difficulty with the text. As in some other ancient texts, certain details are perhaps more part of a past culture than valid facts, such as the concept of Mount Meru as the center of the world, and so on. However, I highly recommend *The Jewel Ornament of Liberation* as a thorough and complete exposition of the stages of mahayana.

As part of the lineage of sGam.po.pa's order of Karma Kagyü, I find it very auspicious to be writing the foreword to this new edition.

CHÖGYAM TRUNGPA
September 1970
Tail of the Tiger
Buddhist Community
Barnet, Vermont

Foreword to Mandala

THE SEARCH FOR knowledge and wisdom by concepts is part of man's confused struggle. Nevertheless, using ideas as a stepping-stone is necessary for the student as a starting point.

Mandala in the broad sense is all-encompassing space which accommodates the self-existing cosmic structure, radiating different energies: pacifying, magnetizing, increasing, destroying.

In this book the authors have worked diligently, delving into many different cultures and studying the expressions of buddha nature in each tradition, particularly in terms of the mandala principle. As such, their work is itself a demonstration of mandala in action.

The paths that the reason will follow going through this book may bring confusion as well as affirmation, but this experience can also be regarded as an expression of mandala in action because both positive and negative experiences are part of the contents of the mandala. The awakening of the underlying intelligence is the only starting point.

It is my hope that this book will give you new insight in transcending the world of psychological and spiritual materialism.

CHÖGYAM TRUNGPA RINPOCHE
Karma Dzong
Boulder, Colorado
February 25, 1972

Foreword to Living Dharma

During its 2,500-year history, Buddhism has manifested itself in a multitude of different schools and styles. Always the dynamic nature of living dharma has brought about, in different cultural and historical environments, new modes of expression. But at the heart of all of these manifestations lies the practice of meditation, as exemplified and taught by the Buddha himself. Only through personal meditative practice is the student of dharma enabled to slow down the speed of neurotic mind and to begin seeing the world with clarity and precision. Without this, he will only be able to increase his confusion and perpetuate his aggressive grasping for self-confirmation. Without meditation, there is no approach to genuine sanity, no path to enlightenment, indeed no dharma.

The practice of meditation presents itself as an especially powerful discipline for the shrinking world of the twentieth century. The age of technology would like also to produce a spiritual gadgetry—a new, improved spirituality guaranteed to bring quick results. Charlatans manufacture their versions of the dharma, advertising miraculous, easy ways, rather than the steady and demanding personal journey which has always been essential to genuine spiritual practice.

It is this genuine tradition which is embodied by the teachers presented in this book. They are holders of an unbroken lineage of transmission which has succeeded in surviving and communicating itself in its pure form. The teaching of these masters and the example of their lives provide the impetus and inspiration for further practitioners to follow, properly and fully, the path of dharma.

Vajracharya the Venerable
Chögyam Trungpa

Foreword to The History of the Sixteen Karmapas of Tibet

THE PRACTICING LINEAGE of the Kagyü tradition remains the crown jewel of the contemplative Buddhist world. The examples and lifestyles of great teachers of this tradition have inspired countless practitioners, such that their lives could be further devoted to meditative disciplines. The Karmapas are particularly the great pillars of the Kagyü tradition, who have enabled the practicing lineage to continue in spite of political, social, and economic obstacles.

Karma Thinley Rinpoche is a very close friend and student of mine. I appreciate his insight and wisdom in revealing to us the true stories of the lineage of the Karmapas. No doubt this book will benefit its readers; they should read it with inspiration and devotion.

I remain a servant and propagator of the Kagyü tradition,

VAJRACHARYA THE VENERABLE
CHÖGYAM TRUNGPA RINPOCHE
Boulder, Colorado
February 21, 1980

Foreword to Buddha in the Palm of Your Hand

PROCLAIMING THE LIVING STRENGTH OF THE PRACTICE LINEAGE

I N ORDER TO CREATE a civilized world, it is very important for one person to trust another. Furthermore, it is very important to impart the wisdom of one human being to another and to trust that wisdom at the same time, knowing that it is immaculate, pure, good, accurate, no nonsense.

In the twentieth century, we talk about democracy, individualism, personal heroism, and all kinds of things like that. While all of those ideals are excellent in one sense, they are the creation of a culture that does not appreciate arduous and long training in a traditional discipline. Throwing away tradition and wisdom that have been developed through many centuries is like tossing the extraordinary exertion and sacrifice that human beings have made out of the window, like dirty socks. This is certainly not the way to maintain the best of human society.

While much of Europe was still quite primitive, tantric Buddhism was flourishing in India. At that time in India, people were less savage. They practiced purification and learned how to treat each other as brothers. Needless to say, such human wisdom evolved by means of compassion and love of the world—love of humanity, animals, plants, flowers, and all the rest. Lord Buddha's message goes along with that: If you feel bad about somebody, don't destroy him; take such bad aggression onto yourself, as if you were in that other person's place. Thus the tradition of exchanging oneself for others was developed by the Lord Buddha.

In this little book, my Regent, Ösel Tendzin, has discussed the principles of the attainment of enlightenment, that is, human decency and human wakefulness. No self-proclaimed wisdom exists in his writings. Ösel Tendzin reflects here only the study and training he has gone through with my personal guidance. These are the identical teachings that I received in the same way from my teacher, Jamgön Kongtrül of Sechen. So everything in this book is according to the tradition. I would certainly suggest that readers pay a great deal of attention to this work that my Regent has produced.

As members of the practice lineage of Tibetan Buddhism, our path and goal are to tame our ego-centered mind, which consists of passion, aggression, and ignorance. As a student and child of mine, Ösel Tendzin has developed his natural ability to respond to the teachings of egolessness. He not only intellectually comprehends these teachings, but he has actually practiced and trained himself in this way. Although I would not say Ösel Tendzin is an enlightened person, he is one of the greatest examples of a practitioner who has followed the command of the Buddha and his guru and the tradition of the practice lineage.

Many Oriental advisers have said to me, "Do not make an Occidental your successor; they are not trustworthy." With the blessing of His Holiness the sixteenth Gyalwa Karmapa, and through working with Ösel Tendzin as my Regent, I have come to the conclusion that anybody who possesses tathagatagarbha is worthy of experiencing enlightenment. Moreover, Ösel Tendzin is my prime student. He has been able to commit himself and learn thoroughly the teachings of vajrayana. I have worked arduously in training him as my best student and foremost leader, and His Holiness Karmapa has confirmed his Regency. With His Holiness' blessing, Ösel Tendzin should hold his title and the sanity of the enlightened lineage. He is absolutely capable of imparting the message of buddhadharma to the rest of the world.

I am extraordinarily happy and joyous that my Regent has made his talks available in the form of a book. This work should be tremendously beneficial to those who would like to follow the path of enlightenment and the practice lineage of the Kagyü tradition.

Dragon thunders:
Rainclouds
Lightning
Power

Strength.
Warrior proclaims:
Gentle
Excellent.
Fruits grow and taste delicious.
As buddha nature blossoms,
The world has no regrets
But experiences the dharma
And rejoices in the Great Eastern Sun.
Let us wake as buddha!

VAJRACHARYA THE VENERABLE
CHÖGYAM TRUNGPA RINPOCHE
Boulder, Colorado
December 16, 1981

Foreword to Women of Wisdom

CONTRARY TO POPULAR OPINION which holds that the vajrayana tradition of Buddhism has been practiced primarily by men, many of the great contemplative teachers and practitioners have been women. In Tibet we found that women practitioners were frequently more diligent and dedicated than men. I am very pleased to see the publication of *Women of Wisdom*, which provides ample evidence to that effect. Tsultrim Allione's work should not be regarded as mere feminism. This collection of stories is a great contribution to spreading the understanding of Tibetan Buddhism in the West.

With blessings,
VAJRACHARYA THE VENERABLE
CHÖGYAM TRUNGPA RINPOCHE

Foreword to Mahāmudrā

I AM SO DELIGHTED that this text is being published in the English language. It will greatly benefit English-speaking students of Buddhism. I myself have used this text in working with my students, and I have always found that it communicates, clearly and simply, the mahamudra teachings of the practice lineage. I am very pleased that now English-speaking students can read and study this book in their own language.

The term *mahamudra* in Sanskrit or *chaggya chenpo* (*phyag rgya chen po*) in Tibetan literally means "the great symbol." Mahamudra refers to an actual experience of realization that we ourselves might have. As this text makes very clear, the ground of mahamudra is experienced in the sitting practice of meditation. So although mahamudra is very deep and profound, it can only be realized through the direct and simple practice of shamatha and vipashyana meditation.

The precision and accuracy of meditation allow us to rest in our natural state of being, and out of that we are able to realize that hopes and fears and emotions of all kinds no longer need be regarded as obstacles or highlights. In meditation practice, there is always some sense of going and not going, some process of thinking and not thinking taking place. Nonetheless, beyond that process of thinking and not thinking, there is some basis of nonthought, nonconceptualization. No matter how confused we might be, there is a dancing ground of experience that is common to everyone. Another way of saying this is that, although the nature of samsara is like a water wheel that turns around and around, constantly creating actions that produce later effects, nonetheless there is a basic state of mind that is clear and pure and natural. The realization of that basic state of mind is what is known as mahamudra.

The English edition of this text is titled simply *Mahāmudrā*. In Tibetan this work is usually referred to as *Moonbeams of Mahamudra* (*Chakchen dawai özer*). The moon is the brightest source of light at night, and it is the light from the moon that illuminates the darkness. We are so grateful to Dagpo Tashi Namgyal for having written this book to illuminate the darkness of beings suffering in samsāra. We are also thankful to the translator and the publisher for bringing this light of wisdom into the Western world. May it benefit countless multitudes of beings.

With blessings,
VIDYADHARA THE VENERABLE
CHÖGYAM TRUNGPA RINPOCHE
Boulder, Colorado
March 7, 1986

GLOSSARY

SINCE NONE of the books in Volume Three included a glossary, this list of terms was compiled to cover some of the basic terms that appear in the volume. For other definitions, please see the index.

abhisheka (Skt., "anointment"): A ceremony or formal experience of vajrayana transmission. The student is ritually introduced into a mandala of a particular tantric deity by a tantric master and is thus empowered to visualize and invoke that particular deity. The essential element of abhisheka is a meeting of minds between teacher and student.

amrita (Skt., "deathless"): Consecrated liquor used in vajrayana meditation practices. The term may also refer to spiritual intoxication.

anuttaratantra (Skt.): The highest of the four tantric yanas ("vehicles"), according to the New Translation school of Marpa and his contemporaries. The first three yanas are kriya, upa, and yoga. The realization of mahamudra is the highest attainment of anuttaratantra.

arhat (Skt.): A "worthy one," who has attained the highest level of realization according to the hinayana teachings.

atman (Skt.): The soul posited by Hindu philosophy, or, as translated by Chögyam Trungpa, the ego.

bhumi (Skt., "land"): One of the ten stages or spiritual levels that a bodhisattva must go through to attain buddhahood: (1) very joyful, (2) stainless, (3) luminous, (4) radiant, (5) difficult to conquer, (6) face-to-face, (7) far-going, (8) immovable, (9) having good intellect, and (10) cloud of dharma.

bodhichitta (Skt.): Awakened mind or heart, or "enlightened mind." Ultimate or absolute bodhichitta is the union of emptiness and compassion, the essential nature of awakened mind. Relative bodhichitta is the tenderness arising from a glimpse of ultimate bodhichitta that inspires one to work for the benefit of others.

bodhisattva path: The mahayana path of compassion and the practice of the six paramitas. The bodhisattva vows to relinquish the quest for personal enlightenment in order to work for the benefit of all sentient beings.

Bön (Tib.; also Pön): The old religion of the Tibetans prior to the coming of Buddhism; a form of shamanism.

dakini (Skt.; Tib. *khandroma*): A wrathful or semiwrathful female deity signifying compassion, emptiness, and transcendental knowledge. The dakinis are tricky and playful, representing the basic space of fertility out of which the play of samsara and nirvana arises. More generally, a dakini can be a type of messenger or protector.

dön (Tib.): A minor Bön demon, often an agent of a larger demonic force. *Dön* has come to be used to refer to being attacked by depression, resentment, anger, or other negative emotions.

five buddha families: Five basic qualities of energy in the tantric tradition. The five families refer to the mandala of the five sambhogakaya buddhas and the five fundamental principles of enlightenment they represent. In the mandala of enlightenment, these are five wisdom energies, but in the confused world of samsara, these energies arise as five confused emotions. The following list gives the name of each family, its buddha, its wisdom, its confused emotion, and its direction and color in the mandala: (1) buddha, Vairochana, all-pervading wisdom, ignorance, center, white; (2) vajra, Akshobhya, mirrorlike wisdom, aggression, east, blue; (3) ratna (jewel), Ratnasambhava, wisdom of equanimity, pride, south, yellow; (4) padma (lotus), Amitabha, discriminating-awareness wisdom, passion, west, red; (5) karma (action), Amoghasiddhi, all-accomplishing wisdom, jealousy, north, green. Some qualities differ slightly in different tantras.

guru yoga (Skt.): A devotional practice in which one identifies with and surrenders to the teacher (guru) in his or her vajrayana form as a vajra master and representative of the lineage of ultimate sanity.

heruka (Skt.): A wrathful male deity.

jnana (Skt.; Tib. *yeshe*): the wisdom-activity of enlightenment, transcending all dualistic conceptualization.

kalyanamitra (Skt.): The spiritual friend or the manifestation of the teacher in the mahayana.

karuna (Skt.): Compassion, a key principle of the mahayana, describing the motivation and action of a bodhisattva.

kaya (Skt.): *See* trikaya.

klesha (Skt.): "Poison" or obscuration. The five main kleshas are passion, aggression, delusion, jealousy, and pride.

lhasang (Tib.): A ceremony, originally taken from the Bön religion of Tibet, in which smoke from juniper branches, combined with offerings and chanting, is used to invoke the power and presence of various deities.

ngöndro (Tib.): The foundational practices that are preliminary to receiving abhisheka.

mahasukha (Skt., "great bliss"): An experience or state of spiritual development that arises from the realization of mahamudra, an advanced stage of realization in the vajrayana teachings, particularly practiced in the Kagyü school.

mandala (Skt.): A total vision that unifies the seeming complexity and chaos of experience into a simple pattern and natural hierarchy. The Tibetan word *khyilkhor* used to translate the Sanskrit term literally means "center and surroundings." A mandala is usually represented two-dimensionally as a four-sided diagram with a central deity, a personification of the basic sanity of buddha nature. Three-dimensionally, it is a palace with a center and four gates in the cardinal directions.

mantra (Skt.; Tib. *ngak*): A combination of words (usually Sanskrit) or syllables that expresses the quintessence of a tantric deity. A mantra may or may not have conceptual content. Recitation of mantra is a vajrayana practice that is always done in conjunction with visualization. Mantra is associated with protecting the mind.

paramita (Skt., "that which has reached the other shore"): The six paramitas, or "perfections," are generosity, discipline, patience, exertion, meditation, and knowledge.

prajna (Skt.; Tib. *sherab*): Literally, "transcendental knowledge." Prajna, the sixth paramita, is called transcendental because it sees through the veils of dualistic confusion.

samaya (Skt.; Tib. *tamtsik*): The vajrayana principle of commitment, whereby the student's total experience is bound to the path.

shamatha (Skt.; Tib. *shi-ne*): Mindfulness practice. A basic meditation practice common to most schools of Buddhism, the aim of which is to tame the mind.

shunyata (Skt., "emptiness"): A completely open and unbounded clarity of mind.

skandha (Skt.): Group, aggregate, or heap. The five skandhas are the five aggregates or psychophysical factors that make up what we generally understand as personality or ego.

skillful means (Skt. *upaya*): Skill in expounding the teaching. The bodhi-sattva guides beings to liberation through skillful means. All possible methods and ruses from straightforward talk to the most conspicuous miracles could be applicable.

skull cup (Skt. *kapala*): A cup that is either made from a human skull or visualized as being made from a human skull. The kapala is used in vaj-rayana rituals and usually contains amrita. It represents conquest over extreme beliefs or the intoxication of extreme beliefs.

trikaya (Skt.): The three bodies of buddhahood. The dharmakaya is enlight-enment itself, wisdom beyond any reference point. The sambhogakaya is the environment of compassion and communication. Iconographically, it is represented by the five buddhas, yidams, and protectors. The nirmana-kaya is the buddha who actually takes human form. In the vajrayana, the teacher's body, speech, and mind are regarded as the trikaya.

Vajrasattva (Skt.): One of the deities visualized at various levels of tantric practice. He is associated with primordial purity.

Vajrayogini (Skt.): One of the principal deities or yidams of the Kagyü school of Tibetan Buddhism. Vajrayogini is the consort of Chakrasam-vara. She represents the principle of nonthought or wisdom beyond con-ceptual mind.

vipashyana (Skt.; Tib. *lhakthong*): Awareness practice. Shamatha and vipa-shyana together constitute the basic practice of meditation. *Vipashyana* also refers to the development of insight and discriminating awareness in meditation practice. It is the hallmark of the development of egolessness in the hinayana.

yidam (Tib.): Vajrayana deities, who embody various aspects of the awak-ened nature of mind.

SOURCES

"Cutting Through," in *Garuda II: Working with Negativity* (Barnet, Vt. & Boulder, Colo.: Tail of the Tiger and Karma Dzong, 1972), pp. 3–6. ©1972 Diana J. Mukpo.

Cutting Through Spiritual Materialism, edited by John Baker and Marvin Casper, illustrated by Glen Eddy (Boston & London: Shambhala Publications, 1987). © 1973 by Diana J. Mukpo.

"Cynicism and Warmth," in *The Vajradhatu Sun* (December 1989–January 1990), p. 11. © 1989 by Diana J. Mukpo.

"Dome Darshan," in *Chögyam Trungpa Rinpoche at Lama Foundation* (San Cristobal, N.M.: Lama Foundation, 1974), pp. 4–11. ©1974 by Lama Foundation. Used by gracious permission of Lama Foundation.

Foreword to *Buddha in the Palm of Your Hand* by Ösel Tendzin, edited by Donna Holm (Boulder & London: Shambhala Publications, 1982), pp. xi–xiii. © 1982 by Diana J. Mukpo.

Foreword to *Living Dharma: Teachings of Twelve Buddhist Masters* by Jack Kornfield. (Boston & London: Shambhala Publications, 1977), p. vii. © 1977 by Diana J. Mukpo.

Foreword to *Mahamudra: The Quintessence of Mind and Meditation* by Takpo Tashi Namgyal, translated and annotated by Lobsang P. Lhalungpa (Boston & London: Shambhala Publications, 1986), pp. xv–xvi. © 1986 Diana J. Mukpo.

Foreword to *The History of the Sixteen Karmapas of Tibet* by Karma Thinley (Boulder: Prajñā Press, 1980), p. vii. © 1980 Diana J. Mukpo.

Foreword to *Women of Wisdom* by Tsultrim Allione (London, Boston, Melbourne & Henley: Routledge & Kegan Paul, 1984), p. viii. © 1984 Diana J. Mukpo.

Foreword to *Jewel Ornament of Liberation* by sGam.po.pa, translated by Herbert Guenther (Berkeley: Shambhala Publications, 1971). p. vi. © 1971 Diana J. Mukpo.

Foreword to *Mandala* by José and Miriam Argüelles (Boston and London: Shambhala Publications, 1995). p. 8. © 1973 by Diana J. Mukpo.

"Freedom Is a Kind of Gyp," *East West Journal* 5, no. 6 (June 15, 1975), p. 15. © 1975 *East West Journal*. Used by permission.

The Heart of the Buddha, edited by Judith L. Lief (Boston & London: Shambhala Publications, 1991). © 1991 by Diana J. Mukpo.

"Report from Outside the Closet," in *Chögyam Trungpa Rinpoche at Lama Foundation* (San Cristobal, N.M.: Lama Foundation, 1974), p. 36. ©1974 by Diana J. Mukpo.

"The Myth of Don Juan: An Interview with Chögyam Trungpa" by Karl Ray, in *Codex Shambhala* 4, no. 1 (1975), pp. 1, 23–24. © 1975 by Shambhala Publications.

The Myth of Freedom and the Way of Meditation, edited by John Baker and Marvin Casper, illustrated by Glen Eddy (Boston & London: Shambhala Publications, 1988). © 1976 by Diana J. Mukpo.

"The Three-Yana Principle in Tibetan Buddhism," in *Sangha: A Bi-annual Journal* 1, no. 1 (Autumn 1974). ©1974 by Diana J. Mukpo.

"The Tibetan Buddhist Teachings and Their Application." Based on two versions: the first published in *The Laughing Man* 1, no. 1 (1976); the second published in *Friends of the Buddhadharma*, Bulletin Number One (Spring 1978). ©2003 by Diana J. Mukpo.

"The Wisdom of Tibetan Teachings," *The American Theosophist* 60, no. 5 (May 1972), pp. 117–19. ©1972 by Diana J. Mukpo.

"Tower House Discussions I and II," in *Chögyam Trungpa Rinpoche at Lama Foundation* (San Cristobal, N.M.: Lama Foundation, 1974, pp. 12–23. ©1974 by Lama Foundation. Used by gracious permission of Lama Foundation.

"Transcending Materialism," in *Garuda I: Tibetan Buddhism in America* (Barnet, Vt. & Boulder, Colo.: Tail of the Tiger and Karma Dzong. *Garuda I* (1971), pp.6–10. © 1971 by Diana J. Mukpo.

ACKNOWLEDGMENTS

I WOULD LIKE TO THANK James Minkin, editor of *Dawn Horse* and *The Laughing Man,* for locating and sending a copy of "The Tibetan Buddhist Teachings and Their Application," and to James Gimian for helping me to locate James Minkin! Tom Bonoma at Shambhala Publications provided photocopies of several forewords that appear in Volume Three. Melvin McLeod, James Gimian, and others at the *Shambhala Sun* magazine provided unfettered access to the archives of both the *Vajradhatu Sun* and the *Shambhala Sun.* Emily Sell loaned me her copy of *Women of Wisdom* so that I might photocopy the foreword. Gordon Kidd at the Shambhala Archives helped me to locate several articles. Amanda Lydon, an editorial intern at *Natural Health* magazine, helped me track down a copy of "Freedom Is a Kind of Gyp," an interview that appeared in *East West Journal* in 1975. Thanks to all these people for their assistance.

I would like to thank John Baker and Marvin Casper for having edited both *Cutting Through Spiritual Materialism* and *The Myth of Freedom.* To John, additional thanks for providing information on the history of the editing of both books. Judith L. Lief, the editor of *The Heart of the Buddha,* deserves thanks for putting together that charming volume. As well, I am grateful for her comments on the editorial history of the book. Thanks also to Lama Foundation, *The Laughing Man,* Routledge, and *Natural Health* for permission to reproduce material by Chögyam Trungpa. Philip Barry at Shambhala Booksellers in Berkeley, California, was exceedingly helpful in getting information on the *Shambhala Codex* and the *Shambhala Review of Books and Ideas.* Sam Bercholz suggested I contact Philip and thus led me to the source of information I was searching for.

To Shambhala Publications, particularly Samuel Bercholz, Kendra Crossen Burroughs, and Emily Hilburn Sell, tremendous thanks for the support of this series. To Diana Mukpo and the Mukpo family, deepest appreciation for their support of this work. And finally, to Chögyam Trungpa himself, the most profound thanks for having given the extraordinary teachings that are published in this book. May we continue to carry high the standard of dharma that he brought to the West.

A BIOGRAPHY OF
CHÖGYAM TRUNGPA

THE VENERABLE CHÖGYAM TRUNGPA was born in the province of Kham in eastern Tibet in 1939. When he was just thirteen months old, Chögyam Trungpa was recognized as a major tulku, or incarnate teacher. According to Tibetan tradition, an enlightened teacher is capable, based on his or her vow of compassion, of reincarnating in human form over a succession of generations. Before dying, such a teacher may leave a letter or other clues to the whereabouts of the next incarnation. Later, students and other realized teachers look through these clues and, based on those plus a careful examination of dreams and visions, conduct searches to discover and recognize the successor. Thus, particular lines of teaching are formed, in some cases extending over many centuries. Chögyam Trungpa was the eleventh in the teaching lineage known as the Trungpa Tulkus.

Once young tulkus are recognized, they enter a period of intensive training in the theory and practice of the Buddhist teachings. Trungpa Rinpoche, after being enthroned as supreme abbot of Surmang Monastery and governor of Surmang District, began a period of training that would last eighteen years, until his departure from Tibet in 1959. As a Kagyü tulku, his training was based on the systematic practice of meditation and on refined theoretical understanding of Buddhist philosophy. One of the four great lineages of Tibet, the Kagyü is known as the practicing (or practice) lineage.

At the age of eight, Trungpa Rinpoche received ordination as a novice monk. Following this, he engaged in intensive study and practice of the traditional monastic disciplines, including traditional Tibetan poetry and monastic dance. His primary teachers were Jamgön Kongtrül of Sechen and Khenpo Gangshar—leading teachers in the Nyingma and Kagyü lineages. In 1958, at the age of eighteen, Trungpa Rinpoche completed his studies, receiving the degrees of kyorpön (doctor of divinity) and khenpo (master of studies). He also received full monastic ordination.

The late 1950s were a time of great upheaval in Tibet. As it became clear that the Chinese communists intended to take over the country by force, many people, both monastic and lay, fled the country. Trungpa Rinpoche spent many harrowing months trekking over the Himalayas (described later in his book *Born in Tibet*). After narrowly escaping capture by the Chinese, he at last reached India in 1959. While in India, Trungpa Rinpoche was appointed to serve as spiritual adviser to the Young Lamas Home School in Delhi, India. He served in this capacity from 1959 to 1963.

Trungpa Rinpoche's opportunity to emigrate to the West came when he received a Spaulding sponsorship to attend Oxford University. At Oxford he studied comparative religion, philosophy, history, and fine arts. He also studied Japanese flower arranging, receiving a degree from the Sogetsu School. While in England, Trungpa Rinpoche began to instruct Western students in the dharma, and in 1967 he founded the Samye Ling Meditation Center in Dumfriesshire, Scotland. During this period, he also published his first two books, both in English: *Born in Tibet* (1966) and *Meditation in Action* (1969).

In 1968 Trungpa Rinpoche traveled to Bhutan, where he entered into a solitary meditation retreat. While on retreat, Rinpoche received[1] a pivotal text for all of his teaching in the West, "The Sadhana of Mahamudra," a text that documents the spiritual degeneration of modern times and its antidote, genuine spirituality that leads to the experience of naked and luminous mind. This retreat marked a pivotal change in his approach to teaching. Soon after returning to England, he became a layper-

---

1. In Tibet, there is a well-documented tradition of teachers discovering or "receiving" texts that are believed to have been buried, some of them in the realm of space, by Padmasambhava, who is regarded as the father of Buddhism in Tibet. Teachers who find what Padmasambhava left hidden for the beings of future ages, which may be objects or physical texts hidden in rocks, lakes, and other locations, are referred to as tertöns, and the materials they find are known as terma. Chögyam Trungpa was already known as a tertön in Tibet.

son, putting aside his monastic robes and dressing in ordinary Western attire. In 1970 he married a young Englishwoman, Diana Pybus, and together they left Scotland and moved to North America. Many of his early students and his Tibetan colleagues found these changes shocking and upsetting. However, he expressed a conviction that in order for the dharma to take root in the West, it needed to be taught free from cultural trappings and religious fascination.

During the seventies, America was in a period of political and cultural ferment. It was a time of fascination with the East. Nevertheless, almost from the moment he arrived in America, Trungpa Rinpoche drew many students to him who were seriously interested in the Buddhist teachings and the practice of meditation. However, he severely criticized the materialistic approach to spirituality that was also quite prevalent , describing it as a "spiritual supermarket." In his lectures, and in his books *Cutting Through Spiritual Materialism* (1973) and *The Myth of Freedom* (1976), he pointed to the simplicity and directness of the practice of sitting meditation as the way to cut through such distortions of the spiritual journey.

During his seventeen years of teaching in North America, Trungpa Rinpoche developed a reputation as a dynamic and controversial teacher. He was a pioneer, one of the first Tibetan Buddhist teachers in North America, preceding by some years and indeed facilitating the later visits by His Holiness the Karmapa, His Holiness Khyentse Rinpoche, His Holiness the Dalai Lama, and many others. In the United States, he found a spiritual kinship with many Zen masters, who were already presenting Buddhist meditation. In the very early days, he particularly connected with Suzuki Roshi, the founder of Zen Center in San Francisco. In later years he was close with Kobun Chino Roshi and Bill Kwong Roshi in Northern California; with Maezumi Roshi, the founder of the Los Angeles Zen Center; and with Eido Roshi, abbot of the New York Zendo Shobo-ji .

Fluent in the English language, Chögyam Trungpa was one of the first Tibetan Buddhist teachers who could speak to Western students directly, without the aid of a translator. Traveling extensively throughout North America and Europe, he gave thousands of talks and hundred of seminars. He established major centers in Vermont, Colorado, and Nova Scotia, as well as many smaller meditation and study centers in cities throughout North America and Europe. Vajradhatu was formed in 1973 as the central administrative body of this network.

In 1974 Trungpa Rinpoche founded the Naropa Institute (now Naropa University), which became the first and only accredited Buddhist-inspired university in North America. He lectured extensively at the institute, and his book *Journey without Goal* (1981) is based on a course he taught there. In 1976 he established the Shambhala Training program, a series of seminars that present a nonsectarian path of spiritual warriorship grounded in the practice of sitting meditation. His book *Shambhala: The Sacred Path of the Warrior* (1984) gives an overview of the Shambhala teachings.

In 1976 Trungpa Rinpoche appointed Ösel Tendzin (Thomas F. Rich) as his Vajra Regent, or dharma heir. Ösel Tendzin worked closely with Trungpa Rinpoche in the administration of Vajradhatu and Shambhala Training. He taught extensively from 1976 until his death in 1990 and is the author of *Buddha in the Palm of Your Hand*.

Trungpa Rinpoche was also active in the field of translation. Working with Francesca Fremantle, he rendered a new translation of *The Tibetan Book of the Dead*, which was published in 1975. Later he formed the Nālandā Translation Committee in order to translate texts and liturgies for his own students as well as to make important texts available publicly.

In 1979 Trungpa Rinpoche conducted a ceremony empowering his eldest son, Ösel Rangdröl Mukpo, as his successor in the Shambhala lineage. At that time he gave him the title of Sawang ("Earth Lord").

Trungpa Rinpoche was also known for his interest in the arts and particularly for his insights into the relationship between contemplative discipline and the artistic process. Two books published since his death— *The Art of Calligraphy* (1994) and *Dharma Art* (1996)—present this aspect of his work. His own artwork included calligraphy, painting, flower arranging, poetry, playwriting, and environmental installations. In addition, at the Naropa Institute he created an educational atmosphere that attracted many leading artists and poets. The exploration of the creative process in light of contemplative training continues there as a provocative dialogue. Trungpa Rinpoche also published two books of poetry: *Mudra* (1972) and *First Thought Best Thought* (1983). In 1998 a retrospective compilation of his poetry, *Timely Rain*, was published.

Shortly before his death, in a meeting with Samuel Bercholz, the publisher of Shambhala Publications, Chögyam Trungpa expressed his interest in publishing 108 volumes of his teachings, to be called the Dharma Ocean Series. "Dharma Ocean" is the translation of Chögyam Trungpa's

Tibetan teaching name, Chökyi Gyatso. The Dharma Ocean Series was to consist primarily of material edited to allow readers to encounter this rich array of teachings simply and directly rather than in an overly systematized or condensed form. In 1991 the first posthumous volume in the series, *Crazy Wisdom*, was published, and since then another seven volumes have appeared.

Trungpa Rinpoche's published books represent only a fraction of the rich legacy of his teachings. During his seventeen years of teaching in North America, he crafted the structures necessary to provide his students with thorough, systematic training in the dharma. From introductory talks and courses to advanced group retreat practices, these programs emphasized a balance of study and practice, of intellect and intuition. *Trungpa* by Fabrice Midal, a French biography (forthcoming in English translation under the title *Chögyam Trungpa*), details the many forms of training that Chögyam Trungpa developed. Since Trungpa Rinpoche's death, there have been significant changes in the training offered by the organizations he founded. However, many of the original structures remain in place, and students can pursue their interest in meditation and the Buddhist path through these many forms of training. Senior students of Trungpa Rinpoche continue to be involved in both teaching and meditation instruction in such programs.

In addition to his extensive teachings in the Buddhist tradition, Trungpa Rinpoche also placed great emphasis on the Shambhala teachings, which stress the importance of meditation in action, synchronizing mind and body, and training oneself to approach obstacles or challenges in everyday life with the courageous attitude of a warrior, without anger. The goal of creating an enlightened society is fundamental to the Shambhala teachings. According to the Shambhala approach, the realization of an enlightened society comes not purely through outer activity, such as community or political involvement, but from appreciation of the senses and the sacred dimension of day-to-day life. A second volume of these teachings, entitled *Great Eastern Sun*, was published in 1999.

Chögyam Trungpa died in 1987, at the age of forty-seven. By the time of his death, he was known not only as Rinpoche ("Precious Jewel") but also as Vajracharya ("Vajra Holder") and as Vidyadhara ("Wisdom Holder") for his role as a master of the vajrayana, or tantric teachings of Buddhism. As a holder of the Shambhala teachings, he had also received the titles of Dorje Dradül ("Indestructible Warrior") and Sakyong

("Earth Protector"). He is survived by his wife, Diana Judith Mukpo, and five sons. His eldest son, the Sawang Ösel Rangdröl Mukpo, succeeds him as the spiritual head of Vajradhatu. Acknowledging the importance of the Shambhala teachings to his father's work, the Sawang changed the name of the umbrella organization to Shambhala, with Vajradhatu remaining one of its major divisions. In 1995 the Sawang received the Shambhala title of Sakyong like his father before him and was also confirmed as an incarnation of the great ecumenical teacher Mipham Rinpoche.

Trungpa Rinpoche is widely acknowledged as a pivotal figure in introducing the buddhadharma to the Western world. He joined his great appreciation for Western culture with his deep understanding of his own tradition. This led to a revolutionary approach to teaching the dharma, in which the most ancient and profound teachings were presented in a thoroughly contemporary way. Trungpa Rinpoche was known for his fearless proclamation of the dharma: free from hesitation, true to the purity of the tradition, and utterly fresh. May these teachings take root and flourish for the benefit of all sentient beings.

BOOKS BY CHÖGYAM TRUNGPA

Born in Tibet (George Allen & Unwin, 1966; Shambhala Publications, 1977)

Chögyam Trungpa's account of his upbringing and education as an incarnate lama in Tibet and the powerful story of his escape to India. An epilogue added in 1976 details Trungpa Rinpoche's time in England in the 1960s and his early years in North America.

Meditation in Action (Shambhala Publications, 1969)

Using the life of the Buddha as a starting point, this classic on meditation and the practice of compassion explores the six paramitas, or enlightened actions on the Buddhist path. Its simplicity and directness make this an appealing book for beginners and seasoned meditators alike.

Mudra (Shambhala Publications, 1972)

This collection of poems mostly written in the 1960s in England also includes two short translations of Buddhist texts and a commentary on the ox-herding pictures, well-known metaphors for the journey on the Buddhist path.

Cutting Through Spiritual Materialism (Shambhala Publications, 1973)

The first volume of Chögyam Trungpa's teaching in America is still fresh, outrageous, and up to date. It describes landmarks on the Buddhist path and focuses on the pitfalls of materialism that plague the modern age.

The Dawn of Tantra, by Herbert V. Guenther and Chögyam Trungpa (Shambhala Publications, 1975)

Jointly authored by Chögyam Trungpa and Buddhist scholar Herbert V. Guenther, this volume presents an introduction to the Buddhist teachings of tantra.

Glimpses of Abhidharma (Shambhala Publications, 1975)

An exploration of the five skandhas, or stages in the development of ego, based on an early seminar given by Chögyam Trungpa. The final chapter on auspicious coincidence is a penetrating explanation of karma and the true experience of spiritual freedom.

The Tibetan Book of the Dead: The Great Liberation through Hearing in the Bardo, translated with commentary by Francesca Fremantle and Chögyam Trungpa (Shambhala Publications, 1975)

Chögyam Trungpa and Francesca Fremantle collaborated on the translation of this important text by Guru Rinpoche, as discovered by Karma Lingpa, and are coauthors of this title. Trungpa Rinpoche provides a powerful commentary on death and dying and on the text itself, which allows modern readers to find the relevance of this ancient guide to the passage from life to death and back to life again.

The Myth of Freedom and the Way of Meditation (Shambhala Publications, 1976)

In short, pithy chapters that exemplify Chögyam Trungpa's hard-hitting and compelling teaching style, this book explores the meaning of freedom and genuine spirituality in the context of traveling the Buddhist path.

The Rain of Wisdom (Shambhala Publications, 1980)

An extraordinary collection of the poetry or songs of the teachers of the Kagyü lineage of Tibetan Buddhism, to which Chögyam Trungpa belonged. The text was translated by the Nālandā Translation Committee under the direction of Chögyam Trungpa. The volume includes an extensive glossary of Buddhist terms.

Journey without Goal: The Tantric Wisdom of the Buddha (Shambhala Publications, 1981)

Based on an early seminar at the Naropa Institute, this guide to the tantric teachings of Buddhism is provocative and profound, emphasizing both the dangers and the wisdom of the vajrayana, the diamond path of Buddhism.

The Life of Marpa the Translator (Shambhala Publications, 1982)
A renowned teacher of the Tibetan Buddhist tradition who combined scholarship and meditative realization, Marpa made three arduous journeys to India to collect the teachings of the Kagyü lineage and bring them to Tibet. Chögyam Trungpa and the Nālandā Translation Committee have produced an inspiring translation of his life's story.

First Thought Best Thought: 108 Poems (Shambhala Publications, 1983)
This collection consists mainly of poetry written during Chögyam Trungpa's first ten years in North America, showing his command of the American idiom, his understanding of American culture, as well as his playfulness and his passion. Some poems from earlier years were also included. Many of the poems from *First Thought Best Thought* were later reprinted in *Timely Rain*.

Shambhala: The Sacred Path of the Warrior (Shambhala Publications, 1984)
Chögyam Trungpa's classic work on the path of warriorship still offers timely advice. This book shows how an attitude of fearlessness and open heart provides the courage to meet the challenges of modern life.

Crazy Wisdom (Shambhala Publications, 1991)
Two seminars from the 1970s were edited for this volume on the life and teachings of Guru Rinpoche, or Padmasambhava, the founder of Buddhism in Tibet.

The Heart of the Buddha (Shambhala Publications, 1991)
A collection of essays, talks, and seminars present the teachings of Budddhism as they relate to everyday life.

Orderly Chaos: The Mandala Principle (Shambhala Publications, 1991)
The mandala is often thought of as a Buddhist drawing representing tantric iconography. However, Chögyam Trungpa explores how both confusion and enlightenment are made up of patterns of orderly chaos that are the basis for the principle of mandala. A difficult but rewarding discussion of the topic of chaos and its underlying structure.

Secret Beyond Thought: The Five Chakras and the Four Karmas (Vajradhatu Publications, 1991)

Two talks from an early seminar on the principles of the chakras and the karmas, teachings from the Buddhist tantric tradition.

The Lion's Roar: An Introduction to Tantra (Shambhala Publications, 1992)

An in-depth presentation of the nine yanas, or stages, of the path in the Tibetan Buddhist tradition. Particularly interesting are the chapters on visualization and the five buddha families.

Transcending Madness: The Experience of the Six Bardos (Shambhala Publications, 1992)

The editor of this volume, Judith L. Lief, calls it "a practical guide to Buddhist psychology." The book is based on two early seminars on the intertwined ideas of bardo (or the gap in experience and the gap between death and birth) and the six realms of being.

Training the Mind and Cultivating Loving-Kindness (Shambhala Publications, 1993)

This volume presents fifty-nine slogans, or aphorisms related to meditation practice, which show a practical path to making friends with oneself and developing compassion for others, through the practice of sacrificing self-centeredness for the welfare of others.

Glimpses of Shunyata (Vajradhatu Publications, 1993)

These four lectures on the principle of shunyata, or emptiness, are an experiential exploration of the ground, path, and fruition of realizing this basic principle of mahayana Buddhism.

The Art of Calligraphy: Joining Heaven and Earth (Shambhala Publications, 1994)

Chögyam Trungpa's extensive love affair with brush and ink is showcased in this book, which also includes an introduction to dharma art and a discussion of the Eastern principles of heaven, earth, and man as applied to the creative process. The beautiful reproductions of fifty-four calligraphies are accompanied by inspirational quotations from the author's works.

Illusion's Game: The Life and Teaching of Naropa (Shambhala Publications, 1994)

The great Indian teacher Naropa was a renowned master of the teachings of mahamudra, an advanced stage of realization in Tibetan Buddhism. This book presents Chögyam Trungpa's teachings on Naropa's life and arduous search for enlightenment.

The Path Is the Goal: A Basic Handbook of Buddhist Meditation (Shambhala Publications, 1995)

A simple and practical manual for the practice of meditation that evokes the author's penetrating insight and colorful language.

Dharma Art (Shambhala Publications, 1996)

Chögyam Trungpa was a calligrapher, painter, poet, designer, and photographer as well as a master of Buddhist meditation. Drawn from his many seminars and talks on the artistic process, this work presents his insights into art and the artist.

Timely Rain: Selected Poetry of Chögyam Trungpa (Shambhala Publications, 1998)

With a foreword by Allen Ginsberg, this collection of poems was organized thematically by editor David I. Rome to show the breadth of the poet's work. Core poems from *Mudra* and *First Thought Best Thought* are reprinted here, along with many poems and "sacred songs" published here for the first time.

Great Eastern Sun: The Wisdom of Shambhala (Shambhala Publications, 1999)

This sequel and complement to *Shambhala: The Sacred Path of the Warrior* offers more heartfelt wisdom on Shambhala warriorship.

Glimpses of Space: The Feminine Principle and Evam (Vajradhatu Publications, 1999)

Two seminars on the tantric understanding of the feminine and masculine principles, what they are and how they work together in vajrayana Buddhist practice as the nondual experience of wisdom and skillful means.

The Essential Chögyam Trungpa (Shambhala Publications, 2000)

This concise overview of Trungpa Rinpoche's teachings consists of forty selections from fourteen different books, articulating the secular path of the Shambhala warrior as well as the Buddhist path of meditation and awakening.

Glimpses of Mahayana (Vajradhatu Publications, 2001)

This little volume focuses on the attributes of buddha nature, the development of compassion, and the experience of being a practiitoner on the bodhisattva path of selfless action to benefit others.

RESOURCES

For information regarding meditation instruction or inquiries about a practice center near you, please contact one of the following:

Shambhala International
1084 Tower Road
Halifax, NS
B3H 2Y5 Canada
Telephone: (902) 425-4275, ext. 10
Fax: (902) 423-2750
Website: www.shambhala.org (This website contains information about the more than 100 meditation centers affiliated with Shambhala, the international network of Buddhist practice centers established by Chögyam Trungpa.)

Shambhala Europe
Annostrasse 27
50678 Cologne, Germany
Telephone: 49-0-700-108-000-00
E-mail: europe@shambhala.org
Website: www.shambhala-europe.org

Dorje Denma Ling
2280 Balmoral Road
Tatamagouche, NS
B0K 1V0 Canada
Telephone: (902) 657-9085
Fax: (902) 657-0462
E-mail: info@dorjedenmaling.com
Website: www.dorjedenmaling.com

KARMÊ CHÖLING
369 Patneaude Lane
Barnet, VT 05821
Telephone: (802) 633-2384
Fax: (802) 633-3012
E-mail: karmecholing@shambhala.org

SHAMBHALA MOUNTAIN CENTER
4921 Country Road 68C
Red Feather Lakes, CO 80545
Telephone: (970) 881-2184
Fax: (970) 881-2909
E-mail: shambhalamountain@shambhala.org

SKY LAKE LODGE
P.O. Box 408
Rosendale, NY 12472
Telephone: (845) 658-8556
E-mail: skylake@shambhala.org
Website: http://ny.shambhala.org/skylake

DECHEN CHÖLING
Mas Marvent
87700 St Yrieix sous Aixe
France
Telephone: 33 (0)5-55-03-55-52
Fax: 33 (0)5-55-03-91-74
E-mail: dechencholing@dechencholing.org

Audio and videotape recordings of talks and seminars by Chögyam Trungpa
are available from:

KALAPA RECORDINGS
1678 Barrington Street, 2nd Floor
Halifax, NS
B3J 2A2 Canada
Telephone: (902) 421-1550
Fax: (902) 423-2750
E-mail: shop@shambhala.org
Website: www.shambhalashop.com

For publications from Shambhala International, please contact:

VAJRADHATU PUBLICATIONS
1678 Barrington Street, 2nd Floor
Halifax, NS
B3J 2A2 Canada
Telephone: (902) 421-1550
E-mail shop@shambhala.org
Website: www.shambhalashop.com

For information about the archive of the author's work—which includes more than 5,000 audio recordings, 1,000 video recordings, original Tibetan manuscripts, correspondence, and more than 30,000 photographs—please contact:

THE SHAMBHALA ARCHIVES
1084 Tower Road
Halifax, NS
B3H 3S3 Canada
Telephone: (902) 421-1550
Website: www.shambhalashop.com/archives

The *Shambhala Sun* is a bimonthly Buddhist magazine founded by Chögyam Trungpa. For a subscription or sample copy, contact:

SHAMBHALA SUN
P. O. Box 3377
Champlain, NY 12919-9871
Telephone: (877) 786-1950
Website: www.shambhalasun.com

Buddhadharma: The Practitioner's Quarterly is an in-depth, practice-oriented journal offering teachings from all Buddhist traditions. For a subscription or sample copy, contact:

BUDDHADHARMA
P. O. Box 3377
Champlain, NY 12919-9871
Telephone: (877) 786-1950
Website: www.thebuddhadharma.com

Naropa University is the only accredited, Buddhist-inspired university in North America. For more information, contact:

NAROPA UNIVERSITY
2130 Arapahoe Avenue
Boulder, CO 80302
Telephone: (303) 444-0202
Website: www.naropa.edu

INDEX

ALL BOOKS, ARTICLES, POEMS, SONGS, AND SEMINARS are attributed to Chögyam Trungpa unless otherwise cited. Owing to the subtle content of the poems, only their titles have been indexed. Illustrations are indicated by page numbers in italics and follow text entries. Titles of books contained within this volume are indicated by initial page number followed by "ff."

INDEX

compassion as, 74–75, 402
as tool for cutting through obstacles, xxiii
world of, 535
Warnings
of dangers on spiritual path, 7
of vajrayana, 366–367, 369–370
Watcher principle (Tib. *dzinba*), 55, 57–58, 145–146, 192, 197, 218, 266, 284–285, 337, 350
awareness without, 58, 264
death of, 192, 197
discriminating knowledge as, 133
ego as, 171
"fixation/holding" as, 285
giving up, 48
Madhyamaka school and, 145–146
negativity and, 235
paranoia as, 58
vajrayana and, 287
Yogachara school and, 145
Water (element), 166, 171, 397, 421
Bön deity of, 487
Watts, Alan, xv
houseboat seminars, xvii
Wealth
Bön god of, 488
compassion as ultimate, 76
mentality of, 76, 81–82
svastika symbol of, 483n
See also Richness
Wellenbach, Polly Monner, xv
Wellenbach, Scott, xiv: n.4
Wesley Foundation, xv
Wheel of dharma
first turning of, 113
second turning of, 145
Wind (element), 169–170, 171, 397, 422
competitiveness of, 207
jealous god realm and, 205
Wisdom(s) (Tib. *yeshe*) 82–83, 86, 232, 321–322, 577
all-accomplishing, 169, 422
all-encompassing, 169–170, 420–421
being vs. knowing, 161
coemergent, 432
discriminating awareness, 168, 287, 415, 421, 439
as "domestic affair," 249
of equanimity, 165, 167, 421
five, of awakened state, 166, 171
vs. knowledge/prajna, 161, 173, 258
of life situations, 173
mirrorlike, 166
as primordial intelligence, 83
rape of Native American, 566–567
spontaneously-existing, 83
tenth *bhumi* as, *paramita*, 267–268
up-to-date, 17
vs. warfare, 86–87
"The Wisdom of Tibetan Teachings" (article), xxii, 503–506

Wishful thinking, 51, 69, 257
eighth *bhumi* as, 266–268
Women of Wisdom (Allione), xxvii, 580
Work, 241–243
as escape from creativity, 241
as meditation, 242
See also Right livelihood
Workability, 396, 522
Working with others, 246–247, 414
World
appreciating phenomenal, 477
creating a civilized, 577
devotion to, 281
as five styles of energy, 166, 420–422
flowing relationship with, 131
guru's, 420
making friends with, 522–523
mystical aspect of, 276, 535–536
nonaggression as, view, 400
phenomenal, as "other," 394
power to change, 394
relative, of split, 553
running, 268
as sacred mandala, 427
of sanity, 268, 431
saving, 480
of self-existing messages, 350, 493
transcending preconceptions of, 133
vajra, 420
Worrying, 81–82
Wrathful *yidam*/deities, 170–173, 239–240, 491
vajra anger of, 173

Yeshe. See Wisdom
Yeshen (Bön deity), 485–486
Yi (sixth sense), 327–328
Yidam (deities), 170–173, 415–417
costumes of, 171
definition of, 416
five buddha families and, 422
peaceful, 170, 239, 438
wrathful, 170–173, 239–240, 438
See also Vajrayogini
Yidam practice, 432–433
Yoga (physical), 162, 286
Yogachara ("mind-only") school, 144–146
theory of enlightenment, 150
watcher and, 145

Za (Bön god), 488
Zen (Buddhism), 40–41
awareness without watcher, 264
boredom and, 223
koan practice, 554
ox-herding pictures, 172
prajna and, 264–266
Zen Center San Francisco, x
Zen Mind, Beginner's Mind (Suzuki), 283
Zero-ness, confirming, 199
Zim, Joshua, xxiv